with the aid of a cane. A youngster with a developmental delay was "awakened," as the doctors described it, by his intense artistic involvement, resulting in an amazing growth spurt at the age of 18. We have many other stories of remarkable transformation. The chapter-opening paintings in this text are a visual testament to these stories.

Much art is predicated on the notion of this separability from life; however, what we advocate is the inseparability of life and art— that the expression of one's most powerful emotions is a process of creating wholeness in both art and self.

Bill Richards, Director
Harlem Horizon Art Studio

Bill Richards expresses the value and inseparability of art and life and how the expressions of powerful emotion can create wholeness in both art and self. This same power of expression can be realized within a classroom where students experience success in learning. Not only can children express themselves through art, as demonstrated in each chapter opener for this text, but educators can encourage expression through the learning process.

This book's title, *Exceeding the Boundaries: Understanding Exceptional Lives*, was selected to reinforce the concept of allowing children to reach beyond artificial boundaries established by society. The basic philosophy of the text is that all children have worth and all children have abilities. Each child is different and each has different potential.

Frequently, boundaries are established educationally and emotionally that prevent a child with disabilities from reaching his or her full potential. Unlocking boundaries is essential for exceptional lives to develop to their fullest.

The boundaries of attitude are the first challenges to overcome before a child with a disability can experience success. As educators, we set the stage and tone for a positive classroom environment. Helping students to exceed the boundary of attitude and making sure our attitudes are positive are the first steps to success. Our hearts must be open to accepting exceptional children despite their level of functioning. When this boundary of attitude exists, breaking educational boundaries is next to impossible. Positive attitudes are essential.

The boundary of accepting the educational level and present skill base of a child is the second step to exceeding boundaries in exceptional lives. We must begin to teach where a child is. One must crawl before he walks. Inclusion must also be infusion. Infusion will only be possible when the child is provided tasks and activities on his present level.

Caring for all children no matter who they are, whether the child has a disability or not, is the third and final step for exceeding boundaries and understanding exceptional lives. We must care for all children. Children's success is our goal, and caring is a stepping stone to success.

All children are different. As my son, Scott, wrote, "If everyone in the world were just alike, we wouldn't miss anyone when they died." To be different is to be special. Only by exceeding the boundaries of attitude, educational level, and the value of caring can we begin to understand exceptional lives.

Judy W. Wood

EXCEEDING THE BOUNDARIES
Understanding Exceptional Lives

JUDY W. WOOD
ANDREA M. LAZZARI

EXCEEDING THE BOUNDARIES

Understanding Exceptional Lives

JUDY W. WOOD

Virginia Commonwealth University

ANDREA M. LAZZARI

Harcourt Brace College Publishers

Fort Worth   Philadelphia   San Diego   New York   Orlando   Austin   San Antonio

Toronto   Montreal   London   Sydney   Tokyo

Publisher	Christopher P. Klein
Senior Acquisitions Editor	Jo-Anne Weaver
Developmental Editor	Tracy Napper
Project Editor	Tamara Neff Vardy
Senior Project Editor	Angela Williams Urquhart
Senior Production Manager	Annette Dudley Wiggins
Art Director	Burl Dean Sloan
Picture Development Editor	Lili Weiner

Address editorial correspondence to:
Harcourt Brace College Publishers
301 Commerce Street, Suite 3700
Fort Worth, TX 76102

Address orders to:
Harcourt Brace & Company
6277 Sea Harbor Drive
Orlando, FL 32887-6777
1-800-782-4479

Harcourt Brace may provide complimentary instructional aids and supplements or supplement packages to those adopters qualified under our adoption policy. Please contact your sales representative for more information. If as an adopter or potential user you receive supplements you do not need, please return them to your sales representative or send them to:

ATTN: Returns Department
Troy Warehouse
465 South Lincoln Drive
Troy, MO 63379

Printed in the United States of America

ISBN: 0-15-501743-8

Library of Congress Catalog Card Number: 96-76432

6 7 8 9 0 1 2 3 4 5 048 9 8 7 6 5 4 3 2 1

PREFACE

Exceeding the Boundaries: Understanding Exceptional Lives is a special text, not because it focuses on individuals with special needs, but because it was carefully developed to remove the boundaries faced by such individuals. It was designed to provide information that will encourage readers to examine their attitudes about individuals with disabilities. By developing the readers' knowledge about specific disabilities and promising practices, this text hopes to promote a future where there are no boundaries to educational, social, vocational and economic opportunities for all individuals with disabilities.

This book was written to provide instructors and students with a practical, user-friendly, easy-to-follow text on individuals with disabilities and the issues and challenges that have shaped the development of services to this population. Written from a "then and now" perspective, the text provides the reader with insight into the many forces that have shaped the field of special education as well as current issues and future trends that will influence its future course. Information is presented from the perspectives of a variety of individuals—professionals, with disabilities, parents and other family members. Throughout each chapter, the authors have strived to provide a realistic view of the needs of individuals with disabilities and the services available to support their full integration into all facets of home, school, and community life.

Each chapter is opened through the artistic expressions of exceptional patrons from the Harlem Horizon Art Studio in New York City (see endpapers). Each stroke of the brush represents special feelings experienced by these hospital patients and youngsters from the community.

The text is divided into 15 chapters, corresponding to the typical number of weeks in a semester course. Each chapter is designed to help the reader develop an understanding of a specific disability or exceptionality or an issue related to disabilities. Chapter 1 sets the stage for the reader by providing brief background information regarding the field of special education, including a general overview of the evolution of attitudes toward and services available to persons with disabilities. Landmark litigation and significant legislation that have served to expand the boundaries for individuals with disabilities are also presented. Chapter 2 provides a look at issues of cultural diversity and how they have influenced and been affected by special education services and practices. Chapters 3–12 address specific exceptionalities such as gifted and talented, learning disabilities, attention deficit hyperactivity disorder, emotional and behavioral disorders, communication disorders, hearing loss, visual impairment, physical disabilities, mental retardation, and autism. Because of the media attention and increasing incidence of AD/HD, an entire chapter has been devoted to this disability, a unique characteristic of this text. Chapters 13 and 14 provide an overview of two special populations—infants, toddlers and preschoolers (early childhood intervention) and young adults moving from school to the workplace (adults in transition). Devoting separate chapters to these populations enabled the authors to look at issues of critical importance to these age groups across disability categories. Chapter 14 presents a cross-categorical look at disabilities across the lifespan as viewed from the perspective of parents and other family members. It also brings to life the facts and figures presented in previous chapters. This chapter was placed after the categorical chapters and the chapters addressing specific age groups in an effort to tie together many of the separate issues discussed in each chapter. The epilogue is intended to give the readers some food for thought as they look ahead to the future of the field of disabilities.

The chapters of this text are organized in a consistent format for ease of use. Each chapter begins with clearly stated objectives for the student and follows a similar format:

historical timeline
historical overview
definitions
characteristics
prevalence
causes
assessment
instructional accommodations
family perspectives
current issues and future trends
five-minute summary
study questions

Each chapter includes a "Real People" box that provides a personal look at each disability from an individual point of view. It serves to remind the reader that individuals from all ethnic, age, gender, and social groups have disabilities, and they are ordinary people who have learned to deal with extraordinary challenges. The "Easy Ideas for Practitioners" box in each chapter provides practical, concrete tips for parents and professionals for each disability area. In the "Innovative Ideas" box, a promising practice or creative approach to each particular disability area is highlighted. At the end of each chapter, a resource list titled "For More Information" provides information on publications and organizations relevant to each disability. Students who wish to pursue further information on a disability, either for research purposes or for personal interest, will find this section helpful. Throughout each chapter, key terms are highlighted, and the most important terms are included in the glossary at the end of the text. References have been placed at the end of each chapter rather than at the end of the book to make it easier for the reader to find them.

Exceeding the Boundaries also offers a complete ancillary package. The Instructor's Manual includes sample lecture outlines, key concepts and terms, activities, assignments, handouts, resources, and overhead masters. The Study Guide offers review questions, summaries, and key terms to help students assimilate and apply the information they have learned. Instructors will also find the printed test bank and computerized test banks very helpful for their courses. Another very exciting feature is the video, which pulls clips from the popular media to illustrate the latest news and advances in the various disability areas. A forward and summary link the video clips to the text itself. We suggest showing the segment related to a specific disability before assigning the chapter in order to familiarize students with that exceptionality and whet their appetites for more information.

ACKNOWLEDGMENTS

Appreciation is extended to the talented, patient, and dedicated educators whose contributions to this book are immeasurable: Mary Beth Bruder, University of Connecticut Health Center; Stephen Conley, Virginia Department of Health; Bonnie Cramond, University of Georgia; Diane Fazzi, California State University, Los Angeles; Nona Flynn and Cherie Takemoto, Parent Education and Advocacy Training Center, Fairfax, VA; Diane Haager, California State University, Los Angeles; Robbie Kendall-Melton, University of Tennessee, Mar-

tin; Rob O'Neill, University of Utah; George Sugai and Timothy Lewis, University of Oregon; Laura Vogtle, University of Alabama, Birmingham; and Paul Wehman, Virginia Commonwealth University.

We are indebted to the reviewers who provided valuable comments and suggestions that helped guide us on our journey: David Alexander, Virginia Polytechnic Institute and State University; David Anderson, Bethel College; David Baker, University of North Texas; Gary Best, California State University, Los Angeles; Barbara Clark, California State University, Los Angeles; Ann Cranston-Gingrass, University of South Florida; Bruno D'Alonzo, New Mexico State University; Debi Gartland, Towson State University; Nancy Halmhuber, Eastern Michigan University; Dona Icabone, Western Michigan University; Earle Knowlton, University of Kansas; Robin Lock, Texas Tech University; Cecil Mercer, University of Florida; August Mauser, University of South Florida; Richard Nowell, Indiana University of Pennsylvania; Bob Ortiz, New Mexico State University; Sandy Parsons, California State University, San Marcos; Alec Peck, Boston College; Carlos Pedraza; Cathy Pratt, Indiana University/Purdue University; Cecil Reynolds, Texas A & M University; Edward Schultz, University of Maine, Farmington; Scott Sparks, Ohio University; Donald Stedman, University of North Carolina, Chapel Hill; Sheela Stuart, New Mexico State University; Maureen Wall, University of Georgia; Doris Williams, Indiana State University; and Richard Whelan, University of Kansas, Kansas City. We also extend thanks to our other friends and colleagues who shared materials, information, and professional expertise.

A very special appreciation is extended to the following staff members at Harcourt Brace College Publishers: Jo-Anne Weaver, Senior Acquisitions Editor, who gave birth to the book; Tracy Napper, Developmental Editor, who so patiently guided us through the process; Angela Urquhart, Senior Project Editor; Tamara Vardy, Project Editor; Susan Kindel, Senior Marketing Manager; Annette Wiggins, Assistant Manager of Production; Burl Sloan, Art Director; and all of the other members of the Harcourt Brace team assigned to this work. We also thank Bill Richards and the artists of the Harlem Horizon Art Studio for their striking chapter-opening and cover paintings, as well as Bill's introductory piece, which so wonderfully explains the mission of this book. We would also like to acknowledge our research assistants/typists—Catharine Robertson, Cheryl Grey, Kathleen Causey, and Kathryn Ullman.

A special acknowledgment goes to an outstanding educator and wonderful person, Dr. Stanley Baker. His gentleness and hand of friendship is extended to all he meets, and his presence makes this world a much better place.

This text is lovingly dedicated to our children: Judy's sons, Eddie, Scott and Jason, and Andrea's daughter, Tamara. Each of you adds support, joy, and blessings to our lives.

ABOUT THE AUTHORS

Judy W. Wood is a professor of special education at Virginia Commonwealth University in Richmond, Virginia. She is core coordinator for the program in mental retardation and director of the Responsive Education Institute. Formerly, she was on the faculty of the University of Southern Mississippi in Hattiesburg, Mississippi, where she was responsible for teaching assignments and in-service training activities for surrounding school districts.

A native of Center, Texas, Dr. Wood received a B.S. degree in English and mental retardation at the University of Southern Mississippi in Hattiesburg. She also holds master's and Ph.D. degrees in special education from the same university. She taught English and special education for a number of years in public schools while she worked on her graduate degrees.

Dr. Wood had conducted in-service workshops for both general and special education teachers, nationally as well as internationally. She is the author of *Adapting Instruction for Mainstream and At-Risk Students* and *Mainstreaming: A Practical Approach for Teachers*.

Andrea M. Lazzari began her career as a speech-language pathologist, later branching out into the field of special education, both as an early childhood special educator and an administrator. She received her Ed. D. from Virginia Polytechnic Institute and State University and has practiced in a variety of settings including college and university, public school, community clinic, private practice, and state education agency.

Dr. Lazzari has published extensive materials in the area of remediation for communication impairments. She is the co-author of the HELP series for language remediation that is widely used by speech-language pathologists across the United States and in other countries. She is the author of *The Transition Sourcebook, HELP for Grammar, HELP for Memory, Just for Adults* and *The HELP Test-Elementary*. She is co-author with Judy Wood of *Test Right* (primary and intermediate levels) and *125 Ways to Be a Better Test Taker*.

The contributing authors:

Robbie Kendall-Melton (Chapter 2) is a full professor and the assistant dean of education at the University of Tennessee at Martin. Her achievements in teaching, research, publications, and presentations in the areas of special education, teaching strategies, technology, distance learning, and learning styles have been recognized nationally and internationally. She was honored as Tennessee's 1995 "Professor of the Year." She is currently chairing a joint international research team for UTM and Hirosaki University in Japan, conducting a comparison study regarding the education of students with disabilities.

Bonnie Cramond (Chapter 3) is an associate professor in the Department of Educational Psychology at the University of Georgia, where she is the coordinator of the graduate program in gifted and creative education. In addition to teaching and parenting gifted children, she has published papers and chapters on giftedness and creativity, is on the editorial boards of three journals in the field, has served in leadership roles in professional organizations, and has presented at local, national, and international conferences.

Diane Haager (Chapter 4) is an assistant professor at California State University, Los Angeles, where she codirects the teacher education and graduate degree programs in mild to moderate disabilities. Prior to this appointment, she taught students with learning disabilities in school, clinical, and university settings for 15 years. Dr. Haager earned a Ph.D. degree in reading and learning disabilities from the University of Miami in Coral Gables, Florida. Her research interests include social factors related to learning disabilities, teachers' adaptations for students with learning disabilities, and classroom-based strategies to facilitate inclusive education.

Timothy J. Lewis (Chapter 6) earned his doctorate in special education at the University of Oregon. Prior to completing his degree, he was a teacher of students with EBD in school and hospital settings. He is currently an assistant professor at the University of Oregon, where he conducts research and teaches courses in EBD. His specialty areas include social skill instruction, functional assessment, and proactive schoolwide systems designed to support children and youth with challenging behavior.

George Sugai (Chapter 6) was a special education teacher for students with EBD in public and private schools before earning his Ph.D. at the University of Washington in Seattle. He is currently an associate professor at the University of Oregon, where he trains teachers and conducts research in the area of EBD. His specialty areas include social skills instruction, applied behavior analysis, behavioral consultation, and comprehensive positive behavioral support systems.

Diane Fazzi (Chapter 9) is an assistant professor in the Division of Special Education at California State University, Los Angeles. She coordinates the orientation and mobility specialist training program and also teaches courses in the teacher education program in blindness and visual impairment. Her publications and presentations include topics on orientation and mobility for children and youth with multiple disabilities, O & M specialists with disabilities, creative concept development, and behavior management for young children with visual impairments.

Stephen Conley (Chapter 10) has extensive teaching, administrative, and research experience in educational programs for children with physical disabilities and health impairments. He has master's degrees in elementary and special education. Presently serving as the director of adolescent pregnancy prevention for the Virginia Department of Health, he is a doctoral candidate for a Ph.D. in education and human resources from Virginia Commonwealth University.

Laura Vogtle (Chapter 10) is an occupational therapist with 23 years' experience working with children who have disabilities at the Kluge Children's Rehabilitation Center in Charlottesville, Virginia. In addition to her clinical work, she has taught pediatric therapy techniques on national and international levels for the last 13 years, as well as teaching in the graduate school of special education at the University of Virginia. In 1991, she received her master's degree in educational research from the University of Virginia and finished her doctoral work in 1995. Currently she is serving as program director of the graduate school of occupational therapy at the University of Alabama at Birmingham.

Robert E. O'Neill (Chapter 12) is an associate professor in the Department of Special Education at the University of Utah in Salt Lake City. His teaching, research, and service efforts focus on developing strategies to support persons with autism and other developmental disabilities that display challenging behaviors in school and other community settings. Dr. O'Neill would like to extend sincere appreciation to Dr. Sally Ozonoff for her

very helpful comments on an earlier version of this chapter.

Nona Flynn, Ed. D. (Chapter 13) is project director at the Parent Educational Advocacy Training Center (PEATC) in Virginia. Her experience encompasses both regular and special education, as well as teaching in graduate programs at two major universities. For the past 12 years she has worked at PEATC, developing parent/professional training programs with national dissemination. She is the director of a four-state project that has established more than 100 parent resource centers in local communities to date.

Cherie Takemoto (Chapter 13) is executive director for the Parent Educational Advocacy Training Center (PEATC) in Virginia. Ms. Takemoto's work at PEATC has focused on inclusion and multicultural issues in early childhood, health care, and special education. Other accomplishments include being a mother to 7-year-old Peter, who approaches his disabilities with a sense of humor and determination, and 9-year-old Margaret, who is a budding poet and scientist.

Mary Beth Bruder (Chapter 14) has been in early intervention for the past 20 years. She began her career as a preschool special educator in Vermont and since then has been involved in the design, provision, and evaluation of early intervention services within a number of states. She received her Ph.D. from the University of Oregon and currently is chief of the Division of Child and Family Studies and a professor of pediatrics at the University of Connecticut School of Medicine. She directs a number of federally funded preservice, in-service, demonstration, and research projects.

Paul Wehman (Chapter 15) is professor at the Department of Physical Medicine and Rehabilitation, Medical College of Virginia and director of the Rehabilitation Research and Training Center at Virginia Commonwealth University. Internationally recognized for his service and scholarly contributions in the fields of special education, psychology, and vocational rehabilitation, Dr. Wehman is the recipient of the 1990 Joseph P. Kennedy Jr. Foundation Award in Mental Retardation and received the Distinguished Service Award from the President's Committee on Employment for Persons With Disabilities in October 1992. He is also editor of the *Journal of Vocational Rehabilitation*. Specific research interests include transition from school to work, supported employment, developmental disabilities, and brain injury.

ABOUT THE ARTISTS

Orville Anderson—Born August 5, 1972
(Chapters 1 and 9)
Orville's paintings evolved from stereotyped landscapes to a personal iconography. Once this happened, he spent 2 years expressing grief over his father's death, which had occurred 10 years earlier. The following 3 years, his paintings predominantly included bird imagery. These paintings represent his psychological exoneration from having shot birds with a BB gun when he was a young boy.

Pierre Anthony—Born April 3, 1983
(Chapters 8 and 15)
Pierre first came to the studio when his parents were in the throes of getting a divorce. Hence, the unity of pairs punctuates his landscapes and seascapes, as seen in the coupling of figures and pairing of inanimate objects such as balloons and trees. His largest painting, *Unity of the World*, appears on the cover of this book.

Abraham Daniel—Born November 2, 1975
(Chapters 2, 7, and 11)
At the age of 9, Abraham fell three stories from a scaffold, sustaining a neurological spinal injury. He was comatose for 33 days and doctors told his mother that his chances of living were slim. Later, she was advised he would live, but would never walk again—that he was quadriplegic. However, Abraham not only won the battle against the odds for survival, but he subsequently overcame wheelchair confinement, initiated while struggling to stand and paint a large canvas. Thus, he has been dubbed by the press as "The Miracle Kid." As Abraham demonstrates, this intensity of focus and concentration on painting simultaneously contribute to his own well-being and to the production of remarkable works of art.

David Hill—Born March 2, 1979
(Chapter 10 and Epilogue)
Soon after coming to the studio, David painted *Red Mountain*, which was his breakthrough painting. Using his vivid imagination to the fullest, he continued to do superb paintings. In 1993, he moved to the state of Washington for a year. Upon his return to Harlem and the art studio, he was out of sync with both his environment and his creative efforts. After about 8 agonizing months, he did his second breakthrough painting, *Lost Paradise*.

Akbar Muhammad—Born July 7, 1979
(Chapter 5)
Akbar was brought to the art studio by her sister, who had been a patient at the hospital. As in this case, many outpatients and ex-patients return to the art studio with their brothers or sisters. Eventually, four of the Muhammad children attended art classes and all were included in exhibitions.

Nelson Rivera—Born July 14, 1978
(Chapters 3 and 14)
Nelson, whose paintings are usually brooding, somber, and poetic, was brought to the studio by a social worker. He has developed a metaphysical and surreal visual vocabulary that usually displays the tranquillity of everyday scenes punctuated with abrupt, unexpected images.

Karima Sappe—Born November 9, 1978
(Chapter 13)
Of all the H.H.A.S. artists, Karima's sensibility is most akin to the typical folk art aesthetic, which combines symmetrical arrangements, patterning, flat spaces, and naive charm. Her subject matter is also personal: her school, her kitchen, her living room.

Gregory Smith—Born October 2, 1969
(Chapters 4, 6, and 12)
Gregory has been attending art classes at Harlem Hospital for 7 years. He is a sickle cell anemia outpatient who had a partially paralyzing stroke as a child in Jamaica. Subsequently, he was developmentally delayed. Doctors attribute Gregory's "awakening"—his physical, mental, and social growth—to his artistic involvement. His paintings are always reinventions of the Jamaican landscape.

TABLE OF CONTENTS

Chapter 1

Harlem of Love, acrylic on canvas, 48″ × 48″ (1993)

SETTING THE STAGE

JUDY W. WOOD
ANDREA M. LAZZARI

After studying this chapter, the reader will:

Be able to trace the historical development of
services for persons with disabilities

Know about some of the most important legal
aspects of special education

Be familiar with different terminology used to refer to disabilities

Define and describe special education and related services

Identify placement options for students with disabilities

Understand the benefits of special education programs

Identify the incidence and prevalence of persons with disabilities

Address the changes in perspectives for persons with disabilities

SETTING THE STAGE

Ancient times–Reformation	Individuals with disabilities were thought to be possessed and were feared, shunned, and often put to death.
Late 1700s	Special schools were established in Europe for some disabilities (deafness, blindness, mental retardation).
Colonial America	Individuals with disabilities were cared for at home, blended into communities.
1800s	Residential programs for people who were deaf or blind were established in the U.S.; special classes for students with mental retardation were developed in some schools.
Early 1900s	The Industrial Revolution brought about the social reform movement and more humane treatment of all individuals with disabilities.
1901	The mental measurement movement began with development of first IQ test; the nature versus nurture debate began.
Post–World War I	The field of rehabilitation began in response to the return of soldiers with disabilities.
1960s	The civil rights movement began, advocating equal rights for everyone, including those with disabilities.
1970s	The normalization movement called for services for people with mental retardation to parallel peers' services.
1973	Section 504 of the Vocational Rehabilitation Act prohibited exclusion of persons with disabilities from programs receiving federal funds.
1975	The Education for All Handicapped Children Act (P.L. 94-142) established the right to a free, appropriate public education in the least restrictive environment for children with disabilities.
1984	The Carl Perkins Vocational Education Act ensured vocational plans for students with disabilities.
1990	The Americans With Disabilities Act (ADA) established accessibility to public transportation and accommodations as well as fair employment for persons with disabilities; P.L. 94-142 was revised and called the Individuals With Disabilities Education Act (IDEA).
1992	Students with attention deficit hyperactivity disorders were added under Section 504 and served with Section 504 plans.

INTRODUCTION

Debbie was born in 1951, part of the post–World War II baby boom. Looking back over her school years during the 1950s and 1960s, Debbie can recall only one fellow student with a disability: a girl who wore a leg brace as a result of polio. Debbie does not remember seeing anyone with a disability in her neighborhood or community, except for the man without legs who sat on a small platform on wheels, collecting spare change from the shoppers downtown.

How different Debbie's experiences are from those of her daughter. Jennifer entered kindergarten in 1985, a decade after the landmark legislation P.L. 94–142 (Education for All Handicapped Children Act of 1975), which mandated public education for students with disabilities. Jennifer is accustomed to interacting with students with disabilities in her school building and some of her classes, as well as during community activities. In restaurants, at church, at the mall, and on the bus, Jennifer sees individuals with disabilities participating in a variety of activities. Persons with disabilities are positively portrayed in books, movies, television shows, and even commercials. While Jennifer notices that these individuals are in some ways different from her, their presence in her environment is not unusual.

Why are Debbie's and Jennifer's experiences so different? What events—social and legal—occurred in the 30-year span between their generations to result in such changes? Are their experiences unique or are these changes evident in all communities? This chapter will provide an answer to these questions, as the stage is set for learning about exceptional individuals.

HISTORICAL OVERVIEW OF SPECIAL EDUCATION

In many endeavors, knowing where you've been is almost as important as knowing where you're going. An awareness of the history underlying a professional field helps us understand why events have unfolded as they have or why more progress has not been made in a certain area. In the field of disabilities, a look at history allows us to realize the powerful influence that political, social, and economic events have had on the treatment of persons with disabilities and the services available to them. It can also prevent us from repeating our mistakes and, hopefully, provide us with some direction for the future. Recognizing the influence that the history of the field of disabilities has on current practice and future directions, each chapter in this text is introduced with a historical overview, allowing the reader to gain a "then and now" perspective.

The history of the field of disabilities is fraught with examples of neglect, abuse, and mistreatment of individuals with disabilities stemming from ignorance, fear, and superstition. In ancient times, many infants with disabilities did not survive. If they did, they were frequently killed or left to die. People feared "catching" disabilities from others. Some individuals with disabilities (e.g., epilepsy) were thought to be possessed and were feared, shunned, and often put to death. Certainly, they were at the mercy of others, often reduced to begging for their subsistence. In some cases, persons with disabilities were used as fools or court jesters to entertain the nobility.

During the Renaissance and Reformation, persecution of people with disabilities continued. They were often thought to be possessed by the devil. They were treated cruelly, and in some cases tortured and killed. Some individuals with

In ancient times, people with disabilities were neglected, abused, or mistreated.

disabilities were placed in hospitals or workhouses, where deplorable conditions resulted in high death rates among the residents.

As Christianity spread throughout Europe some progress was made in developing a scientific understanding of disabilities, but for the most part, people with disabilities continued to be pitied. One positive influence during this period was the development of an ethic of helping those who were less fortunate. As a result, a few religious orders and wealthy citizens established protective homes and residential institutions. During the late 1700s and early 1800s, special schools for some disabilities (deafness, blindness—and later, mental retardation) began to be established in Europe. These schools were headed by medical doctors and followed a medical model of care and treatment.

In the United States, a variety of events supported or interfered with the growth and advancement of services for persons with disabilities. In the colonial period, people cared for their family members with disabilities at home. Since many people were illiterate, many individuals with mild disabilities blended right into their communities. Prior to the early 1800s, many persons with disabilities were not identified as such and, if they were, no special services were available to them. After that time, however, the influence of the development of programs in Europe began to be felt—and residential programs for persons who were deaf or blind began to be established in this country in the early 1800s. By the late 1800s, special classes for students with mental retardation were developed in some school districts. However, it was also during this time that residential facilities were growing in size and number. By the end of the century, the professions of special education and clinical psychology were established and programs to train and certify teachers were beginning.

In the late 1800s and early 1900s numerous events began to lay the groundwork for the development of appropriate services for students with disabilities. The

Industrial Revolution started a landslide of jobs for American workers, including children. As a result of abuses of children in the nation's factories, the social reform movement began. Calls for reform led to child labor laws that were established to prevent the overwork and abuse of the nation's children. The focus of the social reform movement was not, however, limited to children working in factories. Calls for more humane treatment of all individuals, including those with disabilities, were also beginning to be heard.

A look at the status of persons with disabilities in the early part of this century reveals many contrasts. Institutions were still a common placement for many individuals with disabilities, and limited growth of special education classes continued. These classes were primarily found in separate schools and targeted slow learners and children who were deaf or blind.

By 1901, the mental measurement movement, led by Alfred Binet and his student Théodore Simon, began with the development of the first intelligence quotient (IQ) scale. These scientific measurements of intelligence were, however, often misused to prevent children with mental retardation from entering school. During this period, the great controversy of nature versus nurture came to the forefront. How was intelligence determined? Was it determined by heredity (nature) or did the environment (nurture) make the difference? And could the effects of the environment compensate for heredity, or was intelligence a fixed rather than alterable characteristic?

During this same period there was a great interest in heredity and its role in mental illness, mental retardation, and criminal and immoral behavior. This fueled a movement to isolate such individuals from society, typically by placing them in large residential institutions. Many people with disabilities were involuntarily placed in institutions where the mission was not education or rehabilitation but solely that of providing minimal custodial care. Another movement during this period was for sterilization of persons with disabilities to protect society from the spread of deviance. Often, sterilization was performed involuntarily, and in many cases without even informing the individual of the purpose of the procedure.

The focus on these key issues at the turn of the century was interrupted by World War I. After the war, the focus shifted to rehabilitating wounded soldiers, including those with physical disabilities and brain injury. How would Americans care for the physical and emotional wounds received by soldiers in combat? In response to this need, the field of rehabilitation (therapeutic and medical) was begun. Specialized rehabilitation hospitals for veterans were established in several parts of the country and new techniques were developed to meet the needs of veterans with a variety of disabilities.

Unfortunately, the progress that was under way in the fields of rehabilitation and special education came to a halt in the 1920s and 1930s, when the Great Depression paralyzed the country. It brought a standstill in funding for many social and educational programs and services, including those for adults and children with disabilities.

Then, after World War II there was a renewed need for programs and services for individuals with disabilities. Veterans were once again in need of rehabilitation services. As enlisted men and women returned to their communities and began having children, the nation's attention was focused on the needs of children and families, although children with disabilities were still excluded from many of the nation's schools.

By 1960, the civil rights movement began to dominate the need for change in our country. Society began to realize that all citizens, including those with

Table 1.1   **Court Cases Setting the Stage for Change**

CASE	DATE	RULING	SIGNIFICANCE TO INDIVIDUALS WITH DISABILITIES
Brown v. Board of Education of Topeka	1954	Free public education cannot be denied based on race or creed.	A progressive avalanche of legal cases and laws ensued, slowly establishing equal rights for persons with disabilities.
Hobson v. Hansen	1967	Practice of tracking within schools is found discriminatory.	A single IQ score could no longer be used to group (track) students.
Pennsylvania Association for Retarded Citizens v. Commonwealth of Pennsylvania	1972	Commonwealth of Pennsylvania cannot deny any child with mental retardation access to a free public education.	Students with mental retardation previously denied equal access to education based on an IQ score determined by the school psychologist were provided a free and equal education as received by their peers without disabilities.
Mills v. Board of Education of District of Columbia	1972	District of Columbia must extend rights to all students with physical, mental, or emotional disabilities.	Free public education must be provided to all students with disabilities.
		Due process must be provided.	Students are entitled to a hearing before they can be excluded from a class within the school, or placed in an alternative placement.
Burlington School Committee v. Department of Education	1984	Public school systems may be required to pay tuition at private schools.	If it can be proved that a public school system is not providing an appropriate education, tuition for education at a private school may be required.
Honig v. Doe	1988	School systems cannot deny an education to students whose disruptive behavior is related to a disability.	When a school expels a student, this is a change of placement; placement cannot be changed without parental permission.

disabilities, had the basic right of access to equal opportunities. A key issue was not merely the development and provision of services, but also the provision of services to all who were in need of them. Parents became more educated about their rights, resulting in organized advocacy groups for students with disabilities.

Supported by key legislation that was passed in the 1970s, students with disabilities gained the right to equal access to educational opportunities and special education programs began to be widely available in the nation's public schools. Major legislation began to be passed supporting this change (see Table 1.1). The 1970s also saw the beginning of the **normalization movement,** a philosophy calling for services (both settings and procedures) for persons with mental retardation to more closely parallel those provided to their peers in the community. The goal of this movement, which has been extended to other disability areas as well, was for persons with disabilities, regardless of the nature or severity of their disabilities, to be integrated both physically and socially into the mainstream of society (Wolfensberger, 1972).

Because of state and federal legislation, children with disabilities can now be educated alongside their peers without disabilities.

Paralleling the growth of special education programs and services in the nation's public schools was the increased need for trained professionals to provide these services. The decades from the 1970s to the 1990s realized significant growth in the number of personnel preparation programs in special education fields available in the nation's colleges and universities. In 1975, approximately 600 institutions of higher education provided training in education of students with disabilities. By 1995, this number had grown to 713 (National Clearinghouse for Special Education, personal communication, June 1, 1995). In spite of the growth in training programs, however, shortages of trained personnel in special education and related fields have been and continue to be a significant problem in some areas of the country, particularly rural areas.

By 1986, a major movement to include all students with disabilities in regular education settings sounded across the country. This movement became known as the **Regular Education Initiative (REI).** The REI was an organized effort to blend regular and special education or at least reduce the physical and curricular boundaries between the two settings. The responsibility for all students would become a shared responsibility between general and special education teachers. The invisible but solid boundaries, established over many years, would now diminish.

CHANGE AND LEGISLATION

It is helpful to understand how laws are determined. For any federal law, a standard procedure is followed. A bill may originate in either the House of Representatives or the Senate (unless it deals with taxes or spending, in which case it must originate in the House). Very simply, after the bill is introduced it progresses from committee to the full House or Senate. If approved, it goes to the other congressional body; and if approved there, it goes to the President. When a bill is passed by

Congress and officially signed into law by the President, it is given a number. For example, consider P.L. 94-142: The "P.L." stands for Public Law, the "94" indicates that the law was passed by the 94th Congress, and the "142" specifies that it was the 142nd public law that the 94th Congress enacted (National Association of State Mental Retardation Program Directors, 1992).

Why is it important for individuals to be aware of federal laws? According to a Louis Harris (1989) poll, 61% of parents know very little about their rights under P.L. 94-142 and P.L. 93-112 (to be discussed later). A majority of educators, principals, and teachers felt that they were not adequately trained in special education. The National Information Center for Children and Youth With Disabilities stresses that an understanding of laws affecting individuals with disabilities is important for the following reasons:

> Knowledge of the language and intention of these laws empowers families to advocate more effectively for their children and strengthens their ability to participate fully as partners in their children's educational teams.
>
> As independence and self-sufficiency for individuals become increasingly important outcomes of special education, it is important that individuals with disabilities understand the law and its implications for making decisions.
>
> Knowledge of the law can assist professionals in understanding the entire service delivery system, ensure protection of civil rights, and improve collaboration with other agencies and families.
>
> Knowledge of the law can help parents and professionals work together on behalf of children to make the equal education opportunity guaranteed by law a reality. (1993, p. 6)

Major Legislation Affecting Individuals With Disabilities

Numerous laws have been passed that have helped make the United States a better place for individuals with disabilities. Specifically, five pieces of legislation to be discussed here have been the impetus for societal change: Section 504 of the Vocational Rehabilitation Act of 1973 (P.L. 93-112); the Education for All Handicapped Children Act of 1975 (P.L. 94-142), amended in 1990 and called IDEA (P.L. 101-476); the Americans With Disabilities Act of 1990 (P.L. 101-336); and the 1990 reauthorization of the Carl D. Perkins Vocational Education Amendments.

Section 504 of the Vocational Rehabilitation Act of 1973 (P.L. 93-112). Section 504, although only a single paragraph in the text of the law, continues to have a significant impact in the lives of individuals with disabilities. This law applies to all Americans with disabilities, regardless of age; therefore, it applies to all children with disabilities, ages 3 to 21, with respect to their public education. Section 504 states:

> No qualified handicapped person shall, on the basis of handicap, be excluded from participation in, be denied benefits of, or otherwise be subjected to discrimination under any program or activity which receives or benefits from Federal financial assistance. A recipient, in providing any aid, or service, may not, directly or through contractual licensing, or other arrangement, on the basis of handicap, deny a qualified handicapped person the opportunity to participate in or benefit from the aid, benefit, or service. Additionally, a qualified handicapped person may not be limited in the enjoyment of any right, privilege, advantage, or opportunity enjoyed by others receiving an aid, benefit, or service. (Vocational Rehabilitation Act, 1973)

Within the public schools, Section 504 provides additional rights for students with disabilities and also covers students who need assistance but are not covered under P.L. 94-142 or its amendment, IDEA. According to Huefner (1994) these children may be classified into three groups: (1) the age-eligible student who has a physical or mental disability that limits a major life activity such as seeing, hearing, breathing, walking, speaking, caring for oneself, working, or learning (including children with AIDS, attention deficit disorder, asthma, and those who are temporarily homebound); (2) students with a history of physical or mental disabilities (e.g., leukemia); and (3) those children who are wrongly regarded by society as disabled (e.g., students with epilepsy, facial disfigurements, etc.).

According to Huefner (1994) discrimination against students with disabilities in the public school occurs when a student with a disability is barred from any extracurricular services, denied course credit for absenteeism, expelled for misbehavior, refused medication, or refused bus transportation because of the disability. Further, the school must provide information regarding special provisions of college board examinations and modifications in minimum competency or graduation exams, when doing so would allow measurement of proficiency in the competency being measured rather than measurement of the disability itself.

In postsecondary settings, where P.L. 94-142 does not apply, Section 504 has opened doors that have traditionally been closed for students with disabilities. Recruitment, admission, and postadmission treatment for individuals with disabilities must be nondiscriminatory and "reasonable adjustments" must be made. Modifications necessary for academic performance must be provided—such as more time on tests, oral reading of tests, copies of class notes, and other adjustments. Auxiliary aids necessary for the student with a disability to receive the same education as any peers without disabilities must be provided—including taped texts, interpreters, readers, and so forth. All campus programs and activities must be accessible.

Education for All Handicapped Children Act of 1975 (P.L. 94-142). P.L. 94-142, although signed into law 2 years after Section 504, was the wake-up call for public schools in America to serve children with disabilities. The law started into motion a movement that even today continues to impact the lives of students with disabilities and their families.

P.L. 94-142 contains numerous mandates that dramatically changed the delivery of services to students with disabilities. It focuses on individualization of instruction in special education and related services. P.L. 94-142 established five major components that have a direct effect on children with disabilities:

1. Right to a free and appropriate public education

2. Nondiscriminatory evaluation

3. Procedural due process

4. Individualized education program (IEP)

5. Least restrictive environment

Free and appropriate public education means that children with disabilities must be allowed to attend public schools at public expense. In the past, school districts frequently denied this basic right to students with disabilities. After P.L. 94-142, students with disabilities not only have the right to attend a local school, but also to receive services that support their education in general education classes.

Nondiscriminatory evaluation attempts to eliminate errors in the classification and placement of students suspected to have disabilities. The fundamental intent of this provision is to eliminate discrimination based on cultural background, race, or disability. The law requires that agencies involved with the evaluation of students suspected of having a disability ensure the following conditions:

1. Trained personnel must administer validated tests and other evaluation materials, and provide and administer such materials in the child's native language or other mode of communication.

2. Tests and other evaluation material must include those tailored to assess specific areas of education and not merely those designed to provide single, general intelligence quotients.

3. Trained personnel must select and administer tests to accurately reflect the child's aptitude or achievement level without discriminating against the child's disability.

4. Trained personnel cannot use a single procedure as the sole criterion for determining an appropriate educational program for a child.

5. A multidisciplinary team must assess the child in all areas related to the suspected disability.

Procedural due process guarantees safeguards to children with disabilities and their parents in all areas relating to identification, evaluation, and educational practice. Prior to P.L. 94-142, a child with a suspected disability could be evaluated and placed in a special education class without parent notification or permission. A parent may not have even known that the child was in a separate or special class. The law provides for the following due process safeguards:

1. Written parental permission is required for the evaluation of a child for special education services.

2. Written parental permission is required prior to the placement of a child in a special education program—permission that may be withdrawn at any point.

3. Parents have the right to review and question any records on their child.

4. Parents have the right to an independent educational evaluation of their child.

5. Confidentiality in all matters relating to the child must be maintained.

6. Parents, as well as school officials, have the right to a hearing, to present evidence, to have a lawyer present at the hearing, and to call and confront witnesses.

7. Both parents and school authorities have the right to an appeal.

Individualized Education Programs (IEPs) are communication tools used by parents and school personnel and are major vehicles for resolving differences between the school and parent. This written commitment lists resources and related services to be provided and also serves as a compliance/monitoring device for state and local education officials to determine a child's progress toward stated outcomes. Specific components required in an IEP include the following written statements:

WASHINGTON COUNTY PUBLIC SCHOOLS
SPECIAL EDUCATION DEPARTMENT

INDIVIDUALIZED EDUCATION PROGRAM

NAME ___Michael Jones___   Location of Sp. Ed. Program (School) ___Roosevelt___   Grade ___4___

DOB ___6/20/86___   Date of Projected Triennial Evaluation ___3/26/96___   This IEP will be in effect from ___9/5/95___ to ___6/12/96___

Identified Disability ___Learning Disability___   Student Identification Number ___384___   Home School ___Roosevelt___

TYPE OF PROGRAM

___	Mild mental disability
___	Moderate mental disability
_X_	Learning disabilities
___	Visual impairment
___	Speech/language impairment
___	Hearing impairment
___	Severe mental disability
___	Emotional/behavioral disability
___	Preschool (non categorical)
___	Orthopedic impairment
___	Other(s) specify

TYPE OF CLASS

(LEAST RESTRICTIVE ENVIRONMENT)

_X_ Self-contained
(50% or more time in sp. ed. class)

___ Resource
(49% or less of time in sp. ed. class)

___ Other

AMOUNT OF TIME

	MIN/HOURS PER DAY/WK	TIME/ WEEK	% OF TIME IN SP. ED.
	3 hrs./day	5 days/wk	52%

SPECIAL EDUCATION & RELATED SERVICES

	INITIATION/DURATION		LOCATION OF SERVICE	PROVIDER OF SERVICE	MIN/HOURS PER DAY/WK	% OF TIME THIS SERVICES
Self-contained LD	9/5/95	6/12/96	Roosevelt Elementary	LD Teacher	3 hrs./day	52%
	/	/				
	/	/				
					TOTAL:	52%

Transportation _X_ Regular   ___ Special (describe): ___

DESCRIPTION OF EXTENT TO WHICH STUDENT WILL PARTICIPATE IN REGULAR EDUCATION PROGRAMS
(General Education Subjects and/or Nonacademic Activities)

All fourth grade activities   Field Trips
as appropriate.   Assemblies
TAG, SODA, Computer Lab, Art,
Music, Library, Lunch,
Homeroom, Math, Science,
Social Studies, Health/PE,
Family Life

ADAPTATIONS WITHIN REGULAR CLASSROOM

Decrease the amount of written work
Decrease number of vocabulary/spelling words
Allow more time to complete written assignments
Peer tutoring for content area reading
Extra Computer Lab time
Allow oral answers instead of written ones in content
   area tests

Does the program described above ensure 5½ hours of instruction or training per day?   Yes _X_   No ___   If no, state reason: ___

PRESENT ASSESSMENT

Student's Name   Michael Jones

****

PRESENT LEVEL OF EDUCATIONAL PERFORMANCE: Accurately describe the effect of the child's disability on the child's performance in any area of education that is affected including academic areas and non-academic areas written in objective measurable terms. Test scores should be self-explanatory or an explanation should be included. There should be a direct relationship between the present level of performance and other components of the IEP.

EDUCATIONAL TESTING RESULTS (Date of Testing: 5/3/95)

Test Data: Woodcock-Johnson Tests of Achievement-R

Letter Word Identification - 2.0   Applied Problems - 5.8   Science - 6.0
Passage Comprehension - 2.4   Dictation - 2.0   Social Studies - 5.8
Calculation - 4.0   Writing Samples - 2.0   Humanities - 4.2

Strengths: General knowledge and verbal skills are excellent. Has participated in the TAG program for the past two years. He has a very good imagination and uses high order thinking skills. Has a pleasant disposition and is a real joy to work with. He has maintained good grades in math, science, and social studies in the 3rd grade class with minimal assistance from the LD teacher.

Weaknesses: Word attack skills and reading are well below expected levels. His spelling is very weak as well and this interferes with writing ability. Handwriting is legible but he needs to work on size and spacing and letter formation especially in cursive. Needs to work on his multiplication facts to make division and long division easier.

Present Classroom Performance: Reading has improved to allow him to read in the three-two reading book with some assistance. He is attempting larger words with success and comprehension is good. Has maintained a C average in third grade math, and satisfactory grades in science, social studies, and health with minimal help from the LD teacher.

Learning Style: Learns best through a multisensory approach. Visual cues should accompany oral directions. Works best in a structured environment with limited distractions. He has some difficulty staying on task and completing assignments.

Nonacademic Areas/Other: Has low self-esteem. He is very aware of his reading disability. He feels the other students don't like him though no evidence exists to support his feelings. Is very sensitive and emotional. He has a wonderful home environment and lots of family support.

Student's Name _____ Michael Jones _____

ANNUAL GOAL (Indicate goal number only): 3   **Area of Instruction/Activity:** Written Language: will increase his written language skills.

SHORT TERM OBJECTIVE:
Given a weekly spelling list, will spell the words with 80% accuracy.

HOME COMPONENT:

EVALUATION: CRITERIA	80%		**PROCEDURE** dictated spelling tests	
SCHEDULE/FREQUENCY	weekly		**DATE INITIATED** 9/5/95	**DATE MASTERED**
GRADING PERIOD:	1	2	3	4	5	**6 COMMENTS**

****

ANNUAL GOAL (Indicate goal number only): 3   **Area of Instruction/Activity:** Written Language

SHORT TERM OBJECTIVE:
When given a topic, stimulus, or story starter, will write a logical, sequential, multi-sentence story.

HOME COMPONENT:

EVALUATION: CRITERIA	80% before edit		**PROCEDURE** teacher evaluation of stories	
SCHEDULE/FREQUENCY	weekly		**DATE INITIATED** 9/5/95	**DATE MASTERED**
GRADING PERIOD:	1	2	3	4	5	**6 COMMENTS**

****

ANNUAL GOAL (Indicate goal number only): 3   **Area of Instruction/Activity:** Written Language

SHORT TERM OBJECTIVE:
Given reading skills practice activities commonly introduced on the fourth grade level, will complete activities accurately with reading assistance.

HOME COMPONENT:

EVALUATION: CRITERIA	75%		**PROCEDURE** workbook summary quizzes	
SCHEDULE/FREQUENCY	weekly		**DATE INITIATED** 9/5/95	**DATE MASTERED**
GRADING PERIOD:	1	2	3	4	5	**6 COMMENTS**

****

ANNUAL GOAL (Indicate goal number only): 3   **Area of Instruction/Activity:** Written Language

SHORT TERM OBJECTIVE:
When given written work, will write legibly in cursive within a reasonable amount of time.

HOME COMPONENT:

EVALUATION: CRITERIA	teacher assessment		**PROCEDURE** teacher evaluation of written work samples	
SCHEDULE/FREQUENCY	daily		**DATE INITIATED** 9/5/95	**DATE MASTERED**
GRADING PERIOD:	1	2	3	4	5	**6 COMMENTS**

****

Short term objectives will be monitored at each marking period according to the following progress key:
NO MARK – Objective not Initiated   P – Progressing on the Objective   M – Objective Mastered
D – Having Difficulty with Objective (comments to describe difficulty)   M/R – Objective Mastered (but needs review to maintain)

IP CONTACT RECORD:

DATE: 6/6/95

TYPE OF CONTACT letter

COMMENTS meeting held

TEACHER Kamler

I.E.P. MEETING PARTICIPANTS

SIGNATURE	POSITION	DATE SIGNED
Glenet Jones	Parent	6 / 7 / 95
Brenda Brooks	School Administrator/Designee	6 / 7 / 95
Wayne Hart	Special Education Teacher	6 / 7 / 95
P.J. Viger	(General Educational) Classroom Teacher	6 / 7 / 95
	ASE/Designee	/ /
	Student (as appropriate)	/ /
	Other	/ /
	Other	/ /

I understand the contents of this document and I have received a copy of this IEP. I understand that I have the right to review my child's records and to request a change in the IEP at any time. I also understand that I have the right to refuse this placement and to have my child continue his/her present placement pending exhaustion of my due process rights. I have received a copy of procedural safeguards including prior notice and due process. I have been informed of my rights by reading them, or having them read to me, and I understand them as explained to me.

✓ I give permission for my child to be enrolled in the special education program described in this
Individualized Education Program (IEP)

_*Glenet Jones*_____   _6 / 6 / 95_
Signature of Parent(s)/Guardian(s) or Surrogate   Month Day Year

____ I do not give permission for my child to be enrolled in the special education program described in this Individualized Education Program (IEP). I understand that action will not take place without my permission.

_____   _ / /_
Signature of Parent(s)/Guardian(s) or Surrogate   Month Day Year

Parent consent is necessary for the types of the IEPs listed below. Please check as appropriate.

____ Initial Placement

____ Addition of special education services

____ Addition of related services

____ Change in disability

____ Change to or from services outside Washington County

____ Change in placement (service delivery)

✓ Annual review

CONFIDENTIAL PERMANENT RECORD: DO NOT DESTROY THIS DOCUMENT

1. The student's present levels of educational performance (i.e., strengths, weaknesses, and learning styles in academic, social, behavioral and other areas)

2. Annual goals (i.e., what the student can reasonably be expected to achieve in a year)

3. Short-term instructional objectives (i.e., intermediate, sequential steps leading from the present level of performance and ending at the annual goals)

4. Specific educational services to be provided and the extent of the child's participation in regular education settings and programs

5. Specific related services to be provided

6. Projected dates for initiation and anticipated duration of services

7. How progress toward objectives will be evaluated and on what schedule

The IEP must be revised annually for all students receiving special education services. It may be revised more often if necessary.

The **least restrictive environment (LRE)** refers to the physical placement of the student. The law requires that a child be placed with his or her peers without disabilities as much as possible. Over the years, numerous models have been presented of the various settings where a student may receive services.

Individuals With Disabilities Education Act of 1990 (P.L. 101-476). In 1990, P.L. 94-142 was amended and renamed. The requirements of P.L. 94-142 remained and were expanded. Major provisions in IDEA include these:

1. All references to "handicapped children" are changed to "children with disabilities."

2. Two new categories of disabilities were added—"Autism" and "Traumatic Brain Injury."

3. The definitions of "assistive technology device" and "assistive technology service" were added.

4. "Transition services" were added and defined as follows:

A coordinated set of activities for a student, designed within an outcome-oriented process, which promote movement from school to post-school activities, including post-secondary education, vocational training, integrated employment (including supported employment), continuing and adult education, adult services, independent living, and community participation.

The coordinated set of activities shall be based upon the individual student's needs, taking into account the student's preferences and interests, and shall include instruction, community experiences, the development of employment and other post-school adult living objectives, and when appropriate, acquisition of daily living skills, and functional vocational evaluation (Individuals With Disabilities Education Act, 1990).

Additionally, P.L. 101-476 requires that each student's IEP, beginning no later than age 16 (or younger, if appropriate), must include a statement of needed transition services. If appropriate, a statement should also be included of the responsibilities or linkages of all participating agencies before the student exits the school setting (Individuals With Disabilities Education Act, 1990).

Americans With Disabilities Act of 1990 (P.L. 101-336).   Perhaps no other piece of legislation has had the impact on the lives of Americans with disabilities and their families as did the Americans With Disabilities Act (ADA) of 1990. The purpose of the act is stated as follows:

1. To provide a clear and comprehensive national mandate for the elimination of discrimination against individuals with disabilities;

2. To provide clear, strong, consistent, enforceable standards addressing discrimination against individuals with disabilities;

3. To ensure that the Federal government plays a central role in enforcing the standards established in this Act on behalf of individuals with disabilities; and

4. To invoke the sweep of Congressional authority, including the power to enforce the Fourteenth Amendment and to regulate commerce, in order to address the major areas of discrimination faced day-to-day by people with disabilities. (Americans With Disabilities Act, 1990)

The term *disability* in ADA is defined as a physical or mental impairment that substantially limits that person in some major life activity (such as walking, talking, breathing, or working). It can refer to a person with a record of physical or mental impairment, or a person who is regarded as having such an impairment. Individuals who are current users of illegal drugs would not be considered disabled under ADA.

The Americans With Disabilities Act produced sweeping requirements that made life as well as society more accessible to individuals with disabilities. These provisions include the following:

1. Employers of 15 or more employees may not refuse to hire or promote a person with a disability because of that person's disability, when that person is qualified to perform the job.

2. An employer must make reasonable accommodations for a person with a disability if that accommodation will allow the person to perform the essential functions of the job. (Examples of reasonable accommodations would be making existing facilities accessible, instituting part-time or modified work schedules, modifying equipment devices, or providing qualified readers and interpreters.)

3. New vehicles bought by public transit authorities must be accessible to persons with disabilities. One car per train in existing rail systems must be accessible by July 26, 1994.

4. It is illegal for public accommodations (businesses that are used every day by all people—such as hotels, restaurants, dry cleaners, grocery stores, schools, and parks) to exclude or refuse persons with disabilities. Auxiliary aids and services must be provided (e.g., large print materials, tape recordings, and captioning) unless doing so would be too disruptive or burdensome to the business.

The passage of the Americans With Disabilities Act has paved the way for improved accessibility for individuals with disabilities.

The Americans With Disabilities Act established accessibility guidelines or standards so that individuals with disabilities can have access to areas persons without disabilities take for granted. These guidelines apply to parking, exits, doors, elevators, stairs, ramps, alarms, telephones, drinking fountains, restrooms, and operating mechanisms.

Carl D. Perkins Amendments. Vocational education programs have had federal support since 1917. In 1963, the Vocational Education Act (P.L. 88-210) created broad-scale authority for assisting states in developing vocational plans for America's youth. The Carl D. Perkins Vocational Education Act of 1984 expanded this legislation, but in 1990 sweeping changes were made under a new bill, the Reauthorization of the Carl D. Perkins Vocational Education and Applied Technology Amendments (P.L. 101-392).

The 1990 reauthorization designated that federal funds must be used to integrate academics and vocational education. Further, these funds are to be distributed directly to localities instead of the state, and programs must also focus on students who are disadvantaged.

TERMINOLOGY

A variety of terms have been used over the centuries to denote disabilities and to describe persons with disabilities: crippled, defective, feebleminded, disordered, handicapped, disabled, special, exceptional, and physically or mentally challenged. Labels such as these, and others that are more derogatory, have been used to identify people who differ from the norm because of their physical or mental abilities.

In some cases, labels have been used to discriminate against groups or individuals or to exclude them from a range of educational, social, and economic opportunities. Four common labels that continue to be used by the general public are (1) disorder, (2) disability, (3) handicap, and (4) exceptional. Each of these terms has a different connotation. A **disorder** is a broad term used to refer generally to an impairment of mental, physical, or psychological processes, such as a hearing or mental disorder. A **disability** refers to a reduced function or loss of a body part or organ affecting one or more of a person's major life activities, such as a learning disability or blindness. When a person with a disability encounters a problem or limitation when interacting with the environment, the disability becomes a **handicap.** For example, being deaf only becomes a handicap when the smoke alarm cannot be heard, or having a speech impairment may only be a handicap if the person must deliver a lecture. The term **exceptional** is used to refer to individuals who differ from the norm in some way; thus, it can refer to individuals who are gifted as well as individuals with disabilities. These terms are not, however, exclusive of one another. An individual could be both gifted and disabled, such as a student with a learning disability who is also gifted.

Over the years, terminology has changed, as have preferences for use of terms. Many people with disabilities now feel that the term *handicapped* is negative because it implies that a person has a disadvantage, such as when a handicap is allowed in certain sports.

As a result of advocacy and awareness efforts in recent years, a new emphasis has been placed on the use of acceptable terminology—for instance, *disabled* rather than *handicapped* or *disordered*. In addition, use of phrases such as *afflicted with, suffering from,* or *a victim of* in conjunction with the name of a disability is considered inappropriate and thus unacceptable. The success of these efforts is reflected in professional and popular literature as well as in legislation. One of the provisions of the Individuals With Disabilities Education Act of 1990 (P.L. 101-476) was to eliminate the term *handicap* from federal laws and programs and promote use of the term *disability*. Another emphasis in the law is the use of "person-first" language such as these examples:

person *with* a disability, rather than *disabled person*

student *with* a learning disability, rather than *L.D. student*

people *who are* deaf, rather than *the deaf*

person *with* mental retardation, rather than person *afflicted with* mental retardation

By using person-first language, the emphasis is placed on the person, not the disability. Still, some people feel that the term *disability* itself implies a lack of ability and prefer not to use it, instead emphasizing individual abilities. For example, consider the Center for Human disAbilities in Fairfax, Virginia; ABLEDATA; the National Rehabilitation Information Center in Washington, D.C.; or *Ability*, a magazine that focuses on the accomplishments of people with disabilities. Making this change necessitates a constant vigil as people break old habits. However, the change to person-first language is far more than being trendy or politically correct.

The broad term *disability* encompasses numerous types of specific disabilities. As seen in Table 1.2, the U.S. Department of Education recognizes 12 categories of disability that may qualify a student for special education services. The federal definition for each of the 12 category areas is also listed in the table. Beginning with Chapter 3 of this text, the twelve areas, plus the area of giftedness, are presented.

Table 1.2　**Department of Education Definitions of Children With Disabilities**

1. "Deaf-blindness" means concomitant hearing and visual impairments, the combination of which causes such severe communication and other developmental and educational problems that they cannot be accommodated in special education programs solely for children who are deaf or blind.
2. "Hearing impaired" means a hearing loss whether permanent or fluctuating, which adversely affects a child's educational performance, including deafness.
3. "Mental retardation" means significantly subaverage general intellectual functioning existing concurrently with deficits in adaptive behavior and manifested during the development period, which adversely affects a child's educational performance.
4. "Multiple disabilities" means concomitant impairments (such as mental retardation–orthopedic impairment, etc.), the combination of which causes such severe educational problems that they cannot be accommodated in special education programs solely for one of the impairments. The term does not include children who are deaf-blind.
5. "Orthopedic-impaired" means a severe orthopedic impairment which adversely affects a child's educational performance. The term includes impairment caused by malformation (e.g., clubfoot, absence of some member, etc.), impairments caused by deformity (e.g., poliomyelitis, bone tuberculosis, etc.), and impairments from other causes (e.g., cerebral palsy, amputations, and fractures or burns which cause contractures).
6. "Other health impairment" means having limited strength, vitality or alertness due to chronic or acute health problems such as a heart condition, tuberculosis, rheumatic fever, nephritis, asthma, sickle cell anemia, hemophilia, epilepsy, lead poisoning, leukemia, or diabetes, which adversely affects a child's educational performance.
7. "Serious emotional disturbance" is defined as follows:
   a. The term means a condition exhibiting one or more of the following characteristics over a long period of time and to a marked degree, which adversely affects a child's educational performance:
      (1) An inability to learn which cannot be explained by intellectual, sensory, or health factors;
      (2) An inability to build or maintain satisfactory interpersonal relationships with peers and teachers;
      (3) Inappropriate types of behavior or feelings under normal circumstances;
      (4) A general pervasive mood of unhappiness or depression, or;
      (5) A tendency to develop physical symptoms of fears associated with personal or school problems.
   b. The term includes children who are schizophrenic. The term does not include children who are socially maladjusted, unless it is determined that they have a serious emotional disturbance.
8. "Specific learning disability" means a disorder in one or more of the basic psychological processes involved in understanding or in using language, spoken or written, which may manifest itself in an imperfect ability to listen, think, speak, write, spell, or to do mathematical calculations. The term includes such conditions as perceptual disabilities, minimal brain dysfunction, dyslexia, and developmental aphasia. The term does not include children who have learning problems which are primarily the result of visual, hearing, or motor disabilities, of mental retardation, or of environmental, cultural, or economic disadvantage.
9. "Speech or language impairment" means a communication disorder, such as stuttering, impaired articulation, a language impairment, or a voice impairment, which adversely affects a child's educational performance.
10. "Visual impairment" means a vision loss which, even with correction, adversely affects a child's educational performance. The term includes children both with blindness and partial vision.
11. "Autism" means children with a developmental disability that significantly affects verbal and nonverbal communication and social interaction, that is generally evident before age three, and that adversely affects educational performance.*
12. "Traumatic brain injury" may be caused by one or more of the following: traumas from accidents, falls, assaults, and surgical procedures; infections (i.e., meningitis, encephalitis); strokes and other vascular accidents; anoxia injuries caused by reduction in the oxygen supply to the brain from anesthetic accidents, cardiac arrest, choking and near drowning; tumors of the brain; and toxic exposure (e.g., lead and chemical poisoning).*

*These categories were added in 1990 under IDEA.

Sources: *Federal Register* 42, no. 163 (Aug. 23, 1977), pp. 42478–42479; Individuals With Disabilities Education Act of 1990, 20 U.S.C. Chapter 33 § 140-17.

Labeling and Categorizing

Categorizing or labeling persons with specific disabilities is a controversial issue. While all states must use the categories listed in Table 1.3 when reporting numbers

Table 1.3   **Number and Percentage of Students With Disabilities, Ages 6–21 (School Year 1993–1994)**

DISABILITY	NUMBER	PERCENT
Specific learning disabilities	2,444,020	51.1
Speech or language impairments	1,009,379	21.1
Mental retardation	553,992	11.6
Serious emotional disturbance	414,279	8.7
Multiple disabilities	109,746	2.3
Hearing impairments	64,249	1.3
Orthopedic impairments	56,616	1.2
Other health impairments	83,279	1.7
Visual impairments	24,935	0.5
Autism	18,903	0.4
Deaf-blindness	1,372	0.0
Traumatic brain injury	5,295	0.1
All disabilities	4,786,065	100.0

Source: Data from the *Seventeenth Annual Report to Congress on the Implementation of the Individuals With Disabilities Education Act,* p. 11, by the U.S. Department of Education, Office of Special Education Programs, 1995, Washington, DC: Author.

of students with disabilities to the U.S. Department of Education for the purpose of receiving funds, states may use different approaches to categorizing students for the delivery of services. Several states (e.g., Mississippi, Georgia) and local school divisions have adopted a **noncategorical approach.** Instead of specific *categorical labels,* generic terms are used to refer to the population of students with disabilities (e.g., *mild mental disability* rather than *mentally retarded,* or *mild/moderate needs* and *severe/profound needs* for any category of disability).

Negative Effects of Labeling

Some states have opted for a noncategorical approach because of the perceived negative effects of labeling. A drawback to labeling any group is that individual differences are washed out in the process. By its very nature, the process of labeling focuses on a characteristic that all group members share (e.g., a political belief, a cultural background, a physical trait), obscuring individual differences within the group. For many students with disabilities, their individual identities are often lost to the label and they become known primarily by the label (e.g., the deaf girl, the mentally retarded students). This can result in lowered self-esteem and expectations by teachers, parents, and the students themselves. Sometimes, a label becomes a self-fulfilling prophecy whereby a student fulfills only the lower expectations implied by the label.

Another disadvantage of using labels is that it can result in rejection or ridicule from a student's peers. Unfortunately, we can all recall the names used to refer to our classmates who were different (e.g., Four-Eyes, Brace Face, Carrot Top, and worse). Children who are once labeled by peers or teachers may never be able to shed those labels, regardless of their current abilities or future achievements. This negative and sometimes destructive nature of labels has led many to shun the use of labels in identifying and educating children with disabilities.

Positive Effects of Labeling

There are, however, some instances in which the use of labels can be helpful. The use of common labels can enhance communication among professionals. Those in the fields of education, psychology, rehabilitation, and medicine find it helpful to use common labels to describe physical and behavioral similarities and differences among children and adults for the purposes of both research and practice. Labels enable professionals to identify and deliver services that are tailored to an individual's needs. If, for example, we know that a student has a hearing impairment of a specific type and level, we can provide amplification and educational approaches that are known to provide maximum benefit for his specific disability. Or, if a student is referred for an evaluation because her teacher suspects that she has a learning disability, the focus of the evaluation would be different than if the teacher suspected a visual impairment.

Another possible need for categorical labels is that funding of special education programs is often tied to disability categories, as mentioned earlier. Eligibility for certain medical or social programs or services may be limited only to certain groups (e.g., Supplemental Social Security Income benefits, insurance reimbursement for physical therapy), and individuals may have to be identified as qualifying members of those groups to receive benefits.

Regardless of the pros and cons of using categories or labels to identify individuals with disabilities, as you read the chapters in this text and study each disability, keep sight of the fact that a wide variety of differences exist among individuals within any disability group. While the information in each chapter is accurate and factual, the characteristics presented will not necessarily describe any single individual with that specific disability. Rather, an overview is presented of the typical characteristics associated with a disability group.

INCIDENCE AND PREVALENCE OF PERSONS WITH DISABILITIES

Throughout this text, information will be provided on the incidence and prevalence of the various disabilities in our general population. Incidence and prevalence are terms used to report estimates of the frequency of disabilities. These terms are, however, often confused. **Incidence** refers to the number of new cases identified within a population over a certain period of time and is typically reported in terms of a ratio—such as "a 1 in 500 chance." **Prevalence** is the total number of cases throughout the population that exist at a certain time or in a certain place and is typically reported as a percentage—such as "3% of the population" (Ham, 1990; Patton, Payne, & Beirne-Smith, 1981). Because of the differences in definitions used by various agencies collecting data on disabilities and the overlapping nature of some disabilities (e.g., communication impairments and mental retardation), the incidence and prevalence data available for disabilities usually reflect estimates rather than exact numbers.

Table 1.4 **Types and Roles of Special Education and Related Personnel**

TYPE OF PERSONNEL	ROLES
School social worker	Provides homebased services, conducts home visits; completes the sociological report for the screening committee
Occupational therapist	Provides therapy to improve functional motor outcomes, using purposeful activities
Recreational therapist	Teaches recreational activities to students who cannot attend traditional education classes
Physical therapist	Provides therapy to help develop and maintain useful motor movements
Paraprofessional	Assists the teacher in the classroom; may hold review groups, tend to physical needs, etc.
Physical education teacher	Provides regular, modified, or adaptive physical education
Supervisor/administrator (local education agency)	Establishes local policy and oversees teachers at the local level
Psychologist	Completes psychological report for eligibility committee; may provide counseling
Educational diagnostician	Completes the educational assessment for eligibility committee
Audiologist	Conducts hearing screening, assessment, and auditory training
Speech–language pathologist	Conducts speech–language screening, evaluation and therapy
Work-study coordinator	Sets up co-op program
Vocational education teacher	Teaches classes in vocational subjects (e.g., body mechanics, nursing aide, work and family studies, etc.)

DEFINING SPECIAL EDUCATION

Although this text addresses issues in disabilities from birth through adulthood, emphasis is placed on the school-age child. For this reason, it will be helpful to have a basic understanding of the special education process in our public schools.

Special education and related services are provided by numerous persons, depending on the disability area and services needed. Some students receive services in regular class settings. Others receive services in resource rooms or self-contained classrooms alongside other children with the same disability. Some students may receive more than one service (e.g., resource room services and speech–language therapy) in different settings. Different types of special education and related services personnel and their roles are seen in Table 1.4.

Special Education Compared to General Education

To fully understand what special education is and is not, we can compare it to something we are all familiar with—general education. Table 1.5 presents characteristics of general education and special education programs and shows how these characteristics are similar and different. As new laws are passed and society becomes more accepting of individual differences, these characteristics can be expected to grow closer. Perhaps one day, every student will be viewed individually and curriculum will be paced for the students, rather than striving to cover a predetermined amount of curriculum content by the end of the school year.

Table 1.5 **Similarities and Differences Between Special Education and General Education**

CHARACTERISTIC	SPECIAL EDUCATION	GENERAL EDUCATION
Students must be assessed and found eligible for services.	√	
Teachers must meet certain requirements to teach the class.	√	√
By law, services must meet each student's individual needs.	√	
A student's program must be outlined in written form and agreed to by a committee comprising school personnel and parents.	√	
All students are educated alongside same-age peers in their local school building.		√
Parents have the right to a due process hearing if they don't agree with their child's program.	√	
Teachers are certified in the grade level, subject level, or category level of students served.	√	√
Federal and state guidelines mandate that specific services be provided to eligible students.	√	√
Vast changes to curriculum and service delivery models have occurred over the past decade.	√	√

Working Definitions of Special Education

The federal definition provides a starting point for understanding special education. The definitions of special education used by each state are similar to the federal definition. However, educators and parents have added their personal interpretations to these definitions and insisted that an equal education is not separate but that which is the most appropriate for each child.

While working definitions of special education vary, they share some basic tenets. In a recent survey, 65 general and special educators were asked to define special education in their own words. Overall, these practitioners responded that special education means education for students with special needs who have some type of disability, who are behind academically, or whose needs cannot be met in the general education setting. Another common response was that special education is for meeting the individualized needs of all students in a manner that helps each one reach his or her fullest potential. As one educator summed it up, "Special education means equal opportunity to learn, achieve, socialize, accomplish and overcome. It is an individual's right and ability to receive an appropriate education" (Wood & Lazzari, 1994).

Alternate Definitions of Special Education

Special education is alternately defined as a process, a place for receiving special services, or a method (including a curriculum) of providing instruction.

Special Education as a Process. Special education is a process as well as a service and/or a method of delivering individualized instruction. A specific process or procedure involving sequential steps must be followed before a student can begin to receive special education or related services. This process begins at the first indication that a student may have a disability and continues until the disability and resulting special needs are identified and the student is found eligible for special education services or is found ineligible for such services.

Broad steps of this process from the point of initial identification to eligibility determination and placement for special education services or from initial identification to denial of special education services are presented in Figure 1.1.

Special Education as a Place. In the early years, special education was merely a place. This place was frequently at home or in an institution with no systematic instruction or training and no intervention plan. As the twentieth century progressed, special education was still a place separate from students without disabilities, and frequently in a separate building. It was not uncommon to find this "place called special education" located in school basements or trailers detached from the main building's structure. Frequently, speech–language pathologists conducted therapy sessions with students in small rooms that had formerly been broom closets. Students with disabilities were physically separated from their peers without disabilities, rarely joining them in the cafeteria, on the playground, or for special school events.

Today there are numerous placements available for students with disabilities. The regular class setting is the "goal" for placement for many students with disabilities. All students with disabilities, in accordance with federal law, must be educated in the least restrictive environment possible. For many students this will be in regular education classes. Other students may be most appropriately served in separate classes, while a small percentage of students may require more restrictive settings (e.g., separate facilities) to meet their complex needs.

The topic of where special education services are received is one of national interest, discussion, and frequently heated debates. On one side of the debate the regular education classroom is considered the only "place." However, in different states and localities the placement issue is treated differently depending on resources. Possible settings where services are provided include regular class settings, resource rooms, separate classes, separate schools, residential facilities, and home/hospital placements.

Students who receive the majority of their educational programs in a regular classroom and receive special education and related services outside the regular classroom for less than 21% of a school day are considered to have **regular class placements** (U.S. Department of Education, 1993). During the 1992–1993 school

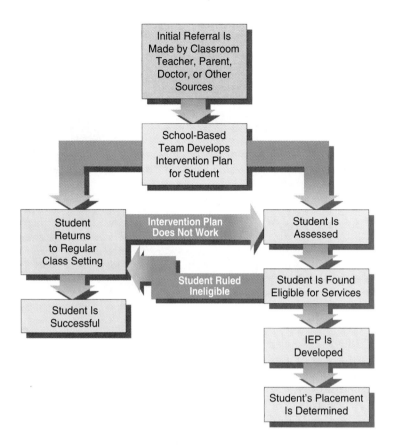

Figure 1.1   **Referral to Placement Process**

year, 39.8% of students with disabilities age 6 through 21 were served in regular class settings (U.S. Department of Education, 1995). Although serving fewer students than resource room placements, this is considered the optimum placement for many students. Students often need modifications or interventions to the regular class curriculum to varying degrees, or they may need a completely different instructional program. However, many consider this placement to be the most desirable because it approximates that which is normal and is more socially appropriate.

Resource room settings, serving 31.7% of students (age 6–21) with disabilities, are the most frequently used settings for delivery of special education services. One reason for this is that many students with learning disabilities—who form the largest special education category—are served in resource rooms. The most common model for resource rooms is the removal of the student to a separate class within the school building to receive services, usually for only a portion of the school day. Students who receive special education and related services outside the regular classroom for at least 21% but no more than 60% of the school day are considered to be served in a resource room setting (U.S. Department of Education, 1995; 1993).

Separate class settings, also known as *self-contained classes,* are located in regular education school facilities, but students receive instruction in separate classes for more than 60% of the school day, usually from a special education teacher (U.S. Department of Education, 1993). This was once a frequently used and popular

Many feel that placement in the regular classroom is the most appropriate environment for students with disabilities.

placement model, yet today is a subject of much controversy. For some students, however, separate class settings provide the lower teacher-to-student ratio and the increased opportunities for individual and small group instruction that they need to succeed. Approximately 23.5% of students with disabilities are served in separate classes (U.S. Department of Education, 1995).

Some students with disabilities (3.7%) receive services in **separate school facilities.** These day schools most commonly are for individuals with significant visual impairments, blindness, deafness, or severe hearing impairments. Students

Some students with disabilities require a self-contained classroom for all or part of their school day.

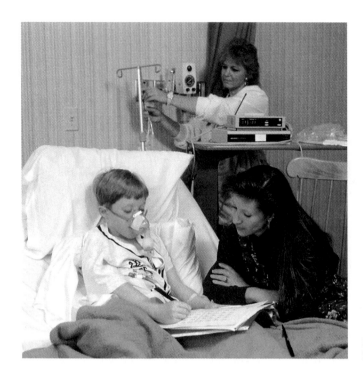

Educational services are brought to students with disabilities who require home or hospital care.

placed in these facilities may need specialized care or services such as training in using braille, mobility training, or intense vocational training. Those who receive special education and related services in a separate school facility for more than 50% of the school day are included in this category (U.S. Department of Education, 1995; 1993).

Residential facilities were once a dumping ground for those with moderate to severe disabilities. Individuals were placed in these facilities without any consideration of their individual needs or the capacity of the institution to meet those needs. Today, these public and private facilities serve students whose needs are extremely intense, who need specialized care, and/or have no appropriate community services available.

Home/hospital placements are used on an as-needed basis. When inbound or homebound medical treatment is required, the educational services are brought to the student. Typically, a teacher will be assigned to come to the hospital or the student's home and provide instruction several hours a day. The goal is for the student to return to school as the student's health status allows.

The ultimate placement goal for all students with disabilities is to be educated in the least restrictive environment (placement) possible. For this reason, each student's placement is reviewed annually (or more often if needed) to determine if it is still appropriate and if the full range of the student's individual needs continue to be met in that setting. Thus, if a student is initially placed in a self-contained classroom at the time he is found eligible for special education and related services, it does not mean that he must remain in that placement for the duration of his school years. Students can and do move from one setting to another, based on their current strengths and needs.

Whereas Table 1.3 provided a breakdown (by disability) of the percentages of school-age students served, Figure 1.2 reports percentages according to placement type.

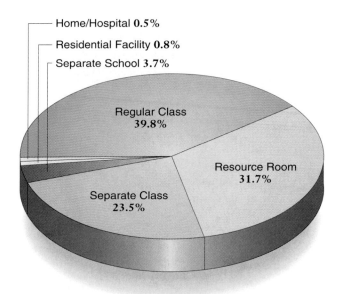

Figure 1.2   **Percentage of Students With Disabilities, Ages 6–21, Served in Six Educational Environments (School Year 1992–1993)**

Source: Data from the *Seventeenth Annual Report to Congress on the Implementation of the Individuals With Disabilities Education Act,* p. 17, by the U.S. Department of Education, Office of Special Education Programs, 1995, Washington, DC: Author.

Special Education as a Method or Curriculum.   For any person to be included in a classroom or in society as a whole, individualization is the key. Classroom curriculum and instructional content must be individualized and all persons must begin to see others as individuals with unique and varied needs.

The 1970s saw special education classes moving physically into regular education buildings, yet curricula remained different. By the 1980s, students in separate special education classes were being carefully and sparsely placed into selected regular education classes. The students who were allowed into the mainstream of general education were typically those with very mild disabilities.

The regular education curriculum slowly began to develop. The transition was under way from "one size fits all" to the possibility of different "sizes" for different students. Modifications to the regular class curriculum became the rule instead of an exception.

The 1990s present the need for vast changes in educational philosophy and practice. Special education and regular education are now aligning not only physically but also instructionally. Increasingly, students with disabilities are receiving their education in regular class settings alongside their peers without disabilities. Students with disabilities are also being included in a range of extracurricular activities, both in school and the community. Perhaps one day America's educational system will be one place for all, yet all will be considered individually.

Mainstreaming, Inclusion, and Individualization

Special education is the where and what of services provided for students with disabilities, and individualization is the key to the where and what. For each student, the place of services as well as the content of services depends on numerous factors.

Initially, when laws were passed in the 1970s and students with disabilities began placements in regular classrooms in the 1980s, the practice of **mainstreaming** began. Students who proved that they could compete with their peers without disabilities were granted the privilege of sitting in regular classes. Individualization of content was not as much a factor as physical placement.

In the 1990s, the concept of mainstreaming evolved to that of **inclusion.** Although greatly debated and widely defined, inclusion is becoming the term of choice and relies greatly on individualization for effective implementation. Inclusion involves students receiving an education in the same place as their peers, bringing needed services to the student and individualizing the information as appropriate for each student. With mainstreaming, on the other hand, students are sent out of the regular class to receive services.

For all students to be totally included within our school systems, each child's program must be individualized and the microsociety of peers within the classroom must be accepting of individual differences. Acceptance of the need for **individualization** by educators within the classroom provides a basis for a more accepting classroom community and, eventually, a more accepting society.

Benefits of Inclusion. Including children who have disabilities provides many benefits to all students: Students with disabilities or those who are gifted may feel more "normal" and develop more friends; students learn to help each other; students learn that all people are more alike than different; and students have opportunities to socialize with classmates with and without disabilities.

Educators also benefit from inclusion. They learn to share various techniques with each other and see that the curriculum for students in general education and that for those with disabilities is not as different as once thought. Most importantly,

Students with disabilities also participate in extracurricular activities with their peers without disabilities.

As service options improve during the school years, many students with disabilities are going on to successful experiences in college.

everyone is learning that removing a student from the mainstream of education may not necessarily be the best option for every student.

The community may reap the greatest benefits of integrating students with disabilities. As students develop more understanding and accepting attitudes, they, in turn, will grow into adults who are more open-minded regarding individual differences. As we wait for this growth of students, we can already see within communities advocacy groups becoming more active and outspoken on issues that have generally been addressed only by PTAs, church groups, and similar organizations. As society recognizes that community inclusion is an extension of the classroom, more jobs are being created and made available to persons with disabilities, day care facilities are becoming more open to accepting children with special needs, community and school involvement is increasing, accountability for service delivery is moving to the forefront, and individual rights are on the front lines of the business world.

CHANGES IN PERSPECTIVE

As a result of the key events that have unfolded since the early part of this century, access to a basic education is now viewed in the United States as a right of every citizen rather than a privilege granted only to a select few. Legislation, litigation, and changing social and cultural attitudes have opened the doors of educational opportunity to all students, including those with disabilities.

Parents, special educators, students with disabilities, and advocates for students with disabilities have realized, however, that access does not ensure success. Along with the expansion of educational opportunities and the increasing diversity of students' needs and goals has come a change in our view of what constitutes an education. The educational curriculum is now defined much more broadly than the three R's. Emphasis on life skills—including vocational training and the ability to function in a diverse society supported by an information-based economy—is now a central theme of much of the curriculum. This broader concept of educational curriculum and the expansion of its legitimate goals and outcomes have enabled many students with disabilities to succeed in programs that can now be more appropriately matched to their projected needs after they leave school and enter the adult world.

Educators are no longer burdened by the question of who can successfully be educated, but have come to realize that everyone can learn to make a meaningful contribution to society at his or her own level and that the public schools are the appropriate and natural setting to help all students reach their individual goals.

Five-Minute Summary

The history of services for persons with disabilities reflects the social attitudes and historical events of the time. In ancient times, persons with disabilities were treated cruelly and often killed or left to die. The Renaissance and Reformation brought about some improvements, but it was not until the 18th and 19th centuries that noticeable progress was evident in the treatment of persons with disabilities. Special schools began to be established in Europe for some disabilities, and interest grew in systematically educating and training persons with disabilities.

The history of services for persons with disabilities in the United States reveals progress in some areas and regression in others. Societal, economic, and political events such as World War I and World War II, the Great Depression, and the civil rights movement affected the status of services available for persons with disabilities. By the 1970s, legislation had established a basis for equal education for all the nation's children, including those with disabilities. Since then, programs and services have expanded and improved. The last decade has seen a movement away from separate facilities, programs, and classes—as students with disabilities become integrated into the mainstream of education.

The history of attitudes toward persons with disabilities is reflected in the terminology used to describe those individuals. Currently, the emphasis is away from "handicapped" terminology, and in favor of person-first language. While the use of labels to categorize both individuals with disabilities and the programs and services for them has been legitimately criticized, there are some instances in which the use of labels may be necessary (e.g., to determine eligibility for benefits or services).

Questions of terminology and definition permeate the field of special education. Federal definitions and working definitions differ, but all have in common the emphasis on providing an appropriate, individualized education to students with disabilities. Special education is alternately defined in terms of the process, the place it is delivered, and the methods of delivery (curriculum). While special education may be defined as distinct from general education, the benefits of special education can be extended to students without disabilities, teachers, and community members. As increasing numbers of students with disabilities receive their education in general education settings, similarities in special and general education are likely to increase and the boundary between them become less distinct. Hopefully, this trend will become more firmly entrenched in society, as children and adults with disabilities have opportunities available to fully participate in all facets of school, home, and community life.

Study Questions

1. What was society's attitude toward persons with disabilities prior to the middle part of this century?
2. How did the civil rights movement in this country affect the rights of individuals with disabilities?
3. Discuss how the Industrial Revolution, World War I, the Depression, and World War II each enhanced or impeded the development of services for persons with disabilities.
4. Why is understanding federal laws important, especially for individuals with disabilities?
5. List the five major components of the Education for All Handicapped Children Act of 1975 (P.L. 94-142).
6. What federal law amended and renamed the Education for All Handicapped Children Act of 1975 (P.L. 94-142)?
7. What did amendments to the Carl D. Perkins Vocational Education Act of 1984 require states to do?
8. What are some common terms that have been used to refer to individuals with disabilities? Why do some individuals dislike use of the term *handicapped?*
9. What are two advantages and two disadvantages of using categorical labels when referring to students with disabilities?

10. Where do the majority of students receive special education services? What is the preferred place for many students to receive special education services? Why?
11. Name two similarities and two differences between special education and general education.
12. Discuss the benefits of special education to different sectors of our society.
13. Discuss the differences in outlook for a child born with a disability in 1920 and one born in 1990.

For More Information

ORGANIZATIONS

Alliance of Genetic Support Groups
35 Wisconsin Circle, Suite 440
Chevy Chase, MD 20815
800-336-4363   301-652-5553
FAX 301-654-0171

Association for Advancement of Rehab
   Technology/RESNA
1101 Connecticut Avenue, NW, Suite 700
Washington, DC 20036
202-857-1199

Beach Center on Families and Disability
The University of Kansas
Bureau of Child Research
4138 Haworth Hall
Lawrence, KS 66045

Clearinghouse on Disability Information
Office of Special Education and Rehabilitative
   Services (OSERS)
Room 3132, Switzer Building
Washington, DC 20202-2524
202-205-8241 (V/TT)   202-205-8723 (V/TT)

Council for Exceptional Children (CEC)
1920 Association Drive
Reston, VA 22091
703-620-3660 (V/TT)   FAX 703-264-9494

National Association of Sibling Programs
Sibling Support Project
Children's Hospital and Medical Center
4800 Sand Point Way, NE
P.O. Box 5371
Seattle, WA 98105
206-368-4911

National Center for Youth with Disabilities
Box 721 UMHC
Harvard Street at East River Road
Minneapolis, MN 55455
800-333-6293   In MN: 612-626-2825
612-624-3939 (TT)   FAX 612-626-2134

National Council on Disability
800 Independence Avenue, SW, Suite 814
Washington, DC 20591
202-267-3846   202-267-3232 (TT)
FAX 202-453-4240

National Information Center for Children and
   Youth with Handicaps (NICHCY)
P.O. Box 1492
Washington, DC 20013

National Institute on Disability and Rehabilitation
   Research (NIDRR)
U.S. Department of Education
400 Maryland Avenue, SW
Washington, DC 20202
202-205-8134   202-205-5479 (TT)
FAX 202-205-8515

National Organization on Disability (NOD)
910 16th Street, NW, Suite 600
Washington, DC 20006
202-293-5960   202-293-5968 (TT)
FAX 202-293-7999

National Rehabilitation Information Center
   (NARIC)
8455 Colesville Road, Suite 935
Silver Spring, MD 20910-3319
800-346-2742   301-588-9284 (V/TT)

Resources for Rehabilitation
33 Bedford Street, Suite 19A
Lexington, MA 02173
617-862-6455 FAX 617-861-7517

Society for Disability Studies (SDS)
Department of Sociology
Gallaudet University
8th and Florida, NE
Washington, DC 20002
202-651-5160

World Institute on Disability
510 Sixteenth Street, Suite 100
Oakland, CA 94612
415-763-4100 (V/TT)

BOOKS AND ARTICLES

Anderson, W., Chitwood, S., & Hayden, D. (1990). *Negotiating the special education maze*. Rockville, MD: Woodbine House.

Baker, E., Wang, M., & Walberg, H. (1995). The effects of inclusion on learning. *Educational Leadership, 52*(4), 33–35.

Biklen, D. (1992). *Schooling without labels: Parents, educators and inclusive education*. Philadelphia: Temple University Press.

Browne, S. E., Connors, D., & Stern, N. (1985). *With the power of each breath: A disabled women's anthology*. Pittsburgh, PA: Cleis Press.

Dickman, I., & Gordon, S. (1985). *One miracle at a time: How to get help for your disabled child—From the experience of other parents*. New York: Simon & Schuster.

Jones, R. L. (1983). *Reflections on growing up disabled*. Reston, VA: Council for Exceptional Children.

Martin, R. (1991). *Extraordinary children, ordinary lives*. Champaign, IL: Research Press.

McGarrity, M. (1993). *A guide to mental retardation*. New York: Crossroad Publishing.

Moore, C. (1990). *A reader's guide for parents of children with mental, physical, or emotional disabilities*. Rockville, MD: Woodbine House.

Peck, C. A., Carlson, P., & Helmster, E. (1992). Parent and teacher perceptions of outcomes for typically developing children enrolled in integrated early childhood programs: A statewide survey. *Journal of Early Intervention, 16*, 53–63.

Pueschel, S. M., Bernier, J. C., & Weidenman, L. E. (1994). *The special child: A source book for parents of children with developmental disabilities*. (2nd ed.). Baltimore: Paul H. Brookes.

Rosenberg, M. S. & Edmond-Rosenberg, I. (1994). *The special education sourcebook: A teacher's guide to programs, materials and information sources*. Rockville, MD: Woodbine House.

Staub, D., & Peck, C. A. (1995). What are the outcomes for nondisabled students? *Educational Leadership, 52*(4), 36–40.

U.S. Department of Education. (1992). *Summary of existing legislation affecting people with disabilities*. Washington, DC: Author.

Weber, M. C. (1992). *Special education law and legislation treatise*. Horsham, PA: LRP Publications.

Wehman, P. (Ed.). (1993). *The ADA mandate for social change*. Baltimore: Paul H. Brookes.

West, M., Kregel, J., Getzel, E. E., Zhu, M., Ipsen, S. M., & Martin, E. D. (1993). Beyond Section 504: Satisfaction and empowerment of students with disabilities in higher education. *Exceptional Children, 59*(5), 1–12.

Wood, J. (1993). *Mainstreaming: A practical approach for teachers*. Columbus, OH: Merrill.

JOURNALS, NEWSLETTERS, AND OTHER PUBLICATIONS

American Rehabilitation
Superintendent of Documents
U.S. Government Printing Office
Washington, DC 20402

Counterpoint
National Association of State Directors of Special Education
10860 Hampton Road
Fairfax, VA 22039
703-239-1557

*Directory of National Information Sources on Handi-
capping Conditions and Related Services*
Superintendent of Documents
U.S. Government Printing Office
Washington, DC 20402

*Directory of Organizations Interested in the Handi-
capped*
People-to-People Committee for the Handicapped
1111 20th Street, N.W., Suite 660
Washington, DC 20036-3470

The Disability Rag
Advocado Press
Box 145
Louisville, KY 40201
502-459-5343

Disability Studies Quarterly
Sociology Department
Brandeis University
Waltham, MA 02254

*Federal Policy on Vocational Education for Exceptional
Students: Q&A Guide to the Carl D. Perkins Act of
1990*
The Council for Exceptional Children
1920 Association Drive, Dept. K2090 1
Reston, VA 22091-1589
703-620-3660

Focus on Exceptional Children
Love Publishing Company
1777 South Bellaire Street
Denver, CO 80222
202-757-2579

Kaleidoscope
United Disability Services
326 Locust Street
Akron, OH 44302
216-762-9755

Mainstream
P.O. Box 370958
San Diego, CA 92137
619-234-3138

*P.L. 94-142, Section 504, and P.L. 99-457—
Understanding What They Are and What They
Are Not*
Joseph Ballard, Bruce Ramirez, and Kathy Zantal-
Weiner
The Council for Exceptional Children
1920 Association Drive, Dept. K2090 1
Reston, VA 22091-1589
703-620-3660

VIDEO AND ELECTRONIC MEDIA

Disabilities Act Video
The Disability Bookshop
P.O. Box 129
Vancouver, WA 98666-0129
206-694-2462 or 800-637-2256

Education for All
Research Press
Dept. G
P.O. Box 9177
Champaign, IL 61826
217-352-3273

References

Americans With Disabilities Act of 1990, 42 U.S.C. 12101, et seq: *Federal Register, 56* (44), 35544–35756.

Ham, R. E. (1990). *Therapy of stuttering.* Englewood Cliffs, NJ: Prentice-Hall.

Harris, L., & Associates. (1989). *The ICD survey III: A report card on special education.* New York: International Center for the Disabled.

Huefner, D. C. (1994). An introduction to Section 504 of the Rehabilitation Act. *The Utah Special Educator, 14*(4), 10–11.

National Association of State Mental Retardation Program Directors. (1992). *Summary of existing legislation affecting people with disabilities* (Rev. ed.). Alexandria, VA: Author.

National Information Center for Children and Youth With Disabilities. (1993). Questions and answers about the IDEA. *NICHCY News Digest, 3*(2), 1–17.

Patton, J. R., Payne, J. S., & Beirne-Smith, M. (1981). *Mental retardation* (2nd ed.). Columbus, OH: Merrill.

U.S. Department of Education. (1995). *Seventeenth annual report to Congress on the implementation of the Individuals With Disabilities Education Act.* Washington, DC: Author.

U.S. Department of Education. (1994). *Sixteenth annual report to Congress on the implementation of the Individuals With Disabilities Education Act.* Washington, DC: Author.

Vocational Rehabilitation Act of 1973.

Wolfensberger, W. (1972). *Normalization: The principle of normalization in human services.* Toronto, Canada: National Institute on Mental Retardation.

Wood, J. W., & Lazzari, A. M. (1994). [General and special educators' perceptions of special education.] Unpublished raw data.

Chapter 2

Unity of Faces, acrylic on canvas, 60″ × 82″ (1992)

CULTURAL DIVERSITY

ROBBIE KENDALL-MELTON

After studying this chapter, the reader will:

Know about the demographic changes in the student population
and the implication of these changes for teaching in
the 21st century

Understand the impact and importance of diversity and
multiculturalism in education

Be prepared for cultural diversity in the classroom—appreciating the
uniqueness of the individual, respecting diversity and culture,
making modifications to curriculum and teaching styles, and
maintaining effective communication between
home and school

Appreciate the effect of learning styles and behavioral styles in
enhancing student achievement and performance

Be aware of the overrepresentation of culturally diverse students
in special education programs and the underrepresentation of
culturally diverse students in programs for students who are
gifted and talented

Be able to outline the educational programs and services for
culturally diverse students, including those with disabilities,
within the continuum of the least restrictive to the most
restrictive educational environment

Recognize the need for bilingual special education

CULTURAL DIVERSITY

1954   The Supreme Court ruled in *Brown* v. *Board of Education* that racial segregation in America's schools is unconstitutional.

1964   The Civil Rights Act of 1964 required school districts receiving federal funding to guarantee nondiscriminatory treatment on the basis of race, color, or national origin. This act ensured access of culturally diverse, limited English proficiency (LEP), and other minority students to public education.

1968   Congress passed Title VII of the Elementary and Secondary School Act, or what is commonly referred to as the Bilingual Education Act. This act ensured the recognition of the special educational needs of the large numbers of LEP students.

1970   A class action suit by nine Mexican American children and their parents (*Diana* v. *California State Board of Education*) resulted in the requirement that evaluations and assessments be in the child's primary language.

1971   In *Larry P.* v. *Riles,* the use of IQ tests with African American children in California public schools was banned due to cultural bias.

1974   The Supreme Court ruled in *Lau* v. *Nichols* that schools must provide an appropriate education for limited English proficiency students, and that there is no equality in treatment merely by providing students with the same facilities, textbooks, teachers, and curriculum.

The Equal Educational Opportunities Act was enacted, mandating that all children enrolled in public schools are entitled to equal educational opportunity without regard to race, color, sex, or national origin.

1978   Congress amended the Bilingual Education Act and added "cultural heritage" to the act, mandating bilingual educational services for those students with a different cultural heritage.

1979 and *Dyrcia S. et al.* v. *Board of Education of the City of New York*
1984   (1979) and *Lora* v. *Board of Education of the City of New York* (1984) mandated the timely identification of children needing special education services with adequate bilingual resources; the establishment of school-based support teams to evaluate children in their own environment with a bilingual nondiscriminatory evaluation process; a comprehensive continuum of services in the least restrictive environment with the provision of appropriate bilingual programs at each level of the continuum for children with limited English proficiency; and the translation of all due process and parental student rights forms, reports, and records into Spanish.

INTRODUCTION

The demographics of American schools are rapidly becoming more diversified. It has been calculated that approximately 25% of the U.S. school-age population is minority, and by the end of the decade the figure should be close to 33% (Chinn & McCormick, 1986). African American and Hispanic American students will make up about 33% of the student population. Others have predicted that by the year 2000, up to 50% of the school-age student population will be from culturally different homes (Perez, 1991; Wilson, 1988). Half of the nation's 22.2 million population increase in the 1990 census was composed of either Hispanics or Asians. According to the 1994 *Statistical Abstract*, published by the U.S. Department of Commerce, one in every four Americans is a member of a minority group. Predictions include the following:

- By the year 2080, Anglo Americans will probably be a minority in the U.S. population (Quality Education for Minorities Project, 1990).

- By the year 2000, Hispanics will make up more than 25% of the school population (Center for Research on Elementary and Middle Schools, 1990).

- More than 30% of today's public school students are from historically underrepresented groups (Perez, 1991).

- By the year 2000, the number of students whose primary language is not English will increase by 75% (Center for Research on Elementary and Middle Schools, 1990).

Thus, the increase in cultural diversity in the schools will bring about school reform such as in the identification of school programs promoting diversity, multicultural activities, diversity among the personnel, value-free curriculum, culturally fair assessments, and an increase in home–school partnerships.

Ironically, the demographics for diversity in the teaching population do not reflect any significant increases in the number of minority teachers by the year 2000. The American Association of Colleges for Teacher Education (1987) reported as follows:

1. Blacks represent 16.2% of the children in public schools, but only 6.9% of the teachers.

2. Hispanics represent 9.1% of the children in public schools, but only 1.9% of the teachers.

3. Asian/Pacific Islanders represent 2.5% of the children in public schools, but only 0.9% of the teachers.

4. American Indians/Alaskan Natives represent 0.9% of the children in public schools, but only 0.6% of the teachers.

5. Whites represent 71.2% of the children in public schools, but 89.6% of the teachers. (p. 15)

The American Association of State Colleges and Universities (1991) calculated that only 10% of today's teachers are from historically underrepresented groups—and that percentage will *drop* to 5% by the year 2000.

The changing demographics in America direct educators to address issues of diversity and multicultural education in order to meet the needs of all students.

Educators must understand the influences and impact of cultural diversity in terms of student performance and achievement, learning and behavioral styles, school environment, and building positive home–school partnerships. Teachers must recognize the need for diversity training in promoting and ensuring quality and equity.

THE NEED FOR DIVERSITY AND MULTICULTURAL EDUCATION

The United States is truly a multicultural nation affected by unparalleled diversity. Chinn and McCormick (1986) noted that the United States is characterized by cultural diversity—a wide range of cultural characteristics and norms and that the United States is one of the most pluralistic nations in the world. Individuals from every ethnic background and nearly every linguistic group make up the mosaic of our country.

The increase in multicultural education arose from the concept that the needs of children from culturally diverse backgrounds that differ from those of white middle-class students were not being appropriately met, thus placing them at risk for academic and social problems. Differences in race, ethnicity, language, and culture can affect school performance and affect the extent to which school experiences are relevant and appropriate for students (Ysseldyke & Algozzine, 1995). Gollnick and Chinn (1994) stated that each student enters the classroom with a set of values and beliefs unique to his or her life situation. These beliefs can be influenced by age, gender, language spoken at home, the religion practiced by the family, socioeconomic level of the family, geographic region of residence, culture, and personal events that have impacted the student's life. These factors, and many

---

REAL PEOPLE   *Rosetta Gonzales*

"My bilingual special education teacher helped me to be proud of who I am regardless of my learning disabilities and culture. In the beginning, I was so confused about reading and writing. The only thing that I could do well was math. At home my parents could not help me because they did not speak English very well. So they were also mixed up and could not help me with my work. My parents felt very bad that they could not help me so they asked the school if someone could. I felt ashamed that I was referred to special education because I felt that it was a punishment because I could not read. However, after being in the class, I found out other ways to learn how to read. The teacher helped me with understanding and translating Spanish words into English. We used a lot of games and learning groups. She did not put any pressure on me or allow the other students to make fun of me. We all worked as a group. Some of us helped others with things and others helped us. My teachers used a lot of things from the community to help us, like posters and pictures. She also sent information to my parents in Spanish. This made them very happy because they could understand things going on in school. She also worked with the other teachers in the school to help them to understand my problems. This helped me when I had to go to the other classroom. Since being in this class, I am not ashamed or embarrassed about my learning disabilities. I now can read and write and when I have trouble, I know where to go and who will help me. The best thing that I like about my class is that the teacher lets me talk about my home and things that we do as a family. She also lets me bring things from my home to show to the other children. I now can help my parents learn words and how to write in English."

The United States has always been a culturally diverse nation.

more, result in the complex diversity of each student. All of these factors must be considered when addressing the educational needs of the student.

Researchers (Franklin, 1992; McIntyre, 1994) have found that traditional school environments often penalize students with values, beliefs, languages, and behaviors at variance with those of "mainstream" American citizens. McIntyre (1995a) noted that "a lack of cross-cultural understanding means that educational personnel are likely to react to culturally determined behavior in ways that are ineffective, inappropriate, counterproductive, insensitive, or offensive" (p. 5). Furthermore, educators who are aware of and use differences in languages, values, cultural norms, and behavioral styles to enrich instruction—and who use appropriate modifications (presenting information in English and in the student's native language, reading stories from other cultures, etc.)—can help students from diverse settings become successful learners. Education has as its major goal the restructuring of the school environment to ensure that students from diverse cultural, social class, racial, and ethnic groups will experience equal opportunities to learn in school.

DEFINITIONS OF CULTURE, DIVERSITY, AND MULTICULTURAL EDUCATION

Banks (1988) delineated that **culture** is a way of perceiving, believing, evaluating, and behaving shared by a group of people. Culture includes institutions, language, values, religions, ideals, habits of thinking, artistic expressions, and patterns of social and interpersonal relationships (Lum, 1986, p. 46). Vontress (1986) believed that people do not reside in one culture, but rather live in five intermingling cultures:

Universal—humans all over the world are biologically alike, e.g., males and females are capable of producing offspring.

Ecological—humans' location on earth determines how its members relate to the natural environment.

National—humans are characterized by aspects such as language, central governments, and world views.

Regional—humans tend to settle in a region, thereby creating cultures specific to an area.

Racio-ethnic—humans have distinct racial and ethnic differences; however, all people are a reflection of their racial and ethnic background. (p. 277)

Ethnic minority groups are categorized according to ethnicity, gender, language, religion, disability, or socioeconomic status. The word **ethnic** denotes the common history, values, attitudes, and behaviors that bind a group of people together (Yetman, 1985). Categories of ethnic minority groups include African Americans, Hispanic Americans, Asian Americans, Native Americans, and so forth. Our cultural and ethnic identities help to shape our beliefs and practices and who we are as individuals and family members. **Ethnocentrism** is the belief in the superiority of one's own culture that inclines us to conclude that those who do not conform to our values (e.g., how we cook, eat, dress, mate, etc.) may be ignorant, irresponsible, and/or inferior.

Spindler (1963) summarized that central to the concept of culture is the fact that any culture is goal oriented and that, "these goals are expressed, patterned, lived out by people in their behaviors and aspirations in the form of values—objects of possessions, conditions of existence, features of personality or characters and states of mind that are conceived as desirable, and act as motivating determinants of behaviors" (p. 132).

Diversity can be viewed in terms of values and behavioral styles, language and dialects, nonverbal communication, awareness of one's own cultural distinctiveness, frames of reference, and identification (Banks, 1988). Diversity also includes gender, age, language, backgrounds, religious beliefs, politics, the work world, physical and mental abilities, and experiences (Tiedt & Tiedt, 1995).

Today's classrooms often represent many ethnicities.

Multicultural education incorporates the idea that all students—regardless of their gender, social class, ethnic, racial, or cultural characteristics—should have an equal opportunity to learn in school (Banks, 1994). In viewing multicultural education from the perspective of teaching, Payne (1984) defined the concept as a process of good teaching where the emphasis is on infusion of ethnic history and ethnic contributors into education. This infusion must take place across disciplines, throughout the curriculum, and be incorporated into methodology and instructional techniques. Multicultural education is viewed by Gollnick and Chinn (1994) as education that values and promotes **cultural pluralism:** "It is not intended to be limited to those of cultural or racial minorities but more appropriately teaches all students about cultural diversity" (p. 29).

FACTORS AFFECTING THE EDUCATION OF CULTURALLY DIVERSE STUDENTS

A large percentage—more than 45%—of culturally diverse families live in poverty. In 1988, the Children's Defense Fund reported that more than half (53%) of all young African American families with children live in poverty, and 40% of all young Hispanic families with children live in poverty; for Native Americans on reservations, the rate of poverty is 42%, and 24% for those living off the reservations (Quality Education for Minorities Project, 1990). According to the Bureau of the Census (1991), poverty is more prevalent in the lives of cultural and ethnic minorities; 20% of all children are considered to be living below the poverty level. However, analyzed by ethnic origin, more than 45% of African American children and more than 39% of Hispanic American children fall below the poverty level, and white children represent 15%.

Poverty can result in hearing, vision, or other physical problems, as well as learning disabilities, mental retardation, and emotional impairments—when the lack of money and programs cannot pay for proper prenatal and postnatal care, improvement of environments, appropriate health and dental care, and proper nutrition. In addition, there is a high degree of lead poisoning, encephalitis, fetal alcohol syndrome (FAS), and fetal alcohol effects (FAE) among poverty-stricken families.

It must be emphasized, however, that not all culturally diverse families live in poverty. Meister (1991) investigated the factor of **migrancy** (frequent mobility and relocating) in relationship to cultural diversity. He noted that the circumstances of migrancy are associated with economic disadvantage, language differences, and social and physical isolation from much of the larger community. Plus, children of migrant workers have a high rate of absentees, and limited continuity and inconsistency in their educational programming. They often have limited access to services due to their short-term enrollments or the schools' limited capabilities to deliver services. It is estimated that migrancy is widespread and involves perhaps 3 million seasonal or migrant workers nationally with a high percentage being of Mexican descent (Vaughan, 1993). These factors must be taken into account when planning instruction for culturally diverse students.

TEACHER TRAINING FOR CULTURAL DIVERSITY

Educators must be able to conceptualize the influence of culture on student performance and how students' cultural styles impact their performance and achievement in school. Gollnick and Chinn (1994) proposed six assumptions to assist educators in designing and implementing cultural competence for cultural diversity and multicultural education:

1. There is strength and value in promoting cultural diversity.

2. Schools should be models for the expression of human rights and respect for cultural differences.

3. Social justice and equality for all people should be of paramount importance in the design and delivery of curricula.

4. Attitudes and values necessary for the continuation of a democratic society can be promoted in schools.

5. Schooling can provide the knowledge, dispositions, and skills for the redistribution of power and income among cultural groups.

6. Educators working with families and communities can create an environment that is supportive of multiculturalism. (p. 29)

Lynch and Hanson (1992) stated that educators must begin to develop **cultural competence,** as well as "respect for differences, eagerness to learn, and a willingness to accept that there are many ways of viewing the world" (p. 356). They found that cultural competence is based on two key skills: awareness and communication. In order to assist students in reaching their maximum potential, teachers must acquire an understanding of students' cultures and backgrounds. In addition, teachers must acquire an appreciation of the differences between cultures and assist students in developing a sense of respect for all cultures. Creating a positive learning environment that promotes students' diversity and individuality will improve school attendance, performance, home–school relationships, and—most noteworthy—prevent mislabeling and inappropriate placement in special education.

Ysseldyke and Algozzine (1995) discussed that teachers can no longer afford to teach from a "monocultural perspective." Rather, cultural diversity must be the teaching force in the classroom and the force that permeates the school curriculum in order to ensure equal educational opportunity and to help each student reach his or her maximum potential.

Taking a Holistic Approach

Using the resources of students' experiences, a teacher can develop multicultural units that are meaningful and relevant. The exchange of knowledge between myself and the students is invaluable.

—Bilingual teacher

Chinn and McCormick (1986) recommended using a holistic approach in the classroom. A holistic teaching method looks at the whole student, in all aspects of his or her environment, bringing the whole range of teaching strategies and support people to the educational process. This includes approaching the educational experience as an integrated whole rather than separate parts. Other educators are advocating a "value-free curriculum" or an "antibias curriculum." Banks (1994) suggested that the curriculum should be modified to reflect "the experiences, cultures, and perspectives of a range of cultural and ethnic groups as well as both genders" (p. 11). Ethnically diverse groups and females are usually underrepresented in textbooks. In addition, stereotyping in books is another factor that educators must be aware of. Too often, educators, textbooks, and films present information only from the position of the dominant culture.

Tiedt and Tiedt (1995) developed specific outcomes for teaching cultural diversity as part of the curriculum design of multicultural education. They advocated that as an end product of effective teaching, students should be able, first, to "identify a strong sense of their own self-esteem and express the need and right of all other persons to similar feelings of self-esteem," and then to "describe their own individual cultures, recognizing the influences that have shaped their thinking and behavior" (p. 27).

Above all, the curriculum must be presented in a climate of acceptance, respect, and caring that guarantees successful learning experiences for all. The conceptual framework of a culturally diverse curriculum should reflect the following:

- Teachers provide a variety of historical and contemporary perspectives of history, social studies, and other curriculum subjects—such as viewing American history through the perspective of the Native Americans and other cultural groups. This will assist all students in learning how to view information objectively and comparing and contrasting information.

- Teachers consider the tremendous diversity among students, rather than categorizing students from a particular culture into one homogeneous group.

- Teachers use test data carefully, remembering that some might be culturally biased.

- Teachers respect and appreciate cultural diversity (language, religion, class, income, and other differences) to the degree that students do not feel their culture is wrong or inferior.

- Teachers eliminate stereotypes, racism, prejudices, and other forms of discrimination from the classroom and school environment.

- Teachers are more sensitive to the learning, social, and cultural styles of their students. Educators must be willing to adjust and modify their instructional methods to find the preferred strategies for their students.

CULTURALLY DIVERSE CHILDREN AND SPECIAL EDUCATION

Overrepresentation in Special Education Programs

A disproportionately high number of students with disabilities come from minority groups or from culturally diverse backgrounds (U.S. Department of Education, 1993), as illustrated in Figure 2.1. Bedell (1989) found that almost 4% of all students receiving special education are from culturally divergent backgrounds. As reported, three times as many African American and four times as many Hispanic American children were being placed in classes for students with mild mental retardation, as compared to their numbers in the general school population. McIntyre (1995b) debated that the overrepresentation of culturally different students in programs for youngsters with mental and emotional or behavioral disorders is typically not a result of intentional or conscious discrimination. Instead, it is usually a consequence of educator ethnocentricity and the difficulty most individuals have comprehending or appreciating behavior that is culturally different from their own.

The most troubling anomaly in special education has to do with mental retardation. More than twice as many blacks as whites are classified as mentally retarded.

Percentage of black, white, and Hispanic special education students with

	Black	White	Hispanic
Mental Retardation	26%	11%	18%
Learning Disabilities	43	51	55
Emotional Disturbance	8	8	4
Speech Impairments	23	30	23

Figure 2.1 **A Breakdown by Race**

Source: From *USN&WR*—Basic data: U.S. Dept. of Education Office of Civil Rights 1990 Survey of Schools.

Underrepresentation in Programs for Students Who Are Gifted and Talented

In contrast, there is a disproportionately low number of these same groups of students in classes for students who are gifted and talented. The identification of students who are gifted is based almost solely on paper-and-pencil instruments and teacher judgments, both of which may be biased toward English language competence:

> Since the common measure of giftedness is also a measure of competence in the English language, one might wonder how we can fairly test students from linguistically diverse backgrounds when they do not have English language competence. The results indicate that these students often are not identified as gifted since identification of giftedness is largely based on reading scores and their reading scores are low. (Garcia, 1994, p. 40)

When criteria other than English proficiency are used to help determine placement in gifted programs, students from culturally diverse backgrounds are more likely to be identified, as shown in Figure 2.2.

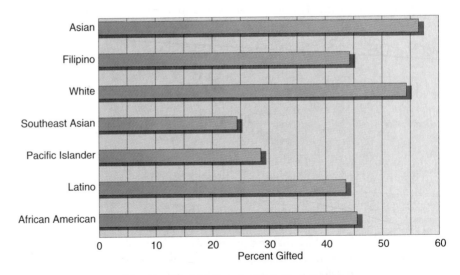

Figure 2.2 **Percent Gifted by Ethnicity Among High Math Performers**

Source: From "Assessment of Asian and Pacific Islander Students for Gifted Programs" by Cheng, L., Ima, K., & Labovitz, G. (1994). In S. B. Garcia (Ed.), *Addressing Cultural and Linguistic Diversity in Special Education* (p. 30), Reston, VA: Council for Exceptional Children. Used with permission.

Numerous students from ethnic backgrounds have gifts and talents that go unrecognized either because educators are unaware these abilities are considered talents in a particular culture, or because they are not valued or nurtured in school. Furthermore, students from culturally and linguistically diverse groups will continue to be unidentified and underrepresented until such time that alternative culturally relevant indicators of giftedness are used in the assessment process (McIntyre, 1993).

Biased Assessment

One of the factors that has caused overrepresentation and underrepresentation in the aforementioned programs has been biased assessment. Jones (1976) maintained that bias is involved at three different levels: (1) at the *content* level where the decisions are first made about what items to include in a test, (2) at the level of *standardization* where decisions are made about the population for whom the test is appropriate, and (3) at the point of *validation* where efforts are undertaken to determine whether or not tests accomplish what they have been designed to accomplish.

One of the assessments that has been identified as being biased is the intelligence test. In *Larry P. v. Riles* (1971), the use of IQ tests for black children in California public schools was banned because the tests were judged to be culturally biased. This led to the California State Department of Education banning or limiting the use of IQ tests for the evaluation and placement of minority children in special education classes.

Another factor that has caused over- and underrepresentation of culturally diverse students in special education is examiner bias. Flanigan and Schwartz (1971) investigated the concept of examiner bias and found that test scores were related more to the rapport and reports of examiners than to the instruments that were administered. Another factor is the ethnic background of the examiner. Researchers found that matching the ethnic and language background of the

Culturally relevant assessments must be used to discern students' gifts and talents.

examiner with a student made a positive significant difference. Chandler and Plakos (1971) found that Hispanic students were placed in classes for students labeled as educable mentally retarded at rates two to three times higher than their Anglo American peers. Yet when properly evaluated by a Spanish-speaking psychologist who used standard instruments translated into Spanish, the IQs of these students who were identified as mentally retarded increased significantly.

To ensure fair evaluations of culturally diverse students, professionals responsible for evaluating students must be trained in the area of diversity and become aware of the influences and impact of the cultures and customs of the students being assessed. The examiners should investigate the adaptive skills of the students in their homes and communities. This additional information will assist examiners in providing a total assessment of the students, as opposed to just an academic point of view. Jones (1976) cited numerous cases where minority students demonstrated significant differences between their performance in school and at home. In addition, evaluations and the testing procedures must be culturally fair. If possible, the examiners should be from the student's ethnic background and/or be competent in speaking the student's language.

Language Diversity

It is hard to keep up in school when you have to think in two languages.

—Bilingual student

Battle (1993) indicated that if language diversity is not considered during assessment and educational planning, the result may be an inappropriate placement in special education. Although poor comprehension, limited vocabulary, and poor syntax may indicate a learning disability in some students, for others these shortcomings may simply indicate a lack of proficiency in English (Ortiz & Polyzoi, 1988).

According to Chinn and McCormick (1986), dialects differ from one another in a variety of ways. For example, dialects that have a lower socioeconomic class basis tend to be viewed negatively, which can have social consequences for the user. Examples include "southern" dialect, black English, and the variety of Hispanic dialects.

In cases where limited English proficiency (LEP) students also have a disability (such as a language disorder or learning disability), professionals must determine the degree to which that disability and the student's language problems contribute to deficiency in academic achievement. It is the responsibility of the multidisciplinary evaluation team to distinguish *diversity* from *disability*. Then, as outlined in Figure 2.3, the Individualized Education Program (IEP) committee must determine whether a child is *linguistically diverse* due to culture or *linguistically deficient* for developmental reasons. If the team determines that a learning or social problem stems only from the student's culture, then placement in special education is not called for and other resources and services should be provided.

LEARNING, BEHAVIORAL, AND CULTURAL STYLES

Educators must first address culturally diverse students as individuals, each being unique. These students, like all other students, hold expectations for themselves. Those expectations are based on past performance, but they also are influenced by the expectations of others (Ysseldyke & Algozzine, 1995). Thus, the way students

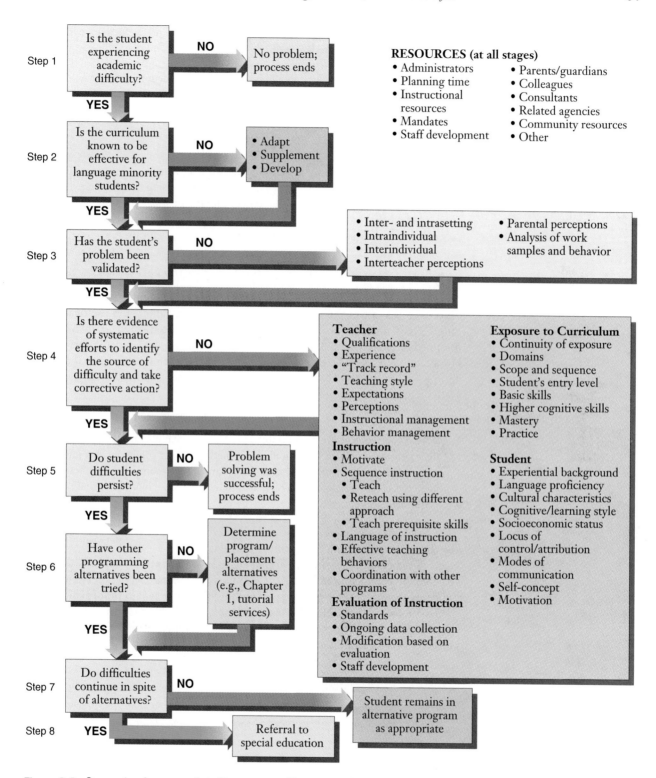

Figure 2.3 **Preventing Inappropriate Placements of Language Minority Students in Special Education: A Prereferral Process**

Source: Adapted from *Preventing Inappropriate Referrals of Language Minority Students to Special Education* (New Focus Series, No. 5), by S. B. Garcia & A. A. Ortiz, 1988, Wheaton, MD: National Clearinghouse for Bilingual Education. Reprinted with permission.

perceive themselves deeply affects their social behavior and performance in school. As noted by Tiedt and Tiedt:

> The aim of all good teaching should be to assist each student in reaching his or her fullest potential. Therefore, the emphasis should not only be for the need to provide multicultural understanding for all students at all levels but also how to teach so as to accommodate individual differences or diversity. (1995, p. 27)

To assist culturally diverse students, as well as all other students, in achieving and performing successfully in school, the practice of *teaching to students' learning style* must be considered. A **style** is a preferred way of using one's abilities. It is not in itself an ability but rather a preference. Hence, various styles are not good or bad—only different (Sternberg, 1994). All students display various degrees and levels of styles and these styles may change according to situations.

Student Learning Styles

Brown and Cooper (1981) defined learning styles as the internal structures and processes that affect the individual's reception, interrelation, and use of information. They concluded that learning styles have three interrelated strands: (1) environmental preferences, (2) information reception modes, and (3) information processing modes (p. 1). Brown and Cooper divided learning styles into three categories—cognitive, social, and expressive—and further subdivided the categories into nine areas, as outlined in Table 2.1.

According to Brown and Cooper:

> If we require students to receive information in a way that does not correspond with their personal dominant learning modes, to perform under conditions that interfere with their learning, or to demonstrate their learning in a manner that does not allow them to use their strengths, we create artificial stress, reduce motivation, and repress performance results. (1981, p. 1)

Thus, achievement increases and frustration decreases when materials are taught by conforming to a student's learning preference.

Teachers can determine learning styles by observing the students' overt behaviors, by conducting informal and formal assessments, and by interviewing the students regarding their perspectives on how they best acquire information. Students can provide valuable information on how they prefer to learn, personal techniques, proven strategies, types of learning environment, and influencing factors such as groups, rewards, and motivation.

Student Behavioral Styles

> *At home I must not look eye-to-eye when adults are speaking to me, but in school the teachers tell me to look right at them. Sometimes I get so confused because I can't remember when to do and say things.*
>
> —Culturally diverse student

It is not uncommon that students who display culturally different behaviors are particularly susceptible to being diagnosed as having a behavior disorder (Hanna, 1988; McIntyre, 1995a; Sugai & Maheady, 1988). McIntyre found that while conscientious educators hold the best interests of their students at heart, the great majority of educational professionals are unaware of cultural differences in behavior.

"This affects their ability to make culturally competent decisions regarding referral and evaluation procedures, services, placement options, and intervention choices" (1995a, p. 5). Certain behaviors that might suggest a learning problem may in fact be the product of a student's cultural background.

Sternberg (1994) outlined types and degrees of behavioral styles that may be displayed in the classroom. These styles, referred to as styles of "mental self-government," tend to parallel the forms of government that exist worldwide: legislative, executive, judicial, monarchic, hierarchic, and oligarchic. (See Table 2.2.)

Cultural Learning Styles

Often, specific learning styles may be displayed by students within a given cultural group. However, to assume that all students from a particular culture have similar learning styles shows a disregard for the diversity of the individual and would tend to stereotype students before they have the opportunity to be assessed on their own merit.

Demographic changes in the last 10 years reveal that schools will encounter their major increase in student enrollment from the following groups: Native Americans, African Americans, Asian Americans, and Hispanic Americans. These groups will be the most populous in our schools, compared to the numerous other culturally diverse groups, as we enter the 21st century. Thus, a brief overview of the learning styles and their implications of these four cultures will be highlighted. Recognizing the cultural learning styles and behaviors of students in these groups can assist educators in understanding some of the impact and influence of a student's culture on his or her education experience. Educators who seek to understand and address cultural diversity can enrich the resources of all students and enhance the climate of the school setting.

However, the following generalizations about these four cultural groups must not be used to stereotype or bias the individual uniqueness of students within those cultures. Therefore, as educators you must always place more emphasis on meeting students' learning and social styles.

Native American Students.   The Native American culture consists of numerous tribes, customs, and languages. The high degree of diversity among Native Americans fosters a complex cross-cultural setting. Richardson (1981) compared the general culture of Native Americans with the cultural norms of Anglo Americans and found that the Native American culture emphasizes honoring elders, a high regard for religious customs, and learning through legends.

African American Students.   Hale-Benson (1986) noted several factors to consider when assessing the learning styles of African American students. Factors to note are that these students tend to respond to things in terms of the whole picture rather than its parts, prefer inferential reasoning to deductive or inductive reasoning, and prefer focusing on people and their activities rather than on things. In addition, Baruth and Manning (1992) pointed out the following:

> Educators will benefit from objective and reliable information about the African American language. Although the child may not experience difficulty at home or in the neighborhood, language differences may result in problems when significant variations exist between home-neighborhood and school languages. African American children are faced with a problem: Their language is "worthy" at home, yet may be "different" and unworthy in school. (p. 71)

Table 2.1   **Categories of Learning Styles**

COGNITIVE STYLE   (preferred mode of taking in information)

Auditory Language

These are students who learn from hearing words spoken. You may hear them vocalizing or see their lips or throats moving as they read, particularly while striving to understand new material. These students will be more capable of understanding and remembering words or facts learned by hearing.

Teaching Techniques: These students will benefit from hearing audiotapes, rote oral practice, lecture, or a class discussion. They may benefit by listening to tape-recorded cassettes, by teaching other students, or by conversing with the teacher. Interaction activities or games for groups of two or more provide the sound of words being spoken, which is essential for pupils with this learning style.

Visual Language

These are the students who learn well from seeing words in books, on the board, and on charts. They may even write words down that have been delivered orally, in order to learn by seeing them on paper. They remember and use information better if they have read it.

Teaching Techniques: These students will benefit from a variety of books, pamphlets, and written materials on several levels of difficulty. Given some time alone with a book, this type of student may learn more than he or she would learn in class. Make sure that important information is given on paper or that notes are taken if you want this student to remember specific information.

Auditory Numerical

These students learn from hearing numbers and oral explanations. They may remember phone and locker numbers with ease, and they are probably successful with oral numbers, games, and puzzles. They may do almost as well in math without their books, for written materials are not as essential. They can probably work problems in their heads. You may hear them saying numbers to themselves or see their lips moving as they read a problem.

Teaching Techniques: These students will benefit from math sound tapes or from working with another person and talking about a problem. Even reading written explanations aloud will help. Games or activities in which the number problems are spoken will help. These students will benefit from tutoring another or delivering an explanation to a study group or to the teacher. Make sure important facts are spoken.

Visual Numerical

These students have to see numbers on the board, in a book, or on paper in order to work with them. They are more likely to remember and understand math facts if they have seen them. They don't seem to need as much oral explanation.

Teaching Techniques: These students will benefit from worksheets, workbooks, and texts. Give a variety of written materials and allow time to study them. While playing games and activities with numbers and number problems, make sure they are visible, printed numbers rather than oral games and activities. Important information should be given on paper.

Tactile Concrete

These students learn best by experience. They need a combination of stimuli. The manipulation of material, along with sight and sound, will make a big difference to them. They seek to handle, touch, and work with what they are learning.

Teaching Techniques: These students must be given more than just a reading or math assignment. Involve each of them with at least one other student, and give activities to relate to the assignment. Or, accompany an audiotape with pictures, objects, and an activity such as drawing, writing, or following directions with physical involvement.

SOCIAL STYLE   (preference for working alone or in a group)

Individual Learning

These students get more work done alone. They think best and remember more when they have learned alone. They do not allow other students' opinions to influence them. They value their own opinions. You will not have much trouble keeping these students from socializing during class.

Teaching Techniques: These students must be allowed to do important learning alone. Socializing should be saved for a non-learning situation. Allow them to go to the library or back in a corner of the room to be alone. Don't force group work on these students. It is distracting and will cause irritability.

Group Learning

These students strive to study with at least one other student and will not get as much done alone. Others' opinions and preferences are valued. Group interaction increases their learning and later recognition of facts. Class observation will quickly reveal how important socializing is to such students.

Table 2.1　**(Continued)**

Teaching Techniques: These students need to do important learning with someone else. The stimulation of the group may be more important at certain times in the learning process than at others, and you may be able to facilitate the timing.

EXPRESSIVE STYLE　(preferred method of giving out information)

Oral Expressive

These students can easily tell you what they know. They talk fluently, comfortably, and seem to be able to say what they mean. After talking to them about their work, you may find that they know more than their tests show. They are probably not shy about giving reports or talking to the teacher or to classmates. The muscular coordination involved in writing may be difficult for them. Organizing and putting thoughts on paper may be a slow, tedious task for these students.

Teaching Techniques: Allow these students to make oral reports instead of written ones. Whether in conference, small group or large, evaluate them more by what they say than by what they write. Reports can be on tape to save class time. Demand a minimum of high-quality written work, and you won't be ignoring the basics of composition and legibility. Grammar can be corrected orally but is best done at another time.

Written Expressive

These students can write fluent essays and good answers on tests to show what they know. They feel less comfortable, perhaps even insecure, when they have to give oral answers. Their thoughts are better organized on paper than when given orally.

Teaching Techniques: These students need to be allowed to write reports, to keep notebooks and journals for credit, and to take written tests for evaluation. Oral transactions should be under nonpressured conditions, perhaps mainly in a one-to-one conference.

Source: From *Learning Styles Inventory for Macintosh HyperCard,* by J. F. Brown & R. M. Cooper, 1981, Freeport, NY: Educational Activities, Inc.

Table 2.2　**Types of Mental Self-Government**

		CHARACTERIZATION OF BEHAVIOR
Style	Legislative	Likes to create, invent, design, do things his or her own way; has little assigned structure
	Executive	Likes to follow directions, do what he or she is told; seeks structure
	Judicial	Likes to judge and evaluate people and things
Forms	Monarchic	Likes to do one thing at a time, devoting to it almost all energy and resources
	Hierarchic	Likes to do many things at once, setting priorities for which to do when and how much time and energy to devote to each
	Oligarchic	Likes to do many things at once, but has trouble setting priorities
	Anarchic	Likes to take a random approach to problems; dislikes systems, guidelines, and practically all constraints
Levels	Global	Likes to deal with the big picture
	Local	Likes to deal with details, specifics, concrete examples
Scope	Internal	Likes to work alone, focus inward, be self-sufficient
	External	Likes to work with others, focus outward, be interdependent
Leaning	Liberal	Likes to do things in new ways, defy conventions
	Conservative	Likes to do things in tried and true ways, follow conventions

Source: Adapted from "Allowing for Thinking Styles," by R. J. Sternberg, 1994, *Educational Leadership, v.52 n.3,* p. 38.

Native American families pass down their culture through the learning of legends.

Hall (1981) summarized that "many African American children come to school equipped with a rich and different dialect ideally suited to the multiple needs of the black culture, only to be told that what they spoke was a degraded, substandard form of English" (p. 32).

Social stereotypes of African Americans being high-risk candidates for crime, pregnancy, and unemployment place these students at risk for predetermined negative attitudes and treatment, which in turn place them at risk for academic failure by the schools. Furthermore, the media reinforce this negative image of African Americans.

Asian American Students.   The diversity among Asian American students requires a consideration of many factors, including geographic location, generational and socioeconomic differences, language, family customs, and ethnic identity. The many nationalities represented in the Asian American culture make overall descriptions difficult. Asian Americans constitute a highly diversified ethnic group and vary greatly in physical characteristics, attitudes, values, and ethnic institutions (Banks, 1988).

Lum (1986) highlighted the general cultural comparisons of Asian American students and found a high adherence to cultural and family traditions, bilingual backgrounds, and strong regard for family priority. Due to the stereotype of Asian American students being the "model minority" (Baruth & Manning, 1992), educators must be careful not to prejudge all students by this measure.

Hispanic American Students.   Mirande (1986) and Fitzpatrick (1987) conducted cultural comparisons of the Hispanic culture. Some general characteristics were a high degree of bilingualism (Spanish as the native language), bicultural orientation, strong commitment to cultural customs, and a tendency toward "male superiority."

Baruth and Manning (1992) highlighted some teaching techniques for working with culturally diverse ethnic students. They recommend the following procedures:

1. Present new or different material in a visual/perceptual/spatial mode; also, remember that many students need to improve their skills in the verbal mode.

2. Present metaphors, images, or symbols, rather than dictionary-style definitions or synonyms when teaching difficult concepts.

3. Present material in a manner that makes the overall purpose and structure clear, rather than presenting information in small, carefully sequenced bits.

LEGAL IMPLICATIONS FOR DIVERSE STUDENTS

Numerous court decisions and laws have addressed the rights of minorities, women, and people with disabilities. The **equal protection clause** of the Fourteenth Amendment to the U.S. Constitution ensures equal rights, privileges, protection, and due process of law for all citizens regardless of race, creed, culture, religion, gender, and age.

In 1954, the Supreme Court ruled in *Brown v. Board of Education* that racial segregation in America's schools is unconstitutional. The Court ruled that the separation of schooling according to race is inherently unequal and does not meet the test of equal protection provided in the Fourteenth Amendment to the U.S. Constitution.

It would be easy to overlook a speech disorder or other disability due to this girl's culturally based reticence.

The Civil Rights Act of 1964 was the first major mandate requiring school districts receiving federal funding to guarantee nondiscriminatory treatment on the basis of race, color, or national origin. In addition, this act ensured access to public education for culturally diverse, limited English proficiency (LEP), and other minority students. Interpretations of the act by the United States Office for Civil Rights (e.g., OCR's May 25, 1970, Memorandum, 35 Fed. Reg. 11595) led to the requirement that such school districts had the obligation to provide specialized instruction to LEP students and to guarantee that nondiscriminatory testing mechanisms are used in evaluating LEP children for placement purposes (Ambert & Melendez, 1987).

In 1968, Congress passed Title 7 of the Elementary and Secondary School Act, or what is commonly referred to as the Bilingual Education Act. This act ensured the recognition of the special educational needs of the large numbers of LEP students. It provided financial assistance to schools to develop programs and provide appropriate services and resources. In 1978, Congress amended the Bilingual Education Act and added the category of *cultural heritage*, mandating bilingual educational services for those LEP students with a cultural heritage that differs from that of English-speaking persons.

In 1970, a class action suit by nine Mexican American children and their parents against the California State Board of Education *(Diana v. California State Board of Education)* resulted in the state supreme court requiring that evaluations and assessments be in the child's primary language. Later, the Department of Health, Education, and Welfare issued a memorandum to school districts requiring their compliance with this mandate and clarified the following issues (Ambert & Melendez, 1987, p. 29) relating to the responsibility of school districts to provide equal education opportunity to culturally diverse, LEP, and national-origin minority children:

- To take affirmative steps to remedy language limitations in order to provide access for these students in the educational programs

- To prohibit assigning national-origin minority group students to classes for the mentally retarded on the basis of English-language limitations, and to require providing students access to college preparatory courses

- To design any ability grouping or tracking system used to remediate the special language needs of these students to meet the language-skill needs of these children as soon as possible, and to prohibit their use as educational dead-ends or permanent tracking

- To hold school districts responsible for the adequate notification of national-origin minority group parents concerning school activities, and to require that such notification be provided in the appropriate language—other than English

In 1974, the Supreme Court ruled in *Lau v. Nichols* that schools must provide an appropriate education for LEP students—and that there is no equality in treatment merely by providing students with the same facilities, textbooks, teachers, and curriculum, for students who do not understand English are effectively foreclosed from any meaningful education. Also in 1974, the Equal Educational Opportunities Act was enacted, mandating that all children enrolled in public schools are entitled to equal educational opportunity without regard to race, color, gender, or national origin.

In 1975, Congress passed P.L. 94-142, the Education for All Handicapped Children Act (also discussed in Chapter 1), which guaranteed a free and appropriate education for students with disabilities between the ages of 3 and 22. As it applies to the area of cultural diversity, the act ensures the following:

1. Students cannot be placed in special education due to their environment, culture, income, race, religion, or creed.

2. Parents have the right to be informed (in their native language) and to give permission to have their child evaluated.

3. Students must be assessed and evaluated in their native language with nondiscriminatory assessments.

4. Parents have the right to due process.

5. Parents must be notified (written or verbal communication) in their native/home language.

Litigation related to both bilingual and special education includes court cases such as *Dyrcia S. et al. v. Board of Education of the City of New York* (1979) and *Lora v. Board of Education of the City of New York* (1984), which required the following:

1. The timely identification of children needing special education services with adequate bilingual resources

2. The establishment of school-based support teams to evaluate children in their own environment with a bilingual, nondiscriminatory evaluation process

3. A comprehensive continuum of services in the least restrictive environment, with the provision of appropriate bilingual programs at each level of the continuum for children with limited English proficiency

4. The translation of all due process and parental student rights forms, reports, and records into Spanish

As discussed in this section, numerous laws and policies have been established to ensure equal educational opportunities for all students. For those students who are from culturally diverse backgrounds, these mandates enforce their rights and equal access to education. However, the responsibility lies with the school personnel who design and deliver the programs. Their sensitivity and understanding are crucial to the practice of respect and appreciation for cultural diversity.

FOSTERING POSITIVE PARENT PARTNERSHIPS

I didn't know what to do when they told me my son was hard of hearing. I knew that he had trouble speaking and reading. I was so happy when I found out that there was a program to help him learn English and to help him with his hearing problems.

—Parent of a bilingual hearing-impaired boy

Numerous studies have documented that effective communication and participation between parents and the school personnel will enhance students' performance in the school. There is a strong, positive relationship between parent involvement and school achievement, increased student attendance, positive parent–child

---

EASY IDEAS FOR PRACTITIONERS

For Working With Culturally Diverse Students:

1. Allow students to use their primary language.
2. Use cooperative learning strategies and learning centers to reinforce academic instruction.
3. Display multicultural posters and charts in the classroom.
4. Provide books representing diversity in gender, race, age, careers, and so forth.
5. Provide tutors who can speak in the student's native language and English.

For Working With Parents of Culturally Diverse Students:

1. Send notes and reports home in both languages.
2. Design parent–school activities that reflect the cultures of the community.
3. Encourage parents and community leaders to assist in the classroom.
4. Incorporate cultural field trips to parents' places of work or homes.
5. Invite parents to host show-and-tell activities in the classroom.

---

communication, improved student attitudes and behavior, and more parent–community support of the schools (Hoover-Dempsey, Bassler, & Brissie, 1987). As concluded in one study: "There is much to be gained in terms of improved overall school achievement and improved cultural and interpersonal relationships between parents, teachers and students when educators accept the challenge of building upon the rich cultural diversity of its school" (Baruth & Manning, 1992, p. 225).

As with students, parents are more likely to become actively involved in the schools when they are respected. They are also more likely to participate in their children's educational programs if the school climate is open, helpful, friendly, and promotes collaboration and partnerships (Ysseldyke & Algozzine, 1995). Planning parent education programs for culturally diverse parents and families requires that educators look at issues, topics, and formats from the perspective of these parents and families (Baruth & Manning, 1992). It has been recommended that to enhance and increase the participation of parents from culturally diverse backgrounds, educators should encourage the following attitudes and actions:

1. Understand the extended family concept and involve educational experiences for both immediate and extended family members when working with culturally diverse groups.

2. Understand culturally diverse parents as individuals with intracultural, socioeconomic, and generational differences.

3. Learn as much as possible about culturally diverse parents and families through firsthand contact, parent surveys, and any other means that provide accurate and objective information.

4. Visit homes of culturally diverse students to gain a better understanding of family backgrounds, values, customs, and traditions.

5. Ensure that communication between the school and family reflects a genuine understanding of the problems that might result from language and communication differences, both verbal and nonverbal.

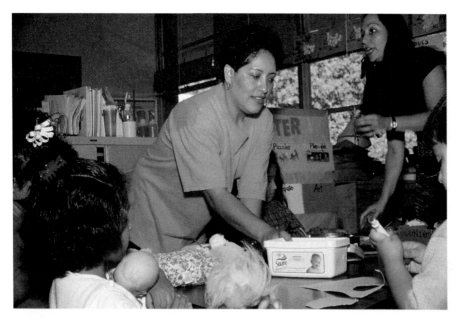

Culturally diverse parents will feel more comfortable becoming involved in the classroom if their language and customs are respected.

6. Ensure the parent advisory councils have a composition that represents the cultural, ethnic, and racial composition of the student body, and that the councils address the specific needs and concerns of culturally diverse parents and families (Baruth & Manning, 1992, p. 283).

In addition, educators must be sensitive to the needs of preparing school documents in the native language of the parents.

According to Light and Martin (1985) an understanding of cultural expectations and roles can contribute to the development of child management techniques specifically designed to eliminate value differences between a child's family, the school system, and the larger society.

VALID ASSESSMENTS FOR CULTURALLY DIVERSE STUDENTS

Court cases such as *Larry P. v. Riles, Lau v. Nichols,* and *Diana v. State Board of Education* established that children, for potential placement in special education, must be assessed in their native or primary language and that children cannot be placed in special education on the basis of culturally biased tests. Cummins (1982) stated that cultural bias is particularly a problem on IQ tests because so many items are designed to meet socialization norms of the culturally dominant group. Reynolds (1993) reported that *measurement bias,* in terms of evaluation tools, refers to errors introduced during testing when results are unfair or inaccurate due to the student's cultural background—reflecting artifacts of the test, or artificial results, rather than actual mental abilities or skills. Hoy and Gregg (1994) reported *test bias* in which some assessment procedures do not test the same level of performance by students from diverse cultures.

In terms of assessing culturally diverse students, **curriculum-based assessments** (also known as *criterion-referenced tests* or *objective-referenced tests*) have been recommended by many educators and evaluators. These tests give the teachers a measure of the extent to which individuals or groups have mastered specific curriculum content. Criterion-referenced testing refers to testing that compares the student's score with some established standard or criterion. Students are not compared to one another or to some norm but to an expected level of performance. This type of test can assist the teacher in determining if a student is ready to advance to another level of instruction. The results of these tests indicate the degree to which the content or skill identified has been mastered, and they assist in describing what each student has learned and needs to learn in a specific content area. Choate and colleagues (1987) listed the following reasons for using curriculum-based assessment:

1. It complies with similar procedural safeguards required by IDEA (see Chapter 1) for assessing students in need of special education.

2. It is efficient.

3. It is a valid, reliable basis for making decisions.

4. It can be used to make different kinds of decisions (e.g., screening, program effectiveness).

5. It increases students' achievements.

6. It helps teachers decide what to teach.

On the other hand, **norm-referenced testing** compares the student with a particular normative group in order to measure performance. Norm-referenced tests are particularly useful in comparing individual differences between children while criterion-referenced assessments are useful in determining whether children have attained various instructional objectives (Baca & Cervantes, 1989).

Assessing Students With Diverse Language

There are more than 2,000 languages spoken in the United States. Students with limited English proficiency are placed at a disadvantage upon entering school due to problems communicating fluently in English. There have been numerous incidents of language-diverse students being mislabeled as having a speech impairment, learning disability, or mental retardation due to their limited English. Thus, the first step in the assessment process is the initial screening of the student's language abilities in both English and the primary language to determine which language should be used for assessment.

Baca and Cervantes (1989) outlined the steps for assessing LEP students. After determining the language for assessment, the second step consists of the evaluation of the student's entire range of communicative abilities. Speech and language evaluations are essential to identify or eliminate suspected communication disorders. The last step is the evaluation of the student's abilities in English. The results of these multiple evaluations will assist the assessment team in determining if the student has a true disorder or needs a bilingual intervention such as ESL (English as a Second Language).

In terms of the assessment tools, examiners must be aware of the linguistic bias of IQ and other tests that are administered in English. In addition, it cannot be assumed that tests available in a minority language will automatically be reliable and valid for use in language assessment. Also, minority language tests should not be a direct translation of an English test because the constructs measured and the difficulty of particular items are often not carried through the translation. Baca and Cervantes (1989) recommended that speech and comprehension tests in minority languages should be used in the evaluation of language skills of LEP children. But they also included a warning:

> However, these tests should not be used indiscriminately by the practitioner simply because they are available. Tests should be screened for the validity of content, format appropriateness, test quality, and usefulness for offering sound judgments regarding the LEP student's need for speech and language services. (p. 135)

Assessment Instruments and Tools for Culturally Diverse Students

The following assessment instruments and tools have been recommended for assessing culturally diverse students. Educators and researchers have found better success with these tools in reducing the presence of culturally biased items:

- The System of Multicultural Pluralistic Assessment (SOMPA) measures and interprets sociocultural variables in a test. The SOMPA provides a set of medical, social, and pluralistic tests that give an extensive profile of the student. This test has had a significant effect in decreasing the number of African American and Hispanic students in special education programs.

- The Brigance Inventory of Early Development and the Brigance Inventory of Essential Skills use a task analysis approach and each subskill is measured.

- The Kaufman Assessment Battery for Children (K-ABC) measures intelligence and achievement but is done with a nominal amount of verbal involvement.

- The Woodcock-Johnson measures cognitive ability, learning aptitude, scholastic achievement, and interest level.

- The Ecological Assessment addresses the whole child and his or her interaction with the social environment.

- Portfolios in the gifted programs can be a useful tool to assist educators with students from culturally and linguistically diverse backgrounds, since the products contained in the portfolio do not have to depend on language or directly reflect academic achievement (Garcia, 1994). The use of portfolios (a collection of student work) has been recognized as an assessment tool that can be used with all students. Research (Johnsen, Ryser, & Dougherty, 1993) has indicated that the predictive validity of portfolios is showing they are a better predictor of future student achievement than most instruments. Among the benefits of the portfolio are its limited use of language, its ability to show student growth over time, its presentation of actual student work, and the documentation of teacher intervention activities.

INNOVATIVE IDEAS   ASSISTIVE TECHNOLOGY

Microcomputer-based technology is now providing the means to maximize students' ability. Computers enable students to work at their own pace, to self-evaluate their work, to problem-solve information, and to use their creative skills. Computers are an equal opportunity teaching tool. As one student stated, "Computers don't laugh at you and the computers will help you regardless of who you are or what learning problem you might have."

My name is Marcus Hagen and I am 13 years old. Last year I was in the seventh grade at Belle Plaine Junior High, in Belle Plaine, Minnesota. The seventh grade was very hard for me in social studies and science. I could not understand the books and sometimes I could not lip-read the teacher. It was so bad that I did not want to go to school at all. My mother learned about computers and asked the school to try Computer Assisted Instruction for me. They said yes, so my mother started writing programs for me to use at school. Things got better right away. The computer helps me learn new words and meanings. I used the computer at least 2 hours a day at school. I am learning how to type with a computer typing tutor and I am writing this story with a word processing system. My mother is writing courseware in science and geography for next year for me and other eighth graders. I like computers because they help me learn. I wish all students could use computers because if they could, it would make life easier for them. You can use a microcomputer to learn for typing, for word processing, for games, or just about anything. You can even use it as a TDD now that the telephone company said it is okay to use the microcomputer as a telecommunication device for the deaf. Sometimes it is hard for me to understand the teachers because they talk very fast. When they talk fast they asked me, "What does that word mean?" I said it all wrong. I felt so embarrassed because my class laughed at me. When I use the computer, the class didn't laugh. The computer does not make fun of me, it just teaches me.

Source: From *Microcomputer Resource Book for Special Education* (p. 20), by D. Hagen, 1984, Reston, VA: Reston Publishing, a Prentice-Hall Company.

SCHOOL PLACEMENT OPTIONS FOR CULTURALLY DIVERSE STUDENTS

Outlined below are some of the major educational programs for enhancing the education of culturally diverse students. Some students might receive all of their services in the regular education setting, whereas some with specific learning and/or language problems might be served better in a more restrictive environment such as a bilingual program or ESL—or for those with disabilities, a bilingual special education program. Again, it must be emphasized that the types of programs and services depend on the individual needs of the student.

Regular Education (With Emphasis on Diversity and Multicultural Education)

The goal of diversity and multicultural education is to promote educational programs, services, and activities that recognize and respect the culture and diversity of *all* students. Banks (1988, 1994) identified four major goals in multicultural education:

1. To increase the academic achievement of all students

2. To help all students develop more positive attitudes toward different cultural, racial, ethnic, and religious groups

Participating in ethnic celebrations allows all students to learn about and appreciate different cultures.

3. To help students from historically victimized groups develop confidence in their ability to succeed academically and to influence societal institutions

4. To help all students learn to consider the perspective of other groups

Bilingual–Bicultural Education

The goal of bilingual–bicultural education is to promote educational programs and services, with the primary focus on assisting students with two or more languages and cultures. The primary emphasis is to teach children concepts, knowledge, and skills in the language they know best and then to reinforce this through the use of English (Baca & Cervantes, 1989). The four general instructional program components for bilingual education, as recommended by Baca and Cervantes, are these:

- Acquisition of concepts and learning skills
- Development of the primary language
- Acquisition of a second language
- Multicultural education (p. 84)

Bilingual education may be justified as (1) the best way to attain the maximum cognitive development of linguistically different students, (2) a means of achieving equal educational opportunity and/or results, (3) a means of easing the transition into the dominant language and culture, (4) an approach to eventual total educational reform, (5) a means of promoting positive interethnic relations, and (6) a wise economic investment to help linguistic minority children to become maximally productive in adult life for the benefit of themselves and society (Baca & Cervantes, 1989, p. 27).

Bilingual Transitional Program. Students are taught in English using ESL strategies and also in their native language until they master enough English.

Bilingual Maintenance Program.   Students are taught both in English and in their native language. However, the goal is to maintain proficiency in the native language and in English.

English as a Second Language (ESL) Programs

English as a Second Language programs promote the acquisition of the English language and customs. Unlike bilingual education, ESL programs are used to assimilate limited English proficiency students into the linguistic mainstream as quickly as possible. Gollnick and Chinn (1994) expressed that in ESL programs, the home language and culture are given less emphasis than the acquisition of the English language.

Bilingual Special Education

You must be innovative in adapting special education materials and lessons into the home language. You must be creative and willing to try new materials and methods. After working with the students, you become more knowledgeable about other cultures and customs.

—Bilingual special education teacher

Bilingual special education incorporates the student's home language and culture, along with English, into an individualized special education program. Bilingual special education considers the student's language and culture as a foundation through which appropriate special education services can be implemented (Baca & Cervantes, 1989). The program consists of special educational programs and related services provided to bilingual students with identified disabilities as documented on the IEP. The program is designed to provide special instruction to enhance the cognitive, academic, and social abilities of the bilingual exceptional

Sometimes a bilingual special education classroom is the most appropriate placement for culturally diverse students with disabilities.

student to the fullest potential. Instruction is provided through the primary language while providing opportunities for learning English. Thus, the remediation of the LEP student with disabilities is conducted in the dominant language that the student can understand, with the student also acquiring the English language skills needed to survive in the school and community.

One of the problems with providing bilingual special education programs is the lack of trained personnel who can deliver the instruction in both languages and who also have special education training for the particular disability. Many programs will employ the use of a bilingual aide to assist the special education teacher. Another problem is modifying the specialized instructions into the home language. In the area of sign language, for example, some signs must be created to reflect terms and words in other cultures. Other problems involve the transition of bilingual special education students into regular education programs. The teacher must be sure that the students are properly integrated in terms of the modifications of their disability, culture, and language.

In developing bilingual special education programs, educators should follow these guidelines:

1. Assess the credentials of the personnel to determine their knowledge and skills in working and teaching culturally diverse special education students.

2. Assess the community in identifying resources such as interpreters, aides, materials, books, and community activities.

3. Assess the skills and talents of parents and community leaders in order to develop a pool of tutors and resource people to enhance the school program.

4. Identify special education teachers who can speak the home language of the students.

5. Provide in-service training for staff and students regarding the impact of students' cultures on school performance and achievement.

6. Provide in-service training for the evaluation teams in order to assist them in determining the most appropriate school placements in the least restrictive environment.

7. Develop teams of regular, special, and bilingual teachers and administrators to review the objectives and problems of delivering bilingual special education services such as grading, scheduling, assignments, and social skills.

8. Develop home–school–community multicultural enrichment activities.

CONCLUSION

Every student deserves the right to a free public education that fosters the student's educational and national rights to equal opportunity. It has been discussed that in order for students to achieve at their maximum educational potential, they must learn in a climate that accepts their individual uniqueness and respects their diversity. To accomplish this goal, teachers must accommodate an array of thinking and learning styles, systematically varying teaching and assessment methods to reach every student: "The key is variety and flexibility—using the full range of styles and resources available" (Sternberg, 1994, p. 38). Teachers who make positive use of the unique learning strengths that students bring from their cultures will help them to be more successful in school (Smith & Tyler, 1995). Students learn best when they can associate new information with their experiences. Students from diverse cultures may feel, justifiably, that their society has been misrepresented, underrepresented, or omitted entirely from the school curriculum (Smith & Tyler, 1995). When teachers do not provide students with the tools necessary to view information from different perspectives, they limit students' abilities to think and solve problems (Smith & Tyler, 1995).

To ensure education commitment to cultural diversity, Baruth and Manning (1992) designed the following self-evaluation checklist for educational professionals to determine their strengths, weaknesses, and overall knowledge of multicultural education:

Making a Commitment to Promoting Cultural Diversity

- The educational professional values and respects cultural diversity in all forms and degrees.
- The educational professional recognizes differences between disabilities and cultural diversity rather than perceiving differences as liabilities or deficiencies in need of remediation.
- The educational professional coordinates the efforts of administrators, faculty, and staff in the provision of the least restrictive environment for culturally diverse learners with disabilities.
- The educational professional supports a racially and culturally diverse faculty and staff for all children with disabilities.
- The educational professional insists that screening and placement procedures recognize cultural diversity but also be in accordance with the legal mandates and guidelines for providing special education experiences.
- The educational professional works with parents and families on a regular basis, helps them understand programs for children with disabilities, and makes referrals to appropriate social services agencies.
- The educational professional provides screening and testing using assessment instruments that do not have racial, cultural, and social class bias.
- The educational professional provides opportunities for culturally diverse children with disabilities to be included with students of all cultural backgrounds in general education settings whenever possible.
- The educational professional plans learning experiences that recognize differences in language and dialectic backgrounds.
- The educational professional supports community recognition and efforts to provide appropriate educational experiences for culturally diverse students with disabilities.

Five-Minute Summary

This chapter presented information and data to highlight the demographic changes in the student population and the implication of these changes for teaching in the 21st century. It clarified the need for addressing cultural diversity in classrooms, curriculum, school activities and programs, and in employing education personnel. It discussed the impact and importance of diversity and multiculturalism in education and the need to prepare teachers accordingly. It highlighted the importance of using learning and behavioral styles of culturally diverse students as an instructional tool to enhance their academic and social achievement in the classroom. It presented strategies on integrating multicultural education into the school environment. It reviewed the mandates and evaluation procedures and assessments used to guarantee equal educational opportunity for all students. It explored cultural diversity—especially in terms of overrepresentation in special education and underrepresentation in gifted and talented programs. Services for culturally diverse students and for LEP (limited English

proficiency students) were discussed, including bicultural education, bilingual education, and ESL (English as a Second Language). It described bilingual special education programs and services and the corresponding need for bilingual special education teachers. It discussed ways of building positive home–school partnerships and teaching strategies for involving parents in the education of their children. It provided a self-evaluation checklist for professionals to determine strengths, weaknesses, and overall knowledge of multicultural education, emphasizing the need to serve as a role model in fostering equal education opportunities for all students.

Study Questions

1. What are the implications of the predicted demographic changes in the student population for teaching in the 21st century?
2. Why is there a need for diversity and multicultural education?
3. What are some of the factors affecting the education of culturally diverse students?
4. Why is it important for teachers to have knowledge and skills in promoting cultural diversity?
5. What are some of the reasons for overrepresentation of culturally diverse students in special education and the underrepresentation of culturally diverse students in programs for students who are gifted and talented?

6. What are some of the major mandates, policies, and procedures that ensure equal educational opportunity for all students?
7. What are the effects of learning styles and behavioral styles in enhancing student achievement and performance?
8. What are some of the programs and services that schools may provide to assist culturally diverse students (including those with disabilities) in learning and performing in a positive environment and in ensuring equal educational opportunities?
9. Why is there a need for bilingual special education?

For More Information

ORGANIZATIONS

Association for Culturally and Linguistically
Diverse Exceptional Learners
The Council for Exceptional Children
1920 Association Drive
Reston, VA 22091

International Council on Disability (ICD)
25 East 21st Street, 4th Floor
New York, NY 10010

BOOKS AND ARTICLES

Baca, L. M., & Almanza, E. (1991). *Language minority students with disabilities.* Reston, VA: Council for Exceptional Students.

Campione, J. C., & Brown, A. L. (1987). Linking dynamic assessment with school achievement. In C. Schneider Lidz (Ed.), *Dynamic assessment: An interactional approach to evaluating learning potential* (pp. 82–115). New York: Guilford.

Chinn, P., & McCormick, L. (1986). Cultural diversity and exceptionality. In N. Haring & L. McCormick (Eds.), *Exceptional children and youth*. Columbus, OH: Merrill.

Derman-Sparks, L. (1989). *Anti-bias curriculum: Tools for empowering young children*. Washington, DC: National Association for the Education of Young Children.

Dunn, R., & Dunn, K. (1978). *Teaching students through their individual learning styles, a practical approach*. Reston, VA: Reston Publishing.

Guild, P. (1994). The culture/learning style connection. *Education Leadership, 51*, 16–21.

Hardman, M., Drew, C. J., & Egan, D. M. (1996). *Human exceptionality: Society, school, and family* (5th ed.). Boston: Allyn & Bacon.

Kappan, P. S. (1996). *Pathways for exceptional children: School, home, and culture*. New York: West.

LaFromboise, T., Coleman, H. L. K., & Gerton, J. (1993). Psychological impact of biculturalism: Evidence and theory. *Psychology Bulletin, 114*, 395–412.

Lasky, B. (1991). How long will they have to wait? The demand for teachers to instruct the LEP student. *Teacher Education Quarterly, 19*(3), 49–55.

Lasky, B. (1994). Language and behavioral disorders. In R. Peterson & S. Ishii-Jordan (Eds.), *Multicultural issues in the education of students with behavioral disorders* (pp. 178–183). Boston: Brookline.

Mercer, J. R., & Lewis, J. F. (1978). *System of multicultural pluralistic assessments: Student assessment manual*. New York: Psychological Corporation.

National Council for Accreditation of Teacher Education (1986). *Standards, procedures and policies for accreditation of professional teacher education units*. Washington, DC: Author.

Ortiz, A. A., & Yates, J. R. (1989). Staffing and the development of individualized educational programs for the bilingual exceptional student. In L. M. Baca & H. T. Cervantes (Eds.), *The bilingual special education interface* (pp. 183–203). Columbus, OH: Merrill.

Pai, Y. (1990). *Cultural foundations of education*. New York: Merrill.

Peterson, R. L., & Ishii-Jordan, S. (1994). *Multicultural issues in the education of students with behavioral disorders*. Cambridge, MA: Brookline.

Sobol, T. (undated). Bills of Rights for children: An education charter for the decade of the child. Drafted by Thomas Sobol, Commissioner of Education in New York: New York State Department of Education.

Stahl, R. L., & VanSickle, R. L. (Eds.). (1992). *Cooperative learning in the social studies classroom*. Bulletin No. 87. Washington, DC: National Council for the Social Studies.

Summer Institute of Linguistics. (1992). *Ethnology of language of the world*. Dallas: Summer Institute of Linguistics.

U.S. Commission on Civil Rights. (1975). *A better chance to learn: Bilingual–bicultural education*. Washington, DC: Clearinghouse Publication No. 51.

Waggoner, D. (1993). 1990 Census shows dramatic change in the foreign-born population in the U.S. *NABE News, 16*, (1), 18–19.

Yao, E. L. (1988). Working effectively with Asian immigrant parents. *Phi Delta Kappan, 70*, 223–225.

JOURNALS, NEWSLETTERS, AND OTHER PUBLICATIONS

Addressing Cultural and Linguistic Diversity in Special Education
S. Garcia, Editor
(A publication of the Division for Culturally and Linguistically Diverse Exceptional Learners)
Council for Exceptional Children
Reston, VA 22090

Teaching Tolerance
400 Washington Avenue
Montgomery, AL 36104
FAX 205-264-3121

VIDEO AND ELECTRONIC DATA

Learning Styles Inventory for Macintosh HyperCard
Educational Activities, Inc.
Freeport, NY 11520

References

Ambert, S., & Melendez, S. E. (1987). *Bilingual diversity: A sourcebook.* NY: Teacher College Press.

American Association of Colleges for Teacher Education. (1987). *Minority teacher recruitment and retention: A public policy issue.* Washington, DC: Author.

American Association of State Colleges and Universities. (1991). Short takes. *AACU Memo to the President, 32*(22), 1. (Citing material from the Education Commission of the States.)

Baca, L. M., & Cervantes, H. T. (1989). *The bilingual special education interface* (2d ed.). Columbus, OH: Merrill.

Banks, J. A. (1988). *Multiethnic education: Theory and practice* (2nd ed.). Boston: Allyn & Bacon.

Banks, J. A. (1994). *An introduction to multicultural education.* Boston: Allyn & Bacon.

Baruth, L. G., & Manning, M. L. (1992). *Multicultural education of children and adolescents.* Boston: Allyn & Bacon.

Battle, D. E. (1993). *Communication disorders in multicultural populations.* Stoneham, MA: Andover Medical Publishers.

Bedell, F. D. (1989). Testimony delivered at hearings conducted by the National Council on the Handicapped, June 7 and 8. Washington, DC.

Brown v. Board of Education of Topeka, 347 U.S. 483 (1954).

Brown, J. F., & Cooper, R. M. (1981). *Learning styles inventory for Macintosh hyperCard.* Freeport, NY: Educational Activities, Inc.

Bureau of the Census (1991). *Final 1990 census population counts.* Washington, DC: U.S. Department of Commerce.

Center for Research on Elementary and Middle Schools (1990). *The changing nature of the disadvantaged population: Current dimensions and future trends.* Baltimore: Johns Hopkins University.

Chandler, J. T., & Plakos, J. (1971). An investigation of Spanish speaking pupils placed in classes for the educable mentally retarded. *Journal of Mexican American Studies, 1,* 58.

Choate, J., Bennett, T., Enright, B., Miller, L., Poteet, J., & Rakes, T. (1987). *Assessing and programming basic curriculum skills.* Boston: Allyn & Bacon.

Cummins, J. (1982). Test, achievement, and bilingual students. *Focus, 1*(9), 19–27. Rosslyn, VA: National Clearinghouse for Bilingual Education.

Diana v. State Board of Education, No. C-70-37 Rfp (N.D. Calif. 1970).

Dyrcia S. et al. v. Board of Education of the City of New York, 79 C. 2562 (E.D.N.Y., 1979).

Equal Educational Opportunities Act of 1974, Section 1701–1703.

Fitzpatrick, J. P. (1987). *Puerto Rican Americans* (2nd ed.). Englewood Cliffs, NJ: Prentice-Hall.

Flanigan, P. J., & Schwartz, R. H. (1971, September). Evaluation of examiner bias in intelligence testing. *American Journal of Mental Deficiency, 56,* 252.

Franklin, M. E. (1992). Culturally sensitive instructional practices for African American learners with disabilities. *Exceptional Children, 59*(2), 115–122.

Garcia, J. H. (1994). Nonstandardized instruments for the assessment of Mexican-American children for gifted and talented programs. In Shernaz B. Garcia (Ed.), *Addressing cultural and linguistic diversity in special education* (pp. 3–12). Reston, VA: Council for Exceptional Children.

Gollnick, D. M., & Chinn, P. C. (1994). *Multicultural education in a pluralistic society* (4th ed.). Columbus, OH: Merrill.

Hale-Benson, J. E. (1986). *Black children: Their roots, culture, and learning styles.* Baltimore: Johns Hopkins University Press.

Hall, E. T. (1981). *Beyond culture.* Garden City, NY: Anchor.

Hanna, J. (1988). *Disruptive school behavior: Class, race and culture.* New York: Holmes & Meier.

Hoover-Dempsey, K. V., Bassler, O. C., & Brissie, J. S. (1987). Parent involvement: Contributions of teacher efficacy, school socioeconomic status, and other school characteristics. *American Education Research Journal, 24,* 417–435.

Hoy, C., & Gregg, N. (1994). *Assessment: The special educator's role.* Pacific Grove, CA: Brooks/Cole.

Johnsen, S. K., Ryser, G., & Dougherty, E. (1993). The validity of product portfolios in the identification of gifted students. *Gifted International: A Talent Development Journal, 8*(1), 40–43.

Jones, R. L. (1976). *Mainstreaming and the minority child.* Minneapolis: Council for Exceptional Children.

Larry P. v. Riles, Civil Action No. C-70-37 (N.D. Calif. 1971).

Lau v. Nichols, 414 U.S. 563 (1974).

Light, H., & Martin, R. (1985). Guidance of American Indian children. *Journal of American Indian Education, 25*(1), 42–46.

Lora v. Board of Education of the City of New York, 587 F. Supp. 1572 (E.D.N.Y., 1984).

Lum, D. (1986). *Social work practice and people of color: A process-stage approach.* Monterey, CA: Brooks/Cole.

Lynch, E. W., & Hanson, M. J. (1992). *Developing cross-cultural competence.* Baltimore: Paul H. Brookes.

McIntyre, T. (1992). A primer on cultural diversity for educators. *Multicultural Forum, 1*(1), 6, 13.

McIntyre, T. (1993). A response to May: Did we read the same article? *Beyond Behavior, 4*(3), 2.

McIntyre, T. (1994). Teaching urban behavior disordered youth. In R. Peterson & S. Ishii-Jordan (Eds.), *Multicultural issues in the education of students with behavioral disorders* (pp. 216–232). Boston: Brookline.

McIntyre, T. (1995a). Entering uncharted waters with tattered sails and a broken rudder. In B. Brooks & D. Sabatino, (Eds.), *Behavior disorders: Personal perspectives on the past, present and future.* PRO-ED.

McIntyre, T. (1995b). *The McIntyre assessment of culture.* Columbia, MO: Hawthorne Educational Services.

Meister, J. S. (1991). The health of migrant farm workers. *Journal of Occupational Medicine, 6,* 503–513.

Mirande, A. (1986). Adolescence and Chicano families. In G. K. Leigh & G. W. Peterson (Eds.), *Adolescents in families* (pp. 433–455). Cincinnati, OH: Southwestern.

Ortiz, A. A., & Polyzoi, E. (1988). Language assessment of Hispanic learning disabled and speech and language handicapped students: Research in progress. In A. A. Ortiz & B. A. Ramirez (Eds.), *Schools and the culturally diverse exceptional student: Promising practices and future directions* (pp. 32–45). Reston, VA: Council for Exceptional Children.

Payne, C. (1984). Multicultural education and racism in American schools. *Theory Into Practice, 23,* 124–131.

Perez, B. (1991). Cultural and linguistic democracy: A challenge for today's schools. *Curriculum Report, 22*(2), 1–4.

Quality Education for Minorities Project (1990). *Education that works: An action plan for the education of minorities.* Cambridge, MA: Massachusetts Institute of Technology.

Reynolds, C. R. (1993). *Cognitive assessment: A multidisciplinary perspective.* New York: Plenum.

Richardson, E. H. (1981). Cultural and historical perspectives in counseling American Indians. In D. W. Sue (Ed.), *Counseling the culturally different* (pp. 225–227). New York: Wiley.

Smith, D. D., & Tyler, N. C. (1995). A focus on diversity and awareness of differences. In Smith and Luckasson. In *Introduction to special education: Teaching in an age of challenge* (2nd ed.). Boston: Allyn & Bacon.

Spindler, G. D. (1963). Education in a transforming America. In G. D. Spindler (Ed.), *Education and culture* (pp. 132–147). New York: Holt, Rinehart & Winston.

Statistical Abstract. (1994). Washington, DC: U.S. Department of Commerce.

Sternberg, R. J. (Nov., 1994). Allowing for thinking styles. *Educational Leadership.*

Sugai, G., & Maheady, L. (1988). Cultural diversity and individual assessment for behavior disorders. *Teaching Exceptional Children, 52*(3), 36–40.

Tiedt, P. L., & Tiedt, I. M. (1995). *Multicultural teaching: A handbook of activities, information, and resources* (4th ed.). Boston: Allyn & Bacon.

U.S. Department of Education. (1993). *Fifteenth annual report to Congress on the implementation of the Individuals With Disabilities Education Act.* Washington, DC: Author.

Vaughan, E. (1993). Individual and cultural differences in adaptation to environmental risks. *American Psychologist, 48,* 673–680.

Vontress, C. E. (1986). Counseling the racial and ethnic minorities. In G. S. Belkin (Ed.), *Counseling: Directions in theory and practice* (pp. 277–290). Belmont, CA: Wadsworth.

Wilson, R. (1988). Recruiting and retaining minority teachers. *Journal of Negro Education, 57*(2), 195–201.

Yetman, N. R. (1985). *Majority and minority: The dynamics of race and ethnicity in American life* (4th ed.). Boston: Allyn & Bacon.

Ysseldyke, J., & Algozzine, B. (1995). *Special education: A practical approach for teachers* (3rd ed.). Boston: Houghton Mifflin.

Chapter 3

Poet's World, acrylic on canvas, 48″ × 38″ (1994)

GIFTED AND TALENTED

Bonnie Cramond

After studying this chapter, the reader will:

Be able to trace the historical ebb and flow of
support for gifted education

Know the major purposes and findings of the
Terman and Hollingworth studies

Differentiate among the definitions of giftedness according to
Terman, Renzulli, and the U.S. Office of Education

Recognize cognitive and affective characteristics and
resultant needs of gifted children

Appreciate the special needs of the highly gifted, the creative,
gifted underachievers, and gifted children with disabilities

Be able to explain the prevalence of giftedness as
determined by the definition used

Understand the roles of nature and nurture in the
development of giftedness

Be familiar with issues and recommendations relative
to the assessment of giftedness

Understand the concept of curriculum differentiation
for gifted students

Have suggestions for teachers to meet the needs of
gifted students in the regular classroom

Have suggestions for parents to develop the
talents of their gifted children

Identify current issues and predict future trends in gifted education

Gifted and Talented

Late 1700s	Jefferson urged the country to select the brightest boys for education at public expense.
1905	Binet developed the first lasting test of intelligence.
1921	Terman began his longitudinal study of gifted individuals.
1920s	Ability grouping and enrichment classes came into use.
1942	Hollingworth published her study of highly gifted children.
1946	The first professional society devoted to the needs of gifted and talented individuals, the American Association for the Study of the Gifted, was established.
1954	The National Association for Gifted Children was established.
1957	Sputnik was launched.
1958	The Association for the Gifted, an affiliate of the Council for Exceptional Children, was established.
1960s	An increase in creativity studies became evident.
1970	Congress passed P.L. 91-230; Section 806 addressed "Provisions Related to Gifted and Talented Children."
1972	The first federal definition of giftedness and the Office of the Gifted and Talented were established.
1981	The Office of the Gifted and Talented was dissolved.
1988	The Jacob K. Javits Gifted and Talented Students Act was passed.
1995	Javits Act appropriation was slashed in half—continued funding for the research center, but no new grants.

HISTORICAL OVERVIEW

In the embryonic democracy of Plato's Greece, little Ari may have been selected for distinctive education because of his ability to detect deceit, recognize superstitions, and profit by trial and error—all abilities seen as helpful to society. In China, young Wang may have been selected for education in the royal court because he showed verbal ability, creativity, and leadership potential. In Sparta, military prowess was cultivated; in Renaissance Europe, it was artistic ability. In Suleiman's Ottoman Empire, the brightest were trained to be leaders. Throughout history and throughout the world, gifts that are valued by the society have been sought out and nurtured, often without regard to social class, and usually at public expense.

So, too, in the early days of our own country, those gifts that were valued and viewed as useful to the society were identified and developed. Thomas Jefferson, who was so heavily influenced by the writings of the Greeks in developing our country's system of government, was also persuaded that a democracy depends on educating its future leaders. He urged the country to select the brightest boys for education at public expense. However, as indicated in a 1794 pamphlet by Ben Franklin (cited in Burdin, 1978), some residents of the United States differed as to just what gifts should be developed. In reply to an offer from the government of Virginia to educate Indian youth at the college in Williamsburg, the spokesman from the Six Nations replied as follows:

> We know that you highly esteem the kind of learning taught in those colleges, and that the maintenance of our young men, while with you, would be very expensive to you. We are convinced, therefore, that you mean to do us good by your proposal and we thank you heartily.
>
> But you, who are wise, must know that different nations have different conceptions of things; and you will not therefore take it amiss, if our ideas of this kind of education happen not to be the same with yours. We have had some experience of it: several of our young people were formerly brought up at the colleges of the northern provinces; they were instructed in all your sciences; but, when they came back to us, they were bad runners, ignorant of every means of living in the woods, unable to bear either cold or hunger, knew neither how to build a cabin, take a dear [*sic*] nor kill an enemy, spoke our language imperfectly, were therefore neither fit for hunters, warriors, nor counsellors: they were totally good for nothing.
>
> We are however not the less obligated by your kind offer, though we decline accepting it; and, to show our grateful sense of it, if the gentlemen of Virginia will send us a dozen of their sons, we will take care of their education, instruct them in all we know, and make men of them. (Burdin, 1978, p. 33)

Brief History of Education for the Gifted in the United States

In the one-room schoolhouse with multiage groupings, it was probably not too difficult for the teacher to allow each child to move through the material at his or her own pace. As schools became larger and more complex, accommodations for rapid learners primarily took the form of flexible promotion (Tannenbaum, 1983). However, in the 1920s, the interest in individual abilities and methods for measuring them that inspired Terman impacted the schools with the beginnings of ability grouping and enrichment classes for the gifted (Tannenbaum, 1983).

In the 1930s and 1940s ability grouping and separate enrichment classes declined in popularity. According to Davis and Rimm (1994, p. 4), the decline can be

REAL PEOPLE   *Maya Angelou*

Even if there had been a program for gifted and talented students in Stamps, Arkansas, when Marguerite Johnson was a young girl, it is unlikely that she would have been selected to participate. Living in the rural South, poor, black, and from a broken home, she epitomized what educators often view as an "at-risk" student. Her rape at age 8 and subsequent psychosomatic muteness would seem to solidify that view. However, inside the body that she herself described as thin and unattractive burned a brilliant mind. Marguerite Johnson grew up to be the poet, playwright, novelist, actress, director, and professor that we know as Maya Angelou.

How did little disadvantaged Marguerite become the much honored Maya Angelou? As for any gifted and talented individual, Maya Angelou's success probably resulted from a combination of inborn talents, role models and mentors, opportunities, and motivation. There is evidence of all of these in the autobiography of her early years, *I Know Why the Caged Bird Sings.*

A quietly intelligent child, Maya read as much for the sheer delight of language as to escape the loneliness and difficulty of her life. Early evidence of the vividness of her memory and imagination is apparent in her rich descriptions of her life in Stamps, St. Louis, and then later in San Francisco.

Her primary role models were her grandmother and mother, two very different women who taught her how to be a strong, independent woman. But her mentor was Mrs. Flowers, a family friend who was able to coax Maya into speaking again 5 years after the traumatic rape. In doing so she also reopened Maya's mind and heart through a mutual love of literature. Mrs. Flowers, who recognized Maya's potential, was described by Maya Angelou this way: "She was one of the few gentlewomen I have ever known, and has remained throughout my life the measure of what a human being can be" (1969/1973, p. 78).

Maya's real opportunity came when she was able to move to San Francisco with her mother. She flourished in the cosmopolitan atmosphere and freedom that city life afforded her. However, it was her iron will and drive that allowed her to make the most of her opportunities. At age 15, setting her sights on becoming a streetcar conductor, Maya fought tradition and bureaucracy, then lied about her age on the application, to become the first black streetcar conductor in San Francisco.

Throughout her life Maya Angelou fought poverty, racism, sexism, and ignorance to become the woman she is today. With the help of strong role models and a good, dedicated teacher, she was able to become an accomplished, eminent individual.

attributed to two main causes: a concern for equity over excellence and the Depression. However, by 1946 the establishment of the American Association for the Study of the Gifted, the first professional society in this field, evidenced a resurgence of interest in gifted students. This interest was further reflected in the report of the Educational Policies Commission in 1950, which decried the waste to society from the educational neglect of gifted students, and the publication of an extensive book on the topic in 1951, *The Gifted Child*, edited by Paul Witty (Tannenbaum, 1983). Then, in 1954, the National Association for Gifted Children was established, followed by The Association for the Gifted (TAG) in 1958, an affiliate of the Council for Exceptional Children.

The burgeoning interest in gifted education was fueled by what may have been the pivotal event of the 1950s—the launch of the Soviet satellite, *Sputnik.* Perceiving an intellectual, technological, and military threat to the United States, the country became convinced that years of anti-intellectualism in the schools had allowed the Soviets to overtake American superiority (Tannenbaum, 1983, p. 20).

The result was expenditures and efforts to ensure that the most able American minds—especially in science and mathematics—were prepared to compete with the Soviets.

The 1960s, marked by turmoil in many areas, witnessed a questioning by gifted youth of the values of their parents and the rationalism of science (Tannenbaum, 1983). The civil rights movement and the women's movement raised social consciousness about equal opportunities and concerns about the elitism of special programs.

However, in 1970 there was a landmark addition to the Elementary and Secondary Education Amendments of 1969 (P.L. 91-230) that addressed the needs of gifted children. This addition, Section 806, titled "Provisions Related to Gifted and Talented Children," determined that the gifted should benefit from existing federal legislation and empowered the commissioner of education, Sidney Marland, to investigate and make recommendations about additional provisions. Marland's report (1972) established the Office of the Gifted and Talented in Washington, D.C., with ten regional offices to coordinate federal efforts. It also included a definition of the gifted and talented for federal education programs that was designed to encompass 3% to 5% of the school population.

In 1981, with federal cutbacks in education and social programs, the Office of the Gifted and Talented was dissolved. However, in 1988, the Jacob K. Javits Gifted and Talented Students Act caused a rebound in the federal initiative (Title 4, Part B, of P.L. 100-297). The Javits Act impacted gifted education in two major ways: First, it established the National Research Center on the Gifted and Talented, based at the University of Connecticut, with collaborative sites at the University of Georgia, the University of Virginia, and Yale University. The purposes of the center are to conduct research on policies and practices in gifted education, and to disseminate and implement findings. Second, the Javits Act provided funding for research, teacher training, establishment of model programs, and technical assistance across the country. The resultant growth of gifted programs has been phenomenal. By 1990, all 50 states had enacted legislation for gifted education, although not all had allocated funds (Davis & Rimm, 1994).

This pattern of waxing and waning support for gifted programs coincides with specific periods in U.S. history. Some of the factors that affect public support are (1) the pervasiveness of the belief that gifted individuals are a valuable asset for the society, (2) the availability of resources, and (3) the current opinion swing on the excellence-versus-equity debate. Whether gifted programs continue to receive support depends on these and other factors; the expansion of the definition of giftedness is one move in the direction of resolving the question of providing for excellence in an equitable manner.

Today, concerns about inclusion and multicultural viewpoints have led to a broadening of the concept of giftedness. In past decades, as society came to recognize the value of educating females, girls were gradually included in schools and classes for the gifted. Now there is a concern for recognizing and developing gifts as they are valued and expressed in various cultures.

In summary, the idea of selection and development of gifts is an ancient one, although what is considered gifted has varied with time and place. The definition of giftedness will no doubt continue to shift as the needs and values of society change; however, the argument for the development of gifts at public expense for potential benefit to the society remains. What has been added is the more modern, Western idea of development of gifts for the good of the individual, as well as movement toward a more inclusive view of giftedness reflecting the multiculturalism of U.S. society. Concurrently, there is growing support for the idea that measuring this array of abilities with a single test score is inappropriate.

DEFINITIONS OF GIFTEDNESS

What does *gifted* mean? As you read in the historical overview, definitions of giftedness vary with time and place. The development of the intelligence test at the beginning of the 20th century promoted the practice of equating giftedness with an IQ score. Ironically, the test that Binet developed to find the children most likely to have trouble learning in the French school system provided the means by which Lewis Terman and his colleagues began the longitudinal descriptive study of a group of gifted individuals.

In a five-volume tome titled *Genetic Studies of Genius* (Vol. 1, 1925; Vol. 2, 1926; Vol. 3, 1930; Vol. 4, 1947; Vol. 5, 1959), Terman and colleagues refuted the commonly held negative myths about gifted children being homelier, sicklier, frailer, and more emotionally unstable than other children (Seagoe, 1975; Shurkin, 1992; Subotnik, Kassan, Summers, & Wasser, 1993). Although now viewed as flawed due to failure to control for teacher selection bias and differences in the students' socioeconomic status, Terman's study retains its place as a landmark because he was able to provide a more encouraging and desirable view of gifted children. The current view is that gifted children are a heterogeneous group that includes individuals normally dispersed along any continuum of health, beauty, emotional stability, and other traits.

Unfortunately, another result of Terman's work was that giftedness was equated with and identified solely by IQ for many years. As concepts of intelligence have broadened beyond something that can be represented by a single score on a single test, so too have recent definitions of giftedness broadened to include more than intelligence.

An example of the broadening of the concept of intelligence is evident in Spearman's (1904) differentiation between general intelligence, which he labeled "*g*," and special task intelligence, such as mathematical ability, labeled "*s*." Broadening it more, Thurstone (1938) divided intelligence into seven factors: number, verbal, space, memory, reasoning, word fluency, and perceptual speed. However, the splintering of the intelligence construct reached an all-time high with Guilford's Structure of the Intellect Model (1967). Conceptualized as a three-dimensional model of intelligence depicting the interaction of the contents, operations, and products of any intellectual activity, it originally comprised 120 cognitive abilities. Later, Guilford subdivided the components, resulting in 180 cognitive abilities (1977).

As more modern theorists such as Gardner (1983) and Sternberg (1985; 1996) have described multiple intelligences, the idea of measuring giftedness with a single IQ score has become suspect. Thus, leaders in the field of gifted education are calling for the use of multiple measures to identify gifted students and a varied curriculum to develop their diverse gifts (e.g., Clark, 1992; Cox, Daniel, & Boston, 1985; Feldhusen, 1996; Frasier, 1987; Renzulli, 1994; Renzulli & Reis, 1986; Treffinger & Feldhusen, 1996). In addition to or in place of IQ tests, districts might also use measures such as parent, peer, and teacher nominations; tests of special abilities or aptitudes such as in creativity, academics, and the arts; checklists of behaviors indicative of motivation and/or leadership; and real-life measures such as products and performances.

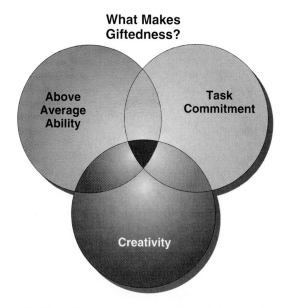

Figure 3.1   Renzulli's Three-Ring Conception of Giftedness

Source: Adapted from *The Schoolwide Enrichment Model: A Comprehensive Plan for Educational Excellence* (p. 24), by J. S. Renzulli & S. M. Reis, 1985, Mansfield Center, CT: Creative Learning Press.

An example of a broadened definition of giftedness, Renzulli's three-ring conceptualization of giftedness includes above average ability, creativity, and task commitment (1978, 1986). This concept is illustrated in Figure 3.1. According to Renzulli, potential can be identified through checklists and other measures of these three areas, although a child need not possess all three to be identified as gifted (Renzulli, 1985, 1986). In Renzulli's words: "Gifted and talented children are those possessing or capable of developing this composite set of traits and applying them to any potentially valuable area of human performance" (1986, p. 73).

The federal definition of giftedness is also much broader than that used by Terman and other early researchers. The definition composed by experts in the field and published in Marland's 1972 report to the U.S. Congress included six areas through which a child could show outstanding potential or achievement:

1. General intellectual ability

2. Creative or productive thinking

3. Specific academic aptitude

4. Leadership ability

5. Visual and performing arts ability

6. Psychomotor ability

In the Educational Amendment of 1978, (Title 9, Part A of P.L. 95-561) the last category was deleted to prevent the money allocated for gifted programs from going to sports programs. The latest definition from the U.S. Department of Education reflects concern for including both a wide range of abilities and children from diverse cultural and economic groups:

College may be the most appropriate academic setting for this gifted student, but he may have trouble adapting socially.

> Children and youth with outstanding talent perform or show the potential for performing at remarkably high levels of accomplishment when compared with others of their age, experience, or environment.
>
> These children and youth exhibit high performance capability in intellectual, creative, and/or artistic areas, possess an unusual leadership capacity, or excel in specific academic fields. They require services or activities not ordinarily provided by the schools.
>
> Outstanding talents are present in children and youth from all cultural groups, across all economic strata, and in all areas of human endeavor. (1993, p. 3)

Although most states have adopted and adapted some version of the federal definition as their *theoretical* definition of giftedness, they still have to determine an *operational* definition. The theoretical definition explains who the gifted are; the operational definition details exactly what criteria will be used to identify them. For example, a state may indicate in its theoretical definition that creativity is part of being gifted. The operational definition must outline how the student will be identified as creative (e.g., a score at or above the 95th percentile on a standardized creativity test).

Partly because of the need to operationalize definitions for implementation, and partly because of the ambiguity inherent in the terms, there is much variability in how people use the terms *giftedness, creativity,* and *talent.* Sometimes giftedness refers to general intellectual ability, and talent to specific ability, such as "a talented mathematician" (Feldhusen, 1986; MacKinnon, 1978). Other times talent refers to a point on the continuum of ability that is less than giftedness—such as when one believes there are many talented musicians, but few truly gifted ones (Cox, Daniel, & Boston, 1985, p. 122). On the other hand, Gagné (1985) conceptualized giftedness as ability, and talent as performance. According to his definitions, a talented mathematician must have a mathematical gift, but not all individuals with mathematical gifts develop their talent. This is more similar to Bloom's (1985) definition of talent as a high level of *demonstrated* ability rather than *aptitude* in a certain field of study or interest.

The same confusion reigns with the concept of creativity. Guilford (1967, 1977) included many creative abilities in his model of intelligence. However, many people assume that creativity is limited to artistic expression and don't consider the creativity inherent in scientific discoveries, the formulation of mathematical algorithms, or even everyday creativity such as stretching a dollar. Although there is wide variation in both popular and academic definitions of these terms, the operational definitions adopted by the schools ultimately determine who will be served through the gifted program.

CHARACTERISTICS OF GIFTED CHILDREN

Cognitive Abilities

Spend some time in a class of gifted children. If it is like most such classes, the children will exhibit a range of physical and personality characteristics. What they will have in common is a set of characteristics related to the operational definition by which they were identified. For example, children identified by an IQ test will typically exhibit an advanced vocabulary, wide general knowledge, an excellent memory, reading proficiency, strong reasoning skills, good visual spatial ability, and solid problem solving ability. That is because these skills are measured on IQ tests.

Children identified by other means may be expected to be similar to each other to the extent that they were identified because of similar traits. For example, children identified for leadership ability might be expected to have good social, communication, and organizational skills. Children who are identified for an advanced language arts class could be expected to be similar in their facility with language, although they may be very different in many other ways.

Behaviors Indicative of Giftedness

According to Hagen (1980, pp. 23–26), one of the authors of the Stanford Binet IV intelligence test, the 15 characteristics in Table 3.1 are observable indicators of potential giftedness. Of course, in order for children to exhibit such behaviors, they must be given opportunities in the school and the home to engage in a variety of activities that allow a high level of challenge and require persistence. Also, there must be an adult willing to interact with the child and observe the child over a period of time. In some classrooms and homes these conditions are not met. However, when they are, these behaviors, indicative of giftedness, are better measured by teacher and parent observations than on formal instruments (Hagen, 1980).

One caveat regarding identification by teacher observation is that the teacher must be willing and able to recognize giftedness in all students regardless of gender, race, or socioeconomic status. Successful identification requires that the teacher be able to see the manifestations of giftedness through the cultural milieu by some

Table 3.1   **Observable Indicators of Potential Giftedness and Related Educational Needs**

CHARACTERISTICS	OBSERVABLE BEHAVIORS	EDUCATIONAL NEEDS
Use of language	Precision in the use of words and complexity of sentence structure, in addition to vocabulary	Exposure to challenging literature in different genres and opportunities to try writing in each
Quality of student's questions	Unusualness and insightfulness of questions in relation to age	Instruction in a wide variety of methods of research and technologies for finding information
Quality of examples, illustrations, or elaborations	Appropriate and original examples, analogies, or translations of information into another format	Opportunities for transforming knowledge from one form to another and availability of resources for doing so
Use of quantitative expressions and quantitative reasoning	Use of abstractions at an early age and translation of situations into mathematical expressions	Instruction in mathematical concepts, problem solving, and mysteries at an early age
Systematic and strategic problem solving	A large repertoire of strategies, the awareness of which to use when, and the flexibility to change when one is not working	Opportunities to use strategic problem solving in a variety of situations and contents
Special skills that are unusual for the student's age or grade	Any talents or skills exhibited during lessons or free activities (artistic ability, grace in movement, dramatic expression, etc.)	A mentor, who may even be an older child, with some expertise in the area of expressed talent
Innovative use of common materials in the classroom or outside of it	Adaptations or combinations of familiar materials for new uses	A rich variety of materials available (may be junk) and opportunities to work with various media
Breadth of information	Indications of a good memory and a variety of interests	Opportunities to "test out" of instruction in areas the student has already mastered
Depth of information in a particular area	Intense interest and memory focused on an area	Content acceleration in the area of expertise (e.g., fifth grade math skills in third grade)
Collections of materials or hobbies	Unusual pastimes or collections and original or systematic organization	Opportunities to create new products and systems with assignments
Persistence on uncompleted tasks	Motivation to find the answer or complete the task, even if during play time (may not be observed on routine school work)	Encouragement for task completion; assistance in learning to prioritize
Absorption in intellectual tasks	Resistance to interruption; losing track of time	Instruction in time management and negotiation skills
Extensiveness of exploratory behavior	Curiosity and attempts to satisfy it	Open-ended assignments that encourage exploration
Criticalness of his or her own performance	Objective, analytical application of standards rather than false modesty	Assistance in setting realistic goals and information about standards in the area of interest; self and peer evaluation
Preferences for complexity, difficulty, and novelty in tasks	Challenge seeking	Opportunities for self-selection of challenging assignments

Source: Characteristics and behaviors adapted from *Identification of the Gifted,* by E. Hagen, 1980, New York: Teachers College, Columbia University.

awareness of the values of children's native cultures. For example, children from some Asian cultures may demonstrate curiosity through intense scrutiny rather than by asking questions because they have been taught not to question their elders.

In the table, each characteristic has been paired with an educational need that is related to it. In general, students exhibiting characteristics of giftedness need modifications in their curriculum according to the characteristics they display and the content areas in which they excel. There will be more discussion of curriculum modifications for the gifted later in this chapter.

Affective Characteristics and the Needs They Create

In the list of behaviors on the table, there is an observable temperament characteristic that has received much attention and support as a key to success in life: **task persistence.** Terman (1947) found that "integration toward a goal" is what differentiated the most successful of his subjects from the least successful, regardless of IQ. Torrance (1979) also found that persistence allowed creative children to hold onto their creativity over the years. This compulsion, or drive, has been noted by others who have studied eminent adults (Albert, 1975) and is reflected in Renzulli's (1978) definition of the gifted. Although not a new idea, the prominent role that affect plays in an individual's achievement has gained widespread acknowledgment with the publication of *Emotional Intelligence* (Goleman, 1995), a book synthesizing 10 years of research into this matter.

Other affective characteristics of gifted students are related to the operational definition that was used to identify them as gifted and the extremity of their gifts. For example, Terman concluded that the children he identified as gifted differed from average children in emotional and moral qualities as well as intellectual and volitional traits (Seagoe, 1975, p. 91). Because of the relationship between intellectual and affective development, his observations about emotional and moral differences may have been related to the children's intellectual precocity. Advanced cognitive development allows children to transcend egocentrism at an earlier age and take into account the viewpoint of others (Piaget & Inhelder, 1969). This empathetic viewpoint facilitates moral development and an advanced sense of justice (Hoffman, 1987). In the words of one researcher: "Giftedness has an emotional as well as a cognitive substructure: cognitive complexity gives rise to emotional depth" (Silverman, 1993a, p. 3).

When the intellectual and affective development are too asynchronous, the result may be problematic (Silverman, 1993a). For example, Hollingworth (1942) noted that the highly intellectually gifted children she studied asked metaphysical questions years before their age peers. However, although they were intellectually capable of pondering the meaning of life and the nature of death at the age of 6 or 7, their emotional control in dealing with such issues remained that of a child: "For instance, a six-year-old boy of IQ 187 wept bitterly after reading 'how the North taxed the South after the Civil War'" (Hollingworth, 1942, p. 281).

The empathy apparent in Hollingworth's example is an indication of how advanced cognitive ability affects emotional characteristics and moral development. It would be unlikely for the average 6-year-old to respond so empathetically to a group of people so far removed from him in place and time. It would be unlikely for the average 6-year-old to be interested in and capable of reading such an account in the first place.

Other problems can result from just feeling different from peers. These problems are exacerbated when the giftedness creates behaviors that are counter to those acceptable in the peer group. For example, gifted girls hide their abilities to be less intimidating to boys. Children from minority groups may also feel peer pressure to hide their gifts. This excerpt from a speech by Jennifer, a gifted African American adolescent, addresses some of these feelings:

> In third grade, I was accused of something called "acting white" by some of my black peers. I could not understand why they could not see that I was just being what I was, not black, not white, just interested in learning. . . . I had few friends in class and lots of enemies on the playground. . . . In terms of relations with my black peers, sixth grade . . . was my worst year. . . . I could no longer have normal conversations with my white friends because mobs of other black students would surround us and shout things. . . . Insults and names began appearing on my locker in black permanent marker. Food was thrown at me in lunch, three of my purses disappeared, and my saxophone was mysteriously broken. . . . Even though I was having all of these problems with my peers, when I was in gifted class, not only was I physically away from the persons causing me distress, but I was mentally away from them also. As they yelled insults my way I was lost in the Odyssey. . . . I found a place where I fit in. . . .
>
> In a perfect school every child would be challenged to his utmost ability, and no group would be put in front of any other group. . . . [The gifted program] would not be associated with any negative images having to do with race, sex, or background. (Jenkins, 1995)

In addition, there may be confusion about the label "gifted" and fear of increased expectations. Jennifer described those fears like this:

> After being accepted into the gifted program, I was not sure how to act. I was under the illusion that from now on everything that came out of my mouth had to be of great significance. I figured gifted kids did not make mistakes, not if they were truly gifted. (Jenkins, 1995)

Sometimes such fears lead to an "imposter syndrome" (Adderholdt-Elliot, 1987) in which the sufferers dread being discovered as the fakes they feel themselves to be.

Other times such fears lead to disabling **perfectionism.** Adderholdt-Elliot (1987) described the touch of perfectionism that drives individuals to do their best work in a healthy pursuit of excellence. She differentiated this from disabling perfectionism that inhibits productivity. Thus, the bright student who continues to work on his science project past the due date may be suffering from disabling perfectionism. As it worsens, he may even refuse to attempt a science fair project the next year. More extreme reactions to disabling perfectionism may include loss of self-esteem, high anxiety, eating disorders, or depression.

SPECIAL SUBGROUPS OF GIFTED CHILDREN

The Highly Gifted

Relatively little is known about highly gifted children. Because they are statistically few in number, studies of students who are highly gifted are difficult to conduct and not conducive to analysis by most statistical methods. A notable exception, Hollingworth's longitudinal case studies of 12 children with IQs above 180 were groundbreaking in their revelations about such rare and extreme cases of intellectual giftedness. Hollingworth recorded the precocious intellectual accomplishments of these children and noted that early ability in talking and reading most clearly distinguished the group from the norm (1942, p. 228).

In general, Hollingworth found that children with very high IQs demonstrated remarkable intellectual accomplishments at an early age. Some experienced social and emotional adjustments due to the challenges of having an adult mind in a child's body, but those whose talents were recognized and nurtured from an early age grew into productive, well adjusted adults.

Hollingworth's study has been criticized for some of the same reasons as Terman's: a narrow definition of giftedness as IQ and a lack of representatives in the study from various socioeconomic and ethnic groups, with the additional concern that her sample was so very small. However, she should be credited with noting that highly gifted children experienced some special adjustment problems related to the extremity of their differences. The children Hollingworth studied suffered with extreme boredom, isolation, and intolerance for peers and teachers if they were not accelerated in school at an early age. When they were accelerated, however, they had to adjust to problems of being the smallest and youngest in the group and the resultant negative impact on dating, playing sports, and vying for leadership roles. Furthermore, in terms of IQ, Hollingworth pointed out that the highly gifted child surpasses the least gifted by as much as the average child surpasses a child with mental retardation (1926, p. 153). Therefore, grouping all gifted children together, conceptually or educationally, makes about as much sense as grouping all children together who score below average on an IQ test. Yet, that is exactly what many programs do with gifted children. Once identified as gifted, all children receive the same services regardless of the area or extremity of their abilities.

Other studies of highly talented individuals have been conducted retrospectively, by identifying eminent people in certain fields and reflecting back on their characteristics and needs in childhood. Several studies (e.g., Goertzel & Goertzel, 1962; Goertzel, Goertzel, & Goertzel, 1978; Walberg, 1982) have emphasized some of the differences in individuals from different fields that make lists of characteristics difficult to generalize to all talented individuals. Some of the findings, for example, include these:

- Artists were more emotional, and scientists more concerned with theories (Walberg, 1982).
- Writers and artists were more independent and unconventional than scientists and statesmen (Goertzel, Goertzel, & Goertzel, 1978).
- Writers were more likely to come from dysfunctional families (Goertzel & Goertzel, 1962).

However, Bloom's study of the development of highly talented individuals in four general fields of endeavor led him to conclude that three qualities are consistent across fields:

1. Strong interest and commitment to a particular talent field

2. Ambition to reach a high level of attainment in the field

3. The work ethic necessary to put in the long hours and effort required to achieve (1985, p. 544)

Highly creative children should be encouraged to fulfill their potential.

In addition, the highly talented individuals studied by Bloom and his colleagues benefited from an encouraging home environment and excellent teachers.

The Creative

Creative children compose another special subgroup. Several studies have indicated that measured intelligence and creativity are separate qualities (Getzels & Jackson, 1962; Ochse, 1990; Restak, 1993; Wallach & Kogan, 1965; Wallach & Wing, 1969). A certain amount of intelligence, not necessarily at a level measured as "gifted," is often seen as a necessary but not sufficient quality of creativity (Ochse, 1990). Creative children may also be intellectually gifted as measured by an IQ test, but often they are not. Therefore, many highly creative children are missed by identification criteria for gifted programs that are heavily dependent on IQ scores.

Much of what we know about the characteristics of creative children is inferred from studies of accomplished, creative adults (Barron, 1969, 1976; Gardner, 1993; MacKinnon, 1978; Roe, 1953). Other studies have focused directly on children, comparing more and less creative individuals in looking for defining characteristics (Getzels & Jackson, 1962; Torrance, 1979).

Although creative individuals are a diverse group, there are some common characteristics that they typically exhibit. Some of these characteristics are related to the thought processes involved in creating: ideational fluency (the ability to think of many ideas), flexibility (the ability to shift direction in thinking), originality (the ability to come up with unusual ideas), and elaboration (the ability to add meaningful details to ideas) (Guilford, 1967; Torrance, 1966). Others are related to personality characteristics or styles of working: tendency to play with ideas, tolerance for ambiguity, risk taking, impulsiveness, aesthetic awareness, unconventional behavior, energy, humor, ego strength, preferring solitary to group activities, intuitiveness, and emotionality (cf. Tardif & Sternberg, 1988). Similarly, Gardner concluded that those whom he termed "Exemplary Creators" are "self-confident, alert, unconventional, hardworking, and committed obsessively to their work" (Gardner, 1993, p. 364). Any one person may not exhibit all of these traits, and the characteristics may not always be seen as positive.

Many of the behaviors indicative of creativity are very similar to the behaviors that may be indicative of attention deficit hyperactivity disorder—particularly daydreaming, impulsivity, high energy, and risk taking (Cramond, 1994). It is no wonder, then, that teachers reportedly prefer the high IQ child over the highly creative child (Getzels & Jackson, 1962)—especially when creative children often engage in "disruptive, attention-seeking behavior" in the classroom (Wallach & Kogan, 1965, pp. 294–295). In fact, examination of the lives of many creative adults indicates that they had learning and behavior problems in school (Thompson, 1971; West, 1991). Therefore, it is important that adults who observe these behaviors realize that many of them can be as indicative of high potential as of problems.

Gifted Underachievers

Perhaps the most perplexing to their parents and teachers are gifted underachievers. The causes of chronic underachievement are many, but they could be generally characterized as problems in the family, school, and/or society that interact with the child's personality to result in a response of underachievement (Rimm, 1986; Whitmore, 1980).

Family causes may include poor role models, disorganized homes, or ineffective parenting. Family counseling is usually needed to break the underachievement pattern. School causes result from incompatible instruction for the child's needs. For gifted children, one of the most frequent problems is an unchallenging curriculum that results in boredom and learned patterns of doing little work to get by. This is a strong rationale for providing gifted children with a challenging, engaging curriculum from an early age. Social causes include responses to gender bias or racial discrimination. Children who are given a message that they "can't" or "shouldn't" often *don't*. This is a far more complex and pervasive problem than the other two, but a strong and facilitative family and school can often overcome negative societal messages (Rimm, 1986; Whitmore, 1980).

Gifted Students With Disabilities

We should expect that gifted children are represented in the same proportions among populations of children who are hard-of-hearing, deaf, speech impaired, visually impaired, seriously emotionally disturbed, orthopedically impaired, or have other health impairments or specific learning disabilities as they are among the general public. Of all of the disabilities listed in P.L. 94-142 (the Education for All Handicapped Children Act of 1975), only one, mental retardation, seems to be incompatible with a coexistent identification of giftedness. Stephen Hawking, the physicist, provides an excellent example of a brilliant mind trapped in a body that is disabled. Since the 1960s he has had to cope with a highly disabling and progressive motor neuron disease.

However, relatively few children with disabilities are served in gifted programs. There are several reasons for this. First, when children are disabled in some way, it is the disability that gets attention. Often educators don't even look for giftedness in a class of students with hearing or visual impairments. Second, many of the identification processes for gifted children are not amenable to testing children with disabilities. Group intelligence tests with a high dependence on reading skills, for example, would not fairly test the abilities of a child with a reading disability. Nor would children with certain physical disabilities be able to fill in the circles quickly. Third, many school systems will not serve a child in more than one area of exceptionality. In other words, the child can get gifted services or special education, but not both. Even school systems that want to serve such children often have difficulty figuring out how to do so.

Gifted children with disabilities will manifest the same characteristics as any other gifted children, except as they are limited by the disability. For example, children with hearing impairments may be expected to have a delay in language development; children with a learning disability in reading won't show reading proficiency; and children with visual impairments won't have good visual spatial skills. Also, these children may have poor self-images because of negative labels, low expectations of teachers and parents, and rejection of peers (Maker, 1977).

The first step in removing the barriers to gifted children with disabilities is to look for them. Then, they should be given opportunities to show their strengths in ways that don't penalize them for their disabilities. For example, a combination of measures—including products, observational checklists, performances, and individually administered assessments—should be included in the identification. Once their talents are identified, children with disabilities should receive the same educational modifications in their curriculum as other children with the same talents: educational emphasis should be placed on enhancing the identified talent(s), expectations should be high, and self-evaluation with reasonable standards should be encouraged.

PREVALENCE OF GIFTEDNESS

The prevalence of giftedness in any group depends on the definitions, both theoretical and operational, that are used. Terman used a definition that included the top 1% of the population based on IQ scores (1925). Most estimates now indicate that individuals who are gifted make up 3% to 5% of the population. This is because most identification systems set the criterion score at about two standard deviations above the mean on standardized tests. By applying the normal curve of scores, one can see that approximately 3% of the population would be expected to score at or above that level. This was the accepted estimate though the 1950s, when the definition of giftedness began to be broadened beyond IQ (Marland, 1972, p. 21).

The Schoolwide Enrichment Model (Renzulli & Reis, 1985, 1991), based on Renzulli's three-ring definition of giftedness (1986), cast a much wider net in identifying the top 15% to 20% of a school population. However, the identified individuals are called "talent pool" members, not gifted. So too, the Pyramid Project (Cox, Daniel, & Boston, 1985) identified "able learners" who may make up 25% of a school population. Therefore, it is impossible to safely say that there is a hard and fast number of gifted and talented individuals in any population; the number varies according to the definition and identification practices used. According to a 1993 report from the U.S. Department of Education, four states identified more than 10% of students as gifted and 21 states identify fewer than 5% (p. 16).

CAUSES OF GIFTEDNESS

What causes giftedness? Is it primarily a function of inheritance or environment? In 1869, Galton attempted to extend his cousin Darwin's theory of the transmission

A stimulating home environment helps to nurture the development of a child's intellectual and creative potential.

of traits to show that genius was inherited (1869/1976). This belief in the primacy of inheritance was also shared by many early researchers such as Terman (1925) and Hollingworth (1926). However, most modern psychologists agree that environment and inheritance interact in the development of intelligence, although they don't always agree to what extent each contributes.

Arguments about the extent of heritability of intelligence range from 80% (Jensen, 1969; Rainer, 1976) to more recent estimates of approximately 50% (Plomin & Neiderhiser, 1991). Given that even the most generous estimates of the heritability of intelligence are correct, there is still a great deal of variance to be affected by environmental factors. For teachers and parents, the opportunity to positively enhance a child's intelligence by 20% is remarkable!

Yet, there is the view that heredity and environment are not merely additive; they interact in ways too complex to predict (Plomin & Neiderhiser, 1991). Gardner (1988) described a system of interactions involved in the development of giftedness that is so complex there are four levels of analysis:

1. *The subpersonal*—genetic endowment, structure of the nervous system, metabolic and hormonal factors, and so forth

2. *The personal*—intelligences, personality traits, and motivation

3. *The extrapersonal*—an area of knowledge or accomplishment

4. *The multipersonal*—the social context

He has argued that all of these factors must coincide in the right combinations for an individual to be optimally productive (pp. 301–304).

Some would argue that it is impossible to separate the effects of heredity from environment because they become intertwined, even in the womb, and complicated by factors such as nutrition, mate selection, parental attitudes, and differential individual reactions to environmental conditions (Plomin & Neiderhiser, 1991; Rainer, 1976). Giving credence to this argument is the observation that an enriched environment can actually cause physiological changes in the brain (Diamond, 1988). According to this argument, it is fruitless to try to separate inherited abilities from environmental effects because we don't know in what ways different environmental factors interact with human abilities and temperament to help or hinder the development of gifts. We don't know what is the most facilitative environment for any given individual. As Renzulli so aptly stated:

> The advantages of high socioeconomic status, a favorable educational background, and early life experiences that do not include hardship, frustration, or disappointment may lead to a productive career for some individuals, but for others it may very well eliminate the kinds of frustration that might become the "trigger" to a more positive application of one's abilities. (1986, p. 84)

ASSESSMENT OF GIFTEDNESS

The assessment of giftedness should be easy. A school system has a theoretical definition of giftedness that is translated into an operational definition. This operational definition determines how children are identified, which in turn is related to the educational programs designed for them. It should be easy, but it isn't.

However, the foregoing scenario is rarely played out in school systems (Hoge, 1988). For example, a system may claim that it is using the federal definition with the five categories of giftedness, yet identify children solely on the basis of IQ. Then the identified children receive instruction designed to nurture their creativity.

Other issues of concern are the inappropriate use of instruments and the practice of combining multiple criteria in unsuitable ways (Richert, 1991). An example of the former would be the case of a school system administering a group IQ test in English to a child who speaks English as a second language. Obviously, the test would not be the best measure of that child's abilities. An example of the latter would be the adding of several test scores from tests with different metrics to get one overall score.

However, the most serious identification problem, also discussed in Chapter 2, is the underrepresentation of minorities in gifted programs (Richert, 1991; U.S. Department of Education, 1993). Largely because they are left out at the nomination phase or are missed through inappropriate identification procedures, many gifted minority children are excluded from gifted programs. In order to minimize this danger and to discover as many talents in need of nurturance as possible, experts recommend the use of a variety of assessment methods, both objective and subjective, for identifying gifted behaviors (Frasier, 1987; Hagen, 1980).

In order to provide guidelines for school systems in designing identification methods, a group of experts wrote the *National Report on Identification* (Richert, Alvino, & McDonnel, 1982, pp. 204–205; Richert, 1991, p. 85), which included the following principles for an identification system for gifted children:

1. *Advocacy:* It is in the best interests of all students.

2. *Defensibility:* It is based on the best available research.

3. *Equity:* It can guarantee that no one is overlooked.

4. *Pluralism:* It uses a broad definition of gifted.

5. *Comprehensiveness:* It serves as many gifted learners as possible.

6. *Pragmatism:* Whenever possible, it uses resources on hand.

Screening

Frequently, the identification process is a two-step process with some type of screening in the first phase, and more extensive testing and/or data collection to make a placement decision in the second phase. The purpose of screening is to narrow the pool of students for whom more extensive information is collected.

System-wide testing is one method that is often used for screening. In school systems where achievement or aptitude tests are routinely given to all students, the scores are readily available for scanning and forming a pool of students on whom more data will be collected. System-wide testing can be an effective and efficient method of screening for gifted students if those doing the screening are alert to several cautions:

- System-wide testing should not be the only screening measure used. Group tests are not as reliable and valid as individual tests and may discriminate against minority children, children with English as a second language, and children with disabilities.
- Eligibility scores on screening measures should be low enough to lessen the probability that children with gifts and talents will be missed.
- Subtest scores as well as composites should be considered. Children who have strengths in specific areas may not have overall high scores.

Another popular method of screening students for further assessment is by nomination. In order to carefully screen the population of students, it is recommended that nominations be elicited from teachers, parents, other school personnel, peers, and the children themselves. There are two important reasons for using the nominations. First, the nominating individuals collectively are likely to have more information about a child's abilities and motivations than any one person alone would have. Such information goes beyond what can be seen on a test or in a typical classroom. Therefore, there is a greater chance that children with special abilities, especially those that are not usually tapped in school, will come to the attention of the gifted program. Second, the process of nominating children, usually solicited in the form of checklists of gifted behaviors, serves to educate teachers, parents, and others about the characteristics of gifted children and open the lines of communication among them. By forging cooperation between the home and school, and respecting the input of all parties involved, it is likely that a better understanding of the child's needs and more investment in meeting those needs will be the result.

Further Assessment for Identification

With the shift away from identifying *children* as gifted and toward identifying *behaviors* indicative of gifts and talents, the need for multiple measures and ongoing assessment becomes clearer. Further assessment may include additional tests as well as ratings of products and performances, grades, checklists, interest inventories, and the like. The key is to assemble evidence by giving students many opportunities to demonstrate their talents and motivations. Ongoing assessment is

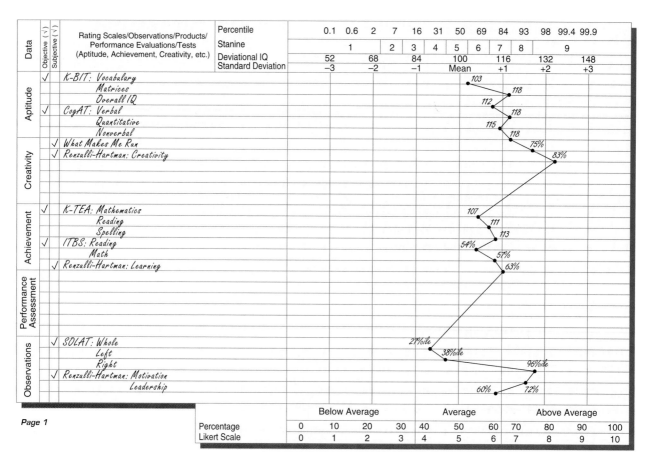

Figure 3.2   Frasier Talent Assessment Profile (F-TAP), pages 1–3

Source: From *The Frasier Talent Assessment Profile (F-TAP): A Multiple Criteria Model for the Identification of Gifted Students* by M. M. Frasier, 1994, Athens, GA: Torrance Center for Creative Studies, University of Georgia.

necessary to continually collect the body of information about students that can be used to adapt and change the curriculum according to students' developing talents and changing interests (U.S. Department of Education, 1993). One system for discovering talents on an ongoing basis is DISCOVER (Maker, 1996), which engages children in developmentally appropriate tasks in the three of Gardner's seven intelligences (1983) most often addressed in school: linguistic, logical–mathematical, and spatial intelligences. Such tasks give children the opportunity to solve authentic problems with appropriate materials. An example of a spatial-logical problem for a child in grades 3 to 5 is "Make a triangle with as many tangram pieces as possible" (p. 45).

Resistance to using an identification system that is multidimensional and continual arises primarily from concern about the practicality of implementing such a complex system. Two methods that have been devised to assist schools with the organization of students' assessment portfolios are the Frasier Talent Assessment Profile, or F-TAP (Frasier, 1994), and the Total Talent Portfolio (Renzulli, 1994). As shown in the example in Figure 3.2, the F-TAP is a method of combining objective and subjective data in categories determined by the district's definition to

QUALITATIVE ASSESSMENT
[Based on Core Gifted Traits, Aptitudes, and Behaviors (TABS)]

Communication – (Highly expressive and effective use of words, numbers, and symbols.)
Strong non-verbal communication abilities as evidenced in his drawings, claymation videos, & playing music by ear.
Has advanced vocabulary for his age.

Motivation – (Evidence of desire to learn.)
Appears to be extremely excited & intrinsically driven by interests but shows little evidence of a desire to participate in general classroom activities or to complete routine tasks.

Humor – (Conveys and picks up on humor.)
Has a keen sense of humor.
Sees humor in situations that may not appear humorous to others.

Inquiry – (Questions, experiments, explores.)
Enjoys seeking information by manipulating & trying ideas. Plays guess. Curious; asks questions. Displays intellectual playfulness; imagines. Plays "I wonder what would happen if . . ."

Insight – (Quickly grasps new concepts and makes connections; sense deeper meanings.)
Intuitive. A keen & alert observer who usually "gets more" out of a story, film, etc. than others.
Looks for relationships between events, people, & things.

Interests – (Intense (sometimes unusual) interests.)
Primary interest lies in the area of cinematography & animation (e.g., clay & computer).
Likes to design & create with hands (e.g., draw, play musical instruments)

Problem Solving – (Effective, often inventive, strategies for recognizing and solving problems.)
Inventive. Uses whatever is available to solve the problem.
Takes material apart & analyzes individual parts. Uses visuals to problem solve.

Memory – (Large storehouse of information on school or non-school topics.)
Strong recall of non-verbal material (e.g., pictures, sounds, & actions).
Possesses a large storehouse of information about a variety of non-school topics.

Reasoning – (Logical approaches to figuring out solutions.)
Responds to questions in a logical manner.
Skilled at summarizing, finding the main idea.

Imagination/Creativity – (Produces many ideas; highly original.)
Highly curious. Nonconforming. Accepts disorder.
Generates a large number of ideas to problems.
Often offers unusual responses. Sensitive to aesthetics.

Page 2

create a profile of a student's strengths and weaknesses. The Total Talent Portfolio is a collection of information about a student's abilities, interests, and style preferences that is accumulated through the provision of learning experiences designed to elicit talents and interests in a broad range of areas. A sheet in the student's folder as presented in Figure 3.3 provides a picture of strengths and preferences at a glance. Both of these systems emphasize that the result of assessment is the design of learning experiences tailored to the child's needs.

In summary, a good identification plan for gifted students is one that matches the school district's theoretical definition with the operational one. It is complex in that the assessment is ongoing, more than one type of assessment is used, and multiple sources of information are sought. All measures are as effective, efficient, valid, and reliable as possible, and there are alternative measures for children with special needs. Throughout the process, the principles of advocacy, defensibility, equity, pluralism, comprehensiveness, and pragmatism apply.

PHASE IV: EDUCATIONAL SERVICE PLAN

Programming Options

- *Mentor preferably in area of cinematography*
- *Involvement in a creative problem solving program with opportunities to invent (e.g., FPSP-visuals, invent America)*
- *Independent study to pursue non-school-related interests*

Curricula Needs

- *Advanced level math (e.g., compacting) and language (e.g., enrichment) courses*
- *Variety of visuals incorporated into learning experiences.*
- *For large, product-based assignments, establish contracts with teachers to provide parameters and guidance while allowing freedom for exploration.*
- *Affective education with students of similar abilities with a focus on topics such as "fear of failure" and developing study habits.*

THE CHILD

Counseling Needs

- *Bibliotherapy*
  - *—biography of highly creative, artistic person*
  - *—Hazel Rye by Cleaver & Cleaver (1983)*
- *Career counseling to gather information on responsibilities of career interests.*

Goals/Outcome Evaluations

- *Complete a minimum of one independent study on topic of choice including final self-facilitator.*
- *Complete a minimum of bibliotherapy exercise per semester.*
- *Establish a relationship with a mentor.*
- *Establish a dynamic portfolio of work important to the student.*
- *Complete a performance assessment incorporating math and language.*

Student Name _____ John

INSTRUCTIONAL CONSIDERATIONS

The logical conclusion to an identification system for a gifted program is the provision of differentiated services. A differentiated curriculum is one that is designed to meet the learning needs of gifted children based on the characteristics that identified them as gifted in the first place (Ward, 1964). For example, gifted students who have a quick grasp of information do not need the amount of practice that some other students may need in learning a new skill. Therefore, a reasonable modification for gifted students would be to accelerate the pace of the instruction.

Maker (1982) has described modification of lessons along four dimensions in order to meet the needs of gifted students: content, process, products, and learning environment.

First, the *content* can be modified to include more complex, abstract topics. For example, an intellectually gifted child may study the philosophy that was current at a certain place and time in a history lesson.

Abilities	Interests	Style Preferences			
Maximum Performance Indicators	**Interest Areas**	**Instructional Style Preferences**	**Learning Environment Preferences**	**Thinking Style Preferences**	**Expression Style Preferences**
Tests • Standardized • Teacher-Made Course Grades Teacher Ratings Product Evaluation • Written • Oral • Visual • Musical • Constructed (Note differences between assigned and self-selected products.) Level of Participation in Learning Activities Degree of Interaction With Others	Fine Arts Crafts Literary Historical Mathematical/Logical Physical Sciences Life Sciences Political/Judicial Athletic/Recreation Marketing/Business Drama/Dance Musical Performance Musical Composition Managerial/Business Photography Film/Video Computers Other (Specify)	Recitation & Drill Peer Tutoring Lecture Lecture/Discussion Discussion Guided Independent Study* Learning/Interest Center Simulation, Role Playing, Dramatization, Guided Fantasy Learning Games Replicative Reports or Projects* Investigative Reports or Projects* Unguided Independent Study* Internship* Apprenticeship*	Inter/Intra Personal • Self-Oriented • Peer-Oriented • Adult-Oriented • Combined Physical • Sound • Heat • Light • Design • Mobility • Time of Day • Food Intake • Seating	Analytic (School Smart) Synthetic/ Creative (Creative, Inventive) Practical/ Contextual (Street Smart) Legislative Executive Judicial	Written Oral Manipulative Discussion Display Dramatization Artistic Graphic Commercial Service

*With or without a mentor

Figure 3.3 Total Talent Portfolio

Source: Adapted from *Schools for Talent Development: A Practical Plan for Total School Improvement* (p. 101), by J. S. Renzulli, 1994, Mansfield Center, CT: Creative Learning Press.

Second, the *process* by which students learn can be modified in a number of ways. One way is by changing the pacing of the lesson so that children can proceed through material rapidly. For example, Chris, a talented fifth grader, was able to complete all of the fifth grade math skills by Thanksgiving and go on to sixth grade skills. Another process modification is changing the level of thought required according to the Taxonomy of Educational Objectives (Bloom, Englehart, Furst, Hill, & Krathwohl, 1956). For instance, because Terry came to school with so much knowledge about the solar system and a comprehension of astronomy beyond her eighth grade classmates, she was able to spend more time applying, analyzing, synthesizing and evaluating the principles of heavenly bodies to find a new star.

Third, the *products* of student learning can be differentiated so that students are expected to complete more sophisticated products if they are able. For example, in a study of poetry, Ali, who is verbally gifted, may make the assignment of writing a poem more challenging by attempting to compose poems in different genres on the same theme into a poetry book.

INNOVATIVE IDEAS

IDENTIFYING GIFTED BEHAVIORS

What if, instead of identifying *students* for the gifted program, we identified gifted *behaviors?* What if the outcome of the identification process were not a decision of yes, the student gets into the program, or no, the student does not? Furthermore, what if those identified behaviors determined what type of program the student would receive?

All of this is possible if we move away from a simplistic identification process and a one-size-fits-all gifted program. Instead, we could amass a variety of information on a nominated child and design a program specifically to suit that child's needs. One way to manage this is with the Frasier Talent Assessment Profile, as you can see in the F-TAP example in Figure 3.2.

The three pages depicted in the figure demonstrate how both quantitative and qualitative data were gathered on John's abilities in order to inform the services recommended for him. Test data are entered by category on page 1 and plotted to create a profile of strengths and weaknesses. Then

teachers' comments are gathered on page 2 in ten key areas representing gifted traits, aptitudes, and behaviors. On page 3, the information from the first two pages is used to make recommendations about John's needs.

This process ties the identified behaviors clearly to the services received. There is not a single "gifted program," but rather a variety of services provided for students based on demonstrated gifts and talents. The concept of the teacher of the gifted meeting all of the gifted students' needs in the part-time program is exchanged for the concept of the teacher of the gifted serving as a teacher and facilitator—providing for some of the students' needs and finding resources within the school or system to meet the others.

Schools systems need not wonder, What if . . . ? This process is being used in several school systems across the country and is providing services for students whose gifts and talents would otherwise not be identified through IQ and achievement tests alone.

Finally, the *learning environment* can be modified so that gifted students are responsible for more of their own learning at an earlier age than are other students. All students need to be independent learners, but students with advanced ability in an area may be ready and able to do so at an earlier age. Students who learn the skills of research and self-evaluation are immunized against an unchallenging curriculum.

Talent Development

Bloom and his colleagues (Sosniak, 1985) observed that students with talents in specific areas needed challenges and different types of teachers, depending on the stage of development of the talent. In the first phase, teachers of the talented individuals the researchers studied were nurturing, playful, patient, and filled lessons with many rewards and incentives. In the second phase of talent development, the teachers were more demanding and exacting to help students perfect their skills, acquire expertise, and discover the job of accomplishment. In the third phase, the teachers expected the students to expend a great deal of time and effort to go beyond learning that which has been done before and develop a personal style or technique. In a school setting, children in the same grade may be at different levels of talent development, and therefore, have different instructional needs.

Acceleration

Acceleration refers to moving the student through the curriculum at a rapid pace so that the result is advanced placement or credit. This advanced placement may result in early enrollment or grade skipping. It may also result in content acceleration whereby a student stays in the same grade but works on more advanced content. However, it is only considered acceleration if it changes the student's placement so that there is continuous progress. For example, a third grader who works on fourth grade math concepts is allowed to take up where he left off when he gets to fourth grade.

An example of an acceleration curriculum model was developed by the Study of Mathematically Precocious Youth at Johns Hopkins University in 1971 (Stanley, 1983) to educate the brightest students in mathematics through fast-paced math classes. The principles have since been applied to instruction in physical and biological sciences, computer science, and language arts (Benbow, 1986). The instructional model used, called DT-PI (for *diagnostic testing* and *prescriptive instruction*), is a method for determining each student's level of knowledge in a specific area and designing an instructional program based on the student's weaknesses. Students are then instructed at a rapid rate in keeping with their abilities, some learning as much as 4 years of course content in 1 year (Benbow, 1986).

Enrichment

Enrichment usually refers to modifications in the curriculum that are made for gifted students to increase the depth and breadth of learning beyond that in the regular curriculum, but that do not result in advanced placement. An example of this would be a psychology minicourse in sixth grade that does not result in credit or placement in higher level psychology.

A well known model for enrichment is the Enrichment Triad Model, as shown in Figure 3.4 (Renzulli, 1977). This model consists of three components that determine the types of enrichment experiences students have.

Enrichment activities, even at the preschool level, provide experiences children might not normally receive.

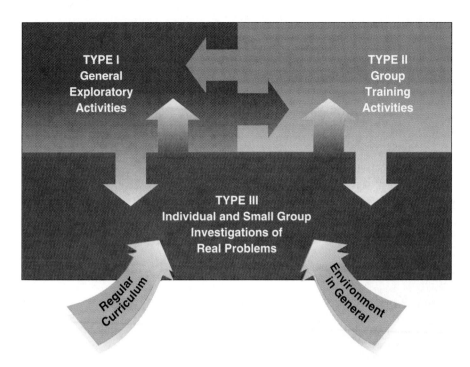

Figure 3.4   Renzulli's Enrichment Triad

Source: From *The Enrichment Triad Model: A Guide for Developing Defensible Programs for the Gifted* (p. 14), by J. S. Renzulli, 1977, Mansfield Center, CT: Creative Learning Press.

Type I experiences are general exploratory experiences designed to expose students to a variety of content that is not part of the regular curriculum and motivate them for further study in the area. These activities are in the form of field trips, speakers, films, experiments, and so forth.

Type II experiences are group and individual training activities that are designed to develop both cognitive and effective processes. They consist of three types of lessons: (1) those planned in advance as part of the curriculum, (2) those that result from student interests, and (3) those that must be taught to enable one or more students to complete projects.

Type III experiences are individual and small group investigations of real problems. These are research and/or creative projects that students engage in to explore an area of interest (Renzulli, 1977; Renzulli & Reis, 1985, 1986).

The arrows in Figure 3.4 that go from one type of enrichment to another demonstrate that students may move among the different types of experiences in different orders. For example, a student may attend a lecture on oceanography as a Type I experience and get an idea to investigate the possibility of underwater cities. For a Type II experience, she may learn some research skills to help her investigate the feasibility of this idea. As a Type III experience, she may construct a prototype of an underwater city that addresses the issues she found in researching the topic. Another student could move from a lesson on interviewing in Type II, to interviewing an astronaut who had been brought in as a Type I speaker, to conducting a debate with some classmates on whether the U.S. should expend resources to continue space exploration.

Enrichment programs should be used to enhance a child's education, not merely add "busy work."

Combining Acceleration and Enrichment

In deciding whether to use enrichment or acceleration as the guiding force in designing curriculum for the gifted, one should keep three things in mind: (1) the terms are overlapping in many cases, (2) good gifted programs provide provisions for both acceleration and enrichment, and in fact (3) both enrichment and acceleration have a part even in the prototypical models such as the ones just described here. In other words, gifted students need both rapid pacing and exposure to content of greater variety, depth, and breadth than in the regular curriculum.

Service Delivery Models

In addition to the concern about what we teach gifted students is the concern for how we deliver the services to them. Service delivery models range from the most exclusive, which employ full-time homogeneous grouping, to the most inclusive, which employ full-time heterogeneous grouping.

Examples of special schools are those such as the Stuyvesant High School in New York; the Louisiana School for Math, Science, and the Arts; and the Illinois Math and Science Academy—all designed for students with high ability in one or more areas. Less inclusive options are the school-within-a-school, special classes, or pull-out programs that allow some time for gifted students to attend classes together, and some time to attend classes with the rest of the students in the school. The most inclusive options, which employ full-time heterogeneous grouping, may use some individualized instruction for gifted students or some cluster groups within the class.

EASY IDEAS FOR PRACTITIONERS

For the Teacher:

1. Learn about the special characteristics and needs of gifted children.
2. Allow some self-selection of content and products, encouraging able students to choose more complex, abstract topics and more sophisticated materials within the topic being studied.
3. Allow some change in pacing whereby able students can opt out of re-learning material they already know and proceed as quickly as possible through new material.
4. Vary large group instruction with small group instruction, individual study, and flexible cluster groupings according to interests and instructional needs.
5. Avoid giving gifted students simply more of the same work to keep them busy or using them as teacher's aides.

For Parents:

1. Be child-centered. Spend time with your children and provide them with experiences in interest areas you both value.
2. Emphasize and model a work ethic that stresses the importance of extended and intense effort to do well.
3. Demonstrate that you value and encourage the pursuit of excellence in a particular field—but do it through motivation and support rather than pushing.
4. Be an advocate for your child. As much as possible, provide resources and teachers to help develop talent in the chosen field.
5. Promote family harmony and respect by recognizing and encouraging each member's gifts and talents without comparing them to each other.

There are pros and cons for all of the options. In general, the more exclusive, specialized options provide more hours of service for gifted students that is appropriate to their special needs. However, there are concomitant concerns about selectivity, practicality, and elitism. On the other hand, the more inclusive options virtually eliminate those concerns—but as the program becomes more inclusive, concerns about differentiating the curriculum to meet the needs of gifted students become salient. In some cases the program becomes so inclusive that it disappears; it is difficult to see what, if any, provisions are made for gifted students.

Suggestions for Teachers

In all but the most exclusive models, gifted children spend most of their time in the regular classroom. What can the regular classroom teacher do to provide for these children?

Learn about the special characteristics and needs of gifted children. Teachers who understand the special characteristics of gifted students are less likely to view normal gifted or creative behaviors as aberrant. Also, they are more likely to be understanding and accommodating of these children's special cognitive and affective needs.

Allow some self-selection of content and products. If children are given some options about what to learn, the gifted children can be encouraged to choose more complex, abstract topics within the theme being studied. Also, those who are verbally gifted may choose more advanced reading materials if given a range and guidance in selection. A key here is that they be given some choices that include *sophisticated* and *novel* content—themes and materials that go beyond the traditional school curriculum in complexity and scope (Gallagher, 1994b).

Allow some change in pacing. When studying new material, gifted students may be given opportunities to proceed as quickly as possible through it. One way to do this is by *telescoping the common core* (Tannenbaum, 1983, p. 429), *curriculum compacting* (Reis, Burns, & Renzulli, 1992; Renzulli & Reis, 1985; Starko, 1986), or using the idea of *diagnostic testing and prescriptive instruction* (Benbow, 1986). These provisions allow students to opt out of relearning material they already know. In the case of gifted students, this can often be a considerable amount; several studies have found that bright children knew between 78% and 93% of the material on a pretest of the year's content before they were taught it (Komoski, 1981; Reis, 1994; Taylor & Frye, 1988). During the time they buy this way, they can do more in-depth study of a related topic.

Adapt the learning environment so that children are given some options about how they learn. Vary large group instruction with small group instruction and individual study. In a homogeneously grouped class, allow some flexible cluster groupings according to interests and instructional needs.

Avoid two practices that are the bane of gifted children: giving them more of the same work to keep them busy, and using them as teacher's aides. In the first case, gifted students who can easily solve 10 math problems need not do 20 more while the rest of the class finishes. They will see this as punishment for being gifted and working efficiently. In the second case, having students work together can be an effective educational and management strategy, but the gifted child should not always have the role of instructor, nor should this be the only educational modification for a bright child.

Addressing Affective Needs.   As indicated earlier, gifted students often have specialized affective needs in addition to their cognitive needs. Many of these affective needs are too specialized and complex for the classroom teacher to handle. In cases where a student exhibits signs of chronic or extreme stress or depression, teachers should see that the appropriate actions are taken for professional psychological intervention.

However, many of the less serious problems can be averted through **preventive counseling** (Silverman, 1993b). An example of a curriculum for gifted students that includes a counseling component was designed by Betts (1986; Betts & Knapp, 1980) and called the Autonomous Learner Model. With this model, students are oriented at the beginning of each year with information to help them understand themselves, giftedness, and the opportunities and responsibilities of the program. There are also opportunities for them to develop personal and interpersonal skills, career awareness, and mentor relationships, as well as other learning skills.

Other preventive measures include teaching students **stress reduction techniques** and problem solving skills. One example of a stress reduction technique has students identify the sources and severity of their stress through an activity in which they write "ME" in a circle in the center of a page surrounded by other circles, as shown in Figure 3.5. They then write possible sources of stress in the surrounding circles. The final step is to draw static lines indicating the severity of the stress caused by each source (Jenkins-Friedman & Anderson, 1985). Once students

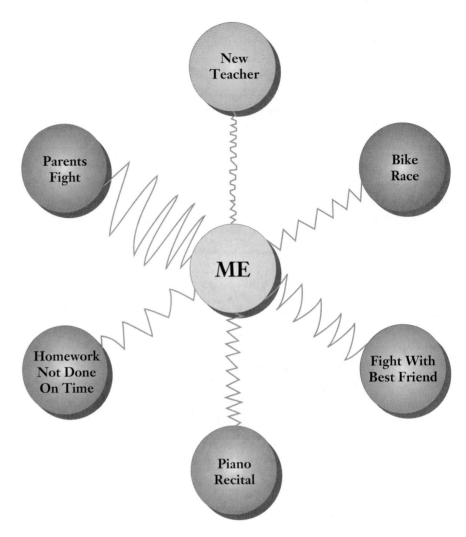

Figure 3.5 **Sample Static Scale**

Source: Adapted from *Gifted Plus: Teaching High Potential Students About Their Abilities,* by R. Jenkins-Friedman & M. A. Anderson, 1985. (Available from Reva Jenkins-Friedman, Educational Psychology and Research Department, 2 Bailey Hall, University of Kansas, Lawrence, KS 66045.)

have identified the sources of stress, they can be taught to relax through systematically tightening and relaxing different muscles in their bodies. They can also be helped to see how slow, careful breathing helps relax the body and mind.

Problem solving instruction can include teaching a systematic problem solving procedure such as Creative Problem Solving (CPS) (Isaksen & Treffinger, 1985). The steps of CPS include identifying the problem, defining it for solution, gathering information about the problem, applying criteria to select the best solution(s), and implementing the solution(s). CPS can be applied to personal and social problems as well as societal ones. In this context, problem solving may also include the skills of negotiation and getting along with others. Some very bright children need direct instruction of social skills that others learn intuitively, just as some children need direct reading instruction while others don't.

Another technique that has been particularly useful with gifted students is **bibliotherapy.** Bibliotherapy is the use of carefully selected reading materials, matched to the child's needs, that enable gifted learners to identify with a character, real or imaginary, who has faced similar problems and resolved them. There are several sources of books for bibliotherapy that are referenced according to the particular problems they address (Bailey, Boyce, & Van Tassel-Baska, 1990; Halsted, 1988). For example, a theme in Louisa May Alcott's *Little Women* is the conflict that a bright female faces when pursuing her career instead of fulfilling the expectations of others.

There are several books on the resource list at the end of this chapter to help students, parents, and teachers address some of the affective issues that gifted students face. Some of these books are suitable for children to read on their own, and others require the guidance of an adult.

Teachers who do the things discussed here will be providing opportunities for all children to make choices and develop their abilities. For gifted children it will mean that they are not just gifted for the time that they are served through the gifted program.

FAMILY PERSPECTIVES

What is the role of the family in the nurturance of gifts and talents? Studies of highly talented individuals (Bloom, 1985; Cox, Daniel, & Boston, 1985; Feldman, 1986) have indicated that the family is instrumental to the development of talent in several ways. The families of talented individuals usually share the following traits:

1. They are child-centered, spend a great deal of time together, and provide children with experiences in valued areas.

2. They emphasize and model a work ethic that stresses the importance of extended and intense effort to do well.

3. They value and encourage the pursuit of excellence in a particular field, but do so through motivation rather than pushing.

4. They regard the talented child as special and provide resources and teachers to help develop talent in the chosen field.

As researchers who have studied talented teenagers conclude, "Families providing both support and challenge enhance the development of talent" (Csikszentmihalyi, Rathunde, & Whalen, 1993, p. 247).

On the other hand, retrospective studies have indicated that the families of highly creative individuals were often troubled by lack of parental harmony, lack of closeness with a parent, loss of a parent through desertion or death, business failings, frequent moving, and the like (Goertzel & Goertzel, 1962; Guilford, 1977; MacKinnon, 1960/1992; Simonton, 1988). Yet with all of the difficulties, the families of creative productive individuals still had a clear expectation of commitment to high achievement and the effort required to reach it (Albert, 1992). There were role models and materials for intellectual and cultural stimulation in the home (Simonton, 1988).

It is clear that the family can have a tremendous impact on the gifted and talented child—but what impact does the presence of such a child have on the family? Research indicates that in most cases there is a mutually rewarding relationship between the parents and the talented child, especially as the parents regard the child as special and value the talent (Bloom, 1985; Cornell, 1983; Feldman, 1986).

The same is not necessarily true of sibling relationships. The gifted child's relationship may be strained with siblings who are not given the special label, time, and teaching. In addition, these siblings may fear being unable to meet what they perceive as very high family standards and pressure to compete with the talented child (Rimm, 1991). Is it any wonder that Cornell and Grossberg (1986) found that some nongifted siblings of gifted students had personality adjustment difficulties?

Parents can mitigate against the negative impact of having a gifted or talented sibling by valuing the unique contributions of all family members in whatever sphere of endeavor, helping each child to find and develop talents and a positive self-image, and keeping the lines of communication open in the family (Donovan, 1992). Parents who avoid comparisons between children and balance the needs of family members are more likely to engender the positive peer relations noted by Feldman (1986).

CURRENT ISSUES AND FUTURE TRENDS

The most controversial issue in the field of gifted education right now centers around the debate over excellence versus equity. This is not a new debate, but rather a continuation of one that has gone on for years (Fetterman, 1988). Whenever the scales have tipped on the side of equity—usually during a time of social awareness and progress—concerns for equal education for all have been predominant and special programs for the gifted eschewed. Whenever the nation has been challenged militarily, technologically, or economically, the scales have tipped to concern for making public schools more academic and competitive (McDaniel, 1993).

On the *excellence* side are those who argue that education in the U.S. should be challenging and competitive with education in other countries. They argue that scores on tests in the U.S. are dropping, the reading levels of the texts are dropping, and this "dumbing down" of the curriculum has resulted in the U.S. ranking far below other industrialized countries on international tests of achievement (Callahan, 1994; McDaniel, 1993; Reis, 1994). They conclude that this is a matter not only of concern for those students who are languishing in an unchallenging curriculum, but also a matter of national concern (Gallagher, 1993, 1994a, 1995).

On the *equity* side are those who argue that exclusivity in identification and special programs for the gifted are elitist (Oakes, 1985, 1994). There is concern that gifted programs result in a "Matthew effect," from the Gospel of Matthew describing how the rich get richer, whereby those children who come from educationally enriched homes are the ones most likely to be identified as gifted and therefore receive enriched educational experiences in school (Walberg & Herbig, 1991). Proponents of equity argue that such practices result in a disparity between the highest and lowest achievers that is unequaled in other industrialized nations (Darling-Hammond, 1994).

This theme of excellence versus equity can be used as a framework through which to view some of the specific issues that are challenging gifted education (and general education) today. Some primary issues are the grouping of children for instruction, fairness of assessments used to identify children for gifted programs, and the effectiveness of curriculum modifications for the gifted. The central question is: How can we achieve both excellence and equity in our schools?

With ability grouping seen as "tracking" and discriminatory to children in the lower tracks, and with homogeneous grouping seen as resulting in a stultifying

Participating in advanced placement classes in high school often allows students to earn college credit.

curriculum that encourages underachievement in gifted children, there seems to be a Solomon's dilemma. Research on the effects of grouping children for instruction is conflicting (Brewer, Rees, & Argys, 1995; Kulik & Kulik, 1991; Rogers, 1991; Slavin, 1987, 1990). The question is: How can we provide challenges for the most gifted and talented students while providing equal educational opportunities for all students?

Most of the concern about identification comes from relying on a single score, often an IQ score, to make a decision based on an arbitrary cutoff point. The simple decision, yes or no, admits some children to a gifted program and relegates others to the regular classroom. According to this model, two children who differ by only a few points on a test get very different educational programs. Because the children who are left out of the gifted program are disproportionately from minority groups, there is an additional concern about the fairness of such an identification system (Frasier, 1987; Richert, 1991). The question is: How can we identify talents in children?

Another issue is the quality of the instruction that children receive in gifted programs and in the regular classroom. The curriculum in gifted programs is too often seen as a hodgepodge of disconnected activities without a grounding in theory or articulation of content. Also, regardless of relative strengths or weaknesses, gifted children in far too many programs are treated as a homogeneous group and all receive the same instruction. In the regular classroom there are few, if any, modifications made for gifted children (Westberg, Archambault, Dobyns, & Salvin, 1993). Perhaps we are expecting too much of teachers to meet the needs of such large and diverse classes. As Gallagher (1993) asked:

> Can the over 1 million elementary teachers, given the resources and their environment setting, provide an exciting and stimulating environment for gifted students who are often three, four, or five grades beyond their age-mates? If they can do it, why have they not been doing it? (p. 20)

The question is: How can we best meet the needs and develop the talents of all children in schools?

Responding to these questions is the challenge of the future for gifted education. The current procedures are long overdue for change. We cannot continue to offer simplistic responses to complex issues. Gifted programs will have to respond to the broadening of definitions of intelligence by broadening their identification procedures. The curriculum will have to respond to the enormous variety in the resulting gifted population by increasing the spectrum of services for children in response to the type and degree of their gifts and talents. There are some curriculum models, such as the Pyramid Project (Cox, Daniel, & Boston, 1985) and the Schoolwide Enrichment Model (Renzulli, 1994; Renzulli & Reis, 1985, 1986, 1991), that allow for broader identification and a range of services to the school population. These and other such complex models, which may incorporate some of the older models, may be the future of gifted education.

Five-Minute Summary

The idea of selection and development of gifts is an ancient one, although what is considered gifted has varied with time and place. The definition of giftedness will no doubt continue to shift as the needs and values in our society change, and broaden as our view of intelligence broadens. Yet, the argument for the development of gifts at public expense for potential benefit to the society remains. What has been added is the more modern and Western idea of development of gifts for the good of the individual, and movement toward a more inclusive view of giftedness reflecting the multiculturalism of our society. Concurrently, there is growing support for the idea that measuring this array of abilities with a single test score is inappropriate. Also, there is emphasis on identifying and developing gifts and talents rather than on identifying gifted students. The difference is the emphasis on serving needs rather than on providing special programs for children with a high IQ. Gifted programs will have to respond to the broadening of definitions of intelligence by broadening their identification procedures.

This change in the way that gifts and talents are defined and identified brings with it a commensurate need for a curriculum change. We cannot continue to serve students with diverse gifts and talents in a single program, treating them as a homogeneous group. The curriculum will have to respond to the enormous variety in the resulting gifted population by increasing the spectrum of services for children in response to the type and degree of their giftedness. There are identification methods and curriculum models that allow for broadened identification and services to the school population.

Regardless of the method of identification or services provided to gifted and talented students, most students will spend the bulk of their time in the regular classroom. Therefore, it behooves every teacher to be aware of the indications of gifts and talents, the special needs these create, and some methods for addressing the needs. Whatever the method of identification and service for the gifted students in the school system, teachers should ask themselves this question: "How can I best meet the needs and develop the talents of children that I teach?" The more we move toward serving all children's needs, the closer we get to attaining both excellence and equity.

Study Questions

1. Draw a graph illustrating the ebb and flow of support for gifted education in the U.S. Can you predict the degree of support for the next 5 years? For the next 10 years?
2. What are some cognitive and affective characteristics that the parent of a gifted child might observe? What are some that a teacher might observe?
3. Make a case for the definition of giftedness that you'd like your school system to adopt. How would your definition affect the number of students served in the program?
4. What are some practical modifications you could make in a classroom to meet the needs of gifted students?
5. What major points would you make in a handbook for parents of gifted children? In a handbook for teachers?
6. In what ways might a gifted program be beneficial to the whole school?
7. Think of the subgroups of gifted students. What are their defining characteristics and special needs?
8. What are some special affective problems associated with gifted students? How might you, as a teacher, help students with these problems?
9. Why have some periods of history such as the Renaissance been marked by a proliferation of genius while other times have been seemingly deficient?
10. What are your opinions on the debate over excellence versus equity? Are both attainable? How?

For More Information

ORGANIZATIONS

American Association for Gifted Children
(Talent Identification Program)
David Goldstein, Executive Director
Duke University
1121 W. Main Street, Suite 100
Durham, NC 27701
919-683-1400

The Association for the Gifted (TAG)
Council for Exceptional Children
1920 Association Drive
Reston, VA 22091
800-336-3278

Mensa, Gifted Children's Program
5304 1st Place, N.
Arlington, VA 22203
703-527-4293

National Association for Gifted Children
1155 15th Street, N.W.
Suite 1002
Washington, DC 20005
202-624-5845

World Council for Gifted and Talented Children
Division of Special Education

California State University, Los Angeles
5151 State University Drive
Los Angeles, CA 90032
213-343-4408

BOOKS AND ARTICLES

Adderholdt-Elliot, M. (1987). *Perfectionism: What's bad about being too good?* Minneapolis: Free Spirit.

Alvino, J. (Ed.). (1985). *Parents' guide to raising a gifted child: Recognizing and developing your child's potential.* New York: Little, Brown.

Baskin, B. H., & Harris, K. H. (1980). *Books for the gifted child.* New York: Bowker.

Bireley, M., & Genshaft, J. (1991). *Understanding the gifted adolescent: Educational, developmental, and multicultural issues.* New York: Teachers College Press.

Cramond, B. (1995). *The coincidence of attention deficit hyperactivity disorder and creativity.* Storrs, CT: National Research Center on the Gifted and Talented. (RBDM 9508)

Delisle, J. (1992). *Guiding the social and emotional development of gifted youth: A practical guide for educators and counselors.* New York: Longman.

Fetterman, D. M. (1988). *Excellence & equity: A qualitatively different perspective on gifted and talented education.* Albany, NY: State University of New York Press.

Galbraith, J. (1983). *The gifted kids survival guide: For ages 11–18.* Minneapolis: Free Spirit.

Galbraith, J. (1994). *The gifted kids survival guide: For ages 10 & under.* Minneapolis: Free Spirit.

Golant, S. K. (1991). *The joys and challenges of raising a gifted child.* New York: Prentice-Hall.

Halsted, J. W. (1988). *Guiding gifted readers from preschool through high school: A handbook for parents, teachers, counselors and librarians.* Columbus, OH: Ohio Psychology.

Perino, S., & Perino, J. (1981). *Parenting the gifted: Developing the promise.* New York: Bowker.

Reis, S. M., Burns, D. E., & Renzulli, J. S. (1992). *Curriculum compacting: The complete guide to modifying the regular curriculum for high ability students.* Mansfield Center, CT: Creative Learning Press.

Rimm, S. B. (1986). *Underachievement syndrome: Causes and cures.* Watertown, WI: Apple.

Saunders, J. (1986). *Bringing out the best: A resource guide for parents of young gifted children.* Minneapolis: Free Spirit.

Schmitz, C., & Galbraith, J. (1985). *Managing the social and emotional needs of the gifted: A teacher's survival guide.* Minneapolis: Free Spirit.

Starko, A. J. (1986). *It's about time: Inservice strategies for curriculum compacting.* Mansfield Center, CT: Creative Learning Press.

Van Tassel-Baska, J. (Ed.). (1990). *A practical guide to counseling the gifted in a school setting.* Reston, VA: ERIC Clearinghouse on Handicapped and Gifted Children.

JOURNALS, NEWSLETTERS, AND OTHER PUBLICATIONS

Gifted Child Quarterly
Provides a mix of research, program, evaluations, and program descriptions for gifted and talented children.
Journal of the National Association for Gifted Children
1155 15th Street, N. W.
Suite 1002
Washington, DC 20005

Gifted Child Today
A magazine published five times a year for teachers and parents of gifted, creative, and talented children.
P. O. Box 637
100 Pine Avenue
Holmes, PA 19043-9937

Journal for the Education of the Gifted
Reports on research, teacher training, and program suggestions for gifted and talented children.
Publication vehicle for TAG (The Association for the Gifted)
University of North Carolina Press
P. O. Box 2288
Chapel Hill, NC 27515-2288

Journal of Secondary Gifted Education
Provides a list of research and program descriptions for students in secondary education (formerly the Prufrock).
Department of Educational Psychology
Teachers College
Ball State University
Muncie, IN 47306

Roeper Review
A quarterly journal focusing on philosophical, moral, and academic issues that relate to the lives and experiences of the gifted and talented.
Roeper City and County Schools
P. O. Box 329
Bloomfield Hills, MI 48303-0329

VIDEO AND ELECTRONIC MEDIA

Little Man Tate [Film]. (1991).
Orion Pictures Corp.

The National Student Research Center provides students from distant schools with the opportunity to participate in cooperative student research teams, interschool research projects, the exchange of scientific data, and the possible publication of research abstracts in one of its print or electronic journals of student research, which now have a worldwide circulation.

Contact:
John I. Swang, Director
Mandeville Middle School
2525 Soult Street
Mandeville, LA 70448
America Online: NSRC MMS
Internet: nsrcmms@aol.com

References

Adderholdt-Elliot, M. (1987). *Perfectionism: What's bad about being too good?* Minneapolis: Free Spirit.

Albert, R. S. (1975). Toward a behavioral definition of genius. *American Psychologists, 30*, 140–151.

Albert, R. S. (1992). *Genius and eminence* (2nd ed.). New York: Pergamon.

Angelou, M. (1969/1973). *I know why the caged bird sings.* New York: Bantam.

Bailey, J. M., Boyce, L. N., & Van Tassel-Baska, J. (1990). The reading, writing, and counseling connection: A framework for serving the gifted. In J. Van Tassel-Baska (Ed.), *A practical guide to counseling the gifted in a school setting* (2nd ed.) (pp. 72–89). Reston, VA: Council for Exceptional Children.

Barron, F. (1969). *Creative person and creative process.* New York: Holt, Rinehart & Winston.

Barron, F. (1976). The psychology of creativity. In A. Rothenberg & C. R. Hausman (Eds.), *The creativity question* (pp. 189–200). Durham, NC: Duke University Press.

Benbow, C. P. (1986). SMPY's model for teaching mathematically precocious students. In J. S. Renzulli (Ed.), *Systems and models for developing programs for the gifted and talented* (pp. 1–26). Mansfield Center, CT: Creative Learning Press.

Betts, G. T. (1986). The autonomous learner model for the gifted and talented. In J. S. Renzulli (Ed.), *Systems and models for developing programs for the gifted and talented* (pp. 27–56). Mansfield Center, CT: Creative Learning Press.

Betts, G. T., & Knapp, J. (1980). Autonomous learning and the gifted: A secondary model. In A. Arnold (Ed.), *Secondary programs for the gifted* (pp. 29–36). Ventura, CA: Ventura Superintendent of Schools Office.

Bloom, B. S. (Ed.). (1985). *Developing talent in young people.* New York: Ballantine.

Bloom, B. S., Englehart, M. D., Furst, E. J., Hill, W. H., & Krathwohl, D. J. (1956). *Taxonomy of educational objectives, Handbook I: Cognitive domain.* New York: McKay.

Brewer, D. J., Rees, D. I., & Argys, L. M. (1995). Detracking America's schools: The reform without cost? *Phi Delta Kappan, 77*, 210–215.

Burdin, J. L. (1978). Factors promoting and constraining inservice education. *Journal of Teacher Education, 29*(3), 31–33.

Callahan, C. M. (1994). The performance of high ability students in the United States on national and international tests. In P. O. Ross (Ed.), *National excellence, a case for developing America's talent: An anthology of readings* (pp. 5–26). Washington, DC: Office of Educational Research and Improvement, U.S. Department of Education.

Cornell, D. G. (1983). Gifted children: The impact of positive labeling on the family system. *American Journal of Orthopsychiatry, 53*(2), 322–355.

Cornell, D. G., & Grossberg, I. N. (1986). Siblings of children in gifted programs. *Journal for the Education of the Gifted, 9*, 253–264.

Cox, J., Daniel, N., & Boston, B. (1985). *Educating able learners: Programs and promising practices.* Austin, TX: University of Texas Press.

Cramond, B. (1994). Attention-deficit hyperactivity disorder and creativity—What is the connection? *The Journal of Creative Behavior, 28*, 193–210.

Csikszentmihalyi, M., Rathunde, K., & Whalen, S. (1993). *Talented teenagers: The roots of success & failure.* New York: Cambridge University Press.

Darling-Hammond, L. (1994, April). *Do the "gifted folks" and the "detracking folks" have anything in common?* Paper presented at the meeting of the American Educational Research Association, New Orleans, LA. (Cassette Recording No. 4-5.64). Chicago: American Educational Research Association.

Davis, G., & Rimm, S. B. (1994). *Education of the gifted and talented.* Boston: Allyn & Bacon.

Diamond, M. (1988). *Enriching heredity.* New York: Free Press.

Donovan, A. (1992). Bridging family and school: A school psychologist perspective. In J. Van Tassel-Baska (Ed.), *Planning effective curriculum for gifted learners.* Denver: Love.

Feldhusen, J. F. (1986). A conception of giftedness. In R. J. Sternberg & J. E. Davidson (Eds.), *Conceptions of giftedness* (pp. 112–127). Cambridge: Cambridge University Press.

Feldhusen, J. F. (1996). How to identify and develop special talents. *Educational Leadership, 53*(5), 66–69.

Feldman, D. H., with Goldsmith, L. T. (1986). *Nature's gambit*. New York: Basic Books.

Frasier, M. M. (1987). The identification of gifted black students: Developing new perspectives. *Journal for the Education of the Gifted, 10*, 155–180.

Frasier, M. M. (1994). *The Frasier Talent Assessment Profile (F-TAP): A multiple criteria model for the identification of gifted students*. Athens, GA: Torrance Center for Creative Studies, University of Georgia.

Gagné, F. (1985). Giftedness and talent: Reexamining a reexamination of the definitions. *Gifted Child Quarterly, 29*, 103–112.

Gallagher, J. J. (1993). Comments on McDaniel's "Education of the gifted and the excellence–equity debate." In C. J. Maker (Ed.), *Critical issues in gifted education: Programs for the gifted in regular classrooms* (Vol. 3, pp. 19–21). Austin, TX: PRO-ED.

Gallagher, J. J. (1994a). Current and historical thinking on education for gifted and talented students. In P. O. Ross (Ed.), *National excellence, a case for developing America's talent: An anthology of readings* (pp. 27–60). Washington, DC: Office of Educational Research and Improvement, U.S. Department of Education.

Gallagher, J. J. (1994b). *Teaching the gifted child*. Boston: Allyn & Bacon.

Gallagher, J. J. (1995). Comments on "The reform without cost?" *Phi Delta Kappan, 77*, 216–217.

Galton, F. (1869/1976). Genius as inherited. In A. Rothenberg & C. R. Hausman (Eds.), *The creativity question* (pp. 42–48). Durham, NC: Duke University Press.

Gardner, H. (1983). *Frames of mind: The theory of multiple intelligences*. New York: Basic Books.

Gardner, H. (1988). Creative lives and creative works: A synthetic scientific approach. In R. J. Sternberg (Ed.), *The nature of creativity* (pp. 298–321). Cambridge: Cambridge University Press.

Gardner, H. (1993). *Creating minds*. New York: Basic Books.

Getzels, J. W., & Jackson, P. W. (1962). *Creativity and intelligence: Explorations with gifted students*. New York: Wiley.

Goertzel, M. G., Goertzel, V., & Goertzel, T. G. (1978). *300 eminent personalities*. San Francisco: Jossey-Bass.

Goertzel, V., & Goertzel, M. G. (1962). *Cradles of eminence*. Boston: Little, Brown.

Goleman, D. (1995). *Emotional intelligence*. New York: Bantam.

Guilford, J. P. (1967). *The nature of human intelligence*. New York: McGraw-Hill.

Guilford, J. P. (1977). *Way beyond the IQ*. Buffalo, NY: Creative Education Foundation.

Hagen, E. (1980). *Identification of the gifted*. New York: Teachers College, Columbia University.

Halsted, J. W. (1988). *Guiding gifted readers from preschool through high school: A handbook for parents, teachers, counselors and librarians*. Columbus, OH: Ohio Psychology.

Hoffman, M. L. (1987). The contribution of empathy to justice and moral judgment. In N. Eisenberg & J. Strayer (Eds.), *Empathy and its development* (pp. 47–80). Cambridge: Cambridge University Press.

Hoge, R. D. (1988). Issues in the definition and measurement of the giftedness construct. *Educational Researcher, 17*(7), 12–16.

Hollingworth, L. S. (1926). *Gifted children: Their nature and nurture*. New York: Macmillan.

Hollingworth, L. (1942, reprinted 1977). *Children above 180 IQ*. New York: Octagon Books.

Isaksen, S. G., & Treffinger, D. J. (1985). *Creative problem solving: The basic course*. Buffalo, NY: Bearly.

Jenkins, J. (1995, March). *Reflections on being gifted*. Speech given at the meeting of the Georgia Association for Gifted Children, Athens, GA. Reprinted in part in the *Newsletter of the Clarke County Supporters for the Gifted*. (Available from Bonnie Cramond, Department of Educational Psychology, University of Georgia, Athens, GA 30602)

Jenkins-Friedman, R., & Anderson, M. A. (1985). *Gifted plus: Teaching high potential students about their abilities*. (Available from Reva Jenkins-Friedman, Educational Psychology and Research Department, 2 Bailey Hall, University of Kansas, Lawrence, KS 66045)

Jensen, A. (1969). How much can we boost IQ and scholastic achievement? *Harvard Educational Review, 39*, 1–123.

Komoski, P. K. (1981). Educational R & D report. *EPIE Institute, 3*(4).

Kulik, J. A., & Kulik, C. C. (1991). Ability grouping and gifted students. In N. Colangelo & G. A. Davis (Eds.), *Handbook of gifted education* (pp. 178–196). Needham Heights, MA: Allyn & Bacon.

MacKinnon, D. W. (1992). The highly effective individual. In R. S. Albert (Ed.), *Genius & eminence*. New York: Pergamon. (Reprinted from *Teacher's College Record*, 1960, *61*, 376–378)

MacKinnon, D. W. (1978). *In search of human effectiveness*. Buffalo, NY: Creative Education Foundation.

Maker, C. J. (1977). *Providing programs for the handicapped gifted*. Reston, VA: Council for Exceptional Children.

Maker, C. J. (1982). *Curriculum development for the gifted*. Rockville, MD: Aspen.

Maker, C. J. (1996). Identification of gifted minority students: A national problem, needed changes and a promising solution. *Gifted Child Quarterly, 40*, 41–50.

Marland, S. J., Jr. (1972). *Education of the gifted and talented: Report to the Congress of the United States*. Washington, DC: U.S. Government Printing Office.

McDaniel, T. R. (1993). Education of the gifted and the excellence–equity debate: Lessons from history. In C. J. Maker (Ed.), *Critical issues in gifted education: Programs for the gifted in regular classrooms* (Vol. 3, pp. 6–18). Austin, TX: PRO-ED.

Oakes, J. (1985). *Keeping track: How schools structure inequality*. New Haven, CT: Yale University Press.

Oakes, J. (1994, April). *Do the "gifted folks" and the "detracking folks" have anything in common?* Paper presented at the meeting of the American Educational Research Association, New Orleans, LA. (Cassette Recording No. 4-5.64). Chicago: American Educational Research Association.

Ochse, R. (1990). *Before the gates of excellence: The determinants of creative genius.* New York: Cambridge University Press.

Piaget, J., & Inhelder, B. (1969). *The psychology of the child* (Weaver, Trans.). New York: Basic Books.

Plomin, R., & Neiderhiser, J. (1991). Quantitative genetics, molecular genetics, and intelligence. *Intelligence, 15,* 369–387.

Rainer, J. D. (1976). Genetics of intelligence: Current issues and unsolved questions. *Research Communications in Psychology, Psychiatry & Behavior, 1,* 607–618.

Reis, S. (1994, April). *Do the "gifted folks" and the "detracking folks" have anything in common?* Paper presented at the meeting of the American Educational Research Association, New Orleans, LA. (Cassette Recording No. 4-5.64). Chicago: American Educational Research Association.

Reis, S. M., Burns, D. E., & Renzulli, J. S. (1992). *Curriculum compacting: The complete guide to modifying the regular curriculum for high ability students.* Mansfield Center, CT: Creative Learning Press.

Renzulli, J. S. (1977). *The enrichment triad model: A guide for developing defensible programs for the gifted.* Mansfield Center, CT: Creative Learning Press.

Renzulli, J. S. (1978). What makes giftedness? Re-examining a definition. *Phi Delta Kappan, 60,* 180–184, 261.

Renzulli, J. S. (1985, November). *Four frequently asked questions about the triad/revolving door model.* Paper presented at the meeting of the National Association for Gifted Children, Denver, CO.

Renzulli, J. S. (1986). *The three-ring conception of giftedness: A developmental model for creative productivity.* In R. J. Sternberg & J. E. Davidson (Eds.), *Conceptions of giftedness* (pp. 53–92). New York: Cambridge University Press.

Renzulli, J. S. (1994). *Schools for talent development: A practical plan for total school improvement.* Mansfield Center, CT: Creative Learning Press.

Renzulli, J. S., & Reis, S. M. (1985). *The schoolwide enrichment model: A comprehensive plan for educational excellence.* Mansfield Center, CT: Creative Learning Press.

Renzulli, J. S., & Reis, S. M. (1986). The enrichment triad/revolving door model: A schoolwide plan for the development of creative productivity. In J. S. Renzulli (Ed.), *Systems and models for developing programs for the gifted and talented* (pp. 216–266). Mansfield Center, CT: Creative Learning Press.

Renzulli, J. S., & Reis, S. M. (1991). The schoolwide enrichment model: A comprehensive plan for the development of creative productivity. In N. Colangelo & G. A. Davis (Eds.), *Handbook of gifted education* (pp. 111–141). Needham Heights, MA: Allyn & Bacon.

Restak, R. (1993). The creative brain. In J. Brockman (Ed.), *Creativity* (pp. 164–175). New York: Touchstone.

Richert, S. E. (1991). Rampant problems and promising practices in identification. In N. Colangelo & G. A. Davis (Eds.), *Handbook of gifted education* (pp. 81–96). Needham Heights, MA: Allyn & Bacon.

Richert, S. E., Alvino, J., & McDonnel, R. (1982). *National report on identification: Assessment and recommendation for comprehensive identification of gifted and talented youth.* Servell, NJ: Educational Improvement Center-South.

Rimm, S. B. (1986). *Underachievement syndrome: Causes and cures.* Watertown, WI: Apple.

Rimm, S. B. (1991). Parenting the gifted adolescent–special problems, special joys. In M. Bireley and J. Genshaft (Eds.), *Understanding the gifted adolescent.* New York: Columbia University.

Roe, A. (1953). *The making of a scientist.* New York: Dodd Mead.

Rogers, K. B. (1991). *The relationship of grouping practices to the education of the gifted and talented learner.* Storrs, CT: National Research Center on the Gifted and Talented. (Number 9102)

Seagoe, M. V. (1975). *Terman and the gifted.* Los Altos, CA: Kaufmann.

Shurkin, J. N. (1992). *Terman's kids: The groundbreaking study of how the gifted grow up.* Boston: Little, Brown.

Silverman, L. K. (1993a). The gifted individual. In L. K. Silverman (Ed.), *Counseling the gifted and talented* (pp. 3–28). Denver: Love.

Silverman, L. K. (1993b). Techniques for preventive counseling. In L. K. Silverman (Ed.), *Counseling the gifted and talented* (pp. 81–109). Denver: Love.

Simonton, D. K. (1988). Creativity, leadership, and chance. In R. J. Sternberg (Ed.), *The nature of creativity* (pp. 386–426). New York: Cambridge University Press.

Slavin, R. E. (1987). Ability grouping and student achievement in elementary schools: A best-evidence synthesis. *Review of Educational Research, 57,* 347–350.

Slavin, R. E. (1990). Achievement effects of ability grouping in secondary schools: A best-evidence synthesis. *Review of Educational Research, 60,* 471–499.

Sosniak, L. A. (1995). Phases of learning. In B. S. Bloom (Ed.), *Developing talent in young people.* New York: Ballantine.

Spearman, C. (1904). General intelligence—Objectively determined and measured. *American Journal of Psychology, 15,* 201–293.

Stanley, J. (1983). Introduction. In E. P. Benbow & J. C. Stanley (Eds.), *Academic precocity* (pp. 1–8). Baltimore, MD: Johns Hopkins University Press.

Starko, A. (1986). *It's about time!* Mansfield Center, CT: Creative Learning Press.

Sternberg, R. J. (1985). *Beyond IQ: A triarchic theory of human intelligence.* New York: Cambridge University Press.

Sternberg, R. J. (1996). Myths, countermyths, and truths about intelligence. *Educational Researcher, 25*(2), 11–16.

Subotnik, R., Kassan, L., Summers, E., & Wasser, A. (1993). *Genius revisited: High IQ children grown up.* Norwood, NJ: Ablex.

Tannenbaum, A. J. (1983). *Gifted children: Psychological and educational perspectives.* New York: Macmillan.

Tardif, T. Z., & Sternberg, R. J. (1988). What do we know about creativity? In R. J. Sternberg (Ed.), *The nature of creativity* (429–440). New York: Cambridge University Press.

Taylor, B. M., & Frye, B. J. (1988). Pretesting: Minimize time spent on skill work for intermediate readers. *The Reading Teacher, 42*(2), 100–104.

Terman, L. M. (1925). *Genetic studies of genius: Vol. 1. Mental and physical traits of a thousand gifted children.* Stanford, CA: Stanford University Press.

Terman, L. M., Burks, B. S., & Jensen, D. W. (1930). *Genetic studies of genius: Vol. 3. The promise of youth: Follow-up studies of a thousand gifted children.* Stanford, CA: Stanford University Press.

Terman, L. M., & Oden, M. H. (1947). *Genetic studies of genius: Vol. 4. The gifted child grows up.* Stanford, CA: Stanford University Press.

Terman, L. M., & Oden, M. H. (1959). *Genetic studies of genius: Vol. 5. The promise of youth: Follow-up studies of a thousand gifted children.* Stanford, CA: Stanford University Press.

Thompson, L. J. (1971). Language disabilities in men of eminence. *Journal of Learning Disabilities, 4,* 34–45.

Thurstone, L. L. (1938). *Primary mental abilities.* Chicago: University of Chicago Press.

Torrance, E. P. (1966). *Torrance tests of creative thinking.* Bensenville, IL: Scholastic Testing Service.

Torrance, E. P. (1979). An instructional model for enhancing incubation. *Journal of Creative Behavior, 13,* 23–35.

Treffinger, D. J., & Feldhusen, J. F. (1996). Talent recognition and development: Successor to gifted education. *Journal for the Education of the Gifted, 19,* 181–193.

U.S. Department of Education (1993). *National excellence: A case for developing America's talent.* Washington, DC: Office of Educational Research and Improvement.

Walberg, H. J. (1982). Child traits and environmental conditions of highly eminent adults. *Gifted Child Quarterly, 25,* 103–107.

Walberg, H. J., & Herbig, M. P. (1991). Developing talent, creativity, and eminence. In N. Colangelo & G. A. Davis (Eds.), *Handbook of gifted education* (pp. 245–255). Needham Heights, MA: Allyn & Bacon.

Wallach, M. A., & Kogan, N. (1965). *Modes of thinking in young children: A study of the creativity–intelligence distinction.* New York: Holt, Rinehart & Winston.

Wallach, M. A., & Wing, C. W., Jr. (1969). *The talented student: A validation of the creativity–intelligence distinction.* New York: Holt, Rinehart & Winston.

Ward, V. S. (1964). Ten cardinal principles. In J. L. French (Ed.), *Educating the gifted* (pp. 171–177). New York: Holt, Rhinehart & Winston.

West, T. G. (1991). *In the mind's eye: Visual thinkers, gifted people with learning difficulties, computer images, and ironies of creativity.* Buffalo, NY: Prometheus.

Westberg, K. L., Archambault, F. X., Jr., Dobyns, S. M., & Salvin, T. J. (1993). *An observational study of instructional and curricular practices used with gifted and talented students in regular classrooms.* Storrs, CT: National Research Center on the Gifted and Talented. (Research Monograph 93104)

Whitmore, J. R. (1980). *Giftedness, conflict, and underachievement.* Boston: Allyn & Bacon.

Witty, P. (Ed.). (1951). *The gifted child.* Lexington, MA: Heath.

Chapter 4

Jamaican Night, acrylic on canvas, 30″ × 50″ (1990)

LEARNING DISABILITIES

DIANE HAAGER

After studying this chapter, the reader will:

Demonstrate knowledge of the major definitions of learning disabilities and how they are operationalized

Understand the controversy surrounding the development of a widely accepted definition of learning disabilities

Be able to list and describe common characteristics of individuals with learning disabilities and their possible implications for educational outcomes

Identify and explain appropriate assessment methods

Recognize the instructional needs of and expectations for students with learning disabilities in elementary, secondary, and postsecondary settings

Know the appropriate instructional adaptations and modifications for students with learning disabilities in traditional and inclusive service delivery settings

Appreciate the impact of learning disabilities on the family

Learning Disabilities

1800–1930 Early research related specific areas of the brain to the ability to read, speak, and write.

1930–1960 Clinical study of perceptual–motor processes in children with brain injuries led to using the term *minimal brain dysfunction* to describe children who have no known brain injury but nevertheless have learning difficulties.

1963 At a national parent conference, Samuel Kirk proposed the term *learning disabilities* to describe children who have difficulty learning.

1964 A parent organization, the Association for Children with Learning Disabilities (now known as Learning Disabilities Association, or LDA), was formed.

1969 Congress recognized the field of learning disabilities by passing the Children With Specific Learning Disabilities Act, providing funding for teacher training.

1975 Congress passed P.L. 94-142, the Education for All Handicapped Children Act, which included learning disabilities as a category of disability and mandated public school services for children with learning disabilities.

1990s Recent developments have included more effective instruction, diagnostic techniques, and genetic research.

HISTORICAL OVERVIEW

Compared to other areas of disability, the field of learning disabilities is little beyond the infancy stage. It was only in 1963 that Samuel A. Kirk, now considered the "grandfather" of the field, coined the term *learning disabilities* to describe the difficulties some children have in school despite no obvious brain damage or other physical cause. In 1969 Congress passed the Children with Specific Learning Disabilities Act, which provided some funding for teacher training. But it was not until 1975, with passage of the Education for All Handicapped Children Act (P.L. 94-142), that learning disabilities were included as a category of disability and public school services for children with learning disabilities were mandated. This act of Congress speeded up efforts of researchers and practitioners who were seeking appropriate methods and techniques for teaching children with presumably unexplainable learning difficulties and can be considered the formal beginning of the field as we know it.

Clinical Study of Brain Trauma

The roots of the field of learning disabilities can be traced to early brain research from the 1800s and early 1900s. During this time scientists began to obtain concrete evidence that different language and motor functions could be attributed to specific areas of the brain. Scientists began to associate perceptual impairment and resultant learning difficulties with brain damage, leading Heinz Werner and Alfred Strauss to study brain-injured children.

Beginning in the early 1930s there was a surge in the clinical study and treatment of children with brain damage as well as children with **dyslexia,** or an inability to read, leading to the conclusion that a link existed between brain damage and learning difficulties. Several clinicians became interested in children who had language and learning difficulties but had not suffered any known brain trauma—thus the term *minimal brain dysfunction* emerged. It was assumed there was some internal brain damage or dysfunction that could not be detected that was impairing their ability to use language or their visual perception. Methods and materials were developed for such children. Strauss and Lehtinen (1947), for example, proposed a learning environment as free as possible from distracting auditory and visual stimuli—resulting in years of special education classrooms designed with isolated cubicles to minimize distractions. Another clinician, Grace Fernald (1943), developed a multisensory method for teaching reading through the use of visual, auditory, kinesthetic, and tactile modes of learning, referred to as the VAKT technique, which is sometimes used today. Samuel T. Orton (1937) hypothesized that a lack of cerebral dominance accounted for children's language disorders, and his multisensory teaching methods later developed into the Orton-Gillingham method for simultaneously teaching reading and spelling. This highly structured method, still in clinical use, emphasizes sequential phonics instruction through tracing and saying the letter sounds and names. The Orton Dyslexia Society today is an active force in promoting advances in the study and treatment of reading disabilities.

Perceptual–Motor Phase

Other theorists hypothesized that disorders of the perceptual–motor processes rather than brain damage were at the core of such unexplainable learning difficulties. The influence of these theorists dominated the field well into the 1970s.

REAL PEOPLE

Yoshiko Izumi is a first-year special education teacher. Like many other new teachers, she is anticipating a year of hard work and many challenges. After all, her students are counting on her to be a teacher, an advocate, a counselor, and a friend. Most of Yoshiko's students have significant learning disabilities that have made a full-time special class placement necessary. Most have other difficulties as well—behavior problems, attention problems, emotional difficulties, or medical conditions. But Yoshiko has an added challenge unknown to most observers. She herself has a significant learning disability that persists in all aspects of her adult life.

When I first met Yoshiko, she was a student in my graduate class in learning disabilities. Though she sat in the front of the room and seemed to pay close attention, she did not have much to say in class and her first written exam was marked down because it was not elaborate or detailed. Soon after this, I learned that she has a learning disability. Throughout the next two years, I became Yoshiko's academic adviser and learned a great deal more about her. She began to work with the Office for Students With Disabilities to develop adaptations for her university courses and they requested additional time for her for the next exam. I learned that she had neared completion of all the coursework to earn both an elementary and a special education teaching credential. However, she would not be allowed to do student teaching until she passed the basic teacher exam, something she had attempted more than once. Yoshiko felt she knew the material on the test, but she was a very nervous and slow test taker. Meanwhile, she was successfully taking courses toward a master's degree. I developed a great admiration for Yoshiko as I began to understand how challenging graduate school must be for her. Our expectations of graduate students are that they will read a tremendous amount, memorize material, synthesize information, write cohesively, and apply their learning to classrooms. How many additional hours it must have taken for Yoshiko to do this in order to succeed in her graduate coursework is difficult to imagine.

As Yoshiko neared completion of the master's courses, she passed the teacher exam and enrolled in her first supervised field experience in special education. During the following 10 weeks, I watched Yoshiko become one of the best beginning teachers I have known. As quiet as she was in my classes, she could establish rapport with young children with sensitivity and ease. She designed appropriate assessments and fascinating lessons. I could see in her a great love and respect for children. And I discovered an area of strength that had not been obvious in my classes: She had a background and degree in art. Yoshiko was using her artistic ability to engage and instruct children.

Marianne Frostig hypothesized that children with learning disorders but no obvious brain trauma had a neurological dysfunction. She developed a widely used diagnostic test, the Developmental Test of Visual Perception (Frostig, Maslow, Lefever, & Whittlesey, 1964), and a set of training materials widely used in special education and remedial school programs (Frostig & Horne, 1964). William Cruickshank developed a set of highly structured lessons focused on teaching arithmetic and reading through the development of perceptual–motor processes such as auditory and visual discrimination or eye–hand coordination (Cruickshank, Bentzen, Ratzeburg, & Tannhauser, 1961).

Educational Perspective

With the development of the Illinois Test of Psycholinguistic Abilities (McCarthy & Kirk, 1961) and related teaching methods (Kirk, 1972), the idea of *psycholinguistic teaching* became the most widely used method in the field of learning disabilities. In

Yoshiko Izumi

Yoshiko remembers that her first indication of having difficulty learning came in first grade when she was not successfully learning to read. Her first grade teacher called her mother in and she was referred to a reading specialist, Mrs. Phillips, "a really nice lady." Following an assessment in reading, Yoshiko was pulled out of class just for reading during the first and second grades. She enjoyed the special reading class and felt pleased to be allowed to take books home for extra practice. By the fourth and fifth grades, Yoshiko remembers the class work getting harder. She says this was her first real indication that her learning problems were significant. In the spelling books, the rest of the class was "on list 32 while I was only on list 10." In the reading kits with individual sequential lessons, she was always far behind the others. By the time Yoshiko got to junior high school, she was substantially behind the other students. She was placed in remedial reading classes instead of regular English. She especially remembers her eighth grade reading teacher. It was in this class that Yoshiko was finally introduced to phonics, an event that she feels was a turning point in her being able to read as an adult. Though she learned phonics in this one year, it took years for her to develop the necessary speed with these skills to be fluent. All through high school she couldn't keep up, and barely graduated with a D average.

It is Yoshiko's singular determination that led her to graduate school and a teaching career despite being told she would never get into graduate school. In order to bring up her grades enough to get into a university, she attended a junior college for 2 years. She began to analyze her learning difficulties and seek ways to succeed. "In elementary school," she says, "I can remember wondering why my teachers weren't teaching me ways to figure out how to do things I couldn't do. I finally figured out ways to work around assignments in college. I guess I developed strategies. I figured out I didn't have to read every sentence, but could pick out the important parts." From junior college, Yoshiko went to a state university and completed a liberal arts degree with a major in art. Though she contemplated a career in jewelry design, others were encouraging her to go into teaching. Finally, at the prompting of her sister and other friends, she entered a graduate teacher education program.

Yoshiko thinks that getting along in life seems easier than it did 10 years ago, although she still considers it tough going. It still takes a great deal of effort to accomplish some things that other people breeze through—such as writing her lesson plans in detail. She always starts out with good intentions and tries to keep up with things, but often has difficulty getting started. In her words: "It's not so much that the task is hard as it is the time factor—trying to get everything done when I know it takes me more time. . . . But, I guess, that's just what I have to do. . . . With practice, tasks seem a little easier and take a little less time."

this approach, **individualized instruction** was based on the idea of finding an individual's learning modality strengths and weaknesses (i.e., auditory, visual, etc.) and then planning instruction accordingly. This test was widely used to plan individualized programs for students with learning disabilities throughout the 1970s. Though other tests are used today, the idea of individualizing instruction by building on students' strengths and remediating areas of weakness remains a central tenet in the field.

Kirk's proposal of the term *learning disabilities* to describe the problems of children with unexplainable learning difficulties marked the formal beginning of the field of learning disabilities. Parents and many educators felt that previously used terms were too medical or clinical and did not adequately describe children in terms of their educational needs. In 1963, Kirk met with a group of parents in Chicago to discuss the educational needs of such children and to mark the formation of a parent organization. In his address, Kirk used the term *learning disabilities,* much to the delight of the parents who had been beleaguered by the clinical obscurity of previous terminology. As a result of the 1963 meeting, the Association of Children With Learning Disabilities (now called Learning Disabilities Association, or LDA) was formed in 1964 and is today a very strong parent and professional group. This group was a powerful force in the effort to foster awareness of and obtain educational services for children with learning disabilities and thus the focus turned away from a medical or clinical perspective toward an educational perspective.

In 1975, Congress included learning disabilities for the first time as a disability in the Education for All Handicapped Children Act, guaranteeing a free and appropriate public education for children with learning disabilities. School systems nationwide found themselves scrambling to develop special education classrooms with trained teachers to serve a rapidly increasing number of identified students with this disorder. This legislation still governs most of what we do to serve children with learning disabilities.

In 1990, Congress reauthorized the original legislation as P.L. 101-476, the Individuals With Disabilities Education Act, or IDEA. It maintained learning disabilities as a category of disability, and the federal definition that governs identification also remained unchanged. This act adopted a **person-first language,** making it preferable to refer, for instance, to a "student with learning disabilities" rather than a "learning disabled student." An important provision of IDEA is the mandate for transition services for all adolescents with learning disabilities, beginning at the age of 16. Because a learning disability does not usually involve physical or intellectual impairment, school programs prior to this legislation had not typically focused on assisting students with learning disabilities in the transition from school to work. However, by the time of this legislation, research had shown that there were a significant number of young adults with learning disabilities who had been served in public school programs and were having difficulty maintaining employment and a satisfactory quality of life. Because of this legislation, schools nationwide have developed transition programs to assist students with learning disabilities in exploring their career options, preparing for postsecondary education, and learning appropriate life skills. In addition, many postsecondary institutions have developed support services for individuals with learning disabilities.

In the years since 1963, we have learned a great deal about how to teach individuals with learning disabilities. We have also begun to understand factors that may lead to early identification and prevention. Some now think that *learning disabilities* may be a generic term that describes several different types of specific disorders and that in the future we may be able to be more specific about effective methods for these different types of learning disabilities. Modern advances may lead to more effective methods for providing optimal services for individuals with learning disabilities.

DEFINITION: A CONTROVERSIAL ISSUE

Most human disorders have easily recognizable characteristics and well defined criteria for identifying those who have a disorder. This is far from true for learning disabilities, leading to ongoing debate regarding the federal definition. Though many agree that the federal definition of learning disabilities is somewhat ambiguous, no one has been able to propose an acceptable alternative that clearly specifies characteristics and criteria for identification. Until this happens, we are left with a definition that is open to interpretation by state and local education agencies.

The federal definition included in the Education for All Handicapped Children Act of 1975 has remained virtually unchanged in subsequent legislation and is

Which student has a learning disability? Unlike other disabilities with recognizable characteristics, students with learning disabilities look no different from their peers.

the definition that governs states' implementation of service delivery. The definition states:

> "Specific learning disability" means a disorder in one or more of the basic psychological processes involved in understanding or in using language, spoken or written, which may manifest itself in an imperfect ability to listen, think, speak, read, write, spell, or to do mathematical calculations. The term includes such conditions as perceptual handicaps, brain injury, minimal brain dysfunction, dyslexia, and developmental aphasia. The term does not include children who have learning problems which are primarily the result of visual, hearing, or motor handicaps, of mental retardation, or emotional disturbance, or of environmental, cultural, or economic disadvantage. (U.S. Office of Education, 1977, p. 65083)

What does this definition tell us about children with learning disabilities? How do we go about distinguishing those who do have this disorder from others who do not? The most important question asked by state education agencies is this: How do we know whom to serve? Let's examine some of the specific components of this definition and how the specific wording influences the identification of children with learning disabilities.

Basic Psychological Processes

> "Specific learning disability" means a disorder in one or more of the basic psychological processes . . .

This phrase specifies a belief that the disorder is a result of some type of intrinsic processing difficulty. However, from this definition, do we know what "basic psychological processes" are? The federal government did not specify what processes are included nor did it determine criteria for measuring these processes. Since the field of learning disabilities grew out of the clinical study of perceptual processes, terms such as *visual–spatial orientation*, *auditory perception*, and a multitude of other perceptual terms have been used in describing children with learning disabilities. In recent years, information processing or cognitive theories have influenced the study of learning. Some have used this interpretation to define the basic psychological processes, using such terms as *short-term* or *long-term memory*, *attention*, *perceptual integration*, and others to describe the psychological processes of children with learning disabilities. This component of the definition seems to many to be fundamental to defining the disorder; yet, despite years of debate, no consensus on its meaning and no concrete guidelines for identification have been established. According to two studies (Chalfant, 1985; Mercer, Hughes, & Mercer, 1985), several states require some type of assessment results indicating a **processing disorder** such as visual–motor, visual-perceptual, auditory–receptive, or expressive language disorders for identification of learning disabilities. Furthermore, Chalfant (1985) recommends direct observation of the student in a learning setting to accompany the assessment results in this area.

Language-Based Disorder

. . . involved in understanding or in using language, spoken or written, which may manifest itself in an imperfect ability to listen, think, read, write, spell, or to do mathematical calculations.

This portion of the definition establishes the category of learning disabilities as a language-based disorder that influences the acquisition of academic skills. It is presumed that fundamental to this disability is a language problem. Individuals with learning disabilities have difficulty using language, but people with other disorders also have language difficulties. From this component of the definition, would you suppose we use a battery of language tests to identify individuals with learning disabilities, or academic tests? Most people look at academic problems as the outcome of the language-based difficulties and, therefore, rely on academic tests to determine the extent of the disability. However, many students with learning disabilities also receive speech and language therapy as a supplement to their basic special education services due to significant difficulties with the use of language.

Discrepancy Criteria

. . . an imperfect ability [to listen, think, read, write, spell or to do mathematical calculations].

The two little words *imperfect ability* have caused the most controversy surrounding the definition. These two little words are also at the heart of how we have identified children for services for the past 20 years. How we interpret "imperfect ability" has a great impact on establishing concrete criteria for inclusion in this definition. Does it mean an individual with learning disabilities is performing below what you would expect for his or her age or grade level? Does it mean an individual with learning disabilities is not performing at his or her individual potential?

The first question, or the idea of being behind in age or grade expectancy, defines what we have always thought of as low achievement. The second question, or the idea of not performing at potential, introduces a measure of aptitude into the equation. In a separate set of guidelines (U.S. Office of Education, 1977), the federal government suggested that both issues should be addressed in determining a learning disability: A child should need the services, or be performing below age or grade level; and a child should not be performing at potential, or have a "severe discrepancy" between achievement and intellectual ability in one or more academic areas. Most states follow these guidelines and primarily use a discrepancy formula to identify children. However, the federal government did not specify what constitutes a severe discrepancy and states or local districts must determine this for themselves. This has resulted in differences in criteria and in the proportion of students identified state by state. Later we will discuss some of the difficulties in determining a severe discrepancy between intellectual ability and academic performance.

Inclusionary and Exclusionary Terms

The term includes such conditions as perceptual handicaps, brain injury, minimal brain dysfunction, dyslexia, and developmental aphasia.

This wording illustrates some of the terms previously used to describe children with this disorder. The purpose here is to consolidate previous clinical terminology into one federally recognized term: *learning disabilities.*

The term does not include children who have learning problems which are primarily the result of visual, hearing, or motor handicaps, of mental retardation, or emotional disturbance, or of environmental, cultural, or economic disadvantage.

This sentence is usually referred to as enumerating the "exclusionary" criteria. It describes what a learning disability is *not.* The intent of this component of the definition is to assure that the learning disability is the primary disability. For example, a child with poor vision might have difficulty learning to read due to vision problems. When corrective lenses are provided, the child may no longer have difficulty, given appropriate instruction. This is not a case of a learning disability. The intent is to identify children who have difficulty learning despite appropriate instruction and opportunity. According to this definition, environmental, cultural, or economic disadvantage might lead to learning difficulties, but this would not constitute a learning disability. The disorder must occur despite adequate opportunity to learn and must not be attributable to some other disorder or condition.

One problem with the exclusionary criteria is the possibility of overlap with characteristics of other disorders. For example, numerous studies have indicated a higher than average rate of behavioral difficulties among students with learning disabilities (Bender & Smith, 1990). Behavioral difficulties also define a serious emotional disturbance. It is then up to the team to specify whether the behavioral difficulties of a certain individual constitute the *primary* disability associated with emotional disturbance or are secondary to the learning difficulties of a learning disability. Attention deficit disorder, behavior disorders, speech and language disorders, visual impairment, hearing impairment, and others are all types of disorders that sometimes co-occur with learning disabilities. If the placement team determines that the learning disability is the primary disability, then the student may be placed into services for students with learning disabilities with secondary support services as needed.

Alternative Definitions

Twice, interdisciplinary committees have convened to develop and propose a new definition to Congress to clarify ambiguity in the federal definition. In 1981, the

National Joint Committee on Learning Disabilities (NJCLD) put forth a definition that was accepted as an improvement by many parents and professionals yet did not fully address some of the problems inherent in the federal definition and was never adopted into federal law. This definition did recognize the heterogeneity of the population of individuals with this disorder and attempted to clarify the term *basic psychological processes* (Hammill, 1990). Again, in 1987, the Interagency Committee on Learning Disabilities (ICLD) proposed a new definition of learning disabilities to Congress following extensive review of current research and literature on various aspects of learning disabilities (Kavanagh & Truss, 1988). However this definition, too, had ambiguous components. Congress did not endorse the ICLD definition and the federal definition of learning disabilities has remained almost unchanged from the 1975 version.

Despite the difficulties inherent in the federal definition of learning disabilities, no one has been able to construct an alternative that has been widely accepted as more operational. Some have proposed eliminating this category of disability from the federal legislation altogether due to the inherent difficulty in definition and the lack of clear distinction between those who truly have learning disabilities and those who have learning problems not related to an intrinsic disorder. However, it is likely that, with time and scientific advances, we will develop a more precise definition. Until that time, it is important to keep in mind the intent of the federal law and to understand specific identification criteria adopted state by state.

CHARACTERISTICS ASSOCIATED WITH LEARNING DISABILITIES

Who are the nearly 2 million children, adolescents, and adults with learning disabilities that make up the largest group of individuals served in special education? What are they like? It is important for teachers and other professionals to understand the characteristics associated with this disorder and their potential impact on the individual and his or her family.

A Heterogeneous Group of Individuals

To characterize the population of individuals with learning disabilities it is important to think in terms of diversity. Individuals with learning disabilities are probably more different from each other than they are different from individuals without disabilities. Though there are certain characteristics that are commonly associated with the disorder, any one individual may have only one or a few of the characteristics and is likely to have a very different pattern of characteristics from others with the disorder. By definition, individuals with learning disabilities have significant difficulty in at least one area of academic functioning. Unexpected underachievement is probably the only characteristic that is common to all individuals with this disorder. Individuals with learning disabilities may be very different from each other in terms of their academic areas of strength and difficulty, specific cognitive abilities, language skills, social and behavioral characteristics, and physical characteristics.

Because we tend to focus on the characteristics that cause learning difficulty for an individual student, it is easy to lose sight of the fact that each individual with this disorder is likely to have areas of strength. For example, Mark, age 15, has tremendous difficulty with reading and writing and this difficulty pervades all his academic work. He struggles to maintain a C average in his classes with the assistance of a special education resource teacher and his supportive parents and older brother. If he does not maintain passing grades, he will not be allowed to participate in the track team. One day when Mark was helping his parents clean out the garage, they noticed that he has a keen spatial sense. He can very easily arrange and organize things in a given space. Mark appears to have two areas of strength: athletic and spatial abilities.

A learning disability is a lifelong disorder. When adults with learning disabilities describe their experiences throughout their lives, they often report that specific characteristics impacted their lives differently at various stages of life. As we discuss the following characteristics that are common to this disability, ask yourself how specific characteristics may impact individuals differently. Also, think about how each characteristic might or might not be detected at an early age.

Cognitive Processes

We think of individuals with learning disabilities as having average or above average intellectual ability because, if they were significantly below average, they would likely be categorized as having mental retardation. By definition, this would exclude them from the learning disabilities category. However, intelligence tests provide numerical scores and are very limited in the information they provide about how an individual thinks and learns. To understand that, we would need to look at **cognition.** Cognition and intelligence are related concepts but are not synonymous. To better understand the learning difficulties of individuals with learning disabilities, researchers have been studying their cognitive processes, or how they think and learn. It is likely that the intent of the wording "basic psychological processes" in the federal definition was meant to depict how an individual takes in, stores, connects, and utilizes information. A disorder in these basic learning processes would certainly result in academic difficulties as the definition indicates.

Metacognition is the ability to control and coordinate the learning process. It is thought to control the processing components of attention, perception, and memory. We generally think of two components of metacognition: (1) self-awareness of the strategies and resources needed to learn; and (2) self-regulation of the learning processes by planning and monitoring the learning process, employing appropriate strategies throughout the process, and self-evaluating learning (Brown, 1980). This might best be illustrated with an example.

Suppose you have a difficult chapter to read for an upcoming test. Being aware of its difficulty, you decide that it would be best to read it when you are wide awake. You plan to read it on Saturday morning, in a quiet room of the house with a notebook and pen available for taking notes. This is an example of your self-awareness of the strategies and resources needed to carry out your cognitive task and your ability to plan your learning. You carry out your plan, but once you get into the chapter, you realize that it is very complex material. You decide to outline the chapter and learn the information in chunks, taking breaks between the main sections. An hour into the study session, you get a phone call. When you get back to the chapter, you realize you've lost your train of thought, so you go back a couple of pages and reread your outline to refamiliarize yourself with it. Your self-monitoring led you to realize that the chapter was more difficult than you had initially realized and you regulated your learning by deciding to outline and learn it in chunks. Your self-monitoring also led you to be aware of your distraction with

Teachers must learn to look for nonverbal cues to discern student understanding or confusion.

the phone call. Your ability to self-regulate, or employ fix-up strategies along the way, led you to decide to outline and reread. When you finish reading, you wonder how well you will remember the important facts, so you plan an additional study session for the next day to go over some difficult terminology and to reread the outline. This is an example of self-evaluation of learning. Because you were not confident that you had mastered the material, you planned some additional time to study.

The 1980s began a period of intense study of the cognitive and metacognitive processes of individuals with learning disabilities. Bernice Wong (1987) was one of the first to bring metacognitive theory into the realm of learning disabilities. Since then, strategy instruction has become an important component of effective learning programs for individuals with learning disabilities, particularly for adolescents. Many students with learning disabilities either lack strategies or have inefficient metacognitive strategies in various aspects of learning such as reading, writing, mathematics, and content area learning. Many studies have shown that when students with learning disabilities are taught metacognitive strategies, their learning increases (Swanson & Ransby, 1994).

Language Processes

Individuals with learning disabilities are likely to have difficulty with language processing or skills. Because language is at the base of all thought and reasoning, it is hard to separate language abilities from the cognitive processes described here. Language processing difficulties are thought to be an underlying cause of the academic difficulties experienced by students with learning disabilities. The federal definition states that a disorder in "the basic psychological processes involved in understanding or in using language, spoken or written" may lead to problems with various language-based abilities such as listening, thinking, and speaking as well as academic difficulties in reading, writing, spelling, or math. It is important for teachers to understand that when students have difficulty learning specific academic concepts, it may be that they are having difficulty processing the language.

Individuals with learning disabilities may have difficulty with **receptive language processing** and/or **expressive language processing.** Receptive language is a person's ability to understand what is being communicated. Students who have difficulty with receptive language might experience problems with following directions, understanding specific concepts and their interrelationship, understanding figurative language or multiple meanings, understanding complex sentences, and following a sequential arrangement of ideas. Expressive language refers to one's ability to produce or convey a message. Difficulties with expressive language will be apparent when an individual has difficulty finding the right words or names for things, using correct grammar or sentence structure, conveying a complete message, or adapting his or her communication style to fit social situations.

Academic Difficulties

We have examined cognitive and language factors that affect the learning process. Academic difficulties are the most likely outcome of such learning difficulties. By definition, individuals with learning disabilities have difficulties in one or more academic areas, usually indicated by a discrepancy between academic performance and intellectual ability, or potential. If these students are not performing academically below what would be expected for their age or grade, they are not eligible for special services. Identification procedures almost always involve an evaluation of academic performance to determine eligibility for services. Individuals with learning disabilities may differ from each other in academic performance in the *specific area(s)* of academic skills affected and in the *severity* of the disability.

SPECIFIC AREAS OF DIFFICULTIES

Reading Difficulties

Approximately 80% of school-age individuals with learning disabilities have difficulty with reading (Lyon, 1985; Norman & Zigmond, 1980). Given that learning disabilities by definition is a language-based disorder, it stands to reason that many individuals with learning disabilities would have difficulty with reading—a skill highly dependent on language ability. After second grade, much of school learning involves reading skill. Thus, if a youngster has difficulty with reading, other academic areas are likely to be affected. Difficulty learning to read is often the first sign that a youngster has a learning disability. This explains why most individuals with learning disabilities are not identified until they reach school age.

Word Identification Skills.   The ability to decode words is a skill central to all others in the reading process. Ease of word identification is a prerequisite to reading comprehension (Vellutino, Scanlon, & Tanzman, 1994). Overwhelming evidence indicates that children identified as having learning disabilities who have word identification problems are likely to have difficulty with **phonological processing** (Vellutino, 1991; Wagner & Torgeson, 1987), a term used to represent a cluster of skills related to interpreting the sounds within words. *Phonemic awareness,* or the knowledge that component sounds make up words, is a fundamental

INNOVATIVE IDEAS

WRITING "POWER"

Middle school and high school pose significant challenges for students with learning disabilities. As the curriculum focus shifts from skill development to building content knowledge, the demand for writing increases. Many students with learning disabilities have extreme difficulty with the mechanics of writing—spelling, grammar, and sentence and paragraph structure—as well as the formulation and organization of ideas. Furthermore, many students at this age have developed a strong reluctance to write. Recently, secondary special education teachers have coupled strategy instruction with technology to provide the support that these students need to be successful.

Strategy instruction in writing helps students break down the task of producing written language into smaller, achievable steps. Using acronyms and easily memorized steps, students learn the process of writing and how to apply it to their written assignments in content area classes. Englert* developed the POWER strategy for expository writing to assist students with learning disabilities through the writing process. Students use "think-sheets" for the preparatory steps of writing. The first step is *Planning*. Students use a Planning Think-Sheet to write down their ideas and the relevant information they need to convey. Next they *Organize* their ideas in a visual format similar to webbing or mapping, using an Organizing Think-Sheet. They focus on the relationships between ideas and think through the best way to present them. They produce some type of visual representation of their ideas to put them into a meaningful framework. Several weeks might be spent learning the different types of relationships (cause and effect, hierar-

chical, etc.) *Writing* is the next step—getting a rough draft on paper. Students then *Edit* their work, looking for spelling, structural, and grammatical errors. *Revising* is the last step of the process to prepare the final draft of the paper.

Secondary teachers have recently been using computers to assist students with learning disabilities through this difficult process. Using standard word processing programs, many students with learning disabilities are able to develop keyboarding skills to compensate for poor handwriting. The capability to edit on-screen and to use a spell-checker, thesaurus, and a dictionary enhances students' writing abilities. For some students, being able to read their own writing on-screen is easier than reading back their own handwriting. Several adaptations have been developed with students with learning disabilities in mind. Some teachers have found speech synthesis software that enables the computer to read back what is written to assist students with learning disabilities. Other software programs suggest words and corrections that may be appropriate, thus providing ongoing assistance and allowing the student to make decisions while writing.

Using strategies and technology together, secondary students with learning disabilities are receiving needed assistance and support. Teachers are finding students with learning disabilities to be more productive and to have more positive attitudes toward writing.

*Englert, C. S. (1990). Unraveling the mysteries of writing through strategy instruction. In T. E. Scruggs & B. Y. L. Wong (Eds.), *Intervention research in learning disabilities* (pp. 186–223). New York: Springer-Verlag.

component of phonological processing. *Phonological coding* involves mapping specific letters or combinations of letters to specific sounds. *Phonemic segmentation* is the ability to break words apart into component sounds; *blending* is the ability to put the component sounds of words together to make words.

As children learn to read, whether in a phonics-based program or a whole language or meaning-based program, these phonological skills develop to the point of becoming automatic, thus allowing the reader to focus attention on the meaning of the words and sentences. For many students with learning disabilities, these skills do not develop easily and reading becomes a very laborious task. Because so much attention is allocated to decoding the words, the process breaks down before meaning is attached. Students with severe reading disabilities usually benefit from intensive training in phonological skills. Some may also benefit from a sight word program that deemphasizes phonics and emphasizes visual memory of whole words. Though early intervention for children with phonological difficulties has been shown to be effective, youngsters with learning disabilities are often not identified until after second grade, thus precluding the possibility of early intervention.

Reading Comprehension and Vocabulary Development. Reading is a process of attaching meaning to written symbols with the ultimate goal being comprehension. For many students with learning disabilities, having difficulty with vocabulary meaning or reading comprehension can be attributed to a lack of automaticity with decoding. Still, many youngsters with learning disabilities in reading also have vocabulary and comprehension difficulties. And, though it is less likely, a few may be good decoders but have difficulty attaching meaning to what they read. Remember that a learning disability is defined as a language-based disorder—thus students with this disorder may have difficulty with word naming in general or with language comprehension in general, not just while reading (Mann, 1994).

Writing Difficulties

Writing and reading are interconnected skills. The difference, of course, is that the reading process involves taking in information, or reception, while writing is an expressive skill, or sending information out. Many individuals with learning disabilities have difficulty with both reading and writing. Both processes involve phonological knowledge, language use, and mechanical skills. Some students with learning disabilities have more difficulty with writing than with reading, probably because writing is an act of production involving the formation of ideas. Even students who have facility with oral language sometimes have difficulty with writing. Many are fearful of making mistakes or of putting forth their ideas. Many have serious difficulties with the component skills. As we examine the components of the writing process, think about how difficulty with writing is the same as or different from the reading difficulties described on the foregoing pages.

Written Expression. The writing process includes planning, organization, composing, editing, and revising. Individuals with learning disabilities often have difficulties with these component skills (Newcomer & Barenbaum, 1991). These difficulties often persist into adulthood (Adelman & Vogel, 1991). Metacognitive abilities—the self-monitoring, self-regulation, and self-evaluation of one's own writing—are inherent in good writers. Students with learning disabilities, whose metacognitive skills are often less well developed than other students, often produce writing that lacks organization and structure. They are less likely to engage in prewriting activities such as planning and idea generation (Wong, Wong, & Blenkisop, 1989). Their writing reflects a lack of knowledge of text structure and a lack of sensitivity to the audience, or being able to consider the perspective of the audience while writing (Englert, 1994).

Extensive practice is essential to the development of writing ability. When students experience serious difficulty with writing, they often refrain from participating, thus limiting their opportunities to practice. Recent research has led to the development of effective writing instruction for students with learning disabilities, drawing on the use of metacognitive strategies. With consistent use of planning, composing, editing, and revision strategies, students with learning disabilities have been able to improve their writing (Englert, 1994; Graham & Harris, 1992).

Mechanics of Writing.   In order to produce written compositions, students must have a cadre of mechanical skills such as spelling, handwriting, sentence structure, and knowledge of grammar rules. Individuals with learning disabilities often have difficulties with these component skills and their self-regulation strategies focus on spelling, punctuation, and other mechanics rather than the higher order processes of planning and idea generation (Wong et al., 1989). In the past, special education programs would teach the mechanics as prerequisite skills to writing compositions and students with learning disabilities would not get beyond the skill instruction to actually engage in composition. Today, you are more likely to find writing process instruction and time for composing occurring in both general and special education classrooms. However, students with learning disabilities are likely to need extensive instruction and practice to develop mechanical skills.

Grammar and Sentence Structure.   There are many rules of writing in the English language that govern how and when to use punctuation, capital letters, and syntax. These rules often pose problems for students with learning disabilities who may already be struggling to find the right words for expression, the right spelling, or an organizational structure for a composition. Good readers who are sensitive to these rules in written text are more likely to understand and use these conventions in their own writing. It is not surprising that students with learning disabilities often have difficulty with grammatical and syntactical rules in written language.

Spelling.   Another area of difficulty for many individuals with learning disabilities is spelling. As you can probably guess, spelling ability is highly related to the phonological knowledge discussed earlier. Individuals with poor phonological processing skills are likely to have difficulty with spelling.

Handwriting.   Handwriting is another skill that is problematic for many individuals with learning disabilities. Poor handwriting could be the result of lack of knowledge of the formation of letters, resulting in mistakes such as writing an *n* for an *m* or perhaps writing a *k* with a part missing. Sometimes students have difficulty remembering the orientation or direction of specific letters, resulting in backward or rotated letters or confusion of similar letter pairs such as *b* and *d*, *p* and *q*, or *n* and *u*. People have often defined dyslexia as "reading backwards" or writing in reverse, saying that such children "see things backward." This is probably not the case. Repeated reversals are more likely to be attributed to confusion as a result of memory, directional, or attention problems. Poor handwriting could be the result of poor fine motor skills, leading to wavy or too-dark lines, not staying on the line, or other problems.

Math Difficulties

Many individuals with learning disabilities have difficulty with mathematics. Math difficulties may occur separately from or along with difficulties in reading, writing, and spoken language (Fleischner, 1994). Achievement difficulties in math are related to several factors. Foremost is inadequate teaching, curriculum, and materials (Carnine, 1991; Russell & Ginsburg, 1984), a problem seen as widespread in

is particularly alarming since low peer acceptance is thought to be a predictor of later life problems such as poor adult adjustment, lack of school success, and employment difficulties (Parker & Asher, 1987).

Individuals with learning disabilities also often have poorer social skills than their peers without disabilities (Hazel & Schumaker, 1988). In the classroom, students with learning disabilities may interact frequently with the teacher, but these interactions are more often intended to correct academic or social behavior than for students without disabilities. In addition, as compared to students without disabilities, students with learning disabilities tend to talk more, provide less elaborate information in conversations, use gestures and expressions less, and are less sensitive to the cues of the listener (Bos & Vaughn, 1994).

When you talk to classroom teachers about students with learning disabilities in their classes, they are often concerned about behavior problems. They feel positive about having students with learning disabilities as long as they don't have serious behavior problems (Schumm & Vaughn, 1992). Some evidence indicates a higher rate of behavior problems for youngsters with learning disabilities as compared to students without disabilities. They are more likely than children without disabilities to be off-task, inattentive, and act out or may exhibit internalizing or withdrawn behavior (Bender & Smith, 1990; Haager & Vaughn, 1995; McKinney, 1989; McKinney & Feagans, 1984; Vaughn & Haager, 1994b; Vaughn, Zaragoza, Hogan, & Walker, 1993).

It is also important to note that there is a significant overlap of learning disabilities and attention deficit disorders. Estimates of the percentage of youngsters with learning disabilities who also have attention deficit hyperactivity disorder range from 30% to 40% (Shaywitz & Shaywitz, 1988). The question of why children with learning disabilities often also have behavior problems is somewhat like the "chicken or egg" question. Do they have learning problems in addition to, or because of, such behavioral difficulties, or do their behavioral difficulties indicate frustration and anxiety stemming from learning problems? Perhaps both are true, or neither, given the heterogeneity of the population.

Individuals with learning disabilities may experience lower self-concept and self-perceptions of competence than their peers without disabilities (Bender & Wall, 1994; Chapman, 1988). It is interesting to note that self-concept or self-esteem is a domain-specific construct. In other words, a person may feel good about himself or herself with regard to areas of strengths and feel poorly about himself or herself only in areas of difficulty. Thus, many students with learning disabilities demonstrate lower self-perceptions in the academic domain, particularly with regard to reading ability, but do not necessarily demonstrate lower self-concepts with regard to other areas (Chapman, 1988; Vaughn & Haager, 1994a).

We know a great deal less about the affective characteristics of individuals with learning disabilities because this is a fairly new area of research. Some evidence suggests a higher rate of depression and suicide for individuals with learning disabilities (Bender & Wall, 1994) as well as a tendency toward loneliness and anxiety (Margalit & Zak, 1984). This is an area in which further research is needed.

PREVALENCE OF LEARNING DISABILITIES

Students with learning disabilities make up the largest group of people served in special education programs. Soon after P.L. 94-142 defined this disability in 1975 and included it in federal guidelines for providing services, approximately 800,000 students were identified. In 20 years, this number has grown to more than 2 million students (U.S. Department of Education, 1991). The number of students identified and placed into school services has grown every year since 1977 when the federal law was implemented. While the number of students identified as having learning disabilities increased 119% from 1977 to 1985, the number of students identified as having need of special services in general rose only 16%. It is likely that the category of learning disabilities began to "pick up" some of the students who might otherwise have been classified into some other category. The number also has steadily increased because other students were identified who would have remained unserved as low achievers if P.L. 94-142 had not mandated service.

It is difficult to determine the exact proportion of the student population classified as having learning disabilities due to the differences in specific identification criteria and procedures from state to state. Generally, the population of students with learning disabilities ranges from 4% to 5% of the school population from year to year. As recent federal laws have extended special education services to the preschool population and up to the age of 22 years, we may see a continued increase in the number of students identified as having learning disabilities at earlier and later ages, thus increasing this population even further.

CAUSES OF LEARNING DISABILITIES

Little is known about the causes of learning disabilities. Years ago, as the field of learning disabilities emerged, there was much speculation about causality. Because the learning difficulties were similar to those of children who had suffered brain trauma, it was thought that these students may have some unknown brain injury or malfunction. Others thought that perhaps the language and learning difficulties experienced by individuals with learning disabilities resulted from neurological problems. Still others speculated that emotional stress might be involved, or that it was really a "teaching disability," meaning that teachers had somehow failed to provide appropriate educational experiences. However, as the field evolved and there was little evidence to support any of these conjectures, the focus turned away from causality to the more pragmatic functions of conducting adequate assessment for identification purposes and providing needed services. As we develop more sophisticated technology for studying the brain function and learn more about genetics, we may gain a better understanding of potential causes of learning disabilities. Until then, it is important to focus on what we can do to better identify and serve individuals with learning disabilities.

ASSESSMENT OF LEARNING DISABILITIES

There is a general lack of consensus regarding what constitutes best practice in the assessment of learning disabilities. Indeed, the field of assessment in general education is rapidly changing as we adopt new ways of measuring growth and change and new ways of authentically representing the curriculum in our assessment materials and procedures. These changes have begun to influence how we identify and assess individuals with learning disabilities. Besides the usual reliability and validity issues of assessment, the main issue in the assessment of learning disabilities relates to the controversy over the definition: deciding *what* to assess. If we don't know how to define it, how do we know how to measure it?

Until the definition is further refined, we can think of assessment of learning disabilities in terms of the purpose of the assessment. Let us examine three purposes of assessment related to serving students with learning disabilities: identification, individual program monitoring, and classroom instruction.

Assessment for Identification

As you can probably guess from the discussion of variability in definition from state to state, there is no single method for identifying students who have suspected learning disabilities. We will discuss principles and guidelines that are generally thought to be "best practice." It is important for teachers to know that they will have to consult their own state and district guidelines for detailed information regarding practices in their own schools.

We learned earlier in this chapter that the main identifying characteristic of individuals with learning disabilities is academic performance below what you would expect for the student's ability and below what you would expect for the student's age and grade level. Remember that, according to the federal definition, the discrepancy only has to occur in one academic area but could occur in more than one. In most states, this is determined by looking at the discrepancy between *expected ability* and *actual achievement*. Some states provide a formula or set of procedures for determining a discrepancy. Others leave it to the local education agencies to put forth a set of procedures to be approved by the state agency. There are three commonly used methods for determining a severe discrepancy between expectancy and ability (Frankenberger & Fronzaglio, 1991):

1. *Discrepancy between scores on an intelligence measure and a standardized academic test of one to two standard deviations.* Scores of both tests are converted to standard scores with the same scale (e.g., mean of 100 and a standard deviation of 15) and then subtracted to determine the amount of discrepancy (how many standard deviations) in each academic area. Generally, a discrepancy of 1.5 or 2 standard deviations is considered a severe discrepancy.

2. *Discrepancy between actual academic scores and expected level for age or grade level* (e.g., performing 2 years below grade level in any one academic area). This method may also take into account intellectual performance by setting a separate criterion that intellectual ability must be within a normal range (i.e., not within range of mental retardation).

3. *Formula-based criteria.* Some states have developed discrepancy-based formulas that include such factors as age or grade level in determining the discrepancy between intellectual ability and academic achievement. Some formulas may also provide a method of correcting for a statistical phenomenon called *regression to the mean* that corrects for extreme scores on either measure.

It is stated in P.L. 94-142 that no single procedure shall be used as the sole criterion for identifying learning disabilities and that the student must be tested in all areas related to the disability. It is standard practice for a battery of tests to be used for identification. At the least, the test battery would include measures of academic achievement in the specific areas listed in the definition: reading, writing, spelling, and mathematical calculations. The definition also lists speaking, listening, and thinking as possible areas of difficulty. These areas might be tested with norm-referenced tests, or criterion-referenced tests. Processing tests are often used to measure the "basic psychological processes" involved. An intelligence test or other test of cognitive ability may also be used. Ecological assessment that includes a contextual description of the student's functioning reveals not only how the student functions within a context but also what contextual factors might be manipulated to maximize the student's success.

What is often left out of an assessment battery is the assessment of contextual variables that may influence student performance and behavior, or an **ecological assessment.** Evans, Gable, and Evans (1993) argue for assessment that is multidimensional and "reflects the significance and complexity of person–environment transactions." Assessment of ecological characteristics and events provides information about the nature of problem situations and assists the development of specialized education programs. Such assessment might include observation tools or anecdotal records, curriculum-based tests, and interviews to provide information about the specific academic demands placed on the student; it should also cover characteristics of the classroom structure such as grouping practices, classroom rules, and teaching approaches. It is also possible to gather information about social factors such as the students' social network, peer acceptance, and the nature of typical peer interactions.

Role of the Teacher and Family in Assessment for Identification. According to federal law, the IEP team serves as decision makers to determine eligibility and to outline an appropriate plan for providing services. Too often, teachers and parents report that their voices are not heard in team meetings where the test scores and numbers are presented and eligibility decisions seem to be routine procedure. All too often, educators whose business it is to test and attend meetings forget that they are making decisions that will affect individual children, their families, and classrooms. Though academic difficulties characterize students with learning disabilities, it is important that the IEP team consider all factors relevant to classroom functioning including social, cognitive, behavioral, and affective considerations. Parents and siblings provide valuable information on such matters as the child's intellectual and processing abilities, adaptive functioning, social-emotional state, language skills, and areas of strength and need. Teachers also provide valuable information regarding the child's day-to-day classroom functioning as well as a perspective on the feasibility of educational planning. Recent efforts have focused on collaborative teaming to more adequately identify and serve individuals with special needs (Givner & Haager, 1995).

Assessment for Monitoring the IEP

Once a student's eligibility has been determined and an appropriate individualized program has been drawn up, it is important to have a manageable and effective plan for monitoring the individual's progress with the objectives outlined in the IEP. The special educator and other designated support personnel usually take primary responsibility for monitoring progress with the IEP objectives. However, with increased inclusion of individuals with learning disabilities in the general education classroom, the IEP may specify certain educational responsibilities for the classroom teacher.

Parents and students (as appropriate) should also participate in the IEP meeting with school personnel.

Performance-based assessment should be designed to assess progress with specific objectives. For example, one of Theresa's IEP goals states that she is to participate in group activities in social studies in the general education classroom. Her teacher uses a great deal of cooperative grouping in social studies. Specifically, the IEP states that Theresa is to (1) complete her homework assignments with 80% accuracy; (2) volunteer to answer questions at least two times a day; (3) pass each chapter test with at least 80% accuracy; and (4) read each chapter with an assigned peer tutor. The classroom teacher, the parents, and the special education teacher collaboratively worked out a progress monitoring plan for each objective. Their main goal was to make a plan that was feasible given the teacher's responsibility to 34 other students. For the first objective, a homework chart was devised that Theresa and her parents were to complete and turn in weekly. For the second objective, the classroom teacher was to keep a chart taped to Theresa's desk. When Theresa raised her hand to answer a question, the teacher would make a tally mark. A student assistant was assigned to help with this in case the teacher forgot. The chapter tests were to be read aloud to Theresa by a parent volunteer. The special educator was to put a form in the teacher's box every 2 weeks requesting the grades. If Theresa's grades went below 80%, the special educator provided extra assistance. The chapter reading with a peer tutor was tracked using a simple chart filled out by Theresa and the peer tutor. Since they completed the end-of-chapter questions together, the teacher kept the papers they turned in as a record for this objective.

There are numerous other methods of implementing performance-based assessment to monitor students' progress with IEP objectives. Charts and graphs of

A homework chart can help a student keep track of his assignments and progress.

student progress with specific skills and student portfolios are examples of performance-based assessment. The main purpose is to provide evidence of progress specific to the IEP objectives.

Assessment for Instruction

Assessment serves a different purpose in ongoing instructional decision making. Teachers need to know how individual students are doing with regard to the curriculum and specific classroom instruction. Students with learning disabilities included in general education classes can be included in whatever curriculum-based assessment is implemented. Evaluation of daily work, quizzes, class performance, projects, unit and chapter tests, competency checklists, and writing samples are all examples of ongoing, curriculum-based assessment. For the purpose of evaluating and designing instruction in the general education classroom, authentic assessment, or assessment that involves real-world tasks, is most informative.

SERVICE DELIVERY OPTIONS FOR STUDENTS WITH LEARNING DISABILITIES

Students with learning disabilities are served across the spectrum of service delivery from the most restrictive to least restrictive settings. The majority are served by a resource teacher, spending at least part of their school day in a general education classroom. Numerous private clinical schools throughout the United States specialize in learning disabilities. They usually provide intensive remedial services and small classes. This represents the most restrictive educational setting and is not the typical placement for students with learning disabilities. Schools may offer self-contained classes for students with learning disabilities where a special education teacher and support personnel provide 100% of the educational services. However, the majority of students with learning disabilities spend at least part of their day in general education classes. The recent inclusion movement in schools has led to the development of alternative service delivery options. Increasingly, students with learning disabilities are placed in the general education classroom either with or without the support of a special education teacher. Though considerable debate has ensued as to whether segregation or inclusion is the best option for students with learning disabilities, the most important issue is not *where* the services are provided. Rather, it is whether the placement is meeting the individual student's needs.

Traditional Service Delivery Models

For years we thought of special education as taking place outside the general education classroom. Students with learning disabilities have traditionally been "pulled out" of the general education setting to receive special education services. Sometimes, this means being sent to a different school if the services are not available at the home school.

Students with learning disabilities are often placed in a special education setting based on severity of need. Students whose learning disabilities are considered severe or those who have accompanying difficulties such as serious attention or behavior problems may be served in a *self-contained special education classroom.* In this setting, the special education teacher and support personnel such as paraprofessionals, speech-language pathologist, and others would be solely responsible for the student's educational needs. When the IEP team decides the student will benefit from placement in the general education classroom, the student may be assigned to a *resource program* on a part-time basis, spending a portion of the day in the general education classroom and a portion in the special education setting.

Self-contained and resource programs might be organized as categorical, cross-categorical, or noncategorical programs. In a categorical model, only students with learning disabilities would be served in one classroom while students with mental retardation would be served in another, students with emotional and behavior problems in another, and so on. In a cross-categorical model, students with different disability classifications may be served together. It is not uncommon for students with learning disabilities to be placed with other students with "mild" disabilities including behavior disorders or mild mental retardation. In a noncategorical approach, students would be placed without regard to disability label but would be placed according to academic and behavioral needs. Noncategorical programs are uncommon in the United States because federal law mandates classifying students for funding purposes. Other countries, such as New Zealand, do not classify students according to disability labels but provide support services for any student who has an educational need.

The majority of students with learning disabilities spend at least part of their school day in the general education classroom and receive services from a resource teacher. One advantage of the resource program is *social:* Students with learning disabilities can receive remedial support while maintaining contact with their same-age peers. Another advantage is *cost-effectiveness:* The resource teacher can serve more students than can a teacher of a self-contained special class. In addition, resource teachers often serve nonreferred students indirectly through consultation with general education teachers. Resource teachers often serve as sources of information to teachers, parents, and other personnel. Some question the efficacy of resource programs and argue that students with learning disabilities need more

Sometimes there is less stigma, and more opportunity for social contact, when a peer tutors a student with a learning disability.

intensive remediation. Others argue that students with learning disabilities served in the resource program are not qualitatively different from low-achieving students with no identified disabilities and that, since the general education classroom serves low achievers, they should also serve students with learning disabilities. Resource programs generally are as effective as self-contained special classes and students served in resource programs tend to do better than students who remain in the general education classroom with no support services at all (Wiederholt, Hammill, & Brown, 1993).

It is important to remember that the decision as to the appropriate placement for students with learning disabilities should be made on a case-by-case basis. The severity of disability may be one factor to consider in choosing between self-contained and resource placement. Behavioral difficulties may also warrant a more restrictive setting for some students. No placement should be considered permanent. The law intended for periodic review and adjustment of educational programs and this disability is no exception to that rule.

Inclusive Service Delivery Models

Arguments against pull-out resource programs and in favor of providing services in the general education setting (e.g., Lipsky & Gartner, 1989; National Association of State Boards of Education, 1992; Reynolds, 1989) have led to an increase in the adoption of inclusive service delivery models for students with disabilities. Though some have envisioned inclusion that would abolish the need for special education services, an inclusive education model that maintains services within the general education context is considered to be the best inclusion model for meeting students' individual needs (Council for Exceptional Children 1993; National Association of State Boards of Education, 1992). This requires new roles for general and special education teachers who must develop collaborative partnerships to make inclusion work.

Some are concerned about what inclusion means for students with learning disabilities and fear it means denial of appropriate services (Division for Learning Disabilities, 1993; Learning Disabilities Association, 1993). Remember that this is a relatively "hidden" disorder and may not be as well understood by peers without disabilities as other, more visible disabilities. What we do know about students with learning disabilities in the general education classroom highlights the reasons for these concerns. Students with learning disabilities generally do not succeed academically in this setting without support (Fuchs, Fuchs, & Fernstrom, 1993). And support is not the norm: Academic instruction in general education classrooms that includes students with learning disabilities is generally undifferentiated, large group instruction (Baker & Zigmond, 1990) and teachers make few if any adaptations for individual needs (McIntosh et al., 1993; Schumm et al., 1995). Thus, if inclusive education is to work for students with learning disabilities, collaborative partnerships between general and special educators need to be formed to reinvent methods for providing support.

What do we know about inclusive education for students with learning disabilities? Vaughn and Schumm (in press) cite several components of responsible inclusion for students with learning disabilities. Based on extensive work with classroom teachers, they developed some guidelines for developing an inclusive education program for students with learning disabilities, as follows:

1. The student's academic and social needs are more important than the place where services are delivered. Ongoing assessment and monitoring must provide evidence that inclusion is beneficial.

2. Teachers should participate voluntarily in inclusive education rather than participating as a result of an administrative mandate.

3. Adequate resources must be considered and provided to develop and maintain inclusive classrooms.

4. The model for inclusive education should be developed at the school level rather than handed down from district or state guidelines—that is, the development, implementation, and evaluation should be a school-based effort.

5. A continuum of services should be maintained. The general education classroom should not be expected to meet the needs of all students with learning disabilities. Therefore, other placement options should be available.

6. The inclusive model should be evaluated and refined on an ongoing basis.

7. Ongoing professional development should be provided to continuously prepare teachers for their role in inclusive education.

8. Teachers and school personnel should develop their own philosophy of inclusion.

9. Curriculum and instruction should be developed that meet the needs of all students.

Many new teachers ask, "What does inclusion look like? What do teachers actually do?" The role of teachers may take several forms. General education teachers will find themselves more intimately involved with assessment and instruction of students with learning disabilities. They will likely be involved with ongoing monitoring and evaluation of program effectiveness. Special educators are likely to wear different hats at different times. They may be consultants, providing information and assistance to teachers, parents, and others. They may provide direct instruction, going into the general education classroom to provide one-to-one or small group instruction with the identified students and even with others who need similar assistance. One advantage of an inclusive program is that the special education resources may benefit other students who also need support. General and special education teachers may co-plan and co-teach, sharing the roles of teacher/facilitator and provider of individual/group support.

INSTRUCTIONAL CONSIDERATIONS FOR STUDENTS WITH LEARNING DISABILITIES

Following are specific components of effective instruction for students with learning disabilities at different ages. Because there are vast differences between elementary and secondary schools, these are discussed separately. The instructional considerations presented here are described as they might occur in either special education or general education classrooms.

Early Identification and Intervention

Children with learning disabilities are usually not identified until they reach the school years. Because this disorder is defined by academic difficulty, it is usually not identified until a child has had an opportunity to learn but demonstrates difficulty. (This is particularly true when the student is learning English as a second language. It is important to determine if the learning difficulties in this case are caused by true learning disabilities or stem from difficulties functioning in English.) Reading difficulties are often the first clue that teachers report. Teachers and parents are reluctant to label a child early in life because of the dangers of the "self-fulfilling prophecy" (Rosenthal & Jacobson, 1968): that labeling a child early in life will set the expectation that the child will have learning difficulties, and thus, he or she is likely to live up to that expectation. For that reason, children are not likely to be labeled as having learning disabilities in the first 2 or 3 years of school. Parents and teachers often report learning difficulties for children with learning disabilities as early as preschool or kindergarten. Even then, the school and parents often want to see if maturity or some type of informal intervention will work before referring the child for an assessment.

The problem with waiting until third grade or so to conduct a formal assessment and consider placement is that early intervention is the most effective approach to correcting reading disabilities. Whether a child in the primary grades is formally identified or not, the important consideration is to provide the earliest and most intensive assistance possible. Most schools have some type of prereferral intervention team or student assistance team made up of teachers and other school personnel (sometimes parents, too). These teams are very helpful in developing interventions and monitoring student progress in the early years.

Intensive, direct instruction is usually the best approach to early intervention. Because the majority of students with learning disabilities have reading difficulties related to phonological processing, early intervention and prevention programs should include phonological training. Intensive instruction in letter names and sounds, auditory discrimination of sounds, sound blending, phonemic segmentation, and rhyming are all elements of early phonological instruction. Early education programs rich in spoken and written language might also benefit children with possible learning disabilities.

Considerations for the Elementary Grades

Elementary classrooms (both special and general education) tend to offer more flexibility in scheduling and curriculum than those of middle and high schools, making the design and implementation of specialized educational programs a bit easier. As students move through the elementary grades, the curriculum demands increase. Difficulty in reading and writing affect all other areas of academic work. It is important for general and special education teachers in the elementary grades to work together to identify children and to develop classroom modifications that are appropriate for the individual student and are feasible for the teacher to implement. These modifications generally include adaptations in the following areas:

1. Classroom structure

2. Time management

3. Grouping structures

4. Student engagement

5. Direct instruction

6. Interactive teaching

Classroom structure is one element that seems to make a difference in the success of students with learning disabilities. The overall design of classroom rules, the flow of events, amount of time allocated to tasks, and the seating arrangement are all elements of the classroom structure. Because learning disabilities comprise a heterogeneous group of disorders, there is no "formula" for designing the perfect classroom. Those classroom characteristics that constitute "best practice" for all students are likely to benefit students with learning disabilities, too, in both traditional and inclusive educational settings. For example, consistency in enforcing classroom rules, but not to the point of rigidity, is generally a good rule of thumb for maintaining an orderly classroom. Maintaining a regular routine (e.g., math is at 10:00 every day) helps students to know what to expect and to perform at their best. Sometimes, making modifications in the classroom structure for individual students is necessary whether or not they have learning disabilities. Some students perform best when they are seated closer to the teacher and they are close to the area of instruction. The teacher is able to give them frequent reminders to stay on-task and to monitor their classwork. For other students, this may prove to be distracting. The teacher's area tends to be one of high traffic and activity.

Efficient *time management* is also an important factor for the success of all students, including those with learning disabilities. Good teachers are scheduling artists. They plan appropriate amounts of time for instruction—enough to accomplish learning objectives, not too much as to produce restlessness. It is important to plan for variation in the time allocated to different types of activities. One pencil-and-paper task after another produces boredom and restlessness for many students with learning disabilities. Teachers may need to make individual modifications for students with learning disabilities related to time management. For example, if one hour of math seems to be too much for an individual student, the teacher may allow the student to take breaks or may design some alternative tasks for the student to do during the last 15 to 30 minutes, such as watering the plants or working on the computer.

Use of *grouping structures* is another element that may facilitate learning for students with learning disabilities. Increasingly, general education teachers are using cooperative grouping to assist students with learning disabilities. Students with reading and writing difficulties may flounder when given individual responsibility for learning tasks. When this responsibility can be shared within a group or pair, the student may be more able to focus on the concepts and ideas being taught. Flexible grouping practices may also allow a teacher to spend some intensive instructional time with an individual or small group of students while other groups are carrying on independently. In the special education classroom, pairing and grouping students allows for student interaction and allows the teacher to provide intensive instruction to groups of students with similar learning needs.

Student engagement is critical for learning. Students with learning disabilities are more likely to be off-task during a lesson than are students without disabilities (Bender & Smith, 1990; McKinney & Feagans, 1984). Students with learning disabilities may also have an inactive or passive learning style (Torgeson, 1987). Teachers do many things to maintain student engagement—they use humor, novelty, pacing, cues, student interest, and many other techniques. However, teachers find the passivity of many students with learning disabilities to be challenging and even frustrating (Schumm et al., 1995). For students who are behind in their learning, engagement is critical to maximizing learning. Englert and Thomas (1982) suggest a simple tally method for measuring the rate of engagement for an entire class during selected time intervals (e.g., writing down the number of students engaged between time A and time B) and then using self-observation to identify teacher behaviors that facilitate engagement (e.g., "Was I giving information, directions, asking questions, or listening to students?" or "Was it a whole class activity, or groups?").

Direct instruction is often effective for students with learning disabilities (Carnine, Silbert, & Kameenui, 1990). Though this is often the thrust of instruction in the special education classroom, direct instruction techniques can also be implemented in the general education classroom. In direct instruction, the teacher specifies the objective or purpose of the learning task, models or describes the problem or task, uses task analysis to identify the critical steps for task completion, provides guidance and feedback while the student performs the task, and teaches to mastery (Bender, 1995).

Interactive teaching is a more constructivist approach than direct instruction and involves teacher–student dialogue during learning (Bos & Anders, 1990). It is based on the assumption that learning is a constructive process in which learners use cognitive strategies to combine what they are learning with what they already know. Learning is enhanced when teachers and students discuss concepts as well as appropriate learning strategies. The teacher, in effect, serves as the mediator of learning, scaffolding instruction and acting as a sounding board as students construct meaning. The advantages of interactive teaching include increased language use and development for students with learning disabilities (who may have inherent language difficulties), opportunities for teachers to know immediately if students understand or not, opportunities for the student to obtain immediate feedback

EASY IDEAS FOR PRACTITIONERS

For the Teachers:

1. Help students with learning disabilities connect new information with previously learned concepts. Make the connections explicit using verbal directions or graphic aids to illustrate.
2. Help students with learning disabilities organize ideas and concepts using semantic maps, flowcharts, outlines, study guides, and other visual representations of knowledge.
3. Strategically seat students with learning disabilities to minimize distractions, provide peer assistance, and provide proximity to the teacher.
4. Use learning strategies such as mnemonic devices, paired association, and verbal rehearsal to provide assistance with memorization of factual material in class.
5. Provide opportunities for students with learning disabilities to demonstrate their understanding in ways that utilize their strengths; for example, allow an oral report or a poster drawing instead of a written book report.

For Parents:

1. Break tasks down into shorter steps. For example, instead of saying "clean your room," explain the steps to be included in the task: Specify picking up all the dirty clothes as the first step; followed by putting away all books, toys, and papers; then emptying the trash; dusting; making the bed; and sweeping.
2. Help your child develop strategies for organizing homework—establishing a time and place to do homework, a system for writing down assignments, the means for obtaining assistance, and a plan for prioritizing assignments and tasks.
3. Provide extra practice and assistance with memorization tasks such as spelling words, math facts, and maps. For example, practice the multiplication tables while driving in the car, spend 15 minutes before going to bed studying maps, or recite the spelling words at breakfast.
4. Provide opportunities for your child to discover and demonstrate areas of strength at home. For example, a youngster who has a good sense of visual organization might make a good family photographer or may be particularly helpful organizing cupboards or bookshelves at home.
5. Provide honest and genuine feedback to your child. Point out errors and shortcomings in an honest, respectful, and straightforward manner and give praise when your child is correct.

regarding learning, opportunities to integrate strategy instruction with conceptual learning, opportunities to build on students' prior knowledge, and opportunities to help them organize knowledge. Interactive teaching strategies include the following (Bos & Anders, 1990, p. 174):

• Activating prior knowledge
• Utilizing cooperative knowledge sharing
• Tying new knowledge to old knowledge
• Predicting and justifying meanings and relationships among concepts
• Confirming and integrating understanding
• Learning concepts in relation to content contexts

The confusion of changing classes in crowded hallways can pose problems for students with learning disabilities.

These ideas could be used in either special education or general education settings and would be appropriate for both elementary and secondary education.

Considerations for Secondary School

The secondary setting (middle and high school) is quite different from the elementary setting for students with learning disabilities (McIntosh et al., 1993; Schumm et al., 1995). Changing classes and teachers from period to period, students must learn the structure and expectations of several different environments. Special and general education teachers are less likely to communicate and collaborate. General education teachers are less likely to make adaptations and modifications for individual students. In fact, many secondary teachers express a strong belief that the general education classroom should get students ready for the "real world" and, therefore, it is wrong to make special accommodations for individuals (Schumm et al., 1995).

Secondary programs for students with learning disabilities include two major components: academic instruction and transition to adulthood.

Academic Instruction. When students go to middle school, they are suddenly confronted with a large school, many students, many teachers, and a new routine to figure out. For any student, this transition can be difficult. For students with learning difficulties, it can be overwhelming. It is important for secondary teachers to be aware of how easy it is for a student having learning problems to get lost in the shuffle of activity in middle school and high school. Academically, the focus is on subject area learning. The demand for reading and study skills increases dramatically. The instructional approaches described for the elementary grades are also appropriate for the secondary setting. Others, specific to secondary instruction, are also effective—including strategy instruction, teaching a parallel curriculum, or life skills.

Strategy instruction is very important for the success of secondary students with learning disabilities. The idea of teaching learning strategies draws on the research in metacognition. A **learning strategy** is a structured approach to a learning task. Learning strategy models have been developed that teach students step-by-step procedures for completing instructional or social tasks. Strategy approaches often use acronyms representing the steps that are used in self-talk or self-regulation throughout the task. An example is the SPOT strategy for understanding story elements when reading (Bos & Vaughn, 1994):

Setting—Who, what, when, where?

Problem—What problem is to be solved?

Order of action—What steps were taken to solve the problem?

Tail end—What was the outcome?

Special education classes in the middle and high schools often provide a *parallel curriculum* (some call it "watered down") that is at a simpler conceptual level and is less demanding in terms of reading and writing. The parallel curriculum approach allows for teaching subject matter that is age-appropriate and prepares students for compulsory competency exams. Critics call this a duplication of services already provided in the general education setting and call for heterogeneous classes that teach to all levels of students.

Special education classes at the secondary level might also use a *life skills curriculum* to teach some students with learning disabilities. A life skills approach would include the necessary skills for adult life within the curriculum of academic classes. In the context of math class, for example, students might learn related job skills or how to manage personal finances. English classes would include how to read technical manuals, use resources such as telephone books, fill out job applications, write letters, and so forth.

Many students with learning disabilities are able to take classes in the general education setting alongside peers without disabilities. These students may need the assistance of a consultant or resource teacher to be successful. General education teachers may find it helpful to consult with the special education personnel to develop a system for monitoring progress and making adaptations. As already stated, secondary teachers are not likely to make specific adaptations in curriculum or instructional activities. However, consultation may help them to understand the student's learning capabilities and to be supportive of the student rather than punitive.

Transition Instruction.   Many high schools employ transition specialists to work with individual students with disabilities to develop an ITP, or Individualized Transition Plan, as a supplement to the IEP. There may be special classes that simulate job settings or students may have opportunities to work in a supervised community setting to develop employment skills. Transition specialists may also prepare students with learning disabilities for postsecondary education opportunities. As the student reaches high school, the need for special education personnel to communicate and collaborate with human service agencies and the community in general increases.

The goal of transition planning is to prepare the student fully for adult life in the community. This includes training in vocational and life skills. The elements generally found in effective transition programs for students with learning disabilities are as follow:

- *Self-assessment:* Students who are nearing adulthood need to be aware of their skill strengths, needs, and interests. Their aspirations and their families' expectations are also important factors in determining the course of their future.

- *Knowledge of postsecondary options:* Transition programs should make students aware of the vocational and educational opportunities available. Transition programs should also provide assistance in obtaining information and making applications to various agencies and institutions as needed.

- *Self-advocacy skills:* We don't generally think of students with learning disabilities as being unable to communicate their needs and desires or to make choices. However, students with learning disabilities generally have a passive learning style that may cause them to follow others' decisions rather than make their own choices. Students need decision-making skills to make their own life choices.

- *Job skills:* Basic academic skills are needed for successful performance on the job. Other skills, too, are important such as social skills, punctuality and dependability, problem-solving skills, and communication skills.

- *Vocational training and opportunities:* Many schools help students with learning disabilities to obtain paid work experience and to explore different vocational choices. They also help students to seek out postsecondary vocational training opportunities.

- *Postsecondary education:* Many students with learning disabilities are finding success in colleges and universities today. Many higher education institutions offer support services for individuals with learning disabilities including academic assistance, diagnostic assessment, counseling, strategy instruction, peer support programs, and others (Mangrum & Strichart, 1988).

CLASSROOM ADAPTATIONS AND MODIFICATIONS

Because the majority of students with learning disabilities in grades K–12 spend at least part of their school day in general education classrooms, it is important for teachers to know how to make adaptations to meet their specific needs. Teachers will make adaptations when they fit into the scope of planning and instructing the class as a whole (Schumm & Vaughn, 1991).

For example, when Ms. Stevens seated Robert where she can make frequent eye contact with him, she made an adaptation that did not require extra planning or instruction. It fit well into her normal teaching routine and provided many benefits for Robert. Because the teacher could see him well, she was more likely to notice when he was confused or lost. They developed a silent signal that indicated when he needed help. Later, Ms. Stevens felt Robert was getting too dependent on her help so she made a rule that he could only signal for her help three times a day. She then worked out a buddy system in which another student helped Robert with the reading assignments during social studies. In return, Robert helped his buddy with math, since this was his strong area. This plan allowed Robert to be the expert for at least one time each day and made him feel valued among peers. These individual plans took no additional time for Ms. Stevens yet they helped Robert to be successful. If Ms. Stevens had tried to provide individual instructional time in social studies for Robert on a daily basis, she would have become frustrated because it is not feasible for her to provide intensive individualized instruction when she has 33 other students.

Following are general suggestions for making adaptations for students with learning disabilities in the general education classroom.

Adapting the Curriculum

General education teachers often worry that the curriculum is too fast-paced and complex for students with learning disabilities. When you add reading and writing difficulties to the complexity of subject matter, it is easy to see that this is a valid worry. The most important principle to keep in mind is that of teamwork. Collaboration and consultation with special education teachers, parents, the students, and even peers can provide valuable assistance in designing curriculum adaptations that are feasible. When teachers share the responsibility, it ceases to be overwhelming. Two additional ideas may help teachers to make feasible adaptations to the curriculum.

The first is the idea of *setting priorities*. When planning a unit and the individual lessons within a unit, teachers should prioritize the concepts to be taught. The most important concepts, those that are essential to a basic understanding of this topic, should be the first priority in instructing students with learning disabilities. Schumm, Vaughn, and Leavell (1994) suggest organizing concepts into three groups: those that are fundamental to the topic (what all students must learn), those that are important (what most students will learn), and those that are incidental or supplementary (what some, but not all, students will learn). They further suggest that teachers focus instruction so that the fundamental concepts are heavily emphasized and every effort is made to make sure that all students understand.

The second idea related to curriculum adaptations is that of *focusing on IEP objectives*. The IEP is a legal document that lays out a design for meeting the student's individual needs. When Mr. Barber, a fifth grade teacher, met with Ms. Levine, a resource teacher, to discuss adaptations for two students placed in his class, they first listed the IEP objectives for each student. They decided that perhaps the entire curriculum was not appropriate for these two students. They spent some time matching the planned lessons and activities with each student's objectives to determine which objectives would be addressed in the planned lessons. They identified some elements of the planned lessons that the students were not ready for and they planned alternative activities for the students. Mr. Barber agreed not to include the missed assignments in the students' grades and to use the alternative assignment grades instead.

Adapting Instruction

Instructional adaptations are most feasible when they can be implemented within the framework of the normal instructional routine. Again, special education resource teachers can provide valuable assistance in designing such adaptations. Experienced resource teachers will say, however, that the most successful adaptations

Computer-assisted instruction can help students feel more competent as well as provide immediate feedback.

are those initiated by the classroom teacher. Only the classroom teacher knows his or her normal routine and comfort level with various adaptations.

There are numerous ways to adjust the instruction for students with learning disabilities. Adapting the seating arrangement is one suggestion that has already been mentioned. Adjusting instructional groups is another means of providing assistance for students with learning disabilities. Groups could be formed so that the student with learning disabilities has a strong and sensitive peer support. Cooperative groups or peer tutors are ways of using peers as resources for assistance. There are also several things teachers can do on an ongoing basis during instruction. For example, making frequent verbal or visual checks with particular students allows for close monitoring of their understanding. Promoting active engagement is an important consideration—and a sensitive one—for students with learning disabilities. Teachers often do not call on students with learning disabilities because they do not want to embarrass them. There are no special methods or formulas for adapting instruction, only the rule of thumb that the adaptations should be feasible and comfortable for the teacher and students.

Assistive technology is a growing trend in instructional adaptations for students with learning disabilities. There are some word processing programs that provide assistance with spelling, grammar, or sentence structure. Some programs make suggestions when students have difficulty finding a word. Some programs also have speech synthesis to read back what has been written. Computer-assisted instruction has been developed for all subject areas and may provide the needed repetition and practice for students to master concepts and skills.

Adapting Evaluation Criteria

Grading is a touchy issue in most schools, particularly when it comes to students with special needs. No one wants to harshly punish students with disabilities by giving them bad grades, yet lowering academic standards is not an acceptable alternative. This is especially true in secondary schools where absolute standards are set for earning a diploma. Grading is an issue that should be addressed with a school-wide policy for special education students. Once a policy is set, teachers must help students to work within it to maximize their success.

FAMILY PERSPECTIVES

We know significantly less about the impact on the families of individuals with learning disabilities than we know about families of children with more severe disabilities. What we do know has to do with parents' attitudes and their needs for support. First, parents see their child with learning disabilities as less capable than their other children and have lower expectations for his or her future success (Bryan & Bryan, 1983). Knowing what a powerful force parental expectation is in child development, this is a critical concern. Parents of children with learning disabilities report more behavior problems in the home than do parents of children without disabilities (Eliason & Richman, 1988; Haager & Vaughn, 1995). Many times in parent conferences, when teachers express frustration with classroom-related problems, parents share the same feelings. Other times, a child will have behavior problems in one setting but not the other.

We know very little about the impact of a learning disability on siblings. We can only guess that, similar to other disabilities, having a brother or sister with learning disabilities might lead to feelings of guilt, resentment, or protectiveness on the part of siblings. Educators must work with parents to set realistic, yet positive expectations for their children with and without learning disabilities and then to communicate about them openly with their children. Ongoing communication among teachers, parents, and other support personnel is the key to facilitating positive changes in students' learning and behavior.

The support needed by parents of children with learning disabilities is similar to that needed by parents of children with other disabilities. Parents may not understand the disability and often feel alienated by the school procedures of assessment, placement, and the IEP development, particularly if there are cultural differences between school personnel and the family (Harry, 1992). First and foremost, parents need information. Second, they need emotional support. Parent support groups such as the Learning Disabilities Association (LDA) have been enormously helpful in linking parents with information sources and in providing various support services. Not all parents will seek out an organization such as LDA. They may turn to the school or other parents for support. Other families see disability as a stigma and do not readily seek information or support from any source. Parents need ongoing communication with teachers and other school personnel.

Adult Outcomes

An increase in follow-up research on adults with learning disabilities in recent years has led to a better understanding of learning disabilities as a lifelong disorder. Unfortunately, the research to date shows that we have far to go to make education for individuals with learning disabilities optimal. The good news is that recent changes in school-based and family service programs are not yet reflected in the follow-up research. Perhaps in 10 years we will learn that recent movements—such as

Groups such as the Learning Disabilities Association provide the support and information parents need to help their children.

inclusive education, intensive academic intervention, transition programming, and metacognitive strategy instruction, to name a few—have led to improved outcomes for adults with learning disabilities. What we currently know about adults with learning disabilities relates to their academic and cognitive abilities, educational attainment, employment status, and personal adjustment.

The academic and cognitive processing difficulties experienced by school-age students with learning disabilities continue throughout the life span. Academically, many adults with learning disabilities report continued difficulty with reading, writing, and mathematics (Adelman & Vogel, 1990; Rogan & Hartman, 1990). Those who go on to college or universities report having difficulty with required competency testing (Wagner & Shaver, 1989). Adults with learning disabilities have continued difficulty with language processing as well as with various nonverbal tasks (Adelman & Vogel, 1991).

School completion is difficult to determine due to differences in sample selection procedures and methods used across research studies. Estimates of the dropout rate for students with learning disabilities range from 30% to 40% (Adelman & Vogel, 1991). There is variability from state to state with a higher dropout rate among minority students with learning disabilities and those of low socioeconomic status. However, individuals with learning disabilities do not necessarily have a higher rate of unemployment than adults without disabilities (Adelman & Vogel, 1990). Though that sounds encouraging, some evidence indicates that adults with learning disabilities have jobs that are less well paying than others, are often underemployed (i.e., part-time employment, do not get promotions), and are less satisfied with their jobs.

Adults with learning disabilities appear to be at social-emotional risk as well. However, it should be noted that we need considerably more research to make sweeping conclusions. Remember the heterogeneity of this population as you examine the findings from the limited number of studies on social and emotional outcomes. Surely, there are many well adjusted adults with learning disabilities as well as adults without disabilities who have considerable personal difficulties. Nevertheless, looking at self-satisfaction, researchers have found lower self-concepts for adults with learning disabilities than for those with no disabilities (Bender, 1995). Generally, adults with learning disabilities have more social and personal adjustment problems than other adults. They engage in less social activity, have a higher rate of depression, have more legal difficulties, and have a lower self-concept than other adults without disabilities (White, 1992). What we do not know is the extent to which these social-emotional difficulties existed prior to school completion or whether they developed in the adult years. We also do not know the extent to which school and other factors influence outcomes.

Several important points are clear from the foregoing findings. First, we need more reliable and extensive follow-up data on individuals with learning disabilities throughout different stages of adulthood. Second, we know that school completion is an issue, but we know very little about the students who drop out. We do not know if these students ever receive a diploma or have successful adult lives. Third, we can see the critical importance of transition programs and the importance of providing academic and vocational support into the adult years. In addition, we can see that social and emotional support are also very important.

CURRENT ISSUES AND FUTURE TRENDS

We can see that the field of learning disabilities has suffered growing pains along the way. We have yet to learn how to clearly define the disorder and reliably classify students. Though we have learned a great deal about effective treatment, the adult outcomes are still less than we would hope. Several issues appear to be critically important for the development of the field in terms of research and practice.

First, we seem to know little about individuals with learning disabilities from a developmental perspective. We do not know how this disorder affects individuals at different life stages or how life events impact the disability. We know relatively little about how to assist the family at different junctures in life. We therefore have a critical need for the development of effective support strategies for families.

The field of learning disabilities has a history of "borrowing" techniques and methodology from other fields. For example, research on the reading process, including metacognitive strategies, has had a tremendous impact on research, identification, and practice. Technology is beginning to be developed specifically for those with learning disabilities. Cognitive psychology has provided a theoretical base for understanding the processing difficulties experienced by many. Thus, we need to continue to draw on multidisciplinary resources as we search for more effective treatments.

Finally, advanced research techniques may lead us into the 21st century with a better understanding of the physiology and etiology of learning disabilities. We may learn to better identify different subtypes of learning disabilities. We may even someday be able to diagnose learning disabilities physiologically or genetically.

The greatest challenge as we make these advances, then, is to apply what we learn. Researchers and practitioners must go beyond classification to match subtypes with practical, school-based interventions.

Five-Minute Summary

The nearly 2 million people in the U.S. who have learning disabilities are a very heterogeneous group. Making up about 4% of the school population, this is the largest group served by special education. Most students with learning disabilities spend at least part of their school day in the general education classroom and are served by resource teachers. The category of learning disabilities is a language-based disorder characterized by academic underachievement. Presumably, a cognitive processing disorder underlies a learning disability, resulting in learning difficulty. Individuals with learning disabilities vary greatly in terms of the characteristics they exhibit. This lifelong disorder impacts learning throughout the different developmental stages of life.

The term *learning disabilities* was coined in 1963 by Samuel Kirk to describe the problems of children who have difficulty learning but have no obvious brain damage or cognitive impairment. Since that time, controversy has surrounded the definition of learning disabilities. In 1975 Congress included learning disabilities as a disability in P.L. 94-142, mandating public special education services for this population. The federal definition is criticized as ambiguous and open to interpretation, resulting in variation from state to state as to how many children are identified and the specific criteria used. Alternative definitions have been proposed but have not been accepted as clearer or more precise. As research yields more information regarding diagnosis and characteristics, the definition may be refined. Some think that learning disabilities may more accurately describe several different types of disabilities.

Individuals with learning disabilities are typically identified once they reach school age and learning difficulties become apparent. Early intervention, particularly with reading disabilities, may hold promise for prevention. Throughout the school years, children and adolescents with learning disabilities typically need support with academic learning. They may also have behavioral, attentional, or social difficulties. Transition programs for those individuals nearing adulthood include vocational and life skills training as well as preparation for postsecondary vocational or higher education opportunities. Many postsecondary institutions now have support services for individuals with learning disabilities.

Study Questions

1. Trace the field of learning disabilities from its roots in early brain research and clinical study, and list the major events that led to the provision of school services for individuals with learning disabilities.

2. List and describe the major components of the federal definition of learning disabilities and how they impact identification procedures. What are the major difficulties with this definition and why is it criticized?

3. Individuals with learning disabilities are described as a heterogeneous group. What are the main identifying characteristics that a teacher or parent might look for? What are some common secondary characteristics?

4. The population of students with learning disabilities served in our public schools has grown tremendously in 20 years. How many individuals with learning disabilities are there and why has this number grown over the years?

5. Explain the different assessment procedures typically used for identification of students with learning disabilities, for monitoring the individual program, and for ongoing instruction. How are these assessment procedures similar to and different from procedures used with students without disabilities?

6. Describe the main service delivery options for students with learning disabilities and the advantages

and disadvantages of each. How would you determine what is an appropriate placement for an individual student?

7. List and describe the major instructional approaches used with individuals with learning disabilities at different ages.

8. Because many students with learning disabilities spend at least a portion of their school day in the general education classroom, it is important for teachers to know how to make adaptations to accommodate their learning needs. What are some considerations in designing appropriate adaptations? How do collaboration and consultation facilitate this process?

9. Summarize the current data on adult outcomes for individuals with learning disabilities. Given the current changes in the field to focus on transition programs and better integrate students into general education classes, how might the data change in the next few years?

10. What suggestions do you have for future research and practice in learning disabilities?

For More Information

ORGANIZATIONS

Council for Learning Disabilities (CLD)
P.O. Box 40303
Overland Park, KS 66204

Division for Learning Disabilities (DLD) of the
  Council for Exceptional Children
1920 Association Drive
Reston, VA 22091

Learning Disabilities Association (LDA)
4156 Library Road
Pittsburgh, PA 15234

Orton Dyslexia Society
724 York Road
Baltimore, MD 21204

BOOKS AND ARTICLES

Armstrong, T. (1987). *In their own way.* Los Angeles: Tarcher.

Harwell, J. (1989). *Complete learning disabilities handbook.* Columbia, MO: Hawthorne.

McCarney, S. B. (1989). *The learning disability intervention manual.* Columbia, MO: Hawthorne.

JOURNALS, NEWSLETTERS, AND OTHER PUBLICATIONS

Journal of Learning Disabilities
Learning Disabilities Research
  and Practice

National Information Center for Children
  and Youth With Disabilities (NICHCY)
Publications List (several publications
  available)
P.O. Box 1492
Washington, DC 20013
800-999-5599

VIDEO AND ELECTRONIC MEDIA

*Understanding Learning Disabilities: How
  Difficult Can This Be? The F.A.T. City
  Workshop* [PBS Video]. (1989).
Produced and narrated by R. D. Lavoie.
For information: 800-424-7963

References

Adelman, P., & Vogel, S. (1990). College graduates with learning disabilities: Employment attainment and career patterns. *Learning Disability Quarterly, 13,* 154–166.

Adelman, P., & Vogel, S. (1991). The learning-disabled adult. In B. Wong (Ed.), *Learning about learning disabilities* (pp. 563–594). San Diego, CA: Academic Press.

Baker, J. M., & Zigmond, N. (1990). Are regular education classes equipped to accommodate students with learning disabilities? *Exceptional Children, 56,* 515–526.

Bender, W. N. (1995). *Learning disabilities: Characteristics, identification, and teaching strategies* (2nd ed.). Boston: Allyn & Bacon.

Bender, W. N., & Smith, J. K. (1990). Classroom behavior of children and adolescents with learning disabilities: A meta-analysis. *Journal of Learning Disabilities, 23,* 298–306.

Bender, W. N., & Wall, M. E. (1994). Social-emotional development of students with learning disabilities. *Learning Disability Quarterly, 17,* 323–341.

Bos, C. S., & Vaughn, S. (1994). *Strategies for teaching students with learning and behavior problems* (3rd ed.). Boston: Allyn & Bacon.

Bryan, J. H., & Bryan, T. S. (1983). The social life of the learning disabled youngster. In J. D. McKinney & L. Feagans (Eds.), *Current topics in learning disabilities* (Vol. 1). Norwood, NJ: Ablex.

Carnine, D. (1991). Reforming mathematics instruction: The role of curriculum materials. *Journal of Behavioral Education, 1,* 37–57.

Carnine, D., Silbert, J., & Kameenui, E. J. (1990). *Direct instruction reading.* Columbus, OH: Merrill.

Chalfant, J. C. (1985). Identifying learning disabled students: A summary of the national task force report. *Learning Disabilities Focus, 1* (1), 9–20.

Chapman, J. W. (1988). Learning disabled children's self-concepts. *Review of Educational Research, 58,* 347–371.

Council for Exceptional Children. (1993). *Statement on inclusive schools and communities.* Reston, VA: Council for Exceptional Children.

Cruickshank, W. M., Bentzen, F. A., Ratzeburg, R. H., & Tannhauser, M. T. (1961). *A teaching method for brain-injured and hyperactive children.* Syracuse, NY: Syracuse University Press.

Division for Learning Disabilities. (1993). *Inclusion: What does it mean for students with learning disabilities?* Reston, VA: Division for Learning Disabilities of the Council for Exceptional Children.

Eliason & Richman (1988). Behavior and attention in LD children. *Learning Disability Quarterly, 11,* 360–369.

Englert, C. S. (1994). Unraveling the mysteries of writing through strategy instruction. In T. E. Scruggs & B. Y. L. Wong (Eds.), *Intervention research in learning disabilities* (pp. 186–223). New York: Springer-Verlag.

Fernald, G. M. (1943). *Remedial techniques in basic school subjects.* New York: McGraw-Hill.

Fleischner, J. E. (1994). Diagnosis and assessment of mathematics learning disabilities. In G. R. Lyon, D. B. Gray, J. F. Kavanagh, & N. A. Krasnegor (Eds.), *Better understanding learning disabilities: New views from research and their implications for education and public policies* (pp. 441–458). Baltimore: Paul H. Brookes.

Frankenberger, W., & Fronzaglio, K. (1991). A review of state's criteria and procedures for identifying children with learning disabilities. *Journal of Learning Disabilities, 24,* 495–500.

Frostig, M., & Horne, D. (1964). *The Frostig program for the development of visual perception: Teacher's guide.* Chicago: Follett.

Frostig, M., Maslow, P., Lefever, D. W., & Whittlesey, J. R. B. (1964). *The Marianne Frostig Developmental Test of Visual Perception: 1963 standardization.* Palo Alto, CA: Consulting Psychologists Press.

Fuchs, D., Fuchs, L., & Fernstrom, P. (1993). A conservative approach to special education reform: Mainstreaming through transenvironmental programming and curriculum-based measurement. *American Educational Research Journal, 30,* 149–177.

Givner, C., & Haager, D. (1995). Strategies for effective collaboration. In M. Falvey (Ed.), *Inclusive and heterogeneous education: Assessment, curriculum, and instruction* (pp. 41–57). Baltimore: Paul H. Brookes.

Graham, S., & Harris, K. R. (1992). Self-regulated strategy development: Programmatic research in writing. In B. Y. L. Wong (Ed.), *Contemporary intervention research in learning disabilities: An international perspective* (pp. 47–64). New York: Springer-Verlag.

Haager, D., & Vaughn, S. (1995). Parent, teacher, peer and self-reports of the social competence of students with learning disabilities. *Journal of Learning Disabilities, 28,* 205–215, 231.

Hammill, D. (1990). On defining learning disabilities: An emerging consensus. *Journal of Learning Disabilities, 23,* 74–84.

Hammill, D. D., & Larsen, S. C. (1974). The relationship of selected auditory perceptual skills and reading ability. *Journal of Learning Disabilities, 7,* 429–435.

Harry, B. (1992). An ethnographic study of cross-cultural communication with Puerto-Rican families in special education. *American Educational Research Journal, 29,* 471–494.

Kulm, G. (1980). Research on mathematics attitudes. In R. J. Shumway (Ed.), *Research in mathematics education* (pp. 356–387). Reston, VA: National Council of Teachers of Mathematics.

Larsen, S. C., & Hammill, D. D. (1975). The relationship of selected visual perceptual skills to academic abilities. *Journal of Special Education, 9,* 281–291.

Learning Disabilities Association. (1993). *Position paper on full inclusion of all students with learning disabilities in the regular education classroom.* Pittsburgh: Learning Disabilities Association.

Lerner, J. W. (1993). *Learning disabilities: Theories, diagnosis, and teaching strategies* (6th ed.). Boston: Houghton Mifflin.

Lipsky, D. K., & Gartner, A. (1989). *Beyond separate education: Quality for all.* Baltimore: Paul H. Brookes.

Lyon, G. R. (1985). Educational validation studies of learning disability subtypes. In B. Rourke (Ed.), *Neuropsychology of learning disabilities* (pp. 228–253). New York: Guilford.

Mann, V. (1994). Phonological skills and the prediction of early reading problems. In N. C. Jordan & J. Goldsmith-Phillips (Eds.), *Learning disabilities: New directions for assessment* (pp. 67–84). Needham Heights, MA: Allyn & Bacon.

Margalit, M., & Zak, I. (1984). Anxiety and self-concept of learning disabled children. *Journal of Learning Disabilities, 17,* 537–539.

McIntosh, R., Vaughn, S., Schumm, J. S., Haager, D., & Lee, O. (1993). Observations of students with learning disabilities in general education classrooms. *Exceptional Children, 60,* 249–261.

McKinney, J. D. (1989). Longitudinal research on the behavioral characteristics of children with learning disabilities. *Journal of Learning Disabilities, 22,* 141–150.

McKinney, J. D., & Feagans, L. (1984). Academic and behavioral characteristics of learning disabled children and average achievers: Longitudinal studies. *Learning Disability Quarterly, 7,* 251–264.

National Association of State Boards of Education. (1992). *Winners all: A call for inclusive schools.* Washington, DC: National Association of State Boards of Education.

Newcomer, P. L., & Barenbaum, E. M. (1991). The written composing ability of children with learning disabilities: A review of the literature from 1980–1990. *Journal of Learning Disabilities, 24,* 578–593.

Norman, C., & Zigmond, N. (1980). Characteristics of children labeled and served as learning disabled in school systems affiliated with child service demonstration centers. *Journal of Learning Disabilities, 13,* 16–21.

Orton, S. (1937). *Reading, writing and speech problems in children.* New York: Norton.

Parker, J. G., & Asher, S. R. (1987). Peer relations and later personal adjustment: Are low-accepted children at risk? *Psychological Bulletin, 102,* 357–389.

Pearl, R. M., Donahue, M., & Bryan, T. (1986). Social relationships of learning-disabled children. In J. K. Torgesen & B. Y. L. Wong (Eds.), *Psychological and educational perspectives on learning disabilities* (pp. 193–254). Orlando, FL: Academic Press.

Reynolds, M. C. (1989). An historical perspective: The delivery of special education to mildly disabled and at-risk students. *Remedial and Special Education, 10,* 7–11.

Rogan, L., & Hartman, L. D. (1990). Adult outcome of learning disabled students ten years after initial follow-up. *Learning Disabilities Focus, 5,* 91–102.

Rosenthal, R., & Jacobson, L. (1968). *Pygmalion in the classroom.* New York: Holt, Rinehart & Winston.

Russell, R., & Ginsburg, H. P. (1984). Cognitive analysis of children's mathematics difficulties. *Cognition and Instruction, 1,* 217–274.

Schumm, J. S., Vaughn, S., Haager, D., McDowell, J., Rothlein, L., & Samuell, L. (1995). General education teacher planning: What can students with learning disabilities expect? *Exceptional Children, 61,* 335–352.

Shaywitz, S. E., & Shaywitz, B. A. (1988). Attention deficit disorder: Current perspectives. In J. F. Kavanagh & T. J. Truss, Jr. (Eds.), *Learning disabilities: Proceedings of the national conference* (pp. 369–523).

Strauss, A., & Lehtinen, L. (1974). *Psychopathology and education of the brain-injured child.* New York: Grune & Stratton.

Swanson, H. L., & Ransby, M. (1994). The study of cognitive processes in learning disabled students. In S. Vaughn & C. Bos (Eds.), *Research issues in learning disabilities: Theory, methodology, and ethics* (pp. 246–275). New York: Springer-Verlag.

U.S. Department of Education. (1991). *Thirteenth annual report to Congress on the implementation of the Individuals with Disabilities Education Act.* Washington, DC: U.S. Government Printing Office.

U.S. Office of Education. (1977). Assistance to states for education of handicapped children: Procedures for evaluating specific learning disabilities. *Federal Register, 42,* 65082–65085.

Vaughn, S., & Haager, D. (1994a). Social assessment of students with learning disabilities: Do they measure up? In S. Vaughn & C. Bos (Eds.), *Research issues in learning disabilities: Theory, methodology, assessment, and ethics* (pp. 276–311). New York: Springer-Verlag.

Vaughn, S., & Haager, D. (1994b). Social competence as a multifaceted construct: How do students with learning disabilities fare? *Learning Disability Quarterly, 17,* 253–266.

Vaughn, S., Hogan, A., Kouzekanani, K., & Shapiro, S. (1990). Peer acceptance, self-perceptions, and social skills of learning disabled students prior to identification. *Journal of Educational Psychology, 82,* 101–106.

Vaughn, S., Zaragoza, N., Hogan, A., & Walker, J. (1993). A four-year longitudinal investigation of the social skills and behavior problems of students with learning disabilities. *Journal of Learning Disabilities, 26,* 404–412.

Vellutino, F. R. (1991). Introduction to three studies on reading acquisition: Convergent findings on theoretical foundations of code-oriented versus whole-language approaches to reading instruction. *Journal of Educational Psychology, 83,* 437–443.

Vellutino, F. R., Scanlon, D. M., & Tanzman, M. S. (1994). Components of reading ability. In G. R. Lyon (Ed.), *Frames of reference for the assessment of learning disabilities: New views on measurement issues* (pp. 279–332). Baltimore: Paul H. Brookes.

Wagner, M., & Shaver, D. M. (1989). Educational programs and achievements of secondary special education students: Findings from the National Longitudinal Transition Study. Paper presented at the annual meeting of the American Educational Research Association, San Francisco, CA.

Wagner, R. K., & Torgeson, J. K. (1987). The nature of phonological processing and its causal role in the acquisition of reading skills. *Psychological Bulletin, 101,* 192–212.

Wiederholt, J. L., Hammill, D. D., & Brown, V. L. (1993). *The resource program: Organization and implementation.* Austin, TX: PRO-ED.

Wiener, J. (1987). Peer status of learning disabled children and adolescents: A review of the literature. *Learning Disabilities Research, 2,* 62–79.

Wong, B. Y. L., Wong, R., & Blenkisop, J. (1989). Cognitive and metacognitive aspects of learning-disabled adolescents' composing problems. *Learning Disability Quarterly, 12,* 300–323.

Chapter 5

Moonwalk, acrylic on canvas, 24″ × 30″ (1994)

ATTENTION DEFICIT DISORDERS

JUDY W. WOOD

After studying this chapter, the reader will:

Be able to trace the history of the AD/HD population

Identify the three subtypes of AD/HD and the five essential
components that define the disorder

Know which law protects the AD/HD population
and provides for services

Recognize the characteristics of people with AD/HD
from infancy through adulthood

Be aware of the prevalence of AD/HD and
the effect of gender on diagnosis

Understand genetic, biological, environmental, and psychological
factors that may contribute to AD/HD

Be familiar with important assessment factors and tools

Know the components of a multimodal treatment
approach for AD/HD

Be able to discuss and compare traditional and
inclusive service delivery models

Understand how AD/HD affects family, peer,
and school relationships

Identify current issues concerning AD/HD and
be aware of future trends

ATTENTION DEFICIT DISORDERS

Early years Adventurers and explorers served society with their restless, inattentive, and impulsive behaviors by continuous geographic movement.

1890 William James related inhibiting control and inattention and determined that they were caused by the same underlying neurological deficit.

1917–1918 Epidemic of encephalitis in America focused attention on surviving children, providing a link to neurological damage or minimal brain damage.

1947 Information on neurological damage was formally reported by Strauss and Lehtinen.

1950s–1960s Researchers began to shift cause of attention deficits from brain injury to brain mechanisms, genetics, and the environment.

1970s Hundreds of studies on ADD emerged.

1987 The American Psychiatric Association changed the term *attention deficit disorder* (ADD) to *attention deficit hyperactivity disorder* (AD/HD).

  Children With Attention Deficit Disorders (CHADD) was established.

1991 The AD/HD population was given rights, protections, and services provided under P.L. 101-476 and Section 504 of the Rehabilitation Act of 1973.

1994 The American Psychiatric Association established three subtypes for diagnostic purposes: AD/HD combined type, AD/HD predominantly inattentive type, and AD/HD predominantly hyperactive-impulsive type.

Researchers speculate that the impulsive behavior of explorers such as the Vikings may have served a purpose for society.

HISTORICAL OVERVIEW

The term *attention deficit hyperactivity disorder* (AD/HD) is relatively new to the field of education. The population of individuals with attention deficit hyperactivity disorder is not new for society, however—but perhaps simply overlooked or mislabeled. Since this population has become of great concern to educators as well as to parents and society as a whole, the following chapter is devoted completely to students and adults with attention deficit disorders (ADD), which may also be referred to as attention deficit hyperactivity disorders (AD/HD).

The labeling of the student population with ADD is relatively new to school systems. However, history reports that this medical condition has probably been with us from society's beginning. Cantwell (1983) has speculated that the adventurers and explorers of the past, with their restless, inattentive, and impulsive behaviors, may have served a purpose to society by continuous geographic movement resulting in population dispersal and the discovery of new worlds and lands.

A comprehensive report of the history of the AD/HD population is provided in the *Utah Attention Deficit Disorder Guide* (Utah State Office of Education, 1992). It reports early references to AD/HD by William James in 1890, when he suggested that inhibiting control and inattention were related and that both were caused by the same underlying neurological deficit. In 1902, a British physician described these same behaviors in 20 children, linking AD/HD behavior to genetics, neurological diseases, and brain injury. The 1917–18 epidemic of encephalitis in America focused attention on surviving children, providing a link to neurological damage or minimal brain damage. This information was formally reported in 1947 by Strauss and Lehtinen.

Other timely events on cause and treatment of AD/HD began to occur. In 1937, a physician was asked to prescribe medication for students' headaches. Although the headaches remained, teachers noticed an improved focus in the students' behaviors. In the 1950s and 1960s, the speculated cause began to shift from brain injury to brain mechanisms, genetics, and the environment. The research of the 1970s saw hundreds of studies published on the disability of ADD. In 1987, and with passage of laws and time, the disorder was referred to by the American Psychiatric Association as *attention deficit hyperactivity disorder* (AD/HD).

The passage of history brought us closer to cause, definition, and treatment suggestions. Even though AD/HD is relatively new as far as the label is concerned, the condition has been present from the beginning of mankind. Technically, who are these persons with AD/HD and how do we define the population?

DEFINITION

Over the years various terms have been used to describe or define students with AD/HD. Some of these terms include *minimal brain dysfunction, minimal cerebral*

REAL PEOPLE

"I was born June 13, 1979, on the first day of my father's classes in Air Force college. I was a perfectly healthy baby girl. I developed much like any other child and was pretty much the average kid. My parents always said that I was a very fast learner. I remember saying the word 'remarkable' and knowing what it meant when I was 4 or 5. Even though I was a fast learner, AD/HD pulled me down.

"AD/HD is very hard to cope with. I have to make a conscious effort to concentrate in almost everything that I do. I don't like to think of only one thing at a time because it will bore me to death. I also remember when I was 5 I had a very hard time learning the alphabet. I know that first grade was very hard for me and that I felt very stupid because I couldn't read and math was nearly impossible. I was teased and bothered almost every day. My parents had me take an IQ test and I tested high, so the school tried to say that all I needed was to be held back. Luckily my parents were dead set against that. The next 3 years I went to a private school named White Oak Academy where all 18 students were like myself—intelligent people who just weren't traditional students. I learned quickly and still do. I began to enjoy school there and I excelled in all of my subjects. By the fourth grade I was told that I was fully capable of handling a public school again and that I would be going to a larger private school. At that point I knew my strengths and weaknesses—my strengths being reading, comprehension, and vocabulary; my weaknesses, spelling and math. I went back to public school instead and have been in public schools since that point.

"My father has always been looking for the 'cure.' It is hard knowing that my father has never accepted my minimal disability as just something to work around. That's all I think of it as. I know that I am smart because I took another IQ test recently and I came out in the superior range—so I just compensate for my weaknesses and do what I can with what I have. If only I could tell my father that. I have tried to tell my father numerous times, but he thinks of AD/HD as a sickness that can be cured. I have always gotten the distinct feeling that he felt as if he were to blame for my disability. I probably will never know how he really feels about it all.

"I am a junior in high school now, and he and I argue a lot over grades. I know I can do better, but it's so hard to concentrate in classes like science and math. I just can't get interested, and if I am not interested, I lose all patience with the subject and I just fade out. Keyboarding is another class that is particularly hard because I can't stand sitting in front of a computer screen for 55 minutes straight. You throw in the hyperactivity and all is lost. At 16, I have learned to control my hyperactivity to a point, but I have to want to first. It's not always easy to think constantly of staying on focus. Sometimes even if I think I have it under control, I catch myself tapping my toe or fidgeting. I have to fight the constant compulsion to get up and do something in the middle of class.

"I am working on getting good grades so that I have good options in the future. I still don't know what I want to do, but I want to have opportunities to do whatever it is that I choose. Upon high school graduation, I plan to attend college.

"As I've grown older, I've learned to compensate better for my weaknesses by utilizing my strengths. I am looking forward to a bright future."

dysfunction, minimal brain damage, hyperkinetic reaction of childhood, hyperkinetic syn-drome, hyperactive child syndrome, and currently *attention deficit disorder with or without hyperactivity.*

DSM-IV Components or Criteria

The American Psychiatric Association's (1994) *Diagnostic and Statistical Manual of Mental Disorders* (4th edition, revised), referred to as *DSM-IV,* is used by medical and mental health professionals to assist in the identification of children and adults with emotional and learning problems; it presents essential features of AD/HD. According to the *DSM-IV,* the following five essential components define AD/HD:

1. Persistent pattern of inattention and/or hyperactivity-impulsivity unlike that of peer groups

2. Symptoms present before age 7

3. Symptoms present in at least two settings (e.g., home, school, and/or work)

4. Condition interferes with developmentally appropriate social, academic, or occupational functioning

5. Condition does not occur exclusively during the course of a psychotic disorder better accounted for by another mental disorder

Criteria established for diagnosing AD/HD also assist in providing definitional boundaries for the disorder. The following 14-step criteria must occur more frequently among persons diagnosed with AD/HD than in other people of the same mental age:

1. Often fidgets with hands or feet or squirms in seat (in adolescents, may be limited to subjective feelings of restlessness)

2. Has difficulty remaining seated when required to do so

3. Is easily distracted by extraneous stimuli

4. Has difficulty awaiting turn in games or group situations

5. Often blurts out answers to questions before they have been completed

6. Has difficulty following through on instructions from others, not due to oppositional behavior or failure of comprehension (e.g., fails to complete chores)

7. Has difficulty sustaining attention in tasks or play activities

8. Often shifts from one uncompleted activity to another

9. Has difficulty playing quietly

10. Often talks excessively

11. Often interrupts or intrudes on others (e.g., butts into other children's games)

12. Often does not seem to listen to what is being said to him or her

13. Often loses things necessary for tasks or activities at school or at home (e.g., toys, pencils, books, assignments)

14. Often engages in physically dangerous activities without considering possible consequences, not for the purpose of thrill-seeking (e.g., runs into street without looking)

In addition, the following three standards must also be met:

1. A disturbance of at least 6 months, during which at least eight of the criteria are present

2. Onset before the age of 7

3. Does not meet the criteria for a Pervasive Developmental Disorder

Generally, while most individuals with AD/HD exhibit inattention, hyperactivity, and impulsivity, some individuals have a predominant pattern. There are three patterns, or subtypes—one of which must be evident for 6 months prior to diagnosis. They are as follows:

Attention Deficit Hyperactivity Disorder, Combined Type: This subtype should be used if six or more symptoms of inattention and six or more symptoms of hyperactivity-impulsivity have persisted for at least 6 months. Most children and adolescents with the disorder have this combined type. It is not known whether the same is true of adults with the disorder.

Attention Deficit Hyperactivity Disorder, Predominantly Inattentive Type: This subtype should be used if six or more symptoms of inattention but fewer than six symptoms of hyperactivity-impulsivity have persisted for at least 6 months.

Attention Deficit Hyperactivity Disorder, Predominantly Hyperactive-Impulsive Type: This subtype should be used if six or more symptoms of hyperactivity-impulsivity but fewer than six symptoms of inattention have persisted for at least 6 months. Inattention may often still be a significant clinical feature in such cases (American Psychiatric Association, 1994, p. 80).

Recognition thus is given to the fact that younger children have higher rates of each of these three characteristics than older children. Hyperactivity, in fact, appears to diminish steadily throughout the school years, and may disappear altogether in adolescence. Attention problems and impulsivity persist. While manifestations of the disorder usually appear in every setting (home, school, with peers, etc.), it is possible that in one-on-one situations, problems of attention will not be evident (e.g., being examined in the clinician's office, or interacting with a video game).

Severity of AD/HD

The severity of AD/HD may range from mild to moderate to severe. Persons with mild AD/HD exhibit only enough characteristics to make a diagnosis and may have minimal or no impairment in school and social functioning. When students show significant and pervasive impairment in school and at home, the symptoms are characteristic of severe AD/HD.

Practical Definition

The *DSM-IV* definition is for use by medical and mental health professionals. Table 5.1 presents practical characteristics that may be more functional for parents and teachers to use in defining AD/HD (Utah State Office of Education, 1992).

Table 5.1   **Practical Definition for AD/HD**

Attention Deficit Disorder is a medical condition of inappropriate developmental degrees of:

INATTENTION

The student is off-task, distractible, or shifts attention from one activity to another.

IMPULSIVITY

The student acts before he thinks, often interrupts, talks excessively, intrudes, and engages in thrill-seeking behavior.

OVERACTIVITY

The student is overactive, out-of-seat, tapping objects, squirmy, or fidgety.

NONCOMPLIANCE

The student does not follow adult requests in a reasonable period of time, often resulting in arguing, delaying, or tantrums.

SELF-MANAGEMENT DEFICITS

The student has difficulty delaying gratification and self-managing his or her behavior.

ACADEMIC DEFICITS

The student is academically behind in subjects, has difficulty with organization and completing class work or homework.

SOCIAL SKILLS DEFICITS

The student has social skill problems that lead to peer rejection. These problems can include poor cooperation, poor friend making skills, resisting peer pressure, and difficulty giving and receiving feedback.

Source: Adapted from *The Utah Attention Deficit Disorder Guide,* published in 1992 by the Utah State Board of Education, Salt Lake City, UT.

LEGAL REQUIREMENTS FOR ELIGIBILITY

Even though from early years the AD/HD dilemma was manifest in children and adults, a definition of consensus was not reached by the American Psychiatric Association until 1987. It has only been in the 1990s that laws have supported services to this population. Early on it was unclear how states were going to serve students with AD/HD. Since this population was not specifically referred to under P.L. 94-142 (the Education for All Handicapped Children Act of 1975), nor under P.L. 101-476 (the Individuals With Disabilities Education Act of 1990), many students with AD/HD were receiving inappropriate services and many received no services.

Congress ordered a Notice of Inquiry. On September 16, 1991, after reviewing more than 2,000 written comments from across the nation from professionals, parents, organizations, and persons with AD/HD, a memo was issued from the U.S. Department of Education to the chief state school officers defining the rights, protections, and services for students with AD/HD under P.L. 101-476 (IDEA) and also under Section 504 of P.L. 93-112 (the Rehabilitation Act of 1973). Students with AD/HD would be served under IDEA in the Other Health Impaired category, and, since Section 504 protects the rights of persons with physical and mental impairments, they must be served in any program receiving federal funds. Students with AD/HD could qualify for services for 504 protection without being eligible for IDEA services (Fowler, 1992; Murray, 1991).

Children sometimes daydream in class to escape a discussion or lesson they can't follow.

CHARACTERISTICS ASSOCIATED WITH AD/HD

In his early years, a baby with AD/HD may cry or scream for unknown reasons or experience difficulty eating and sleeping. The toddler with AD/HD is in perpetual motion, prone to frequent accidents and exhibiting frequent temper tantrums. When the child with AD/HD begins school he or she is inattentive, talkative and may daydream. Handwriting is sloppy, letters are reversed, and math or reading becomes an apparent weakness (Nichamin & Windell, 1984). Children with AD/HD may also have learning disabilities. AD/HD crosses over IQ levels and can exist among students who are gifted as well as those in the average and subaverage IQ ranges.

By the middle and high school years, physical hyperactivity may have diminished, but the accumulation of academic and social failures may result in low self-esteem among students with AD/HD. College may be a reality for some, but the greater academic demands may result in the student dropping out of school and depression resulting from career goal changes. Adults with AD/HD may show fewer of their earlier characteristics, yet short attention span, distractibility, and impulsivity are lifelong problems (Nichamin & Windell, 1984). Job tenure may be short for some while others learn to compensate for their weaknesses and maintain their employment.

More specifically, the characteristics of students with AD/HD focus on problems with inattention and hyperactivity-impulsivity.

Students With AD/HD Who Are Inattentive

Many students with AD/HD do not exhibit the characteristic of hyperactivity. In their case, the disorder is characterized primarily by **inattentiveness.** These children may often be described as lazy and unmotivated. They are usually not disruptive in the classroom, but successive academic failure begins to cause low self-esteem. Individuals with AD/HD who are inattentive have difficulty attending to details, make careless mistakes in schoolwork or on the job, and may have difficulty sustaining attention to tasks. They may not listen when spoken to, fail to follow through or understand instructions, have difficulty organizing, avoid and/or dislike tasks that require sustained mental effort, lose items, are easily distracted, and are often forgetful.

Students With AD/HD Who Are Hyperactive-Impulsive

Some children with AD/HD begin to lose the active overtones after age 3. Many may show no hyperactivity in adolescence, while for others behavior problems begin to surface during this period. Symptoms of **hyperactivity** (which must persist for at least 6 months) include fidgeting or squirming in seat, inability to stay in seat, running or climbing excessively where this behavior is inappropriate, having difficulty playing quietly or participating in leisure activities, always being "on the go," and often talking excessively. Symptoms of **impulsivity** include blurting out answers, having difficulty awaiting turn, and interrupting others or ongoing activities. This behavior can be extremely trying to teachers, parents, and later in life, to employers.

Components of Attention

In order to better understand students with AD/HD, a further look into specific types of attentional weaknesses is warranted. Attention can be divided into two categories: encoding and selection (Rooney, 1993). **Encoding** problems of attention refer to "problems with incoming stimuli and the storage of this stimuli for processing" (Rooney, 1993, p. 2), and **selection** focuses on the further processing of stimuli.

Table 5.2 presents the two categories and related attention types to each. An understanding of these categories helps in intervention planning.

Table 5.2   **Specific Types of Attention**

ENCODING		SELECTION	
Attention span:	Length of time on a task or activity	*Selective attention:*	Ability to choose appropriate stimuli for processing
Focusing attention:	Ability to tune out distracting or irrelevant stimuli	*Involuntary attention:*	Automatic response to a stimuli
Divided attention:	Ability to split attention between two or more tasks	*Voluntary attention:*	Deliberate attention
Intensity of attention:	Affects focus as well as memory storage	*Filtering:*	Weeding out irrelevant from relevant stimuli
Sequential attention:	Focusing on tasks in necessary order to complete the tasks	*Filtering (response set):*	Selecting stimuli for further processing based on the similarity between the stimuli and the conceptual expectation

Source: Adapted from "Classroom Interventions for Students With Attention Deficit Disorders," by K. J. Rooney, 1993, *Focus on Exceptional Children, 26*(4), p. 3.

Other Characteristics of AD/HD

In addition to deficits in attention, numerous other characteristics are exhibited by the student with AD/HD. Table 5.3 presents an overview of these characteristics, some of which are discussed below.

Problematic Social Skills. Appropriate social skills are necessary for functioning in daily activities and for interaction with peers (Barkley, 1990). Deficits in social skills are frequently problematic for individuals with AD/HD. Many of these children are described as immature, demanding, and overly sensitive. Many of the individual's behaviors are inappropriate for the occasion.

Disorganization. Children and many adults with AD/HD lack organizational skills. Younger and school-age children have difficulty keeping their rooms clean, organizing school notebooks, keeping track of school materials and books, and following directions. When the child with AD/HD reaches adulthood, the same lack of organization spills into adult life. Bills go overdue, checkbooks are unbalanced, items are lost, and job tasks are disorganized.

Academic Deficits. Many students with AD/HD experience difficulties with basic academic skills. Hinshaw (1992) estimates that between 40% and 80% of all students with AD/HD have problems learning. Difficulty in learning only compounds the problem of low self-esteem. If, however, these students have no cognitive deficits (e.g., learning disability, mental retardation) and can learn to focus their attention, they are usually capable of learning academic material.

Distractibility. Frequently you will hear someone say that students with AD/HD are distracted, that they do not pay attention. **Distractibility** means paying attention to everything around you rather than focusing on the task at hand.

Table 5.3 **AD/HD Fact Sheet**

- Impulsivity occurs in approximately 40% to 60% of individuals with AD/HD, particularly in boys.
- Research has indicated that more adolescents with hyperactivity fail academic subjects, have difficulty getting along with teachers and peers, and drop out of school at a higher rate than any other group of adolescents.
- Approximately 15% of the children who are medicated for AD/HD may need to continue the medication through adolescence and adulthood.
- An estimated 50% to 80% of AD/HD children are likely to exhibit problems with inattention and impulsivity into adulthood.
- The number of children and adolescents in the United States affected by AD/HD ranges from 1.4 to 2.2 million.
- 60% to 70% of children with AD/HD have another immediate family member who evidences similar symptoms.
- Approximately 60% to 70% of children with AD/HD begin to show symptoms of the disorder during infancy, although it usually goes unrecognized until the child starts school.
- In 25% of AD/HD cases, a learning disability is evident.
- Approximately 33% of the children with learning disabilities also have AD/HD.

Source: Information compiled by Ann Welch of Fairfax, VA, chosen the 1993 National Teacher of the Year by the Council for Exceptional Children.

A child with AD/HD may not have acquired the social skills necessary to successfully join group play.

Staying organized is sometimes very difficult for students with AD/HD.

Students with AD/HD focus on everything in the environment and cannot "zoom" in on one specific detail. For example, as the teacher explains how to do a math problem, not only is the student with AD/HD focusing on the math problem—but also on a bird outside the window, the smell coming down the hall, and the boy wiggling in the next desk.

PREVALENCE OF AD/HD

Estimates of the incidence of AD/HD vary widely. Some experts estimate that 3% to 20% of the school-age population are affected. The range from 3% to 5% is the most widely accepted estimate (U.S. Department of Education, 1994). Boys tend to be diagnosed more readily, while girls may not be diagnosed until their symptoms are severe. About 25% of students with AD/HD also have learning disabilities, and 30% to 65% are diagnosed as having emotional disturbance.

CAUSES OF AD/HD

Currently, the etiology of AD/HD is unknown, although some facts are clear. AD/HD may be attributed to multiple causes. Parents alone do not "cause" AD/HD. AD/HD is a biological condition affecting educational progress; certain environmental factors may intensify the condition (Utah State Office of Education, 1992).

Genetic and Biological Factors

Research suggests that AD/HD can be genetically transmitted. As early as 1983, researchers began to see inherited traits, such as basic temperament, in young infants. Temperament is considered an inherited disposition. Chess and Thomas (1983) found that 10% of newborn infants were temperament-sensitive, while 40% were easy in temperament. They also noted that 70% of the temperament-sensitive infants had behavior problems in childhood and later life. In a 1990 landmark study by Zametkin and colleagues, it was found that significant differences in the brain's utilization of glucose as an energy source differed in individuals with AD/HD as compared to individuals without AD/HD.

Between 60% and 70% of children with AD/HD also have another family member who is diagnosed or has similar symptoms. It is not uncommon for a child to be diagnosed and during the assessment process, or shortly thereafter, one parent recognizes that he or she has the same symptoms as the child.

Environmental and Psychological Factors

Environmental factors such as trauma during pregnancy or birth, lead poisoning, prenatal alcohol and drug exposure (Rief, 1993), divorce, weak parenting skills, or a poor school environment (Utah State Office of Education, 1992) may contribute to AD/HD but do not serve as a primary source. Little evidence supports environmental factors as a cause, although they may contribute to the problem in some cases.

ASSESSMENT OF AD/HD

Since many preschoolers are impulsive, inattentive, and physically very active, children with AD/HD are usually not identified until their school years. School personnel most commonly initiate the assessment of a child for AD/HD. The assessment must also include an evaluation by a physician. The actual assessment of the AD/HD child is still in debate. According to the Connecticut Task Force on

AD/HD (Connecticut Department of Education, 1993), before a consensus is reached on the actual label three factors should be considered: (1) the use of multiple sources of information, (2) the collection of information in numerous settings, and (3) the assessment of all three dimensions of AD/HD (attention, impulsivity, and hyperactivity).

Use Multiple Sources of Information.   The assessment process should include numerous sources. Appropriate tests and observations must be made. Information should be gathered from parents, teachers, and others who have contact with the child.

Collect Information in Numerous Settings.   At one time it was thought that a student with AD/HD exhibited the same characteristics in all environments. Now we know that the characteristics may vary from situation to situation. A child may not attend to tasks in the classroom, but may sit for long periods watching a TV program of interest. Therefore, it is imperative that the student be observed in a number of settings while interacting with different people (e.g., other children, adults).

Assess All Three Dimensions of AD/HD.   The characteristics of inattention, impulsivity, and hyperactivity should all be considered in the assessment process. Even though these may overlap, each is a complex construct. Any assessment of AD/HD should consider the following behavioral components (Connecticut Department of Education, 1993, p. 12):

1. The ability to focus, or come to attention

2. The ability to choose which stimulus to focus on ("selective attention")

3. The ability to resist distractors in the environment

4. The ability to sustain attention over a reasonable period ("attention span")

Types of Assessment Data

A comprehensive assessment of AD/HD includes numerous components: medical reviews, case history, school records, interviews, observations, rating scales, academic assessment, portfolio assessment, and social skills assessment.

Interviews.   Assessment interviews may be conducted with parents, teachers, and the student. Parents hold valuable information regarding their child. They frequently know what will and will not reinforce positive behaviors. Teachers can provide useful information about behavioral characteristics in the classroom and how the student interacts with peers. An interview of the student with AD/HD provides a perspective from that student's point of view. *What subjects are difficult? What do you like best in school? What motivates you to learn?* These and numerous other questions can be answered by the student. Interview scales may be constructed by professionals, or numerous structured interviews are available from commercial sources.

Observations.   Observations may be done at home or in the school setting. It is helpful when observing at school that careful planning be made as to when the observation will be done (e.g., during which activities, at what time of day, etc.). Observations should be systematic and structured.

Table 5.4   **Behavior Checklists for Assessing AD/HD**

Behavior Rating Profile (Teacher Form)
L. Brown & D. Hammill
PRO-ED Publishing Co.
8700 Shoal Creek Boulevard
Austin, TX 78757-6897

Child Behavior Checklist, 1991 Edition
(Teacher, Parent, Youth Report Form)
T. M. Achenbach
University Associates in Psychiatry
1 South Prospect Street
Burlington, VT 05401

Conners Behavior Checklist
K. Conners
Multi-Health System, Inc.
908 Niagra Falls Boulevard
North Tanawanda, NY 14120-2060

Problem Behavior Checklist—Revised
R. Quay
Department of Psychology
University of Miami
Coral Gables, FL 33124

Wilker Problem Behavior Identification—Revised
(Grades P– 6)
Western Psychological Services
12031 Wilshire Boulevard
Los Angeles, CA 90025

Source: Data from *The Utah Attention Deficit Disorder Guide* (p. 22), published in 1992 by the Utah State Office of Education, Salt Lake City, UT.

Rating Scales.   Rating scales are inexpensive, time conservative, and may be completed by teachers and/or parents. It should be noted, however, that this evaluation measure should not be the sole form of assessment. Selected rating scales to use for identifying AD/HD may be found in Table 5.4.

Psychoeducational Tests.   Since a vast majority of students with AD/HD also experience difficulties in learning, tests that measure academic strengths and weaknesses are useful assessment measures. These may include the *Wechsler Intelligence Scale for Children—Revised* (WISC-R), the *Wechsler Preschool and Primary Scale of Intelligence* (WPPSI-R), and the *Wechsler Adult Intelligence Scale—Revised* (WAIS-R). These tests have subtests that measure a "Freedom from Distractibility" factor. The *Woodcock Johnson Psychoeducational Battery—Revised* and the *Kaufman Test of Educational Achievement* (K-TEA) assess multiple areas of functioning (Connecticut Department of Education, 1993).

Social Skills Assessment.   Social interactions are extremely important for all individuals. However, students with AD/HD often have great deficits in the areas of school-related social skills, school relations, and peer-to-peer social skills. Numerous checklists are available to assist in assessing specific social skill deficit areas. A list of social skills checklists is presented in Table 5.5.

Table 5.5　**Social Skills Checklists for Assessing AD/HD**

School Social Skills
L. Brown, D. Black, & J. Downs
Slosson Educational Publications
P.O. Box 280
East Aurora, NY 14052

Social Skills Rating System (SSRS)
F. Gresham & S. Elliot
American Guidance Services
Publisher's Building
P.O. Box 99
Circle Pines, MN 55014-1796

Walker-McConnell Scale of Social Competence and Social Maladjustment
PRO-ED Publishing Co.
8700 Shoal Creek Boulevard
Austin, TX 78757-6897

Source: Data from *The Utah Attention Deficit Disorder Guide* (p. 22), published in 1992 by the Utah State Office of Education, Salt Lake City, UT.

INNOVATIVE IDEAS

A SCHOOL TO FILL THE GAP

What happens when the public school cannot provide what you feel is an appropriate education for your child, and private schools refuse to accept your child? Dr. Dennis Garvin, a neurologist with no experience in education, discovered the answer: He established a school to meet the unique needs of children who fall "between the cracks" of the educational system, children who are not mentally retarded or emotionally disturbed, who are not classified as "bright" students with dyslexia or other learning disabilities—but rather, students with average to slightly less than average potential who nonetheless have special needs.

With strong faith, extreme love for children, and enormous energy, Dr. Garvin launched the Northstar Academy, a day school that enrolls students from the Richmond, Virginia, area who share a common background of difficulties in academics. Many of these children also have difficulties with peer relationships; they may have language disorders and/or attention deficits. These students often do not qualify for traditional special education programs, or if they are in such a program they are achieving inconsistently.

Seeking private corporate funding and the donation of a daytime facility from a local church, and starting with a few creative teachers who wanted the freedom to teach children using a developmentally appropriate reality-based curriculum, Dr. Garvin began putting into place the ingredients necessary for his school. Northstar's curriculum was developed by experts who have worked with nontraditional learners and have studied the curricula of successful private schools. It was designed to provide individual and small group instruction, allowing for each student's individual learning preferences and style.

Grade levels are eliminated and the student population is divided into "constellations" according to chronological age (I: ages 7–9, II: ages 10–12, III: ages 13–15, etc.). There are no more than 10 students in each constellation. Other features of the school include a curriculum centered around thematic units; emphasis on cooperative learning, problem solving, and critical thinking; and the enhancement of self-esteem by emphasizing independent functioning.

Small classes, devoted teachers, community volunteers, support from local businesses, and a father's vision turned a dream into reality. At the Northstar Academy, children with diverse needs not being met by other educational facilities can find love, success, and hope.

Peer Assessment.   Peers are quick to assess one another. This holds true for students with AD/HD and for their classmates without the disorder. Schaughency and Rothlind (1991) found that peers are able to help in the identification of AD/HD since they can identify social problems and attentional deficits. The negative behaviors frequently associated with AD/HD can be pinpointed from peers as well.

Portfolio Evaluation.   An excellent source for tracking academic progress is the portfolio evaluation file. Samples of the student's work may be collected over time and filed for parents, teachers, and the student to see the progress being made. The portfolio method is an excellent vehicle for student self-monitoring.

TREATMENT AND INTERVENTION CONSIDERATIONS FOR AD/HD

AD/HD is not just a school problem but a problem for parents, siblings, physicians, and the child (Fowler, 1991). A total management approach or multimodal treatment is recommended for the treatment of AD/HD, including the following areas: (1) knowledge of the disorder and its effects on the child, home, school, and peers; (2) medication; (3) educational intervention; and (4) behavior management (Fowler, 1992; Lerner & Lowenthal, 1992). In addition, family training and counseling is also recommended.

Knowledge of the Disorder

Knowledge is power. Just as in sports: The best defense is a good offense. Parents, physicians, educators, siblings, and the child with AD/HD need information on the disorder and how it affects the total environment. Parents must learn that AD/HD is not their fault. It is no one's fault. Parents need information in order to work effectively with the school, child, and family as a whole. Physicians will identify the problem of AD/HD more readily when they are also educated in the characteristics manifested in children with AD/HD. Knowing appropriate resources and guiding the family to these resources is of extreme importance. Since AD/HD can be noticed at birth or soon after, the child's physician can be of tremendous help during the first few years prior to the beginning of school.

It is imperative that educators have the necessary knowledge for appropriate identification of AD/HD and strategies for implementing appropriate educational plans. Siblings, through an understanding of the disorder, learn how to live in better harmony with a brother or sister with AD/HD. Of the greatest importance, the child with AD/HD needs an arsenal of information on the disability and self-coping strategies. Learning that AD/HD is "not their fault" can bring great relief and reduce the anxiety level for students.

Medication

"I have looked through an out-of-focus camera my whole life . . . now my world is in focus." These words were spoken by an articulate student describing the effects of medication taken for AD/HD. Instead of focusing on everything at once, with medication the focus can be zeroed in on one or two things and the remaining stimuli filtered out. Even though it is a controversial treatment, medication is the most widely used intervention for children and youth with AD/HD. Approximately

60% to 90% of individuals diagnosed with AD/HD will be placed on a medication program (U.S. Department of Education, 1994). An improvement in students with AD/HD is shown in 70% to 80% of students if they are given appropriate doses of stimulants (Barkley, 1990). However, Gadow (1992) warns that while stimulant medication may help students focus on tasks, it does not "cure" the disability. The three medications most often used are Ritalin, Dexedrine, and Cylert. One of these may work better with one child than another.

Professionals who administer medications at school to students who have AD/HD must be sure to follow the dosage schedule and maintain confidentiality of the student. Most often the school nurse keeps all medications in the clinic and the student goes to the clinic for administration of medication. The dosage may need to be modified when the student reaches adolescence. For an excellent review of the literature on the effects of stimulant medication on children with AD/HD, see Swanson, McBurnett, and Wigal (1994).

Educational Interventions

Students with AD/HD, if identified and served under IDEA or Section 504, are entitled to an Individualized Educational Program (IEP). This mandate was an important educational step for these individuals.

Wood (1992) presents the SAALE (A Systematic Approach for Adapting the Learning Environment) model, which provides a three-prong approach for planning and teaching all at-risk students including those with AD/HD. The model, visually presented in Figure 5.1, provides a framework for (1) breaking down the school day into manageable environments, (2) helping educators organize all of the strategies learned for teaching at-risk students, and (3) finding the specific "mismatch" between the student and his or her environment. The model and accompanying intervention checklist are designed to assist the educator in becoming "intervention mismatch specific." The model helps to identify specific areas for intervention to be included in the IEP.

Specific skill area modifications in the areas of reading, math, and written language may be helpful in intervening academically with students with AD/HD. Before considering academic modifications, the overall stress level should be monitored. If the educational tasks are not on the instructional level of the student, frustration closely follows. Stress levels must be reduced and one of the best ways to reduce stress is to teach at the student's instructional levels. Following are some proven effective management strategies for the specific characteristics of AD/HD—inattention, hyperactivity, impulsivity, disorganization, and distractibility.

Managing Inattentiveness.   Inattentiveness may occur at home, school, or work. At home tasks are left unfinished and directions missed. In school, assignments are incomplete or homework is left at home; materials and texts necessary for class are left in the locker; directions are missed and assignments for the next day are not recorded. Actually, unless assisted, students with AD/HD probably will not even use an assignment pad. On the job, important details of the job are overlooked, projects left unfinished, and mistakes made. Strategies that are helpful in working with inattentive individuals (Braukman) include these:

1. Give directions slowly, one at a time. Have the child repeat the instructions.

2. Give "alerting" messages such as "Look here" or "Everyone listen."

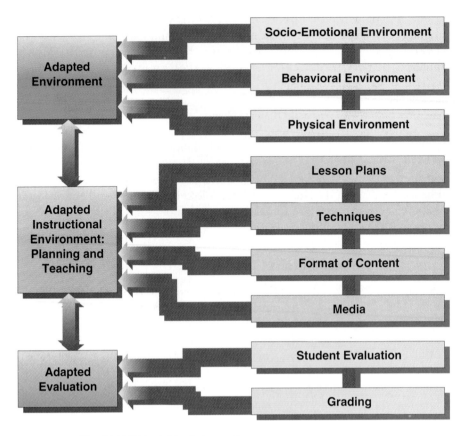

Figure 5.1   **The SAALE Model for Intervention**

Source: From *Adapting Instruction for Mainstream and At-Risk Students* (p. 2), by J. W. Wood, 1995, Columbus, OH: Merrill.

3. Use eye contact and proximity control:

   • Touch the child gently, and give instruction to the eyes, not the back of the head or the ears.

   • If the child is not attending, stop talking until eye contact is reestablished.

4. Use a prearranged signal to regain the child's attention.

5. Appeal to visual and tactile learning channels:

   • Write instructions, schedules, assignments, and so forth.

   • Encourage active participation, not passive listening.

   • Minimize words and maximize actions when giving instructions.

6. Use a timer to encourage longer periods of focused attention and reward frequently.

7. Structure tasks to enhance attention:

   • Divide assignments into small parts.

   • Cut out a "window" that isolates one problem at a time.

   • Pace the work: 12 five-minute assignments are more effective than 2 half-hour assignments.

A checklist or chart provides the child who has AD/HD with a tangible method for recording progress and planning new goals.

- Vary the work frequently: Eliminate the child's focus on the inability to sustain effort.

8. Reward systematically:

  - Positively reinforce on-task behavior.
  - Positively reinforce effort: Reward after completion of each part of a command or task.
  - Give non-attention to off-task behavior by attending to the appropriate on-task behavior of classmates.
  - Set predictable intervals of "no-work" periods as rewards that can be earned for effort.
  - Use a system of checkmarks or some other visible, tangible method whereby the child can directly measure his or her own success. .

View the length of attention as a level of skill development. Determine the child's current length of attention and proceed toward a terminal objective. The child's tolerance should increase little by little (Braukman).

Managing Hyperactivity. The inability to remain still—including fidgeting, squirming, running, or climbing excessively—is seen in approximately 50% of students with AD/HD. Hyperactivity appears to diminish as the student progresses throughout the school years. Effective strategies for working with students with attention deficit with hyperactivity (Braukman) include the following:

1. Accept a higher level of activity from these students.

2. Observe the students and identify conditions that appear to trigger hyperactive behavior. Avoid as many as possible.

3. Provide appropriate times to burn up energy in vigorous activities.

4. Allow work to be done standing up or at the chalkboard.

5. Teach alphabet, math, and other activities while students that are hyperactive bounce a ball or swing one leg.

6. Have a rocking chair in the room for reading and other activities.

7. Teach counting, days of the week, and other sequenced lessons while climbing stairs or having the students do push-ups.

8. Take daily field trips within the school or around the school grounds for lessons such as teaching listening skills, nature and science, or finding parts of speech (such as verbs or nouns, etc.).

9. Channel annoying behavior into more acceptable behavior. For instance, ask a student not to tap the desk with a pencil but instead to tap fingertips together, or tap an eraser or a sponge.

10. Use coupons for allowing students to go to the restroom, pencil sharpener, and so forth, so they begin to think and plan before engaging in random movement.

11. Set a timer for 5 minutes. Reward students if they stay in their seat and/or work for that time. Increase time gradually.

12. Alternate sitting and moving activities. Divide tasks into small parts and reward completion of each part.

13. If students roam the room, reward them when they stay near their desk; then reward if they stay within arm's length of the desk, then touching the seat, and so on, using successive approximations.

14. Prepare these students for unusual events immediately before their occurrence. Discuss exactly what will happen, how to behave, where to stand, and

Students with AD/HD can be very successful with the one-on-one interaction provided by a computer.

when to talk. Practice some behaviors with walk-throughs and talk-throughs.

15. Provide a sanctuary where students can work away from distractions.

16. Avoid team games. Individual or pair games and activities will reduce excitability.

17. Use tactile and kinesthetic activities such as air writing, forming clay letters, and use of tactile boards.

18. Avoid activities with a time deadline.

Managing Impulsivity.   Problems with impulsivity, unlike hyperactivity, tend to persist as the student with AD/HD grows older. This impulsive behavior continues even into adulthood. The student reacts suddenly to an event without considering the consequences of the act. Effective strategies to use with impulsive students (Braukman) include these:

1. Use time-out for punishment. When impulsive students become upset, remove them from the situation. Don't expect them to "shape up" or "calm down" while they are upset.

2. Notice and reward appropriate behavior. Find activities these children can succeed at.

3. Establish rules by priority (safety first, most annoying acts next, etc.) and hold to them consistently. You will probably need to discuss problems of these students with classmates.

4. Use rewards such as smiles, pats, stars, and free time frequently.

5. Use behavior checklists, contracting, and other behavior management controls. Involve these children in their own improvement.

6. Establish routine schedules for the day and for the activities within the day.

7. Don't let impulsive students interrupt. Have them wait a brief time before you give permission to speak.

8. Work on consistent home–school management programs.

9. Use visual cues such as a sign on the desk that says "Think Before You Act."

10. Think through the worst-case scenario before taking field trips. Plan ahead to prevent behavior problems before they happen.

11. Intersperse known tasks with unknown or new tasks to reduce frustration.

12. Develop signals to let students know where to begin and where to stop.

13. Establish routines for taking role, collecting papers, and other routine activities—and stick to them.

14. Handle inappropriate behavior promptly. Deal with it calmly, quickly, and consistently.

15. When impulsive students try to argue, become a broken record, calmly repeating your original request until they stop talking back.

A physical reminder, such as a hand on the shoulder, can redirect a child from misbehavior.

Managing Disorganization.   Organization requires a student to bring objects and/or ideas into a logical sequence in order to reach a specific goal. Organizing information and objects is a difficult task for many students. They cannot decide where, when, or with which part to begin. Lost work, messy rooms, incomplete assignments—all become common occurrences. Strategies for assisting with organizational problems (Braukman) include the following:

1. Use faint line graph paper for arithmetic computation problems or use dark line graph paper under regular sheet for writing to help keep numbers in correct order.

2. Have students leave every other line blank when writing.

3. Have a sample organized page laminated for these students to keep on their desk—including heading, date, name, column, and sample paragraph form. On the back list criteria: no single letters or numbers touching each other, all letters and numbers on the line, and so on.

4. Mark off paper for arithmetic problems into squares or rectangles. Each problem goes into its own box. Fade boxes.

5. Establish firm rules, consistently adhered to with consequences understood. Avoid subtleties and innuendoes.

6. Structure daily schedule, length of task; provide routines.

7. Reduce choices in instructional tasks; avoid open-ended assignments.

8. Provide opportunities for choice in noninstructional situations.

9. Provide comparing, categorizing, sorting of information.

10. Provide concrete assignments and monitor progress.

11. Set specific objectives for and with disorganized students; divide longer tasks into sub-objectives; assign priorities.

12. Phonetic reading programs may be less useful with these children. Total language arts approaches that organize spelling/writing/reading/listening into a whole are more appropriate.

13. Avoid complicated systems to be followed for an assignment.

14. Break down directions into short parts, giving only one part at a time.

15. Keep the environment free of distracting stimuli.

16. Keep the emotional climate calm.

17. Watch for signs of "early" frustration. Break up lengthy tasks by giving something else, not similar, to complete.

18. It is only after you have established the controls that these students can later accept self-control. Self-control can take place only after they have performed the behavior many times under your control.

19. Do not postpone reinforcement or grades. Remember, these students have a basically impulsive nature. They find it difficult to wait until the end of the month to get a mark for their work.

20. Explain and give directions in simple terms. Once you have given an explanation or direction, don't change your wording when you repeat it. Merely repeat your remarks slowly.

21. Develop a standard outline. Avoid timed tests.

22. Expect to see day-to-day (or even minute-to-minute) fluctuations in performance.

23. The speed of thought processing (reception, integration, and expressive elements) is vastly different with these students. You should be aware of this and make necessary allowances by speaking slowly, in thought units, and checking comprehension.

Managing Distractibility. Distractibility refers to the lack of ability to focus on one significant stimulus. Students who are distracted focus on all stimuli so attention is distributed instead of focused. Strategies helpful with students who are distractible (Braukman) include these:

1. Organize the workspace to reduce distractions:

    • Keep everything off the desk that is not needed for the task.
    • Use a brightly colored blotter for background.
    • Place these children where there are the fewest distractions (in the front row, away from windows, etc.).

2. Allow the use of headphones, ear plugs, or cotton in the ears to reduce auditory distractions.

3. Use worksheets with black or green print if blue causes figure–ground confusion.

4. Keep the physical arrangement of the room as constant as possible. Frequent changes in the location of desks and materials create distracting stimuli.

5. Minimize schedule changes:

Using headphones helps this girl to avoid the distraction of her chatting neighbors.

- Prepare lists of the daily and weekly schedule, which are kept at each child's desk.
- Assign a "buddy" to help these students with unplanned situations such as a fire drill.
- Physically orient these children in their space: Use partitions, carrels, and "offices" that you offer in a positive way without negative associations.

6. Prepare these students for transitions:

- Use a prearranged signal or "stop sign" to alert them to clean up, turn in work, and so forth.
- Allow plenty of time to get organized: Rushing creates multiple distractions.
- Provide advance warning of any schedule changes.

7. Reward systematically; praise persistence.

Behavior Management Techniques

The fourth component in treatment/interventions for students with AD/HD is behavior management. Lerner and Lowenthal (1992), discuss techniques that may be used with all students and specifically those with AD/HD.

Contingent reinforcement is based on the principle that a behavior can be either weakened or strengthened depending on the consequence that immediately

Chapter 6

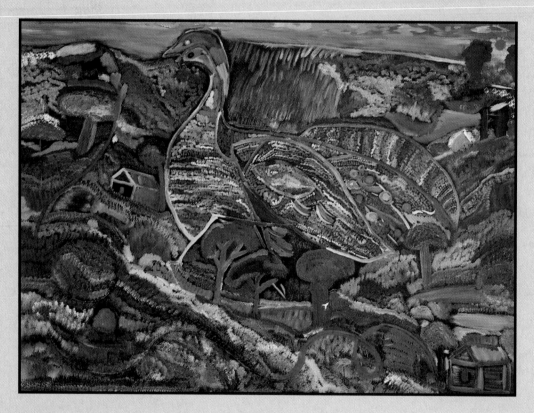

Sea Duck, acrylic on canvas, 60″ × 82″ (1992)

EMOTIONAL AND BEHAVIORAL DISORDERS

GEORGE SUGAI AND TIMOTHY J. LEWIS

After studying this chapter, the reader will:

Know the strengths and weaknesses of the terminology and
definitions used to characterize students with
emotional and behavioral disorders

Be familiar with the educational and behavioral characteristics
and prevalence rates of students with emotional
and behavioral disorders

Identify the historical themes that characterize how Western
societies have identified, defined, and responded to
individuals with deviant behavior

Be able to outline the special education provisions, regulations, and
protections that have been established for students who have been
identified as having emotional and behavioral disorders

Be able to describe the preferred assessment and evaluation
practices used with students who display emotional
and behavioral disorders

Be able to describe the preferred educational practices used with
students who display emotional and behavioral disorders

Recognize the challenges and unanswered questions associated
with educating students who have emotional
and behavioral disorders

EMOTIONAL AND BEHAVIORAL DISORDERS

2000 B.C.   First written accounts of persons with EBD were recorded in Egypt.

1547   St. Mary's of Bethlehem Asylum (later widely known as "Bedlam") was founded in London to house persons with EBD.

1728   Daniel Defoe wrote of deplorable conditions in asylums, which prompted England's Parliament to pass an act regulating "madhouses" and gave rise to the moral treatment movement.

Early 1800s   Benjamin Rush established Pennsylvania Hospital (first in the United States) to "restore the mentally ill back to work." Harsh treatments such as straitjackets, rotator chairs, and food deprivation were used to "calm" patients.

1840s   Dorothea Dix created 30 new hospitals in the United States and reformed mental health care in Europe. Focus began to shift from "cure" to humane treatment.

1894   Juvenile court systems were established in Chicago and Denver.

1920s   Cases of post–World War I "shell shock" (psychoneurosis) shifted the mental health focus from organic to psychological factors.

1946   New York opened the 600 School for disturbed youth; Redl and Wineman established Pioneer House in Detroit for delinquent and disturbed youth.

1964   The Council for Children With Behavior Disorders was founded.

1967   Frank Hewitt developed the "engineered classroom" for children with EBD.

1987   The National Mental Health and Special Education Coalition was formed to rewrite the federal definition of SED.

1990   New EBD definition proposed by the Mental Health and Special Education Coalition.

1994   Office of Special Education Programs, U.S. Department establishes a national agenda for improving the outcomes of children and youth with EBD and their families.

INTRODUCTION

This chapter is about children and youth with emotional and behavioral disorders and the teachers who work with them. These students in our schools are recognized as being different from their peers because of things that they say and do. In fact, these children and youth are so different that they are "marked" as emotionally disturbed, behaviorally disordered, emotionally disabled, socially maladjusted, and a variety of other terms that help us characterize their unique profiles. This chapter is about a disabling condition in special education that traditionally has been called **seriously emotionally disturbed (SED)**. We prefer the term **emotional and behavioral disorder (EBD)**, and we will refer to the children and youth to whom we give this label as *children and youth with emotional and behavioral disorders*.

The EBD field is exciting, challenging, and ever changing. Other disabling conditions have more clearly distinguishable features that are physical (e.g., orthopedic impairment), sensory (e.g., speech or language impairment, visual impairment, hearing impairment), cognitive (e.g., mental retardation, autism), or learning (e.g., specific learning disabilities) in nature. The purpose of this chapter is to provide a foundational framework for understanding what special education for students with EBD looks like and what we currently know about educating students with EBD.

For ease of presentation, the chapter is divided into eight overlapping sections that present a historical overview, the definition, characteristics of EBD, its prevalence, its causes, assessment and evaluation criteria, instructional considerations, family perspectives, and current issues and future trends. Although the content in each of these sections provides a general overview, we focus on two primary kinds of educational practices: preferred practices that have been investigated systematically (research), and promising practices that are untested but have been applied in the field and show potential (Peters & Heron, 1993).

HISTORICAL OVERVIEW

P.L. 94-142 (the Education for All Handicapped Children Act of 1975) revolutionized how the public schools conceptualized students whose social behaviors were determined by educators and families as being markedly different from their peers' behaviors or seriously in violation of social norms of acceptable behavior. After 1975, as mentioned in Chapter 1 and elsewhere in this text, students with EBD were formally identified as having a disability that interfered with their opportunities to succeed in the public schools without specially designed instruction. However, it is important to remember that emotional disturbance is not just a 20th-century educational phenomenon. Written references to persons with EBD can be traced back as far as 2000 B.C. The following section provides a Western chronology of the historical events that have shaped present-day views of emotional and behavioral disorders.

Early History (2000 B.C.–300 A.D.)

Prior to written records, deviant behavior was hypothesized as being caused by evil spirits that possessed the human body. Written records of the first communities found in Egypt around 2000 B.C. also point to a strong belief in spiritual causation of aberrant behavior.

REAL PEOPLE   Tracy and Scott

Tracy describes herself as "one of the lucky ones who got out." During much of her adolescent years she attended school within the confines of a state youth detention center. Growing up, she was described as "incorrigible," routinely breaking school, family, and societal rules. "I used to break into cars and houses, steal small stuff mostly for money for drugs and alcohol," she says. During middle and high school, Tracy says she was easily frustrated with school. "It was a lot easier to raise hell and get kicked out or cut school altogether than struggle through my classes." In school, Tracy often broke school rules—such as those prohibiting smoking and fighting—and was typically noncompliant with teacher directions, often engaging adults in heated arguments. Unfortunately, Tracy was not entitled to receive special education since she attended school prior to the passage of P.L. 94–142. "Some of my teachers would try to work with me, but they typically became as frustrated as I was and passed me along just to get rid of me. My parents also had a hard time with me. My friends and I would sneak out late at night to steal, get high, or just cause trouble, like breaking windows." Why is Tracy now a graduate student studying special education? "When I was locked up, one of my friends was raped and beaten to death. I decided then that this wasn't the life for me." Through a combination of specialized tutoring, counseling, and learning to stay within family rules, Tracy was able to earn her G.E.D. and continue her education at the state university. Tracy is now working on a graduate degree with the aspiration to work with students who have emotional and behavioral disorders. "It's interesting," she reflects, "once I did my time and started cleaning up my act, no one I met at college ever knew that I was once a student with a behavioral disorder."

Scott is currently working at a fast-food restaurant. His earlier life as a student is decidedly different from Tracy's. "I was the kid nobody knew was there. I sat in the back, never talked, avoided the cafeteria, and stayed to myself as much as possible." During elementary school Scott showed difficulties in math, was tested, and was found eligible for special education under the learning disabilities category. However, during middle school, his learning problems worsened. "I was having a real hard time with lots of my classes and I learned real early, with so many students, if you just lay low the teachers won't bother you." Scott also started having difficulty with his peers. "In grade school, I had a few friends, but once I reached middle school, I just didn't seem to get along with anyone, especially girls." During his triennial reevaluation, the multidisciplinary team determined that Scott had a secondary disability, "seriously emotionally disturbed." Scott received social skills instruction in the resource room and saw a counselor twice a month. "I liked going to social skills class and doing the role plays. I learned to make a few new friends." How is he doing now? "Okay," he replies, and shrugs his shoulders. "I still have a hard time sometimes talking with people. I still have a hard time with math, but I can read okay." And the future? "I don't know. I like working here, but my parents want me to go to the junior college and study for a better job. I'm not sure if I'll do it or not."

Around the 7th century B.C., Greece rose to the forefront of Western civilization. At this time, somatic (i.e., physical) explanations for deviant behavior emerged in the writings of Hippocrates, who postulated that aberrant behavior was caused by imbalances within the body's systems. Exercise, diet, and massage treatments were used to restore a healthy balance between mind and body. Although they did not write directly to the causes of emotional and behavioral problems, the Greek philosophers (Socrates, Plato, and Aristotle) had a profound and lasting effect on how we view, discuss, understand, and respond to human behavior. For example, Socrates was one of the first to use science and logic as tools to examine and acquire knowledge about human behavior. Plato added to our understanding by hypothesizing that man was controlled by desires, emotions, reasons, and experiences.

Middle Ages (300–1600)

Following the decline of Greek civilization, history entered the Dark Ages, often characterized by the increased power held by the church to influence the political and social character of the time. Spiritual explanations replaced the mental or sensory process interpretations of Greek philosophical query into the "truth" of man's existence. But now, unlike previous spiritual explanations involving multiple gods, only one God was said to exist and to give man divine insight into truth. Those who failed to gain truth or attempted to gain truth through revelation were thought to be influenced by God's counterpart, the devil.

During the earlier periods of the Middle Ages, monks continued many of the Greek somatic treatments. Children who displayed aberrant behavior were viewed as special because they were thought to be communicating with God. Because their abnormal behavior was believed to be evidence of being touched by God, they received relatively humane treatment. However, benevolent understanding and treatment were replaced with fear, harassment, and ultimately torture as explanations shifted to devil possession. By the high Middle Ages, "reason" was replaced by church dogma, and persons who did not behave as "Christians" were perceived to be possessed by the devil.

Scientific Revolution and the Age of Reason (1600–1700)

As the nations of Europe grew, the reformation movement continued, especially in the colonies of America. The scientific community, however, began to mount stronger opposition to spiritual explanations of deviant behavior. During the 17th century two important trends emerged in the area of EBD. The first was a shift away from explanations that emphasized imbalances of body systems and toward interpretations that focused on diseases as the cause of deviant behavior. The second was the development of a classification system of abnormal behavior, the *Praxis Medica*, that was based on "reason" or rational versus irrational thought. These two trends set the stage for modern psychological explanations of normal and abnormal behavior. Treatment of choice during this period became hospitalization in asylums.

The 18th and 19th Centuries

During the Enlightenment in the 18th century, empiricism replaced rationalism as the primary method of inquiry. Philosophers such as Hume and Kant laid the foundation for modern scientific inquiry into the nature of aberrant behavior. For the first time, deviancy was viewed as a proper subject for objective medical investigation, and the first university-based medical research was conducted in cities such as Edinburgh and Vienna. Behavioral deviance was now believed to be caused by disease, and medical intervention became the treatment of choice.

During the first half of the 19th century, the medical model continued to develop, and physicians postulated that all abnormal behavior was due to organic causes. Unfortunately, immediate cures were not evident, and persons who displayed abnormal behavior typically continued to be warehoused in asylums where the newly conceived medical "cures" remained harsh. For example, in efforts to calm patients, Benjamin Rush, who is considered the father of American psychology, used rotator chairs to spin patients ("curing" the illness by increasing blood supply to the brain), in addition to straitjackets, food deprivation, and immersion in cold water.

Using torture as a cure: the Fool's Tower, Vienna.

In response to the harsh conditions found in most U.S. asylums in the mid-1800s, Dorothea Dix helped create 30 new hospitals to provide a humane place for, in her words, "helpless incurables." During this time and in spite of Dix's pessimistic view of incurability, educational programs began to emerge within institutions with a treatment focus on self-help and daily living skills.

Although Darwin's theory of evolution pushed the scientific community into the next century, the outcome of "social Darwinism" had the opposite effect on persons with EBD. Since behavior was argued to be genetically predetermined, no cure was possible for aberrant behavior. Proponents of this position called for the end of any government support that might be used for persons who were "genetically inferior." During the late 19th century, Charles Davenport lobbied for and helped several states pass sterilization laws for persons who engaged in "anti-social" acts. Known as *eugenics*, this philosophy led many to extreme solutions to preventing the transmission of disturbed behavior.

The 20th Century

The 20th century is marked by the development and refinement of somatic and psychological explanations and treatment of behavior. Freud's notion that behavior was controlled by unconscious mental processes brought renewed interest in psychological explanations of behavior. As a result of Freud's work and other 19th-century psychologists and physicians, three major psychological paradigms—

psychoeducational, ecological, and behavioral—emerged during the 20th century as explanations for aberrant behavior and became the foundation for the treatment of disturbed behavior. These paradigms are significant because of the direct impact they have had on the nature of education and treatment of children with EBD. A more detailed analysis will be presented in the sections discussing characteristics and causes, later in this chapter.

The 20th century also is marked by medical advances and the disease model of aberrant behavior. For example, in 1913 Noguchi and Moore located the site in the brain that is attacked by the syphilis spirochete. In 1938 Cerletti and Bini used electroshock therapy to "realign" the central nervous system and to "cure" schizophrenia. In 1935, Moniz performed the first lobotomy to break the neurological cycle of "morbid ideas." At the same time, the use of pharmacological treatments to treat abnormal behavior increased.

In another important development at the turn of the century, the establishment of juvenile courts and mandatory school attendance laws created a separate focus on the treatment of children and adolescents. During the second half of the century, child-specific educational interventions emerged as the field began to establish itself as a separate entity from medicine and psychology. For example, schools and programs were established specifically to educate children and youth with EBD—such as Carl Fenichel's League School in 1953 and Nicholas Hobb's Project Re-ED in 1960. In 1964, the Council for Children with Behavior Disorders (CCBD) became the first educationally focused professional organization in the field.

DEFINITION OF EBD

In the 1990s, philosophical, educational, medical, and psychological debates regarding the nature of deviance continue. In this section, we narrow our focus to the educational context and describe how EBD is defined.

Students with EBD look like any other students in school. In fact it is difficult, if not impossible, to look at a class picture or a yearbook and identify a student

Without the evidence of inappropriate behavior, it is difficult to identify who is labeled as having an emotional or behavioral disorder.

who is labeled as having EBD. The feature that sets students with EBD apart from other students, however, is the display of externalizing (e.g., acting out) and internalizing (e.g., social withdrawal) behaviors that are chronic, severe, and disturbing to the school community, are particularly resistant to standard or typical classroom and behavior management practices, and interfere with the student's educational performance. Like Tracy and Scott, the students portrayed at the beginning of this chapter, these students tend to display behaviors that extend beyond the acceptable social norms of the classroom and require highly specialized, individualized, and intensive interventions to succeed in school. More significantly, students with EBD fail to benefit from typical classroom opportunities and from their overall school experience.

Although it can seem relatively simple to identify students with EBD and to say that they behave in ways that are significantly different from their larger peer group, attempts to develop a functional definition of EBD have been largely unsuccessful and controversial. Before 1975 when Congress enacted P.L. 94-142, EBD identification formally did not exist. Before P.L. 94-142, these students were characterized as "incorrigible," "in need of supervision," "mentally ill," "delinquent," or were labeled with a variety of other psychiatric or sociologic terms, and educational identifiers and programs were typically not developed or required by law.

Federal Definition

When the need to provide educational safeguards for students with EBD became apparent, the authors of P.L. 94-142 needed a definition that would help educators to discriminate students with EBD from the rest of the student population. The definition used by Eli Bower (1981) to screen for students with emotional disabilities was modified and adopted. The current federal definition of "serious emotional disturbance" is as follows:

> (i) The term means a condition exhibiting one or more of the following characteristics over a long period of time and to a marked degree, which adversely affects educational performance:
> (A) An inability to learn which cannot be explained by intellectual, sensory, or health factors;
> (B) An inability to build or maintain satisfactory interpersonal relationships with peers and teachers;
> (C) Inappropriate types of behavior or feelings under normal circumstances;
> (D) A general pervasive mood of unhappiness or depression; or
> (E) A tendency to develop physical symptoms or fears associated with personal or school problems.
> (ii) The term includes children who are schizophrenic. The term does not include children who are socially maladjusted, unless it is determined that they are seriously emotionally disturbed.

When the federal government adopted the Bower definition, four changes were made in the wording: (1) "emotionally handicapped" was replaced by "seriously emotionally disturbed," (2) "which adversely affects educational performance" was added, (3) "children who are schizophrenic" was included, and (4) "children who are socially maladjusted, unless it is determined that they are seriously emotionally disturbed" was added as an exclusionary provision.

Although the current SED definition represents a reasonable effort to delineate who should and should not receive special education services, the definition generally has been viewed as inadequate. For example, the SED terminology and the definition tend to be stigmatizing, overly focused on intrapsychic disturbances, excessively focused on the most severe problems, biased toward noneducational-based interventions, and unclear about the distinction between social maladjust-ment (especially conduct disorders) and SED. Bower himself (1982) has indicated that the current definition is flawed because his original definition was medically/clinically based (i.e., disability perspective) and is now being applied to a school context (i.e., deviance perspective). This criticism of the federal definition has been echoed by many in the field (e.g., Bower, 1982; Council for Children With Behavioral Disorders, 1987; Forness & Knitzer, 1990; Kauffman, 1993; Knitzer, Steinberg, & Fleisch, 1990; Walker & Fabre, 1987).

Proposed Definition

A promising step forward was initiated in the late 1980s when the National Mental Health and Special Education Coalition was formed to consider and develop a new terminology and definition to replace SED (Forness & Knitzer, 1990, 1992). Initial efforts by the coalition were approved by the 1991 Council for Exceptional Chil-dren delegate assembly, and subsequently were revised into a form that is being considered in reauthorization of the Individuals With Disabilities Education Act (IDEA). The proposed definition is as follows:

(i) The term "emotional or behavioral disorder" means a disability characterized by behavioral or emotional responses in school programs so different from ap-propriate age, cultural, or ethnic norms that they adversely affect educational performance, including academic, social, vocational or personal skills. Such a disability

   (A) is more than a temporary, expected response to stressful events in the envi-ronment;

   (B) is exhibited in two different settings, at least one of which is school-related; and

   (C) is unresponsive to direct intervention applied in the general education set-ting or the child's condition is such that general education intervention would be insufficient.

(ii) Emotional or behavioral disorders can co-exist with other disabilities.

(iii) This category may include children or youth with schizophrenic disorders, af-fective disorders, anxiety disorders or other sustained disorders of conduct or adjustment when they adversely affect educational performance in accordance with section (i). (Forness & Knitzer, 1990, 1992)

Although still vulnerable to disciplinary debates, the new revised definition offers greater clarity and specificity, with fewer redundancies. For example, propo-nents (e.g., Forness & Knitzer, 1990, 1992; Kauffman, 1993) argue that this new terminology and definition reduces the disciplinary distinction associated with "emotional" and "behavioral" disturbance; increases the school and educational focus; increases specificity regarding number of settings and behavioral transience; acknowledges the impact of age, cultural, and ethnic differences; stresses the unre-sponsiveness to general education direct interventions; acknowledges the possibil-ity that EBD might overlap with other disabilities; and includes consideration of psychopathologically defined disorders.

CHARACTERISTICS OF EBD

Regardless of the definition that is applied, all students have a range of behavioral characteristics, both strengths and weaknesses. Whether a student is or should be labeled as having EBD is often a function of a multitude of contextual and cultural factors. Consider the following:

> A young man decorates his face with paint, and dances around a neatly organized pile of broken stones and twigs, his head bobbing in a slow jerking motion. As others approach him, he quickly steps aside and raises his arm over his head. He utters unintelligible remarks, and repeats sounds in a ritualistic manner.

Are these behaviors acceptable or unacceptable? Is this a person with EBD? What society would view these actions as "normal"? Our view of whether the young man's behavior is normal or acceptable would vary depending on whether he is an Aboriginal leader from Western Australia who is dancing the life of the emu, a homeless youth performing on a street corner in Seattle, the shaman from a native tribe in western Brazil purifying the ground for the spring planting season, a junior high school student who has ingested a psychotropic substance, or a youth playing in an isolated section of an elementary school playground. The point is that no single episode of behavior or particular characteristic equals an emotional and behavioral disorder. Rather, the amount, the outcome, and the context or culture within which behaviors occur must all be taken into consideration.

In addition, each of us develops his or her own way of characterizing students who are identified as having EBD based on our individual disciplinary biases and experiences. Three conceptual models for describing students with EBD are the most prevalent in the field (Cullinan, Epstein, & Lloyd, 1991). First, the **psychoeducational model** generally focuses on internal causation, past events, formal explanatory principles, and a wide range of interventions. Second, the **ecological model** generally emphasizes holistic views of causation (multiple factors) and intervention (multiple perspectives). Third, the **behavioral model** highlights causal explanations and formal principles, replicable and effective interventions, and a scientific approach.

Because of societal and disciplinary traditions, noneducational labels and characterizations are also common within the area of EBD. For instance, charac-

A behavior that is appropriate in one context (yelling at a sports event) may not be appropriate in another (yelling at a girl walking by).

Table 6.1   Common Mental Health Labels

LABEL	CHARACTERISTICS
Schizophrenia	Student displays behaviors that represent a split from reality (not multiple or dual personalities) such as incoherence in verbal responses, delusions, and hallucinations.
Conduct disorder	Student displays extreme noncompliance with societal and legal rules and norms.
Attention deficit hyperactivity disorder (AD/HD)	Student spends the majority of time off-task, poorly focused, with high rates of motor responses.

terizations that reflect the mental health (psychoeducational) approach to describing disturbing behavior frequently are heard or read in our society. A sample of the mental health labels and associated behavioral characteristics commonly associated with students with EBD are presented in Table 6.1. Although the characterizations in the table may be commonplace, widely accepted by certain disciplines, and useful to describe broad classes of behavior, they are limited in their applicability to educational environments. Criticisms of these characterizations include stigmatization, excessive blame placed on the student, reduced educator responsibility and accountability, limited empirical support, and limited usefulness in educational contexts.

Given these considerations, we prefer to describe students with EBD from an educational and behavioral perspective. We endorse this perspective for three major reasons. First, by law (IDEA) special education for students with EBD emphasizes specialized individual educational programming. Second, the behavioral approach focuses on what educators can see and manipulate within the context of the learning and teaching environment. Finally, the behavioral approach has more distinct, definable, and functional empirical support than the psychoeducational and ecological approaches (Cooper, Heron, & Heward, 1987; Epstein, Foley, & Cullinan, 1993; Kauffman, 1993; Kerr & Nelson, 1989; Kerr, Nelson, & Lambert, 1987; Knitzer et al., 1990; Ninness, Glenn, & Ellis, 1993; Peacock Hill Working Group, 1991; Wolery, Bailey, & Sugai, 1988).

In the following sections, we describe from an educational/behavioral perspective the kinds of behaviors students with EBD are likely to display and the correlates or risk factors that accompany these behaviors. It is important to remember that these behaviors, in and of themselves, do not equal an emotional and behavioral disorder, but rather the frequency and duration of these behaviors are significant enough to adversely affect educational performance and differentiate the student from his or her peers.

EBD Behaviors

Students with EBD display a wide range of behaviors that can be organized into three broad categories: normal, internalizing, and externalizing. It is important to remember that even students with the most challenging behavior patterns will display some behaviors at some times that can and should be viewed as socially acceptable. Similarly, many students who usually present ideal patterns of normal behaviors will display at some time behaviors that can and should be considered deviant. Issues of intensity, frequency, location, quality, and timing can cause a shift in judgment about a behavior from acceptable to unacceptable.

For example, David is talking quietly with Nicolas and Emilie. As the focus of the conversation continues, a disagreement about an earlier altercation surfaces. David's voice rises, profane words are uttered, Nicolas stands and moves toward David, and tables and chairs are pushed aside. In David's case these episodes occur once a day. Nicolas, however, rarely displays these behaviors, and Emilie always leaves the scene unnoticed. Behavior that was once acceptable has become unacceptable; behavior that is common for one student is rare in the other. These behaviors also are judged differently if they are observed in the library, in the classroom, on the bus, in the cafeteria, on the playground, or at home. The point is that what we label as normal or acceptable is relative to (1) place, time, and context, (2) features or dimensions of the behavior (i.e., rate, duration, latency, topography, locus, intensity), and (3) the labels previously assigned to the individual. Table 6.2 further illustrates the sample and range of behaviors that students with EBD display.

Social Skill Problems

As the current and proposed definitions of SED and EBD indicate, students with EBD typically have social interaction problems. Social skill problems may be between the student and his peers, teachers, or other adults. Social skill problems cover the range from verbal and physical aggression directed toward others to extreme social withdrawal with no verbal communication.

Social skill problems typically fall into one of two categories (Lewis, 1992; Lewis & Sugai, 1993). The first is a *social skill deficit*. As implied by the name, a student who displays a social skill deficit has failed to learn the skill. For example, when Laura needs help with a project, she yells and screams until the teacher assists her. Laura may not have learned that the rule in school when you want assistance is to raise your hand or ask a peer quietly. Intervention for this type of problem focuses on teaching the necessary skills, providing several opportunities to practice, and acknowledging appropriate displays of the skill.

The second and much more common type of social skill problem is a *performance problem* (Lewis, 1992). Students with performance social skill problems can display and describe the correct skill under some conditions (e.g., during instruction) but display inappropriate behavior in other conditions (i.e., in the natural setting). If we ask Laura to state the rule for getting help and conduct a role play, we might find that she can state the rule and can display it accurately in a role play. With performance problems the intervention must be preceded by functional assessment (discussed more fully later in the chapter) to discover why she displays the skills in some settings but not others. With this assessment information an intervention can be developed to increase the likelihood that Laura can get what she wants (e.g., assistance from others) by using the appropriate social skill rather than the inappropriate problem behavior.

Academic Performance

Given that students with EBD display high rates of inappropriate behavior, and by definition do not succeed in general education environments without specialized services, there are—not surprisingly—associated learning problems (Kauffman, 1993). According to Gottlieb, Alter, and Gottlieb (1991), up to 74% of students with EBD display some form of academic difficulty. The need for a carefully planned curriculum and predictable student success is obviously warranted. More discussion about academic interventions is provided later in this chapter.

Table 6.2   **Examples of Characteristics and Behaviors Displayed by Students With EBD**

	ACCEPTABLE	EBD EXTERNALIZING	EBD INTERNALIZING
Academic/Academic Related	Raises hand to speak in class during group instruction Cooperates with peers during small group projects; waits for turn Works independently on tasks Comes to class prepared and ready to learn Begins tasks on cue or independently Follows teacher directions Finds acceptable activity when done with work; uses free time appropriately Leads peer group in classroom tasks	Talks out, interrupts others, makes rude comments about peer responses; demands peer and adult attention or help Participates out of turn; bullies peers to get way; does not attend to comments of others Does not complete or return homework Comes to class unprepared to begin and complete work Talks back or openly ignores teacher directions Engages in or displays inappropriate sexual behaviors	Rarely contributes to class discussion; fails to respond to teacher or peer initiations Rarely volunteers; allows others to answer Comes late to class; frequently calls in ill Cries easily, runs away, or hides face when asked to answer in the presence of peers Is easily intimidated by peers and teachers
Social	Talks and jokes with peers in hallway between classes, before and after school, and during recess breaks Sits with peers and talks Accepts criticism and feedback from adults Follows school and classroom rules Manages conflicts and anger appropriately Problem-solves appropriately and without assistance Participates in appropriate games and sports Makes friends easily; is sensitive to the needs of others	Runs and bumps into peers in the hallway Throws objects; destroys property; is disrespectful of property of others; grabs property of others Handles anger and conflicts by verbal arguments, intimidation, and physical force Uses profane language Fails to follow school and classroom rules Leads peers to inappropriate acts Takes property of others without permission Does not tell the truth	Lingers in the classroom to avoid social contact Walks close to hallway walls; keeps head and eyes down; does not initiate or respond to social contacts by peers or adults Sits by self in classroom and lunchroom, or on the bus Cries easily when confronted by peers or adults Is easily influenced by others; follows others Uses excuses of physical illness to avoid social activities; has frequent physical illnesses and complaints Has poor sleep, eating, and self-care habits Plays alone; displays lack of interest Reports auditory or visual hallucinations Pouts and sulks Talks about hurting self; abuses self Displays poor eating habits; vomits after eating

PREVALENCE OF EBD

Each year since 1975 when P.L. 94-142 was enacted, the federal government has required states to provide data about students with disabilities. Based on current federal terminology and definitions, these data provide information about how individual states and the nation have identified and served students with disabilities. For example, the *Seventeenth Annual Report to Congress on the Implementation of the Individuals With Disabilities Education Act* (U.S. Department of Education, 1995) provides data about students with EBD. In 1993–94, there were 384, 261 students between the ages of six and 21 that were served as EBD under Part B of IDEA.

Relative to students with specific learning disabilities (52.1%), with speech or language impairments (21.6%), and with mental retardation (11.0%), students with EBD represented 8.3% of the total. This percentage represents a 50% increase from the period 1976–77 and a 1.03% increase from 1992–93. Boys are four times as likely to be identified with EBD as girls (Cullinan, Epstein, & Kauffman, 1984; Cullinan, Epstein, & Sabornie, 1992).

The report also indicates the EBD identification rates within the estimated resident population of students ages 6 to 21 ranged from 0.03% to 1.7% and averaged 0.70%. Although this number might seem acceptable, conservative estimates from epidemiological research indicate that about 7% of all school-age students may be eligible for special education under the EBD category (Brandenburg, Friedman, & Silver, 1990; Forness, Kavale, & Lopez, 1993). Why 5% to 6% of students with behavioral problems severe enough to require specialized educational programming have not been identified and served in special education has been the focus of much concern and speculation (Kauffman, 1993). Explanations for this discrepancy include reluctance of school personnel to identify students with EBD, lack of adequate screening and identification criteria and instruments, shortage of personnel, limited service delivery options, inadequate funding, and limited range of disciplinary options at the schoolwide level. Whatever the reasons, students with EBD are clearly underidentified, and many of these students are clearly not receiving the free appropriate public education to which they are entitled.

CAUSES OF EBD

As illustrated in the discussions on definition and characteristics, EBD remains an elusive construct relying primarily on professional judgment to determine its existence. The field's inability to reach consensus on a single definition with clear characteristics to a large degree is derived from the multiple interpretations of causation. Although IDEA dictates that EBD is largely an educational construct (i.e., behavior interferes with learning), service provision cuts across several agencies with differing views on definition, causation, and treatment. In addition, no single causal agent, or for that matter a combination of causes, can be identified as the "cause" of EBD. In general, the debate is based on one's perspective about behavior. Newcomer (1980) suggests that central to the core of the issue is determining whether disturbance is viewed as a "disability" or a "deviancy." From the disability perspective, disturbance is seen as being caused by factors that are internal to the student (e.g., psychic conflict, hindered psychological development, emotional trauma), that give rise to symptomatic behaviors (e.g., tantrums, crying), and that are fixed and developmental in nature (e.g., earlier childhood experiences). In contrast, the deviance perspective considers disturbance to be caused or affected by factors that are external to the student (e.g., school environment, societal factors, peers, family), that are directly and primarily reflected in the student's behaviors, and that are variable in nature.

Disability Perspective

Within the **disability perspective,** EBD is believed to be caused by intrapsychic or biological phenomena. For example, the psychodynamic model puts forth a view in which problem behavior is said to be the symptom of unresolved conflicts that were established during the child's early development. Other mental health or psychological explanations of causation generally explain the presence of problem behavior as an indicator of internal or external conflicts or trauma, such as failure to establish a relationship with one's parents, the death of a sibling, or the child's failure to develop a positive self-image.

Through medical research, correlates of physical symptoms and problem behavior have been documented. For example, children born with fetal alcohol syndrome (FAS) often exhibit poor impulse control, agitation, and noncompliance. However, not all children who are prenatally exposed to alcohol or other toxins demonstrate similar behavior patterns. FAS studies (e.g., Rossett & Weiner, 1984) simply indicate a higher probability of behavior problems if the child is born with a particular medical condition, is exposed to environmental toxins, or experiences a physical trauma.

Deviance Perspective

In contrast to the disability perspective, proponents of the **deviance perspective** explain behavior problems as being the manifestation of experience and the subjective difference between what is viewed as "normal" versus "deviant" behavior. For example, behavioral psychology views problem behavior as learned, and in many cases, adaptive. The student who sells drugs to buy food has learned an adaptive behavior within his personal context and experiences. Although the larger society views the buying of food as appropriate, the behavior chosen by the student to earn the money is viewed as inappropriate or deviant.

Children have multiple opportunities throughout their lives to learn inappropriate and appropriate behavior. When determining the cause of problem behavior from a deviance perspective, four institutions typically are investigated. The first is the family. Researchers such as Gerald Patterson and his colleagues have documented a high correlation between children being labeled as having EBD and parents who engage in harsh punishment and set inconsistent limits for their children (Patterson & Reid, 1984; Patterson, Reid, & Dishion, 1992). The second institution is the larger society in which the child lives. For example, research has demonstrated a strong correlation between factors such as poverty, high crime, and violence and EBD (Kauffman, 1993). The third institution is the student's peer group culture. As children mature, particularly during adolescence, a high correlation is found between EBD and associations or friendships with peers who also engage in antisocial or deviant acts such as drug use, casual sex, and crime (Walker, Colvin, & Ramsey, 1995). Finally, schools themselves are viewed as possible causal EBD agents. The expectation for high behavioral compliance and academic excellence found in most schools is often in direct conflict with the child's experiences outside the school setting. The mismatch between the teacher's expectations for the student (e.g., follow teacher directions, work cooperatively with peers) and behavior displayed by the student is often enough evidence (i.e., professional judgment) to label a student (Gersten, Walker, & Darch, 1988).

Evaluating Causal Explanations

Neither the disability nor deviance perspective can pinpoint with confidence that an event or factor is the "cause" of EBD. We believe these factors are more appropriately characterized as correlates or contributors to EBD. Most research looks at children who are already labeled as having EBD and traces their history to look for key events or factors (e.g., Duncan, Forness, & Hartsough, 1995). However, causal

Table 6.3   **Comparison of Deviancy and Disability Perspectives of Disturbance**

	DISABILITY PERSPECTIVE	DEVIANCE PERSPECTIVE
Causation	Internal factors Symptomatic behaviors Underlying causes	External factors Inferred from community judgments Deviation from social norms
Diagnosis	Internal, person-specific functioning Specialized assessment Fixed condition	Assessment of environmental circumstances Nonspecialized techniques Range of length of condition
Intervention	Specialized interventions Cure underlying causes Specialized settings	Nonspecialized teaching interventions Manipulation of environmental influences Nonspecialized settings
Disadvantages	Nonverifiable causes Labeling oriented Blame on student	Normality is conformity Disturbance is nonconformity Value-laden judgments Diminishment of individual differences
Advantages	Culture and environment-free Early intervention focused Specific problem-intervention model	Attention to what is accessible and manipulable Diminishment of labeling Emphasis on environmental manipulation

explanations have important implications concerning which services are provided for the student. For example, while deriving a prescription or intervention to address problem behavior, the physician will look to medications (e.g., Ritalin for hyperactive behavior), the psychologist will look to insight or cognitive therapy to work through the problem, and the majority of special educators who have been trained within behavioral psychological models will look to teach children alternative behaviors that are adaptive and socially appropriate for the school environment. Table 6.3 provides a comparison of the disability and deviance perspectives of causation within four areas: diagnosis, common treatments, advantages, and disadvantages.

ASSESSMENT AND EVALUATION OF EBD

Given the often disruptive nature of the academic and social behavior problems displayed by students with EBD, the identification of students who would be appropriate recipients of special education services under the EBD category would seem to be easy. In reality, however, the identification of students with EBD remains one of the most difficult determinations to make. As mentioned earlier in the chapter, the major obstacle in evaluating students for special education under the EBD label is a lack of clearly defined criteria for making assessment decisions. To increase understanding of special education assessment and evaluation for students who are identified as having EBD or who are at risk of becoming so identified, this section discusses the purposes and methods of assessment. We focus the discussion on behavioral assessment procedures because they are more directly applicable to special education assessment and evaluation practices than are psychologically based assessment tools (e.g., personality inventories, projective assessments) (Sugai & Maheady, 1988; Sugai, Maheady, & Skouge, 1989; Walker & Fabre, 1987).

Purposes of Assessment

Schools typically engage in assessment activities for one of four purposes:

1. Screening for students with potential learning and/or behavioral challenges

2. Evaluating for special education and triennium reviews

3. Determining present level of performance for IEP development

4. Planning for instructional programming

Each of these activities is discussed briefly relative to the assessment and evaluation of students with EBD.

Screening. The most common screening method for EBD relies on teacher judgment and report. For example, teachers are asked to examine their class lists and to rank order their students from most to least socially competent, or from most to least likely to display antisocial behavior. A less formal method of screening involves asking teachers to develop a list of students who should be referred because they are not succeeding in their classroom and who require more intensive and systematic assessment. By law, school buildings and districts are required to conduct a systematic screening to identify students who might be eligible for special education services and should be assessed for potential learning and/or social behavior difficulties. These assessments should be systematic to avoid overlooking students whose behaviors occur at low rates or are less socially disruptive. For example, the Systematic Screening for Behavior Disorders scale (SSBD) (Walker & Severson, 1992) is a three "gate" or step screening system that assists teachers to identify students who are at risk of social behavior failure. The SSBD provides a systematic screening sequence in which both externalizing and internalizing behavior problems are examined.

Evaluating. The purposes of periodic evaluations are to determine if the student displays one or more of the characteristic problem behaviors listed in the official definition, if the behaviors of concern interfere with the student's opportunities to benefit from available educational experiences, and if the behaviors are displayed over a long period of time and are not in response to any recent significant stressor (e.g., parent divorce, death in family). Eligibility evaluations for services under the EBD label continue to rely primarily on the use of standardized instruments (e.g., Behavior Dimension Rating Scale, Child Behavior Checklist) and anecdotal teacher reports. Unfortunately, direct observation of student behavior often is not conducted or is only undertaken for one or two brief periods (e.g., one hour of observation in the referring teacher's classroom). Ideally, several direct observations should be undertaken across settings and time to assist in making eligibility decisions (Peacock Hill Working Group, 1991; Sugai & Maheady, 1988; Sugai & Tindal, 1993; Walker & Fabre, 1987).

Determining Present Level of Performance. Whereas eligibility assessments are more formal in nature to ensure accurate identification based on a list of requirements mandated by IDEA, the determination of present level of performance is left to educators who are working with the student. In the case of annual updates of present level of performance (i.e., annual IEP review), the determination is made by the special education teacher or with regular education faculty. Because attention is primarily focused on the student's present level of *academic* performance, the student's current level of functioning in the area of social behavior often is not addressed with the necessary detail and focus to enable a team to determine specific and appropriate behavioral goals and objectives (Epstein, Patton, Polloway, & Foley, 1992; Lynch & Beare, 1990). As a result, incongruities between information about the student's present level of performance and the proposed annual goals and objectives are often found (Epstein et al., 1992; Smith & Simpson, 1989). The Peacock Hill Working Group (1991) suggests that this problem can be avoided by implementing systematic, ongoing, direct observation assessment practices across a comprehensive domain of educational skill areas. For example, in addition to typical academic areas (e.g., reading, math, spelling) present level of performance in the

Table 6.4   School-Based Methodologies for Assessing Social Behavior

METHOD	SOURCE OF DATA	ADVANTAGES	DISADVANTAGES	EXAMPLES
Archival search: A review of student files and past records	Student files Grade reports Office referrals Attendance records Past IEPs	Provides quick sample of past behavior Provides index of pervasiveness of problem Provides index of successful and unsuccessful interventions	Is an indirect source of information, contingent on viewpoint of person completing record at the time May not reflect current behavior patterns	The School Archival Record Search (SARS)[1]
Rating scales: Standardized instruments in which raters check those items that describe student behavior or check the degree to which behavior patterns occur	Teachers Parents Peers Student	Usually provides normative scales to compare target student to same-age/sex peers Assesses current perceptions of student behavior	Relies on others' perceptions, subject to biases Uses normative criteria that can become outdated Uses normative criteria that often fail to take into account ethnic and cultural diversity Requires raters to recall information and experiences to rate the student	Walker-McConnell Scale of Social Competence and School Adjustment[2] Systematic Screening for Behavior Disorders (SSBD)[3] Behavior Evaluation Scale[4] Child Behavior Checklist[5] Walker Problem Behavior Identification—Revised[6]
Interviews: Formal or informal conversations with those who have first-hand knowledge of student behavior	Teachers Parents Peers Student	Allows interviewees to expand on responses (vs. rating scales) Is helpful in organizing a more formal assessment (e.g., where to observe, what rating scale appropriate)	Is time consuming Relies on indirect sources of data (i.e., interviewee's perceptions of behavior) Has possibility that interviewee's responses may be biased	Interview resources and examples[7]

following areas also should be assessed: academic-related skills (e.g., following directions), interpersonal skills (e.g., maintaining friendships), conflict resolution (e.g., anger management and problem solving), self-management skills (e.g., self-recording, self-administration of consequences, self-instruction), and vocational/career-related skills (e.g., applications, interviews, workplace social skills).

Planning.   The final level of assessment practices focuses on designing and evaluating specific individualized instructional interventions. When planning for instruction and to determine where instruction should begin and be provided, how it should be designed and presented, and what performance criteria the student must meet for learning to be demonstrated, detailed information is needed about the student's current level of performance and his or her specific weaknesses and strengths. Assessment practices should focus on direct observation strategies that produce baseline information about the student's present level of performance, and should continue during intervention. By maintaining assessment consistency before and during instruction, educators can assess student progress by comparing performance data before and after instruction was initiated.

Table 6.4   Continued

METHOD	SOURCE OF DATA	ADVANTAGES	DISADVANTAGES	EXAMPLES
Direct observation: An observer (teacher, school psychologist, administrator) watches the student across several academic and nonacademic settings and records verbatim what occurs	Trained observer	Provides actual data on student performance. Provides information on: • What the problem behavior looks like (topography) • How often the problem behavior occurs (rate) • Under what conditions the problem behavior is more likely to occur or not occur (function) • How the student's problem behavior compares to the behavior of other students who are similar by age, sex, and ethnic status	Is time consuming. Requires that observer be trained to collect accurate data	Direct observation resources and examples[8]

[1]See Walker, Block, Todis, Barkley, & Severson, 1988.
[2]See Walker & McConnell, 1988.
[3]See Walker & Severson, 1992.
[4]See McCarney, Leigh, & Cornbleet, 1983.
[5]See Achenbach, 1991.
[6]See Walker, 1983.
[7]See Kern, Childs, Dunlap, Clarke, & Falk, 1994; Lewis, Scott, & Sugai, 1994; O'Neill, Horner, Albin, Storey, & Sprague, 1990; Sugai & Tindal, 1993.
[8]See Cooper, Heron, & Heward, 1987; Kerr & Nelson, 1989; Sugai & Tindal, 1993; Wolery, Bailey, & Sugai, 1988.

Methods of Assessing Social Behavior

Several methods of gathering information about student behavior can be utilized; however, the selection of a particular assessment method depends on the purpose of the assessment, the theoretical perspective held by the person doing the assessment, and the experience and level of training of this person. Unlike academic behaviors that often produce a permanent product (e.g., test score, writing sample, number of problems completed), social behaviors usually are represented by observable responses that do not result in a permanent product (e.g., verbal aggressions, anger management responses, running away, cooperative play, verbal intimidation). Therefore, the methodology for assessing social behavior relies on (1) systematic reviews of archival or past records, (2) rating scales completed by persons who are familiar with the student, (3) interviews with persons who are familiar with the student, and (4) direct observations of the student in natural or analogue situations. Each method is briefly described in Table 6.4.

Matching Assessment to Intervention

The final outcome of all assessment activities is the development and provision of specialized instruction to students with disabilities who are not succeeding in the general education curriculum. Curriculum-based assessment has proven to be an effective methodology for pinpointing student academic needs within the school's curriculum (Howell, 1985; Howell, Fox, & Morehead, 1993; Sugai & Tindal, 1993; Tindal & Marston, 1990). An analogous assessment methodology for social behaviors is known as **functional assessment.**

Functional assessment determines what function or purpose the problem behavior serves (e.g., to gain attention, to escape or avoid an aversive situation). Once the function of a problem behavior can be determined, interventions can be developed that establish a competing alternative behavior (i.e., serves the same function but is more appropriate for the context). For example, Michael hits peers during recess when they tease him. In the past, we would develop a punishment procedure for when he hits (e.g., lose the rest of recess). Unfortunately, these kinds of strategies were only effective in the short term, and when the intervention was removed, the problem behavior would reappear—often with greater intensity. However, with functional assessment the emphasis has moved from implementing interventions that focus on decreasing problem behavior to understanding what function the problem behavior serves, and then teaching a prosocial alternative that serves the same function (Iwata, Vollmer, & Zarcone, 1990). In our example with Michael, a functional assessment indicates that his hitting behavior serves effectively to gain peer attention (e.g., they hit and tease him back) and entry into preferred playground activities (e.g., he joins ball games). Knowing this information, interventions are developed that focus on teaching him alternatives to hitting (e.g., asking permission to join games, waiting in line for a turn) that result in the same outcome (e.g., joining games, playing with peers).

By observing the conditions under which problem behavior occurs and does not occur and looking for common events, hypotheses can be made regarding the function of the behavior. Common antecedent events often associated with problem behavior include task difficulty, time of day, disruptions in schedule, and transitions. Common consequent events include peer and teacher attention or escape from or avoidance of difficult tasks or aversive persons. Once a hypothesis regarding the function is developed, the teacher's task is to teach a functional alternative to the problem behavior (e.g., raising hand for teacher attention versus calling out,

Rather than just punishing a behavior, teachers can try to discover the function the behavior serves and provide an appropriate alternative.

asking for help to avoid difficult tasks versus throwing books in an attempt to be sent to the office). To be successful, the functional alternative behavior must make the problem behavior irrelevant, inefficient, and ineffective (Horner & Day, 1991). Figure 6.1 provides an overview of possible functions of problem behavior and related interventions.

INSTRUCTIONAL CONSIDERATIONS

Without question, students who display challenging behaviors pose serious educational challenges for their teachers and families. However, displays of those behaviors alone are insufficient for claiming the need for special education. This section reviews the special education service delivery procedures, programs, and placement practices for students with EBD. Then, it briefly outlines instructional interventions designed to impact the education of students with EBD.

Special Education for Students With EBD

Provisions, Regulations, and Protections.   The Individuals With Disabilities Education Act of 1990 (IDEA) provides a clear, specific three-step process for determining special education for students who present serious behavior problems (Bateman, 1992). Using the definition and characteristics described previously, the first step in determining the need for special education for an individual student is to apply the evaluation and identification provisions of IDEA. These evaluation and identification procedures must be conducted by a multidisciplinary team (MDT) that assesses all areas related to the suspected EBD. Once this evaluation team determines that the student is eligible for an individualized education program (IEP) and determines which specific and unique student needs must be

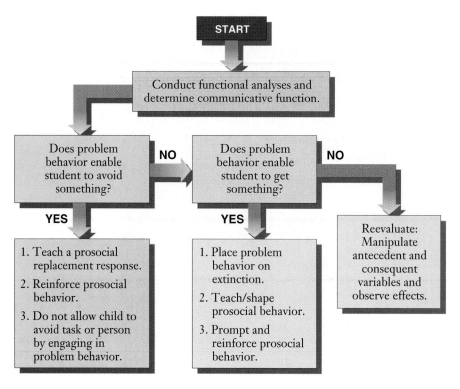

Figure 6.1   **Typical Functions of Problem
Behavior and Matched Intervention Strategies**

addressed by the IEP, the second step is the development of an IEP that is specially designed to meet the individual needs of the student with EBD. Finally, the IEP team determines an educational placement that is free, appropriate, *and* based on the individual student's IEP: "Specifically, the IDEA clearly stipulates that educational goals and objectives and placement decisions are based on each student's needs and not available space or prevailing trends" (Lewis, Chard, & Scott, 1994, p. 279).

According to the provisions of IDEA, special education is defined as specially designed *instruction* and not simply placement in a special education classroom or program. The delivery of special education is based on student need and the IEP team's judgment. IDEA and the federal courts have mandated that decisions regarding where to deliver special education should be guided by two principles:

1. Procedures and requirements for placement in the least restrictive environment (LRE) must be applied.

2. A full continuum of services and alternative placements must be available and considered.

LRE refers to the educational environment where the student can experience the greatest benefit from instruction, and IDEA mandates that the placement decision be individualized and based on the unique needs of the student. LRE requirements also dictate that placement decisions enable students to be educated with peers without disabilities whenever possible, removed from general education only when services cannot be implemented in that setting satisfactorily, and placed in their home school unless the IEP indicates differently (Bateman, 1992). The mandate for a full continuum of services requires school districts to provide a range of possible placements from general education classrooms with consultation to segregated settings, at no cost to the parents, and based on MDT decisions (Vergason, 1991).

Unfortunately, many school districts fail to comply fully with IDEA when providing special education for students with EBD and continue to assume that services must be delivered in "the BD classroom" or segregated facility without individualizing the placement decision (Lewis, Chard, & Scott, 1994). Once a child is identified with a disability, that "label" simply serves as a method to access special education and related services. Development of a legally correct IEP should be based on student need and *not* student label (Davila, 1991; Will, 1987). All decisions regarding special education services and delivery (placement) should be made independently of the student's label, the services presently available in the district, and the current practice for similarly identified students. Rather, services and placement decisions should follow these guidelines:

1. They must be based on each student's individual educational needs.

2. They must be based on the full continuum of educational placements.

3. They must be consistent with the principles of the least restrictive environment (Bateman & Chard, in press).

Current Special Education Programs.   It is useful to examine how states and schools have actually implemented federal regulations for educating students with EBD. In a survey of programs that serve students with EBD, Epstein, Foley, and Cullinan (1993) grouped prevailing program curricula across the continuum of placements into five types. In the first type, the emphasis is on "social and school survival skills." As the name implies, the curriculum emphasizes teaching behavioral versus academic skills. In the second program type, "individualized communication and instruction" are stressed. A specific curriculum area is not emphasized; instead, curriculum is built and based on each student's needs. The third curriculum type focuses on "mainstreaming" and relies on general education to set the curriculum. Special education is provided to assist students in meeting the demands of this general education curriculum. In the fourth type, "instruction in nontraditional content" covers curricula that depart from the common academic and social curriculum found in most schools, and focuses on alternative curriculum areas such as vocational training or outdoor school. The final curriculum group focuses on building and maintaining "classroom structure"—that is, the control and management of student behavior through highly structured small group classrooms.

In a separate national survey, Knitzer and colleagues (1990) found that most programs serving students with EBD overemphasized the "classroom structure" type of curriculum. In these programs, the establishment of behavioral control eclipsed the teaching of appropriate social, academic, or vocational skills. Regardless of curriculum type, most programs serving students with EBD are characterized as lacking well planned interventions and systems to monitor progress and make data-based decisions (Hallenbeck, Kauffman, & Lloyd, 1993; Kauffman & Lloyd, 1992; Peacock Hill Working Group, 1991).

Given this disparate picture of current services, student outcomes are predictably poor. Approximately 50% of students labeled with EBD drop out of school, the highest rate among all disability categories (U.S. Department of Education, 1994). Of those who remain in school, only 42% graduate with a diploma

(Wagner, 1991). Research reveals that 20% of students with EBD are arrested at least once before they leave school, and 35% are arrested within a few years of leaving school (Wagner et al., 1991). Additional information about the school experience of students with EBD was compiled by Wagner and her colleagues (Wagner, 1991; Wagner et al., 1991) at SRI International through a contract from the U.S. Department of Education. Their data suggest that students with EBD present increasing, significant, and exceptional challenges to public schools and communities (U.S. Department of Education, 1994). For example:

> Students with SED have lower grades than any other group of students with disabilities. They fail more courses, and they more frequently fail minimum competency examinations than do other students with disabilities. . . . Forty-four percent received one or more failing grades in their most recent school year—compared with 31 percent for all students with disabilities. (p. 109)

> Although African American and white students represent 16 and 68 percent of the school-age enrollment respectively, they represent 22 and 71 percent of the students classified as SED. On the other hand, Hispanic Americans and Asian Americans represent 12 and 3 percent of the school-aged population respectively, but only 6 and 1 percent of the students classified as SED. (p. 110)

> Data also suggest that there is a high disproportion of students from disadvantaged socioeconomic backgrounds and a low disproportion of female students among those identified with SED. (p. 110)

Current Placement Practices. According to data collected by the U.S. Department of Education (1994), students with EBD continue to represent the largest group of students with disabilities served outside of general education settings. Of all students identified with EBD, 20% are served in separate facilities (versus 5% of students with other disabilities), and 30% of students receiving homebound instruction are students with EBD (U.S. Department of Education, 1994). Koyangi and Gaines (1993) found that more than half of all students in residential placements were identified as EBD. Of those students with EBD who are served in general education settings, more than half receive special education in segregated settings (37% in separate classrooms and 28% in resource rooms) (U.S. Department of Education, 1994). Data from a national survey of special education administrators indicate that self-contained classrooms remain the most prevalent service delivery option for students with EBD (Grosenick, George, George, & Lewis, 1991).

The explanations for the disproportionate number of students who are educated outside of their home schools or within separate classrooms vary. One explanation is that most general education school personnel simply are not trained to address the often challenging nature of behavior displayed by students with EBD (Kauffman & Wong, 1991). In fact, Kauffman and Wong argue as follows:

> Many of the practices known to be effective . . . with children who are difficult to teach are not widely accepted by general educators . . . [and furthermore] many proposals for educational reform advocate adoption of instructional strategies known to fail with many difficult students. (1991, p. 233)

It also has been suggested that segregated placements facilitate comprehensive multidisciplinary treatment programs (e.g., mental health, family services, juvenile

Students with EBD who remain in regular classrooms may need more structure in order to succeed.

justice) by providing one location for several students and thereby reducing costs of several agencies traveling to multiple sites (Epstein, Nelson, et al. 1993; Koyangi & Gaines, 1993; U.S. Department of Education, 1994). However, data on the effectiveness of psychiatric hospitalization and residential programs that incorporate multitreatment programs are inconclusive (Epstein, Nelson, et al., 1993). In addition, little coordination and communication are found between segregated settings and the schools into which most students return, leading to poor follow-through and fragmented services (U.S. Department of Education, 1994).

Data on outcomes associated with educational placement are mixed. For example, Schneider and Leroux (1994) reported that students in self-contained classrooms experienced greater achievement gains than students in resource rooms. In contrast, Meadows, Neel, Scott, and Parker (1994) reported the opposite. The data also are mixed on the kind of behavioral gains students make across placements (Schneider & Leroux, 1994). One of the biggest problems in any analysis of outcomes is the wide range of abilities and needs of students served in various settings. No specific evidence exists to show that any one service delivery model is inherently or empirically better than the next. If anything, the mixed data add further support to the need for individualized service delivery decisions that should be guided, first and foremost, by empirical evidence of the effectiveness of specific educational strategies regardless of placement, and second, by the principles of least restrictive environment and a full continuum of placements.

Instructional Interventions for Students With EBD

Students with EBD require an educational experience that is specially designed to meet their individual learning needs. By definition, students with EBD have learning and behavioral characteristics that interfere with their opportunities to benefit from "typical" academic and social behavior instruction. In other words, these students fail to learn and perform in independent and group instructional contexts and are not responsive to schoolwide, specific setting (e.g., cafeteria, bus, hallway, classroom), and individual disciplinary expectations. We now provide a brief review of preferred practices for teaching students with EBD. The strategies are applicable for any educator (general or special teacher, counselor, educational assistant, etc.) who is responsible for educating these students. However, the special educator frequently must have additional specialized skills that involve working with others as a consultant (see Colvin, Kameenui, & Sugai, 1993; Sugai & Horner, 1994; Sugai & Tindal, 1993).

Academic Interventions.   Because social behavior problems tend to be the defining characteristic of students with EBD, it is easy to overlook the importance of

EASY IDEAS FOR PRACTITIONERS

When Teaching Students With EBD:

1. Focus on what the student does, not on labels.
2. Build educational programs that:
   a. Are proactive and positive
   b. Emphasize the teaching of functional social skills
   c. Consider the total student (i.e., family, community, school)
   d. Are based on functional assessment information
   e. Have been empirically and socially validated
   f. Are individualized to meet the student's unique learning and social needs
   g. Include the student to the greatest extent possible in the least restrictive environment
3. Create learning environments where success is maximized and celebrated.
4. Proactively involve others (e.g., peers, family members, teachers) in the planning and implementation of educational programs.
5. Anticipate problem behaviors by planning and implementing proactive prevention plans.

When Working With Parents of Students With EBD:

1. Use understandable and objective language to describe the student's behaviors.
2. Include the family in planning, implementing, and evaluating academic and social behavior programming.
3. Plan and implement regular and positive communications (e.g., meetings, telephone conversations, written notes) about the student's progress.
4. Prepare a list of resources (e.g., counseling, respite, medical/health) that might be helpful to families.
5. Establish a parent support group that meets on a regular schedule.
6. Avoid blaming parents for the student's behavior challenges.

building academic competence. However, high rates of academic engagement and learning are powerful interventions, in and of themselves, for reducing problem behavior and setting the occasion for the practice of and feedback for appropriate social engagement and on-task behavior. Consistent use of effective academic practices is an important prerequisite to effective classroom and behavior management (Kameenui & Darch, 1995).

Effective academic interventions for students with EBD consist of appropriately arranged learning environments and opportunities, carefully designed and delivered curricula, consistent use of effective teaching practices, and reliable and valid assessment and evaluation procedures (Kameenui & Simmons, 1990). When teaching students with EBD, the learning environment must be specially designed to meet each student's individual needs. Therefore, when planning an academic program for a student with EBD, the full range of service delivery options and environments should be considered. The teaching environment might be the regular classroom, the special education resource room, a segregated setting, or some other location. The important consideration is identifying which environment is most likely to enable the student to achieve his or her individual education plan objectives.

The effective teaching literature has a long developmental history, and we can define the qualities of a competent and productive teacher. In general, this teacher arranges the learning and teaching environment to maximize student academic engagement and learning time for learning outcomes specified for the student on his or her individual education program. This teacher develops and presents an integrated curriculum where facts, concepts, skills, and strategies are applied across content areas. This teacher blends academic and social behavior interventions into a seamless curriculum. Except for the ability to develop specially designed academic and social behavior instructional plans, the general skills this teacher displays are no different from those that characterize any other effective general or special education teacher.

Social Skills Instruction.   Every educational program for a student with EBD should have a social skills instructional component. By definition, students are

Teachers who arrange the environment to maximize learning will have active, engaged students.

identified as having EBD because they exhibit behavioral excesses and deficits that interfere with their ability to benefit from typical instructional programs and to be successful in peer and adult interactions. If special and general educators are to be successful in reducing and eliminating behavioral excesses and improving behavioral deficits, they will need to teach alternative responses (i.e., social skills) that compete with the undesirable behavior. With an effective competing alternative behavior, undesirable behaviors will be remediated effectively and efficiently.

For example, Manuella talks out in class, initiates and engages in fights with peers, and plays alone at recess time. Her teachers have used time-out techniques to reduce her interrupting, behavioral contracts to control her fights with peers, and time with an educational assistant to decrease the amount of time she plays alone at recess. However, none of these problem behaviors has been eliminated completely, and whenever these interventions are reduced or removed, the problem behaviors increase in frequency and intensity. The problem is that Manuella has not been taught appropriate alternative responses (i.e., social skills) to replace and compete with her presenting problem behaviors. From a functional assessment, we learn that Manuella uses her disruptive behavior to obtain teacher attention and to get assistance to complete tasks. We use this information to teach her to raise her hand (or ask a peer, or look up the answer) instead of talking out. We also teach her to tell the teacher if the work is too difficult or if she does not understand what to do on a given task. If we learn that she engages in fights to manage conflicts and express her anger, we can work on teaching her different ways to manage her anger (e.g., walk away, ask for an adult to mediate, talk about it). Finally, if our functional assessment indicates that Manuella plays alone because she has not learned how to share and wait her turn in cooperative games, she should be taught those skills.

This example illustrates the importance of using functional assessment information to build effective programs that are designed to reduce problematic behavior and to teach a more acceptable alternative response. Many published social skills programs provide a general rating scale for determining the presence or absence of a particular social skill, and then present a general lesson for teaching that skill, without consideration of the problem behavior's function. We believe that published social skills programs are useful for creating a consistent and solid foundation of social competence for all students; however, we also believe that these programs, in general, are inadequate for meeting the special needs of students with EBD (Lewis, 1992, 1994). See the "For More Information" section at the end of this chapter for some published general social skills programs.

In addition, many social skills programs are developed and presented as if the student does not have the social skill in his or her repertoire. Instruction is designed for acquisition or beginning learning (e.g., model, lead, test; demonstrate, practice, probe), when in fact the student has the skill, but emits the problem behavior because it is more efficient and effective in producing desired outcomes (Lewis, 1994, Lewis & Sugai, 1993, 1996). For these students with EBD, social skills instruction should be focused on teaching skill discrimination and transfer (Lewis, 1994). Again, emphasis is placed on teaching and strengthening acceptable functional alternative behaviors (social skills) that are more likely to be emitted than the problem behavior.

Social Behavior Interventions.   We have stressed throughout this chapter that all students with EBD should have a specially designed social skills program that directly addresses their problem behavior. However, despite our best social skills instructional efforts, some students may continue to display chronic inappropriate behavior. Social behavior interventions designed to reduce and/or eliminate these problem behaviors abound in the special education literature. At the end of this chapter is a list of excellent resources for identifying, developing, implementing, and evaluating social behavior interventions (see "For More Information"). In general, programs designed to change social behavior fall into four major categories: (1) prevention, (2) pre-correction, (3) intervention, and (4) crisis prevention.

Prevention approaches for students with EBD focus on the academic and social skill instructional strategies described earlier. We know that using effective teaching strategies increases the likelihood of student success. We also know that when students are successful they are less likely to misbehave (Kameenui & Darch, 1995). Therefore, classrooms should emphasize and focus curricula to ensure student success, thereby preventing behavior problems from occurring.

Pre-correction strategies are commonly applied in academic instruction to increase the likelihood that students will make correct responses and decrease the likelihood of errors (Engelmann & Carnine, 1982; Kameenui & Simmons, 1990). In a typical academic sequence, students are given information about a correct response, asked to practice with their new skill, and then asked to demonstrate or show their acquisition of that skill. If a student provides a correct demonstration, provide positive acknowledgments. If the student makes an error, provide more instruction or reteach the more appropriate academic response.

On the other hand, educators generally tend to respond differently to social behavior errors (i.e., displaying an undesirable or inappropriate behavior) than to academic errors (Colvin, Sugai, & Patching, 1993; Sugai, 1992). When a student makes a social behavior error, we assume that student should "know better" and will remember to do it right the next time if we apply a swift and intense aversive consequence. For example, when Melba comes late to class, the teacher tells her that she is late, is supposed to be in her seat when the bell rings, and will receive 20 minutes in-school detention if she is late again. If Melba comes in late the next time, the teacher provides the detention consequence.

A pre-correction strategy for chronic social behavior errors would be the same as that used with chronic academic errors. For example, when Melba comes in late for the *first* time, her teacher assumes that Melba has not learned the correct response, and has Melba verbally repeat the on-time rule and demonstrate or role-play the correct sequence of behaviors required to be on time. This instructional sequence helps the teacher know if the student has the required behavior in her repertoire. If coming to class late becomes *chronic*, Melba's teacher would provide pre-corrections that would assist Melba in coming to class on time—for example, providing a verbal reminder 3 minutes before the bell rings, assigning a peer helper who would prompt her to be on time, or meeting Melba in the hallway and escorting her to class before the bell rings. In each of these pre-correction strategy examples, the teacher attempts to arrange the environment so Melba can succeed, and then can be acknowledged for engaging in the correct social behavior.

When social behavior problems are unresponsive to prevention and pre-correction strategies, more intrusive *intervention* procedures may need to be considered. A discussion of the full range of intervention procedures that could be considered goes beyond the scope of this chapter (see "For More Information" for additional resources). However, we believe that educators must engage in informed, positive, and effective social behavior change procedures. In general, preferred intervention practices are empirically derived and supported, are non-aversive in nature, are focused on teaching and strengthening prosocial alternative behaviors to problem behaviors, and are monitored and evaluated on an ongoing basis (Colvin, Sugai, & Patching, 1993; O'Neill et al., 1990; Sugai & Tindal, 1993; Wolery et al., 1988). In addition and more importantly, the process of selecting and developing intervention strategies must be guided by information collected from functional assessments. Examples of effective intervention strategies are presented in Table 6.5.

If educators conduct systematic functional assessments, we find that most social behavior problems displayed by students with EBD tend to be predictable and understandable. However, we also can predict that some behavioral events will be unexpected or will escalate to a crisis level despite our best prevention and precorrection techniques. A **crisis** is any situation in which a student or adult displays behaviors that are not responsive to standard or typical classroom or behavior management strategies, are associated with the potential for personal injury or property damage, are the most severe and intense for that individual, and require an immediate response from the environment.

Crisis prevention refers to strategies that are designed to avert episodes of severe behaviors and to interrupt sequences of problem behaviors from escalating to more intense forms. In general, crisis prevention consists of three major strategies (Walker et al., 1995). The first is to avoid using or to remove any prompts or stimuli that might cause the problem behavior to escalate to unsafe levels. Early problem behaviors are likely to escalate if, for example, a student is confronted in a hostile, aggressive manner; is not given a choice; is touched or physically threatened; is the target of nagging, loud voices, accusations, or blame; or is drawn into an argument. The second crisis prevention strategy is to "maintain calmness, respect, and detachment" (Walker et al., 1995, p. 108)—that is, approach and communicate with the student in a neutral and nonjudgmental manner. The third strategy to interrupt an escalating chain of behavior is to inform the student about the expected behaviors and the consequences for inappropriate behaviors and for escalation of those behaviors. This information should be given in a way that provides the student with a choice or decision to be made.

In addition to the three strategies proposed by Walker and colleagues (1995), we suggest that educators who work with students with EBD assume that crisis situations are likely to occur and therefore should be prepared. To be prepared means

Table 6.5 **Examples of Effective Intervention Strategies**

Set-Up Strategies	Ecobehavioral assessment
	Functional assessment
	Curriculum-based assessment
	Curriculum modifications
	Effective academic instruction and management
Behavior Strengthening Strategies	Positive reinforcement
	Social skills instruction
	Anger management/conflict resolution
	Functional communication training
	Behavioral counseling
	Behavioral contracting
	Token economy
	Peer mediation; class-wide peer tutoring
	Self-management strategies
Behavior Weakening/Elimination Strategies	Type I punishment (e.g., presentation of aversive, verbal reprimands; overcorrection)
	Type II punishment (e.g., response cost; time-out)

Students can learn acceptable alternatives for gaining the teacher's attention.

arranging the physical environment so that escalating stimuli are minimized and establishing procedures that inform and involve others in responding to potential crisis situations.

Educators must be aware that crisis prevention and intervention strategies are not designed to teach students more appropriate ways of behaving, to decrease future occurrences of the problem behavior, or to take the place of prevention, pre-correction, or proactive intervention techniques. Crisis prevention and intervention strategies are designed solely to reduce and eliminate the likelihood of injury or property damage and de-escalate and interrupt escalating chains of problem behavior.

Systems-Level Interventions. Teaching students with EBD does not occur in a vacuum. Typically, it occurs in a public school building, with hundreds of other students who present the full range of learning and behavioral skills and deficits, and with educators who have varied levels of teaching expertise and specialization. Educating students with EBD requires a team-based, schoolwide collaborative effort that includes the student, his or her family, all building staff, and community agents (Sugai & Horner, 1994). If students with EBD or students who are at-risk of EBD are enrolled in a school, a systems-level approach that includes the following features must be considered.

First, a proactive, instructional-based schoolwide system of classroom and behavior management for all students must be developed and implemented (Colvin, Kameenui, & Sugai, 1993). Second, a systems-level approach to educating students with EBD must have specialized accommodations for specific school building settings (e.g., cafeteria, playground, hallways, restrooms, assemblies, bus) where increased opportunities for displays of problem behavior exist. Third, a systems-level approach requires that all building staff participate in the education of individual students with severe behavior problems, both students identified as EBD and those who are at-risk of EBD. A fourth feature of a systems-level approach to educating students with EBD is the inclusion of individualized,

INNOVATIVE IDEAS   EFFECTIVE BEHAVIOR SUPPORT

New methods of educating students with EBD involve active collaborations between special and general educators—placing high demands on the time and resources of educators. To increase efficiency and effectiveness, efforts must focus on the school building as a collective of systems that work in harmony to educate and assist all students with severe problem behaviors. Developed in the College of Education at the University of Oregon (Sugai & Horner, 1994), the Effective Behavior Support (EBS) approach provides practices and processes for supporting and responding to students who display severe problem behaviors. The approach has five main features.

A system approach is taken. EBS is represented by four major overlapping and integrated systems: (1) the schoolwide system, consisting of the structures and procedures that guide the actions of all staff members and students in a building; (2) the specific setting system, focusing on structures and procedures for common areas of school buildings (e.g., cafeteria, playground, hallways, bus); (3) the classroom system, emphasizing the behavior support practices within the classroom context; and (4) the individual student system, providing structures and procedures for developing individualized programs for those students with the most severe emotional and behavioral problems.

A team-based approach is required. EBS consists of two major teaming structures. The first is a formally constituted schoolwide team that oversees the development, implementation, and monitoring of the four EBS systems. This team must have equitable teacher and support staff representation; active administrator support, participation, and representation; parental input and involvement; and total building staff consensus. To be effective, this team must meet on a regular basis (at least monthly) and have administrative authority and building priority. The second team is the action team. When a request for assistance is made, all teachers who have regular interactions with the target student meet within 10 school days to build, implement, and oversee a behavior support plan. Usually a member of the schoolwide EBS team facilitates action team meetings by keeping everyone on-task with the agenda, providing technical assistance, and ensuring that tasks and procedures are completed as planned. The action team also develops a short-term support plan that can be implemented immediately while the comprehensive behavior support plan is being put in place.

A proactive approach is promoted. Although some students have learning histories that enable them to benefit from their behavioral errors, students with EBD tend not to benefit from punishment-oriented approaches and require practices that teach more acceptable prosocial replacement or social skills. The EBS approach takes a proactive (i.e., positive and preventive) stance across all four systems, but especially at the individual student level—providing opportunities to practice and succeed at desired skills, to receive positive feedback, and to benefit from frequent reminders or prompts to increase the probability of student success.

A commitment to improving behavior support is focused and long-term. The development, implementation, and management of a systemic approach to effective behavior support for students with EBD requires a strong commitment. Changing habitual behavior patterns—of students' and educators—does not occur overnight; it takes time, energy and focused attention. For the EBS approach to function efficiently, building staff must agree that the improvement of behavior support systems for all students must be a top school improvement goal and that a sustained focus will be maintained for at least 2 years.

Emphasis is placed on increasing the behavioral capacity within the school building. The EBS approach focuses on increasing the behavioral capacities that are available on a continuous basis within the school building. This behavioral capacity includes a specified amount of time (e.g., 10 hours per week), designated EBS persons, and specialized skills (e.g., functional assessment, individualized behavior support planning, social skills instruction, staff training proficiencies). Without this behavioral expertise, programming for students with EBD cannot be specialized, efficient, effective, or relevant.

The EBS approach has been introduced, developed, and implemented in various forms in schools across the state of Oregon. Although its long-term impact has not been evaluated, its procedures, policies, and perspectives hold great promise for educating students with EBD.

comprehensive educational programming that systematically connects and includes the school, family, and community (McLaughlin, Leone, Warren, & Schofield, 1994; Nelson & Pearson, 1991).

Community-Level Interventions. Students with EBD typically display challenging behavior beyond the classroom, often necessitating community-based services (e.g., family-based training and support, vocational and career planning and training, juvenile justice and corrections, recreation and leisure activities and opportunities, mental health counseling and support, and medical, health, and welfare assistance). At the extreme are students who are placed in residential treatment facilities to maximize service coordination 24 hours a day (e.g., psychiatric placements). Others may receive counseling or social services outside of school hours. For the majority of children receiving community support services, the primary goal of the school should be coordination and information sharing. This requires educators to be familiar with the types of services various agencies provide, the theoretical approach they take, the goals and objectives they are working toward, and establish a common language (Nelson & Pearson, 1991). Educators should continue to teach children social behaviors that allow them to benefit from instruction within the classroom setting using strategies they have been trained to use, regardless of external services provided. At the same time, establishing open communications with external agencies to develop strategies that will carry over any benefits gained outside of school will increase the overall benefit for the child.

FAMILY PERSPECTIVES

Family members of students with EBD represent important allies to special and general educators because when families, educators, and students can work together, more consistent and comprehensive educational programming is possible. Unfortunately, family members, like teachers, are entwined in processes that often result in disruptions of school and family functioning, failures to benefit from educational opportunities, and expressions of severe problem behaviors. In addition, families are often unjustly blamed for their child's academic learning and social behavior problems. Problems are compounded when behavioral patterns are difficult to understand (e.g., schizophrenia, depression) or tolerate (e.g., aggression, social maladjustment, juvenile delinquency).

Unlike other disabilities that one can see (e.g., orthopedic disability), that have academic labels (e.g., learning disability), or that can be attributed to a clear causal factor (e.g., mental retardation caused by a genetic error), having a child labeled "seriously emotionally disturbed" leaves parents with more questions than answers. In addition, parents' normal emotional reactions to learning their child has a disability are compounded by the fact that the disability often is identified only after there have been repeated interactions between school and home around negative behavior incidents. Parents may spend a great deal of time and energy trying to find out "why" their child behaves the way he does in hopes that they can then "cure" the problem. At the other extreme are those parents who deny that there is a disability and who perceive that the school has the problem and not their child.

The majority of parents want as much information and commonsense strategies as they can get from educators to help their child. Parents often team up with educators to extend behavior management systems into the home. For example, the

Parents often find it difficult to understand the cause of their child's misbehavior and how to help.

parents of an elementary student with EBD made privileges such as riding his bike and watching television contingent on receiving a certain number of earned points during school. Other parents simply replicate successful strategies used at school. For example, the family of a high school student set up a self-management system similar to the one the student used in school to earn the use of the family car.

At the same time, parents and siblings have been dealing with the child's behavior, in some cases for the duration of the child's life, and therefore expect educators to be equally interested in receiving information from them. Parents often voice their frustrations about educators who appear not to listen or to ignore what they have to say about their child, particularly regarding strategies they have used successfully at home.

"It's tough," reports a mother of a middle school child with EBD, "we always are waiting for the phone call to say come and get your kid, he is out of control again." Having a family member with a disability potentially adds stress. Having a family member with an emotional or behavioral disability is almost certain to add stress. The often aggressive or violent nature of EBD and the likelihood that children with EBD will be noncompliant sets the stage for ongoing battles. Parents and siblings often report "giving up" or "choosing their battles carefully" to avoid further problems. Compounding the stress is the misunderstanding society has about EBD. "When we are in public, and Larry starts acting up, people look at me like, 'Can't you control your kid?' If he was in a wheelchair, people would understand: 'Oh, he is disabled'—but you can't see a behavior disability so people just assume it's your fault." While the family focus is typically directed toward the child with EBD, family members also have to remember to take care of themselves. Says one parent: "We spend so much energy to make sure Valerie is doing okay, we forget to make sure her brother is doing all right." Parents and family members often seek help from peers (e.g., family support and advocacy groups, respite care) or professionals (e.g., family counseling) to provide needed support. "Just knowing there are other families dealing with the same problems we are helps," reports the sister of a child with EBD, "I don't feel like we are different or weird any more."

CURRENT ISSUES AND FUTURE TRENDS

The purpose of this chapter was to describe special education for students with EBD. Instead of focusing our attention on the characteristics of students who acquire this label, we presented a comprehensive look at the educational context in which they are educated. In particular, we tried to characterize general and special education for the student with EBD from a perspective of preferred and promising practices—that is, what do we know about educating students with EBD and students who are at-risk of being identified as having EBD. In this presentation, we emphasized the difficulty educators have in characterizing who these students are, the poor immediate and long-term prognosis for those students who are identified, and the individualized and comprehensive nature of the educational programs that are necessary to serve these students.

Clearly, the job of educating students with EBD is simultaneously challenging and embracing, rewarding and punishing, and encouraging and frustrating. We believe that educating students with EBD is a critical element of general and special education, and that these students are entitled to a free, public, and appropriate education. However, despite good intentions, laws and regulations, research on effective practices, and educational progress, there are many questions whose answers could improve the capacity to educate students with EBD. To conclude this chapter, we provide a brief discussion of these issues.

First, educating students who enter school with diverse cultural, learning, and behavioral histories pose a number of unanswered questions. For example: How do cultural differences affect the identification, placement, and education of students with EBD? How can cultural differences and diversity be used productively to educate students with EBD? What changes need to be made in identification and assessment procedures to ensure equitable, reliable, and valid identification of students with EBD across culturally diverse populations of students? Answers to these questions must be developed because more students are entering school with English as their second language, with cultural and racial backgrounds that are different from the culture of the school and its staff, and with family backgrounds that have different values and child-rearing practices from the traditional family unit. Clearly, all students deserve an educational experience that maximizes their learning potential and accommodates their individual characteristics. Similarly, the impact of cultural and linguistic diversity must be considered when determining whether a student needs specialized educational programming because of emotional and behavioral disorders.

Second, although major advances have been made in how we educate students with EBD, we have been relatively unsuccessful in producing significant long-term gains. Answers to the following questions are needed: How can the long-term prognosis for students with EBD be improved? How can the dropout rate, arrest and police-contact numbers, and mental health contact rates be decreased? How can high school graduation rates for students with EBD be improved? How can the employment status for students with EBD be improved? Fortunately, efforts at the national level have been initiated to address these questions. In 1994, the Office of Special Education Programs of the U.S. Department of Education contracted with the Chesapeake Institute to establish a national agenda that would lead toward better outcomes for students with EBD. This agenda consists of six strategic targets designed to create "a reorientation and national preparedness to foster the emotional development and adjustment of all children and youth, including those with SED, as the critical foundation for realizing their potential at school, work, and in the community". The strategic targets are to (1) expand positive learning opportunities and results, (2) strengthen school and community capacity, (3) value and address diversity, (4) collaborate with families, (5) promote appropriate assessment, (6) provide ongoing skill development and support, and (7) create comprehensive and collaborative systems. Efforts to achieve these targets are under way and should lead to improved outcomes for students with EBD.

Third, the impact of students with EBD unfortunately often extends into the community and involves the juvenile justice system. A question that has not been answered fully is this: What is the status of special education services for students with EBD within the juvenile justice system? Although improvement of special education in correctional settings has been attempted, efforts have been labor intensive and not widespread. Differences in disciplinary focus, practice, and outcomes have slowed efforts to bring special and correctional educators to a common ground. In addition, efforts must be directed toward preventing initial delinquent and antisocial behavior and for increasing the likelihood that students with EBD who leave correctional facilities do not return. Special and general educators, correctional educators, mental health personnel, and other community agents will need to build, implement, and evaluate comprehensive "wraparound" programs for students with EBD to answer this question.

Finally, technological advances are appearing in every aspect of our daily lives. Multimedia hardware and software, advanced communication systems, portable computers, the information highway (Internet), high-density read and write compact discs, virtual reality hardware, and interactive instructional curricula are becoming commonplace in many public school classrooms. However, a number of questions remain unanswered: How can and will technological advances be used to improve the academic and social behavior outcomes of students with EBD? How will we ensure that these technologies will become available in all general and special education classrooms? How will we know what works and does not work with students with EBD? Although to date, relatively little attention has been directed toward the development, study, and application of new technologies to educating students with EBD, the potential for improving academic and social behavior outcomes is evident. For example, one could imagine a virtual reality–based social skills lesson in which students would practice alternative and interactive ways of responding to a full range of conflict situations with other students at multiple sites around the world. Or, Internet-based, high-interest academic experiences could be arranged so individualized goals could be achieved with high rates of successful responding. If opportunities for academic success can be increased, the emotional and behavioral status of students with EBD also could be improved.

Five-Minute Summary

Educating students with EBD is an exciting and ever changing challenge, although EBD is clearly not a new phenomenon. References to persons with EBD have existed since the beginning of written records. Debate about the nature of deviance continues today at multiple levels: philosophical, educational, medical, and psychological.

Interestingly, parents, teachers, students, and others have little difficulty identifying students with EBD—but we have not developed a terminology and definition that have descriptive and educational utility. Students with EBD display a wide range of emotional, behavioral, and educational characteristics. Although general similarities exist across these characteristics, what we see and how we describe and explain what we see are affected by environmental, conceptual, cultural, experiential, and disciplinary standards. These same standards also affect our educational assessment, identification, programming, and evaluation practices.

Federal and state mandates (e.g., the Individuals With Disabilities Education Act) provide important provisions, regulations, and protections for all students with disabilities. Educators note, however, that students with severe emotional and behavioral problems present significant challenges to their ability to implement these mandates. Fortunately, educators have access to many promising and preferred practices that enable them to enhance academic, personal, interpersonal, and life skills and to provide a comprehensive and positive system of support for students with EBD and their families.

Although we know quite a bit about educating students with EBD, we also have many questions that encompass the school, family, and community contexts. For example, we need to learn more about how factors like culture, gender, race, and socioeconomic status affect the education of these students. We need to know how we can improve the long-term prognosis for students with EBD. We need to know how to incorporate early identification and prevention into the regular repertoire of practices in elementary grades. We need to determine how to coordinate services of the school, family, and community in order to improve the educational outcomes for these students. Clearly, we have made significant progress—yet we also have many exciting challenges ahead.

Study Questions

1. Identify one strength and one weakness of the current definition of emotional and behavioral disorders.
2. Using three dimensions of behavior (i.e., frequency, topography, locus, latency, intensity, duration) define a problem and replacement behavior that might be displayed by students with emotional and behavioral disorders.
3. Identify two paradigms for characterizing EBD and list key historical events that support the paradigms in their current form.
4. List three key elements mandated in IDEA that ensure a free and appropriate education for students who have been identified as having an emotional and behavioral disorder.
5. List two assessment methodology practices used with students who display emotional and behavioral disorders and describe instruments and techniques commonly associated with those methodologies.
6. List and describe three preferred educational practices used with students who display emotional and behavioral disorders.
7. Identify one remaining challenge or unanswered question associated with educating students with emotional and behavioral disorders and provide suggestions on how you would attempt to resolve the issue.

For More Information

ORGANIZATIONS

The Council for Children with Behavior Disorders (CCBD)
1920 Association Drive
Reston, VA 22091
800-845-6232

The Council for Exceptional Children
1920 Association Drive
Reston, VA 22091
800-845-6232

Educational Resource Information Clearinghouse (ERIC)
800-538-3742

The Federation of Families for Children's Mental Health
1021 Prince Street
Alexandria, VA 22314-2071

BOOKS AND ARTICLES

Alberto, P.A., & Troutman, A. C. (1995). *Applied behavior analysis for teachers* (4th ed.). Columbus, OH: Merrill.

Carr, E. G., Levin, L., McConnachie, G., Carlson, J. I., Kemp, D. C., & Smith, C. E. (1994). *Communication based intervention for problem behavior: A user's guide for producing positive change.* Baltimore: Paul H. Brookes.

Dunlap, G., Kern, L., dePerczel, M., Clarke, S., Wilson, D., Childs, K. E., White, R., & Falk, G. D. (1993). Functional analysis of classroom variables for students with emotional and behavioral disorders. *Behavioral Disorders, 18,* 275–291.

Durand, V. M., & Carr, E. G. (1991). Functional communication training to reduce challenging behavior: Maintenance and application in new settings. *Journal of Applied Behavior Analysis, 24,* 251–264.

Durand, V. M., & Crimmins, D. B. (1988). Identifying the variables maintaining self-injurious behavior. *Journal of Autism and Developmental Disorders, 18,* 99–117.

Ehrenwald, J. (Ed.). (1976). *The history of psychotherapy: from healing magic to encounter.* New York: Aronson.

Gunter, P. L., Jack, S. L., Shores, R. E., Carrell, D. E., & Flowers, J. (1993). Lag sequential analysis as a tool for functional analysis of student disruptive behavior in classrooms. *Journal of Emotional and Behavioral Disorders, 1,* 138–148.

Iwata, B. A., Dorsey, M. F., Slifer, K. J., Bauman, K. E., & Richman, G. S. (1982). Toward a functional analysis of self-injury. *Analysis and Intervention in Developmental Disabilities, 2,* 3–20.

Jones, V. F., & Jones, L. S. (1995). *Comprehensive classroom management: Creating positive learning environments for all students* (4th ed.). Boston: Allyn & Bacon.

Kameenui, E. J., & Darch, C. B. (1995). *Instructional classroom management: A proactive approach to behavior management.* White Plains, NY: Longman.

Kerr, M. M., & Nelson, C. M. (1989). *Strategies for managing behavior problems in the classroom* (2nd ed.). Columbus, OH: Merrill/Macmillan.

Kerr, M. M., Nelson, C. M., & Lambert, D. L. (1987). *Helping adolescents with learning and behavior problems.* Columbus, OH: Merrill/Macmillan.

Patterson, G. R. (1982). *Coercive family process.* Eugene, OR: Castalia.

Reichle, J., & Wacker, D. P. (Eds.). (1993). *Communicative alternatives to challenging behavior: Integrating functional assessment and intervention strategies.* Baltimore: Paul H. Brookes.

Sugai, G., & Tindal, G. (1993). *Effective school consultation: An interactive approach.* Pacific Grove, CA: Brooks/Cole.

Wagner, M. (1991). *Dropouts with disabilities: What do we know? What can we do?* Menlo Park, CA: SRI International.

Wagner, M., Newman, L., D'Amico, R., Jay, E. D., Bulter-Nalin, P., Marder, C., & Cox, R. (1991). *Youth with disabilities: How are they doing? The first comprehensive report from the National Longitudinal Transition Study of special education students.* Menlo Park, CA: SRI International.

Walker, H. M., Block-Pedego, A., Todis, B., & Severson, H. (1991). *School Archival Records Search (SARS).* Longmont, CO: Sopris West.

Walker, H. M., Colvin, G., & Ramsey, E. (1995). *Antisocial behavior in school: Strategies and best practices.* Pacific Grove, CA: Brooks/Cole.

Wolery, M., Bailey, D. B., & Sugai, G. M. (1988). *Effective teaching: Principles and procedures of applied behavior analysis with exceptional students.* Boston: Allyn & Bacon.

Wolfensberger, W. (1975). *The origin and nature of institutional models.* Syracuse, NY: Human Policy Press.

JOURNALS, NEWSLETTERS, AND OTHER PUBLICATIONS

Behavioral Disorders
Council for Children with Behavioral Disorders
1920 Association Drive
Reston, VA 22091-1589

Education and Treatment of Children
Pressley Ridge Schools
530 Marshall Avenue
Pittsburgh, PA 15214

Journal of Applied Behavior Analysis
Society for the Experimental Analysis of Behavior, Inc.
Department of Psychology, Indiana University
Bloomington, IN 47405

Journal of Behavioral Education
Human Sciences Press, Inc.
233 Spring Street
New York, NY 10013-1578

Journal of Emotional and Behavioral Disorders
PRO-ED, Inc.
8700 Shoal Creek Boulevard
Austin, TX 78758-6897

Journal of Emotional and Behavioral Problems
National Educational Service
P. O. Box 8
Bloomington, IN 47402

OTHER SOURCES

This list provides a sample of published programs for teaching social skills.

Elliott, S. N., & Gresham, F. M. (1991). *Social skills intervention guide: Practical strategies for social skills training.* Circle Pines, MN: American Guidance Service.

Goldstein, A. P., Sprafkin, R. P., Gershaw, N. J., & Klein, P. (1980). *Skillstreaming the adolescent: A structured learning approach to teaching prosocial skills.* Champaign, IL: Research Press.

Jackson, N. F., Jackson, D. A., & Monroe, C. (1983). *Getting along with others: Teaching social effectiveness to children.* Champaign, IL: Research Press.

McGinnis, E., & Goldstein, A. P. (1990). *Skillstreaming in early childhood: Teaching prosocial skills to the preschool and kindergarten child.* Champaign, IL: Research Press.

McGinnis, E., Goldstein, A. P., Sprafkin, R. P., & Gershaw, N. J. (1984). *Skillstreaming the elementary school child: A guide for teaching prosocial skills.* Champaign, IL: Research Press.

Walker, H. M., McConnell, S., Holmes, D., Todis, B., Walker, J., & Golden, N. (1983). *The Walker social skills curriculum: The ACCEPTS program.* Austin, TX: PRO-ED

Walker, H. M., Todis, B., Holmes, D., & Horton, G. (1983). *The Walker social skills curriculum: The ACCESS program.* Austin, TX: PRO-ED.

References

Achenbach, T. M. (1991) *Child behavior checklist.* Burlington, VT: University of Vermont, Department of Psychiatry.

Bateman, B. D. (1992). *Better IEPs.* Creswell, OR: Otter Ink.

Bateman, B. D., & Chard, D. J. (1995). Legal demands and constraints on placement decisions. In J. W. Lloyd & J. M. Kauffman (Eds.), *Issues in the educational placement of pupils with emotional or behavioral disorders* (pp. 285-316). Hillsdale, NJ: Erlbaum

Bower, E. M. (1981). *Early identification of emotionally handicapped children in school* (3rd ed.). Springfield, IL: Thomas.

Bower, E. M. (1982). Defining emotional disturbance: Public policy and research. *Psychology in the Schools, 10,* 55–60.

Colvin, G., Kameenui, E. J., & Sugai, G. (1993). School-wide and classroom management: Reconceptualizing the integration and management of students with behavior problems in general education. *Education and Treatment of Children, 16,* 361–381.

Colvin, G., Sugai, G., & Patching, W. (1993). Pre-correction: An instructional strategy for managing predictable behavior problems. *Intervention, 28,* 143–150.

Cooper, J. O., Heron, T. E., & Heward, W. L. (1987). *Applied behavior analysis.* Columbus, OH: Merrill/Macmillan.

Council for Children with Behavioral Disorders, Executive Committee. (1987). Position paper on definition and identification of students with behavioral disorders. *Behavioral Disorders, 13,* 9–19.

Cullinan, D., Epstein, M. H., & Kauffman, J. M. (1984). Teacher's ratings of students behaviors: What constitutes behavior disorders in school? *Behavioral Disorders, 10,* 9–19.

Cullinan, D., Epstein, M. H., & Lloyd, J. W. (1991). Evaluation of a conceptual model of behavior disorders. *Behavioral Disorders, 16,* 148–157.

Cullinan, D., Epstein, M. H., & Sabornie, E. J. (1992). Selected characteristics of a national sample of seriously emotionally disturbed adolescents. *Behavioral Disorders, 17,* 273–280.

Davila, R., 18 *IDELR* 594 (OSERS, 1991).

Duncan, B. B., Forness, S. R., & Hartsough, C. (1995). Students identified as seriously emotionally disturbed in school-based day treatment: Cognitive, psychiatric, and special education characteristics. *Behavioral Disorders, 20,* 238–252.

Engelmann, S., & Carnine, D. W. (1982). *Theory of instruction: Principles and applications.* New York: Irvington.

Epstein, M. H., Foley, R. M., & Cullinan, D. (1993). National survey of educational programs for adolescents with serious emotional disturbance. *Behavioral Disorders, 17,* 202–210.

Epstein, M. H., Nelson, M., Polsgrove, L., Coutinho, M., Cumblad, C., & Quinn, K. (1993). A comprehensive community-based approach to serving students with emotional and behavioral disorders. *Journal of Emotional and Behavioral Disorders, 1* (2), 127–133.

Epstein, M. H., Patton, J. R., Polloway, E. A., & Foley, R. (1992). Educational services for students with behavior disorders: A review of individualized education programs. *Teacher Education and Special Education, 15,* 41–47.

Forness, S. R., Kavale, K. A., & Lopez, M. (1993). Conduct disorders in school: Special education eligibility and comorbidity. *Journal of Emotional and Behavioral Disorders, 1* (2), 101–108.

Forness, S. R., & Knitzer, J. (1990, June). *A new proposed definition and terminology to replace "serious emotional disturbance" in Education of the Handicapped Act.* Workgroup on Definition, the National Mental Health and Special Education Coalition. Alexandria, VA: National Mental Health Association.

Forness, S. R., & Knitzer, J. (1992). A new proposed definition and terminology to replace "serious emotional disturbance" in Individuals With Disabilities Act. *School Psychology Review, 21,* 12–21.

Gersten, R., Walker, H. M., & Darch, C. (1988). The relationship between teachers' effectiveness and their tolerance for handicapped students. *Exceptional Children, 54,* 433–438.

Gottlieb, J., Alter, M., & Gottlieb, B. W. (1991). Mainstreaming academically handicapped children in urban schools. In J. W. Lloyd, A. C. Repp, & N. Singh (Eds.), *The regular education initiative: Alternative perspectives on concepts, issues, and models* (pp. 95–112). Sycamore, IL: Sycamore Press.

Grosenick, J. K., George, N. L., George, M. P., & Lewis, T. J. (1991). Public school services for behaviorally disordered students: Program practices in the 1980's. *Behavioral Disorders, 16,* 87–96.

Hallenbeck, B. A., Kauffman, J. M., & Lloyd, J. W. (1993). When, how, and why educational placement decisions are made: Two case studies. *Journal of Emotional and Behavioral Disorders, 1* (2), 109–117.

Horner, R., & Day, H. M. (1991). The effects of response efficiency on functionally equivalent competing behaviors. *Journal of Applied Behavior Analysis, 24,* 719–732.

Howell, K. W. (1985). A task-analytical approach to social behavior. *Remedial and Special Education, 6* (2), 24–30.

Howell, K. W., Fox, S. L., & Morehead, M. K. (1993). *Curriculum-based evaluation: Teaching and decision making* (2nd ed.). Pacific Grove, CA: Brooks/Cole.

Iwata, B. A., Vollmer, T. R., & Zarcone, J. R. (1990). The experimental (functional) analysis of behavior disorders: Methodology, applications, and limitations. In A. C. Repp & N. N. Sigh (Eds.), *Perspectives on the use of nonaversive and aversive interventions for persons with developmental disabilities* (pp. 301–330). Sycamore, IL: Sycamore Publishing.

Kameenui, E. J., & Darch, C. B. (1995). *Instructional classroom management: A proactive approach to behavior management.* White Plains, NY: Longman.

Kameenui, E. J., & Simmons, D. C. (1990). *Designing instructional strategies: The prevention of academic learning problems.* Columbus, OH: Merrill/Macmillan.

Kauffman, J. M. (1993). *Characteristics of behavior disorders of children and youth* (5th ed.). New York: Merrill Publishing.

Kauffman, J. M., & Lloyd, J. W. (1992). Restrictive educational placement of students with emotional or behavioral disorders: What we know and what we need to know. In R. B. Rutherford & S. R. Maher (Eds.), *Severe behavior disorders of children and youth* (vol. 15, pp. 35–43). Reston, VA: Council for Children With Behavioral Disorders.

Kauffman, J. M., & Wong, K. L. H. (1991). Effective teachers of students with behavioral disorders: Are generic teaching skills enough? *Behavioral Disorders, 16,* 225–237.

Kern, L., Childs, K., Dunlap, G., Clarke, S., & Falk, G. D. (1994). Using assessment-based curricular intervention to improve the classroom behavior of a student with emotional and behavioral challenges. *Journal of Applied Behavior Analysis, 27,* 7–19.

Kerr, M. M., & Nelson, C. M., (1989). *Strategies for managing behavior problems in the classroom* (2nd ed.). Columbus, OH: Merrill/Macmillan.

Kerr, M. M., Nelson, C. M., & Lambert, D. L. (1987). *Helping adolescents with learning and behavior problems.* Columbus, OH: Merrill/Macmillan.

Knitzer, J., Steinberg, Z, & Fleisch, B. (1990). *At the schoolhouse door: An examination of programs and policies for children with behavioral and emotional problems.* New York: Bank Street College of Education.

Koyangi, C., & Gaines, S. (1993). *All systems failure: An examination of the results of neglecting the needs of children with serious emotional disturbance.* Washington, DC: National Mental Health Association.

Lewis, T. J. (1992). Essential features of a social skills instructional program. In J. Marr & G. Tindal (Eds.), *The Oregon Conference '92 Monograph* (pp. 32–40). Eugene, OR: College of Education, University of Oregon.

Lewis, T. J. (1994). A comparative analysis of the effects of social skills training and teacher directed contingencies on the generalized social behavior of pre-school children with disabilities. *Journal of Behavioral Education, 4,* 267–281.

Lewis, T. J., Chard, D., & Scott, T. (1994). Full inclusion and the education of children and youth with emotional and behavioral disorders. *Behavioral Disorders, 19,* 277–293.

Lewis, T. J., Scott, T., & Sugai, G. (1994). The problem behavior questionnaire: A teacher based instrument to develop functional hypotheses of problem behavior in general education classrooms. *Diagnostique, 19* (2–3), 103–115.

Lewis, T. J., & Sugai, G. (1993). Teaching communicative alternatives to socially withdrawn behavior: An investigation in maintaining treatment effects. *Journal of Behavioral Education, 3,* 61–75.

Lewis, T. J., & Sugai, G. (1996). Descriptive and experimental analysis of teacher and peer attention and the use of assessment based intervention to improve the pro-social behavior of a student in a general education setting. *Journal of Behavioral Education, 6,* 7–24.

Lynch, E. C., & Beare, P. L. (1990). The quality of IEP objectives and their relevance to instruction for students with mental retardation and behavioral disorders. *Remedial and Special Education, 11,* 48–55.

McCarney, S., Leigh, J., & Cornbleet, J. (1983). *Behavior Evaluation Scale (BES).* Vernon, AL: Associated Management Systems.

McLaughlin, M. J., Leone, P., Warren, S. H., & Schofield, P. F. (1994). *Doing things differently: Issues and options for creating comprehensive school linked services for children and youth with emotional and behavioral disorders.* College Park: University of Maryland and Westat, Inc.

Meadows, N. B., Neel, R. S., Scott, C., & Parker, G. (1994). Academic performance, social competence, and mainstream accommodations: A look at mainstreamed and nonmainstreamed students with serious behavioral disorders. *Behavioral Disorders, 19,* 170–180.

Nelson, C. M., & Pearson, C. A. (1991). *Integrating services for children and youth with emotional and behavioral disorders.* Reston, VA: Council for Exceptional Children.

Ninness, H. A. C., Glenn, S. S., & Ellis, J. (1993). *Assessment and treatment of emotional or behavioral disorders.* Westport, CT: Praeger.

O'Neill, R. E., Horner, R. H., Albin, R. W., Storey, K., & Sprague, J. R. (1990). *Functional analysis of problem behavior: A practical assessment guide.* Pacific Grove, CA: Brooks/Cole.

Patterson, G. R., & Reid, J. B. (1984). Social interactional processes within the family: The study of the moment-by-moment family transactions in which human social development is imbedded. *Journal of Applied Developmental Psychology, 5,* 237–262.

Patterson, G. R., Reid, J. B., & Dishion, T. J. (1992). *A social learning approach: Vol. 4. A coercion model.* Eugene, OR: Castalia.

Peacock Hill Working Group. (1991). Problems and promises in special education and related services for children and youth with emotional or behavioral disorders. *Behavioral Disorders, 16,* 299–313.

Peters, M. T., & Heron, T. E. (1993). When the best is not good enough: An examination of best practice. *Journal of Special Education, 26,* 371–385.

Rossett, H. L., & Weiner, L. (1984). *Alcohol and the fetus.* New York: Oxford University Press.

Schneider, B. H., & Leroux, J. (1994). Educational environments for the pupil with behavioral disorders: A "best evidence" synthesis. *Behavioral Disorders, 19,* 192–204.

Smith, S. W., & Simpson, R. L. (1989). An analysis of individualized education programs (IEPs) for students with behavior disorders. *Behavioral Disorders, 14,* 107–116.

Sugai, G. M. (1992). The design of instruction and the proactive management of social behaviors. *Learning Disabilities Forum, 17*(2), 20–23.

Sugai, G. M., & Horner, R. (1994). Including students with severe behavior problems in general education settings: Assumptions, challenges, and solutions. In J. Marr, G. Sugai, & G. Tindal (Eds.), *The Oregon conference monograph* (pp. 102–120). Eugene, OR: University of Oregon.

Sugai, G. M., & Maheady, L. (1988). Cultural diversity and individual assessment for behavior disorders. *Teaching Exceptional Children, 21*(1), 28–31.

Sugai, G. M., Maheady, L., & Skouge, J. (1989). Best assessment practices for students with behavior disorders: Accommodation to cultural diversity and other individual differences. *Behavioral Disorders, 14*(4), 263–278.

Sugai, G. M., & Tindal, G. A. (1993). *Effective school consultation: An interactive approach.* Pacific Grove, CA: Brooks/Cole.

Tindal, G. A., & Marston, D. B. (1990). *Classroom-based assessment: Evaluating instructional outcomes.* Columbus, OH: Merrill.

U.S. Department of Education. (1994). Achieving better results for children and youth with serious emotional disturbances (pp. 109–130). In *To assure the free appropriate public education of all children with disabilities: Sixteenth annual report to Congress on the implementation of the Individuals With Disabilities Education Act.* Washington, DC: Author.

Vergason, 19 *EHLR* 471 (OSERS, 1991).

Walker, H. M. (1983). *Walker Problem Behavior Identification—Revised (WPBI—R).* Los Angeles: Western Psychological Services.

Walker, H. M., Colvin, G., & Ramsey, E. (1995). *Antisocial behavior in school: Strategies and best practices.* Pacific Grove, CA: Brooks/Cole.

Walker, H. M., & Fabre, T. R. (1987). Assessment of behavior disorders in the school setting: Issues, problems, and strategies revisited. In N. G. Haring (Ed.), *Assessing and managing behavior disabilities* (pp. 198-243). Seattle: University of Washington Press.

Walker, H. M., & McConnell, S. R. (1988). *The Walker-McConnell scale of social competence and school adjustment: A social skills rating scale for teachers.* Austin, TX: PRO-ED.

Walker, H. M., & Severson, H. (1992). *The Systematic Screening for Behavior Disorders scale.* Longmont, CO: Sopris West.

Will, M., *EHLR 211:442* (OSERS, 1987).

Wolery, M. R., Bailey, D. B., Jr., & Sugai, G. M. (1988). *Effective teaching: Principles and procedures of applied behavior analysis with exceptional students.* Boston: Allyn & Bacon.

Chapter 7

Mug Warrior, acrylic on canvas, 40″ × 30″ (1991)

COMMUNICATION DISORDERS

ANDREA M. LAZZARI

After studying this chapter, the reader will:

Know the history of the development of the field of
speech–language pathology

Distinguish speech disorders from language disorders

Be able to identify and define the three
categories of speech disorders

Be able to identify different methods of intervention
for speech and language disorders

Understand the normal course of language
development in young children

Know the basic components of language

Be familiar with common causes of speech and language disorders

Appreciate families' concerns regarding communication disorders
and the role of family members in prevention

COMMUNICATION DISORDERS

Ancient Greece
c. 350 B.C.
Demosthenes, a notable Greek orator, improved his speech by putting pebbles in his mouth and projecting his voice above the sound of ocean waves.

Ancient Rome
1st century A.D.
Balbus Blaesus, a stutterer, would amuse the crowd by trying to speak so they would throw coins into his cage.

1600s
Medieval physiology (four humors—four temperaments) was used to account for communication problems (i.e., stuttering).

1700s
J. C. Amman emerged as one of the first scientists in Europe to specialize in the practice of speech pathology.

1850s
Publications on speech disorders written by physicians began to appear in Europe, as remediation of speech was viewed as a medical issue. The elocutionary movement began in England.

Early 1900s
Practitioners who had trained in Europe began providing treatment in the United States.

1910–1916
Speech correction teachers were hired in some U.S. school systems.

1957
Chomsky presented a psycholinguistic theory of the psychological processes underlying language.

Skinner and other behaviorists stressed the importance of selective reinforcement and parent modeling in language acquisition.

1960s
Language intervention as an organized professional field began to emerge.

1978
The name of the American Speech and Hearing Association was changed to the American Speech–Language–Hearing Association, to reflect the increased emphasis by the profession on language disorders.

1980s
Language intervention shifted from teaching specific speech and language skills to enhancing children's social communication.

1990s
Speech–language professionals became involved in collaborative consultation with classroom teachers and in integrated therapy.

INTRODUCTION

A dog scratches at the door and its owner lets the dog out . . . a baby whimpers and his mother comforts him . . . a quarterback forms a T with his hands and the game clock is stopped . . . a driver sees a flashing light behind her and pulls over . . . a child raises his hand and his teacher goes to him . . . a father frowns and his child stops tipping back in her chair . . . the mail carrier notices a red flag raised on a mailbox and stops to pick up the mail . . . Each of these is an act of communication. Although no words have been exchanged, in each instance a message has been sent and received.

Almost everything we do, undertake, or strive for involves communication. We communicate almost constantly in a variety of ways, both consciously and unconsciously, with or without using spoken language. While language is just one form of communication, it is the one that is uniquely human.

Language may be defined as a rule-governed system of communication shared by a group of speakers. Language can be oral, written, or gestural. It mediates our thoughts, feelings, relationships, experiences, and memories. It enables us to learn new things, to relate new knowledge to past experience, and to think abstractly. On a broader scale, language fulfills a social function. Society depends on language as a means of conveying information, ideas, values, and rules among its members and to record and pass on its history and heritage to subsequent generations.

Speech may be defined as an audible means of expressing a language. It conveys the messages of the language. Speech and language combined form *oral communication.*

Even nonverbal signals send a message commonly understood by the receiver.

REAL PEOPLE   *Robert Merrill*

"Growing up in Brooklyn, I was shy and stuttered badly. I dreaded being asked to speak in front of the class. On days I knew I would be called upon, I played hooky from school; when it couldn't be avoided, I stood with my back to the class and read. The kids made fun of me.

"So I was actually relieved when, during the Depression, at age 15, I had to quit school to deliver dresses and shoes for my father and uncle in Manhattan. They couldn't afford to pay me, but running those errands literally changed my life.

"The starting point was my growing love of opera—which came from my mother, an amateur singer with a beautiful voice. Hearing me sing around the house, she took me to a voice instructor whose studio was in the Metropolitan Opera House. I was awe-struck. We could not afford to pay him, but he agreed to teach me on scholarship.

"I went for lessons at lunch time, my arms full of shoe boxes and dresses, or after work, when I was exhausted. Mother and I kept the lessons secret from my father because we knew he wouldn't understand.

"One day when I came home late after a lesson, my father demanded to know why. I couldn't keep the secret anymore. I broke down and told him that I was taking voice lessons. Though he had no idea what voice lessons were, he didn't try to stop me.

"Not long after, while making a delivery on 57th Street, I saw a crowd in front of Steinway Hall. Auditions were being held for a summer job at an Adirondack Mountain resort called Scaroon Manor.

"I sang and got the job, beating out more than 40 others. Eighteen years old, I was very nervous because I had no real experience. But that didn't last long, since I had to do everything in that job. I sang show tunes and backup songs for the chorus girls and was the straight man for a young comedian named Red Skelton. The first time I heard the audience applaud, I knew this was the business for me.

"Incredibly, when I got up onstage and sang, my stutter disappeared. I gained assurance each time I faced a new audience. My shyness disappeared as well. I learned the vital lesson that it's possible to overcome a debilitating handicap.

"If I hadn't been making a delivery that day, I never would have known about the auditions and gotten my first break. The experience taught me that only by being out there in the world, confronting it every day, can you learn of the infinite opportunities available to you."

Robert Merrill, a baritone, has given nearly 800 performances at the Metropolitan Opera House. He has sung for nine Presidents.

The importance of speech and language competence is underscored when we consider that communication is the root of many other skills. Children use speech and language to develop competence across skill domains—cognitive, social, artistic, athletic. Even mathematics, a skill that at first glance would seem removed from language, uses language as its basis.

Because communication is central to so many of our actions, the failure of a child to acquire speech and language normally can be viewed as a "developmental disaster" (Warren & Kaiser, 1988). The effects of a communication disorder or delay are not limited to the child's linguistic proficiency but affect all other areas of the child's development and achievement in both educational and social domains. When one considers the far-reaching effects of a communication delay or disorder, the responsibility of parents and educators to provide optimum opportunities for speech and language acquisition as well as to identify delays or differences early and provide timely and appropriate intervention becomes paramount.

This chapter explores the many facets of communication and the characteristics of the various communication disorders. For each disorder, possible causes, characteristic behaviors, and assessment and intervention approaches are presented.

One of the milestones of early childhood is learning to speak; parents encourage this development and worry if their child doesn't seem to be progressing.

HISTORICAL OVERVIEW

Accounts of individuals with communication disorders are found among the earliest examples of recorded history. Moses, Aesop, Virgil, Demosthenes, and several of the kings of France reportedly suffered from "defective speech." Accounts of cures for speech disorders are abundant as well. Hippocrates believed that stuttering was due to problems of the digestive tract and could be overcome by treating the digestive problems. Francis Bacon's view was somewhat more creative. He believed that stammering was caused by refrigeration of the tongue, which made it less apt to move freely. His prescription was to drink wine in moderation, "because it heateth" the tongue.

Unusual views of speech disorders persisted into this century. In *The Practical Treatment of Stammering and Stuttering*, George A. Lewis (1902) stated that "stammering is undoubtedly a mental disease" (p. 58). He noted the greater incidence of stuttering among males, concluding that "a greater proportion of [men] have the nervous strain of business, and are more often brought into the trying relations of life" (p. 17).

Up until the 1930s, speech disorders were perceived as medical concerns requiring medical treatment. In the early part of this century, practitioners who had trained in Europe began to provide treatment of speech disorders in the United States. During this time, speech correction teachers were hired in some U.S. school systems to work with students who stuttered or had problems with speech sounds.

By the 1920s, speech professionals began to meet and discuss techniques for treatment. In 1924, Lee Edward Travis (the first nonmedical doctor—with a Ph.D. degree rather than an M.D.—trained to work with speech and hearing disorders) began to study stuttering from a neurological perspective. The American Speech and Hearing Association (now the American Speech–Language–Hearing Association), the first professional organization for communication specialists, was established in 1969.

Over the years, professionals who deliver direct diagnostic and therapeutic services have been referred to as logopedists, communicologists, speech or voice teachers, correctionists, therapists, clinicians, or pathologists. The current preferred terminology for certified professionals who diagnose communication disorders and provide therapy is **speech–language pathologist.**

The practice of speech–language pathology has undergone many changes, moving from an almost exclusive focus on articulation and fluency disorders to diagnosis and treatment of disorders formerly thought to be outside of the realm of speech pathologists (e.g., voice, language, swallowing functioning). Currently, clinical practice extends to developmental language disorders, written language, learning disabilities, cognitive–communicative disorders, myofunctional disorders, aural rehabilitation, augmentative and alternative communication, and dysphagia (swallowing disorders) (Paul-Brown & Zingeser, 1994). These services are delivered in a variety of settings: hospitals, public and private schools, community or private clinics, nursing homes, individuals' own homes, and rehabilitation centers.

CLASSIFYING COMMUNICATION DISORDERS

Communication disorders are classified according to the broad categories of speech, voice, and language—although voice disorders can actually be said to form one subcategory of speech disorders. An individual may have a disorder in any or all of these areas.

For discussion purposes in this chapter, speech and voice disorders will be grouped together and are discussed separately from language disorders. Keep in mind, however, that because speech is one means of producing language, there is substantial overlap among the categories.

DISORDERS OF SPEECH

According to the American Speech–Language–Hearing Association (1982), a **speech disorder** is "an impairment of voice, articulation of speech sounds, and/or fluency. These impairments are observed in the transmission and use of the oral symbol system." More simply stated, a speech disorder is a problem with producing the sounds (phonemes) and words of oral language.

Before turning to the three types of speech disorders, a basic review of the mechanics of normal speech production is in order.

The Mechanics of Normal Speech Production

Speech production is a mechanical act that is set in motion by air generated by the lungs. As the airstream moves up through the larynx, the vocal folds are set into motion. These rapid vibrations are the sound source for speech production. The 10 intrinsic muscles of the larynx open and close the vocal folds, changing their tension and shape, producing different types of vocalization.

The sound produced by the larynx then moves into the oral cavity where it is shaped into speech sounds by the articulators: the lips, teeth, tongue, and palate. The lips shape the sound by stopping the airstream (as when the sounds /p/, /b/, or /m/ are produced) or partially obstructing it (as when the sounds /f/, /v/, /w/, or /wh/ are produced). The lips are also used to produce vowels (e.g., rounded for /oo/ and spread for /ee/). The teeth help direct the airstream within the mouth—for example, toward the front of the mouth for /sh/. They also provide friction for production of some sounds (/s/, /z/, /sh/, /zh/) and construct the airstream for others (/f/, /v/). The tongue shapes the airstream, as when it is pointed for production of /l/ or flattened for /sh/. It also closes off the oral cavity and then allows the air to be released quickly, as when /g/, /k/, /t/, or /d/ are produced. The alveolar ridge, the bony ridge behind the upper incisors, serves as a stopping point for the tongue for production of certain sounds (/t/, /d/, /n/). The back of the tongue presses against the hard palate when /k/, /g/, and /ng/ are produced. The soft palate helps open the passage between the oral and nasal cavities. The entire oral cavity (the inside of the mouth) serves as a resonating chamber for the voice (Calvert & Silverman, 1983). Figure 7.1 displays a simplified cross section of the structures involved in speech production. Speech disorders occur when one or more of the foregoing steps does not occur properly.

Articulation Disorders

An **articulation disorder** occurs when a person cannot correctly produce one or more sounds of his language. Articulation difficulties are the most common speech

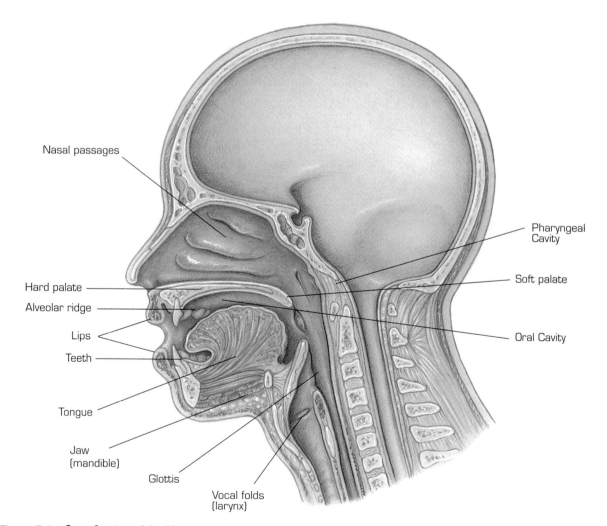

Figure 7.1   Cross Section of the Neck and Head

disorder, making up approximately 75% of all speech disorders (Newman, Creaghead, & Secord, 1985). Articulation disorders are most common among young children, especially those of preschool age. As illustrated by Figure 7.2, articulation development must be judged within the context of a child's age. For example, 90% of children typically are able to produce the sounds /p/, /m/, /h/, /n/, and /w/ by age 3. Therefore, a 4-year-old child who is unable to produce these sounds consistently in connected speech would be considered to have delayed articulation development. But, if the same child had difficulty producing /sh/, /j/, and /th/, this would not be of concern since 90% of children do not produce these sounds consistently until age 7.

Articulation disorders can be classified according to the type of error made when attempting to produce the sounds. For example, if the speaker leaves out sounds from words—as when a child says "ite" for *bite*, "wa" for *want*, or "coo-ie" for *cookie*—it is an *omission* error. Omissions can occur when pronouncing single words or in connected speech ("I wa a ite a you coo-ie" for "I want a bite of your cookie"). Most children will omit the same sounds consistently, although not necessarily in all positions of the word (beginning, middle, end). A child may produce the /b/ sound in the beginning of words but omit it from the middle and final word positions. In a *substitution* disorder, a sound that belongs in a word is replaced with a different sound. A child who says "allwight" for *all right*, "balentine" for *valentine*, or "wake" for *lake* displays substitution errors. Substitution errors also occur in connected speech ("Top weading me wibary book" for "Stop reading my library book"). Other types of articulation errors are *distortions*, in which a sound is

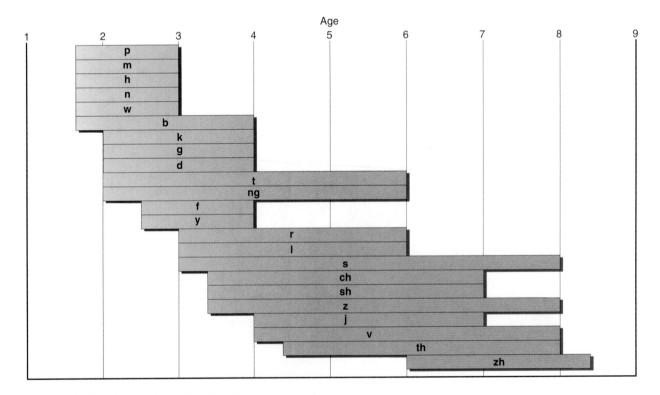

Figure 7.2 **Developmental Articulation Chart**

Source: Adapted from "When Are Speech Sounds Learned?," by E. K. Sander, 1972, *Journal of Speech and Hearing Disorders, 37,* p. 62. Used with permission.

produced incorrectly (a slushy /s/ sound), and *additions*, in which an extra sound is added to a word ("flinger" for *finger*).

A speaker may display one or all of these types of articulation errors. The more errors displayed and the greater the number of word positions in which the errors occur, the less intelligible is the person's speech. A small number of children exhibit so many errors that their speech consists of a string of connected vowels with a few consonants, making it almost impossible for them to speak intelligibly. However, most children with articulation disorders can be understood when using connected speech, as the listener fills in the appropriate sounds and uses context cues to help supply meaning. Unless their articulation disorders are severe, most young children will not need intervention. Parents and teachers can help them by providing correct speech models and not reinforcing errors because they sound cute.

It should be noted that many speakers produce the sounds of a language differently due to regional, social, cultural, or ethnic dialects or the influence of their native languages (American Speech–Language–Hearing Association, 1982). Consider the added /r/ of a Boston accent ("idear" for *idea*), the rounded vowels of Virginia's eastern shore ("oat and aboat" for *out and about*), or the soft /r/ of Lousiana's Cajun residents. Few listeners would judge this speech as impaired in any way and many would appreciate the richness that accents and dialects add to the spoken language. Unless the speaker has a specific reason for modifying his or her dialect (e.g., wanting to become a network broadcaster), a regional accent is considered a communicative variation and not a reason for professional intervention. It is, however, possible for an individual to have a communication disorder concomitant with speaking in a dialect. Therefore, it is important for speech–language professionals to be able to "distinguish between dialectical differences and communicative disorders" (American Speech–Language–Hearing Association, 1982).

Causes of Articulation Disorders.   Articulation disorders can result from an *organic* impairment such as a cleft palate, cerebral palsy, or malocclusion (dental malformation). Others are *functional* in nature, meaning that there is no identifiable organic or structural cause for the problem.

Chromosomal Disorders.   Some organic impairments are genetic or chromosomal in nature. There are a variety of genetic syndromes that can result in articulation disorders. If a syndrome causes structural variations, for instance, the child may have difficulty achieving proper placement of the articulators. Also, some syndromes result in developmental delays and cognitive impairment that contribute to slower development of speech. For example, articulation disorders are present in many children with Down syndrome; anatomical differences (e.g., unusually high larynx, unusually small oral cavity), low muscle tone in and around the mouth and face, and the prevalence of conductive hearing losses could account for the high rate of articulation disorders among this group (Kumin, 1994). Other chromosomal disorders that can result in articulation impairment, often in conjunction with language impairment or delay, include cri du chat syndrome, fragile X syndrome, Turner syndrome, Pierre-Robin syndrome, and Prader-Willi syndrome. Single gene disorders that can result in articulation and language disorders include Hunter's syndrome, Treacher-Collins syndrome, and Cornelia de Lange syndrome (Rosetti, 1996; Sparks, 1984).

Cleft Palate and Other Malformations.   A cleft lip or palate (roof of the mouth) is the failure of the lip or palate to join properly. As the embryo develops, the face, lips, and palate are formed when several components fuse together during the first trimester of the pregnancy. In 1 of every 700 births, this fusion is not completed and a cleft lip, with or without cleft palate, results. In about 1 in every 2,500 births, a cleft palate alone occurs. In many cases, there is a family history of cleft palate and/or lip. Recent research indicates that the gene causing cleft deformities can be triggered by a mother's smoking during pregnancy (American Cleft Palate–Craniofacial Association, personal communication, October 19, 1995; "Study Links," 1995).

A cleft can take the form of a unilateral (one-sided) or bilateral (both sides) cleft lip, a unilateral or bilateral cleft palate, or both. Surgical repair of a cleft lip usually begins around 3 months of age, while cleft palate repair usually begins between the ages of 9 and 18 months (Setliff, 1994). Even after surgery, there may not be complete separation of the oral and nasal cavities. As a result of this organic impairment, the child may have difficulty building and sustaining sufficient air pressure to produce pressure consonants (/p/, /b/, /s/, /z/, /ch/). When the child attempts these consonants, excess air escapes through the nose and results in excess nasal emission (a snorting-like sound that interferes with clear speech production) (Moran & Pentz, 1995).

Malformations of the jaw, teeth, or palate can also cause articulation disorders. For example, an open bite, in which the back teeth come together when the mouth is closed but there is a large open area between the upper and lower front teeth, can cause difficulty producing /s/ and /z/ sounds.

Hearing Impairments.   Another organic cause of articulation disorders is hearing impairment. Many of the sounds of our language are not visible on the lips as they are produced. Individuals with hearing impairment have difficulty producing sounds they can neither hear nor see. Levels of intelligibility can be correlated with the severity of the loss. For example, studies of speech intelligibility in persons with

Child with a cleft lip before surgery

Child with a cleft lip after surgery

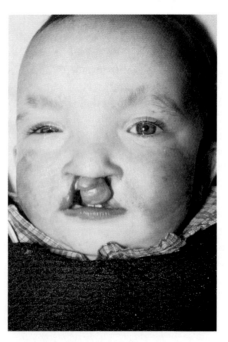
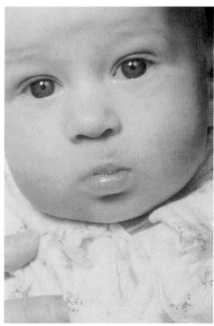

hearing impairment have reported that the average intelligibility of speakers with profound levels of hearing impairment is approximately 20% (Carney, 1986).

Motor Impairments.   Most young children with unclear speech have not yet developed the fine motor skills needed to move their tongue, lips, and jaw with enough speed, accuracy, and coordination to produce the sounds and words of their language. As their motor skills develop, they become increasingly proficient with speech production. Most children can produce the sounds of their native language with few or no errors by age 6 or 7. Many misarticulations produced by children before this age are developmental in nature and, therefore, not true speech disorders.

A small number of children's articulation difficulties, however, result from neuromotor impairment caused by a dysfunction in the motor control center in the central and/or peripheral nervous systems—resulting in another example of articulation difficulties with an organic basis. Children whose speech is *dysarthric* exhibit abnormal motor movements when attempting to speak. Abnormal muscle tone may cause their movements to be weak or slow, unsteady, and uncoordinated. **Dysarthria** of speech is characteristic of many children with cerebral palsy and neuromuscular injuries, and adults who have suffered strokes (Love, 1992).

Apraxia.   Some children lack the voluntary control of the oral mechanism needed for clear speech production. Their speech disorders, functional in nature, may be identified as **developmental apraxia of speech (DAS).** The errors of children with DAS differ from those of other children with developmental articulation disorders in that they may produce extra sounds in words, may prolong syllables in words, and repeat sounds and syllables in words. Further, their speech is inconsistent and their errors are often unpredictable, not following any set pattern (Hall, Jordan, & Robin, 1993).

Assessment of Articulation Disorders.   All assessments of speech–language disorders have components in common: a history of the individual's communication status, formal (standardized) evaluation instruments, an informal sample of the individual's communication skills, examination of the individual's oral peripheral speech mechanism to reveal any structural anomalies, and a hearing test to rule out hearing loss as a possible cause of the communication impairment.

For children with impaired articulation, a single-word, standardized articulation test should be used to provide an opportunity for the child to produce all the consonant phonemes of a language in initial, medial, and final word positions, as well as many vowels and blends. Typically, the child is shown a picture and asked to name it (without a verbal model). The speech–language pathologist then notes which sounds were produced incorrectly and in which word positions. Since such tests may not always reflect the child's production of sounds in connected speech, a sample of spontaneous speech should also be taken.

Intervention for Articulation Disorders.   The beginning point for therapy for articulation disorders is based on the child's unique speech patterns. Many approaches begin by making the child aware of the sounds within words that he may be omitting, distorting or for which he is substituting other sounds. Auditory discrimination activities are used to help the child hear the differences between words (e.g., "Do the words *shoe* and *chew* begin with the same sound?" or "Are the words *bit* and *bet* the same or different?").

INNOVATIVE IDEAS　　THE CHALLENGE OF DIVERSE POPULATIONS

Communication between the speech–language pathologist and client is the basis of effective intervention for speech and language disorders. But what happens if the speech–language pathologist and the client do not speak the same language? As our society becomes increasingly multicultural, more and more school systems are faced with the challenge of providing diagnostic and therapeutic speech-language services to children whose native language is not English.

In Virginia, the Arlington Public Schools in the suburbs of Washington, D.C., face this challenge on a daily basis. There are more than 50 different languages spoken by students in this school system. The largest non-English-speaking group of students is Hispanic. To meet the needs of this population, Arlington public schools have developed Spanish immersion programs at three elementary schools and one middle school. Through this program, "first language" support (e.g., instruction in Spanish) is provided to students in an effort to prevent the need for speech–language services. Parent outreach programs are also available to help parents of preschool and elementary children in stimulating their children's home language.

A long-standing problem throughout the nation has been assessment of non-English-speaking students who have been referred for special education services. If these students are assessed in English, their test scores could reflect a limited proficiency in English rather than a deficit in cognitive skills and they might be erroneously identified as needing special education services. Arlington public schools meet this challenge by providing bilingual examiners for speech–language, psychological, and educational evaluations.

The support provided to non-English-speaking students goes beyond prevention and assessment. Most preschoolers who are found eligible for speech–language services received their therapy in Spanish. At one high school, bilingual students with communication impairments and/or other disabilities are taught by a bilingual special education teacher. Bilingual counselors provide individual and group counseling to students who exhibit emotional and/or behavioral difficulties. In many cases, counseling prevents the need for special education services. In addition, teachers come together to brainstorm ideas for materials, techniques, and strategies in reaching the second language student with special needs.

These are just some of the approaches that Arlington Public Schools have tried to meet the needs of their diverse student population. They continue to look for new and effective ways to provide the needed support to their non-English-speaking students and their parents, continually revising their approaches as their student population changes.

Some children can benefit from training nonspeech movement patterns of the articulators (Hall, Jordan, & Robin, 1993; Robin, 1992). This is typically done in the form of tongue and lip exercises, with mirror work to provide visual feedback. Children with severe articulation disorders may begin working on sound production in isolation or in syllables (e.g., /ba/, /be/, /bi/, /bo/), rather than beginning at the word level. Others may begin working at the word level, progressing to the phrase and sentence levels, and finally to conversation.

Most articulation programs will target early developing consonants (/p/, /b/, /m/) or easily visible consonants (/p/, /b/, /m/, /f/, /v/, voiced and voiceless /th/, /l/, /d/, /ch/, /sh/, /s/, /z/) for initial intervention efforts. Some experts feel that voiceless consonants (/p/, /f/, /t/, voiceless /th/, /sh/, /s/) are easier to teach because they require fewer motor skills (Blakeley, 1983; Marquardt & Sussman, 1991). Vowels are usually not selected as initial therapy targets because differentiated vowel production depends on finely graded movements of the jaw, which many children find difficult, and because most vowels are not easily visible when produced nor is their

Children with articulation disorders may do mirror work with a parent or therapist to develop their speech.

manner of production easy to describe. To illustrate this point, try to instruct someone to produce a short /e/ sound as in the word *pet* using only placement cues for the articulators (not the name of the letter or sound) in your instructions. No doubt, you will have difficulty eliciting the sound. Now, try the same task but instruct the individual to produce the /m/ sound. The placement cues for /m/ (e.g., "Press your lips together") along with a cue to turn the voice on provide clear instructions on how to produce the sound.

Phonological processing is an approach that has proven successful with children who are highly unintelligible. This approach focuses on the basic system of sound production. The underlying premise is that a child may produce the same sound incorrectly in different words for different reasons. As Hodson and Paden explain, "Failure to produce /s/, for example, may be the result of different processes in different word situations" (1983, p. 4). In some instances the child may produce an /s/ incorrectly because she reduces consonant clusters (/str/ in the word *string* becomes /tr/). The same child may omit /s/ at the end of words because she deletes single consonants following the vowel in a syllable (*bus* becomes /bu/). Rather than teach the correct production of individual sounds in words, the phonological processing approach teaches the process of production (e.g., producing consonant clusters).

Voice Disorders

Voice disorders occur when the two vocal folds do not come together smoothly along the entire length of their surfaces. Voice disorders are defined as "the absence or abnormal production of voice quality, pitch, loudness, resonance, and/or duration" (American Speech–Language–Hearing Association, 1982). Each type of voice disorder has unique aspects that will be reviewed separately.

Disorders of Voice Quality. A voice quality that is unusual or abnormal may be described as strained, breathy, harsh, shrill, strident, hoarse, raspy, flat, nasal, or denasal. Vocal abuse is a primary cause of voice disorders. Abusive behaviors include screaming, talking excessively or for long periods of time, talking in a noisy environment, singing out of one's natural pitch range, excessive coughing or throat clearing, and smoking. Children abuse their voices through excessive crying, by making repetitive noises when playing (e.g., car noises, battle noises, voices of pretend characters), or by screaming when playing games outside. High school cheerleaders experience a higher than normal incidence of voice problems due to the prolonged and strenuous use of their voices (Aaron & Madison, 1991). Adults are more likely to experience voice problems as a result of their vocations. Voice problems are prevalent among singers, aerobics instructors (trying to be heard above loud music), preachers, politicians, college lecturers, and character actors and comedians who imitate others' voices.

Persistent hoarseness can indicate a more serious problem such as benign growths on the vocal folds (vocal nodules) or tumors. A strained or breathy voice can result from a physical condition (a paralyzed vocal fold) or it can be a learned behavior, as can an excessively harsh voice. Other causes include deafness, systemic disease (asthma or emphysema), or hormonal imbalance; neurological problems such as cerebral palsy, degenerative neuromuscular diseases, or damage to the nerves supplying the larynx as a result of injury or surgery; or vocal abuse.

Disorders of resonance occur when air does not resonate in the nasal passages when the nasal sounds (/m/, /n/, /ng/) are produced, or when too much air resonates in the nasal passages when non-nasal sounds are produced. A *hyponasal* (or denasal) voice sounds flat or hollow due to a lack of nasal resonance. It can result from obstruction of the nasal passages (enlarged adenoids, deviated septum, stuffy nose due to chronic allergies, sinus infections, or a foreign object placed in the nose by a child) or can be a learned manner of speaking characteristic of some regional dialects. A *hypernasal* voice is the result of too much resonance in the nasal cavity. It can be a learned pattern—or it can result from an organic cause such as a cleft palate that allows excess air to enter the nasal passages when speaking, or perhaps from a severe closed head injury (Murdoch, Stokes, & Chenery, 1993). Reduced sensory feedback can result in hypernasality among speakers who are deaf (Calvert & Silverman, 1983).

A person may have a **disorder of pitch** if he speaks in a voice that is too high or low for his age, size, or gender, speaks in a monotone, or has excessive or limited variation in pitch. *Pitch breaks* (abrupt shifts in pitch) are common among adolescent boys and can occur among girls as well. Pitch breaks may indicate a voice problem if they occur at other ages. Pitch disorders can cause social problems if the person's voice is unusually high or low (such as when a male with a high-pitched voice answers the telephone). A *monopitch* or monotone voice can result from a hearing loss, from structural abnormalities, or it can reflect a person's depressed affect. Deafness is another cause of abnormal pitch. Young persons who are deaf tend to speak with a higher fundamental pitch than do persons of the same age with normal hearing (Calvert & Silverman, 1983).

Disorders of loudness or intensity result in excessive or inadequate volume or limited or excessive variation in loudness. Intensity differences can reflect a person's personality (assertive versus reticent) or body size (small people have softer, higher-pitched voices and larger people have louder, lower-pitched voices), or can result from structural differences of the vocal mechanism or from chronic disease (e.g., emphysema). Low volume can result from inadequate breath supply from the lungs. Speakers who are deaf may not use adequate volume in certain situations because they are unaware of the need to vary the intensity of their voices to account for ambient noise in the environment (Calvert & Silverman, 1983). Variations in loudness are considered disorders only when the person's voice is inappropriate for the speaking context, prevents the person from performing job-related duties, or causes concern or embarrassment.

Loss of Voice.   In cases of **aphonia,** a person loses his voice. The loss can be temporary, such as when laryngitis results from inflamed vocal folds. In cases of hysterical aphonia, there is no apparent organic cause of voice loss.

Permanent voice loss can result from accidents and injuries or as a result of surgery for cancer of the larynx. If the larynx is surgically removed, an alternate means of voice production can be learned. One technique is *esophageal speech,* whereby the speaker takes in air through his mouth, swallows it, "burps" it back into the oral cavity, and uses the vibrating airstream to form words with his mouth. Many individuals are able to learn this technique and some become very proficient esophageal speakers. An alternative to esophageal speech is to use an electro-mechanical device for voice production. The *electrolarynx* is a hand-held instrument placed on the neck, which causes vibrations of the air within the vocal tract. The speaker then shapes these vibrations into words using his mouth, thereby producing audible speech. For individuals who cannot use an electrolarynx held on the neck due to tissue damage or swelling, another type is available that delivers sound directly to the oral cavity through a tube that is placed in the mouth. The speaker then forms the vibrations into words using his mouth.

Assessment of Voice Disorders.   As a first step in assessing voice disorders, the client will be asked to provide a history of the voice problems and identify any abusive vocal behaviors (Shipley & McAfee, 1992). A medical history should be taken to rule out any organic problems. Because the cause of a voice disorder can be temporary and because the quality of voice production can vary with environmental factors (e.g., abusive speaking behaviors, exposure to environmental irritants), it is essential to observe someone with a voice disorder over the course of several weeks to obtain a true picture of the customary voice. The appropriateness of a speaker's voice must be judged in the context of the person's gender, age, and body size and the environment in which the person typically communicates.

Intervention for Voice Disorders.   Direct intervention usually focuses on increasing the individual's awareness of proper voice production. Therapeutic techniques include relaxation exercises to reduce tension of the vocal mechanism, breathing exercises to increase breath support for speech, development of the speaker's awareness of proper and improper levels of loudness or pitch, and biofeedback techniques used to train individuals in better voice production. If the voice disorder is caused by vocal abuse, therapy goals will include changing inappropriate patterns of vocalizing (e.g., refraining from shouting or straining the voice to sing) or modifying the environment (e.g., using a microphone for lecturing). In some cases, treatment may also include medical intervention (e.g., surgery, medication).

Fluency Disorders

A **fluency disorder** is defined as "the abnormal flow of verbal expression, characterized by impaired rate and rhythm which may be accompanied by struggle behavior" (American Speech–Language–Hearing Association, 1982). Fluency can be viewed on a continuum from normal fluency (easily flowing speech with few repetitions or hesitations) to disfluency (halting speech with many pauses, silence, and repetitions). Individuals who are disfluent may frequently hesitate, pause, and/or repeat sounds, syllables, or words in connected speech.

While we all experience disfluency at one time or another (e.g., when tired, frightened, or when speaking in front of a group), **stuttering** occurs when a person's speech is notably disfluent much of the time and in many different speaking situations. Some professionals feel that stuttering should be a target for intervention only if it is accompanied by struggle behavior and causes distress for the speaker (*not* the listener). Unless a person feels that his own disfluent speech is a significant handicap in his daily life, he is not necessarily communicatively impaired. There are, after all, variations in both individual and societal acceptance of speech differences. Charles Van Riper illustrates this point in his classic text, *Speech Correction: Principles and Methods* (1978):

> Once, on Fiji in the South Pacific, we found a whole family of stutterers. As our guide and translator phrased it: "Mama kaka; papa kaka; and kaka, kaka, kaka, kaka." All six persons in that family showed marked repetitions and prolongations in their speech but they were happy people, not at all troubled by their stuttering. It was just the way they talked. No hurry, no frustration, no stigma, indeed very little awareness. We could not help but contrast their attitudes and the simplicity of their stuttering with those which would have been shown by a similar family in our own land, where the pace of living is so much faster, where defective communication is rejected, where stutterers get penalized all of their lives. (pp. 6–7)

Some degree of disfluency is normal in very young children as they try to imitate adult words and sentence lengths and to communicate in new ways. Most preschoolers, unaware that they repeat words or sounds, do not exhibit tension and struggle behaviors as a result of their speech. Parents and teachers are advised to avoid drawing the child's attention to these repetitions and to listen patiently.

Typically, a person who is disfluent will have more difficulty with certain sounds, words, or phrases, especially in the beginning of sentences and in certain speaking situations. In addition, there are many secondary behaviors associated with stuttering. One category of secondary behaviors is verbal mannerisms. A common verbal mannerism is to use fillers or stallers (e.g., "let me see," "well uh," "you know"). The speaker might use a sound before a problem word to ease into the word (e.g., "uh give me the change") or he may use a word or phrase to buy time while mentally rearranging his sentences to avoid problem words or to change the positions of words in sentences (e.g., "Let me see . . . I'll take the change"). As a result, many speakers who are disfluent develop excellent vocabulary skills, being very adept at finding synonyms quickly. The pressure of thinking so quickly can, however, increase the speaker's level of stress. Another verbal mannerism is repetition of a word or phrase until the speaker feels comfortable saying the word (e.g., "Why don't you, don't you, give me the change?"). Some speakers pretend to think about an answer until they feel they can speak fluently (Leith, 1984).

Nonverbal struggle behaviors are characteristic of many speakers who stutter. These include eye movements (e.g., eye blinks), tongue movements and clicks, mouth movements (e.g., opening the mouth very wide), head movements (e.g., nodding or moving the head from side to side), body movements (e.g., rhythmic finger or foot tapping), increased muscle tension, and irregular breathing patterns (Leith, 1984).

Causes of Disfluency.   A variety of causes of disfluency have been set forth over the years. As postulated by Benjamin Bogue (1939), for many years the causes of disfluency were thought to be the result of traumatic events or illness (see Table 7.1). If the reasons for stuttering set forth by Bogue were all valid, it is surprising that anyone can speak fluently.

Although Bogue's causes have systematically been ruled out, research to date has not revealed a definitive cause of stuttering. Contributing factors include neurophysiological, psychological, social, and linguistic factors. For many years, researchers have been interested in the role that heredity plays in stuttering. Family studies have revealed a genetic predisposition for stuttering, although the exact pattern of transmission has not been established. Studies of twins reveal that stuttering occurs more often in identical twin pairs (who have identical genes) than in fraternal twin pairs, leading to the conclusion that stuttering is inherited. However, the fact that in some of the identical twin pairs only one twin stuttered implies the influence of environmental factors as well. Although a child may be predisposed to stuttering if he has family members who stutter, he may not necessarily become a stutterer (Ham, 1990; Howie, 1981; Kidd, 1983; Peters & Guitar, 1991).

Assessment of Fluency Disorders.   To begin the assessment process, information is obtained about the client's perception of the fluency problems, the situations and events that lead to fluent or disfluent speech, feared speaking situations, the particular sounds and words or word positions that pose difficulty, and the reactions of others to the client's speech. Physiological factors such as respiration, phonation, and articulation should also be assessed. Speech and disfluency rates are calculated, reflecting the number of words per minute the speaker uses in connected speech and the number of words on which he stutters. Specific disfluent speaking behaviors such as word repetitions, part-word repetitions, phrase repetitions, prolongations, pauses, and stops are counted. Accompanying struggle behaviors (e.g., body movements, eye blinks) and avoidance behaviors (e.g., use of starter phrases) are noted as well.

Throughout the assessment, the speech–language pathologist looks for a pattern of disfluencies. Questionnaires or interviews can be used to assess the speaker's

---

Table 7.1   Causes of Stammering and Stuttering* According to Benjamin N. Bogue

1. It is an *acquired* condition. Stammerers are not born, . . . they are actually made.

2. *Fright* is, in fact, a common cause of stammering and stuttering. [There was a] child who was so badly frightened when boarding a train for the first time that stammering developed.

3. *Threats* of playmates to throw a boy on a railroad track in front of an approaching train – fear of a savage dog – a sudden plunge into cold water – these have produced shocks that have led to stammering.

4. *Injury:* Almost any kind of blow on any part of the body may be a prime cause in a case stammering or stuttering. . . . A small boy went down into the cellar. . . . As he came back the door fell and struck him on the head. . . . He stammered from then on. Another boy fell off a horse; the horse stepped upon him, and stammering resulted almost immediately. . . . One boy swallowed his sister's ring and stammered from that time on.

5. *Illness:* Many cases . . . have an illness as the basis or predisposing cause. . . . Diphtheria, scarlet fever, typhoid fever, influenza, measles, chicken pox, bronchitis, whooping cough, meningitis, mumps, often serve as inciting causes of stammering or stuttering.

---

*Bogue used *stammering* as a broad term that encompassed stuttering. The term is no longer used by professionals.

Source: Adapted from *Stammering: Its Cause and Correction* (pp. 58; 71–79), by B. N. Bogue, 1939, Indianapolis: Author.

feelings and attitudes about his speech. All of the information obtained will be used to rate the individual's disfluencies on a continuum from mild to severe, and recommendations for intervention will be made accordingly (Ham, 1990; Peters & Guitar, 1991).

Intervention for Fluency Disorders.   One outcome of the many misconceptions about stuttering that have proliferated over the years is the development of a wide range of treatments. Almost everything has been tried or prescribed—including surgery (e.g., slitting or notching the patient's tongue), hypnotism, electrical stimulation, medication, tongue exercises, psychotherapy, behavior modification using aversive stimuli, and ignoring the disfluencies (Bogue, 1939; LaBlance, Steckol, & Smith, 1994). In addition to differences in approaches, there is also considerable variation in the intensity, timing, and duration of therapy sessions (American Speech–Language–Hearing Association, 1995a).

Current therapy approaches may be classified under one of two categories: *stuttering modification therapy* or *fluency shaping therapy*. Both approaches attempt to teach the speaker a different speech pattern that results in speech that sounds fluent to listeners.

Stuttering modification therapy, which is sometimes referred to as cognitive therapy, teaches the speaker to monitor his own speech production and to use new speech patterns and control techniques to maintain fluent speech in a variety of speaking situations. The goal is not to teach the person to speak normally, but rather to stutter in a more fluent manner. The focus, therefore, is on modifying the symptoms of the stuttering behavior. Cognitive approaches have in common the development of the speaker's awareness of the mechanics of speech production (i.e., breath support, vibration of the vocal folds, using articulators to shape speech sounds) as well as internal and external factors that affect the ability to produce fluent speech. Even young children can be taught the difference between "hard" speech and "easy" speech, as well as techniques (e.g., diaphragmatic breathing) that will enable smoother speech production (Ham, 1990; Leith, 1984; Peters & Guitar, 1991; Van Riper, 1973).

In contrast, the purpose of **fluency shaping therapy** is to replace the moments of stuttering with fluent speech. The speaker is taught to prolong the production of speech sounds, reducing speech to a very slow rate. Using auditory and visual feedback from machines, the speaker modifies the speech pattern at the syllable, word, phrase, and sentence levels until fluent speech is achieved. This fluent pattern is then generalized to conversational speaking situations in the clinic and then to daily speaking environments. The rate of speech is gradually increased until it approaches a normal rate. Thus, the new, fluent speech pattern learned in the clinic is transferred to the individual's natural environment (Peters & Guitar, 1991; Ryan, 1974; Webster, 1980).

One of the greatest hurdles in fluency therapy is carryover of fluent speech to situations outside the therapy setting. As therapy progresses, factors in the environment (the therapy room and the speech–language pathologist) become cues to fluency and the speaker has little difficulty speaking fluently. Problems may arise when the speaker leaves the safe environment of the therapy setting and tries to communicate in other settings. For this reason, it is essential that steps to achieve carryover are built into any therapy plan and that therapy continues beyond the point when the speaker is fluent in the therapy setting. Communication partners can help a speaker who is disfluent by being patient, responsive listeners. The Stuttering Foundation of America offers suggestions, which are presented in Table 7.2.

Table 7.2   How to React When Speaking With Someone Who Is Disfluent

- Refrain from making comments like "Slow down," "Take a deep breath," or "Relax." Such advice can be demeaning and it is not helpful. It can even have the opposite effect of increasing the speaker's level of tension.

- Refrain from interrupting the speaker to finish sentences or fill in words. Let the speaker express himself.

- Maintain natural eye contact and try not to appear embarrassed or impatient. Try to wait patiently and naturally until the speaker is finished.

- Speak with a relatively slow, relaxed rate but not so slow as to sound unnatural.

- Let the person know by your manner, actions, and verbal responses that you are listening to *what* he says, not *how* it is said.

- Be aware that those who are disfluent usually find talking on the telephone difficult. If you answer the phone and hear nothing, wait to see if it is a disfluent caller before you hang up.

Source: Adapted with permission from the Stuttering Foundation of America.

DISORDERS OF LANGUAGE

A **language disorder** is "the impairment or deviant development of comprehension and/or use of a spoken, written, and/or other symbol system" (American Speech–Language–Hearing Association, 1982). Individuals with language disorders have difficulty using the language code to communicate. They may have problems in both expressing and receiving messages of the language code, as manifested by difficulty in any or all language modes (i.e., listening, speaking, reading, writing).

Before discussing language disorders in more detail, an overview of normal language development follows.

Normal Language Development

An understanding of normal language acquisition is needed to understand language impairments. Children do not acquire language overnight. They learn to talk in a sequence of overlapping stages, acquiring **receptive language skills** (understanding the language) and **expressive language skills** (producing the language). (See Table 7.3 for a checklist of normal language development in infants and young children.)

Infants begin developing oral communication skills from the time they are born. Over the past two decades, research has revealed that infants possess communication abilities that are much more sophisticated than previously thought. This is demonstrated by infants' differentiated cries when wet, tired, hungry, and so forth, and their abilities to discriminate their mothers' voices from others. During the first 3 months, most of the vocalizations of infants are vowel-like. By the age of 6 or 7 months, most infants can produce a full range of front, middle, and back vowel sounds. Over the next 3 months, infants begin to combine consonant sounds (/p/, /b/, /m/, /t/, /d/, /n/) with vowels to produce repetitive sound chains ("ba-ba-ba," "doe-doe-doe"). These two stages (vowel production and repetitive consonant-vowel sound chains) are known as **babbling** (Fowler, 1990; Miller, 1983).

Beginning at about 9 months, infants enter the **jargon** stage. Repetitive babbling decreases and children begin to imitate adult speech patterns of stress and intonation, although without using actual words. Children at this stage sound as if they are talking. For instance, they may raise their voices at the end of a "sentence" as if asking a question, or they may speak loudly and emphasize certain "words" if

Table 7.3 **Checklist for Normal Language Development**

BIRTH TO 3 MONTHS	3 TO 6 MONTHS	6 TO 9 MONTHS	9 TO 12 MONTHS	12 TO 18 MONTHS
Communicates with different cries—for example, when wet, hungry, or in pain Uses vowel-like sounds in vocal play Likes to take turns vocalizing with caregivers Smiles in response to a familiar voice	Uses vowels and consonants in vocal play Begins to imitate sounds Responds to his/her name Babbles using repetitive sound chains	May produce his/her first true word Looks at common objects when named Responds with gestures to words such as "bye-bye" Begins to imitate sounds and intonation of parents' utterances	Understands simple questions and commands ("Where's Grandma?" "Give me the ball.") Uses several (2–4) words Uses exclamations such as "uh-oh" or "huh" Uses single words to represent a whole sentence	Babbles with tone and inflection that imitates sentences (jargon) Uses 20–25 real words Uses one-word sentences—for example, "Drink" for "I want a drink" Responds to simple commands Shakes head in response to yes/no questions

18 TO 24 MONTHS	2 TO 3 YEARS	3 TO 4 YEARS	4 TO 5 YEARS	5 YEARS+
Uses 200–300 words Combines words into short phrases Uses "no" frequently Refers to self by name Uses two-word phrases	Uses four- to five-word sentences Asks many questions ("Why?" "What?" "Where?") Talks about something that has just happened Uses pronouns (I, me, mine, you) Understands simple concepts of size and quantity	Uses over 1,500 words by age 4 Can relay events and retell stories Uses four- to five-word sentences Uses regular past tense and regular plural forms Uses prepositions (on, in, under)	Uses over 2,000 words by age 5 Talks in complete paragraphs Uses possessive pronouns, future tense verbs, and contracted negatives (can't) Can carry out two or three unrelated commands Likes to retell stories	Relates a complex story about future plans Identifies all primary colors States own address Has little difficulty with multisyllabic words Understands concepts of time (before/after; yesterday, today, last week)

Sources: Information derived from *The Language of Toys,* by S. Schwartz & J. E. H. Miller, 1988, Rockville, MD: Woodbine House; *Assessment in Speech–Language Pathology,* by K. G. Shipley & J. G. McAfee, 1992, San Diego: Singular Publishing Group; *Parent Helper,* by the U.S. Department of Education, 1982, Washington, DC: U.S. Government Printing Office.

they are angry. Children of this age also demonstrate their understanding of language by pausing for a moment in response to "no-no" or their names, looking for objects that are named, and responding with gestures to "up," "pat-a-cake," and so forth.

By around 11 or 12 months of age, real words begin to appear in a baby's jargon. Although children at this stage are only capable of using single words in isolation, each word may have several different meanings. For example, the child may say "dirty" when her diaper needs to be changed, when her hands become messy eating a banana, when she sees her father writing with a pen, or when her mother gets out the vacuum cleaner. In each instance, she uses "dirty" to represent a different concept—"I need to be changed," "This banana is messy," "Daddy's using that thing that makes marks on the wall," or "Mama's getting out the noisy machine

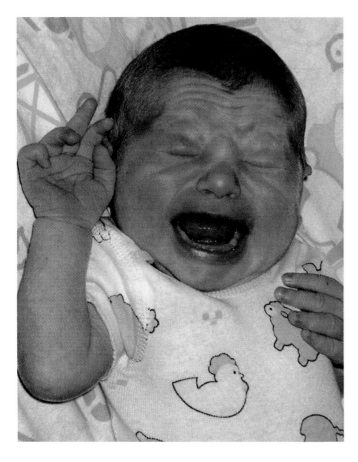

This 3-day-old infant is expressing his displeasure quite clearly.

that picks up dirt." Over the next 6 months, the child continues to learn new words and refine their meanings, until by the time she is 18 months old, the typical child possesses an expressive vocabulary of approximately 50 words. During this period, the child's receptive language develops rapidly as well. By 18 months of age, the child can respond to simple commands ("Wave bye-bye"; "Give me the ball"), will shake his head in response to yes/no questions ("Are you sleepy?"; "Do you want more juice?"), and can point to several body parts when named.

From the period of 18 months to 3 years, children develop mastery of longer utterances using a variety of syntactical forms (nouns, verbs, adjectives, prepositions, and adverbs combined in simple sentences using present and past tense; pronouns; possessives) and increase their vocabulary exponentially. By the time a child is 3 years old, his expressive vocabulary will have grown to several thousand words. Continued expansion of the child's linguistic skills will continue until the child reaches age 5 or 6. During the preschool period, children learn to use a variety of question types and sentence types. New syntactical forms appear in their expressive language (e.g., future tense verbs, contracted negatives, possessive pronouns). Vocabulary continues to increase while syntactical (grammatical) errors decrease.

By age 5, a child's language development is essentially complete in terms of style and format, although there will be occasional errors. As children grow to adulthood, they continue to refine their language use—learning new ways to use language (e.g., written format) and adding more complex forms and content. For example, at age 5, children will have mastered use of the conjunctions *and* and *but*.

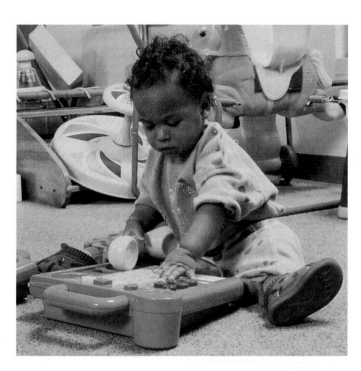

Young children enjoy using jargon and engaging in pretend play.

Full acquisition of conjunctions takes place over the next several years: *if* at 6 years, *because* at 7 years, *unless* at 9 years, and *although* at 12 years. Similarly, although most children at age 5 have a range of modifiers (adjectives and adverbs) within their repertoires, it is not until they become teenagers that they master subtle distinctions between modifiers (e.g., *slightly, somewhat, quite*) (Haynes, 1989).

Thus, in just 5 short years, without formal or direct instruction, most children who are developing normally are able to master a very complex system that incorporates many inconsistent rules, subtleties of meaning, and variations in use. The fact that most children do this without difficulty is amazing. The instances when children do not develop language normally can be devastating to the child and his family.

Characteristics of Language Disorders

As enumerated in Table 7.4, there are five basic components of language. An individual with a language disorder may have difficulty with any or all of these components. Speakers who have problems with phonology may find it difficult to distinguish between similar sounding words (e.g., "lie" and "light," or "pail" and "bail"), a problem that may also affect the person's articulation. Individuals with semantic deficits may have limited vocabulary skills and categorical knowledge. They may have difficulty expressing thoughts and comprehending what is said, especially if the speaker uses abstract forms of expression such as idioms and figurative language. Deficits in syntax and morphology result in the production of utterances that are grammatically incorrect; for example, the speaker may have difficulty with subject–verb agreement, verb tense, and pronouns. Individuals with deficient pragmatic skills will have difficulty with the social context of language—for example, initiating, maintaining, and terminating conversations; maintaining appropriate

The language development of these 5-year-olds is essentially complete.

conversational distance; and knowing when to use formal conversation, humor, or slang (Thomas, 1990). (See Table 7.5 for examples of pragmatic language skills.)

Another approach to categorize the elements of language was set forth by Bloom and Lahey in 1978. They identified three interrelated components of language, as follows:

1. *Form:* The elements that connect the sounds or the symbols of language with its meaning (that is, the form the language takes); incorporates phonology, morphology, and syntax

2. *Content:* The meanings of words; knowledge of the relationships among objects, events, and people

3. *Use:* Rules for the social use of language for communication

Table 7.4   **Components of Language**

COMPONENT	DESCRIPTION
Phonology	The sounds of a language and the rules that determine their use (i.e., which sounds can be combined and in what order)
Semantics	The meaning of the words of the language to individuals
Syntax	The rules for sequencing words into phrases, clauses, and sentences to convey meaning
Morphology	The rules for deriving various word forms and internal structure of words (i.e., adding prefixes and suffixes and changing verb tenses and number)
Pragmatics	The rules for how language is to be used to communicate in different social situations

Sources: Information derived from *Effective Intervention With the Language Impaired Child,* by M. L. Cole & J. T. Cole, 1989, Rockville, MD: Aspen; *An Introduction to Children With Language Disorders,* by V. A. Reed, 1994, New York: Macmillan.

Table 7.5 **Pragmatic Language Skills**

- Initiates communication appropriately
- Carries out communicative intents (e.g., greeting; requesting objects, information, or actions; making requests; making choices; stating reasons; predicting; protesting)
- Establishes and maintains appropriate conversational distance
- Establishes and maintains normal eye contact during conversations
- Uses and interprets body language appropriately
- Initiates conversations appropriately
- Chooses conversational topics appropriate for the conversational partner(s) and situation
- Uses a variety of conversational devices (e.g., answering questions, attending to the speaker, requesting clarification, providing clarification)
- Specifies, maintains, and changes conversational topics appropriately
- Interrupts another speaker politely
- Terminates conversations appropriately
- Elaborates on a topic chosen by self or conversational partner
- Takes turns with other speakers in conversation
- Shares personal information appropriately
- Discusses current events

Sources: Information derived from *Functional Communication Profile,* by L. I. Kleiman, 1993, Moline, IL: LinguiSystems; *Assessment in Speech–Language Pathology,* by K. Shipley & J. McAfee, 1992, San Diego: Singular Publishing Group.

Using Bloom and Lahey's model, consider a child with normal language development. He is tired of shopping with his mother and says, "I want to go home now." He has conveyed the meaning of his message (appropriate content), he has used an understandable means of formulating his message (appropriate form), and he has followed the rules for conveying his message to his mother at a critical time (appropriate use). But consider a child whose language is delayed or disordered. In the same circumstance he says, "Him doe tee vee-a-vur." Although his mother can translate this message to mean "I want to go see Christopher,"—from which she can infer that her child is tired and wants to leave the store and go see his brother Christopher at home—the child has not followed the rules of the language for conveying his message with appropriate or conventional form and content. And, if he directed his request to a stranger, rather than his mother, he would also be demonstrating inappropriate use of language.

Causes of Language Disorders. Language disorders can be developmental or acquired. The language delays of children who have not yet attained normal language skills may be viewed as *developmental* in nature. Loss of language skills after they have been learned may be viewed as *acquired* language disorders. Causes of acquired language disorders include stroke, traumatic brain injury, and neuromuscular diseases. Most cases of acquired language disorders occur among adults, but a relatively small number of children are included in this group. In many cases, the exact cause of a language disorder is unknown. Children with no organic impairment, injury, or other disability fail to develop language or exhibit delayed language.

Language disorders are salient features of many other disabilities such as mental retardation, hearing impairment, learning disabilities, autism, and emotional disorders. Acquired language disorders can result from a traumatic brain injury, a stroke, or as a result of a convulsive disorder. Delayed language is more prevalent in children with cleft palate, perhaps due to the higher incidence of hearing loss among this population and the great deal of time spent in the hospital and at home recovering, where language learning opportunities and the desire to communicate orally may be diminished (Moran & Pentz, 1995). Since vision plays an important role in normal language development (e.g., pairing word meanings with events and objects that are observed, learning nonverbal language through gestural cues, developing cognitive skills through observing and interacting with the environment), preschool children who are blind or visually impaired may also experience language delays. If alternate language acquisition strategies are provided to young children who are blind, however, they can acquire language skills commensurate with age level expectations (Evans & Johnson, 1988).

Another common causal factor of language disabilities is environmental. Children who are raised in environments that are impoverished linguistically (e.g., lack of appropriate language models, experiences, or materials to explore and discuss)—especially during the preschool years—may exhibit language delays that persist into their school years and beyond. The relationship between children's linguistic environments and language development is, however, variable. Hearing children of parents who are deaf often develop oral language in accordance with developmental norms, while some children in enriched environments fail to develop adequate language skills for no apparent reason.

Assessment of Language Disorders. The primary purposes of assessment for language disorders are (1) to determine whether a language disorder exists, (2) to determine possible causes of the disorder, (3) to identify specific areas of deficit, (4) to establish goals for intervention, and (5) to project a prognosis for intervention (Swisher, 1985). Within this framework, diagnostic approaches are tailored to each individual's needs, age, and communication status.

Informal observation and interviews are important sources of information about an individual's communicative status. Broen (1988) explains that during assessment, "an attempt is made to understand the performance of an individual in the environment in which that individual functions" (p. 301). Language assessment should begin with an interview with a child's parents or, for an adult, with someone who is familiar with the person's use of language in his or her environment.

Infants and very young children should be assessed within the context of the family system (Comfort, 1988). The infant's prenatal and neonatal history will provide relevant assessment information. And, since the primary targets of infant communication are the caregivers, young children should be assessed while interacting with them. Use of playlike settings in naturalistic environments to assess infants and young children can yield valuable diagnostic information (Rossetti, 1996). School-age children may respond better to school-like tasks (i.e., describing pictures, defining words, pointing to pictures as named).

Valuable diagnostic information can be obtained from a language sample during which the individual's responses to questions, to pictures, or when telling a story are tape-recorded and later transcribed. The sample is then analyzed to determine the individual's mean length of utterance (average length of phrases or sentences used) or the number and types of grammatical and syntactical forms used.

As illustrated by the following two examples, a language sample can provide an in-depth picture of an individual's expressive language skills, which can supplement data from standardized tests.

"How do you do a somersault?"

Response of 10-year-old boy with a language disorder:

"Put our hands on the mat and put your legs on your shoulders. Put your hand way back. Put your head way forward. Roll back on floor and go like a . . . I can't do it very good. I do something else. I show you a different one."

Response of 10-year-old boy with normal language development:

"First you stand up. And then you sort of squat down. Next, put your hands flat on the ground in front of your knees. Then you push off with your legs . . . put your head down . . . and then you push off with your feet and tumble . . . You just go!"

While both of these children knew what a somersault was, the sample from the boy with a language disorder reveals difficulty in both describing and sequencing the steps of the somersault. Such valuable information might have been missed if a vocabulary test had been used on which the boys were asked only to point to a picture of someone doing a somersault. Both of them would have pointed to the correct picture, but, as can be seen in the samples, their language skills are quite discrepant.

The varied components of language and the many contexts in which language is used makes the assessment of language disorders a difficult task. While some components (e.g., receptive or expressive vocabulary, response to simple questions, ability to follow verbal directions) can be assessed easily, others (e.g., pragmatic skills, comprehension, and use of abstract forms) may be difficult to accurately assess. For this reason, assessment of an individual's language status must be viewed as an ongoing activity, rather than one that can be completed in one diagnostic session.

While helpful diagnostic information can be obtained from standardized instruments, such tests should be used cautiously when evaluating the linguistic skills of children who speak nonstandard dialects of English (e.g., "black English"). Tests standardized on midwestern white students can result in an overidentification of children with language and articulation disorders among different populations (e.g., Hispanics, Native Americans). Therefore, speech–language pathologists should choose tests that take language and dialectical differences into account and avoid tests that are not valid for nonstandard speech patterns (Vaughn-Cooke, 1989).

If the individual's expressive language skills are limited, a functional language assessment can provide useful information. Functional assessments tap basic language functions such as the individual's verbal status (e.g., verbal or nonverbal), his typical level of expressive language (e.g., single words, phrases, sentences), the means he typically uses to communicate (e.g., sounds, speech, facial expressions, signs, writing), how he uses communication (e.g., to express basic needs, emotions, interests, feelings), and the effectiveness of his communication (e.g., consistently communicates his intent, communicates intent sporadically, is unable to communicate intent). As shown in Figure 7.3, which displays one section of the *Functional Language Profile* (Kleiman, 1994), a functional language assessment attempts to provide information on all methods an individual might use to communicate.

Intervention for Language Disorders.   The frontline approach to intervention for language disorders is prevention. As illustrated in Table 7.6, parents, other fam-

Type	Communicates Choices	Expresses Pleasure/ Discomfort	Expresses Name	Labels Objects
attempts speech				
speaks				
imitates speech				
sign language				
fingerspells				
alphabet set				
writes				
types				
picture system				
word system				
eye gaze				
communication device				
facilitation				
vocalizes				
points/gestures				
facial expression				
takes object of choice				
body movements				
shows I.D. tag or card				
not expressed				
other				

Figure 7.3   Functional Language Skills

Source: From *Functional Communication Profile* (p. 5), by L. I. Kleiman, 1994, Moline, IL: LinguiSystems. Copyright © 1994 by LinguiSystems, Inc. Used with permission.

ily members, and caregivers can foster a young child's language acquisition by providing an enriched linguistic environment, good speech and language models, and appropriate encouragement and reinforcement of the child's attempts at speech and language production. Research has demonstrated that an enriched early environment has a positive effect not only on a child's verbal language development but on cognitive and social development as well (Fowler, 1990). Children with significant developmental disabilities, however, may not interact with their environments the way other children do. Even in an enriched linguistic environment, their learning experiences and outcomes may be vastly different (Schiefelbusch, 1988). For these children, a more direct approach to facilitating communication development is needed.

The primary goals of language intervention programs are to enable an individual to communicate basic needs, feelings, and opinions and to comprehend the basic meanings expressed through the language of his or her culture. Beyond this primary goal, the desired outcomes of language intervention programs will vary

Table 7.6   **Enhancing Children's Communication Development**

- Interact with infants and toddlers on their developmental levels, using objects and activities that are interesting to *them*.

- Have a variety of interesting objects (e.g., toys, noisemakers, household items, picture books, containers to hide things in and under) available to play with and talk about. Periodically put some away and bring new ones out.

- Take turns initiating and responding to one another as you play (e.g., baby hits a block with a rattle, parent hits a block with a rattle). Imitate baby's sounds as well as his actions.

- Label objects and actions in a natural manner as you play (e.g., "I like the blue car. It goes fast.").

- Make noises when playing with toys and objects (e.g., "bam-bam" for the toy hammer, clicking noises with your tongue as the toy horse runs). Imitate the child's noises.

- Use good speech and language models consisting of short, complete sentences, with a minimum of "baby talk."

- Stress key concepts and labels as you talk (e.g., "The cup is empty. You have an empty cup.").

- Ask simple questions that the young child can respond to with a word or phrase or by demonstrating the correct response (e.g., "Where is the duck?" rather than "Why does the duck go in the water?").

- Expand on the child's utterances. If the child says, "Ball red," respond with "The ball is red" or "I see the red ball."

- Give the child a chance to talk. When adults "take charge" of play, children miss opportunities to initiate language and try out new forms. They also may lose interest in the activity.

- Take advantage of the many opportunities throughout a typical day to talk to your child about what you are doing, where you are going, who you see, and so forth. The ideal situations for language learning are those that occur naturally.

- Turn off the television and get the child actively involved in a pleasurable activity. Remember, something as simple as washing the dishes can be exciting if an adult is interacting positively with the child.

- Look at picture books, magazines, and family photos—and talk about each picture. Read children's books daily to the child and let the child "read" them back to you using her own language and story line. Make a special book for the child of her favorite pictures.

- Let the child know that you enjoy communicating with him by stopping what you are doing, looking at the child, and showing interest in what he is saying. Refrain from interrupting the child to correct his speech or language, to talk for him, or to hurry him along.

according to the individual's age, cognitive level, and the demands of the communication environments (e.g., home, school, community, workplace).

Appropriate language development programs for infants, toddlers, and preschool children (Warren, 1992) have several distinctive features:

1. *Parents and other caregivers as central players:* Parent-initiated language intervention programs are effective in helping young children develop language skills. The potential of parents as effective language facilitators is based on several premises. First, parents usually serve as initial language teachers for their children. Thus, involving parents as facilitators in language intervention programs enables them to fulfill a natural role. Second, parents are able to promote generalization of language use that is not as easily achieved in formal language training programs. And third, parents are invested in their children's language development and are usually better able to interpret their children's communicative acts than are other adults who may not be as familiar with the children (Kaiser, 1993). But by far the most compelling reason for involving parents as participants in their children's language intervention programs is that it works. As McDade and Varnedoe (1987) conclude from the results of a dozen accounts of parent training programs, "Simply put, programs that involve parents produce greater gains than those that do not" (p. 150).

2. *Language training in a natural context:* The importance of implementing language training to young children in a natural context cannot be overemphasized. In their book *Natural Language*, Hatten and Hatten (1981) state that "children normally do not learn the complicated rules of language and the complex processes of speech in formal teacher–student lessons. They learn language best in the usual give-and-take of everyday life" (p. 6). For this reason, effective language intervention programs for young children involve a lot of play activities in which the child is having fun as well as learning new communication skills.

3. *Arrangement of the environment to meet the child's communication needs:* Typically, the initial objective of communication intervention programs for young children is learning labels for common objects and actions (Warren, 1992). As the child's single word vocabulary grows, the focus shifts from primarily teaching the child new words to combining words into meaningful utterances and developing basic concepts for grouping vocabulary words into meaningful schema. Table 7.7 displays some of the basic concepts frequently targeted in communication intervention with young children. You will notice that they are the same concepts that preschool children with normal language development acquire naturally. Table 7.8 presents a chronological record of the progress of a 3-year-old boy over the course

Table 7.7 Basic Categories and Concepts for Communication Intervention With Young Children

CATEGORY	CONCEPTS
People/objects	Body parts and facial parts, clothing, food, animals, toys, family members, belongings
Descriptive words	Colors, temperature (hot, cold), size (big, little), appearance (dirty, wet, broken), emotions (happy, sad)
Sound words	Animal sounds, toy sounds, car and train sounds
Action words	Daily activities (eat, sleep), body movements (push, jump), actions of toys (bounce, shake), actions of animals (run, hop)
Location words	Prepositions (on, in, under)
Names of daily activities	Breakfast, playtime, bath, nap
Incidental words	More, all gone, uh-oh, bye-bye, mine

Table 7.8 Language Sample Demonstrating Progress of a 3-Year-Old Boy Receiving Speech–Language Therapy

9/94	move on truck car up glue tree
10/94	more ball ball in balloon
11/94	put in leaf in put leaf pull off nut open here where high hole cut
1/95	read book out here horse stick marker house yes turn page read book where book? big cow little cow
2/95	cut hair look mom pull out pull cotton squeeze glue up high cut more hold leg hurt glue here put cotton here put in hole alligator ma more purple green hat one more
3/95	hold hand hippo jump in put glue hand green scarf baboon jump out jump in cut more bed up there close sleepy jumping mama hold that your hand got two purple two eye jump rope tear off sitting that playhouse read book

of 7 months of language therapy. Note how this child's sample utterances reflect many of the basic concepts presented in Table 7.7 and how his utterances systematically increased in length, number, and complexity over the therapy period.

INCIDENCE AND PREVALENCE OF COMMUNICATION DISORDERS

Communication disorders have historically been the most frequently occurring disabilities (Gerber, 1990). It is estimated that communication disorders (including hearing disorders) affect 1 of every 10 persons in the United States (National Information Center for Children and Youth With Disabilities, 1993) and that 5% of school-age children have speech and language disorders.

Students with speech and language impairments represent 21.1% of the students aged 6 to 21 receiving special education and related services under Part B of IDEA. This is the second largest disability category receiving special education services in our public schools, exceeded in number only by the category of learning disabilities (U.S. Department of Education, 1995).

Within the general category of speech and language disorders, articulation disorders make up the largest subgroup, affecting approximately 75% of individuals with communication disorders and approximately 5% of the general population (Newman, Creaghead, & Secord, 1985; Palmer & Yantis, 1990).

Voice disorders are a small portion of speech–language disorders, affecting only 1% of the total population (Zangari, 1991). Estimates of the percentage of school-age children with voice disorders range from 3% to 9%, with only about 1% of those children being seen for treatment (Kahane & Mayo, 1989). The peak period for prevalence of voice disorders is from 4 to 14 years of age (Marge, 1991).

Although stuttering is probably the most commonly recognized speech disorder, it occurs relatively infrequently. Stuttering and other fluency disorders constitute a small subgroup of all speech disorders, affecting approximately 1% of the U.S. population (Shames, 1986), with disfluent males outnumbering females at a ratio of more than 4 to 1 (Stuttering Foundation of America, 1993). Incidence figures (how many people have stuttered at some time in their lives) indicate that as many as 15% of people have stuttered at some point in their lives (Bloodstein, 1987), with 5% of them experiencing stuttering for longer than 6 months (Andrews et al., 1983). As interpreted by Peters and Guitar (1991), the difference between the prevalence (1%) and incidence (5%) figures indicate that most individuals who stutter at some point in their lives eventually regain fluent speech.

Approximately 1% of the total population exhibits language disorders (Palmer & Yantis, 1990), with the greatest concentration among young children. Due to the substantial differences in definitions of language impairment and the overlap of language disorders with other disability categories (e.g., learning disabilities, mental retardation), precise estimates of the exact numbers of children with language disorders are difficult to make. However, current estimates are that 5% to 10% of the child population experience these difficulties (Zangari, 1991).

AUGMENTATIVE AND ALTERNATIVE COMMUNICATION SYSTEMS

Approximately 2 million Americans have severe communication disorders that prevent them from speaking adequately to meet their communication needs (American Speech–Hearing–Language Association, 1991). Although some of them have limited verbal output (i.e., speech), it is not sufficient to meet their communication needs in all situations. Their speech may not be clear enough to be understood by most listeners; they may not be able to sustain vocal output long enough to produce more than isolated words; or the time they need to express a thought verbally may be too long to allow efficient communication. Some individuals may be nonverbal and/or unable to use gestures or written language as a communication mode.

The need for adaptive assistance to communicate can result from a variety of congenital or acquired impairments. Congenital causes of severe communication disorders include cerebral palsy, severe or profound mental retardation, developmental disabilities, autism, deafness, and multiple disabilities such as deaf-blindness. Acquired impairments include traumatic brain injury, multiple sclerosis, amyotrophic lateral sclerosis (ALS), myasthenia gravis, stroke, spinal cord injuries, laryngectomy, and elective mutism (Beukelman & Mirenda, 1992; Musselwhite & St. Louis, 1988).

Augmentative Systems

Augmentative communication systems serve as alternatives or supplements to communication skills of individuals whose speech is inadequate (American Speech–Language–Hearing Association, 1982). For some individuals, the use of an augmentative or alternative communication (AAC) system may be temporary, as in the early stage of recovery from traumatic brain injury. Others may use an AAC system only in some situations, such as when answering questions in the classroom, where speed and accuracy of communication are important. Still others may use an AAC system in all or most communication attempts.

AAC systems may be unaided (not requiring use of any equipment or devices) or aided. Examples of *unaided systems* are sign language (e.g., American Sign Language), educational sign systems (e.g., Signed English), formal gestural systems (e.g., finger spelling to represent the English language code), or natural gestures (such as beckoning someone to come closer). Although sign language has traditionally been viewed as the primary means of communication for individuals who are hearing impaired or deaf, it has proven successful as an alternative system for other nonverbal individuals as well (Shenk, 1994). Studies have shown that sign language training can help some children in effecting a transition from sign to oral (verbal) communication (Kouri, 1989; Meier & Newport, 1990).

Depending on which unaided system is used, a certain level of motor control will be needed to use it (e.g., good fine motor control of the arms, hands, and fingers of both hands to use American Sign Language). The individual's degree of motor control, along with her cognitive skill level for learning and recalling signs, are primary considerations when selecting which unaided system she will use or when determining whether an unaided system will meet her communication needs.

Some individuals may not have the level of fine motor control or cognitive abilities necessary to use unaided systems. For them, aided systems are more practical and efficient. *Aided systems* include object communication systems (using actual objects or replications), representational symbol systems (using pictures, photos, or pictographs), abstract symbol systems (using symbols that do not directly represent or suggest the meaning of the word), and symbolic language codes (using alphabets, words, Braille, etc.) (Musselwhite & St. Louis, 1988).

With aided systems, the objects, pictures, symbols, and so forth are displayed on some type of board, which the person uses to communicate his message by

Augmentative communication systems have allowed people with limited motor control to converse with others.

indicating the desired symbol. The format of the board, the complexity of the layout, and the number and type of available symbols depend on the interests and abilities of the user. The symbols chosen for display on a communication board should reflect the individual's specific needs relative to his environment. The display in Figure 7.4 is for use with a young child at bedtime. The display would be changed as the environment changes. For example, in the morning, a display for getting dressed or eating breakfast would be used. Prior to presenting a new display, the individual who will be using it should be trained in its use. Rather than using displays solely as command boards (e.g., child points to symbol, person receiving message carries out request), Goossens', Crain, and Elder (1994) stress the importance of carrying out training for the displays in an interactive format of give and take.

Of prime importance in the development of any aided system is the identification of a selection mode. With *direct selection* techniques, the user selects the desired symbol from the display board by directly pointing to the symbol, by depressing a key, by applying pressure to a touch-sensitive pad, by using a headstick or head light, by eye-gaze or other body motions, or by sonar or infrared signals activated by moving the head. *Scanning selection* offers another means of choosing options from a board. In scanning, the items are presented on the board and an electronic device (scanner or cursor) moves across or around the board. The user stops the scanner at the desired symbol. Although scanning is a good option for individuals who cannot use direct selection, it decreases efficiency of communication (Beukelman & Mirenda, 1992).

Another important component to consider when designing an AAC system is a method of signaling that can be used to attract or redirect the attention of others (King, 1991). If this option is not made available to AAC and other non-oral communicators, they are unable to participate on an equal basis with their communication partners because they are unable to initiate communication, interrupt communication, or redirect the conversation. Thus, they are placed in the position

Figure 7.4 Sample Display for a Child's Communication Board

Source: Reprinted with permission from *Communication Displays for Engineered Preschool Environments* (p. 43), by C. Goossens', S. Crain, & P. Elder, 1994, Solana Beach, CA: Mayer-Johnson.

of a dependent rather than independent communicator. Signaling devices can be relatively simple, such as an electronic hand signal that a student can use instead of raising his hand in the classroom.

Facilitated Communication

Facilitated Communication (FC) is another type of assisted communication technique that has received considerable media attention over the last several years in *Time* magazine and on *Prime Time Live, Front Line, 60 Minutes,* and elsewhere. To use FC, a "facilitator" provides support to the communicator's forearm, wrist, and/or fingers as the communicator types responses on a keyboard or points to pictures or words.

Initially, FC was perceived as a significant breakthrough and even a "miracle" by some (Bennett, 1994). Professionals have become skeptical of FC, however, because of a lack of controlled studies validating the technique (Cummins & Prior, 1992; Shane, 1993; Trace, 1994; Wheeler, Jacobson, Paglieri, & Schwartz, 1993). Anecdotal reports support the success of FC with some individuals, but there are insufficient data to support the initial claims of its effectiveness. In many cases, the message has been found to originate with the facilitator. Until the validity and reliability of FC has been established, the American Speech–Language–Hearing Association recommends that "information obtained through or based on Facilitated Communication should not form the sole basis for making any diagnostic treatment decisions" (American Speech–Language–Hearing Association, 1995b, p. 22). (See Chapter 12 for further discussion of FC.)

Synthetic and Digitized Speech

Synthetic or digitized speech is produced either through input into a computer and output from an electronic voice synthesizer, or through prerecorded natural speech. Both methods have shown promise for use by individuals with severe impairments of oral communication. With *synthetic speech*, data are received from a computer software program (when either a letter key or a symbol key is accessed by the communicator), translated into a phonetic code, and articulated (spoken) by the synthesizer. Although the output may not always be easily intelligible to the listener, synthetic speech requires little computer memory and can adequately meet the communication needs of many individuals. *Digitized speech* comprises natural speech that has been recorded. Although it requires a great deal of computer memory and, therefore, is expensive, the intelligibility and quality of the speech output is very good.

These types of systems reduce the listener's burden in the communication exchange, allow communication with partners who cannot read or who have visual impairments (as opposed to systems that use printouts of the message), and allow communication to take place from a distance. They also eliminate the need for a signaling device to attract the attention of the listener. A disadvantage of these systems is that they are not easily affordable or accessible by everyone (Beukelman & Mirenda, 1992; Romski, Lloyd, & Sevcik, 1988).

ACCOMMODATING STUDENTS WITH COMMUNICATION DISORDERS IN INCLUSIVE ENVIRONMENTS

The majority of students with communication impairments as their sole or primary disability are served in general education settings. More students with communication impairments are educated in regular classes than are those in any other disability category. For example, during the school year 1991–92 (the most recent year for which data are available), 85.5% of students with speech or language impairments were served in regular classes, with 9.1% served in resource rooms and only 3.9% served in separate classes (U.S. Department of Education, 1994).

Most students who are eligible for speech–language therapy services receive weekly small group or individual therapy sessions. Students with mild impairments and those who are in the carryover stages of therapy may receive consultative rather than direct therapy services. In this model, the speech–language pathologist sees the students intermittently to check on their communication status and advises the classroom teacher on strategies to support the students in the regular classroom. The frequency, length, and type of intervention services are determined for each student on an individual basis by his IEP team members.

Teachers fill an important role in the identification and referral of students with speech–language disorders as well as in promoting carryover of communication skills to the classroom. Teachers of students with communication impairments can promote their success in general education settings by establishing comfortable, nonthreatening communication environments and providing clear and correct speech–language models.

Teachers must also be aware of the effects of their students' disabilities on classroom performance and academic achievement. For example, teachers of students who stutter should be aware of problem speaking situations for each student and structure the learning environment to avoid placing students in these high-stress situations or provide alternative ways of participating. Teachers of students with articulation impairments need to become familiar with the students' patterns of speech to help interpret their comments as well as to provide opportunities for carryover of target sounds in the classroom. For example, if a student is working on producing /sh/ at the word level in therapy, the teacher could draw the student's attention to this sound as it occurs in spelling and reading words. Teachers of students with voice disorders should be aware of the students' target behaviors for correct voice production (e.g., refraining from screaming on the playground) and should reinforce the desired behaviors. Teachers of students with language disorders must be aware of the pervasive effects of a language impairment on a student's academic performance. If a student with a language impairment is having difficulty in math, is it because he cannot perform the operations, or because he does not understand the math language (e.g., "some," "all," "each," "average")?

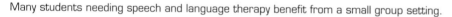

Many students needing speech and language therapy benefit from a small group setting.

EASY IDEAS FOR PRACTITIONERS

For the Teacher:

1. Plan small group learning activities that allow children to communicate with and learn from one another.
2. Use varied questioning techniques that elicit more than yes/no answers.
3. Help students develop cross-categorical knowledge by pointing out different characteristics of objects (e.g., an orange could be grouped with other fruit, round objects, things that grow on trees, etc.).
4. Let students know that you are interested in what they say and not only in how they say it (in both oral and written communication).
5. Work closely with your school's speech–language pathologist to maintain an awareness of therapy objectives for individual students and to get suggestions for promoting carryover to the classroom.

For Parents:

1. Show your child that you are interested in what he or she has to say, remembering to make eye contact while your child speaks and to show your interest with facial expressions and body language.
2. Give your child enough time to respond to questions and statements, rather than jumping in and talking for your child during conversations with one another.
3. Pause occasionally when reading to your child—to ask questions about the story, point out interesting things in the pictures, and let your child ask questions and make comments.
4. Help your child learn different forms of language by talking about what happened yesterday, what is planned for tomorrow, as well as what your child is doing right now.
5. Provide clear, consistent speech and language models for your child.

Collaboration between the classroom teacher and the speech–language pathologist can enhance these students' chances of success in both the classroom and the therapy setting. As discussed more fully later in the chapter, in the section covering issues and trends, many speech–language pathologists in the public schools are moving toward an integrated therapy model that enables closer communication between teachers and the speech–language pathologist by delivery of intervention services in the classroom setting.

FAMILY PERSPECTIVES

Parents of children with communication disorders are concerned about their children's ability to function at school and at home, their future outcomes, and their abilities to function independently and successfully in the adult world. If their children's communication disorders are severe, parents may be concerned about their own and others' abilities to communicate with their children. They also often have questions about how to react to their children's frustration when they cannot be understood or when they are ridiculed or ignored by others.

Since communication is so broad and encompasses so many subskills, parents are often unsure about what is reasonable for them to expect. Because of the great variation in individual achievement and the wide latitude for error in predicting communication outcomes, professionals are often unable to provide a definitive prognosis.

A broad-based concern of many parents is the perceptions others hold of children who have speech–language disorders. As already mentioned, speech–language disorders are often the result of, or exist simultaneously with, other disabilities (e.g., hearing impairment, autism, mental retardation). Although this is not always the case, some individuals incorrectly assume that speech–language disorders always represent other functional limitations (e.g., behavioral, social, academic). For example, Rice, Hadley, and Alexander (1993) studied the social consequences of speech–language disorders for kindergarten children. They found that teachers and other adults were likely to assume that the children had other impairments as well—including cognitive and social limitations, a lack of social maturity, and weak school readiness skills. Such biases can affect the interaction between students and teachers—resulting in curtailed academic and social success for individual students—and raise legitimate concerns on the part of parents regarding their children's chances for success during their school years.

Parents of children with communication disorders are also concerned about the attitudes of peers. Studies have shown that students across age groups have negative attitudes toward their peers who have only *mild* communication disorders (e.g., only one or two articulation errors) (Hall, 1991; Silverman & Falk, 1992). Understandably, the concerns of parents of children with more severe communication impairments (e.g., severe stuttering) are even greater.

Through her interaction with thousands of families of children with speech–language impairments and the professionals serving them, Crutcher (1993) compiled a list of common parental concerns about speech–language intervention, including the following:

1. Overemphasis on articulation skills as opposed to the social use of language and pragmatic skills for conversation

2. Lack of carryover from the therapy setting to the classroom and home, and a lack of systematic strategies for skill generalization in everyday life

3. Underemphasis on speech intelligibility (e.g., rate, volume, eye contact)

4. A limited range of therapeutic options offered to families

5. Inappropriate judgment by professionals that a family is "dysfunctional," and definition of a "functional" family only in the traditional sense (e.g., two parents, middle-class, etc.)

6. A lack of established protocols for determining the age at which therapy can be beneficial, for identifying and intervening with children who are at risk for hearing loss, for identifying and treating auditory and visual processing problems that are related to speech and language acquisition and use, for facilitating transitions from one program to another, and for modifying interventions to include surgical alterations (e.g., tongue reduction)

Family members of adults with communication disorders experience similar concerns. This is particularly true if the communication impairment has been acquired as a result of a stroke, traumatic brain injury (TBI), or progressive neurological disease (e.g., amyotrophic lateral sclerosis). If the onset of the communication impairment has been sudden, as in the case of stroke or TBI, family members must deal with the medical aftereffects of the illness or accident at the same time they are trying to reestablish communication with their family member. This can be very frustrating, especially if the family member is unable to communicate verbally and has also suffered neuromotor impairment that prevents him from writing or communicating by gesturing. The psychoemotional effects of the sudden loss of communication often exacerbate the frustration experienced by the patient and family when they attempt to communicate with one another. Professionals involved in the patient's recovery and rehabilitation can help family members cope with the impact of a communication loss by sharing an understanding of the nature of the disorder with family members, providing the patient with an alternative communication method to use as early as possible (e.g., a temporary communication board), and involving the family in the rehabilitation process as their resources and interests allow.

CURRENT ISSUES AND FUTURE TRENDS

Some of the parental concerns addressed by Crutcher are shared by professionals in the field of communication. One issue that is related to the concerns expressed by parents is that of caseload size, particularly for speech–language pathologists practicing in the public schools. The national average of the number of students a therapist sees weekly for therapy is 53, which translates to approximately 50 or more 30-minute sessions per week. Some states allow up to 75 students in a caseload, or even more (American Speech–Language–Hearing Association, 1990; Blachman, Garrett, Higbe, & Recantus, 1991). Added to the other duties involved in delivering speech–language services—evaluation and screening, travel time, planning time, report writing, attending IEP meetings, serving on interdisciplinary teams, meeting with teachers and parents, observing students in their classrooms, and record keeping—the ability of speech–language pathologists to provide appropriate services to 75 or more students per week is diminished.

One solution to the problem of caseload size is that of training paraprofessional support personnel to work with the students, thereby enabling speech–language pathologists to spend more time carrying out assessment, developing individualized programs, and consulting with teachers and parents. Professional speech–language pathologists support this practice only when the paraprofessionals perform activities that are an *adjunct* to the primary intervention efforts of the professionals, and only with appropriate training and supervision by a certified speech–language pathologist (American Speech–Language–Hearing Association, 1995c).

Personnel shortages are a problem in some areas. One solution that has been proposed is to use interactive video to deliver services in rural and remote areas (Dublinske, 1995).

Assessment is another issue currently of concern and interest to many speech–language pathologists. Speech–language pathologists are moving away from formal, standardized assessments as the mainstay of their assessment batteries. The language samples they have been collecting for many years as a basis of assessment and evaluation of progress have been forerunners in the move toward authentic assessment in education. As the field looks to the future, functionally based assessment tools administered in natural settings such as the classroom or the home will predominate (Montgomery & Herer, 1994).

Integrated therapy (i.e., delivering speech–language therapy services in classroom settings instead of in isolated therapy rooms) is beginning to have a noticeable impact on the delivery of speech–language services in the schools. The move toward integrated therapy has been spurred by two factors: the increasing demands for speech–language services, and the move toward delivering all special education services in more inclusive environments (Fad, 1995). As more children are being identified with language-based learning disabilities and more children with severe communication disabilities are being served in neighborhood schools, the demand for speech–language services has grown. In many schools, this has resulted in fewer individual and small group therapy sessions. The increasing caseloads of speech–language pathologists is not, however, the only factor that has led to fewer pull-out therapy sessions. Speech–language pathologists, teachers, parents, and other IEP team members have begun to realize that the classroom may be a more natural communication environment. Delivering speech–language therapy sessions in the more inclusive classroom environment has the added benefit of enabling the therapists and teachers to consult on the students' communication needs, sharing resources and strategies. An integrated therapy approach does, however, require new skills and attitudes on the part of both the classroom teacher and the speech–language pathologist. For integrated therapy to be successful, both parties must be willing to give up some of their own turf and alter traditional roles and practices.

Advances in technology have resulted in significant changes in the field of communication disorders. Augmentative and alternative communication systems continue to be upgraded and improved. Microcomputers and related applications are enabling individuals with severe communication impairments to communicate in a variety of ways. In addition to augmenting communication, microcomputers serve as a learning aid, enable the individuals to control their environments, provide recreational opportunities, and permit successful communication through a variety of channels (e.g., mail, telephone, face-to-face) (Silverman, 1987).

Speech–language pathologists are using microcomputers in a variety of ways. These include report writing, clinical record keeping, administering diagnostic tests, analyzing clinical data (such as language samples), developing augmentative communication systems, and administering language stimulation and other types of therapy exercises (Silverman, 1987).

Changes in service delivery will continue to take place as the needs of individuals with communication impairments change. Increasingly, services will be delivered in an individual's natural environment (e.g., home, work, community, school), and services will be made to accommodate the work and lifestyles of the individuals who use them (Dublinske, 1995).

A societal change that is beginning to affect many professionals in the field of communication disorders is that of an increasingly multicultural society. Changing demographics are resulting in changes in the people that speech–language professionals are serving. According to the 1990 census, one in seven persons speak a language other than English in their home (American Speech–Language–Hearing Association, 1994). The American Speech–Language–Hearing Association estimates that approximately 10% of individuals of racial or ethnic minority groups have communication disorders—which translates to at least 6 million individuals with communication disorders from culturally and linguistically diverse populations.

The effects of linguistic diversity, however, are not limited to verbal communication. Communication skills are central to the education process. Many students at-risk for school success have speech–language delays or disorders. Many students with language disorders also develop reading problems. Students whose first language is not English may not be proficient in the language of the school (i.e.,

COMMUNICLOCK® "TALKS" FOR SHAWNA

NEW MODEL - Can reverse direction of pointer with flipper switch.

Flipper Switch

Plate Switch

SHAWNA KOCH, of Billings, MT, tells people what she wants by using the Communiclock® and the Plate Switch. At 17, she broke through her communication barrier. She has cerebral palsy and is deaf and nonverbal. In three months time she quadrupled her vocabulary to 200 words and is still using it today with various overlays.

Frustration from the inability to communicate one's needs can be eased by Communiclock®. Nonverbal children and adults express their thoughts easily with one finger operation in seconds. By pressing the built-in large button, the pointer moves clockwise. Release the button to stop the pointer at the desired picture or word. Has standard ⅛" miniature jack outlet. Those unable to press the button, like Shawna, can use the Jumbo Plate Switch. The Jumbo Plate Switch (not included) requires only a light touch and is ideal for people with limited motor control (item

3097, page 17). Communiclock® is lightweight, portable with carrying handle, and free standing. Includes battery.

Comes with 6 blank overlays for use in designing various situations. Includes 246 stickers: 96 pictures from Talking Pictures® Kit I, 50 words, 50 numerals and alphabet, and 50 blanks. Those with visual difficulties can use Talking Picture® cards. 6 mo. warranty.

U.S. Patent No. 4,761,633

3055 Communiclock®, 6 Overlays, 246 Stickers **$214.95**
3097 Jumbo Plate Switch (See page 17)....... **$80.00**
3057 SPECIAL OFFER - SAVE $35 Communiclock® PKG. Communiclock®, 6 Overlays, 246 stickers and Jumbo Plate Switch....... **$259.95**
3058 6 Additional Overlays **$19.95**

Technology has provided many advances in communication for people with disabilities.

English). The complex relationship between communication delays, disorders, and differences is summed up by Futrell (1989):

> At the heart of the successful school experience is the ability to master the components of communication. The most dedicated, the most effective classroom teacher cannot teach the child who has not developed adequate communication skills to learn. (p. 2)

The importance of ensuring adequate communication skills among diverse student populations will continue to present new challenges. Professionals seek to make certain that assessment and intervention approaches for communication disorders are nonbiased and take into consideration the wide variety of cultural values, norms, social beliefs, and learning styles represented by various cultures (Scott, 1994). Another implication of this multicultural shift in the population of persons with communication impairments is the need to increase diversity among the group of professionals serving them.

Five-Minute Summary

Communication impairments have been a source of interest and a target of ridicule for centuries. Early accounts of speech impairments present a medical orientation focusing primarily on articulation and fluency disorders. The practice of speech pathology in this country dates back to the early 1900s, when speech correction teachers were employed by some public schools. As the profession grew, practice expanded to include voice and language disorders.

Communication disorders can be categorized as either speech or language disorders, although some individuals have deficits in both areas. Speech impairments include disorders of articulation, voice, and fluency. Language impairments are disorders of comprehension or use of spoken or written language.

Communication disorders can result from organic impairments such as hearing loss, cleft palate, dental malocclusion, or a genetic syndrome (e.g., Down syndrome, fragile X syndrome, Turner syndrome, etc.). Strokes and traumatic brain injuries also result in communication impairments. In many cases, the exact cause of a communication impairment is unknown, although inherited tendencies for development of communication disorders is a possible cause.

Assessment of communication impairments includes a variety of formal and informal procedures designed to present a well rounded picture of an individual's communication status. Formal tests can provide information relative to norms regarding an individual's communication abilities, while interviews with the person and family members and informal observation can provide information relative to the individual's typical communication performance (i.e., strengths and weaknesses).

A variety of intervention techniques for communication impairments are used. Therapeutic approaches vary depending on the individual's age, the nature of the disability, the setting in which the intervention is provided (e.g., hospital, public school, speech–language clinic, rehabilitation setting), and the desired outcomes of the intervention. Most students with communication impairments are placed in integrated settings (e.g., in regular classrooms) in public schools. Integrated therapy, in which the speech–language pathologist delivers intervention services in the classroom, is a new trend in some schools.

Parents of children with communication disorders have concerns about the eventual status of their children's communication development as well as the effects of a communication disorder on the child's social and academic skills. Family members of adults with communication disorders, especially if they are acquired as a result of stroke or traumatic brain injury, are concerned about the immediate and long-term prognosis for their family member to regain lost skills.

As the field of speech–language pathology continues to evolve, new challenges arise: reducing caseload size, making trained professionals available in all areas of the country, providing options for integrated therapy, keeping up with and developing technological applications, and meeting the needs of an increasingly multicultural society.

Study Questions

1. Prior to the early 1900s, what types of services were available for remediation of communication impairments?
2. Provide differential definitions of speech, language, and communication. How are they related?
3. What are four common organic causes of articulation impairments?
4. List six behaviors that you would try to display when talking to someone who is disfluent.
5. What is a common means of remediating voice disorders that are a result of vocal abuse?
6. Language disorders often occur in conjunction with other disabilities or syndromes. Name five of these.
7. Discuss the possible effects of a language impairment on a child's academic and social development.
8. When assessing speech and language disorders, what assessment techniques are used? Why is it important to obtain a sample of the individual's connected speech in informal conversation?
9. What role does personal and professional judgment play in determining if an individual has a communication impairment?

10. What advice would you give to parents of a new baby for enhancing her communication development during her preschool years?
11. What are three things teachers of students with communication impairments can do to enhance the students' chances of success in the regular education setting?
12. React to this statement: The goal for all individuals with language impairments should be to acquire oral language.
13. Discuss common concerns of parents of children with communication impairments.
14. Provide three examples of how technology is being used to enhance the abilities of individuals to communicate.
15. Why is the shift of our society to increasing multiculturalism of particular concern to speech–language pathologists?

For More Information

ORGANIZATIONS

American Cleft Palate–Craniofacial Association (ACPA)
1218 Grandview Avenue
Pittsburgh, PA 15211
800-242-5338   412-481-1376
FAX 412-481-0847

American Speech–Language–Hearing Association (ASHA)
10801 Rockville Pike
Rockville, MD 20852
301-897-5700 (V/TT)   FAX 301-571-0457

Division for Children With Communication Disorders
c/o The Council for Exceptional Children
1920 Association Drive
Reston, VA 22091

National Center for Stuttering
200 East 33rd Street
New York, NY 10016
800-221-2483   (In NY) 212-532-1460

National Easter Seal Society
70 East Lake Street
Chicago, IL 60601
312-726-6200

National Institute of Neurological and Communicative Disorders and Stroke
National Institutes of Health, HHS
Building 31, Room 8A–06
Bethesda, MD 20205

National Stuttering Project
2151 Irving Street, Suite 208
San Francisco, CA 94122
800-364-1677   415-566-5324
FAX 415-664-3721

Stuttering Foundation of America
P.O. Box 11749
Memphis, TN 38111-0479
800-992-9392

U.S. Society for Augmentative and Alternative Communication (USSAAC)

P.O. Box 12440
Pittsburgh, PA 15231
412-264-2288

BOOKS AND ARTICLES

Adler, S., & King, D. (Eds.) (1994). *Oral communication problems in children and adolescents* (2nd ed.). Needham Heights, MA: Allyn & Bacon.

Barach, C. (1983). *Help me say it: A parent's guide to speech problems.* New York: New American Library.

Fletcher, P. (1992). *Specific speech and language disorders in children.* San Diego: Singular.

Josephs, A. (1993). *The invaluable guide to life after stroke: An owner's manual.* Long Beach, CA: Amadeus.

Lazzari, A., & Peters, P. (1993). *The handbook of exercises for language processing (Elementary).* Moline, IL: LinguiSystems, Inc.

Niemeyer, S. (1994). *Caregiver education guide for children with developmental disabilities.* Gaithersburg, MD: Aspen Press.

Oyer, H., Crowe, B., & Haas, W. (1987). *Speech, language and hearing disorders: A guide for the teacher.* Boston: Allyn & Bacon.

Schwartz, S., Miller, J. E. H. (1988). *The language of toys: Teaching communication skills to special-needs children.* Rockville, MD: Woodbine House.

Weitzman, E. (1992). *Learning language and loving it.* Toronto: CA: Hanen Center Publication.

JOURNALS, NEWSLETTERS, AND OTHER PUBLICATIONS

Fraser, J. (Ed.). (1988). *If your child stutters.* Memphis, TN: Stuttering Foundation of America.

Letting Go (monthly)
National Stuttering Project
4601 Irving Street
San Francisco, CA 94122

VIDEO AND ELECTRONIC MEDIA

The Healing Influence: Guidelines for Stroke Families [Videotape]
Produced in cooperation with the American Heart Association

Available from Danamar Productions
106 Monte Vista Place
Santa Fe, NM 87501
800-578-6508

References

Aaron, V. L., & Madison, C. L. (1991). A vocal hygiene program for high-school cheerleaders. *Language, Speech, and Hearing Services in Schools, 22,* 287–290.

American Speech–Language–Hearing Association. (1982). Definitions: Communicative disorders and variations. *Asha, 24,* 949–950.

American Speech–Language–Hearing Association. (1990). *Research division report, Omnibus survey.* Rockville, MD: Author.

American Speech–Language–Hearing Association. (1991). Report: Augmentative and alternative communication. *Asha, 33*(Suppl. 5), 9–12.

American Speech–Language–Hearing Association. (1994, April). Let's talk: Children and bilingualism. *Asha, 36,* 57–58.

American Speech–Language–Hearing Association. (1995a, March). Guidelines for practice for stuttering treatment. *Asha, 37*(Suppl. 14), 26.

American Speech–Language–Hearing Association. (1995b, March). Position statement facilitated communication. *Asha, 37*(Suppl. 14), 22.

American Speech–Language–Hearing Association. (1995c, March). Position statement for the training, credentialing, use and supervision of support personnel in speech–language pathology. *Asha, 37*(Suppl. 14), 21.

Andrews, G., Craig, A., Feyer, A.-M., Hoddinott, S., Howie, P., & Neilson, M. (1983). Stuttering: A review of research findings and theories circa 1982. *Journal of Speech and Hearing Disorders, 48,* 226–246.

Bennett, C. (1994). Facilitated communication: Witchcraft & fantasy. *Journal of the Speech–Language–Hearing Association of Virginia, 34*(1), 21–23.

Beukelman, D. R., & Mirenda, P. (1992). *Augmentative and alternative communication.* Baltimore: Paul H. Brookes.

Blachman, L., Garrett, C., Higbe, J., & Recantus, T. (1991). Position statement: Public school speech and language caseload reduction. *Journal of the Speech–Language–Hearing Association of Virginia, 32*(1), 34–35.

Blakeley, R. W. (1983). Treatment of developmental apraxia of speech. In W. H. Perkins (Ed.), *Dysarthria and apraxia* (pp. 25–33). New York: Thieme-Stratton.

Bloodstein, O. (1987). *A handbook on stuttering.* Chicago: National Easter Seal Society.

Bloom, L., & Lahey, M. (1978). *Language development and disorders.* New York: Wiley.

Bogue, B. N. (1939). *Stammering: Its cause and correction.* Indianapolis: Author.

Broen, P. A. (1988). Plotting a course: The ongoing assessment of language. In R. L. Schiefelbusch & L. L. Lloyd (Eds.), *Language perspectives: Acquisition, retardation and intervention* (pp. 299–320). Austin, TX: PRO-ED.

Calvert, D. R., & Silverman, S. R. (1983). *Speech and deafness.* Washington, DC: Alexander Graham Bell Association for the Deaf.

Carney, A. E. (1986). Understanding speech intelligibility in the hearing impaired. *Topics in Language Disorders, 6*(3), 47–59.

Comfort, M. (1988). Assessing parent–child interactions. In D. B. Bailey & R. J. Simeonsson (Eds.), *Family assessment in early intervention* (pp. 65–94). Columbus, OH: Merrill.

Crutcher, D. M. (1993). Parent perspectives: Best practice and recommendations for research. In A. P. Kaiser & D. B. Gray (Eds.), *Enhancing children's communication* (pp. 365–373). Baltimore: Paul H. Brookes.

Cummins, R., & Prior, M. (1992). Autism and facilitated communication: A reply to Biklen. *Harvard Educational Review, 62,* 228–241.

Dublinske, S. (1995). Professional practices: Perspective on change. *Asha, 37*(1), 26.

Evans, C. J., & Johnson, C. J. (1988). Training pragmatic language skills through alternate strategies with a blind multiply handicapped child. *Journal of Visual Impairment & Blindness,* 109–112.

Fad, K. (1995). Communication disorders. In T. Smith, E. Polloway, J. Patton, & C. Dowdy (Eds.), *Teaching children with special needs in inclusive settings* (pp. 248–285). Boston: Allyn & Bacon.

Fowler, W. (1990). *Talking from infancy.* Cambridge, MA: Brookline.

Futrell, M. H. (1989). With literacy and justice for all: America's unfinished revolution. In B. A. Stewart (Ed.), *Partnerships in education: Toward a literate America* (pp. 4–7). Rockville, MD: American Speech–Language–Hearing Association. (ERIC Document Reproduction Service No. ED 373 488)

Gerber, S. E. (1990). *Prevention: The etiology of communicative disorders in children.* Englewood Cliffs, NJ: Prentice-Hall.

Goossens', C., Crain, S., & Elder, P. (1994). *Communication displays for engineered preschool environments.* Solana Beach, CA: Mayer-Johnson.

Hall, B. J. C. (1991). Attitudes of fourth and sixth graders toward peers with mild articulation disorders. *Language, Speech, and Hearing Services in Schools, 22,* 334–340.

Hall, P. K., Jordan, L. S., & Robin, D. A. (1993). *Developmental apraxia of speech.* Austin, TX: PRO-ED.

Ham, R. E. (1990). *Therapy of stuttering.* Englewood Cliffs, NJ: Prentice-Hall.

Hatten, J. T., & Hatten, P. W. (1981). *Natural language.* Tucson, AZ: Communication Skill Builders.

Haynes, C. (1989). Language development in the school years—What can go wrong? In K. Mogford & J. Sadler (Eds.), *Child language disability: Implications in an educational setting* (pp. 8–21). Clevedon, Avon, England: Multilingual Matters Ltd.

Hodson, B. W., & Paden, E. P. (1983). *Targeting intelligible speech.* San Diego: College-Hill Press.

Howie, P. M. (1981). Concordance for stuttering in monozygotic and dizygotic twin pairs. *Journal of Speech and Hearing Research, 24,* 317–321.

Kahane, J. C., & Mayo, R. (1989). The need for aggressive pursuit of healthy childhood voices. *Language, Speech, and Hearing Services in Schools, 20,* 102–107.

Kaiser, A. P. (1993). Parent-implemented language intervention. In A. P. Kaiser & D. B. Gray (Eds.), *Enhancing Children's Communication: Research Foundations for Intervention* (Vol. 2) (pp. 63–84). Baltimore: Paul H. Brookes.

Kidd, K. K. (1983). Recent progress on the genetics of stuttering. In C. L. Ludlow & J. A. Cooper (Eds.), *Genetic aspects of speech and language* (pp. 197–213). New York: Academic Press.

King, T. W. (1991). A signalling device for non-oral communicators. *Language, Speech and Hearing Services in Schools, 22,* 277–282.

Kleiman, L. I. (1994). *Functional communication profile.* Moline, IL: LinguiSystems.

Kouri, T. (1989). How manual sign acquisition related to the development of spoken language: A case study. *Language, Speech, and Hearing Services in Schools, 20,* 50–62.

Kumin, L. (1994). *Communication skills in children with Down syndrome.* Rockville, MD: Woodbine House.

LaBlance, G. R., Šteckol, K. F., & Smith, V. L. (1994). Stuttering: The role of the classroom teacher. *Teaching Exceptional Children, 26*(2), 10–12.

Leith, W. R. (1984). *Handbook of stuttering therapy for the school clinician.* San Diego: College-Hill Press.

Lewis, G. A. (1902). *The practical treatment of stammering and stuttering.* Detroit: Author.

Love, R. J. (1992). *Childhood motor speech disability.* New York: Macmillan.

Marge, M. (1991). Introduction to the prevention and epidemiology of voice disorders. In T. S. Johnson (Ed.), *Seminars in Speech and Language, 12,* 49–72.

Marquardt, T. P., & Sussman, H. M. (1991). Developmental apraxia of speech: Theory and practice. In D. Vogel & M. P. Cannito (Eds.), *Treating disordered speech motor control* (pp. 341–390). Austin, TX: PRO-ED.

McDade, H. L., & Varnedoe, D. R. (1987). Training parents to be language facilitators. *Topics in Language Disorders, 7*(3), 19–30.

Meier, R. P., & Newport, E. L. (1990). Out of the hands of babes: On a possible sign advantage in language acquisition. *Language, 66,* 1–23.

Miller, J. F. (1983). Identifying children with language disorders and describing their language performance. In J. Miller, D. Yoder, & R. Schiefelbusch (Eds.), *Contemporary issues in language intervention,* ASHA Reports 12 (pp. 61–74). Rockville, MD: American Speech–Language–Hearing Association.

Montgomery, J. K., & Herer, G. R. (1994). Future watch: Our schools in the 21st century. *Language, Speech, and Hearing Services in Schools, 25,* 130–135.

Moran, M. J., & Pentz, A. L. (1995). Helping the child with a cleft palate in your classroom. *Teaching Exceptional Children, 27*(3), 46–48.

Murdoch, T. D., Stokes, P. D., & Chenery, H. J. (1993). Hypernasality in dysarthric speakers following severe closed head injury: A perceptual and instrumental analysis. *Brain Injury, 7*(1), 59–69.

Musselwhite, C. R., & St. Louis, K. W. (1988). *Communication programming for persons with severe handicaps.* Boston: College-Hill Press.

National Information Center for Children and Youth With Disabilities. (1993). *General information about speech and language disorders* (Fact Sheet Number 11). Washington, DC: Author.

Newman, P. W., Creaghead, N. A., & Secord, W. (1985). *Assessment and remediation of articulatory and phonological disorders.* Columbus, OH: Merrill.

Palmer, J. M., & Yantis, P. A. (1990). *Survey of communication disorders.* Baltimore: Williams & Wilkins.

Paul-Brown, D., & Zingeser, L. (1994, November). Professional practices perspective on . . . New diagnostic and treatment methods. *Asha, 36,* 14.

Peters, T. J., & Guitar, B. (1991). *Stuttering: An integrated approach to its nature and treatment.* Baltimore: Williams & Wilkins.

Rice, M. L., Hadley, P. A., & Alexander, A. L. (1993). Social biases toward children with speech and language impairments: A correlative causal model of language limitations. *Applied Psycholinguistics, 14*(4), 445–471.

Robin, D. A. (1992). Developmental apraxia of speech: Just another motor problem. *American Journal of Speech–Language Pathology: A Journal of Clinical Practice, 1,* 19–22.

Romski, M. A., Lloyd, L. L., & Sevcik, R. A. (1988). Augmentative and alternative communication issues. In R. L. Schiefelbusch &

L. L. Lloyd (Eds.), *Language perspectives: Acquisition, retardation and intervention.* Austin, TX: PRO-ED.

Rossetti, L. M. (1996). *Communication intervention: Birth to three.* San Diego: Singular.

Ryan, B. P. (1974). *Programmed therapy of stuttering in children and adults.* Springfield, IL: Thomas.

Schiefelbusch, R. L. (1988). Introduction. In R. L. Schiefelbusch & L. L. Lloyd (Eds.), *Language perspectives: Acquisition, retardation and intervention* (pp. 1–15). Austin, TX: PRO-ED.

Scott, D. M. (1994). Are we ready for the 21st century? *Asha, 36,* 47.

Setliff, M. (1994, August 11). Surgery for clefts begins early in life. *Richmond Times-Dispatch,* p. E3.

Shames, G. H. (1986). Disorders of fluency. In G. H. Shames & E. H. Wiig (Eds.), *Human communication disorders* (3rd ed.) (pp. 187–220). Columbus, OH: Merrill.

Shane, J. (1993). Facilitated communication: Look before you leap. *The Clinical Connection, 7*(2), 1–5.

Shenk, K. K. (1994). Sign language: Not just for the hearing-impaired. *Journal of the Speech–Language–Hearing Association of Virginia, 34*(1), 6–14.

Silverman, F. H. (1987). *Microcomputers in speech–language pathology and audiology.* Englewood Cliffs, NJ: Prentice-Hall.

Silverman, F. H., & Falk, S. M. (1992). Attitudes of teenagers who have a single articulation error. *Language, Speech, and Hearing Services in Schools, 23,* 187.

Sparks, S. N. (1984). *Birth defects and speech–language disorders.* San Diego: College-Hill Press.

Study links smoking to birth defect gene. (1995, April 2). *Richmond Times-Dispatch,* p. A14.

Stuttering Foundation of America. (1993). *Did you know . . . .* Memphis, TN: Author.

Swisher, L. (1985). Language disorders in children. In J. K. Darby (Ed.), *Speech and language evaluation in neurology: Childhood disorders* (pp. 33–96). Orlando, FL: Grune & Stratton.

Thomas, P. J. (1990). Tips for assessing speech and language: A checklist of common errors. *Diagnostique, 16,* 29–31.

Trace, R. (1994). Research findings fail to support early claims by advocates of FC. *Advance, 4,* 6–21.

U.S. Department of Education. (1995). *To assure the free appropriate public education of all children with disabilities: Seventeenth annual report to Congress on the implementation of the Individuals With Disabilities Education Act.* Washington, DC: Author.

Van Riper, C. (1973). *The treatment of stuttering.* Englewood Cliffs, NJ: Prentice-Hall.

Van Riper, C. (1978). *Speech correction: Principles and methods* (6th ed.). Englewood Cliffs, NJ: Prentice-Hall.

Vaughn-Cooke, F. B. (1989). Speech–language pathologists and educators: Time to strengthen the partnership. In B. A. Stewart (Ed.), *Partnerships in education: Toward a literate America* (pp. 67–70). Rockville, MD: American Speech–Hearing–Language Association. (ERIC Document Reproduction Service No. ED 373 488)

Warren, S. F. (1992). Facilitating basic vocabulary acquisition with milieu teaching procedures. *Journal of Early Intervention, 16*(3), 235–251.

Warren, S. F., & Kaiser, A. P. (1988). Research in early language intervention. In S. L. Odom & M. B. Karnes (Eds.), *Early intervention for infants and children with handicaps.* Baltimore: Paul H. Brookes.

Webster, R. L. (1980). Evolution of a target-based behavioral therapy for stuttering. *Journal of Fluency Disorders, 5,* 303–320.

Wheeler, D., Jacobson, J., Paglieri, R., & Schwartz, A. (1993). An experimental assessment of facilitated communication. *Mental Retardation, 31,* 49–60.

Zangari, C. (1991). Individuals with communication difficulties. In S. W. Schwartz (Ed.), *Exceptional people* (pp. 253–273). New York: McGraw-Hill.

Chapter 8

Boat Outing, acrylic on canvas, 24″ × 30″ (1993)

HEARING IMPAIRMENTS

Andrea M. Lazzari

After studying this chapter, the reader will:

Identify the basic parts of the ear and understand how sound is
transmitted from the environment to the brain

Know the different types of hearing impairments

Recognize signs, symptoms, and causes of hearing loss

Understand the methods used to assess hearing impairment

Have a rationale for the early identification of hearing impairment

Know simple steps that can be taken to prevent hearing loss

Be familiar with the possible benefits and restrictions of hearing aids

Know how to implement recommended intervention strategies
and modifications of educational experiences for
students with hearing impairments

Be aware of current issues in the identification, treatment, and
education of persons who are hard-of-hearing or deaf

Demonstrate awareness of specialized equipment and materials
used by persons with hearing impairments

HEARING IMPAIRMENTS

1st century — Early historian Pliny the Elder recorded deafness among people living near the waterfalls along the Nile.

6th century — Roman legal system accorded some rights to people who were deaf, but not to those who were deaf, blind, and mute.

1680 — Dalgarno (and much later, Alexander Graham Bell) developed the first finger spelling techniques.

1760 — Abbe de l'Epee established the first school for the deaf in Paris and developed a sign system.

Early 19th century — Publicly funded schools for the deaf began to open in the United States.

1864 — The Lexington School for the Deaf was opened in Manhattan; the National Deaf-Mute College, which later became Gallaudet University, was founded in Washington, D.C.

1880 — Congress of Milan, an international meeting of educators, affirmed "superiority" of speech over sign.

Early 20th century — Max Goldstein established the Central Institute for the Deaf in St. Louis; the first hearing aids were used there.

1910–1920 — The Industrial Revolution brought about widespread noise pollution and noise-induced hearing loss among workers in the United States.

1960s — The trend toward bilingual/bicultural deaf education began.

1970 — "Total Communication"—which combines the use of voice, signs, finger spelling, and hearing—became widely used.

1990 — U.S. Food and Drug Administration first approved the use of a cochlear implant with children aged 2 to 17.

INTRODUCTION

Most people with normal hearing have difficulty understanding the enormous impact of the auditory sense on human development and learning as well as the integral role it plays in activities of daily living. When imagining what it would be like to live in a world without sound, we think about missing the obvious noises of daily living—the ringing of the alarm clock or doorbell, a baby's cry or a dog's bark, a conversation with a friend, or listening to favorite music. But consider the background noises that add to the texture of the environment—the hum of the refrigerator, the beating of rain on the roof, the grating of sandpaper on wood, the click of someone's heels as she walks down the hall, or even the annoying buzz of a mosquito around your ear. These sounds are also missed by many individuals who are hard-of-hearing or deaf.

This chapter will explore the world of hearing loss from various perspectives. The implications of various types of hearing impairment on an individual's educational, vocational, and personal life will be considered. Suggestions will be given for teachers of students with hearing impairments to enable them to support integration of these students in inclusive education settings. As you read the chapter, try to consider the potential effect of a hearing loss on your life, especially on the activities that you enjoy.

HISTORICAL OVERVIEW

Hearing impairment has been a source of interest for many centuries. One of the first historical accounts of hearing loss was recorded in the 1st century A.D., when Pliny the Elder noted deafness among people living near the waterfalls of the Nile, no doubt due to the loud and constant noise of the water. The earliest documentation of instruction of students who were deaf dates to the 1500s. Ponce de León established a school in Spain around 1578 for deaf children. By 1680, Dalgarno developed the first standard finger spelling techniques. Bonet published the first manual for instruction of deaf students during the 17th century. During the 18th century, schools for students who were deaf were established in many European countries.

Several significant developments in education of individuals with hearing impairments occurred in the 19th century. Thomas Braidwood in the United Kingdom worked on oral language acquisition for people who were deaf, and Thomas Gallaudet began to develop a combined method of manual and oral communication. In the early part of the 19th century, publicly funded schools for the deaf began to open in the United States, some using an oral method and others using only manual communication (signing and finger spelling). In 1817, the American Asylum for the Education of the Deaf and Dumb opened in Hartford, Connecticut, its name reflecting the commonly accepted view that people who were deaf were also dumb, or mute. President Abraham Lincoln signed a bill in 1864 establishing the National Deaf-Mute College (which later became Gallaudet University) in Washington, D.C. That same year the first oral school, the Lexington School for the Deaf, opened in Manhattan. Shortly after, in 1880, an international meeting of educators known as the Congress of Milan affirmed the "superiority" of oral speech over manual sign, thus beginning the dominance of **oralism** in the education of students who are deaf. At the close of the 19th century, the Industrial

REAL PEOPLE

"It was the most exciting moment of my entire life," said Curtis Pride, an outfielder in the Montreal Expos organization. "It was the middle of a pennant race, and there I was, pinch-hitting with runners on first and second base against the Philadelphia Phillies. I hit the first pitch I saw for a two-run double. I got my first standing ovation. I was overwhelmed. As I stood on second base and saw all those people cheering, I reflected back on life, on how I'd come a long way."

Curtis Pride is deaf, born with a 95% hearing loss. A hearing aid enables him to hear certain muffled sounds. In spite of his disability, Pride has always been persistent in the pursuit of his dream. He made it to Montreal after 8 years in the minor leagues. His first major league hit, on September 17, 1993, helped boost the Expos to a surprise victory over the first-place Phillies.

Curtis's deafness was diagnosed when he was 6 months old. He was immediately enrolled in a program for children with hearing loss at a nearby hospital. After 3 years there, he entered the Montgomery County, Maryland, public schools. At the same time, his parents, Sallie and John, were busy educating themselves on how to help Curtis succeed academically and socially. "We read a lot," says Sallie. "We talked a lot, especially to other parents with deaf children. That was really helpful. They tell you the truth."

Sallie and John decided early that their son would not learn sign language; they felt it would exclude him from his peers. Instead, they wanted Curtis to rely on oral communication. Curtis received speech–language therapy throughout his school years. His parents also helped teach him to talk. "There were days my mom would hold up a ball," Curtis recalls, "and she would say the word 'ball' over and over. I would read her lips, and I could sort of 'hear' what it sounded like. I'd put those two things together until I could say the word."

Curtis remembers his first few years of school as being the most difficult period of his life. He grew frustrated by the constant teasing from other children about the unusual way he talked and about his hearing aid. But Curtis found that his talent as an athlete was the key to acceptance from his peers: "People wanted me on their team." Later, Curtis's reputation was so great that if an opponent resorted to making cruel remarks, that person's own teammates would ostracize him.

Curtis Pride was drafted by the New York Mets after high school, but he also received a basketball scholarship from the College of William and Mary. He knew it was important that he get an education. "There's no guarantee of making it in professional sports. So I worked out an agreement with the Mets that allowed me to go to college full-time and play in the minor leagues in the summers." Curtis decided to pursue baseball full-time after graduating from college in 1990 with a degree in finance.

After enduring a mediocre batting average of .251 that plagued him for 7 years while with the Mets, Curtis Pride became a minor league free agent at the end of the 1992 season. The Expos signed him that December. He is now playing for the Ottawa Lynx, a Montreal farm team.

Curtis maintains that his deafness can be an advantage at bat. Because he can't hear the noise of the crowd, his concentration is 100%. When he plays center field, Curtis says, he and his teammates communicate with hand signals.

Curtis Pride wants to inform people that they can do anything they want. "I want inner-city children to know they have no excuse for not being successful," he says. "They see people like me, and they see that I overcame a handicap. I never let my deafness hold me back. I never feel sorry for myself. Never. I know I have a disability. I've accepted it. I can't worry about it. I want to make the most of my life. And I am."

Source: Adapted and reprinted with permission from "I Know What I Can Do," by S. Flatow, August 7, 1994, *Parade Magazine*, pp. 16–17.

Revolution was in force in England and just beginning in the United States. With it came widespread noise pollution and noise-induced hearing loss among workers.

One of the most significant developments in the first half of this century was the development of electronic hearing aids. Although nonelectronic listening de-

Table 8.1   **Levels of Hearing Loss (Average Hearing Loss in Best Ear)**

MILD	MODERATE	SEVERE	PROFOUND	TOTAL
25–40 dB loss	40–60 dB loss	60–80 dB loss	80–120 dB loss	No measurable hearing
• May have difficulty hearing in noisy situations	• May have difficulty hearing normal conversation	• May understand speech with hearing aids and auditory training	• May be able to hear the rhythm and tone of speech through aided hearing	• Is unable to benefit from hearing aid
• May have difficulty hearing some sounds (such as unvoiced consonants)	• Is likely to develop auditory skills	• May have good rhythm, tone, and articulation of speech	• May recognize vowels and discriminate some consonants in connected speech	• Can learn to recognize some environmental sounds by touch and rhythm
• May be frustrated when communicating	• Is likely to acquire speech and language spontaneously without hearing aids		• Has limited perception of speech—often distorted, even with hearing aids	
• May not need a hearing aid unless loss approaches the 30–40 dB range				

vices had been available 100 years earlier, electronic aids were not widely used until the early 20th century. The second half of the 20th century brought about new approaches to communication. In 1966, Dr. R. Orin Cornett developed cued speech, a system in which hand signals provide a visual cue to the sound of speech. In 1970, in reaction to a century of oralism, Roy Holcomb gave the label "Total Communication" to a system that combines voice, signs, and finger spelling. Technological advances were made during this period as well—one of the most significant being the cochlear implant, an electronic device implanted in the inner ear, which was approved in 1990 for use with children aged 2 to 17.

DEFINITION OF TERMS

Hearing loss is a broad term that includes all degrees and types of hearing impairment. The term **hard-of-hearing** is used to refer to losses in the mild to moderate range. **Deaf** is the term used to refer to losses in the severe and profound range (see Table 8.1).

Often, the term *deaf* has been used to refer to a person who cannot understand speech with the ear alone, either with or without a hearing aid, or a person who cannot hear any sounds at all. However, most people who are deaf have some residual hearing. They can hear some sounds at certain frequencies.

Some people prefer the terminology *person with hearing loss* to refer to individuals who are either hard-of-hearing or deaf. Other terms that have been used are *hearing impaired, hearing handicapped, hearing disordered,* and *aurally or auditorily disordered.*

TRANSMISSION OF SOUND

Hearing is a very complex process. Sound waves must travel through intricate pathways and undergo many changes to reach the brain. A break in the chain at any

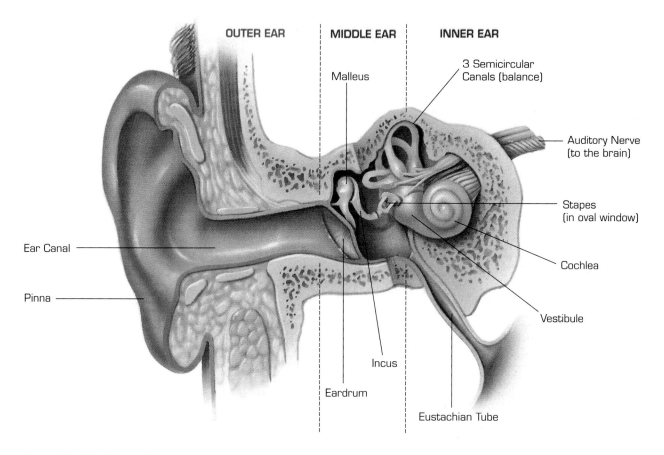

Figure 8.1   The Human Ear

point can result in a hearing loss. Because the nature and degree of an individual's hearing loss is directly related to where the breakdown in the processing of sound occurs within the ear, a brief review of the anatomy of the ear is helpful. There are three main parts of the ear: the outer ear, the inner ear, and the middle ear. (See Figure 8.1.)

Outer Ear.   As shown in Figure 8.1, the outer ear consists of the *pinna* (auricle), the *ear canal*, and the *eardrum* (tympanic membrane). Sound waves of varying frequencies are generated by a multitude of sources in the environment. As these waves travel through the air, some of them are "caught" by the pinna and are channeled into the external ear canal. Thus, the pinna serves as a funnel for sound waves. When we cup our hand behind our ear to hear better, we help the pinna do its job by forming a larger funnel. The sound waves then move through the ear canal and are transmitted to the middle ear via the eardrum.

Middle Ear.   The middle ear contains three small bones or *ossicles:* the *malleus* (hammer), the *incus* (anvil), and the *stapes* (stirrup), as shown in Figure 8.1. As sound waves passing through the outer ear hit the eardrum, it vibrates. These vibrations are then transferred to the ossicles, which convert the sound energy into mechanical energy. Since intensity is lost as the sound waves travel through the air, the middle ear acts as an amplification system for the sound waves as they travel on to the inner ear.

Inner Ear.   The inner ear contains a coiled structure called the *cochlea*, also shown in Figure 8.1. The cochlea is a circular chamber filled with fluid and lined with 20,000 to 40,000 *hair cells* (sensory fibers). Sound travels from the middle ear to the inner ear via the *oval window*. When the stapes moves, the oval window vibrates and waves are sent through the fluid of the inner ear. Thus, in the inner ear, sound waves are changed into waves of fluid. The movement of this fluid causes the hair cells to vibrate, producing an electrostatic current. This current is transmitted to the auditory center in the brain via the *auditory nerve.* The message then travels to higher centers of the brain where meaning is attached to it.

Although most of the sounds in the environment are picked up by and transmitted through the outer ear via the ear canal and the eardrum, we also hear some sounds through the bones of the skull. These sounds (such as when we hum or chew crunchy food), are conducted by our bones rather than by the ear. This explains why our own voices sound somewhat flat to us when we hear a recorded version. A comparison of a person's response to sounds presented via bone conduction versus air conduction is used in the diagnosis of some types of hearing loss (discussed more fully later in the chapter).

CHARACTERISTICS OF INDIVIDUALS WITH HEARING LOSS

The characteristics displayed by an individual with a hearing impairment will depend on the particular type and extent of loss, the person's ability to benefit from amplification, and the type of auditory training, education, and family support received. There are, however, characteristics that many individuals with hearing loss share.

Behavioral changes may be among the first signs that a person is experiencing a hearing loss. People with undetected losses may say "What?" often, watch the speaker's face intently, turn up the volume of the television or radio, confuse similar-sounding words (e.g., *messed* for *nest*), and have difficulty understanding a speaker who is in another room (Gallaudet College, 1986).

Many people with hearing losses in the moderate to profound ranges also have speech and language disorders. Since the individual often cannot hear the sounds of the language clearly, he may be unable to produce them clearly when speaking—especially those sounds that are not readily visible on the speaker's lips, such as /k/, /g/, or /j/. If the loss is in the high-frequency range, the individual may have particular difficulty producing high-frequency sounds such as /s/, /z/, and /ch/. This person's speech may sound slurred and include sound omissions and substitutions of one sound for another (see Chapter 7).

Voice production is also affected by hearing loss. Because they cannot hear their own voices as they speak, individuals with severe hearing loss or deafness typically have a flat quality to their voices. Their voices tend to lack resonance, and they are unable to use intonation to add meaning and emphasis to their messages.

Language deficits are common among children and adults with significant hearing impairments. Limited or slow development of vocabulary may be the first sign that a young child has a hearing loss. As the child grows older and the language of her peers with normal hearing becomes more complex and abstract, her language deficits will become increasingly obvious. And, because language is the medium through which many of our social skills, customs, and mores are learned and friendships are made, children with significant hearing loss may also have problems with social and emotional development.

INCIDENCE AND PREVALENCE OF HEARING LOSS

The lack of standard terms and definitions in describing hearing loss—and the overlap between different levels of impairment—leads to differences in reported incidence and prevalence data. The following statistics reflect the numbers of individuals with hearing loss and deafness in various segments of the population:

- One baby in 1,000 in the United States will be born deaf or become deaf before age 3.
- An additional two children in 1,000 will become deaf during their early childhoods.
- Approximately one child in five experiences a conductive hearing loss at some point in time.
- In 1993–94, there were 64, 249 students with hearing loss, from age 6 through 21, who received special education services in the nation's public schools—representing 1% of the total special education population.
- More than 7 million aged persons have some degree of hearing loss.
- From 28 to 30 million people in the U.S. have a hearing loss (American Academy of Audiology, 1991; Freeland, 1989; National Information Center on Deafness, 1986; U.S. Department of Education, 1995; Webster & Wood, 1989).

A look at the foregoing figures underscores the significance of hearing loss in the nation today. While true deafness is a low-incidence disability, hearing loss is a disability that cuts across all age groups and educational and socioeconomic levels. In spite of preventive measures and educational and technological advances, the number of persons with hearing loss continues to increase.

TYPES OF HEARING LOSS

Hearing loss can be classified in several ways. The first consideration is whether it affects only one ear (*unilateral* loss) or both ears (*bilateral* loss). Typically, a bilateral loss would be more of a handicap than a unilateral loss.

Hearing loss may also be categorized according to when it occurred. If a hearing disorder is present at birth, it is referred to as *congenital*. An *adventitious* loss is one that is acquired later in life. Sometimes losses are referred to as **prelingual** (occurring before the acquisition of language) or **postlingual** (occurring after language development has been attained). Obviously, a prelingual or congenital loss will have a more serious effect on the individual's speech and language development than one acquired later in life. The vast majority (more than 90%) of children who are deaf in the United States today were born deaf or acquired their hearing loss prior to learning to speak (Dolnick, 1993).

Hearing loss is also classified by the location of the disruption in the auditory chain, as described earlier. The three primary types of loss based on site are *conductive*, *sensorineural*, and *central auditory*.

Conductive hearing loss is the result of damage, disease, or injury to the external ear, the ear canal, the eardrum, or any part of the middle ear. A conductive loss occurs when something prevents the sound waves from being mechanically conducted from the environment through the outer and middle ear. The effects of prolonged or persistent conductive losses on a child's speech and language development can be significant, especially if they occur at critical developmental stages. Conductive losses have been associated with delays in speech and language development and also with later problems in reading and spelling. For this reason, children with a history of middle ear disease should be observed periodically for possible communication and reading problems.

Sensorineural hearing loss results from damage to the inner ear; it can be unilateral or bilateral. With this type of loss, there is a problem in reception of sound by the inner ear. Although the sound waves travel from the middle ear to the inner ear, they are not transmitted correctly because of damage to structures in the inner ear (e.g., sensory fibers or the auditory nerve). Even with amplification (hearing aids), the sounds may be distorted when received by the brain. Sensorineural losses can range from mild to profound. Most losses of this type are permanent because once any of the sensory fibers (hair cells) are destroyed, they do not regenerate. Sensorineural losses may affect some frequencies more than others, particularly the higher ones. Fortunately, the prevalence of sensorineural hearing loss is much less than for conductive losses.

It is possible for an individual to have a mixed hearing loss in which problems occur in both the outer or middle and the inner ear. In such cases, the outer or middle ear problem would be treated medically, and amplification (a hearing aid) would be considered to help overcome the effects of the inner ear problem.

Hearing loss can also occur if there is damage to the auditory nerve leading from the inner ear to the brain or in the brain itself. This type of loss is called a *central auditory hearing loss* or a **central auditory dysfunction.** Central losses occur infrequently and the cause is often unknown. Hearing aids are typically not helpful with this type of loss.

CAUSES OF HEARING LOSS

Conductive Hearing Impairments

A child with malformed outer ears may have a conductive loss if the external opening of the ear canal is small or completely filled with tissue. Surgery to remove the tissue or widen the canal enables the sound waves to travel through the outer ear to the middle ear. A child who blocks the ear canal with a small object like a marble, raisin, or stone will experience a temporary conductive loss until the object is removed. A ruptured or perforated eardrum—due to an accident or a foreign object such as a pencil or cotton swab stuck in the ear—can also cause a conductive loss, as can an accumulation of excess wax in the external ear canal.

Otitis media, a buildup of fluid in the middle ear, is the most common cause of conductive hearing loss in young children. Approximately one in five children will experience a conductive hearing loss at some point in time (Murphy, 1976). The peak age for middle ear problems is before age 2. By age 3, more than two thirds of children have had a middle ear infection (Teele, Klein, & Rosner, 1984). It has been estimated that up to 95% of children have had one or more episodes of middle ear infection by the age of 10 (Fielleau-Nikolajsen, 1983). Thus, the group of individuals most vulnerable to middle ear infections and the conductive hearing loss that often results—young children—is also the group that is least likely to be aware of and report symptoms to anyone. For this reason, otitis media often goes undetected and untreated for days or weeks, especially among very young children. Treatment alternatives for recurrent otitis media include low dosage antibiotics or a minor surgical procedure (tympanostomy) in which tiny tubes are inserted in the eardrum to ventilate the middle ear.

Sensorineural Hearing Impairments

Impairments of Genetic Origin.   Many cases of sensorineural hearing loss are genetic in origin. More than 200 types of genetic deafness have been identified. Genetic hearing disorders can be inherited from one or both parents, who may have normal hearing or a hearing loss (National Information Center on Deafness and the National Association of the Deaf, 1984).

Currently, for most types of genetic hearing loss, there is no reliable test that pinpoints the presence of a defective gene or chromosome. However, hearing loss may be associated with certain genetic syndromes for which genetic testing is possible (e.g., Down syndrome, Turner's syndrome). Genetic evaluation and counseling is a helpful service for many families in which genetic hearing loss is present or suspected.

In most cases (90% to 95%), genetic hearing loss occurs without problems in other body systems. In a small number of cases, genetic hearing loss is part of a syndrome (e.g., Treacher-Collins syndrome, Alport's syndrome, Usher's syndrome) that involves problems with other body systems such as the head and face, eyes, or kidneys.

Impairments Due to Viral or Bacterial Illness.   Maternal viruses such as German measles (rubella) and cytomegalovirus (CMV) can also result in sensorineural hearing loss among newborns, especially if the mother acquires the virus during the first 3 months of pregnancy when the sensory organs are forming. In the 1960s, rubella epidemics swept across the United States and Canada and many babies were born with impairments of vision, hearing, and the heart and central nervous systems. Widespread immunization has resulted in a decrease in the number of women who acquire rubella during pregnancy and the number of infants born with birth defects as a result. Cytomegalovirus is a very common infection that children and adults acquire easily and may have without any noticeable symptoms. It can affect an infant's hearing and other body systems if the mother acquires the virus prior to the baby's birth. Babies can also incur hearing loss if they pick up CMV during the birth process.

Other viral or bacterial illnesses can have a profound effect on an infant's hearing. Some childhood diseases can also result in sensorineural hearing loss. The leading cause of adventitious hearing loss is meningitis, an infection that may be viral or bacterial, causing an inflammation of the membranes covering the brain and spinal cord. Measles, mumps, scarlet fever, and other illnesses associated with prolonged high fever can also result in irreversible sensorineural hearing loss. Early

Musician Eddie Van Halen, his wife, actress Valerie Bertinelli, and their son Wolfgang. Eddie has suffered hearing loss due to noise exposure.

diagnosis and treatment are extremely important factors in the prevention of hearing loss caused by illness.

Impairments Due to Medication.   Some medications can have an **ototoxic** effect, causing harm to the organs or nerves concerned with hearing and balance. The ototoxic effect of drugs can occur prior to birth if the mother takes certain medications (e.g., "mycin" type antibiotics, quinine, thalidomide) or at any time throughout a person's life. Common drugs such as aspirin, methyl salicylate (a substance in heat ointments), antibiotics (e.g., neomycin), and diuretics—as well as less frequently prescribed medications—can damage one's hearing and cause *tinnitus* (ringing in the ears), especially if they are taken in large doses or over prolonged periods of time. These drugs can also affect the vestibular system, causing vertigo (dizziness) and balance problems. The benefit of such drugs, especially in life-threatening situations, must be weighed against their potential damaging effects on hearing (Suss, 1993).

Impairments Due to Noise and Other Factors.   Noise exposure is one of the most common causes of sensorineural hearing loss. This occurs when the hair cells in the inner ear are damaged or destroyed and the nerve endings atrophy and die. As shown in Table 8.2, many common objects in the environment are excessively loud and can lead to permanent hearing loss with prolonged or repeated exposure.

Performers and fans of rock music are particularly at-risk for hearing loss due to noise exposure. Hearing specialists note the increase in sensorineural loss, often accompanied by tinnitus, among persons in their twenties and thirties. Performers who acknowledge their hearing losses include Pete Townshend, Ted Nugent, Eric Clapton, and Eddie Van Halen. The implications of hearing loss to musicians are summed up by Townshend:

Table 8.2   **Sources of Noise-Induced Hearing Loss**

OCCUPATIONAL	RECREATIONAL	ENVIRONMENTAL
Factory noise (machinery and equipment)	Music (rock bands, marching bands, symphonies, stereo headsets, crowd noises)	In and around the home (power tools, lawn mowers, chain saws)
Construction noise (jackhammers, bulldozers, other heavy equipment)	Sports (crowd noises, rifles, car and motorcycle racing)	Traffic (ground and air traffic near homes, schools, offices)
Office noises (copy machines)	Toys (cap pistols)	
Transportation noises (trains, buses, subways, airplanes, city traffic)	Other (firecrackers)	
Military noises (guns and rifles, aircraft, vehicles)		

Table 8.3   **Warning Signs of Noise-Induced Hearing Loss as a Result of Exposure to Loud Music**

- Ringing or buzzing in the ears immediately after exposure to loud music
- Slight muffling of sounds after exposure to loud music
- Difficulty in understanding speech after exposure—you can hear all the words, but you can't understand them
- Over time and multiple exposures, difficulty hearing conversation in groups of people, when there is background noise, or in rooms with poor acoustics

Source: Information from HEAR (Hearing Education and Awareness for Rockers), University of California, San Francisco, Center on Deafness.

> The real reason I haven't performed live for a long time is that I have very severe hearing damage. It's manifested itself as tinnitus, ringing in the ears at the frequencies that I play the guitar. It's very difficult for me to work at music. . . . It hurts, and it's painful, and it's frustrating when little children talk to you and you can't hear them. (quoted in Murphy, 1989, p. 101)

Hearing loss due to noise exposure is not, however, limited to rock music. Members of marching bands and symphony orchestras are also at-risk. Even a piccolo can reach levels of 110 dB, which is in the danger zone for noise-induced hearing loss. (See Table 8.3 for warning signs of noise-induced hearing loss.)

Presbycusis is the sum of hearing loss that results from physiological degeneration of the hair cells in the inner ear over a person's life span. This includes loss due to noise exposure, ototoxic medication, and other agents and medical disorders (Committee on Hearing, Bioacoustics, and Biomechanics, 1988). While presbycusis can be partially prevented by avoiding excessive noise and ototoxic medications, everyone will experience some degree of hearing loss as they grow older.

ASSESSMENT OF HEARING LOSS

Early identification of hearing loss is very important. As shown in Table 8.4, there are many symptoms that may indicate hearing loss in children and adults—but these symptoms are not displayed by the one in every 1,000 babies in this country who are born with deafness or hearing loss. How can these hearing losses be detected early enough to prevent or reduce the effects of problems in speech and language development that result from congenital hearing losses?

Table 8.4 **Symptoms of Hearing Loss**

- Is inattentive
- Has difficulty understanding conversation in a group or in noise
- Needs repetition of conversational speech
- Complains of earache, full or "popping" ears, head noises, or ringing in ears
- Speaks with louder or softer voice than others
- Sits close to sound source or turns up volume on television, radio, etc.
- Is slow in responding to simple verbal instructions and responds to questions inappropriately
- Has immature speech and language that is limited in vocabulary and syntax (among children)
- Has slurred speech, sound omissions, or substitutions and a lack of intonation (among adults and children)
- Turns head to one side when listening
- Relies on visual cues to interpret speech
- Is reluctant to speak in group discussions

Table 8.5 **Checklist for Normal Hearing Development**

BIRTH TO 6 WEEKS	BY 3 MONTHS	3 TO 6 MONTHS	6 TO 10 MONTHS
Is startled by loud, sudden noises	Recognizes parents' voices; looks toward person who is speaking	Turns head toward source of sound	Responds to own name; likes toys that make noise; begins to imitate sounds

BY 12 MONTHS	1 TO 2 YEARS	2 TO 3 YEARS	4 TO 5 YEARS
Associates words with the objects they represent; responds to simple requests	Enjoys songs, rhymes, and stories; can point to objects named in a book; understands simple questions and commands	Can follow a 2-step direction; answers when called from another room; listens to a familiar voice on the telephone	Understands most of what is said at home and school; can answer simple questions about a story read aloud; repeats songs and jingles

One answer is routine hearing screening at birth for all infants. Although experts recommend routine screening of infants, it is not standard practice in most hospitals. Parents, family members, and caregivers are often the first to suspect that a young child has a hearing loss.

Although there is variation in the typical course of child development, there are early milestones in the development of listening skills that parents can look for (see Table 8.5). If an infant is not responding to sound appropriately or is not babbling and cooing, there should be a hearing evaluation without delay. A difference of even a few months can have a critical effect on the child's development of speech and language. A child diagnosed with a hearing loss prior to the age of 6 months has a distinct advantage over a child diagnosed at 18 months (Freeland, 1989). By 18 months, a child with a hearing loss will have missed many of the critical periods of speech, language, and hearing development.

Another important practice in early detection of hearing loss is to identify those children who are at high risk for hearing loss and to assess them early and

Even very young children can be tested for hearing problems.

periodically for possible hearing problems. Common risk factors for hearing loss include the following:

- Family history of hearing loss
- Low birth weight (under 5 pounds)
- History of maternal illness (e.g., rubella, diabetes, cytomegalovirus infection)
- Maternal ototoxic drug intake (e.g., certain antibiotics, quinine)
- Presence of other head, facial, or external ear abnormalities
- Prolonged neonatal jaundice
- Fetal distress and lack of oxygen during birth
- Poor APGAR rating (rating of vital signs of newborn)
- Admission to neonatal intensive care unit
- Infant history of meningitis (Schwartz, 1987)

Parents and professionals also need to be aware of certain groups of children who are at-risk for developing conductive hearing losses. Children with Down syndrome often have narrow ear canals that tend to become blocked with wax. They are also prone to ear infections, with up to 78% having experienced a significant conductive hearing loss (Bond, 1984). For these reasons, some parents and educators support the practice of fitting children who have Down syndrome with low-gain hearing aids, to ensure that they are not missing out on valuable language experiences.

The majority of children with cleft palate (estimates of up to 90%) have conductive hearing losses (Northern & Downs, 1978). Because the muscles in their palates do not enable their eustachian tubes to operate effectively, these children are very likely to have middle ear infections resulting in conductive losses. Since children with cleft palate are already at-risk for abnormal speech development, they must be followed carefully for signs of middle ear infections.

Identification efforts should not, however, be limited to infants and children who are at-risk: Half of all infants with hearing loss are otherwise healthy and have no known risk factors. Hearing screenings should be a routine part of all well-child checkups during the preschool years, and parents should insist that their children receive a full audiological evaluation by an accredited audiologist at the first sign of a hearing loss, even if the child is very young (American Academy of Audiology, 1988).

Measurement of Sound

Sounds are measured by intensity (loudness) and frequency (pitch). The standard unit used to measure sound intensity is the **decibel (dB).** Sounds above 125 dB will be painful to the average person. Sounds in our environment range from 10 dB for a whisper to 140 dB for a jet aircraft upon takeoff (see Figure 8.2). Conversational

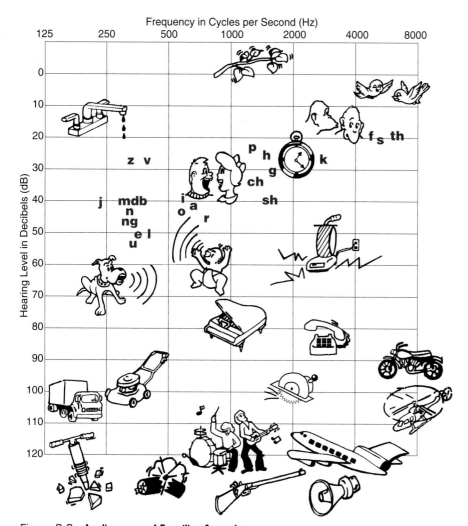

Figure 8.2 Audiogram of Familiar Sounds

Source: American Academy of Audiology, Arlington, VA. Reprinted with permission.

NOW HEAR THIS!

Some people with a hearing loss are not even aware of it. According to the Occupational Hearing Services (OHS), approximately 28 million Americans suffer from some type of hearing disorder. The OHS has established the Dial-a-Hearing Screening Test to enable people to have their hearing screened over the telephone.

Call the National Information Center (NIC) at 1-800-222-EARS between 9:00 a.m. and 5:00 p.m. EST (Monday through Friday) to obtain a local number for a free hearing test. During the test, eight tones will be presented. If you don't hear all eight of them, you should undergo a more complete hearing exam. The NIC can also refer you to a qualified hearing specialist in your locality.

---

speech ranges from 30 to 60 dB while a rock concert may register at 110 dB or louder.

The frequency of sound is measured by the number of cycles (vibrations) per second. The standard unit of measurement is the **hertz (Hz),** with one hertz equal to one cycle per second. The human range of hearing is from 20 to 15,000 Hz but the majority of sounds in our environment fall between 300 and 4,000 Hz.

Measurement of Hearing

Hearing is assessed on the parameters of intensity and frequency. Specialized procedures are carried out by an **audiologist,** a professional trained to assess hearing problems. Commonly used methods of measuring hearing include pure tone audiometry, speech audiometry, tympanometry, and electrical response audiometry.

Pure Tone Audiometry.   An **audiometer** is the most common instrument used to assess hearing. It produces pure tones at various frequencies and intensities, which are received by the listener through earphones (air conduction) or via a vibrating device placed on the skull (bone conduction). Ideally, an audiometric evaluation is conducted in a soundproof booth that blocks out all extraneous noise. Each ear is tested separately. The person responds to each pure tone by raising a hand or pushing a button. Preschool children can be taught to respond to the tones behaviorally by putting a ring on a peg or a block in a container when they hear the sound. The sounds are presented in small increments to determine the person's *threshold of hearing* for each frequency. This threshold, which is the quietest sound heard at a particular frequency, is then plotted on an *audiogram*, as shown in Figure 8.3.

An **audiogram** is a graphic representation of the different levels of sound a person can detect at each frequency tested. As shown in Figure 8.3, the sound frequencies, ranging from 125 to 8,000 Hz, are displayed on the horizontal axis. The decibel levels, ranging from 0 to 120, are displayed on the left vertical axis.

An individual's responses to the hearing test are plotted on the audiogram separately for each ear. The audiogram displayed in Figure 8.3 is that of a person with essentially normal hearing. The responses to the pure tones presented to both ears fall within the 0 to 20 dB range. The audiogram in Figure 8.4 shows a moderate bilateral hearing loss while that in Figure 8.5 shows a severe bilateral hearing loss in the high frequencies.

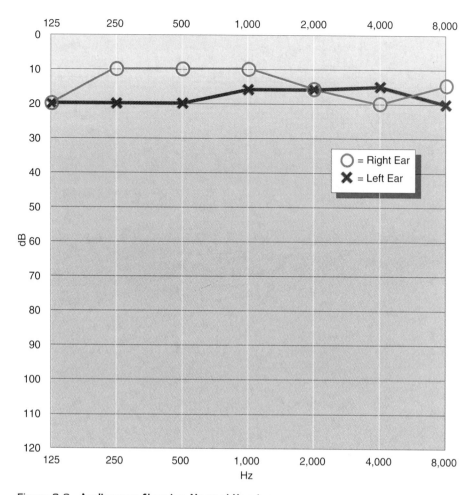

Figure 8.3 **Audiogram Showing Normal Hearing**

Speech Audiometry. Speech audiometry is a form of testing that determines an individual's response to speech at different intensity levels. To determine a person's **Speech Reception Threshold (SRT),** the audiologist presents two-syllable words (e.g., football, hot dog) to find the loudness level at which the person can just barely hear the stimuli. A person with an SRT of 20 to 25 dB or lower should easily hear speech in most situations. When determining **speech discrimination,** the audiologist reads aloud from a list of phonetically balanced words (e.g., "Say the word *bat.* Now say the word *hat.*") and asks the person to repeat the words heard (correctly discriminated). The percentage of words the person hears correctly represents that person's speech discrimination score.

Tympanometry. **Tympanometry** or *impedance audiometry* is used to determine how well the middle ear is functioning. An instrument called a *tympanometer* is used to transmit a low-frequency sound to the eardrum and measure how much of the sound is reflected, indicating the elasticity of the eardrum. If there is fluid in the middle ear, the eardrum will be inelastic. This information is very useful in diagnosing otitis media (middle ear infection) (Freeland, 1989).

Electrical Response Audiometry. Brainstem audiometry or **auditory brainstem response (ABR)** is an objective assessment that does not require a voluntary

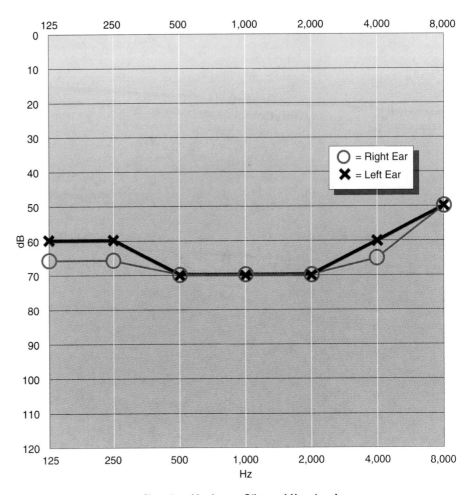

Figure 8.4 Audiogram Showing Moderate Bilateral Hearing Loss

response from the person being tested. By placing electrodes on the scalp, neural responses to sound can be detected. ABR is used to test individuals who are very young, cognitively impaired, or unable to voluntarily respond to pure tone testing.

AMPLIFICATION AND ELECTROMECHANICAL INTERVENTIONS

After the nature and extent of hearing loss are determined through the foregoing assessment methods, the next step for some individuals is to explore options for amplification of sounds. The two most common devices are hearing aids and cochlear implants.

Hearing Aids

There are several types of hearing aids. They are classified according to where they are worn: body aids (strapped to the chest; typically worn by young children), behind-the-ear aids, and in-the-ear-aids. The type of aid that is best for an individual is determined by several factors including the type and extent of the hearing loss, the person's age, and individual preferences.

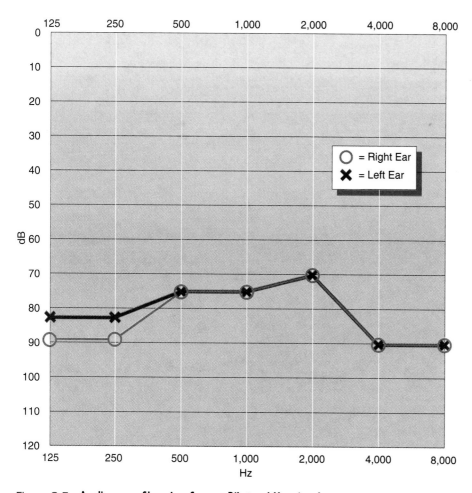

Figure 8.5   Audiogram Showing Severe Bilateral Hearing Loss

A hearing aid is quite simply what it proclaims to be: an aid to hearing. Contrary to what many people believe, a hearing aid does not restore normal hearing to the wearer. Rather, a hearing aid amplifies sound, making it easier to hear speech and other noises, but it doesn't necessarily make it clearer. You can compare it to turning up the volume on a radio—a hearing aid makes the sounds louder but the words don't become easier to understand. Hearing aids pick up and amplify all sounds in the environment, regardless of their importance to the listener. Thus, the noise of a motorcycle passing by the window will be amplified the same as music from a tape player, and the noise of papers and feet being shuffled in the classroom will be amplified along with the teacher's voice.

Even though hearing aids cannot restore normal hearing or provide solutions to all of the problems associated with hearing loss, they are an indispensable resource in the management of hearing loss (Webster & Wood, 1989). Not all individuals with hearing loss can benefit from using an aid (e.g., those with profound sensorineural loss), but many will benefit a great deal.

Recent technological advances have resulted in marked improvements in hearing aids. Not only are they smaller and lighter, but they also are more powerful. Hearing aids can now be programmed to match the specific configurations of a person's hearing pattern. Much like eyeglasses are made to individual specifications

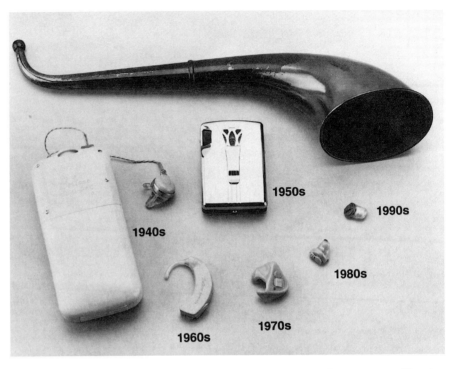

It is easy to see how technology has improved the capabilities and appearance of hearing aids.

for a person's vision, hearing aids can be programmed to provide amplification for those frequencies in the person's range of loss.

Cochlear Implants

A **cochlear implant** is an electronic device that provides useful sound information to the listener by directly stimulating the auditory nerve fibers in the inner ear. It has been designed for a specific group of individuals with hearing loss, specifically "adults and children who have a profound sensorineural hearing loss (nerve deafness) in both ears and show no ability to understand speech through hearing aids" (Cochlear Corporation, 1994).

The device consists of internal components implanted under the skin behind the ear and in the cochlea, and external components that are worn by the individual. An external microphone picks up sounds in the environment, which are amplified, then digitized into coded signals. These signals are then transmitted to the implanted receiver, which stimulates the implanted electrodes in the cochlea. The resulting electrical sound information is then sent to the brain for interpretation.

Although the implant does not restore normal hearing, with training, recipients of the implants can learn to attach meaning to these new stimuli. It has been estimated that 10,000 children and adults who are deaf have been assisted by this technology (Ubell, 1995). Benefits include an improved ability to hear conversation and environmental noises, improved lipreading skills, and improvement in general communication abilities.

Because it has only been since 1990 that the device has been approved by the FDA for use with children, the field remains in a "pioneering" period regarding the technology. Further research is needed to establish the criteria for candidates for the implant and to determine the effects of the device on recipients' speech perception and production (Allen, Rawlings, & Remington, 1993).

Brainstem Implants. A related technology that is being tested is the **multi-channel auditory brainstem implant.** This implant bypasses the ear, transmitting sound via electrodes directly to the auditory region of the brainstem. Potential recipients of this device are people whose auditory nerve has been severed, such as during removal of a tumor (Ubell, 1995).

INSTRUCTIONAL CONSIDERATIONS

Identifying the presence, type, and extent of hearing loss and determining the need for amplification may be all the intervention needed by most persons with mild to moderate hearing impairments. Individuals with severe losses, however—especially those in the profound range (deafness)—will need to select a communication system and receive training in using the system.

Historically, there have been two general schools of thought on the type of communication system that should be taught to young children who are deaf. This controversy has been labeled *oralism* versus *manualism*. One group insists that use of a manual sign language is the only acceptable method of communication for people who are deaf. The other group advocates an oral method that relies on auditory training and speechreading. This controversy has been going on for more than two centuries. There are other considerations as well—all of which are presented in the following discussion. As you read, bear in mind that no single means of communication has been proven effective for all persons with severe hearing loss or deafness. What is certain is that the controversy over approaches and the search for a universal method will continue.

Oral Communication Techniques

Speechreading is the basis of oral communication methods. People with hearing losses in the severe to profound range must rely on speechreading (lipreading) to supplement the sounds they are able to pick up with their hearing aids. Speechreading is difficult to learn, considering that some sounds of the English language are not visible on the lips (/k/, /g/, /r/, /h/) and some resemble others when they are spoken (/s/ and /z/, /p/ and /b/, /f/ and /v/, /sh/ and /ch/). Thus, when spoken, "caught" will look like "hot," and "shoe" will be hard to distinguish from "chew." People who speech-read must also rely on the context of the word, facial expressions, gestures, and situational cues to understand conversational speech. They often miss intonational cues that help convey the speaker's intent (e.g., "*You* didn't tell me that!" versus "You didn't tell me *that!*").

For these reasons, the typical person who is deaf will have difficulty speechreading and will be guessing at almost half the words she sees on a speaker's lips. Another disadvantage of speechreading is that it is exhausting—requiring sustained, intense concentration on the speaker's mouth movements and gestures, as well as awareness of changes in the conversation's context. And, individuals with combined sensory impairments (e.g., low vision coupled with hearing loss) may not be able to receive enough input to speech-read (Karp, 1988). In spite of these drawbacks, with appropriate training, many individuals with hearing loss become excellent speech-readers, enabling them to participate in a wide range of cultural and educational activities.

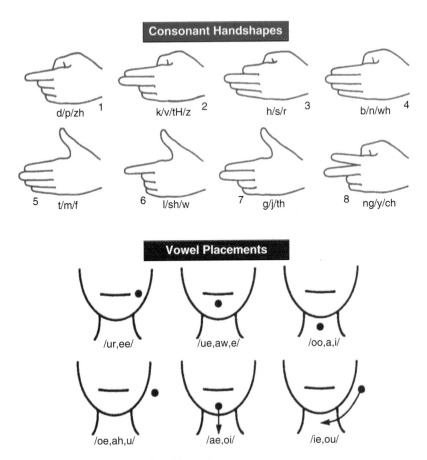

Figure 8.6 Handshapes for Cued Speech

Source: *Choices in Deafness: A Parent's Guide* (p. 26), by Sue Schwartz (Ed.), 1987, Rockville, MD: Woodbine House. Used with permission.

Auditory training is an important adjunct to speechreading. Auditory training consists of activities to help children learn to use their residual hearing, thus improving their listening abilities and their recognition of environmental and speech sounds. While planned auditory training activities are carried out in the classroom or therapy room, auditory training should also take place in the child's natural environment. For example, a parent could direct a young child's attention to the noise of a car pulling into the driveway before the doorbell is rung, or they can play games in which the child discriminates between the mother's and father's voices. Although auditory training is a cornerstone of oral communication methods, it is useful for all children with hearing loss, regardless of their chosen communication method.

Cued speech is a method of visually supplementing oral communication. It was developed at Gallaudet University in the mid-1960s but is not widely used in the United States today. It consists of eight handshapes that are placed near the mouth (to cue consonants) in four different positions (to cue vowels) (see Figure 8.6). The objective of cued speech is to eliminate much of the guesswork involved in speechreading. The cued speech hand signals must be used to accompany the spoken word. Standing alone they have no meaning. For example, the handshape for /d/ (raised index finger) would be used as a cue when saying "done," to help the listener distinguish it from "ton," which requires a different handshape (open palm with thumb extended). The location of the handshape for "done" (to the right of speaker's chin) helps the listener distinguish it from words that start and end the same, yet have a different vowel sound in the middle (e.g., dawn, den, Dan, dean). Although the system appears difficult to learn and use, it reportedly can be learned in approximately 20 hours of instruction.

Manual Communication Systems

Various signed language systems are used around the world. Each employs a system of formal finger, hand, and arm movements to express thoughts and convey messages. **American Sign Language (ASL),** the most widely used system in the country, is the daily language of half a million Americans. Advocates of manual sign suggest that early exposure to signing can result in much richer and earlier language development among children who are deaf (Webster & Wood, 1989).

As displayed at the top of Figure 8.7, many ASL signs are *iconoclastic* (the sign looks like the object it represents). Iconoclastic signs are understood even by people who do not know sign language. Other signs, such as those at the bottom of Figure 8.7, are not as obvious in their meaning. Meaning is conveyed not only by the sign itself, but also by the manner of its delivery (speed, size, direction, place in relation to body, facial and body expressions). Words that do not have a sign, such as proper names, are finger-spelled using the *American Manual Alphabet* (see Figure 8.8).

One disadvantage of ASL is that many of the signs require the use of both hands, which may prohibit its use by individuals who do not have good motor control of both hands or a good range of motion in both arms. Also, if the person is to receive signs using ASL, he must have good visual acuity—although individuals who are deaf-blind can receive signs by placing their hands on the sender's hands.

It must be pointed out that ASL is not a word-for-word representation of spoken English. Research that was begun in the 1950s has demonstrated that ASL is a legitimate language with its own grammar and syntax. For example, to sign "circus," the shape of a circus ring is traced on the back of the hand. To sign "I am going to the circus," one forms the signs "me go circus." If one signs "eat finish," it means the person already ate. ASL also has its own humor and idiomatic expressions, as illustrated by the book title *Train Go Sorry*, which is the ASL equivalent of "you missed the boat" (Cohen, 1994).

Total Communication

The **Total Communication (TC)** philosophy represents a move away from the either/or stance of the manual versus oral controversy. It incorporates a variety of methods for receiving and sending messages: speech, speechreading, writing, gesturing, American Sign Language, and finger spelling. A person who uses Total Communication chooses the appropriate communication modes to fit the situation. For example, a child may choose to use simultaneous voice and manual communication in the classroom but may choose to use only signs when "talking" to a classmate on the playground.

The success and practical utility of Total Communication was realized within a decade of its introduction in this country when, by 1978, approximately 62% of all educational programs for children who were deaf reportedly were using this approach (Schwartz, 1987). The initial optimistic outlook for TC has, however, waned somewhat. Critics claim that TC is not only cumbersome but unworkable. How, they ask, can someone simultaneously speak English and sign in American

rabbit
H shape, both hands palms in, right tips left, left tips right. Cross wrists and flick H's toward body.

lipstick
Mime applying lipstick to lips.

Iconoclastic Signs

The signs for "rabbit" and "lipstick" are easy to interpret because the signs present a visual image of the objects.

mail
Place thumb of right A on mouth. Change to M shape and place tips in upturned left palm.

pretty
Five shaped RH palm in, tips up. Circle face from right to left ending in flat O.

Noniconoclastic Signs

The signs for "pretty" and "mail" are not obvious to a person who does not know manual sign language.

Figure 8.7 Sample ASL Signs (Iconoclastic and Noniconoclastic)

Source: Adapted from *The Comprehensive Signed English Dictionary* (pp. 169, 220, 298–299), by H. Bornstein, K. Saulnier, & L. Hamilton (Eds.), 1983, Washington, DC: Gallaudet University Press. Copyright © 1983 by Gallaudet University. Used with permission of the publisher.

Sign Language when the grammar and word order differ? What often happens is that a teacher speaks English while signing a few key words. Thus, the student must rely more on speechreading than on manual signs to decode the teacher's message. Many students who are trained in Total Communication do not develop

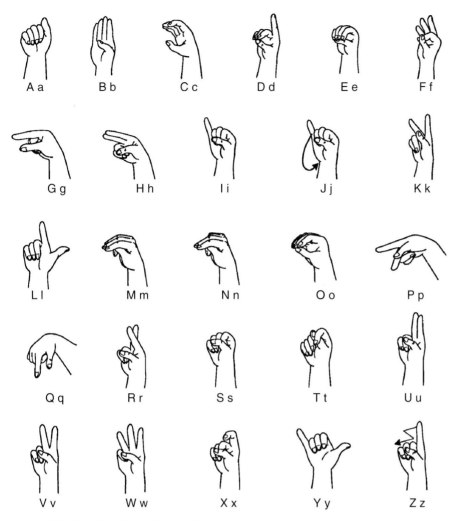

Figure 8.8   **The American Manual Alphabet**

sufficient skill in sign language to use it as a primary mode of communication (Dolnick, 1993).

Bilingual/Bicultural Considerations

Since the 1960s, there has been a growing trend toward **bilingual/bicultural deaf education** (known as DBiBi education). It is a move away from monolingual/monocultural approaches, in which students who were deaf were expected to communicate orally in the classroom and were often instructed by hearing teachers who were not fluent in American Sign Language. DBiBi recognizes that many students who are deaf communicate in both ASL and printed English, making them bilingual. And, because they must adapt to both hearing and deaf cultures, they are bicultural as well. DBiBi upholds ASL as a legitimate language that is a viable means of communication and classroom instruction, rather than a "second language" for students who are deaf. It also recognizes and incorporates the values of both the hearing and deaf cultures (Grossjean, 1992; Mason, 1994).

American Sign Language has its own grammar and syntax.

Students in DBiBi classrooms are free to communicate in ASL or use oral or written English. Spoken and written English is viewed as a second language that students need to acquire, rather than the primary language of instruction. In some DBiBi schools, teachers who are deaf team-teach with hearing teachers (Mason, 1994). Critics of DBiBi are concerned that it discourages the use of voice and spoken language by children who are deaf, thereby delaying the child's introduction to English (Stuckless, 1991).

ACCOMMODATING STUDENTS WITH HEARING LOSS IN INCLUSIVE ENVIRONMENTS

One of the provisions of Public Law 94-142 is that all children with disabilities are educated in the least restrictive environment (LRE) (see Chapter 1). Currently, students with hearing loss are served in a variety of educational placements. During the 1992–93 school year, 29.5% of students with hearing loss were served in regular classes, 19.7% were served in resource rooms, and 28.1% were served in separate classes. The remaining students (22.7%) were served in separate schools, residential facilities, or homebound/hospital settings—as compared to an overall rate of only 5.3% of all students in special education served in these settings (U.S. Department of Education, 1995).

Why aren't a higher percentage of students with hearing loss served in regular classes or schools? One explanation is the wide range in the severity of hearing loss and the students' resulting needs. Another factor may be the past reliance on separate settings to serve this group (U.S. Department of Education, 1994). Historically, the LRE for many children with severe hearing impairments or deafness had been a public or private residential institution. Then, along with the movement to mainstream or integrate students with disabilities into general education settings came the call to move children out of institutions and into their local communities.

Table 8.6   Establishing a Favorable Listening Environment

Keep Out Unwanted Sound	• Locate classroom away from heavy road traffic, the gym, cafeteria, playground, or a busy hallway. • Provide soundproof doors and windows.
Reduce Noise Within the Classroom	• Use sound-absorbent materials such as padded carpets, draperies, acoustic or cork tiles on ceiling and walls, padded seats, rubber-tipped chair and desk legs, felt strips on door closures. • Encourage other students to speak one at a time, to make it easier for students with hearing loss to follow the discussion. Remind others to stay within the student's field of vision.
Select Seating Position Carefully	• Position students who have hearing loss away from busy areas such as bathrooms, storage areas, or pathways through the class. • Position these students in close proximity to the speaker (usually the teacher). • Enable students with hearing loss to see the speaker's face as often as possible. Front and center may not always allow this; better a few rows back and to the side. • Provide adequate illumination to enable students with hearing loss to see the speaker's face for speechreading.

In large school districts, children with severe hearing loss or deafness were placed into special education classes or in general education classes with an interpreter. In small school districts, this was not always possible. The small number of students who needed self-contained placements precluded grouping students with same-age peers. For this reason, many classes for students with hearing loss were composed of students of varying ages, needs, and preferred methods of communication. Often, students had to travel long distances to be taught by a qualified teacher. The scarcity of qualified interpreters in small communities prevented some children from participating in general education classes.

The movement toward total inclusion has major implications for children with hearing loss. As Moores (1993) points out, placing a student who is deaf in a classroom in physical proximity to hearing children does not automatically provide equal access to information. This is especially true as the student moves to higher grades, where the methods of instruction and curriculum content require good skills in listening or responding orally. As noted by Stinson and Lang (1994), full-time placement in general education classes of students with hearing loss or deafness may result in social isolation for some of these students. Several recent court decisions have upheld segregated placement of children with hearing loss because of their need to be taught with other students with hearing loss (McCarthy, 1994). Clearly, the total realm of a student's needs, both academic and social, should be considered when determining the most appropriate placement.

A basic but very important step in accommodating students with hearing loss in inclusive settings is to ensure that there is a minimum of extraneous noise in the classroom. As shown in Table 8.6, a listening environment that reduces or blocks out as much unwanted noise as possible will enable the students to attend to the more important auditory signals in the classroom—namely, teacher's and classmates' voices. Table 8.7 provides some helpful tips that both students and teachers can use when communicating with their classmates who have hearing impairments. Table 8.8 provides some practical tips for teachers of students with hearing loss in integrated settings.

Table 8.7   Tips for Communicating With Persons Who Have Hearing Loss

- Look at and speak directly to the person rather than to an interpreter who may be present.
- Do not exaggerate mouth movements to a person who is speechreading. Look directly at the person. Keep your hands away from your mouth and avoid smoking, eating, or chewing gum while speaking. Make sure a light source shines on your face.
- Speak clearly and slowly in a normal tone of voice. Do not yell. This distorts your speech and draws others' attention to your conversation.
- Substitute a different word or phrase if the person with a hearing loss is having trouble understanding you. This may be more helpful than repeating the same word.
- Never pretend to understand the speaker if you do not. Repeat what you have understood and allow the person to respond.
- To get the attention of a person with a hearing loss, tap the person on the shoulder or wave your hand.
- Don't be embarrassed if you use an expression such as "Wait until you hear this!" when talking to a person with a hearing loss.
- Use natural gestures and facial expressions to support your speech. Don't use exaggerated pantomimes.
- Do not attempt to communicate for the person with a hearing loss. Give the person an opportunity to take part. It may be helpful to cue the person with the topic of conversation (e.g., "We're talking about the exam.").
- Try to answer questions with more than a one-word response. This provides additional context cues to the person with a hearing loss.
- When talking to an adult with a hearing loss, use adult language.
- Write any important parts of your message that are missed, using simple, direct language.

Table 8.8   Strategies for Teaching Students Who Have Hearing Loss

- Use written directions, outlines, and summaries to provide visual structure for assignments.
- Provide students with key vocabulary words and definitions prior to new assignments so that they can learn the new words before class.
- Use visual aids such as overhead transparencies, chalkboard, flip charts, photographs, diagrams, three-dimensional models, and maps as visual supplements to discussions.
- Stay within the range of the student's hearing aid (10 feet or less) when presenting information orally.
- When another student in the class is speaking, indicate who is speaking by pointing to the student or saying the student's name.
- Arrange for a classmate to share notes with the student who has a hearing loss. It is very difficult to lip-read and take notes simultaneously.
- Communicate regularly with specialists (e.g., speech–language pathologists, itinerant teacher, audiologist) about special needs and accommodations for students with hearing impairments.
- If you are wearing an FM transmitter, be sure that the receiver's opening faces outward and is not covered with clothing. Try not to drop it or put it in a hot place.

In spite of these accommodations, the classroom environment may still prove too noisy for a student who wears hearing aids. Extraneous noise in the environment (e.g., scraping of chairs on the floor, hum of an air conditioner) can interfere with the student's reception of the teacher's voice. One solution to this problem is the use of a closed-loop transmitting system whereby the teacher's voice is picked up by a wireless microphone worn around the neck and transmitted via an FM radio signal directly to earphones worn by the student.

Students with hearing losses in the severe to profound range who are not able to benefit from a hearing aid may need an interpreter to function successfully in an integrated setting. If such an accommodation is needed, it should be specified on the student's IEP. The interpreter should be fluent in the child's chosen communication method (American Sign Language, cued speech, etc.).

EASY IDEAS FOR PRACTITIONERS

For the Teacher:

1. Encourage the student to keep the hearing aid on and help or remind the student to check each day to make sure it is working.
2. Realize that students with hearing loss may have language deficits, including limited vocabulary and syntax. You may need to rephrase statements to help the student understand.
3. Remember that listening is a tiring activity for students with hearing loss. Provide frequent breaks and alternate listening activities with "thinking and doing" activities.
4. Use captioned films whenever possible.
5. Send home advance notice of material you will cover in class so that parents can assist the student with preview work.

For Parents:

1. Observe your children in response to different noises and seek immediate medical attention if you suspect your child is having difficulty hearing.
2. Remember that your child is a child first and a child with a hearing loss second.
3. Encourage your child to wear his or her hearing aid during all waking hours to receive optimum benefit from it.
4. Create a hearing environment in which your child can develop his or her listening skills, beginning with an awareness of and attention to sound.
5. Have your child's vision checked periodically, because children with hearing loss rely on their vision for communication cues.

Source: Adapted from *Listen! Hear! For Parents of Hearing-Impaired Children,* available from the Alexander Graham Bell Association for the Deaf, Washington, DC.

Some relatively simple modifications in teaching style can also promote the successful integration of students with hearing loss. The pacing and style of the teacher's delivery of the content material can have a significant effect on the student's ability to comprehend. If material is presented primarily in a lecture type of format, the students will have difficulty listening for long periods of time as well as grasping the key points. Multimedia presentations that include many visual cues (e.g., pictures, models, diagrams, flip charts, key word lists) will help *all* students in the classroom improve their comprehension skills (Webster & Wood, 1989).

Students who are deaf may present special challenges to teachers in integrated settings. A primary reason is the vast differences in their development of reading and writing skills. Even those who have well developed oral language skills continue to have difficulty with reading and writing. The Commission on Education of the Deaf (1988) has targeted reading achievement of students who are deaf as a major problem in their education. Whereas children with normal hearing internalize the rules of English by the time they are 6 years old, children who are deaf—due to vast experiential differences in hearing and speaking English—do not have a solid base on which to build their reading and writing skills. If they use manual communication, the differences in syntax and grammar between English and manual sign language can pose additional problems. As a result, they experience difficulties with these skills, which persist into adulthood.

A closed-loop transmitting system can eliminate extraneous environmental noise and allow this student to focus on the lesson.

Most students who are deaf apply a left-to-right rule when processing written language (subject-verb-object). As a result, particular sentence structures can be difficult for them to process when reading. Consider the sentence "The baby was pushed by its mother." If the subject-verb-object rule is used, this sentence will be interpreted to mean the baby pushed its mother. Embedded clauses are also difficult. The student may understand "The girls left with their teacher" and "The girls were late" but may not understand "The girls who left with their teacher were late" (Webster & Wood, 1989).

The written language of students who are deaf lacks the complexity of that of their same-age peers. They will use shorter sentences, more content words (nouns, verbs, objects), and fewer articles, prepositions, and conjunctions. Figure 8.9, a writing sample by a 9-year-old girl with profound hearing loss, illustrates this difference in written language development (Webster & Wood, 1989).

Computer-assisted learning has shown promise in helping students who are deaf improve their reading and writing skills. Individualized instruction, opportunity for repetition, and the provision of immediate feedback are features that are aptly suited to the learning needs of many students who are deaf. Software programs for checking grammar and spelling are particularly useful for older students.

Postsecondary Education

The unique educational needs of students with hearing loss or deafness do not end with graduation from high school. In the past, options for postsecondary education for students who are deaf were very limited. The student could apply to Gallaudet

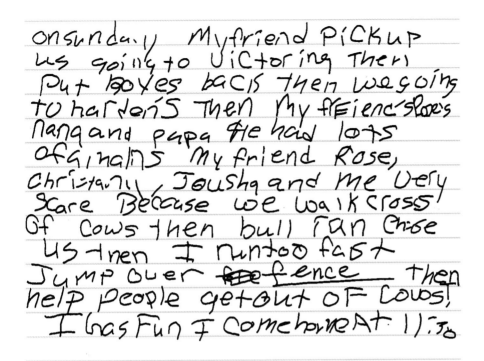

Figure 8.9 Writing Sample of 9-Year-Old Female With Profound Hearing Loss

In this writing sample, a girl tells about the fun she had on Sunday. First, she helped pack boxes for a friend. Then she went to a farm. As she and her friends walked across a field where there were cows, a bull chased them. She jumped over a fence and helped her friends get away too. She came home at 11:30.

University or could try to enter a program at other colleges and universities without special support services.

As a result of legislative efforts and federal financial support, things began to change in the 1960s. The National Technical Institute for the Deaf (NTID) in Rochester, New York, was established in 1968 by public law as a technical college to promote postsecondary technical training and education for persons who are deaf. Today, students who are deaf have access to a variety of postsecondary education programs with a range of options for support services. Results of a study of 4,000 graduates of educational programs for students who are deaf revealed that approximately 50% of these graduates participated in some type of postsecondary education program within 10 years of graduating from high school (Walter & MacLeod-Gallinger, 1989). Prior experience in a mainstream educational environment appears to be a determining factor in participation in postsecondary education for students who are deaf (Kasen, Ouellette, & Cohen, 1990).

Success in postsecondary education often depends on how the student's unique characteristics and needs match those of the institution. Cornett and Daisey (1992) have identified characteristics of postsecondary institutions that are critical to a student's success, as follows:

1. Availability of an institutional text telephone (TT) and a telephone with an amplifier in an easily accessible location

2. Policies and traditions conducive to adapting to the individual needs of the student

Although more students with hearing loss attend college today, they will not benefit from higher education if their school experiences don't give them the academic preparation they need.

3. Prior experience with students who have deafness or hearing loss and a record of sensitivity to their needs and interests

4. Presence of a sizable group of students on campus with deafness or hearing loss

5. Evidence that the other students are interested in learning to communicate with the students who have deafness or hearing loss

Institutions with even the most ideal characteristics cannot compensate for some students' inadequate academic preparation and their deficient English reading and writing skills. These deficits may prevent them from benefiting from higher education. As Moores (1994) observes, access to higher education does not guarantee a successful outcome for all students with deafness or hearing loss.

FAMILY PERSPECTIVES

From the moment parents suspect that their child has a hearing loss, they are faced with a multitude of questions and decisions. Can the hearing loss be treated? Is it permanent, or reversible? Is our child a candidate for amplification? What type of communication system can best meet our needs and those of our child? How will we communicate? What is the best school and classroom placement? How will our child learn if our child cannot hear? Can our child grow up to be independent?

Clear-cut answers to these questions are not always available. Parents of children with hearing loss come into contact with a wide range of professionals—pediatricians, audiologists, ear-nose-throat specialists, speech–language pathologists, teachers of students with hearing loss, and educational psychologists, among others. The recommendations received from these varied individuals may not always be compatible (Webster & Wood, 1989). Edward C. Merrill, the fourth president of Gallaudet College, observed that parents "experience the double trauma of having a child with a severe disability and being confused about how to meet the child's need to learn and to relate to the family and society at large" (1992, p. viii).

Choosing a Communication System

One of the most difficult decisions facing parents of children who are deaf is the choice of a communication system: oral, manual, or a combination. For deaf parents of children who are deaf, this decision is not as difficult. They usually choose the same communication system they use, typically American Sign Language.

However, the oral-versus-manual controversy goes beyond the selection of a method of education and communication. In recent years, the deaf community has emerged as a culture. Many deaf people now claim they form a subculture whose members, like those in other subcultures, speak their own language—namely, American Sign Language. They oppose the view that deafness is a disability, instead viewing it as a culture worth upholding and preserving. Advocates from the deaf culture shun not only spoken language and Total Communication but also sign systems that mimic the grammar and word order of English. They view the exclusive use of manual communication, specifically American Sign Language, as a means of upholding their cultural history and traditions and passing them on to future generations. Some people in the deaf culture criticize the view that medical treatment and technological developments are welcome, viewing them as unnecessary "cures" for a condition that they do not perceive as a handicap, but rather an essential part of their being (Dolnick, 1993).

Consider, however, that the majority of the 2 million Americans with hearing loss are not culturally deaf (Cohen, 1994). Furthermore, 90% of all children who are deaf are born to parents with hearing. Understandably, these parents want to be able to communicate with their children using their own mode of communication (oral speech). Logically, their preferred mode of communication for their children is often oral speech or Total Communication.

Another factor that undermines the perpetuation of the deaf culture and, as a result, limits the selection of manual communication as the method of choice for all children who are deaf, is the deinstitutionalization movement that began in the 1960s. The call to educate all students with disabilities in their home communities whenever possible has significantly decreased the enrollment in residential institutions.

In his autobiographical account, *A Child Sacrificed to the Deaf Culture* (1994), Tom Bertling discusses the drawbacks of the segregated environment of residential schools, citing broken bonds with the child's family and lack of preparation for the students to live as adults in the mainstream of the hearing world. Bertling stresses that parents of children who are deaf "must explore all possibilities, then weigh all the advantages against the disadvantages to make the best decision for *their* child" when deciding where and how their child will be educated.

Parents' critical role in the education and development of their children with hearing loss is underscored by Schwartz (1987), who attributes many of the significant advancements in the field of hearing loss to movements that were spearheaded by parents. As Schwartz points out:

> It was the mother of Luis de Cordoba who first implored Juan Pablo Bonet to find a tutor for her deaf son . . . the father of Alice Cogswell who sent Thomas Hopkins Gallaudet to England to learn how to teach his deaf daughter . . . and Louise Tracy who was the first parent to speak before the Convention of American Instructors of the Deaf in 1947 to tell of her work with her deaf son, John. (p. 123)

Adult-Onset Hearing Loss

When considering the effects of a family member who is deaf on other family members and the family unit as a whole, it is important to consider the unique needs of adults who become deaf or acquire significant hearing losses after many years of normal hearing. These individuals may gradually or suddenly become unable to carry out many activities of daily living that they always took for granted—such as conducting business on the telephone, enjoying musical and dramatic performances, relaying information to other family members, or doing errands in the community. In some cases, the hearing loss may be a threat to the family member's personal safety, because she is unable to hear warning signals such as sirens, car horns, smoke alarms, doorbells, and telephones. These new limitations may prove frustrating to the person with the hearing loss as well as other family members, who see the need to provide assistance with these tasks, yet are apprehensive about compromising the individual's independence.

As the nation's aged population continues to grow, an increasing number of individuals and families will be faced with the challenges of a family member with adult-onset hearing loss. One of the biggest obstacles for family members and professionals alike is convincing the person that his hearing is diminishing and that he is in need of a hearing evaluation. Although a number of screening tools are available to reliably detect hearing loss in aged persons, the rate of follow-up for further audiometric evaluation among this group can be as low as 50%. And, due in part to misconceptions about hearing loss and hearing aids and the fact that hearing aids aren't covered by Medicare, only 10% to 20% of aged persons obtain hearing aids after their impairment has been identified. As a result, many aged persons suffer negative social, emotional, and functional consequences of their hearing losses (American Academy of Audiology, 1991).

CURRENT ISSUES AND FUTURE TRENDS

Underemployment of Adults With Severe Hearing Loss

Adults with severe hearing loss or deafness are more likely than their peers with normal hearing to be unemployed or underemployed (Phillippe & Auvenshine, 1985; Walter & MacLeod-Gallinger, 1989). Those who are employed typically earn less than their hearing counterparts. One reason may be that their limited language and reading abilities causes a high percentage of adults who are deaf to enter manual occupations rather than professional occupations (Cornett & Daisey, 1992). Other contributing factors are the differences in educational outcomes, the attitudes of employers toward hiring persons with disabilities, and the lack of appropriate vocational/career preparation and counseling for students with deafness or hearing loss. Postsecondary technical training has been found to have a positive effect on the socioeconomic status, lifetime wages, and work lives of persons who are deaf (Welsh & Walter, 1988).

Recent legislative mandates have improved the outlook for successful long-term employment of adults with hearing loss or deafness. For example, the Individuals With Disabilities Education Act of 1990 (P.L. 101-476) requires transition planning from school to the workplace for all students with disabilities. And the Americans With Disabilities Act of 1990 (P.L. 101-336) prohibits employers from discriminating against "a qualified person with a disability" and further requires them to provide "reasonable accommodations" for employees with disabilities.

This adult's employer provided the accommodations he needs to be successful at his job.

Mass Screening and Education

Most public schools conduct hearing screenings of all children entering school for the first time and at least one additional time during the child's elementary school years. This practice helps identify children who need further audiological testing and detects some with hearing losses. The gap of several years between routine screenings can, however, result in missing those children who have fluctuating hearing losses.

Industries are another prime location for conducting hearing screening and education for the prevention of hearing loss. In many large factories where there is potential damage to workers' hearing from exposure to noise, periodic screenings are conducted at no cost to workers. Prevention efforts also include the provision of ear protectors to workers and the enforcement of requirements for their use.

Various public agencies, industries, and private foundations attempt to disseminate information to the general public about the potential for hearing loss resulting from noise exposure, inadequate prenatal care, and medical conditions. Through public service announcements, public awareness campaigns, and distribution of information through the mass media, warning signs of hearing loss and means of prevention are publicized. Regardless of the quality of the information or the breadth of its distribution, however, the effectiveness of any such campaign is limited to the willingness of individuals to heed the warnings.

Technological Advances

The influence of technology on the field of hearing loss has been greater than on most other disabilities. Some of the most useful technology has been available for some time. Other technologies are newer. Not surprisingly, many technological devices are related to two of our most prevalent communication modes, the telephone and television (Boothroyd, 1990; Lynch, 1990; "Now the Deaf Can Listen," 1991; Suss, 1993), including the following:

This text telephone enables communication without oral conversation.

Telephone Assistive Devices

- Amplification wheels contained in a special telephone handle, capable of increasing volume by 80%
- Portable telephone amplifiers capable of increasing volume by 30%
- Telephone adapters that channel the incoming message through the person's hearing aids, enabling binaural hearing of telephone conversations and increasing understanding
- Telephones that allow the user to select the best volumes for different frequencies, tailoring the input to the individual's unique hearing pattern
- Telephone ringers that can amplify the ring up to 90 dB
- A tactile speech indicator that enables a person who is deaf and blind to obtain information by telephone
- **Teletypewriters (TTY),** also called **text telephones (TT),** consisting of a keyboard with a display screen that shows the message being sent and the message being received, which enable communication via the telephone without oral conversation (Relay centers enable communication with hearing persons who do not own TTs.)

Other Assistive Listening Devices

- FM systems that transmit sound directly from the speaker to the listener, thereby reducing interference from extraneous noise in the room
- Infrared systems that use a light beam to transmit sound, useful in multiple theaters or courtrooms where it is not desirable for the message to travel beyond the room
- LOOP systems that use electromagnetic transmission to transmit a message to an individual's hearing aid, useful in a contained listening area such as a small conference room or car

- The Tickle Talker, a small device that sends electronic vibrations to a person's hand to supplement lipreading (Sounds picked up by a microphone are sorted by the Tickle Talker's processing chip and sent to ringlike bands worn on one hand. Specific spots on each band correspond to certain sounds, providing additional cues to the listener.)

Television Decoders

- Devices connected to television sets, which display on-screen subtitles for closed-caption television programs (As of 1993, all new television sets with 13-inch screens or larger must, by federal law, have built-in decoders.)

Other recent technological advances have resulted in significant improvement in the quality of life and greater ease in performing daily activities for many individuals with hearing loss or deafness. For instance, electronic mail (E-mail) and

INNOVATIVE IDEAS   TRAINED HEARING DOGS SERVE AS "EARS"

Seeing Eye dogs have been available to assist people who are blind since 1929. Now, many agencies train hearing ear dogs to alert people with severe hearing loss or deafness to sounds in their environment. One such agency is Dogs for the Deaf. Located in Oregon, this nonprofit agency chooses dogs from Humane Society adoption shelters. Certified Hearing Dogs are trained to alert owners to doorbells, alarm clocks, smoke alarms, telephones, crying babies, oven buzzers, and other important daily life signals. Like guide dogs for people who are blind, these dogs have total public access rights. Paul Henkel (1994), a recipient of a hearing dog, expresses how the dogs enrich their owners' lives:

> Micah has changed my life by returning my independence. I am free to be alone without worry that I will not hear a smoke or fire alarm, or miss an important telephone call, but Micah has changed many lives. Many of the students I work with have difficult lives, some are recovering from substance abuse, some do not fit the traditional mold of a conventional school, some have social or legal problems, and some are simply not accepted anywhere but here.
>
> Micah, as a Certified Hearing Dog, accompanies me to work each day, and each day, without regard to race, socioeconomic status, appearance, or past history, gives my students love, acceptance, and something to care about. His boundless enthusiasm is infectious, and while my life has been enriched by his help, my students have gained as much, if not more, by his presence. He may be my "ears," but he is the "heart" for many others.

Even though many resources for assisting persons who have hearing loss can be classified as high-tech, sometimes the most useful assistance comes in the form of "low-tech, high-enthusiasm."

facsimile (FAX) machines have expanded the opportunities for quick interpersonal communication. An advantage of using FAX machines is that input is not limited to a keyboard. They also enable communication with individuals and businesses that would not typically have a TTY (Jensema, 1994).

There are also various alerting systems that assist persons with hearing loss. For example, some smoke detectors have built-in strobe lights powerful enough to wake someone who cannot hear an alarm horn. There are doorbell and telephone systems that flash a lamp or strobe light when the doorbell or telephone rings or when someone knocks on the door. Also available are clocks and other wake-up devices that flash a light or vibrate the bed or pillow at the set time.

Five-Minute Summary

The field of hearing loss has a rich history that is not without conflict and controversy. The debate over which method of communication—oral or manual—is preferable has been going on for decades and no doubt will continue.

Hearing loss is not a homogeneous disorder. Differences exist not only in the type of hearing loss (conductive, sensorineural, central auditory, mixed) but also in the extent of loss (mild to profound). There are also a variety of causes of hearing loss, only some of which are amenable to medical treatment (e.g., middle ear infection).

Causes of hearing loss are varied. Maternal illness during pregnancy (e.g., exposure to certain viruses) can result in significant hearing loss in newborns. Genetic factors are probable causes in about half of all cases of deafness. Noise exposure, injuries, and exposure to ototoxic medication can also result in hearing loss.

Individuals with hearing losses that are not amenable to medical intervention may be helped by amplification (hearing aids) and auditory training to enable them to make the most of their available hearing. For some individuals, hearing aids can provide sufficient sound amplification to enable them to communicate well. Individuals with more significant losses (including deafness), will need intensive training to learn to communicate by either oral or manual communication methods or a combination of both. New technologies such as cochlear implants and auditory brainstem implants can provide some degree of hearing to individuals who are profoundly deaf. Some members of the deaf community, however, reject these new devices, feeling that they undermine their identities as deaf persons.

The movement to include students with hearing losses in mainstream educational environments has been growing in recent years. Since there is so much variability within the population of students with hearing loss or deafness, the unique needs of each child must be carefully considered before the child is integrated into a classroom with hearing peers.

As with other disabilities, prevention is the key to reducing the number of persons with hearing loss. Parents are invaluable resources in the identification of early signs of hearing loss among their children. Public education and awareness are critical in prevention efforts. Although some loss of hearing inevitably occurs as we age, reducing exposure to loud noises can help preserve our hearing.

Study Questions

1. Identify three key historical figures in the education of students with hearing loss. Identify the contributions of each to the field and their significance.

2. What are the two general types of hearing loss discussed in this chapter? Name at least two causes of each.

3. What are some behaviors or characteristics a child might display that would cause you to suspect a hearing loss?
4. Why is it difficult to report exact incidence and prevalence data for hearing loss and deafness?
5. Identify the major cause of hearing loss among young adults and discuss strategies for prevention.
6. Which pattern of hearing loss is most likely to have a detrimental effect on speech and language: a moderate loss in the high frequencies (8,000 to 10,000 Hz) or a moderate loss in the middle frequencies (500 to 2,000 Hz)? Why?
7. List two advantages and two disadvantages of American Sign Language as the primary language for a school-age student who is deaf.
8. Why is a typical classroom environment not an ideal setting for a student who wears a hearing aid? What can be done to make this environment more favorable for listening with an aid?
9. How might members of the deaf culture react to the following statement: Medical science is on the verge of developing a "cure" for many cases of deafness?
10. What is meant by the term *dual sensory impairment?*

For More Information

ORGANIZATIONS

Alexander Graham Bell Association for the Deaf
3417 Volta Place, N.W.
Washington, DC 20007
202-337-5520 (voice/TTY)

American Academy of Audiology
1735 North Lynn Street, Suite 950
Arlington, VA 22209-2022
800-222-2336 (voice only)

American Society for Deaf Children (ASDC)
814 Thayer Avenue
Silver Spring, MD 20910
800-942-2732 (V/TT)   301-585-5400
301-585-5401 (TT)

Association of Late-Deafened Adults (ALDA)
P.O. Box 641763
Chicago, IL 60664-1763
708-445-0860 (TT/FAX)

Better Hearing Institute
Box 1840
Washington, DC 20013
800-327-9355   703-642-0580

Dogs for the Deaf
10175 Wheeler Road
Central Point, OR 97502
503-826-9220 (V/TT)

Gallaudet Research Institute (GRI)
Gallaudet University

800 Florida Avenue, N.E.
Washington, DC 20002
202-651-5400 (V/TT)

Helen Keller National Center for Deaf-Blind Youths and Adults (HKNC)
111 Middle Neck Road
Sands Point, NY 11050
516-944-8900 (V/TT)   FAX 516-944-8751

John Tracy Clinic
806 West Adams Boulevard
Los Angeles, CA 90007
213-748-5481 (voice only)
800-522-4582 (voice/TTY)

Lexington Rehabilitation Engineering Center on Technological Aids for Deaf and Hearing-Impaired Individuals
30th Avenue and 75th Street
Jackson Heights, NY 11370
718-899-8800 (V/TT)   718-899-3030 (TT)
FAX 718-899-9846

National Association of the Deaf (NAD)
814 Thayer Avenue
Silver Spring, MD 20910-4500
301-587-1788 (voice)   301-587-1789 (TTY)

National Cued Speech Association
P.O. Box 31345
Raleigh, NC 27622-1345
919-828-1218 (voice/TTY)

National Information Center on Deafness (NICD)
Gallaudet University
NICD, Dept. P-94
800 Florida Avenue, N.E.
Washington, DC 20002
202-651-5051 (voice)   651-5052 (TTY)

National Institute on Deafness and Other
   Communication Disorders
National Institutes of Health
Building 31, Room 1B-62
9000 Rockville Pike
Bethesda, MD 20892
301-496-7243   301-492-0252 (TT)

National Technical Institute for the Deaf
   (NTID)
Rochester Institute of Technology
Lyndon Baines Johnson Building
P.O. Box 9887
Rochester, NY 14623
716-475-6400   716-475-2181 (TT)
FAX 716-475-6500

Telecommunications for the Deaf
8719 Colesville Road
Silver Spring, MD 20910
301-589-3786   301-589-3006 (TT)
FAX 301-589-3792

Tripod Grapevine
955 North Alfred Street
Los Angeles, CA 90069
800-352-8888 (voice/TTY)

Self Help for Hard of Hearing People, Inc.
   (SHHH)
7800 Wisconsin Avenue
Bethesda, MD 20814
301-657-2248 (voice)   301-657-2249 (TTY)

BOOKS AND ARTICLES

Batson, T. (1976). *Angels and outcasts.* Silver Spring, MD: T-J Publishers.

Christensen K., & Delgado, D. (1993). *Multicultural issues in deafness.* White Plains, NY: Longman.

Fletcher, L. (1987). *Ben's story: A deaf child's right to sign.* Silver Spring, MD: T-J Publishers.

Flexer, C., Wray, D., & Leavitt, R. (1990). *How the student with hearing loss can succeed in college.* Washington, DC: Alexander Graham Bell Association for the Deaf.

Gannon, J. R. (1989). *The week the world heard Gallaudet.* Silver Spring, MD: T-J Publishers.

Long, G., & Harvey, M. *Facilitating the transition of deaf adolescents to adulthood: Focus on Families.* Little Rock, AR: RRTC.

Luterman, D. (1987). *Deafness in the family.* Austin, TX: PRO-ED.

National Center for Law and Deafness. *Legal rights: The guide for deaf and hard of hearing people.* Washington, DC: Gallaudet University Press.

Owens, E. (1989). *Cochlear implants in young deaf children.* Austin, TX: PRO-ED.

Schein, J. D. (1989). *At home among strangers.* Silver Spring, MD: T-J Publishers.

Schwartz, S. (Ed.). (1987). *Choices in deafness: A parents' guide.* Rockville, MD: Woodbine House.

JOURNALS, NEWSLETTERS, AND OTHER PUBLICATIONS

Alerting and Communication Devices for Hearing Impaired People
National Information Center on Deafness
Gallaudet University
800 Florida Avenue, N.E.
Washington, DC 20002
202-651-5051   202-651-5052 (TT)
FAX 202-651-5054

Specialized Audio, Visual, and Tactile Alerting Devices for Deaf and Hard of Hearing People
by Carl J. Jensema
Gallaudet Research Institute
Publication Series—Fay House
Gallaudet University
800 Florida Avenue, N.E.
Washington, DC 20002
202-651-5400 (V/TT)

*Visual Devices for Deaf and Hard of Hearing People:
    State-of-the-Art*
by Judith E. Harkins
Gallaudet Research Institute
Gallaudet University
800 Florida Avenue, N.E.
Washington, DC 20002
202-651-5400 (V/TT)

VIDEO AND ELECTRONIC MEDIA

Captioned Films/Videos for the Deaf
Modern Talking Picture Service
5000 Park Street North
St. Petersburg, FL 33709
800-237-6213 (V/TT)

Children of a Lesser God [Film]
Paramount Pictures, 1986.

Lipreading Made Easy [Video]
Alexander Graham Bell Association for the Deaf
3417 Volta Place, N.W.
Washington, DC 20007-2778
202-337-5220 (V/TT)

On the Other Hand [Video]
South Carolina ETV Marketing
Box 11000
Columbia, SC 29211
800-553-7752   803-737-3441
FAX 803-737-3503

See What I'm Saying [Video]
Fanlight Productions
47 Halifax Street
Boston, MA 02130
800-937-4113   617-542-0980

References

Allen, T. E., Rawlings, B. W., & Remington, E. (1993). Demographic and audiological profiles of deaf children in Texas with cochlear implants. *American Annals of the Deaf, 138,* 260–266.

American Academy of Audiology. (1988). *Position statement: Early identification of hearing loss in infants and children.* Arlington, VA: Author.

American Academy of Audiology. (1991). *Position statement: Task force on hearing impairment in aged people.* Arlington, VA: Author.

Bertling, T. (1994). *A child sacrificed to the deaf culture.* Wilsonville, OR: Kodiak Media Group.

Bond, D. E. (1984). Aspects of additional impairment and multiple handicaps. *Journal of the Association of Educational Psychologists, 6*(5), 50–61.

Boothroyd, A. (1990). Impact of technology on the management of deafness. *Volta Review, 92*(4), 73–82.

Cochlear Corporation. (1994). *Issues and answers.* Englewood, CO: Author.

Cohen, L. H. (1994). *Train go sorry.* New York: Houghton Mifflin.

Commission on Education of the Deaf. (1988). *Toward equality: A report to the President and Congress of the United States.* Washington DC: U.S. Government Printing Office.

Committee on Hearing, Bioacoustics, and Biomechanics (CHABA): Working Group on Speech Understanding. (1988). Speech understanding and aging. *Journal of the Acoustic Society of America, 83,* 859–895.

Cornett, R. O., & Daisey, M. E. (1992). *The cued speech resource book.* Raleigh, NC: National Cued Speech Association.

Dolnick, E. (1993). Deafness as culture. *The Atlantic Monthly, 272*(3), 37–53.

Fiellau-Nikolajsen, M. (1983). Tympanometric prediction of the magnitude of hearing loss in pre-school children with early recurrent middle ear disease. *Annals of Otology, Rhinology and Laryngology, 92,* 249–253.

Freeland, A. (1989). *Deafness: the facts.* New York: Oxford University Press.

Gallaudet College. (1986). *The ear and hearing.* Washington DC: Author.

Grossjean, F. (1992). The bilingual and bicultural person in the hearing and in the deaf world. *Sign Language Studies, 77,* 307–320.

Henkel, P. (1994, Summer). Teacher's aid and hearing dog. *The Canine Listener, 49,* 8.

Jensema, C. (1994). Telecommunications for the deaf. *American Annals of the Deaf, 139,* 22–27.

Karp, A. (1988). Reduced vision and speechreading. *Volta Review, 90*(5), 61–74.

Kasen, S., Ouellette, R., & Cohen, P. (1990). Mainstreaming and postsecondary educational and employment status of a rubella cohort. *American Annals of the Deaf, 135*(1), 22–26.

Lynch, M. R. (1990). Tactile speech indicator: Adaptive telephone device for deaf-blind clients. *Journal of Visual Impairment & Blindness, 84*(1), 21–22.

Mason, D. G. (1994). Bilingual/bicultural deaf education is appropriate. *Occasional Monograph Series, Number 2.* Toronto: Association of Canadian Educators of the Hearing Impaired, York University. (Available from ERIC Document Reproduction Service ED 378 720)

McCarthy, M. M. (1994). Inclusion and the law: Recent judicial developments. *PDK Research Bulletin, 13,* 1–4.

Merrill, E. C. (1992). [Foreword]. In R. O. Cornett & M. E. Daisey, *The cued speech resource book* (pp. vii–viii). Raleigh, NC: National Cued Speech Association.

Moores, D. F. (1993). Total inclusion/zero reject models in general education. *American Annals of the Deaf, 138,* 251.

Moores, D. F. (1994). Postsecondary education: A success story. *American Annals of the Deaf, 139*(2), 75.

Murphy, E. (1989, July 13–July 27). Townshend, tinnitus and rock & roll. *The Rolling Stone,* p. 101.

Murphy, K. P. (1976). Communication for hearing-handicapped people in the United Kingdom and the Republic of Ireland. In H. H. Oyer (Ed.), *Communication for the hearing-handicapped: An international perspective.* Baltimore: University Park Press.

National Information Center on Deafness. (1986). *Educating deaf children: An introduction.* Washington, DC: Gallaudet College.

National Information Center on Deafness and the National Association of the Deaf. (1984). *Deafness: A fact sheet.* Washington, DC: Gallaudet College.

Northern, J. L., & Downs, M. P. (1978). *Hearing in childhood.* Baltimore: Williams & Wilkins.

Phillippe, T., & Auvenshine, D. (1985). Career development among deaf persons. *Journal of Rehabilitation of the Deaf, 19*(1–2), 9–15.

Schwartz, S. (Ed.). (1987). *Choices in deafness: A parents' guide.* Rockville, MD: Woodbine House.

Stinson, M. S., & Lang, H. G. (1994). Full inclusion: A path for integration or isolation? *American Annals of the Deaf, 139*(2), 156–159.

Stuckless, E. R. (1991). Reflections on bilingual, bicultural education for deaf children: Some concerns about current advocacy and trends. *American Annals of the Deaf, 186*(3), 270–272.

Suss, E. (1993). *When the hearing gets hard.* New York: Plenum.

Teele, D. W., Klein, J. O., & Rosner, B. A. (1984). Otitis media with effusion during the first three years of life and development of speech and language. *Pediatrics, 74*(2), 282–287.

Ubell, E. (1995, January 15). New devices can help you hear. *The Washington Post,* p. A14.

U.S. Department of Education. (1995). *To assure the free appropriate public education of all children with disabilities: Seventeenth annual report to Congress on the implementation of the Individuals With Disabilities Education Act.* Washington, DC: U.S. Government Printing Office.

Walter, G., & MacLeod-Gallinger, J. E. (1989). *Employment attainments of deaf adults one and ten years after graduation from high school.* Rochester, NY: Office of Postsecondary Career Studies and Institutional Research, National Technical Institute for the Deaf.

Webster, A., & Wood, D. (1989). *Special needs in ordinary schools—Children with hearing difficulties.* London: Cassell Educational Limited.

Welsh, W. A., & Walter, G. G. (1988). The effect of postsecondary education on the occupational attainments of deaf adults. *Journal of the American Deafness and Rehabilitation Association, 22*(1), 14–22.

Chapter 9

Harlem Hospital/Crisis Center, acrylic on canvas, 48″ × 48″ (1994)

VISUAL IMPAIRMENTS

DIANE FAZZI

After studying this chapter, the reader will:

Know the legal definition of blindness

Identify common causes of visual impairment in children

Differentiate between the terms *congenital* and *adventitious*
in regard to visual impairment

Know the following terms: *verbalism, echolalia,*
and *tactual defensiveness*

Be able to list three responsibilities of the teacher credentialed
in the area of visual impairment

Be able to list three responsibilities of the orientation
and mobility (O&M) specialist

Identify three components of the specialized curriculum
for students who are blind

Understand ways in which general educators can support visually
impaired students' access to the curriculum

Be able to name two critical events or transitions that may be
stressful for the family of a child with a visual impairment

Be aware of issues of current importance in the field of
visual impairment and blindness

Visual Impairments

1784   First school for students who were blind opened in Paris by Valentin Huay, with emphasis on reading embossed letters, vocational training, and music study.

1832   Perkins School for the Blind, the first U.S. school for students who are blind, opened in Boston; directed by Samuel Howe, it would eventually be the first school to successfully educate individuals who are deaf-blind.

1834   A system of embossed dots, known as the Braille Literary Code, was perfected by Louis Braille.

1900   Classes for blind children in the public schools were begun in Chicago.

1904   Helen Keller became the first individual who was deaf-blind to earn a college degree.

1904   The "Act to Promote the Education of the Blind," the first U.S. legislation to support educational efforts for persons with disabilities, established funds for the American Printing House for the Blind to distribute books and materials.

1913   The cities of Boston and Cleveland started classes for students who were partially sighted.

1929   Dorothy Eustis helped establish the first U.S. dog guide school—Seeing Eye, Inc.

1930   The Pratt-Smoot Act designated the Library of Congress as distributor of braille materials and phonograph recordings for readers who were blind.

1940s   Richard Hoover formalized the use of the long cane as a mobility device for veterans who were blind.

1964   Natalie Barraga researched the development of visual efficiency skills in children with low vision.

1970   The first National Conference on Low Vision was held.

1980   National Association of Parents of the Visually Impaired (NAPVI) was formed.

1984   AAWB and AEVH merge to form the Association for Education and Rehabilitation of Blind and Visually Impaired (AER).

1990s   Numerous states adopted laws to promote braille literacy in the schools.

HISTORICAL OVERVIEW

Long before the educational potential of blind persons was fully realized, individuals who were blind made meaningful contributions to society. As early as 700 B.C., Homer created the *Iliad* and the *Odyssey*. Nicholas Saunderson, who studied under Isaac Newton, served as a professor of mathematics at Cambridge University in the early 1700s (Roberts, 1986). Many individuals who are blind have made contributions in the field of music. For instance, in 1939 Joaquin Rodrigo, a prominent Spanish composer, wrote one of the most famous classical guitar concertos, *Concierto de Aranjuez*. In modern music, George Shearing became a legendary jazz pianist in the 1950s and still performs today. Ray Charles and Stevie Wonder are notable for their contributions, as singers and composers, to today's popular music.

The first formalized education for students who were blind occurred in Paris in 1784 when Valentin Huay established the *Institution des Jeunes Aveugles* (Institution for Blind Youth). Students at this first school were taught to read raised letters by touch. Valentin Huay also emphasized vocational training and music study with his students. Louis Braille, once a student at the Institution for Blind Youth, experimented with a system of raised dots, which he believed would make reading more efficient for people who were blind. By 1834 he had perfected the system into what was known as the Braille Literary Code.

Originally known as the New England Asylum for the Blind, the *Perkins School for the Blind* was the first school for students who were blind in the United States. Established in Boston in 1832, under the direction of Samuel Howe, the school emphasized individualized education within a curriculum framework fashioned after the public schools. Music study and crafts were an integral part of the school's program (Roberts, 1986). The residential school received national and international recognition for its success in educating students who were deaf-blind, including Helen Keller.

Helen Keller as a young girl.

REAL PEOPLE

On Tuesday, June 27, 1995—the 115th anniversary of Helen Keller's birth—Erik Weihenmayer completed an 18-day ascent to the summit of Mt. McKinley. His triumph proved that dreams can be realized in spite of obstacles. Erik is a 27-year-old elementary school teacher from Phoenix, Arizona, who happens to be blind.

Erik undertook the climb on behalf of the American Foundation for the Blind (AFB) and carried with him a green-and-white flag representing the millions of persons in the United States who are blind and visually impaired. The AFB HighSights '95 ascent team included Erik Weihenmayer, Sam Epstein, Ryan Ludwig, Jeff Evans, and Jamie Bloomquist. The team trained extensively for the ascent of Mt. McKinley by climbing Mt. Ranier in Washington and Longs Peak in Colorado. Erik began trekking and rock climbing in 1986. For Erik, "the climb was a metaphor for the obstacles that . . . confront people who are visually impaired [each and every day]." Rather than dwelling on any possible limitations imposed on him by his blindness, Erik has succeeded by exploring and fully realizing his potential as an individual.

At age 13, Erik was faced with blindness as his field of view narrowed and vision grew more spotty every day. "New skills, new strategies, and new ways of viewing the world were needed to fill the void," Erik recalls, "but I could not start until my mind relinquished its desperate grip on sight. It wasn't the sight itself that I wished to hold on to, but the confidence and freedom that came with it." As a motivated teenager, Erik began to acquire the speciaized skills necessary for the independence he desired. With the support of his parents, Erik developed the confidence to try many things—including high school and college wrestling. Erik explains: "My parents helped me to accept my blindness as a part of me. . . . With their love and support surrounding me, I came to know that blindness would often be a nuisance, would always make my life more challenging, but would never be a barrier in my path."

Erik currently teaches English and math to fifth grade students in Phoenix. Although his climbing and hiking endeavors include a 60-mile trek across the Andes Mountains along the Inca Trail, a climb of the Karakuram Mountains of Pakistan, a crossing of the Batura glacier (the second largest glacier in the world), and a 65-mile trek through the Bailine Valley of Indonesia, he still considers teaching and capturing the attention of a classroom full of fifth graders, 180 days a year, to be the greatest challenge of all.

Source: Information from American Foundation for the Blind press release, 1995.

As early as 1900, children who were blind were educated in public schools in Chicago, in response to parents' requests for a residential school closer to home. In these first integrated programs, children received a portion of their instruction alongside their sighted peers and instruction in skills such as braille and typing from specially trained teachers. With the continued emphasis on individualized student needs, it was determined that this structure would not be appropriate for all learners (Roberts, 1986), and so the concept of maintaining an array of program options to assure quality education for all children with visual impairments was born.

In 1913, classes for students with partial sight were established in Boston and Cleveland. Over time, educational programs for students with partial sight changed from "sight-saving" classes to those with an emphasis on maximizing the use of vision. In 1947, the American Printing House for the Blind began to distribute large-print materials along with braille materials for students classified as legally blind. In 1964, Natalie Barraga conducted research with learners who were visually impaired and determined that visual efficiency could be trained. The *Barraga Visual Efficiency Scale* was released in 1970 and provided teachers with the first formal assessment of visual efficiency. Functional low vision assessments were formalized in the late

This girl can read even storybooks with braille.

1970s and early 1980s as a respected addition to the information gathered in clinical assessments of visual functioning. Corn (1983) developed a three dimensional model of visual functioning in which visual abilities (e.g., visual acuity), environmental cues (e.g., illumination), and stored and available individuality (e.g., psychological makeup) interact to determine actual functioning. The model successfully explains why two people with the same visual acuity might function very differently and why one individual's visual functioning may vary in different settings (e.g., home vs. office). By understanding these contributions professionals can make crucial suggestions for enhancing visual functioning by altering appropriate variables.

In the mid-1980s professionals and consumers witnessed a dramatic nationwide decline in the braille literacy of individuals who were blind. Recognizing the significance of the matter, professionals and consumers worked together to develop strategies to improve the viability of braille as a reading and writing medium. Numerous states passed legislation in the 1990s to promote braille literacy in the schools, and efforts are currently under way to assure that teachers credentialed to teach students with visual impairments are competent in braille and the teaching of braille reading and writing.

Another important aspect of the education of individuals with blindness and visual impairments is the ability to move about the environment independently, with safety and efficiency. As early as the late 18th century, dogs were being trained in Europe to serve as guides for persons who were blind. The systematic training of dog guides in Germany in the early 20th century was largely in response to the needs of veterans blinded in World War I. In 1929, Dorothy Eustis, who had observed the dog guide training programs in Germany, traveled to America and helped to establish the first U.S. dog guide school, known as *The Seeing Eye, Inc.* An alternative mobility device known as the *long cane* was formalized by Richard

Hoover at the Valley Forge Army General Hospital. The science of "foot travel" (now known as orientation and mobility training) evolved in response to the needs of U.S. veterans blinded in World War II (Bledsoe, 1980)—although it was nearly two decades before formalized orientation and mobility (O&M) instruction was made available for school-age children. In the 1970s, O&M specialists began to work with students with low vision and students with multiple disabilities. In the 1980s and 1990s, O&M services expanded to include work with visually impaired infants, toddlers, and preschoolers.

Throughout history the training and education of individuals who are blind and visually impaired has evolved, as new programs to meet the dynamic needs of this heterogeneous population are developed.

DEFINITIONS

While legal definitions of visual impairments are commonly used to determine eligibility for funding and a wide range of services, benefits, and materials, these guidelines prove less useful in educational settings. Considerations of actual visual functioning are more important for making educational decisions such as the selection of an appropriate reading medium.

Legal Definitions

Legal definitions of visual impairments are based on clinical measurements of visual acuity and visual fields. Legal blindness encompasses a wide range of visual abilities (Corn & Koenig, 1996). Individuals are determined to be **legally blind** if they have a visual acuity of 20/200 or less in the better eye with best correction (such as prescribed glasses or contact lenses). **Visual acuity** is a measurement that refers to the distance from which an individual can clearly see an object. An individual with typical vision has a visual acuity of 20/20. A person who is legally blind (with a visual acuity of 20/200) must stand at a distance of 20 feet in order to clearly see the very same object that a person with typical vision is able to see from 200 feet away.

Individuals are also classified as legally blind if their field of vision is restricted to 20 degrees or less. An individual with typical vision has a **visual field** of approximately 180 degrees. A severely restricted visual field limits the area that can be seen while gazing directly forward; depending on the size of the remaining field, it may be described as tunnel or pinhole vision. Individuals with restricted visual fields may have a central visual acuity of 20/20 and still be considered legally blind if that field is 20 degrees or less.

In addition to definitions for legal blindness, there is also a legal definition for individuals categorized as **partially sighted.** Individuals are determined to be partially sighted if they have a visual acuity between 20/70 and 20/200 in the better eye with correction.

Individuals who are identified as legally blind are eligible for many services and benefits, including supplemental social security benefits, an additional income tax deduction, free postal service titled "Free Matter for the Blind," free telephone directory assistance through some phone companies, vocational training, and access to "talking books" on tapes and records. School-age children who are legally blind are eligible for a wide range of educational services, materials, and equipment. A federal quota system allocates funds for necessary specialized materials to states and local school districts for each pupil who is legally blind. The American

Printing House for the Blind provides specialized materials and equipment that are not available commercially (braillers, braille and large-print books, raised-lined paper, etc.). Specialized materials and equipment are necessary to ensure that each pupil who is legally blind has appropriate access to both special and general education curriculum.

Educational Definitions

In general, educators place little emphasis, beyond eligibility status, on legal classifications of visual impairment. Teachers and specialists serving children who have visual impairments are most concerned with how each child's individual visual functioning impacts his or her growth and development. Legal classifications, therefore, are often replaced with functional classifications in educational settings.

Students who are unable to benefit from visual modes of learning and/or visual educational materials are referred to as **functionally blind.** Students who are functionally blind must rely primarily on their tactile and auditory senses for learning. They are typically "braille users" and rely on a mobility device (e.g., long cane) for safe and independent mobility.

Students who have visual impairments but can benefit from visual modes of learning are commonly referred to as having **low vision.** Students with low vision are often "print users." Some students with low vision may be able to use regular-size print with magnification, while others utilize various sizes of enlarged print known as **large print** (see Figure 9.1). Although many students with low vision are able to utilize printed materials, there are also students with low vision for whom braille use is more appropriate. Some students with visual impairment may eventually use both print and braille reading mediums. These decisions, made by the educational team, are done on an individual basis.

TYPES AND CAUSES OF VISUAL IMPAIRMENT

There are numerous potential causes of blindness and visual impairment. Some causes are associated with the aging process; some causes are more prevalent in adults. The causes of visual impairment discussed in this chapter are those common to children. Note that definitions of visual impairment do not include "visual perceptual or visual motor dysfunctions resulting solely from a learning disability" (California Department of Education, in press, p. 24). As you read this section, refer to the parts of the eye shown in Figure 9.2.

Refractive Errors

Refractive eye problems are very common, but in most cases they can be corrected with prescription lenses and do not result in visual impairments. In refractive errors the size or shape of the eyeball prevents refracted light rays from being focused directly on the retina.

Individuals who have **myopia** (nearsightedness) have an elongated eyeball (football-shaped). This elongation causes light rays to fall short of the retina, resulting in images that are out of focus. Persons with myopia can clearly see objects that are close up, but distant objects are out of focus. Individuals who are high myopics are at a higher risk for retinal detachment because the retina is stretched thin in the elongated eyeball. Participation in contact sports is typically discouraged for these individuals. Individuals who have **hyperopia** (farsightedness) have a shorter

8 POINT TYPE

INDIVIDUALS WITH LOW VISION MAY REQUIRE DIFFERENT FONTS OR SIZES.

10 POINT TYPE

INDIVIDUALS WITH LOW VISION MAY REQUIRE DIFFERENT FONTS OR SIZES.

12 POINT TYPE

INDIVIDUALS WITH LOW VISION MAY REQUIRE DIFFERENT FONTS OR SIZES.

14 POINT TYPE

INDIVIDUALS WITH LOW VISION MAY REQUIRE DIFFERENT FONTS OR SIZES.

18 POINT TYPE

INDIVIDUALS WITH LOW VISION MAY REQUIRE DIFFERENT FONTS OR SIZES.

24 POINT TYPE INDIVIDUALS WITH LOW VISION MAY REQUIRE DIFFERENT FONTS OR SIZES.

36 POINT TYPE

48 POINT TYPE

Figure 9.1   Sample Type Sizes and Fonts, Including Large Print

than normal eyeball that causes light rays to fall beyond the retina. Persons with hyperopia can clearly see objects at a distance, but are unable to clearly focus on near objects. Individuals with **astigmatism** have an irregularly shaped cornea (eye surface) and may have difficulty clearly seeing both near and distant objects. A person may have an astigmatism alone or in conjunction with myopia or hyperopia.

Most refractive errors are correctable with lenses, but school children with uncorrected myopia will typically experience difficulty with tasks such as chalkboard work or ball sports. In contrast, the child with uncorrected hyperopia will typically have difficulty with more detailed tasks such as reading and writing. It is important that all refractive errors be identified and corrected as early as possible to avoid potential vision-related school difficulties.

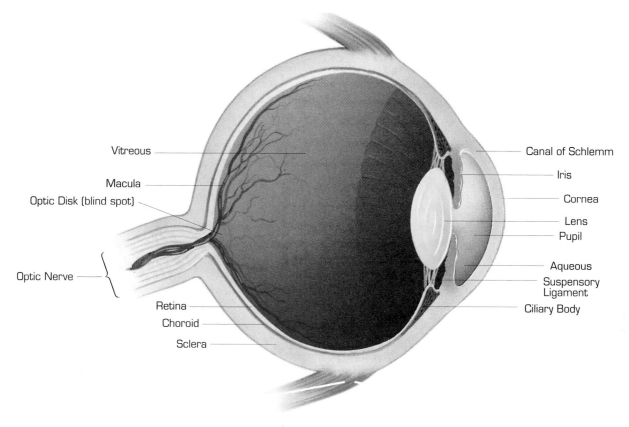

Figure 9.2   **Horizontal Section of a Right Eyeball**

Genetically Determined Impairments

There are a wide variety of genetically determined and hereditary-linked causes of visual impairment. A few of the more common causes in children will be discussed here.

Although the eye's lens is typically clear, **cataracts** are a cloudiness that develops, which blocks light entering the eye and results in reduced visual acuity. Looking through a cataract is often compared to looking through semiopaque glass or a dirty windshield. Individuals with cataracts often experience a great deal of difficulty with glare, as light rays are scattered by the opaque lens. Cataracts may be **congenital** (present from birth) or **adventitious** (acquired later in life). They commonly develop in both eyes. Cataracts may be the primary cause of a visual impairment, or may be a secondary condition to another eye pathology. Cataracts are most common in older adults, but hereditary disorders may result in cataracts in infancy. Cataracts in infants may also be associated with specific syndromes, systemic diseases, and infections (Isenberg, 1989). In children, opaque lenses must be surgically removed as early as possible to maximize restoration of vision. Intraocular lens implants, commonly used with adults to replace the function of the lens following surgical removal, are being considered for use with children with increased frequency. Data regarding the long-term safety and efficacy of pediatric intraocular implants are still being collected. Contact lenses are commonly used with infants who have had lenses surgically removed. Contact lenses, which must be maintained by the parents, are typically more comfortable and cosmetically appealing than heavy, thick, bifocal spectacles. Contact lenses also provide the young child with a greater visual field and improved depth perception than can be supplied with traditional bifocal glasses (Isenberg, 1989).

Glaucoma, which is the result of increased pressure in the eye, causes a loss of vision. If left untreated the increased intraocular pressure will damage the optic nerve and lead to a loss in peripheral vision and the potential for blindness (Isenberg, 1992). Glaucoma may also be congenital (occurring in less than 0.05% of newborns) or adventitious; it is more likely to occur in adults over the age of 40 in which there is a family history of glaucoma. Glaucoma is also more common in individuals who are very nearsighted, in diabetics, and in African American adults (Isenberg, 1989). Typical symptoms of glaucoma may include the appearance of an enlarged cornea in children, frequent eye rubbing, redness and pain, excessive tearing, the gradual loss of peripheral vision, general blurry vision, and halos seen around lights (Isenberg, 1992). Treatment for glaucoma may be surgical to improve the drainage of fluids from the eye, or may use medicated eye drops to reduce the intraocular pressure. In order to reduce the potential for vision loss, early detection and treatment are crucial.

Retinitis pigmentosa (RP) is a hereditary condition in which the retina gradually degenerates over time. Although retinitis pigmentosa may be diagnosed in young children, symptoms such as tunnel vision and night blindness rarely surface prior to adolescence (Isenberg, 1992). Degeneration of the retina affects the peripheral vision first, resulting in a narrowing field of vision (tunnel vision) and difficulty seeing in dimly lit areas (night blindness). There is no treatment for retinitis pigmentosa and over time it may eventually lead to total blindness.

Anophthalmia is a relatively rare phenomenon that is characterized by an absence of the globe of the eye. In some cases anophthalmia is inherited, but it may also occur sporadically or in association with other congenital anomalies (e.g., central nervous system defects). **Microphthalmia** also involves the globe of the eye and is characterized by a small eyeball that is about two thirds the normal size. Together, these two causes of visual impairment only represent approximately 0.6% of the cases of legal blindness in the United States (Ward, 1986).

Acquired Impairments

Beyond genetically determined visual impairments, there are a wide variety of acquired visual impairments. Trauma, tumors, infections, and inflammations are among the most common causes of acquired impairments. A visual impairment can be acquired in utero, during the birth process, in early or later childhood, or in adulthood.

Retinopathy of prematurity (ROP), formerly known as *retrolental fibroplasia*, was the leading cause of blindness in children during the 1940s and 1950s, increasing the school-age population of children with visual impairments by 39% (Spungin & Taylor, 1986). ROP is the result of too much oxygen being administered to premature, low birth weight infants placed in incubators for extended periods of time. After the babies are removed from the oxygen-rich environment, retinal blood vessels and fibrous scar tissue may develop in the retina and vitreous, causing the retina to stretch and lead to possible retinal detachment (Isenberg, 1992). After reaching epidemic proportions in the 1950s, levels of oxygen used in incubators were significantly reduced, decreasing the incidence of ROP. However, the incidence of ROP experienced a resurgence in the 1980s as medical technologies advanced and greater numbers of very small, medically fragile babies (less than

2 lbs.)—who required higher concentrations of oxygen for survival—were being saved. Although ROP does not always result in blindness, approximately 2,100 infants per year in the United States have severe visual impairments due to ROP (Trief, Duckman, Morse, & Silberman, 1989).

Head trauma may also lead to an acquired visual impairment. A direct blow to the eye during sporting activities such as boxing, racquetball, or fishing has the potential for causing severe vision loss. Brain injuries—such as those caused by gunshot wounds, stroke, or physical abuse—may also lead to visual impairment in combination with other neurological complications.

Cortical visual impairment (CVI) is bilateral vision loss associated with damage to the occipital lobes of the brain and/or visual pathways to the brain. Most children with CVI have additional neurological and/or medical problems associated with the brain injury (Good et al., 1994). CVI can be caused by asphyxia, perinatal or postnatal hypoxia-ischemia, head trauma (e.g., "shaken baby syndrome"), severe seizures, infections of the central nervous system, certain drugs or poisons, and other associated metabolic or neurologic conditions. While the child with CVI may show a normal pupillary response and a normal eye health examination, the actual impairment may affect visual fields, visual acuity, or both. Visual functioning will typically fluctuate and in some cases the child may be misdiagnosed as malingering (Good et al., 1994). Depending on age of onset and intervention, cause and location of the insult, and type of brain damage, it can be expected that many children with CVI will recover some visual functioning (Good et al., 1994) through rewiring of neural connections in the visual cortex (Isenberg, 1989). Rehabilitation efforts may be focused on the use of vision and interpretation of visual information with real objects in natural environments.

Retinoblastoma, a malignant tumor in the retina, is among the 10 most frequent causes of visual impairment in children in the United States. Retinoblastomas occur with the incidence of 1 in 17,000 births; early detection leads to a survival rate of 75% (Isenberg, 1989). Retinoblastoma may be transmitted through an autosomal dominant gene (Goldberg, 1993) and may affect one or both eyes. In children with retinoblastoma the affected pupil will commonly appear white in color. Radiotherapy and chemotherapy may be used to treat the tumor(s), but in some instances the eye and tumor must be removed (enucleated) to save the patient's life. Children with enucleated eyes must be fitted with appropriately sized prosthetic eyes. The prosthetics are important for cosmetic appearance and also to ensure that the eye socket maintains its size and shape.

Inflammations and infections in the eye should be treated with care. *Trachoma*, a corneal scarring caused by chlamydial infection, is relatively uncommon in the United States yet is a leading cause of blindness in the world (Goldberg, 1993). At birth, babies are particularly susceptible to infections carried in the birth canal (e.g., gonorrhea and chlamydia) as well as to systemic infections such as herpes and rubella. Eyedrops or ointments (e.g., silver nitrate, erythromycin, or tetracycline) to reduce the incidence of eye infections in newborns have been in use since 1880 and are now mandated by law in many states (Isenberg, 1989). However, silver nitrate is irritating to mucous membranes and can cause a chemical conjunctivitis in some newborns.

Other Visual Impairments

An easily recognizable eye disorder characterized by involuntary rapid eye movements is **nystagmus.** The most common form of nystagmus is a side-to-side jerking movement (Goldberg, 1993). Nystagmus may cause dizziness and nausea. Most people with nystagmus are able to establish a *null point* to look through that will somewhat reduce the rapidity of eye movements. The null point is simply a particular gaze position that lessens eye movements for the individual, hence improving visual acuity. Infants and young children will often find and assume their own head or gaze position to improve their visual acuity.

Another visual impairment that is attributable to an eye muscle imbalance is known as **strabismus.** Strabismus is a misalignment, or turning of the eyes, either inward or outward. With strabismus, the brain receives mixed signals because the muscle imbalance prevents the eyes from working together to focus clearly on one single image. Strabismus may be treated by correcting refractive errors or by prescribed eye patching to equalize visual acuity in both eyes. In some cases eye exercises may be prescribed to strengthen the weaker eye (Ward, 1986). Surgical adjustments to the eye muscles that control eye alignment are another option in some cases of strabismus. Early detection is important because more severe cases of strabismus may result in double vision. **Amblyopia,** commonly known as *lazy eye*, can result from untreated strabismus. In amblyopia, the brain may suppress the use of one eye in order to eliminate confusing signals to the brain caused by unequal acuities or misalignment of the eyes. In other instances, amblyopia in a healthy eye may be a sympathetic response to obstructed vision in the other eye (e.g., congenital cataract or glaucoma). In either case, early detection and treatment are essential to full recovery of vision.

MEASUREMENT OF VISUAL IMPAIRMENT

Measurement of Vision

Most aspects of vision measurement are considered to be subjective because they depend on the ability or desire of the patient to respond accurately to examinations. Keeping in mind that classifications of visual impairment address two aspects of visual functioning—visual acuity and visual field—eye examinations must include measurements of both central vision (near and distance) and peripheral vision.

Measurement of Central Acuity.   Central visual acuity is commonly measured with a *Snellen chart* test. The Snellen chart has rows of letters that become progressively smaller as you move from the top to the bottom of the chart. Typically, the person being tested stands at a distance of 20 feet from the chart and is asked to read letters that are randomly pointed to. Acuity is determined by the distance that corresponds to the smallest row of letters that can be identified accurately. For example, in an acuity measurement of 20/40, the first number represents the distance the person was standing from the chart and the second number represents the smallest row of letters read. *Tumbling E charts* and charts with pictorial symbols (e.g., New York Lighthouse Screening Cards) can be substituted to measure the visual acuity of preliterate children, children with multiple disabilities, and children who are nonverbal. If a child is unable to visually identify the symbols on the largest 20/200 line, the child moves closer to the chart until he or she is able to recognize it. A visual acuity reading is taken from that distance (e.g., 5/200 if the person is able to identify the 20/200 line from a distance of 5 feet). Figure 9.3 provides examples of some commonly used eye charts.

The *Feinbloom Distance Test* chart can be used effectively for individuals who have low vision (for those who cannot identify the 20/200 line on the Snellen

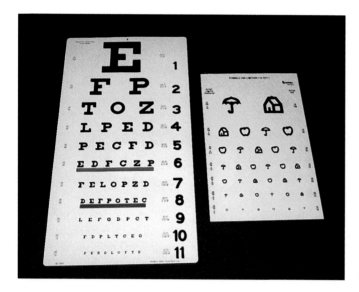

Figure 9.3 **Commonly Used Eye Charts**

chart). The Feinbloom chart may be used at a distance of 10 feet and has increments of visual acuity beyond 20/200 (e.g., 10/700). If the person is unable to read the chart from any distance, then the distance from which the person is able to count fingers that are being held up is measured (e.g, CF at 3 feet). From there, hand motion (HM) recognition, followed by light perception (LP) or no light perception (NLP) is noted.

Near visual acuity should also be assessed because many tasks require our near vision (e.g., reading, writing, keyboarding, making models, and applying makeup). Near-point test charts may be used for this purpose (e.g., Rosenbaum Near Acuity, New York Lighthouse Near Acuity, and Keller Near Reading Cards). Near visual acuity assessment may also be used to help determine the most appropriate print size for a child who has low vision, and will take into consideration lighting and positioning of reading materials.

Measurement of Peripheral Vision.   Peripheral vision (or side vision) is commonly screened using a *confrontation test.* In confrontation testing the person faces the examiner and one eye is covered while the examiner briefly holds up a number of fingers in the peripheral field of vision for the person to identify. The same procedure is used for the other eye. More sophisticated peripheral field testing can be done using a *tangent screen,* a *Goldman perimeter,* or a *computerized automated perimeter.* A tangent screen is simply a black screen across which a black wand with different sized white pins on the tip can be moved. The wand is moved to test the visual field, primarily in the central 30 degrees. The Goldman perimeter is a hollow white bowl in which lights of varying intensity and size are presented to the individual in order to test the full peripheral field of vision. Computerized perimeter testing is similar to the Goldman test except that it is automated and numerical scores are generated.

Early Screening

Early screening of visual functioning is important for detection of visual abnormalities or irregularities. In young children, the early detection of congenital cataracts and glaucoma is crucial to appropriate surgical intervention. Muscle imbalances respond best to treatment when discovered early. Screenings are also important for detecting refractive errors in children, because visual problems due to refractive errors may not be otherwise noticeable until the child reaches school and begins formalized reading and chalkboard tasks. Hyperopia may not be detected in some children until the third grade, when print sizes used in their reading materials become considerably smaller. Vision screenings are also important for adults—especially for individuals who are diabetic and for persons with a family history of glaucoma.

Signs of Visual Impairment

Children who have a visual impairment that is not easily recognizable from physical appearance may exhibit functional signs of visual difficulties. If a combination of the signs in the lists that follow are exhibited by an individual child, it is recommended that the child be referred for a thorough eye examination by an ophthalmologist or optometrist.

General Signs of Vision Problems

- Has red or inflamed eyes
- Has excessive watery eyes
- Eyes have a crusty appearance
- Rubs eyes frequently
- Eyes look dull or cloudy
- Pupil in one or both eyes appears gray or white
- One or both eyes turn inward or outward
- Eyes do not move together
- Often turns or tilts head when viewing something
- Squints to look at something
- Covers one eye to get a better look at something

Signs in Infants, Toddlers, and Preschoolers

- Exhibits a startle response when approached quietly
- In general, does not show an interest in people's faces
- Shows little interest in objects beyond arm's reach
- Is unable to visually follow a moving target
- Exhibits a decreased interest in exploration

Signs in School-Age Children

- Holds books and reading materials close to the face
- Has difficulty following boardwork
- Exhibits frequent, inadvertent bumping into people and things
- Has difficulty with ball sports
- Complains that glare and shadows cause great discomfort
- Complains of headaches, eyestrain, or fatigue following periods of reading or other visual tasks

- Cannot discriminate between letters
- Misses details in pictures

PREVALENCE

Visual impairment is considered to be a **low incidence disability** because the disability is present in less than 1% of the population. Nelson and Dimitrova (1993) estimated that there were a total of 4,293,360 severely visually impaired civilian, noninstitutionalized persons in the nation in 1990, with the majority (68%) being 65 years of age or older. Other estimates contend that two thirds of the population with visual impairments is over the age of 50 (Federal Register, 1991).

It is estimated that 0.1% of the school-age population is visually impaired, with the ratio of blind to low vision students being 1 to 10. According to the American Printing House for the Blind's Annual Report (1995) 54,783 students, classified as legally blind, received specialized services in the public schools. This number does not include school-age students with low vision who are not classified as legally blind, nor does it include infants with visual impairments. It is also difficult to obtain accurate census data within the educational system due to confusing pupil count procedures used for students with multiple disabilities. Nelson and Dimitrova (1993) estimated that in 1990 there were more than 95,000 children with severe visual impairments nationwide aged 17 and under.

Regardless of which estimates you use, students with blindness and visual impairments still make up only a small portion of the student population. Yet even with these relatively small numbers of students, personnel shortages in the field of visual impairment and blindness are prevalent. Many students with visual impairments receive an inadequate quantity and quality of specialized services due to the profession's inability to train enough qualified teachers and specialists to meet the dynamic needs of this low incidence population.

CHARACTERISTICS

The population of individuals who are blind and visually impaired is extremely heterogeneous. The age range spans from birth to older adulthood. For many individuals, visual impairment is a "single" disability, but approximately one third of the populations with visual impairments has additional or multiple disabilities such as Down syndrome, multiple sclerosis, or cerebral palsy. Caution should be taken to avoid drawing too many generalizations about the characteristics of individuals who are visually impaired; the range of personalities, skills, and abilities varies as greatly as it does in the sighted population.

Age at Onset

The age at onset has a tremendous impact on the effects of visual impairment in one's life. Visual impairment early in life impacts development and learning, while visual impairment in adulthood is associated with a tremendous adjustment process. Young children who acquire a severe visual impairment before age 2 typically maintain relatively little visual memory and may learn in much the same way as a child who is born functionally blind. In older children, they may maintain a visual reference from which to develop conceptual understanding for more abstract learning.

Degree of Impairment

The degree of a child's visual impairment, including the visual acuity and size of the visual field, is significant to the child's overall development. The more vision a child has and the more efficiently the child is able to utilize that vision, the greater likelihood that the child will be a visual learner (Scholl, 1986). A child with a mild visual impairment (e.g., 20/80 visual acuity) will likely develop in ways that are very similar to his or her siblings and peers who have a visual acuity of 20/20—climbing trees, riding a bicycle, watching television, and reading books. The child who is functionally blind may also learn to climb trees and ride a bicycle—but will need to learn different skills and overcome more obstacles to be able to do so with as much safety and grace as his or her sighted siblings and peers.

Sensory–Motor Development

Vision plays a major part in the development of sensory–motor skills. While children who are blind are similar to peers who are sighted in the establishment of postural milestones (i.e., sitting and standing), they often lag behind in the initiation of locomotion (i.e., crawling and walking). It is not unusual for children who are blind to skip the crawling stage altogether. While there is no apparent physical reason for not crawling, researchers and practitioners have speculated that a combination of low muscle tone, lack of visual motivation for exploration, and the safety hazard of moving about the environment headfirst without being able to see obstacles in the path may act as powerful disincentives for crawling (Lampert, 1992). Low muscle tone is not an uncommon characteristic of children who are congenitally blind and may contribute to the use of atypical gait patterns.

While children who are blind must rely more heavily on the senses of touch and hearing, it is a mistake to assume they have been given an "extra" special sense or ability. In fact, children with visual impairments may exhibit varying degrees of **tactual defensiveness.** Tactual defensiveness is typified as a negative or emotional response to the sensation of touch (Ayres, 1979). A multisensory approach to intervention is recommended so that children who are visually impaired are able to fully benefit from tactual information. A lot of thoughtful planning and training is necessary to assure that children with visual impairments are able to maximize the use of their sensory and motor capabilities.

Cognitive Development

It is estimated that 80% of what we learn is through our visual sense. Children who are visually impaired have the same range of capacities for cognitive growth and development, but they must learn about the world through their remaining senses. In some instances, the tactual and auditory senses are less efficient for learning tasks, especially when the learner has a limited visual frame of reference.

Practical knowledge of the world may be related to the number and range of concrete experiences sometimes afforded to children with visual impairments. When children with visual impairments have a more limited range of experiences, have less ability to move about, and have fewer opportunities to exhibit control over the environment, they are at a disadvantage for the development of concepts and means to learn about the world around them. This disadvantage may result in slower intellectual development, or development that is uneven across areas of intellectual functioning (Scholl, 1986). For example, children who are blind or who have low vision typically score lower on tests of spatial conceptual understanding and measures of practical knowledge (Warren, 1984). Spatial concepts (i.e., in front of, behind, above, and below) are challenging to develop with a limited visual context—without the ability to see the whole picture.

Development of Speech and Language

Although many children with visual impairments appear to be highly verbal, both the overall quality and use of language may be different from that of their same-age sighted peers. Language patterns may be more egocentric, with more references to self-interest and activities and less emphasis on the interests of peers (Anderson & Kekelis, cited in Kekelis, 1992). Questions may be used more frequently and may be unrelated to current activities or conversations (Chernus-Manfield, Hayashi, & Kekelis, 1985; Erin, 1986).

It is not uncommon for children with congenital blindness to show preference for engaging adults in conversation. Adults tend to be more tolerant of the child's verbal behaviors than are peers. Peers expect appropriate dialogue and will quickly end a communication that is not interactive or responsive.

A degree of **echolalia** may be present in the speech patterns of some children with visual impairments, more commonly in children with additional disabilities. Echolalic speech is characterized by "parroting" the speech patterns of other people. Phrases that have been heard may be repeated on a frequent basis. Children exhibiting the most severe degrees of echolalia rely almost totally on repetitious speech and rarely use their own words to express themselves.

Children who are blind may develop language without a visual context and experiential base to associate spoken words. This can result in the use of **verbalisms,** defined by Warren (1984) as statements made "without adequate experiential referents" (p. 172). It is important to realize that what these children say may not represent what they have actually experienced or what they truly understand. For example, a child who is blind may say "The Arco Building is 65 stories tall" without ever having been in a multistory building and without having any real concept of the height of the building or what is meant by a "story" of a building. On first impression one might think that the child is very knowledgeable—but upon further questioning it might be realized that the child is simply repeating a fact without understanding what it means. The more concrete experiences that a child with a visual impairment has and conceptually understands, the less need there will be to use verbalisms in conversation.

Social Development

Many social norms and skills are learned incidentally through our observations of people around us, and from the verbal and nonverbal feedback we receive regarding the appropriateness of our own behavior. Children who are blind and children with low vision have more limited opportunities for observation of social behaviors and typically receive less feedback regarding the appropriateness of their own behavior. Nuances associated with body language, such as hand gestures, are often missed. Nonverbal forms of communication (e.g., facial expressions) go unnoticed by children who are blind, and in turn, are not easily incorporated within interpersonal communications.

Some children with visual impairments may also develop **stereotypic behaviors,** often referred to as *mannerisms.* Mannerisms such as body-rocking, eye-poking, and finger-flicking have been observed and are thought to develop initially to meet a need for additional sensory stimulation. Over time, these behaviors may become habitual and difficult to extinguish. Stereotypic behaviors are mentioned in this section because of the potential disruption to social development. Sighted peers may have a difficult time interpreting such self-involved movements and may be less likely to initiate social interactions with a child who exhibits mannerisms. Similarly, the child engaged in stereotypic behavior is less able to respond to the interests of peers.

ASSESSMENT AND INSTRUCTION

Roles of Professionals in Assessment

Each child who is diagnosed with a visual impairment and qualifies for specialized services should be seen by an appropriately credentialed/certified teacher of children with visual impairments *and* by an orientation and mobility specialist. The specially trained teacher assesses the child's strengths and needs in the following areas: functional vision (appropriate for all children with any amount of functional vision); cognition and concept development; language development and communication skills; fine motor skills; self-help skills; social skills; and play skills. For preschool children, the teacher may also assess the child's reading readiness (braille or print). The family should also be an integral part of the assessment process for infants, toddlers, and preschoolers. Information sharing between families and professionals helps to establish a more accurate and holistic view of each child's capabilities for positive interactions within a variety of educational and social contexts.

With school-age students, the teacher of children with visual impairments must assess skills in the area of vocational development, use of specialized skills such as braille reading, and use of specialized equipment and materials such as closed circuit television (CCTV), Braille 'n Speak, typoscope, or books recorded on tape—as well as overall academic achievement. Assessment of academic achievement may be completed in conjunction with general educators, or may be the primary responsibility of the general educator with consultation from the specially trained teacher. Assessment roles may vary and should be flexible in order to meet the needs of each individual child.

The orientation and mobility (O&M) specialist assesses the child's strengths and needs in the following areas: functional vision (appropriate for all individuals with any functional vision); motor capabilities (often done in conjunction with an occupational/physical therapist or an adaptive physical educator); movement and travel skills; environmental orientation; the use of prescribed mobility devices; and concept development related to body imagery, spatial and environmental awareness, and independent movement in dynamic environments. Assessments should include information from both home and school environments, and it is most helpful for the O&M specialist to observe the child's functioning in both settings. Family members are often a good source of information regarding the child's movement and exploration patterns in the familiar home environment.

The orientation and mobility specialist should begin working with a child who has visual impairments as early as possible.

When assessments pertaining to the functional use of vision are in question, the O&M specialist and the teacher of children with visual impairments should both be involved. In order to obtain a full picture of the child's visual functioning across settings, the two professionals should work together. The teacher of children with visual impairments is responsible for conducting a functional vision assessment related to the child's ability to use his or her vision in indoor environments as related to growth, development, and academic achievement. This assessment may be used as one factor in determining the most appropriate reading medium (print or braille) for the child. The O&M specialist is responsible for a functional vision assessment related to the child's ability to move about the environment safely while maintaining a sense of orientation. The major portion of the assessment conducted by the O&M specialist is typically conducted in an outdoor environment. This assessment may be used as one factor in determining the necessity for the child to use a mobility device (e.g., long cane) during travel. Together, the two assessments inform and complement one another for the benefit of the child being assessed.

Selecting and Adapting Educational Assessments

Infants, Toddlers, and Preschoolers. Many of the standardized assessments available to measure cognitive development in young children rely on tasks requiring good manual skills and spatial representation (Brambring & Troster, 1994). Both areas rely heavily on visual skills, and so it is difficult to compare the cognitive development of young children who are blind with those who are sighted. To date, no one has successfully been able to develop a standardized developmental assessment that is free from visual biases. There are, however, specialized assessments commercially available for use with young children who are visually impaired (e.g., Brigance diagnostic inventory of early development and Oregon project for preschoolers with visual impairments and blindness).

Interdisciplinary team assessments are probably more appropriate for use with young children who are blind or visually impaired. Team members may include family members, the ophthalmologist or optometrist, the O&M specialist, the teacher credentialed in the area of visual impairment, the occupational therapist, the physical therapist, and the speech–language pathologist. The most effective interdisciplinary teams are those that share an interest in learning about the behavior of young children with visual impairments and who are motivated to explore the unique capabilities of each individual child (Bolduc, Gresset, Sanschagrin, & Thibodeau, 1993).

School-Age Children.   While there are assessment tools specially designed for use with school-age students who are blind or visually impaired, there are general assessment considerations that should be adhered to regardless of the instrument used. For instance, when possible it is best to use measures that do not have time limits or restrictions. Students who are blind and students who have low vision require additional time to complete many types of assignments and tests. The use of enlarged print and/or magnification devices can be tedious and reduce overall reading speed, creating physical and mental fatigue. Time restrictions, when required, are typically increased by an extra 50% to accommodate students with low vision (Duckworth, 1993). Similarly, students who use braille as their reading medium should be given double time in testing situations. Efforts should also be taken to ensure that students have access to the same specialized equipment and materials in testing situations that they use to complete their everyday assignments (Bradley-Johnson, 1986).

Many standardized educational assessments incorporate the use of pictures. In some cases, simple diagrams or shapes can be enlarged and/or produced in a comprehensible tactual format for the student with a visual impairment; in other cases, such reproductions may leave the student with something that is either visually confusing or tactually unrecognizable. For example, the student may not be able to tactually identify a raised line drawing of a bird, and would have even greater difficulty distinguishing the difference between two birds. Care should be taken to eliminate from assessment measures items that rely heavily on visual processing of information. In standardized testing, the majority of items omitted come from the math, science, and social science areas (Duckworth, 1993).

The teacher credentialed to teach children with visual impairments should be consulted regarding educational assessments. The specially trained teacher can suggest assessment adaptations, as well as select and administer norm-referenced or criterion-referenced assessments that have been specially designed for use with students with visual impairments.

Instructional Considerations

Array of Program Options.   Children and youth with visual impairments are an extremely heterogeneous group. Educational needs vary across individuals and according to current developmental needs of each child. Educational placement decisions must be made on an individual basis through a team process that includes the full participation of the family in concert with educators, specialists, and administrators. The educational needs of the child may vary over time and placement options include residential and special schools, home teaching, special classes with opportunities for interaction with sighted peers, resource room support for participation in varying amounts of general education, full participation in general educa-

As many concrete experiences as possible should be given to the child with visual impairment.

tion with support services provided on an itinerant basis, or full participation in general education without specialized support. The **most appropriate placement (MAP)** (Curry & Hatlen, 1988) for each child includes consideration of both developmental needs and disability-specific needs, and may change over time.

Roles of Professionals in Instruction. The teacher credentialed in the area of visual impairment must be trained to carry out many different duties and be prepared to serve in a variety of capacities ranging from full-time classroom teacher to an itinerant consultant. Teachers of students with visual impairments have been providing such flexible individualized services across settings since the early 1900s.

The orientation and mobility (O&M) specialist provides individualized services to children and youth with visual impairments who can benefit from instruction in concepts and skills related to independent movement and orientation. The O&M specialist typically provides services to students on a one-to-one basis and is usually an itinerant, traveling between various school and home environments.

Specialized Curriculum. Children who are blind and visually impaired require a specialized curriculum that includes an emphasis on developing listening skills, visual efficiency skills, tactual discrimination skills, and the use of applicable technology. Students who will use braille must learn a literary braille code that contains two grades of braille, and also a separate math code known as the Nemeth Code. (There are additional braille codes for music, computers, and foreign languages.) There are numerous contractions to learn. Braille contractions are combinations and sequences of dots that represent whole words (e.g., *can*) or word parts (e.g., *-tion*). Contractions are a part of grade 2 braille. They help to reduce the bulkiness of the text and increase overall reading efficiency. The rules that coincide with braille reading and writing do not readily map onto the reading curriculum found in general education primers, and so beginning braille readers may be more successful when using the specialized reading curriculum developed for them. For this reason, many primary grade students who are blind are often best served in a special day class or resource room where they can receive intensive instruction in braille reading and writing. A strong foundation in braille and other specialized skills will ultimately contribute to their success in general education and later independence in adulthood.

There is also much to learn about specialized materials, equipment, and technology. Students who use braille as a reading medium must also be taught to write or produce braille. Braille students may potentially use a brailler, slate and stylus, and/or Braille 'n Speak. Students who read enlarged print may need to be taught to use magnification devices such as hand-held magnifiers, stand magnifiers, or close

SPECIALIZED EQUIPMENT FOR BRAILLE USERS	
Brailler	The brailler is a six-keyed device that enables a person to produce the embossed dots for the braille code. Various sizes of paper can be used with the brailler. The brailler is portable, but somewhat bulky to carry.
Mountbat Brailler	The Mountbat brailler is an electronic brailler that has computer interface capabilities. The keys require less manual strength to operate because it is electric. The Mountbat brailler is considered to be portable, but does weigh approximately 15 lbs. Accessories include a computer keyboard attachment for input.
Slate and Stylus	The slate and stylus also enables the person to produce the embossed dots for braille; however, they must be punched out by hand using the stylus. The dots can only be produced one at a time, but many individuals are able to use the slate and stylus very efficiently. The slate and stylus is lightweight and can be easily carried in a purse or backpack.
Braille 'n Speak	The Braille 'n Speak (manufactured by Blazie Engineering) is a portable device that enables braille users to input information using a braille keyboard. For output, the Braille 'n Speak is able to translate grade 2 braille into either synthesized speech or print. The user can listen to the speech output through an earplug or produce print by connecting the device to a printer. With the correct accessories, the Braille 'n Speak can be used to enter text or read the screen of a host computer, read any IBM disks, or serve as a fax/modem. The Braille 'n Speak is available in 11 languages and is a popular technology for both school-age children and adults.
Computer Access	Computer magnification systems (hardware) and screen magnification software are used to magnify text and graphics on computer screens. In addition, some computer users who have low vision may choose to use speech synthesis hardware and software for additional optional support. Several components of specialized technology can be combined to provide access to computers for individuals who are braille users. A typical computer can be used with the following adaptations: a speech synthesizer and appropriate voice access software; a refreshable computer access braille display; software for braille translation and production; and a braille embosser or printer.
Reading Machine	The reading machine (manufactured by Kurzweil, IBM, and Arkenstone) are sophisticated computers that use synthesized speech to "read" printed materials to individuals with visual impairments. The speed and voice tone can be adjusted by the individual. Current technological advances have made this type of device more portable, more effective in reading a variety of printed materials (e.g., bills, recipes, and junk mail), and the synthetic voices have become more appealing.
SPECIALIZED OPTICAL DEVICES	
Closed Circuit Television (CCTV)	Closed circuit television is an electronic magnification system used by individuals with low vision for a variety of reading tasks. The system incorporates high–intensity illumination, a special closed

Figure 9.4 **Specialized Equipment for Students With Visual Impairments**

circuit television (CCTV). Keyboarding skill is important to most students with visual impairments because it provides greater access to computer technology and supplies another means for producing written materials that can be read by individuals who cannot read braille. Figure 9.4 presents many of the commonly used materials designed to assist instruction for students who have visual impairments.

Students with visual impairments also have a need for specialized instruction beyond academics. Many of the skills needed for independent living (i.e., personal hygiene, cooking, cleaning, and personal management) are typically learned incidentally by children who are sighted. Children who are visually impaired often need instruction in and opportunities to develop specialized techniques for independent living.

Another important component of the specialized curriculum for students with a range of visual impairments is the area of orientation and mobility. Academic preparation and vocational training can be meaningless if the individual is unable to

	circuit television camera, an adjustable lens, monitor and gliding viewing table to provide a versatile low vision device. The individual is able to adjust the size of the image, the brightness of the image, and the contrast to meet their own visual needs. Many students prefer the image when it is white print on a black background. CCTVs come in a variety of shapes and sizes, including desktop, portable and computer compatible versions. The newer systems enable the user to enlarge photographic images with good quality and color.
Monocular	The monocular is a hand-held prescribed telescope that can be used primarily for enlargement in distance viewing tasks. In the classroom, students may use a monocular to read the chalkboard or view a wall clock. In the outdoor environment, students may use a monocular to read street signs or view a traffic light. With increased magnification, the device will have a smaller viewing area and increased distortion. Individuals will need training in the use of the monocular, as well as opportunities to incorporate its use within the daily routine.
Magnifiers	Magnifiers come in many forms, including hand-held magnifiers of various strengths, page magnifiers, stand magnifiers, and magnifiers with lights. Some magnifiers may be prescribed, while others can be commercially purchased. The advantage of most magnifiers is that they are portable and relatively inexpensive. Magnifiers are used for near-distance tasks such as reading.

SPECIALIZED ELECTRONIC TRAVEL DEVICES

Mowat Sensor	The Mowat sensor is a hand-held electronic travel device that translates high-frequency auditory output into vibrotactile feedback for the user. It is a secondary travel device that should be used in combination with a long cane or dog guide. The feedback enables the traveler to detect the presence of an object in the travel path.
Laser Cane	The laser cane is a primary mobility device that incorporates the use of laser beams to detect the presence of obstacles directly in the traveler's path, as well as overhanging objects (e.g., branches). In addition, the laser cane has a third beam that is able to detect drop-offs in the traveler's path (e.g., a curb). The laser cane can be used in place of the long cane because of its capability for detecting drop-offs. The laser beams are translated into both auditory and tactile feedback. The laser cane is used in the same manner as the long cane, but requires additional training.
Sonic Guide	The sonic guide is a secondary mobility device that should be used in conjunction with a long cane or dog guide. This device is worn like glasses, with connected ear tubes. The high-frequency auditory output is translated into auditory signals that can be interpreted by the traveler. The feedback enables the individual to detect the presence of obstacles in the travel path, as well as providing information regarding the quality of the material of the object (i.e., wood vs. metal vs. glass). The sonic guide has also been used to assist congenitally blind children in developing spatial concepts.

This high school student can participate fully in the classroom with his brailler.

move about the workplace freely or travel independently within the community. Orientation and mobility training includes instruction in safe and efficient movements within the home, school, workplace, and greater community. O&M specialists may work with infants, toddlers, and preschoolers in order to facilitate exploration and ensure safe movement at an early age. O&M specialists work with school-age children on school campuses, helping them design and execute routes between classrooms, restrooms, offices, cafeterias, and playgrounds. Orientation and mobility training reaches far beyond the immediate school campus, however. The curriculum addresses orientation in community travel and safety in simple and complex street crossings. Instruction and travel experiences in residential, light business, rural, and downtown urban areas may all be included in the O&M curriculum. The effective use of public transportation and/or paratransit systems is another important component of O&M training. The instruction is individualized and based on the abilities and eventual travel needs of each student.

One method of travel involves the use of a human guide (often referred to as *sighted guide*). O&M specialists assume responsibility for teaching students the techniques and appropriate use of a guide. They also typically provide in-service instruction in guiding procedures for interested family members, professionals, peers, and other individuals who may have occasion to serve as a guide for the student who is blind. The O&M specialist may prescribe a mobility device (e.g., long cane), depending on the child's visual functioning, to provide protection from obstacles in the travel path and to supply additional tactual or auditory environmental feedback. Some adults may choose to use a dog guide for mobility, but it is not typically recommended that school-age students be trained to use a dog guide unless they have very good mobility skills, exceptional maturity, and a need for a sufficient amount of daily independent travel.

Orientation and mobility curriculum also addresses the travel needs of individuals with low vision. The curriculum incorporates the use of mobility devices

Orientation and mobility training in community travel and safety is essential.

and low vision devices (e.g., monocular) for travel in the home, school, work, or community environments. Visual efficiency skills such as systematic scanning, eccentric viewing, and blur interpretation may be emphasized as appropriate. Instruction in *systematic scanning* helps the child with low vision to use her vision more efficiently while traveling through the environment. For instance, a traveler who is visually impaired may be taught to look far and near, then left and right. This simple system assures that the traveler will not miss important elements in the environment and can anticipate obstacles along the travel path. For example, a person with a severely restricted visual field may be able to see visual targets at a distance better than close-up. When looking for the entrance to a store, the traveler will be able to locate the door when looking "far" and can then anticipate where to find the door even though it seems to vanish as she gets close. *Eccentric viewing* is a technique used to look around scotomas (blind spots) so that the person's most usable vision can be directed forward along the travel path. *Blur interpretation* requires the traveler to use educated guessing together with contextual clues to identify visual targets that may be blurred. For example, by identifying location (near the street corner), determining general shape (octagonal), and noting color (red), the traveler can determine that he is looking at a stop sign even if he cannot see it clearly.

Supporting Access to General Education Curriculum

Many students with visual impairments are able to successfully participate in and learn the general education curriculum. Students are more likely to succeed if they have a strong foundation in specialized skills, an ability to appropriately use specialized materials and equipment, and the confidence to communicate and assert their needs in the general education setting. For example, Victor is able to manage his academic courses at Montclair High School. Victor has low vision and is able to use large-print materials or magnification for many materials with regular print. He

INNOVATIVE IDEAS   HELP WITH THE GROCERIES

The next time you go grocery shopping, make a mental note of the vast array of items that are packaged in cans. Fruits, vegetables, soups, juices, and dog food can all be found among the canned goods. Next, wander through the aisles that have boxes of cereal, cookies, and crackers. Imagine trying to locate your favorite cereal or soup without being able to clearly see the labels. Supermarket shopping can be a frustrating experience for individuals who are blind or visually impaired. Although assistance can be requested for shopping, the individual with a visual impairment still has the challenge of organizing or labeling packages of food in the kitchen cabinets at home for easy access.

Christina Baer, fourth grade student in a Gifted and Talented class, gave this challenge a great deal of thought. While shopping with her mother she wondered if the same scanners used at the check-out stands could be modified to read the information out loud. With the help of her father and Spectra Physics, a company in Eugene, Oregon, she designed a hand-held device that scans bar codes on packaged items and says the name of the product out loud. The prototype, called the HandiScan, has been field tested at the Sensory Access Foundation in Palo Alto. The anticipated distribution price is estimated to range between $1,500 and $1,700.

Originally, Christina thought the device could be attached to shopping carts, but now she thinks it would be more useful in the individual's home. Either way, this innovative idea should help people with visual impairments gain a little more independence.

Source: Information from *San Francisco Chronicle*, October 16, 1995, pp. B–2.

---

keeps a closed circuit television (CCTV) in his language arts classroom, because he does the most reading in that class. He sits up front for class discussions and board-work, but always moves to the station with his CCTV for independent reading. His math materials are typically enlarged and he uses a monocular to follow math problems completed on the board. Victor reminds his social studies teacher that he would like a print copy of the information on the overhead projector. His ability to use specialized materials and equipment and his ability to assert his needs to his teachers have enabled Victor to succeed in the mainstream of high school academics.

It is important that the teacher credentialed in the area of visual impairment be informed as early as possible as to the books, readers, and textbooks that will be used during the year. Books may need to be specially ordered or produced in large print or braille. When possible, teachers should place the orders in the spring of the preceding year, so they will have the needed materials in September at the same time as materials are available for sighted students. During the school year, general educators will be using supplementary materials such as handouts, worksheets, and tests. These materials should also be given as early as possible to the teacher credentialed in the area of visual impairment so that they can be adapted in time for use. Assuring that students with visual impairments have timely access to the general education curriculum requires a good deal of organization, communication, and coordination between the general educator and the teacher credentialed in the area of visual impairment.

Some students who have low vision may use regular print, with or without the use of an optical device. The general educator can assist the student with low vision by using materials with high contrast, easily readable print or font, and even spacing. Avoid giving students with visual impairments purple dittos. A photocopy of the original is much easier to read. If the original is not available, the purple ditto can be darkened by tracing the print with a dark marker, or a filter may be used to increase the contrast and make the print easier to see. Pages that are visually cluttered are difficult to manage. In general, common sense should be used when preparing materials for students with visual impairments.

Teachers will need to clearly verbalize the information that is contained on chalkboards or overheads. Students with low vision may have a great deal of difficulty copying boardwork; it is helpful if the teacher can provide the student with a print copy. Individual classmates can help by describing scenes from movies or plays that are viewed at school.

Students with visual impairments may need additional time to complete in-class assignments and tests. While extra time for testing should be allotted in the schedule, in-class assignments can also be adjusted by reducing the number of exercises, to help keep the student with visual impairments on pace with classmates. Similar considerations may be made for homework assignments, as students with visual impairments may spend twice the time as sighted classmates in completing homework assignments. Expectations for performance should not be lowered, but busywork should be kept at a minimum.

General educators who have a student with a visual impairment placed in their classroom should expect the addition of specialized equipment within the classroom. The teacher credentialed in the area of visual impairment will assume the responsibility for securing the appropriate equipment, and may make suggestions for the most advantageous placement and use of the equipment in the general education setting. General educators can support student access by fostering a

EASY IDEAS FOR PRACTITIONERS

For the Teacher:

1. Organize instructional materials and coordinate ordering of specialized materials with the teacher credentialed in visual impairment.
2. Use printed materials with high contrast, even spacing, and easily readable font for students with low vision.
3. Minimize auditory distractions during instructional time by eliminating unnecessary noises.
4. Provide additional time as needed for the completion of in-class assignments.
5. Foster a sense of respect for the student's specialized equipment and materials among classmates, and encourage students with visual impairments to make their unique educational needs known.
6. Maintain high expectations for student success and work closely with family members and appropriate specialists to assure that opportunities for achievement are being fully realized.
7. Talk to families about opportunities for concrete experiences and concept building within the home and on family outings.

For Parents:

1. Be sure to openly express your expectations and concerns at teacher conferences and IEP, IFSP, or ITP meetings.
2. Be informed about your child's visual impairment so that you can more easily discuss functional implications with the child's teachers.
3. Be aware of the tendency to be overly protective of your child and encourage small steps towards increasing independence.

Some students with visual impairments may need to spend time in a resource room for special instruction.

sense of respect for the specialized equipment in classmates and by encouraging the appropriate use of the equipment suggested by the specially trained teacher.

Suggestions will also be made regarding optimum seating arrangements, to maximize use of natural lighting and to minimize glare. These suggestions are made according to the student's individualized visual and learning needs. For example, a student with a central acuity loss may need to sit near the front in order to increase her ability to use the chalkboard, while a student with a restricted field may need to sit further back so that he can see a larger portion of the board in one glance. In general, all students with low vision should be seated so that illumination is optimum, glare is minimized, and functional use of vision is maximized.

The general educator should also be prepared for the inclusion of other professionals in the student's educational program. On occasion, other specialists (e.g., the O&M specialist) may need to schedule individualized lessons during academic periods. These lessons are equally important to the student's long-term success, and teachers and specialists should work together in developing a schedule that will accommodate all of the student's needs.

FAMILY PERSPECTIVES AND LIFE SPAN ISSUES

While much attention is paid to the development of the individual child with a visual impairment or the adjustment of the adult with an acquired visual impairment, it is important also to consider the relationship between the individual and the social network. The family constitutes one of the most intimate networks, and so the presence of a disability becomes a shared experience (Nixon, 1994). Through the life span, families will experience many transitions and critical events that may prove to be stressful, but ultimately rewarding. For instance, consider this family's experience:

The Johnson family was anxiously awaiting the arrival of triplets. The family of three was soon to become a family of six and there was much to do to prepare. Everyone was greatly surprised when the triplets were born 2 months early. The premature newborns were placed in incubators because of their very low birth weight. Monica, the smallest of the three infants, was the last to come home. Upon her first checkup she was diagnosed with retinopathy of prematurity (ROP). The ROP resulted in severe visual impairment, leaving Monica with only light perception in both eyes.

The Johnson family, who had been so diligent in preparing for the arrival of triplets, was not prepared for this. They rolled through waves of emotions, sometimes with a crash of anger: "How could this have happened?!" Sometimes they simply felt inadequate, wondering how they would be able to take care of a child who is blind. They wondered if Monica would grow up happy and healthy alongside her brothers and sister.

The Johnsons felt isolated from family and friends, and all of their energies seemed to be devoted to the care of the children and finding services for Monica. At first, they were hesitant to attend a family support group for parents and siblings of children with visual impairments. In the end, they were glad they went. Not only had they formed lifelong friendships, but they also received much needed support and important information on advocating for their child's needs in the educational system.

Families With Infants, Toddlers, and Preschool Children

Upon the birth of a child with a visual impairment, the family begins a complex adjustment process, wading through a flood of changing emotions. The diagnosis of blindness, whether it is at birth or in later years, is a critical event for the family. The reality of the disability and its impact on the family sets in when the child is brought home from the hospital. Some families experience a sense of isolation and must deal with the reactions of extended family, friends, and persons in the community. Families must also deal with the myriad of potential medical and early intervention services that are available. The **Individualized Family Service Plan (IFSP)** was instituted to assist families of infants and toddlers in the coordination of early intervention services and is developed with family members to assure that their needs are being met. Many families benefit from parent and sibling support groups organized by other parents of children with visual impairments. While early intervention and family support services are commonly home-based for very young children and their families, center-based programs for infants, toddlers, and preschoolers are also available. All too soon the family will begin the search for an appropriate educational setting for their growing child. The home-to-school transition can be a very stressful time for many families of children who have visual impairments.

Families With School-Age Children

One of the first things that the family must become accustomed to in the school system is the process of developing the **Individualized Education Program (IEP).** Parents are essential members of the IEP team and their active participation should be encouraged and always respected. Over the course of the child's education, there will be many decisions to make, many professionals to work with, and many adjustments to make when transitioning between classroom and school placements.

Puberty may be a particularly stressful critical event for families of children who are blind or who have low vision. Issues associated with dating and sexuality can be stressful for any family, but when the child is blind parents may have

Children with visual impairments can participate in household chores.

additional concerns or fears: "Will my child be able to develop a social network of peers?" "Who will date my son or daughter?"

Another critical event that may evoke a good deal of stress in the teenager who is visually impaired occurs around age 16 when peers start driving. Driving is an integral part of American culture. For teenagers, cars are equated with prestige. Driving is also associated with more successful dating, improved social skills, and increased sense of control. In a survey of 2,500 students between the ages of 14 and 18, it was found that obtaining a driver's license was identified as the most important event in high school, followed by attendance at the senior prom (Corn & Sacks, 1994). Being a nondriver, with its associated hassle and frustrations, is an issue that will stay with an individual with visual impairments throughout the life span.

Families Preparing for Their Child's Transition to Adulthood

Families prepare their children for adulthood when personal and family responsibilities are established. Secure relationships within the family set the stage for realistic expectations in future relationships with peers and other significant people. The same is true for families with children who are visually impaired.

It is important for families to expect children who are visually impaired to have personal and family responsibilities. Participation in household chores should be encouraged early on, and as the child matures he or she should be given opportunities for increasing personal responsibility in preparation for independence in adulthood.

The transition from school to work, from childhood to adulthood, is challenging to say the least. The **Individualized Transition Plan (ITP)** is a formalized approach to support families and prepare students with disabilities for that transition. The ITP encourages a representative from the Department of Vocational Rehabilitation to participate in the teenager's educational and vocational planning. This is especially important for students with visual impairments who will utilize rehabilitation services for support in postsecondary education, vocational training, independent living, and employment.

This middle school student may need a little extra time to negotiate busy hallways.

CURRENT ISSUES AND FUTURE TRENDS

Maintaining Specialized Services

The educational needs of children who are visually impaired are diverse yet unique. Their needs can only be fully met by maintaining an array of program options within which high-quality specialized services, equipment, and materials are made available. In light of the current fiscal climate at both the federal and state levels, budgetary cuts in general education and special education may be imminent, and low incidence disability areas will certainly feel the effect.

　　Recruitment and training of professionals will most likely continue to be an important issue well into the future. Silberman, Corn, and Sowell (1996) have validated the threat to personnel preparation, in the area of visual impairment, brought about by fiscal cutbacks and balanced budget initiatives. Personnel shortages directly impact the quantity and quality of specialized instruction received by students who are blind and visually impaired. In order to appropriately serve students from culturally and linguistically diverse backgrounds, recruitment efforts must also attract individuals from underrepresented cultural groups into the field of visual impairment and blindness.

Braille Literacy

Braille is the basic reading and writing medium for individuals who are blind and is the primary means for developing literacy. There has been a national decline in braille literacy. The American Printing House for the Blind (cited in Wittenstein,

1994) has reported a recent dramatic increase in persons with visual impairments registered as "nonreaders." While professionals and consumers have recognized the problem, little agreement has been reached on the causes of this increased braille illiteracy in the United States (Wittenstein, 1994).

In the 1990s approximately 14 states have passed legislation to promote braille literacy in the schools for children who are legally blind. Efforts have been aimed at assuring that all students who are legally blind be provided with the opportunity to learn to read and write braille. An important aspect of assuring this opportunity is to also ensure that appropriately trained teachers are available to teach braille. A portion of the responsibility rests with university personnel preparation programs. Universities that train teachers to teach children who are blind and visually impaired must impart competence in the use of braille and, more importantly, competence in teaching braille to students with visual impairments. However, merely training teachers to be highly skilled in teaching braille is not sufficient unless more materials are accessible in braille format.

Unemployment Rates

While there are individuals with visual impairments who are successful doctors, lawyers, teachers, sports broadcasters, corporate executives, homemakers, salespersons, and entrepreneurs, it has been estimated that as many as 70% of working-age persons who are visually impaired are either unemployed or underemployed (Kirchner & Peterson, 1989). The unemployment rate for persons with congenital visual impairments is estimated to be even higher—80% to 90%. Career development and transition planning must start earlier and become a more integral part of the educational program of each child with visual impairments. There must be stronger linkages between the areas of education and rehabilitation. Communities must work together to support greater opportunities for quality employment for individuals who are blind and visually impaired.

Technology

Technological advances seem to make larger and larger strides, sometimes surpassing the capabilities of the individuals for whom the technology was originally designed. Many recent advances in technology have benefited individuals with visual impairments, including the increased portability of technology in general, the capability of interfacing synthesized speech and braille technology with computer technology, and the ability to convert and exchange reading and writing materials from braille to print to speech in various combinations.

Individuals who are visually impaired now have access to computer screens by using screen magnification products, by interfacing synthesized speech technology to read the text on screens, or by inputting braille into computers and translating the code into print. However, on the information superhighway there are accessibility issues. With the current emphasis on multimedia presentations, graphic displays present a new challenge to computer users who are visually impaired. For individuals who use synthesized speech technology for computer access, the challenge is how to develop programs that can coherently translate Windows-based visual operating systems. Programs must be able to effectively identify application and document windows, translate dialogue boxes, read multiple-column menus, and identify visual icons. An efficient alternative for use of the mouse (which is dependent on eye–hand coordination) is also needed (Leven-

There are many products which accommodate computer use by people with visual impairments.

thal, 1995). Computer users with low vision are also faced with accessibility challenges within the Windows work environment. Screen magnification products are available, but they do not alleviate all of the problems associated with graphical user interface systems (Shragai, 1995; Shragai & Uslan, 1995). Poor screen color contrasts, icons that are difficult to decipher, and mouse pointers that are tedious to track across the computer screen present additional obstacles.

It is also a challenge for teachers to maintain current knowledge in the expanding realm of specialized technology. By the time that a new piece of specialized equipment can be purchased and the teacher and student become trained in its use, it may have been replaced by a newer version. It is always a challenge to keep pace with the changing face of technology in our society; the challenge is even greater when that technology is specialized for a low incidence population.

Five-Minute Summary

The field of visual impairment and blindness has a rich history in providing a range of educational programs to meet the individualized needs of this heterogeneous population. There are many potential causes of visual impairment, and early screenings are crucial to providing timely medical interventions. While clinical measurements of vision are important for legal classifications and for the prescription of optical devices, functional vision assessments are used to form decisions regarding the education of students with visual impairments.

The most appropriate placement (MAP) for any student with a visual impairment should be based on both developmental needs and disability-specific needs. Educational placements are a team decision, made on an individualized basis. Success in general education settings is supported by a strong foundation in specialized skills taught by the teacher credentialed in the area of visual impairment and by the orientation and mobility (O&M) specialist. Families are an integral part of the educational process and deserve both respect and support in their efforts to work with their children with visual impairments through the many critical events and transitions to come.

Study Questions

1. Identify three key figures who have made contributions to the field of visual impairment and blindness. Discuss how their contributions have impacted the education of children with visual impairments.
2. What is the legal definition of blindness? What are the two areas of visual functioning that must be considered in the legal classification?
3. Identify three possible causes of visual impairment common in children.
4. How is central visual acuity commonly measured? Explain in words what is meant by a visual acuity of 20/100.
5. What are the major effects of congenital blindness on social development, language development, and motor development?
6. Why is visual impairment considered to be a low incidence disability?
7. Which two professionals should perform a functional low vision assessment, and how are the orientations of the two assessments different?
8. Describe the elements of a general education environment that is supportive of access for students with visual impairments.
9. Why might age 16 be a particularly stressful time for students with visual impairments and their families?
10. Identify some of the current issues in the field of visual impairment and blindness.

For More Information

ORGANIZATIONS

American Council of the Blind
1010 Vermont Avenue, N.W., Suite 1100
Washington, DC 20005
202-393-3666

American Foundation for the Blind
11 Penn Plaza, Suite 300
New York, NY 10001
212-502-7600   800-AFB-LINE

Association for Educational and Rehabilitation of the Blind and Visually Impaired
206 North Washington Street
Alexandria, VA 22314
703-548-1884

Division for the Visually Handicapped
Council for Exceptional Children
1920 Association Drive
Reston, VA 22091
703-620-3660

National Association for Parents of the Visually Impaired
2180 Linway Drive
Beloit, WI 53511-2720
608-362-4945   800-652-6265

National Federation of the Blind
1800 Johnson Street
Baltimore, MD 21230
301-659-9314

BOOKS AND ARTICLES

Bernstein, J. (1988). *Loving Rachel: A parent's journey from grief.* Boston: Little, Brown.

Bradley-Johnson, S. (1986). *Psychoeducational assessment of visually impaired children and blind students.* New York: American Foundation for the Blind.

Corn, A. L., & Koenig, A. J. (1996). *Foundations of low vision: Clinical and functional perspectives.* New York: American Foundation for the Blind.

Dodson-Burk, B., & Hill, E. W. (1989). *An orientation and mobility primer for families and young children.* New York: American Foundation for the Blind.

Ferrell, K. A. (1985). *Reach out and teach: Meeting the training needs of parents of visually and multiply handicapped young children.* New York: American Foundation for the Blind.

Goldberg, S. (1982). *Ophthalmology made ridiculously simple*. Miami, FL: Medical Master.

Harrell, L., & Akeson, N. (1987). *Preschool vision stimulation: It's more than a flashlight!* New York: American Foundation for the Blind.

Hazekamp, J., & Huebner, K. M. (1989). *Program planning and evaluation for blind and visually impaired students: National guidelines for educational excellence.* New York: American Foundation for the Blind.

Isenberg, S. J. (1989). *The eye in infancy.* Chicago: Year Book Medical Publishers.

Jose, R. T. (1983). *Understanding low vision.* New York: American Foundation for the Blind.

Mangold, S. S. (1982). *A teacher's guide to the special education needs of blind and visually impaired children.* New York: American Foundation for the Blind.

Pogrund, R. L., Fazzi, D. L., & Lampert, J. S. (1992). *Early focus: Working with young blind and visually impaired children and their families.* New York: American Foundation for the Blind.

Scholl, G. T. (1986). *Foundations of education for blind and visually handicapped children and youth.* New York: American Foundation for the Blind.

Swallow, R., & Huebner, K. M. (1987). *How to thrive, not just survive.* New York: American Foundation for the Blind.

Tuttle, D. W. (1984). *Self esteem and adjusting with blindness.* Springfield, IL: Thomas.

Vaughan, D. G., Asbury, T., & Riordan-Eva, P. (1992). *General ophthalmology* (13th ed.). East Norwalk, CT: Appleton & Lange.

Warren, D. H. (1984). *Blindness and early childhood development* (2nd ed. rev.). New York: American Foundation for the Blind.

JOURNALS, NEWSLETTERS, AND OTHER PUBLICATIONS

Journal of Visual Impairment & Blindness
AFB Press

49 Sheridan Avenue
Albany, NY 12210

RE:view
Heldref Publications
1319 18th Street, N. W.
Washington, DC 20036-1802

OTHER SOURCES

AFB Press
American Foundation for the Blind
49 Sheridan Avenue
Albany, NY 12210

American Printing House for the Blind (APH)
1839 Frankfort Avenue
Louisville, KY 40206
502-895-2405

Exceptional Teaching Aids
20102 Woodbine Avenue
Castro Valley, CA 94546
415-582-4859

Helen Keller National Center for Deaf-Blind Youths and Adults
111 Middle Neck Road
Sand Points, NY 11050
516-944-8900 (voice and TDD)

Howe Press
Perkins School for the Blind
175 North Beacon Street
Watertown, MA 02172
617-924-3434

National Library Services for the Blind and Physically Handicapped
Library of Congress
1291 Taylor Street, N.W.
Washington, DC 20542
202-707-5100   800-424-9100

Recordings for the Blind and Dyslexic
20 Roszel Road
Princeton, NJ 08540
609-452-0606

References

American Printing House for the Blind (1995). *Annual report: June 1, 1994–June 30, 1995*, Louisville, KY: Author.

Ayres, A. J. (1979). *Sensory integration and the child*. Los Angeles: Western Psychological Services.

Bledsoe, C. W. (1980). Originators of orientation and mobility training. In R. L. Welsh & B. B. Blasch (Eds.), *Foundations of orientation and mobility* (pp. 581–624). New York: American Foundation for the Blind.

Bolduc, M., Gresset, J., Sanschagrin, S., & Thibodeau, J. (1993). A model for the efficient interdisciplinary assessment of young visually impaired children. *Journal of Visual Impairment & Blindness, 87*(10), 410–414.

Bradley-Johnson, S. (1986). *Psychoeducational assessment of visually impaired and blind students: Infancy through high school*. Austin, TX: PRO-ED.

Brambring, M., & Troster, H. (1994). The assessment of cognitive development in blind infants and preschoolers. *Journal of Visual Impairment & Blindness, 88*(1), 9–18.

California Department of Education. (in press). *Program guidelines for students who are visually impaired*. Sacramento: California Department of Education.

Chernus-Manfield, N., Hayashi, D., Kekelis, L. S. (1985). *Talk to me II: Common concerns*. Los Angeles: Blind Children's Center.

Corn, A. L. (1983). Visual function: A theoretical model for individuals with low vision. *Journal of Visual Impairment & Blindness, 77*, 373–377.

Corn, A. L., & Koenig, A. J. (1996). Perspectives on low vision. In *Foundations of low vision: Clinical and functional perspectives* (pp. 1–21). New York: American Foundation for the Blind.

Corn, A. L., & Sacks, S. Z. (1994). The impact of nondriving on adults with visual impairments. *Journal of Visual Impairment & Blindness, 88*(1), 53–68.

Curry, S. A., & Hatlen, P. H. (1988). Meeting the unique educational needs of visually impaired pupils through appropriate placement. *Journal of Visual Impairment & Blindness, 82*(10), 417–424.

Duckworth, B. J. (1993). Adapting standardized academic tests in braille and large type. *Journal of Visual Impairment & Blindness, 87*(10), 405–407.

Erin, J. N. (1986). Frequencies and types of questions in the language of visually impaired children. *Journal of Visual Impairment & Blindness, 80*, 670–674.

Federal Register. (1991, November 18). Department of Education proposed funding priorities for the National Institute on Disability and Rehabilitation Research for fiscal years 1992–93 (Vol. 58, No. 222, pp. 58280–58290). Washington, DC: U.S. Government Printing Office.

Goldberg, S. (1993). *Ophthalmology made ridiculously simple*. Miami: MedMaster.

Good, W. V., James, E. J., DeSa, L., Barkovich, A. J., Groenveld, M., & Hoyt, C. S. (1994). Cortical visual impairment in children. *Survey of Ophthalmology, 38*(4), 351–364.

Isenberg, S. J. (1989). *The eye in infancy*. Chicago: Year Book Medical Publishers.

Isenberg, S. J. (1992). Vision focus: Understanding the medical and functional implications of vision loss in young blind and visually impaired children. In R. L. Pogrund, D. L. Fazzi, & J. S. Lampert (Eds.), *Early focus: Working with young blind and visually impaired children and their families* (pp. 19–23). New York: American Foundation for the Blind.

Kekelis, L. S. (1992). Peer interactions in childhood: The impact of visual impairment. In S. Z. Sacks, L. S. Kekelis, & R. J. Gaylord-Ross (Eds.), *The development of social skills by blind and visually impaired students: Exploratory studies and strategies* (pp. 13–35). New York: American Foundation for the Blind.

Kirchner, C., & Peterson, R. (1989). Employment: Selected characteristics. In C. Kirchner (Ed.), *Blindness and visual impairment in the U.S.* New York: American Foundation for the Blind.

Lampert, J. S. (1992). Movement focus: Orientation and mobility for young blind and visually impaired children. In R. L. Pogrund, D. L. Fazzi, & J. S. Lampert (Eds.), *Early focus: Working with young blind and visually impaired children and their families* (pp. 88–94). New York: American Foundation for the Blind.

Levanthal, J. D. (1995). Accessing Microsoft Windows with synthetic speech: An overview. *Journal of Visual Impairment & Blindness News Service, 89*(3), 14–18.

Nelson, K. A., & Dimitrova, E. (1993). Severe visual impairment in the United States and in each state, 1990. *Journal of Visual Impairment & Blindness, 87*(3), 80–85.

Nixon, H. L., II (1994). Looking sociologically at family coping with visual impairment. *Journal of Visual Impairment & Blindness, 88*(4), 329–337.

Roberts, F. K. (1986). Education for the visually handicapped: A social and educational history. In G. T. Scholl (Ed.), *Foundations of education for blind and visually handicapped children and youth* (pp. 1–18). New York: American Foundation for the Blind.

Scholl, G. T. (1986). What does it mean to be blind? In G. T. Scholl (Ed.), *Foundations of education for blind and visually handicapped children and youth* (pp. 23–34). New York: American Foundation for the Blind.

Shragai, Y. (1995). Access to Microsoft Windows 95 for persons with low vision: An overview. *Journal of Visual Impairment & Blindness News Service, 89*(6), 5–9.

Shragai, Y., & Uslan, M. M. (1995). Access to Microsoft Windows for persons with low vision: An overview. *Journal of Visual Impairment & Blindness News Service, 89*(5), 13–16.

Silberman, R. K., Corn, A. L., & Sowell, V. M. (1996). Teacher educators and the future of personnel preparation programs for serving students with visual impairments. *Journal of Visual Impairment & Blindness, 90*(2), 115–124.

Spungin, S. J., & Taylor, J. L. (1986). The teacher. In G. T. Scholl (Ed.), *Foundations of education for blind and visually handicapped children and youth* (pp. 255–264). New York: American Foundation for the Blind.

Trief, E., Duckman, R., Morse, A. R., & Silberman, R. K. (1989). Retinopathy of prematurity. *Journal of Visual Impairment & Blindness, 83*(10), 500–504.

Ward, M. E. (1986). The visual system. In G. T. Scholl (Ed.), *Foundations of education for blind and visually handicapped children and youth* (pp. 35–64). New York: American Foundation for the Blind.

Warren, D. (1984). *Blindness and early childhood development* (2nd ed. rev.). New York: American Foundation for the Blind.

Wittenstein, S. H. (1994). Braille literacy: Preservice training and teachers' attitudes. *Journal of Visual Impairment & Blindness, 88*(6), 516–524.

Chapter 10

Red Mountain, acrylic on canvas, 16″ × 20″ (1991)

PHYSICAL DISABILITIES AND OTHER HEALTH IMPAIRMENTS

Stephen Conley and Laura Vogtle

After studying this chapter, the reader will:

Have an awareness of a variety of conditions that affect general physical functioning and cognitive capacities of persons with disabilities

Gain an appreciation of the social impact of various physical and health impairments

Know the basic history of educational and legal events in the U.S. affecting persons with disabilities

Know the causes of the most common conditions that affect physical and health status of children and young adults with disabilities

Understand the importance of regular and ongoing communication among allied health professionals, educators, and parents regarding persons with disabilities, and the importance of including the student in decision making

Acquire an overview of information important for those who work with persons having physical challenges

Identify current trends and developments in the educational and treatment realm for persons with disabilities

Be familiar with sources of additional services and material on specific diagnostic categories

Physical Disabilities and Other Health Impairments

2000 B.C. Egyptian engravings depicted individuals with obvious physical disabilities.

1770 B.C. Chinese literature described epileptic seizures.

460–370 B.C. Hippocrates and his followers described epilepsy diagnosis and treatment.

1407 Medical descriptions of cerebral palsy were included in texts for physicians.

1852 A few public schools in Massachusetts included special classes for "crippled" children.

1904 Meyer reported slowness of thought and difficulty with concentration as symptoms of traumatic brain injury (TBI).

1918 Neurosurgery became recognized as a medical specialty as a consequence of World War I. The first hospital to specialize in head injury rehabilitation was established in Cape May, New Jersey.

1949 The United Cerebral Palsy Association was founded.

1988 Technology-Related Assistance for Individuals With Disabilities Act was passed.

1990 The cystic fibrosis gene was isolated.

1990 Traumatic brain injury was added to list of impairments covered under the Individuals With Disabilities Education Act (IDEA).

1994 Technology-Related Assistance for Individuals With Disabilities Act was reauthorized.

INTRODUCTION

This chapter examines some of the most commonly seen physical disabilities and health impairments in children and young adults. Each condition is discussed in terms of its definition, cause and incidence, types and distribution, associated problems and challenges, and specific issues for teachers of these children. We begin with the neurological impairments of cerebral palsy and spina bifida and then review Duchenne's muscular dystrophy, one of the most familiar neuromuscular diseases. Next we discuss other health impairments and disabilities that result from trauma.

HISTORICAL OVERVIEW

Individuals with physical disabilities and health impairments such as epilepsy and cerebral palsy have been documented in art and written works throughout the earliest development of civilization. Egyptian engravings from around 2000 B.C depict individuals with obvious physical impairments. One sculpture has been reported to show an individual with *spastic diplegia*, a specifically identifiable type of cerebral palsy (Christensen & Melchior, 1967). Mayan sculptures have also been discovered with representations of physical disablilities.

Late in the 4th century B.C. (460–370), Hippocrates (the father of medicine) and his followers described epilepsy as a brain disorder in a series of writings titled *On the Sacred Disease*. Penfield, an early researcher of epilepsy, described this series of observations as the most accurate descriptions of the brain until the work of John Hughlings Jackson—known as the father of English neurology—in the 19th century (Bennett, 1992). The development and use of bromide as a treatment for epileptic seizures was documented in 1857 in England by Edward Sieveking; and in 1912, Hauptmann, a German, described the use of barbiturates as a treatment for epilepsy.

The first extensive medical writing on cerebral palsy is generally attributed to William J. Little (1861), the senior physician of London Hospital and founder of the Royal Orthopaedic Hospital. He has been recognized as the first to describe cerebral palsy as a multiple disabling condition (Wolf, 1969). Little was one of the original developers of modern physical rehabilitation treatments for those with cerebral palsy. More than 130 years ago he developed a treatment regimen that included manipulations, massage, baths, gymnastics, and mechanical instruments (braces, splints, belts, etc.) in addition to surgery (Wolf, 1969). For a while these neurological conditions were even identified in the literature with his name: *Little's disease*. As medical observations and academic debate increased it became obvious that the condition wasn't a progressive disease and Little's name was also subsequently dropped as the diagnostic term for this group of physical disabilities.

Society has struggled throughout history with individuals who have distinct variations in physical appearance and behavior. Scheer and Groce (1988) point out that some cultures, believing that such children represented evil spirits, would place infants with disabilities in unprotected environments so that they would die. Today in some countries children with disabilities are put out on the street to beg in hopes that their disability will engender sympathy; and children without disabilities have sometimes been maimed by their guardians to increase their income potential on the street.

"By far the most difficult obstacle I have been forced to overcome is having cerebral palsy, a physical disability that impairs my walking, speech and motor control. When I was diagnosed with CP at the age of 15 months, nobody knew if I would ever be able to walk, communicate effectively, or have the intellectual capacity that I do today. By the age of 2, my parents were taking me, multiple times each week, to speech, physical and occupational therapy at a local rehabilitation center. Although I have sufficiently decreased the amount of time I spend at the rehab center, I continue to improve my skills as a result of being treated by my lifelong therapy team of occupational, physical, and speech therapists.

"Most children start walking when they are about a year old and begin talking before they are 2. I could not really communicate with people other than my parents until I was 5, and I couldn't walk without assistance until I was 8 years old. I did not learn how to fully dress myself and wash my hair until I was 9 and 10. I have only just recently been able to put on my own shoes and cut up my food. Perhaps the most important lesson I have learned from having CP is that people, especially those with disabilities, can continue learning and improving their skills throughout their lives.

"An equally important lesson to learn is that being disabled didn't interfere with reaching my academic potential. My family was fortunate enough to be able to send me to small schools (in which I was usually the only disabled student) where teachers and administrators could cater to my individual needs. They didn't allow me to 'get lost' in the midst of many other students. Instead of creating an entirely different academic plan for me, they helped me where my physical limitations made it difficult to do the work at the same speed as the other kids. At an early age I learned how to operate a computer in order to compensate for my poor handwriting skills. As my speech improved, I verbalized answers on worksheets and short assignments so that I wouldn't have to take the time to type (though I have gradually learned to become a fairly proficient typist). My parents, teachers, and I soon realized that I could be held to the same academic standards as everyone else.

"Finally, I have learned to accept my disability and to ignore those people who won't. This is partly because I have been in small schools where I am valued as a person and not ridiculed because of a birth defect that I have no control over. I feel that I am living proof of the statement: 'It's what's on the inside that counts.' I now understand that people who don't know the real me don't have a right to make fun of me. Most people who poke fun at people based on appearances are really unhappy and insecure about themselves. Although every teenager has moments of insecurity and often wishes they were different, I am able to look anyone in the eye and say that I am happy to be Kelly."

Kelly, age 18, is a high school student.

More positive views of individuals with physical disabilities have existed in other cultures. Some societies have honored those with disabilities as having special powers, although Scheer and Groce (1988) indicate that this practice was probably not as widespread as commonly believed. They cite a number of examples of less modernized cultures in which people with disabilities were valued members, giving support to the World Health Organization's view that a disability becomes a handicap only when the larger society assigns limitations to people with disabilities.

Throughout history, crises have brought significant social change, and often wars have provided the stimuli for rehabilitation and vocational services. For instance, the U.S. Civil War, with all of its destruction, nonetheless advanced surgical techniques for traumas and fostered extensive use of adaptive devices for individuals with physical disabilities. Federal laws to facilitate the rehabilitation and vocational training of individuals with disabilities were instituted after World War I in efforts aiding veterans injured in the war. In 1917 the Vocational Education (Smith-Hughes) Act (P.L. 64-347) created the Federal Board for Vocational Education. This law was amended to provide for planning of vocational retraining for injured veterans. In 1918 the Soldiers (Veterans) Rehabilitation Act (P.L. 65-178) was passed, providing additional emphasis for the development of medical rehabilitation services for those injured while serving in our armed services (Reed, 1992).

Recognition of the physical and behavioral effects of injury to the brain is relatively recent. Specialized care for people with brain injuries first began during World War I. This was when neurosurgery arose as a recognized medical specialty. In the 1930s, educators recognized that some students who had been labeled as mentally retarded had suffered traumas that could be the cause of their learning problems. The diagnostic category of *minimal brain damage (MBD)* was used to label large numbers of children until the mid-1980s, when *attention deficit disorder (ADD)* replaced the term.

The first reported efforts to remediate or rehabilitate children with disabilities began early in the 20th century. The first physicians and therapists to take an active interest in rehabilitative treatment of children with cerebral palsy and other physical disabilities were located in Boston. At the turn of the century in the neurology department of Children's Hospital of Boston, Jennie Colby directed the original treatment clinic for children with physical disabilities. Colby, a gymnast by training, is considered the mother of cerebral palsy treatment and a pioneer in modern physical therapy (Wolf, 1969). Winthrop Phelps, another principal contributor to medical and therapeutic interventions for individuals with neurological impairments, trained at Children's Hospital of Boston. In 1937 he founded the Children's Rehabilitation Institute at Cockeysville, Maryland. Phelps is credited with popularizing the term *cerebral palsy*. He observed improvements in the functioning of children with physical disabilities when they received comprehensive rehabilitative interventions through surgical, bracing, and other therapeutic treatments. Phelps and his innovative staff prescribed medical and surgical intervention for children with cerebral palsy. These prescriptions were carried out by the child's parents, who received training at the facility, or by therapeutic professionals in the child's home community. From the late 1930s to the early 1960s, it continued to be necessary for children with cerebral palsy and other physical disabilities and their families to travel long distances for rehabilitative assessment and treatment.

The movement to provide special education services for children with physical disabilities and health impairments has been uneven, at best, across the nation. Although compulsory education for general education students had expanded to all states by 1918, children with complex health care needs have historically been educated outside regular classrooms and schools with home-based instruction. In 1852, Massachusetts had a few public schools that included special classes for "crippled" children (Mullins, 1986). In Chicago, day programs for "crippled children and youth" began in 1896 (Mullins, 1986). Nevertheless, formal facilities and programs for students with physical disabilities or multiple disabilities were not common until well into the 20th century. However, in the past several years children with severe physical disabilities have been served alongside their peers without disabilities. This development was initially driven by the Education for All Handicapped Children Act of 1975 (P.L. 94-142) and its support for the least restrictive environment. Students with special needs—including tube feeding, manual or machine suctioning, apnea monitoring, mechanical ventilation, supplemental oxygen, or other medically-related interventions—are now attending regular classes

Students who use wheelchairs are now being accommodated in mainstream classrooms.

within public schools (Lehr, 1993). This movement has rapidly and significantly changed the standards expected of all educators both within and outside of special education.

Lehr (1993) has identified several factors influencing the increase in school-based education of children with complex health care needs. These factors include medical technological advances, greater acceptance of the principle of normalization, expanding school services for children with communicable diseases, and increasing numbers of programs for young children with severe disabilities. Technological advances have increased the portability of many devices for specific health care needs. Ventilators are now routinely attached to powered wheelchairs. Oxygen tanks are much lighter than previous models and may be carried with children almost anywhere they wish to travel. In addition, battery packs allow children with special health care needs to travel outdoors and into their communities without need for direct electrical connections.

Advances in medical technology have also enabled children with severe health-related conditions, who in years past were hospitalized for their care, to be treated in their own homes. Furthermore, new medical and pharmaceutical technologies have allowed more children to survive conditions that were previously fatal at infancy. But while more of these infants are surviving, they are surviving with serious physical or health-related impairments. The special education and rehabilitation needs of such children and young adults are now being addressed in integrated environments. Educational services are advancing in tandem with the medical and technological sciences.

Twentieth-century Western culture places much importance on personal appearance and autonomy (Hahn, 1988). There is also evidence that children in particular prefer to be with others who are similar to themselves, either by race, ethnicity, or gender. Studies (Bromfield, Weisz, & Messer, 1986; Graffi & Minnes, 1988; Howes, 1988; Weinberg, 1978) have shown that by age 4 to 5 years, children are aware that there are differences in how physical differences impact on play skills, and they tend to choose playmates without such differences. Cole (1986) noted that children without disabilities chose to interact more with other children who had cognitive disabilities than those with severe physical disabilities. His study showed that more effort and patience were necessary for the children without disabilities to interact with other children who had more difficulty with vocalizations. These findings reflect a continuing level of intolerance within our society for people with physical disabilities or mental retardation.

DEFINITIONS

Physical disabilities are acquired or congenital impairments of the body's neurological or muscular systems that affect basic movement functions. Some examples of specific physically disabling diagnoses include cerebral palsy, spina bifida, muscular dystrophy, and juvenile rheumatoid arthritis. **Health impairments** under IDEA, the Individuals With Disabilities Education Act of 1990 (P.L. 101-476), are defined as conditions that require ongoing medical attention. Medical attention may be provided for children with limited strength, vitality, or alertness due to chronic or acute health problems. Examples of health impairments include leukemia and other cancers, AIDS, epilepsy, and asthma. Students in today's classrooms may have physical disabilities in combination with complex health impairments, such as the child with spina bifida who may also have a spinal curvature and respiratory difficulties.

    Developmental disabilities as a category of individuals with disabilities first appeared in federal legislation in 1970 with the Services and Facilities Construction Act (Reed, 1992). The definition opened eligibility for services to include individuals with cerebral palsy, autism, epilepsy, and mental retardation. The definition identified developmental disabilities as a severe chronic disability with the following characteristics:

1. Attributable to a mental or physical impairment or combination of mental and physical impairments

2. Manifested before the person attains age 22

3. Likely to continue indefinitely

4. Resulting in substantial functional limitations in three or more of the following areas of major life activity: self-care, receptive and expressive language, learning, mobility, self-direction, capacity for independent living, and economic sufficiency

5. Reflective of a need for a combination and sequence of special interdisciplinary or generic care, treatment, or other services, which are of lifelong or extended duration and are planned and coordinated

    Individuals with health impairments and physical disabilities often face emotional and environmental challenges at an early age. Pain, surgeries, and other invasive procedures, restrictions to activity and diet, and continual medication (often with unpleasant side effects) are some of the trials that persons with physical disabilities and other health impairments must regularly endure.

    Children with physical disabilities and health impairments grow up with influences and stresses different from their peers without disabilities. Children born with special needs are usually involved in lifelong medical treatment. Socially, this may mean that these children are exposed to adults more than to other children. This may affect how they engage with children at large. Their social cues may vary, altered by differences in communication modes and exposure to intense life experiences. Many studies document social skill deficits in children with severe disabilities. Societal attitudes may push children with special health needs or physical disabilities to meet norms for which they are not socially prepared.

Part of the impact of severe physical disabilities on the socialization of young children is the high degree of physical dependence on parents or caretakers. Many of these conditions require parental assistance throughout the child's developmental years. Achieving emotional independence from parents who are by necessity in a position of power over their children is not easy; neither is the development of a satisfactory level of self-esteem. In most societies individuals are not judged as competent if they cannot perform routine tasks such as eating independently or changing position without assistance.

The following sections of this chapter will cover specific diagnoses and categories of the most common physical disabilities. Children with these medically-driven diagnostic labels often have need for specific educational and rehabilitative approaches to foster their development. Understanding the range of abilities within each diagnostic category should enable teachers to devise innovative and efficient teaching strategies. Recognizing characteristics of students with each distinct condition should also increase awareness of the uniqueness of individual children with these physical disabilities.

NEUROLOGICAL DISABILITIES

Cerebral Palsy

Cerebral palsy is a condition caused by an injury or insult to the brain. The injury may occur before, during, or soon after birth, and causes disorganized communication between the brain and muscles. Cerebral palsy is not a disease, because the brain lesions do not get progressively worse. Problems with posture (the ability to hold the body upright) and control of movement result from the damage to the brain. These problems cause functional limitations such as problems with walking, talking, hand use, grooming, hygiene, dressing, and feeding activities. A broad range of disability exists within the condition, from minimal to profound effects. There is no cure for cerebral palsy, but therapy interventions (occupational, physical, and speech therapy), medical treatments and surgeries, and technological adaptations can increase the functional abilities of persons with the condition.

Cause and Incidence. The general consensus is that 2 to 3 of every 1,000 live births will have cerebral palsy (Capute & Accardo, 1991; Molnar, 1991). There is a higher incidence in multiple births (Laplaza, Root, Tassanawipas, & Cervera, 1992), in part because these pregnancies tend to be delivered before term.

A variety of factors have been implicated as causes for cerebral palsy. Up to 45% of children with cerebral palsy are born prematurely or are classified as smaller than expected at birth. Loss of oxygen to the brain after birth accounts for about 25% of the population (Blackman, 1990). Other contributing factors in descending order of frequency are perinatal and congenital infections, exposure to toxins, genetic factors, brain malformations, and endocrine disorders. In many cases the exact cause of the disorder cannot be identified.

Cerebral palsy itself is not fatal. However, severely affected children may have associated conditions that can cause death—such as respiratory complications,

Table 10.1   **Types of Cerebral Palsy**

DEGREE OF SEVERITY	DESCRIPTION
*monoplegia**	One extremity is primarily affected, with mild involvement in other body parts.
hemiplegia	Primary involvement is on one side of the body.
diplegia	The entire body is affected, but the legs more than the arms.
*paraplegia**	Only the legs are involved (very rare).
*triplegia**	Three extremities are more severely involved; one extremity is mildly impaired.
quadriplegia	All of the body is affected, including the head, arms, legs, and trunk.

*The pure conditions of monoplegia, paraplegia, and triplegia are rarely seen.

feeding problems, epileptic complications, or choking from inhalation of liquids or food. The frequent operations performed on individuals with cerebral palsy carry the anesthetic risks that are always associated with surgery.

Types and Distribution.   Children with cerebral palsy can have distinctly different types of movement disorders, depending on where in the brain the lesions occur. Movement disorders involve muscle tone which is either too stiff or loose for easy movement. These disorders cause involuntary motion or difficulty in voluntary movements. The most common types of movement disorders are described in the following paragraphs. Table 10.1 describes the degrees of severity of the condition.

Spasticity refers to increased stiffness or tension in the muscles, which is seen more with activity than during rest. Usually those muscles that bend the joints in the arms and straighten the lower limbs are most affected. Emotional distress, exertion, and efforts by another person to manually force movements of the individual with cerebral palsy can temporarily increase the stiffness, which will lessen once the source of stress is gone. Children who have spasticity are more likely to develop contractures or deformities of the limbs and spine than are children with other manifestations of cerebral palsy. A contracture is deformity at a joint that prevents it from moving within the normal degree of flexibility. Severe contractures result in the loss of functional abilities such as dressing, walking, and eating without help.

Extrapyramidal disorders are a group of movement disorders referring to problems with too much movement, rather than the movement stiffness that is seen in spasticity. These include *athetosis* (slow, writhing movements of the extremities), *choreoathetosis* (fast, abrupt, unintentional motion), *dystonia* (slow, rhythmic, and uncontrolled movements), and *ataxia* (fast movements characterized by inaccuracy, such as several tries to reach before successfully grasping an object). All extrapyramidal disorders are usually accompanied by a decrease in normal muscle stiffness, although in some children increased stiffness may be found.

In direct contrast to the stiffness of people with spasticity, persons who have extrapyramidal cerebral palsy display uncontrolled and excessive movement that interferes with their ability to move and function in a purposeful manner. Contracture deformities are less common in children having this type of movement impairment.

Children with *mixed* cerebral palsy have combinations of movement problems, with one type (i.e., spasticity, athetosis, etc.) usually being more noticeable. For instance, persons with spasticity may have low levels of muscle tone at rest. Similarly, children who generally have low muscle tone may have a limb or side of their body that is stiff.

The level of severity of cerebral palsy is classified as mild, moderate, or severe, depending on the degree of physical limitation. Individuals with *mild* cerebral palsy may be able to walk, but can have difficulty with hand use and/or speech. Individuals with *moderate* cerebral palsy can walk to a limited degree using orthotics (braces) and cane, crutches, or a walker. They may have more severe problems with hand use, and often need help with dressing, bathing, getting in and out of cars, and so forth. Problems with speech may also be present. Those individuals with *severe* cerebral palsy have a degree of motor impairment that doesn't allow them to walk independently. Individuals with this level of cerebral palsy commonly have limited hand use, limited or absent speech, and need complete assistance with self-care activities. Also note that people with severe motor problems can be cognitively intact, while those having mild movement dysfunction can have severe mental retardation.

Children who have cerebral palsy may have other kinds of problems associated with the condition—including difficulties with speech, visual and/or hearing impairments, seizure disorders, mental retardation, learning disabilities, dental problems, poor growth, feeding and/or eating disorders, deformities of involved joints, respiratory difficulties, and behavior problems. Perception of sensations (touch, position of an extremity in space) may also be affected.

Issues for Teachers.   The variation of motor impairments seen with this disability is often confusing for teachers. Expectations regarding performance may be based on experiences with just one child, while another child with the same diagnosis of cerebral palsy may have very different movement and functional abilities.

Children with cerebral palsy often have difficulty performing simultaneous motor tasks. For example, a child may drool when writing or cutting, even though this isn't the case when his hands are quiet. Problems with balance in walking may be observed when a child is asked to carry items from one place to another. Task modifications can minimize such difficulties. Extra support from cushions in a desk chair can help a child perform fine motor tasks. Limiting the distance a child has to carry objects and altering the size or weight of items can facilitate better balance.

The effort required to perform a motor task can also influence attention. For instance, a child who has difficulty walking may hear but not attend to peers when they speak, because of the focus needed to maintain balance while walking. Attending skills may falter at the end of the school day because of fatigue from the effort needed to manage physically during daily activities. Schedules and expectations may need to be adapted in such situations.

Children with cerebral palsy often have difficulty on timed tasks. Speed requirements can have an adverse effect on their performance and skills. Eliminating timed tests is often necessary, but such concerns need to be assessed on an individual basis.

Position change is often needed for children who are in wheelchairs. Prolonged sitting can create discomfort and make other body parts stiffer and harder to move, as well as creating deformities in the limbs and body. School staff should create alternatives to sitting during the day, such as lying down for short periods of time, or sometimes standing in a supportive device.

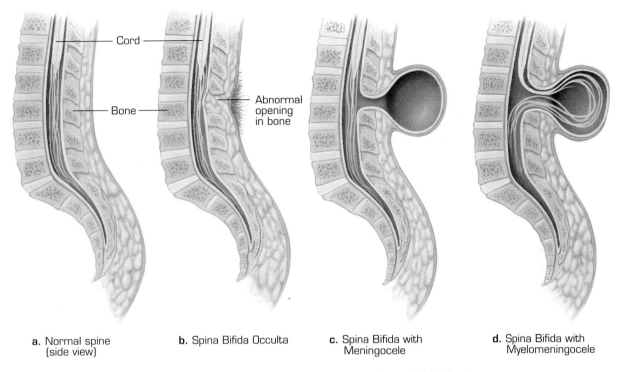

a. Normal spine (side view)

b. Spina Bifida Occulta

c. Spina Bifida with Meningocele

d. Spina Bifida with Myelomeningocele

Figure 10.1 **Side Views of a Normal Spine, Spina Bifida Occulta, and Spina Bifida Cystica**

Adaptive devices are frequently used to help students perform different activities. Built-up spoons and pencil modifications are two examples of "low-tech" adaptations. Adapted computers, electronic or computerized communication devices, and special power wheelchair drives are "high-tech" equipment that can enable a child with cerebral palsy to function at optimum levels in the classroom.

Spina Bifida

Spina bifida refers to a group of disorders that affect the spinal column, spinal cord, and skin. This birth defect occurs in the developing fetus during the first month of life. The spinal cord and vertebrae do not form properly, resulting in a range of severity from *spina bifida occulta*, a mild disability often not visible to *encephalocele*. In cases of encephalocele, the brain protrudes from the skull. In other types of spina bifida, the membranes covering the spinal cord and elements of the cord itself bulge out through the skin of the back. Because the spinal cord is involved, partial or complete paralysis of the muscles and sensory organs occurs at and below the lesion. How much of the body is impaired depends on where the sac is located (see Figure 10.1). The higher on the spine the opening, the more body area is affected. Most defects occur in the mid-back (thoracic area), or low back (lumbar and sacral areas) (Blackman, 1990).

Cause and Incidence. Approximately 1 of every 1,000 children born will have a form of spina bifida. The exact cause is not known. There is an increased risk for having a child with this disorder when there is a family history of such disorders. Environmental factors have been suspect since certain locations (e.g., Wales and northern Africa) have increased incidence of neural tube defects. A recent study has found that mothers of children with this problem had more health problems themselves, took more medications, had poorer nutrition, and took more hot baths during pregnancy than mothers in a control group (Sandford, Kissling, & Joubert, 1992). The cause of this condition seems likely to be from an interaction of environmental and genetic factors. Taking folic acid prior to conception has been proven to decrease the incidence of neural tube defects (Mills & Simpson, 1993; Rush, 1994; Wald, 1994). Folic acid use in the first trimester after conception has also reduced the risk to the infant, but to a lesser degree (Shaw, Schaffer, Velie, Moreland, & Harris, 1995).

Types and Distribution. The mildest defect, spina bifida occulta is often diagnosed by an odd tuft of hair above the child's affected vertebrae or by spinal X-rays. Diagnosis before birth is possible by means of several different procedures, including a blood test called an alpha-fetoprotein test, and sometimes ultrasound (sonogram) or amniocentesis. Women who have given birth to one child with spina bifida have a higher risk of having a second child with the same problem. For this reason, diagnostic procedures are recommended when another child is expected.

Associated Problems. Children who have spina bifida are likely to have a combination of associated problems. The most common of these are described here.

Control of the urinary tract and bowel systems occur at the very end of the spinal cord, so more than 95% of children with spina bifida have a degree of difficulty controlling the elimination of body wastes (Bailey, 1991). Alternative solutions must be used, such as wearing a diaper full-time, a colostomy (surgical revision of the colon so that waste goes into an external bag at the child's side rather than out the rectum), or intermittent self-catheterization (insertion of a tube into the bladder at regular daily intervals to drain urine). Infections of the urinary system are frequent. Children with spina bifida may have malformations of the urinary tract systems at birth, or develop them (Bailey, 1991). Bowel and bladder incontinence can lead to social concerns such as odor, the need for a private place in schools and on job sites to take care of urine and fecal elimination, and the need for assistance in these matters.

Hydrocephalus is caused by blockage of the normal flow of cerebrospinal fluid in the brain. Because the opening in the spine of children with spina bifida results in a disruption of spinal fluid flow, which normally circulates through the brain and spinal cord, hydrocephalus (the accumulation of excess fluid in the ventricles of the brain) can result. The size of the skull and the ventricles are enlarged by the increased volume of fluid, and parts of the brain (the cerebral cortex) are compressed. About 80% to 90% of children with spina bifida develop hydrocephalus (Rekate, 1991; Wolraich, 1990) and have an increased risk for mental retardation. Hydrocephalus is usually corrected by a procedure in which one end of the tube is permanently inserted into the brain, and the other end into the abdomen, to drain the excess fluid (see Figure 10.2). The tube, called a *shunt*, can become infected or otherwise blocked and need replacement, especially as the child grows and the tube needs lengthening. Loss of function, such as cognition and motor skills, can develop with an infected shunt.

Issues for Teachers. Children with spina bifida can also have mental retardation, seizures, visual impairments, learning disabilities, or psychosocial problems. Their

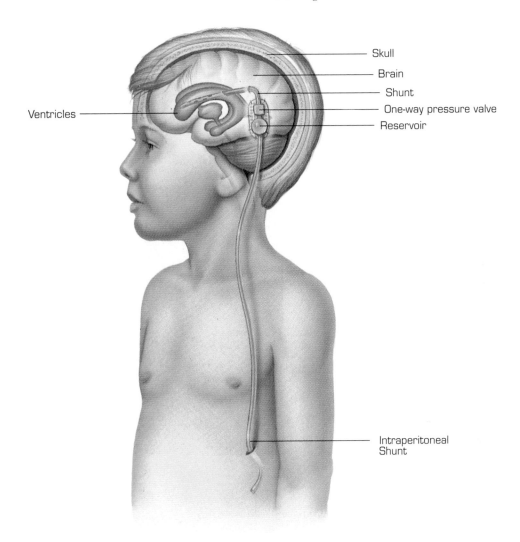

Figure 10.2   **Using a Shunt to Draw Fluid From the Brain**

frequent hospitalizations often result in family and financial stresses that can further complicate the multiple disabling factors already seen with spina bifida.

Recently a high incidence of latex allergies was found in persons with spina bifida (Pearson, Cole, & Jarvis, 1994). Nonlatex gloves should be used when gloves are needed, as during intermittent catheterizations, and care should be used to keep balloons away from children with this disorder. Reactions to this allergy can be fatal.

Shunt infections and other complications can occur in children with treated hydrocephalus. Symptoms of shunt malfunctions include headache, fever, vomiting, or stomachache. If a child appears lethargic and complains of any of these symptoms at school, parents should be notified.

A swollen or reddened area, especially on a leg, should also be reported to the parents. This could be a broken bone or a skin infection. When braces are put on incorrectly, pressure sores can result.

Some children use a standing table in order to participate in classroom activities.

NEUROMUSCULAR DISEASES

Some neuromuscular diseases are the result of an illness such as polio, but more
commonly they are inherited. Neuromuscular diseases are often degenerative or
progressive, with increasing weakness and functional disability over time.
Duchenne's, Becker's, Emery-Dreifuss, and fascioscapulohumeral dystrophies are
in the same family of diseases. Some of the diseases such as Duchenne's muscular
dystrophy are ultimately fatal. Since there are so many different diseases in this category, only the most familiar, Duchenne's muscular dystrophy, will be discussed.

Duchenne's Muscular Dystrophy

The disease is an X-linked disorder, carried by the mother and passed on to sons. It
may also be the result of a genetic mutation. About one third of all cases have no
family history of the disease. The disease is caused by the absence of a specific protein, *dystrophin*, which is required by muscle cells for normal motor function. In
most cases, the diagnosis is made between the ages of 2 and 5. The child may be
observed falling frequently and may appear to weaken over time. Certain muscle
groups appear enlarged, particularly the muscles of the calves. The diagnosis is
made by family history, muscle biopsies, and measuring CPK, the blood protein
found in elevated amounts in persons with muscular dystrophy (Brooke, 1986;

Dubowitz, 1989). The incidence of Duchenne's dystrophy is about 3 per 100,000 (Brooke, 1986).

Associated Problems.   Duchenne's dystrophy causes a waddling style of walking that includes standing on the toes, a lordosis of the lower back (swayback), frequent falls, and difficulty standing and climbing stairs. Contractures of the limbs and spine often occur as muscle strength is lost.

Cognitive limitations can also be found in children with muscular dystrophy (Miller, Tunnecliffe, & Douglas, 1985). These are considered to be related to the disease itself rather than from other causes, such as loss of education, or socioeconomic factors (Appleton, Bushby, Gardner-Medwin, Welch, & Kelly, 1991). In contrast to the progression of the disease, cognition does not steadily worsen (Sollee, Latham, Kindlon, & Bresnan, 1985).

Currently there is no cure for Duchenne's muscular dystrophy. The disease is progressive, with loss of ability to walk and confinement to a wheelchair by 9 to 12 years of age. Death usually occurs by the late teens or early twenties. Recent aggressive management of breathing and spinal problems has increased the possible life span for some of these children (Dubowitz, 1989). Some young men are choosing to sustain life by means of mechanical ventilation (Miller, Colbert, & Osberg, 1990). Technologies such as voice-activated computers, portable externally powered wheelchairs and ventilators, and household environmental controls have accentuated the quality of life for persons with advanced muscular dystrophy.

Issues for Teachers.   School-age children with Duchenne's and other neuromuscular diseases may fatigue more quickly than their classmates and may fall easily. Moving from one part of the school to another and carrying items can be difficult, especially as the child begins to weaken. Early computer access and training as well as computer modifications in the later stages of the disease can facilitate academic achievement as endurance for handwriting lessens.

Psychosocial development issues for children and parents also need to be considered. Children with this condition are faced with the loss of skills they once had, such as walking, and must deal with the idea of early mortality. Such factors can impact on classroom performance and social interactions with peers and teachers.

OTHER HEALTH IMPAIRMENTS

It has been estimated that the number of children in this country with chronic health impairments is 10% to 15% of the population. And many children with chronic health impairments also have physically disabling conditions (Kahn & Battle, 1987).

Diabetes

Diabetes is characterized by the continuous presence of increased glycogen in the body and disturbance of the metabolism of carbohydrate, fat, and protein from poor insulin secretion (Bennett, 1992). Diabetes-related diseases account for a large percentage of the costs of health care, both in the United States and Europe, as well as in developing countries. Stroke, heart disease, and hypertension from diabetes are leading causes of death in the United States. Diabetes is the leading cause of blindness in persons between the ages of 20 and 74 (Davidson, 1991).

About 40% of persons with insulin-dependent diabetes mellitus (IDDM) and probably non-insulin-dependent diabetes mellitus (NIDDM) have kidney disease that requires dialysis and ultimately kidney transplantation, if a matching donor can be found (Davidson, 1991). Other problems include nerve damage, most frequently in the legs and at times to the internal organs. People with diabetes often have psychological problems such as depression and difficulty with adjustment to life transitions, especially in their adolescent years. The relationship between mental and physical states can affect the management of the disease, since stress and depression can alter body chemistry and cause problems with diabetic control (LaGreca, Satin Rapaport, & Skyler, 1991).

Cause and Incidence.   Many researchers agree that there appears to be a genetic predisposition to the disease that is activated by environmental factors (Cavan & Barnett, 1993; McCarthy & Hilmen, 1993). Others cite the presence of epidemic years, strongly suggesting an environmental origin (Tajima, Matsushima, & La Porte, 1993).

     The current incidence of diabetes in the United States is about 2.9 per 1,000 persons and is considered to be increasing (Centers for Disease Control, 1990). Females are more commonly affected than males, and the incidence of diabetes increases with age. Caucasians are more often affected than persons of African or Asian origin. Risk factors for diabetes include glucose intolerance, a family history of diabetes, obesity, a low activity level, and possibly dietary factors. People living in urban areas also seem to have a heightened risk over those who live in more rural communities (Knowler, McCance, Nagi, & Pettitt, 1993).

Types and Distribution.   The World Health Organization has recognized five kinds of diabetes. The two most commonly occurring are *insulin-dependent diabetes mellitus (IDDM)*, also called Type I or juvenile-onset diabetes, and *non-insulin-dependent diabetes mellitus (NIDDM)*, also referred to as Type II, adult-onset, or ketosis-resistant diabetes. The term *non-insulin-dependent* can be misleading, since about 25% of persons with NIDDM use insulin to control their disease. The majority of people with diabetes in the United States have NIDDM (Davidson, 1991).

     Some symptoms of diabetes are excessive thirst, otherwise unexplained weight loss, and frequent urination. In NIDDM, which usually occurs later in life, these symptoms may be absent. As a result, many persons with NIDDM go undiagnosed. IDDM, in contrast, occurs mostly in children and young adults and is easily diagnosed.

Issues for Teachers.   It is important for teachers to know if any of their students have diabetes and to be aware of the symptoms of diabetic crisis. An imbalance of insulin modulation (ketoacidosis) often follows poor insulin treatment monitoring, trauma, or severe infection. While these episodes occur infrequently, immediacy of care is vital when ketoacidosis does develop. Symptoms are complaints of abdominal pain, nausea, or vomiting. The child may appear sleepy with a slow, deep breathing pattern. Untreated, the crisis can result in the child dehydrating and then lapsing into a coma. When children experience this acute diabetic condition, they must have prompt medical attention.

     Since care of the child with diabetes is a complex and intrusive type of medical management, the student's parents should provide the instructional leadership for the teaching staff in this area. It is the younger student's family who will routinely test the blood and monitor insulin injections when they are necessary. As diabetic children approach adolescence, they should begin to monitor themselves for appropriate dosages. As with most serious health impairments, children with diabetes may have frequent absences from school.

Dietary restrictions may prove difficult for children with diabetes, especially during adolescence. The support of peers can be very helpful. Education programs for classmates can build understanding and support.

Cystic Fibrosis

Cystic fibrosis (CF) affects the endocrine system and is characterized by production of abnormal mucus, progressive lung damage, and impaired absorption of fats and proteins. Ultimately fatal, the disease is progressive in nature. Most persons live an average of 26 years. As care improves, life spans are increasing. Up to 80% of children with CF now reach young adulthood (Mulherin & Fitzgerald, 1992).

At present, there is no cure for cystic fibrosis. New treatments under investigation target the accumulation of secretions in the lungs that leads to bacterial infections and progressive lung destruction (Shak, Capon, Hellmiss, Marsters, & Baker, 1993). Introduction of healthy cells into the lungs with cold viruses is a new treatment that shows promise. It is hoped that the healthy cells will remain in the lungs and eventually decrease mucus production and lung damage. Since 1990, recombinant human DNA has shown effectiveness in reducing the viscosity of mucus in the lungs of children with CF. Recombinant DNA is used medically in a process of gene therapy where DNA is injected into the cells in order to change their genetic structure.

Cause and Incidence.   The disease is inherited as an autosomal recessive trait, which means that both parents must be carriers of the problem gene for a child to have cystic fibrosis. Children of those with CF have a 1 in 4 chance of developing the disease. People who are carriers can be identified, and prenatal diagnosis may be done if a history of the disease is known within a family.

Diagnosis of CF is made through the use of a sweat test. Cystic fibrosis is suspected in children who fail to grow, who taste "salty" when kissed, who have chronic respiratory infections, or who exhibit a combination of these symptoms. About 5% to 10% of children with cystic fibrosis also have an intestinal blockage at birth (Blackman, 1990).

The incidence of cystic fibrosis is about 1 per 1,000 births. The rate is lower among African Americans (1 in every 20,000 births) and lower yet in people of Asian descent (1 in every 100,000 births) (Blackman, 1990).

Associated Problems.   As the child with cystic fibrosis gets older, pneumonias become more frequent, accompanied by frequent wheezing and coughing. Parts of the lungs become blocked over time and the heart can become stressed by a lack of oxygen. These children take many medications, including enzymes to help the digestion of fats and proteins, mineral supplements, antibiotics, and drugs to enhance respiratory function. In spite of their regular antibiotic use, death is usually due to respiratory complications.

Issues for Teachers.   As with most complex health care conditions, children with cystic fibrosis have frequent absences from school. They catch infections easily, especially in the later stages of the disease. Fatigue may be a problem, especially in children who have more lung involvement. These students may need a period of their day in which they can recline in an inverted position for postural drainage. Many children may receive daily percussive chest therapy to loosen the mucus in their lungs. Parents, teachers, and instructional aides can be trained by therapists to provide this routine procedure for CF. The same concerns regarding early mortality that were noted in children with muscular dystrophy are faced by children with cystic fibrosis.

Epilepsy

Epilepsy is defined as unprovoked, recurrent seizures of a chronic nature (Murphy & Dehkharghani, 1993). A *seizure* is an involuntary neurological event with sudden, rapid, and abnormal discharge of cortical neurons (Murphy & Dehkharghani, 1993). There are phases to some seizures, including the initial *aura*, the anticipatory, sensory perceptions that people with epilepsy often experience just prior to a seizure. *Postictal* aspects, the state of an individual after a seizure, can vary. It is also possible for seizures to occur without having epilepsy, such as during high fevers. Some children with behavior disorders have been reported to be capable of inducing their seizures.

Classification of epileptic seizures falls into three categories: *partial* (focal or local) seizures, *generalized* (convulsive or nonconvulsive) seizures, and *unclassified* seizures (Dreifuss, 1989). Partial and generalized groupings are further broken down into subcategories. The major difference between partial and generalized seizures is the area of the brain involved. Partial seizures can become generalized seizures (Hermann, Desai, & Whitman, 1988).

Epilepsy is further broken down into a series of syndromes that are classified in several ways: Some are according to the type of seizure involved, by the kind of EEG findings accompanying the seizures, or by the cause of the syndrome. The syndromes can be anatomically defined according to where in the brain the seizures occur, or they can be classified by what causes them (Dreifuss, 1989).

Cause and Incidence.   The causes of epilepsy are numerous. A number of inherited conditions have seizures associated with them (Anderson & Hauser, 1988). Children with other conditions, such as cerebral palsy and spina bifida, have a high incidence of epilepsy. There is also a hereditary factor, as women who have epilepsy have a slightly greater risk of having children with the condition, especially if the mother is on medication (Hermann et al., 1988). Trauma to the brain, such as head injury, child abuse, or stroke, can also result in seizures, as can lack of oxygen during birth or other birth traumas, and tumors. Epilepsy has been noted to occur with higher prevalence in low-income communities (Hermann et al., 1988), indicating a possible link with unsatisfactory prenatal care, nutritional intake, or birthing conditions.

The treatment of epilepsy depends on the underlying cause. Tumors and vascular malformations may respond to surgery. In cases where such options are not possible, the treatment is by medication using anti-epileptic drugs (AEDs). The goal of drug therapy is to achieve the best result for the person with epilepsy. This does not always mean complete seizure control. Some medications may control seizures but leave the child or adult sedated. In these cases, partial control with alertness is a more satisfactory goal (Berent & Sackellares, 1989). In some cases, combinations of drugs are necessary to manage the seizures.

The incidence of epilepsy appears to be about 20 to 50 per 100,000, with males having a higher incidence than females (Zelinski, 1988). Studies indicate that the onset of epilepsy is highest in the first 10 years of life (Hermann et al., 1988; Zelinski, 1988).

Table 10.2 **Procedures for Handling Generalized Tonic-Clonic Seizures**

The typical seizure is not a medical emergency, but knowledgeable handling of the situation is important. When a child experiences a generalized tonic-clonic seizure in the classroom, the teacher should follow these procedures:

Keep calm. Reassure the other students that the child will be fine in a minute.

Ease the child to the floor and clear the area around him of anything that could hurt him.

Put something flat and soft (like a folded coat) under her head so it will not bang on the floor as her body jerks.

You cannot stop the seizure. Let it run its course. Do not try to revive the child and do not interfere with the child's movements.

Turn him gently onto his side. This keeps his airway clear and allows saliva to drain away.

DON'T try to force the child's mouth open. DON'T try to hold on to her tongue. DON'T put anything in her mouth.

When the jerking movements stop, let the child rest until he regains consciousness.

Breathing may be shallow during the seizure, and may even stop briefly. In the unlikely event that breathing does not begin again, check the child's airway for obstruction and give artificial respiration.

Some students recover quickly after this type of seizure; others need more time. A short period of rest is usually advised. If the student is able to remain in the classroom afterwards, however, he should be encouraged to do so. Staying in the classroom (or returning to it as soon as possible) allows for continued participation in classroom activity and is psychologically less difficult for the student. If a student has frequent seizures, handling them can become routine once teacher and classmates learn what to expect.

If a seizure of this type continues for more than 5 minutes, call for emergency assistance.

Source: Information from *Epilepsy School Alert,* by the Epilepsy Foundation of America, 1987, Washington, DC.

Associated Problems. There are many seizure medications available today, but almost all medications used in the treatment of epilepsy have negative side effects. The positive and negative aspects of the medications must be weighed against the needs and quality of life of the person having seizures. Medications require careful monitoring and must be adjusted over time, especially as a child grows. It may take several weeks, and in some cases longer, to obtain an optimum dosage to manage seizures. Special diets have also been used in an effort to establish seizure control. A ketogenic diet, high in fats and low in protein and carbohydrates, has been useful in children with hard to manage seizures (Schwartz, Eaton, Bower, & Aynesley-Green, 1989).

Issues for Teachers. It is important for teachers to know which of their students have epilepsy, what the possible side effects of medication may be, and what to do if a student has a seizure at school (see Table 10.2). Many children will show some physical or behavioral change prior to the onset of a seizure, such as urination in the clothing, loss of consciousness without warning, or contractions of the muscles in the limbs, trunk, or head. Parents can often inform the child's teachers about behaviors exhibited just prior to the actual beginning of a seizure and its general physical manifestations. Changes in attention or in physical and intellectual status should be reported to the family, as these may indicate a change in the child's response to medication or in the seizure disorder itself.

A number of children with epilepsy experience difficulties in academic achievement. It is estimated that 20% of children who are epileptic have severe deficits in reading, arithmetic, and spelling (Seidenberg, 1989). No single group of variables has been shown to be the primary cause of this problem.

Children with epilepsy have a high incidence of psychological and behavioral disorders associated with various aspects of the condition. These can be manifested in a variety of ways, including lack of compliance with medication, fear of seizures, and concern about acceptance by their classmates. Teachers can be instrumental by helping other students understand the condition of epilepsy (Interstate Research Associates, 1992).

HIV Infection and AIDS

The first reports of AIDS (acquired immunodeficiency syndrome) were published in 1981, followed by establishment of clinical criteria for diagnostic purposes in 1982 (Schoub, 1994). Since that time, diagnostic blood tests have been developed and research into treatment and possible vaccines commenced. Human immuno-deficiency virus (HIV), which precedes AIDS, has been contracted by persons from a broad range of lifestyles.

Cause and Incidence.   Efforts at documenting this epidemic continue, complicated by the differences in HIV transmission around the world. The disease is transferred in different ways, including sexual intercourse between homosexual men, intravenous drug use, and in some countries blood transfusions (a decreasing group due to improved screening procedures). In other nations, heterosexual intercourse is the primary method of disease transmission, with men and women affected in equal numbers.

Contact with body fluids (blood, semen, vaginal fluid, urine, and feces) is determined to be the primary cause for the spread of infection. High-risk behaviors and other factors such as same-sex partners (primarily in males), anal intercourse, large numbers of sexual partners, frequent unprotected sexual encounters with infected persons, intravenous drug use, and the coexistence of other sexually transmitted diseases are the most consistent means of transmission for the virus (Schoub, 1994; Stine, 1993).

Women are presently the fastest growing group with HIV infection, and the incidence of the infection in children is also rising (Centers for Disease Control, 1995). Infants born to mothers who are HIV-positive have a 30% chance of contracting the disease, in contrast to an 80% chance of becoming infected if the mother has AIDS (Schoub, 1994).

Associated Problems.   HIV infections are the most relentless of diseases or conditions affecting children or adults. The immune system and the central nervous system are always affected (Schoub, 1994). As the immune system is invaded, the body's ability to fight off infections is diminished—resulting in frequent and pernicious illness, with susceptibility to certain forms of cancer (Butler & Pizzo, 1992; Unsworth & Howard, 1994). The disease in its active form (AIDS) is ultimately fatal. Persons who are HIV-positive have a 65% to 100% chance of developing AIDS within 10 to 12 years of infection. Death usually occurs within 2 to 5 years of the development of active disease (Stine, 1993).

The course of the disease in children is more rapid, although survival rates are improving with better treatment techniques. Infants diagnosed with AIDS rarely live beyond 2 years of age (Stine, 1993), although children found to be HIV-positive can live as long as 10 years.

Infections are seen recurrently. Pneumonia, drug-resistant tuberculosis, Karposi's sarcoma, skin diseases, mouth and eye lesions, kidney and gastrointestinal diseases, and central nervous system diseases such as meningitis, encephalitis, and AIDS dementia complex are some of the infections seen in persons with HIV.

Issues for Teachers. In keeping with the general observational skills of teachers, it is important to recognize the symptoms of AIDS. The general symptoms of AIDS in children and adults are as follow:

- Unexplained, persistent fatigue, fever, chills, or shaking
- Unexplained weight loss of 10 pounds or more
- Swollen glands for 2 months or more
- Pink-purple, flat or raised blotches/bumps on or under the skin
- Persistent dry cough caused by respiratory infection (Quackenbush & Sargent, 1990)

According to the Centers for Disease Control, HIV is *not* spread by sneezing, by kissing, through the sweat of infected persons, or from contact with utensils, toilet seats, or clothing of persons having the virus. Regular hygiene—including washing surfaces and items that have been exposed to body fluids of persons with HIV in a 1:10 solution of bleach and water—is a reasonable preventive measure. Protective clothing and gloves should be used during diapering and wound care, two activities that might be necessary in educational settings. Otherwise, use of such items only contributes to the stigma felt by the persons having this disease.

Emotional traumas can lead to diminished performance in any phase of life, such as educational and work settings. Active support from teachers and guidance staff is essential for these students. Psychosocial concerns are paramount with adults and children with HIV infection. Few diseases have mobilized fear in communities as HIV has, resulting in rejection and stigma for those infected and their families. Particularly for children—where other members of the family unit may also be infected, dying, or already deceased—support and concern for such stresses must be available.

The Maternal and Child Health Bureau of the U.S. Department of Health and Human Services has established "Best Practices Guidelines" to assist schools in coping with the challenges faced by children with HIV. These guidelines are published in the *Journal of School Health* (Crocker et al., 1994). Duplication and distribution of the material is actively encouraged in the journal.

Cancer

Cause and Incidence. Cancer causes more deaths than any other disease in children between ages 1 and 15. The estimated incidence for all childhood cancers is 1 in 10,000 (Leventhal, 1987). Multiple causes for cancer exist. Environmental factors, exposure to some drugs in utero, viruses, and genetic mechanisms have all been implicated. There are also medical conditions that carry an increased risk of cancer. These include AIDS, Down syndrome, and neurofibromatosis (a highly variable inherited syndrome with tumors at the end of the nerves).

Early diagnosis and treatment are critical for the best chances of successful outcomes. Some kinds of malignancies have better long-term survival rates than others. The treatment of cancer in children has improved over recent years, with more than 50% of children initially diagnosed with cancer regarded as cured (Leventhal, 1987). The primary treatment technique is to attempt the removal or destruction of as much malignancy, with as little damage to normal cells, as possible.

These middle school students shaved their heads in solidarity with their friend who was undergoing chemotherapy.

Treatments vary according to the type of tumor. Surgery is an option in some cases, while chemotherapy and radiation are used in other kinds of cancer. In some cancers, all three options are used. Bone marrow transplantation is performed with leukemia in some specific situations, and can substantially improve survival outcomes.

Associated Problems.   All cancer treatments have possible side effects. Fatigue and irritability can last for awhile after each treatment episode. Some side effects can cause long-term complications, such as the need for prosthetic devices after amputations. Radical surgeries performed on some young children with some types of cancers can include hip operations or amputation above the knee. This type of life-saving medical intervention obviously calls for increased social and emotional support for the child who suddenly needs adaptive prosthetics to regain independent ambulation.

Issues for Teachers.   The challenge to the teacher of children with cancer, as for those with other complex health care needs, is to use creative methods to adapt classroom activities. Children receiving treatment for cancer continue to attend school whenever they are strong enough. Absences during chemotherapy or radiation treatment may be frequent, making it difficult for the student to keep up with schoolwork. The side effects of drugs, such as hair loss or bloating, can be uncomfortable for both the student and peers. Preparation of teachers and classmates for such eventualities can make the adjustment easier for everyone. Remember that the emotional stress engendered by life-threatening conditions is considerable, and the support of friends and classmates is important to the coping abilities of all concerned. Letters from classmates while the student is in the hospital can also help to ease the child's loneliness during absences from friends at school.

Juvenile Rheumatoid Arthritis

The term **juvenile rheumatoid arthritis (JRA)** refers to one of a group of diseases. JRA is a chronic disease involving one or more joint structures and is characterized by pain and swelling in the joints. In severe cases there is eventual destruction of the joint structures. Classification of JRA is usually divided into three groups: polyarticular, pauciarticular, and systemic. *Polyarticular* involves five or more joints in any location of the body. *Pauciarticular* cases have four or fewer joints involved, but they are usually the larger joints (knees, hips, elbows). *Systemic* cases have any number of joints affected, and other symptoms may include high fever, rash, and chills (Holt, 1990). This is a disease of flare-ups and remissions, with periods of pain and swelling interposed with dormant times. In some children JRA seems to "burn out" or disappear, while others experience lifelong disease.

Cause and Incidence.   The disease usually occurs more in girls, with a male-to-female ratio of 1 to 2. It occurs in two age groups: 1 to 3 years, and 8 to 12 years. The number of cases varies, with a range of 11 to 17 cases per 100,000 (Vandvik & Hoyeraal, 1993). There is no known cause for the disease, but certain predisposing factors do exist—such as family history of the disease, chronic family stress, and viral and/or bacterial infections. Like many of the medical conditions reviewed in this chapter, an interaction of genetic and environmental disorders is suspected to cause the disease.

Associated Problems.   Care of JRA involves management of symptoms and treatment of the disease processes. Swollen, painful joints can result in deformed joints and loss of flexibility over time. As movement flexibility is lost, functional limitations (difficulty walking, inability to manage daily care needs) can occur. Use of heat and/or cold applications, paraffin dips, and physical and occupational therapies are helpful in limiting such problems and maintaining the child's independence. Medications that reduce pain and swelling are used to control the disease and preserve the joints. Aspirin is most commonly used, with corticosteroids, gold injections, and other drugs employed in more severe cases. Side effects from medications, such as ulcers and fragile bones, can develop. Children with severe arthritis can also suffer hearing loss, both from medications (prolonged aspirin use) and from arthritis in the bones of the ear. Children with severe JRA disease may have surgeries such as joint replacement for hips and knees if joint flexibility is limited enough to necessitate surgical intervention.

Issues for Teachers.   Children with arthritis may have increased absences during periods of active disease when pain is great and movement difficult. Fatigue can be a problem, especially if frequent classroom changes and walking distances are part of the school routine. Joint pain and inflexibility can cause some students to move slowly, needing extra time in moving between their classes. Carrying heavy items such as book bags can be difficult and painful. Arrangements for dual sets of books at home and school can help. Some children with JRA are able to participate in physical education with only minor adjustments, while others need modified progams.

Hand involvement is common in JRA. If this is the case, alternatives to handwriting may be necessary, such as computer use or taped dictation for written assignments. Other students might assist these students by sharing copies of their class notes.

Asthma

Asthma is defined as a respiratory condition with resistance to airflow in the lungs for short periods of time. It is also referred to as *reactive airway disease*. The symptoms are reversed by treatment (Sears, 1991).

Cause and Incidence.   There are many causes of asthma. Genetic and environmental factors appear to interact, resulting in active disease. Environmental features that seem to cause the disease include dust mites, tobacco smoke, pet dander, emotional stress, industrial pollutants, seasonal changes, and cold air. Exercise and viral respiratory infections can also induce asthmatic episodes.

Incidence reports vary, but there seems to be a consistent estimate of 5% of children and 2% to 3% of adults with asthmatic symptoms (Weinberger, 1990). There seems to be a worldwide increase in the occurrence and mortality of persons with asthma. Males younger than 14 years of age have an increased incidence, with the ratio of males to females leveling out through adolescence (Coultas & Samet, 1993). Persons of African American descent have a higher probability of having the disease, as do people from lower socioeconomic levels.

Associated Problems.   There is a range of involvement in this disease. Some persons have mild and moderate symptoms, while others demonstrate severe, frequent asthmatic events. An event may begin slowly with wheezing, coughing, tightness in the chest, and anxiety from the shortness of breath. The episode may end quickly or continue for days.

The management of asthma is twofold, including treatment of symptoms and environmental modifications. A variety of medications are available for management of asthmatic episodes, including use of anti-inflammatory and bronchodilator drugs. Environmental measures may include the use of dust covers, careful and regular housecleaning, exclusion of tobacco smoke, and removal of pets.

Some people do "outgrow" or cease to have asthma. The chances of this happening are better if the disease onset is before age 10, if the symptoms are mild to moderate, and if there is a family history of another member outgrowing the disease (Crockett, 1993).

Issues for Teachers.   Students with asthma need to be identified to their teachers. If regular use of inhalers is necessary, the teacher should have this information and know where the equipment is kept. Older pupils should be encouraged to take the responsibility for keeping such items, while staff working with younger children should be in charge of inhalers and medications (Weinberger, 1990).

Although asthma symptoms can be brought on by exercise, this does not mean that children with asthma should avoid physical education. However, physical education teachers should be aware when exercise may act as an asthmatic trigger, and should listen to students who complain of shortness of breath or wheezing during activity.

Children with asthma are often absent due to hospitalizations or illness. Severe asthma can result in listlessness and decreased energy, affecting classroom participation and possibly achievement.

IMPAIRMENTS CAUSED BY TRAUMA

Childhood traumas are a major source of disability and death in children, causing more deaths among children aged 1 to 19 years than all diseases combined. Permanent disability is seen in an estimated 30,000 children nationwide, impacting all aspects of life for these children, their families, and society as a whole. The United States has one of the highest death rates from trauma in the world—suggesting that an emphasis on prevention could dramatically decrease this figure (Rodriguez & Brown, 1990).

Spinal Cord Injuries

Persons with **spinal cord injury (SCI)** suffer a trauma to the spinal cord, which results in paralysis of movement and loss of sensation. Functionally, the use of the legs, arms, and/or hands as well as control of bowel and bladder can be lost or impaired. The physical and functional impacts of SCI are similar to those caused by spina bifida. SCI can happen to people from any walk of life. Former governor George Wallace of Alabama developed paraplegia after a shooting attempt on his life severed his spine; Christopher Reeve, the actor who portrayed Superman in the movies, broke his neck in a horse-riding accident and survived with quadriplegia. Jill Kinmont, a promising Olympic ski racer, crashed in a practice run and survived with quadriplegia. Her story was depicted in the 1975 movie, *The Other Side of the Mountain.*

Cause and Incidence. There are many causes of SCI, including (in order of frequency) motor vehicle accidents, falls (much more common in persons older than 45), acts of violence, and sports injuries (National Spinal Cord Injury Association, 1994). The estimated incidence of SCI for the total population is 32 per million each year. Many of these injuries occur in teenagers, and 82% of persons with this disability are males (National Spinal Cord Injury Association, 1994).

SCI can be complete or incomplete. *Complete* injuries refer to those that result in total loss of muscular control and sensation at and below the level of spinal injury, while *incomplete* injuries are those that cause partial loss of sensation and muscle control. SCI is categorized by the spinal segment at which the injury occurs and is further divided into paraplegia and quadriplegia. Persons having **paraplegia** lose partial or total use of the lower half of the body. Those with **quadriplegia** have partial or complete loss of control over both legs, both arms, and the trunk.

Associated Problems. Muscle spasms, especially in higher level and complete injuries, can be a problem. Other complications are the same as seen in spina bifida—notably obesity, fractures, pressure sores, and urinary tract infections. Respiratory tract infections among those with injuries at higher levels on the spinal cord are a special concern and can be fatal, since the respiratory system is affected in higher level injuries.

Currently, persons with complete lesions in the spine presently have little hope of regaining control of movement or sensation. The course of rehabilitation

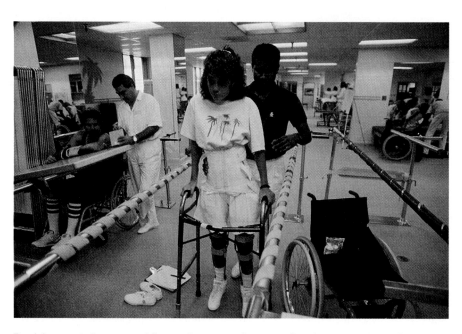

Partial or sometimes even full use of motor and sensory functions can return after extensive physical therapy.

is geared to developing the maximum possible level of independence. The higher the cord injury, the less independence may be attainable. Generally persons with an injury at C8 (the last cervical vertebra) or lower can drive, transfer to and from wheelchairs, and perform all self-care tasks. Full-time employment is very possible for higher level injuries, but assistance is needed with transfers, positioning, and other activities of daily living.

People with incomplete lesions have a more optimistic outlook. Partial or (sometimes) full return of motor and sensory functions can occur, depending on the degree of the injury and the quality of medical and therapeutic care after the trauma.

Issues for Teachers.   Students need extra support when first returning to school after injury. Having lived previously without paralysis, postinjury adjustment to losses of function can be difficult. Some classmates may avoid their peer with a spinal cord injury, or perhaps help too much. An information sharing session with the class prior to the injured student's return to school can be useful.

Architectural adjustments may need to be made to accommodate a wheelchair. Extra time is sometimes needed between classes if the student is in a power chair or is slow with pushing a manual chair. Special bathroom facilities are necessary for intermittent self-catheterization, a method of bladder control used in both spinal cord injury and spina bifida.

Traumatic Brain Injury

The National Head Injury Foundation has defined **traumatic brain injury (TBI)** as an insult to the brain caused by an *external force* that results in significant impairment of cognitive, physical, or psychosocial functional abilities (National Head Injury Foundation, 1986). As with cerebral palsy, TBI is not a progressive condition. The lesions generally remain static after the injury.

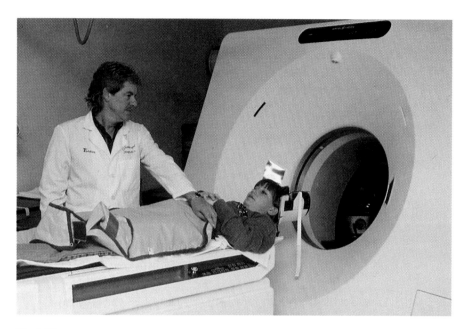

The MRI can assess the extent of trauma an injured brain has received.

Cause and Incidence. Head injuries resulting in TBI commonly occur from motor vehicle accidents, bicycle accidents, collisions during sporting events, physical violence, or falls. Approximately half of serious TBIs are the result of motor vehicular accidents (THINK FIRST Foundation, 1993). A disturbing trend in the United States has been the increase in physically abused children who develop TBI from the actions of their parents or other caretakers. (See Table 10.3 for additional causes of brain injury and other traumas and strategies for prevention.)

The National Institute of Neurological Disorders and Stroke (NINDS) estimated in 1989 that 2 million people annually receive TBIs. Approximately 500,000 people are admitted to U.S. hospitals each year with head injuries, and 70,000 to 90,000 survivors of TBI will have a disability for the remainder of their lives. TBI is considered the main cause of death and disability of youth in the United States (Senelick & Ryan, 1991) and is the fastest growing disability group in this country.

Most people who sustain brain injuries are between 15 and 24 years of age. Risk-taking behaviors in relation to motor vehicle accidents, contact sports, and exposure to firearms violence are all factors in this statistic. Use of alcohol and drugs and failure to take preventive precautions (such as wearing seat belts in automobiles and helmets when riding bicycles, motorcycles, and horses) also contribute to TBI. Preschool children make up the next highest age group with one fourth of the injuries to children less than 2 years of age being inflicted by another person (Michaud, Duhaime, & Bateshaw, 1993).

In the U.S. general population, there are two males with TBI for every female who receives a traumatic brain injury and male children die of their injuries two to four times more often than females. The gender differences in TBI, as in spinal cord injury, support in part the assumption that males engage in risky behavior more frequently than females. Minority children constitute a disproportionate majority of the number of deaths and injuries (Rodriguez & Brown, 1990), with minority males much more highly represented—a statistic graphically illustrated by the high incidence of death from TBI among African American males under the age of 21.

Table 10.3   **Causes of Trauma and Strategies for Prevention**

CAUSE OF TRAUMA	CURRENT STRATEGY	RECOMMENDED STRATEGY
Motor vehicle accidents	• Mandated seat belt wear (in 40 states) • Child safety seats (all states and D.C.) • Air bags (voluntary) • Driver education programs mandatory in some states	• Mandate in all states (currently fines for violation exist in only 10 states) • Mandatory air bags • Raise the driving age to 17 • Mandatory curfews for drivers under age 21 • Alcohol treatment programs and harsher penalties for drunk driving • Universal driver education programs
Burns	• Parent education, voluntary use of smoke detectors, and controls on hot water heaters • Legally mandated flame retardant clothing for children	• Mandatory smoke detectors and hot water controls in all homes • Installation of heat activated sprinklers in homes • Community education on family escape routes in case of fire
Playground equipment	• Parental monitoring at playgrounds • Teacher and school personnel monitoring at schools and day care	• Mandatory type of surface and depth of surface under playground equipment
Drowning	• Locally mandated fencing around pools and use of pool covers • Swim programs for infants and young children • Use of life vests • Boat safety training programs	• More universal mandates for fences and pool covers • Required boat safety courses upon purchase of boats
Bicycle accidents	• Use of helmets (voluntary) • Use of bike paths • Cycling safety programs	• Required use of bike helmets for all riders • Increase bicycle paths and lanes • Increase riding safety programs
Pedestrian injuries	• School and local training programs	• Increase walking safety programs at schools and in local agencies • Parent awareness and training • Mandatory driver education courses • Harsher penalties for drunk drivers
Firearms and violence	• Gun control legislation (in some states) • Mandatory registration of handguns (in some states) • Firearms safety training • Drug and alcohol education programs • School education programs on violence • School use of metal detectors and locker searches to find firearms and weapons • Committees to investigate violence on television • Treatment programs for parents who abuse children, and for victims of abuse • Neighborhood Watch programs	• Restrictions on the manufacture and distribution of guns • Increased funding for education programs dealing with violence in schools and at home • Increased funding of alcohol and drug treatment programs • More local recreational programs and jobs for young people

Associated Problems.   Traumatic brain injury by itself is a complex phenomenon, occurring from impact or inertial forces, and possibly accompanied by skull fracture. The area of the brain affected and the type of lesion give some indication of the possible long-term consequences. Damage can be in motor, speech, or cognitive domains, or combinations of all three. The duration and depth of coma following the injury are believed to give some indication of the possible outcome. The longer and deeper the coma, the less optimistic the prognosis. Traumatic brain injuries are often accompanied by multiple fractures in other areas of the body. The number and severity of the fractures can further complicate the rehabilitation of the person with a head injury.

Issues for Teachers.   Like the other complex disabilities discussed previously, the array of impairments seen in students with TBI calls for an intensive and coordinated team approach. These students often need therapeutic rehabilitation from a multitude of specialists for a lengthy period of time. When the injury is new, neurosurgeons, orthopedic surgeons, neurologists, and nurses are involved. Once the individual is stabilized medically, physical, occupational, and speech-language therapists as well as psychologists, neuropsychologists, social workers, and others begin the rehabilitation process. Commonly, some therapy begins even while the person with TBI is in a deep coma, such as moving the limbs to prevent contractures of the joints.

Students with disabling traumatic injuries, like others with severe health-related impairments, enter into unique joint environments of medical care and educational services. It is often difficult for the child's rehabilitation and educational team to determine when the rehabilitation phase of recovery (with its accompanying medically necessary treatments) has ended or when the individual is no longer so medically fragile that participation in educational programs and resumption of other normal life functions would be harmful or life-threatening.

Teachers are a vital part of the team and must coordinate the student's educational needs along with other professionals treating the child. Children who have received a head injury often return to school with cognitive deficits that may not have been present prior to the injury, such as slower motor and cognitive processing or impairments of memory and attention. Many of these students will require special education services. Neurobehavioral changes may continue to occur for 2 years and possibly longer after the initial injury, making frequent reassessment important. Behavioral changes may necessitate management programs if the behaviors interfere with classroom interaction.

Children with severe injury may require a wheelchair for mobility, necessitating architectural modifications, and may require physical and occupational therapies. They may also need assistive technology support, such as computers and communication aids.

Students with TBI may have impairments that cross all special education categories; they do not fit snugly under any one label (Ball, 1988). Learning and language disabilities often result from TBI, and behavioral problems are common as well. Sensory impairments and the loss of physical skills can also lead to changes in personality and complicate the student's recovery.

Burns

There are four levels of burns: first, second, third, and fourth degree. First degree burns, which usually heal quickly without incident, are characterized by redness and pain. Second degree burns are broken into two groups—*superficial* and *deep partial-thickness*. They commonly heal in 14 to 17 days. Third degree burns, also called *full-thickness burns*, involve total destruction of an area of the skin. They can only heal with surgical grafting of healthy skin. Fourth degree burns refer to those

Hospitals try to make their children's wards as friendly as possible.

where the underlying fat, bone, fascia, and muscle tissue are destroyed as well as the skin. The more of the body surface that is burned, the lower the chances of survival.

Third and fourth degree burns are treated with skin grafting. Hospital stays for severe burns are prolonged, often requiring a number of surgeries for grafting to succeed. Once the initial burn heals, intensive care is needed to help the skin heal and regain elasticity through the use of special creams, splints and braces, pressure garments, and ongoing physical and occupational therapy. These treatment regimes are painful. Severe itching may also develop as the skin heals.

Associated Problems.   People who have extensive third and fourth degree burns are at risk for a number of complications, including kidney failure, drug-resistant infections, amputations, contractures, and stress ulcers. Severe burns, particularly to the face, can result in a difficult readjustment after the initial treatment. Societal responses to disfigurement are often negative, further complicating an already stressful situation for the person who is burned.

Issues for Teachers.   Persons with burns may need to wear special pressure garments for up to 18 months after injury and may require splints or braces for longer periods. There may be frequent absences due to the need for ongoing therapy and surgery. Individuals with burns of the upper and lower limbs may have difficulty walking, reaching, and holding on to objects. Adaptive equipment can help with these problems.

Classmates in school may not understand the need for such care. If severe disfigurement results, this can make readjustment to the changes very difficult. Peers may respond negatively, and students with burns often develop self-esteem problems and become depressed.

ASSESSMENT

Multidisciplinary Assessment

Children who have physical disabilities and/or health impairments present intriguing challenges in the area of educational assessment. Allied health professionals such as physical therapists, occupational therapists, and speech–language pathologists can provide unique approaches to assist with functional skill training and adaptations of teaching approaches for these children. The quality of life for the child in educational settings can be significantly impacted by the goals decided on by the therapeutic team members in conjunction with teachers, instructional aides, family, and (whenever possible) the student. Each person who comes into contact with the child with special needs can shape behavior toward the mutual goals decided on by the team.

Physical Therapy. **Physical therapists (PTs)** are concerned with a person's mobility skills, strength, endurance, and movement at the joints. Mobility refers to a person's ability to move in the environment. When walking without assistance is not possible, physical therapists assist in decisions regarding types of assistive aids to help in walking or moving, such as the types of crutches, canes, walkers, braces, and wheelchairs that are most appropriate. Strength, endurance, and joint motion are all important to moving in space, whether by independent walking or with devices. Physical therapists also train persons using wheelchairs to transfer in and out of their chairs. They may also teach caretakers the safest and easiest ways to lift persons who cannot move themselves. PTs perform developmental assessments of gross motor skills.

Occupational Therapy. **Occupational therapists (OTs)** assess strength and joint motion, primarily of the hands and upper limbs. OTs assess and treat sensory perception, processing, organizational skills, activities of daily living (i.e., dressing, feeding, and hygiene), manipulative skills, and computer access. Construction of splints for better gripping abilities and adaptive devices such as extenders for reaching are part of occupational therapy services as well. OTs perform developmental assessments of fine motor skills.

Speech–Language Therapy. **Speech–language pathologists (SLPs)** evaluate speech and receptive and expressive language, and the age appropriateness of language skills. They suggest and design alternative modes of communication and prescribe specific augmentative communication devices and aids for individuals with physical disabilities or other health impairments. Assisting students to adapt and best use the sounds they can produce in order to expand their expressive language skills is also an important part of the speech–language pathologist's role.

Additional Assessment Considerations

The population of individuals who are physically disabled and severely health-impaired are so varied that comparison with a standardized mean of student performance is not very helpful in modifying a curriculum or selecting the best teaching objectives. The primary use of standardized or norm-referenced tests should be for diagnosis and eligibility determination. Changes in the child's health can change functional abilities quickly. Teachers are encouraged to measure the student against his or her own performance over time. Multiple observations and teacher-made curriculum-based assessments give a better picture of the student and can be accomplished with the assistance of the other specialists involved with the student.

With these students, fatigue is often a limiting factor that the team must take into account. Spreading the assessments over time can give a better view of the child and avoid misconceptions of the student's condition. Likewise, after even a short hospitalization, students may perform more poorly than before the hospital admission. For example, a student who could accurately recite multiplication tables before a minor surgery may not perform the same task as effectively after the hospitalization. When the student returns after each of these absences from school, it is important to conduct another short assessment to see if skills have been maintained and to determine the current energy level of the child.

Similarly, transition planning with the medical and therapeutic staff should begin before the child is discharged and returns to school. A preliminary visit to the new setting prior to the placement change can help all involved to assess the need for modifications. It may also serve to lessen the apprehensions of the educational staff, family, and student.

TEAM APPROACH AND INTERACTIONS

Students with physical or health impairments have to interact with numerous professionals in medical and educational settings. Children with mental retardation may have a teacher, pediatrician, and speech–language pathologist as major influences in their lives. Children with spina bifida often have a teacher, neurologist, urologist, orthopedist, nutritionist, physical and occupational therapists, and an instructional aide that they regularly encounter. The increased numbers of adults involved in their health care and educational training can increase the chances of miscommunication. Therefore, these teams must be encouraged to use collaborative processes based on principles of cooperative group learning. This approach recommends five elements for effective team functioning:

1. Face-to-face team interaction on a frequent basis

2. An "all for one, one for all" feeling of positive interdependence

3. A focus on the development of small group interpersonal skills in trust building, communication, leadership, creative problem solving, decision making, and conflict management

4. Regular assessment of the team's functioning and goal setting for improving relationships and task achievement

5. Methods for holding one another accountable for personal responsibilities and commitments (Thousand & Villa, 1993)

A coordinated team approach looks at the whole student from health, family, and educational perspectives. It is fundamental to communicate with families in the assessment, planning, and development of a unified approach to the individualized program for each child with health or physical impairments.

Many teams have found it effective to assign one team member to communicate changes in health and plans to all of the other members of the child's team. Often it has been the child's mother who has taken this role, since she generally has

EASY IDEAS FOR PRACTITIONERS

For the Teacher:

1. Encourage students with health impairments to discuss their needs and the characteristics associated with their condition with peers. For instance, a description of a routine seizure in advance of seizure occurrence can help to lessen the anxiety of other students.
2. Discuss the characteristics of the student's learning and abilities in small doses and do not be afraid to repeat information.
3. In discussions with parents, always leave them with some hope that improvement may be seen in their child's development.
4. Push students with physical disabilities and other health impairments to attempt difficult or unfamiliar tasks. Many adults with disabilities look back on their schooling with disappointment that they were not challenged to work harder on reading, writing, and other basic skills.
5. Wash your hands frequently when working in close contact with several students to avoid spreading germs to children with health problems.

For Parents:

1. Communicate regularly with the school staff—especially during periods when your child is too sick to attend school. Be sure they know when to tentatively expect your child's return and any relative changes in his or her functioning.
2. Be sure several teachers and educational aides who interact with your child know how to provide routine health procedures so your child is covered during staff absences.
3. Identify to the educational staff symptoms that may require emergency medical attention, and meet regularly as a group with the student's therapists and educational staff.
4. At initial placement into school, advocate for transition planning for the next two phases of your child's program.
5. Seek counseling and support for brothers and sisters who have responsiblities for caring for their sibling.

the most contact with the student and regularly receives all of the communications from the other health and educational team members (Shapiro & Shumaker, 1987). One person can update the other team members on changes more efficiently and call for team meetings when necessary to develop additional plans or change programs.

Successful teams need flexibility in educational bureaucracies and open support from the principal's office to allow children with physical disabilities to have the rich social and learning experiences available in public schools. The benefits of full inclusion are many; however, there may still be instances when a child with physical disabilities can be better served with part of the educational/therapeutic program administered outside of the regular classroom.

Caldwell, Todaro, and Gates (1989) described four components necessary for developing individualized educational programs for children with special health care conditions, as follows:

1. Methods for assuring communication between and among family, school personnel, and medical providers

2. Provisions for transition from hospital or home to school

3. Identification of resources for technical assistance, health care, and emergency plans

4. Provision of training and monitoring of education personnel

Educational staff also must learn when to call the child's physicians about an emergency event and how to perform initial emergency procedures.

Team Interactions

Children with the special needs described in this chapter are necessarily involved with a large number of professionals who are available to help in a variety of ways. Physicians, nurses, and therapists in medical settings see the child less often than teachers do and focus more closely on the health care needs of the child. While both groups are important players in the life of the child, the family system is central and must be involved with all the major decisions about the child that are made in either setting.

The Cayuga-Onondaga Assessment for Children with Handicaps (COACH) was created by Giangreco, Cloninger, and Iverson (1990) to assist family members and school educational staff with joint planning of educational objectives and inclusive school and community activities. Now in its sixth revision, COACH assumes six facts regarding families of severely involved children:

1. They know aspects of their children better than anyone else.

2. They have the greatest vested interest in their children's education.

3. They are the only adults involved in their child's entire school career.

4. They have unique access to information about their children in the home as well as the community.

5. They can benevolently influence the quality of community services.

6. They must live with the outcomes of educational decisions.

Though the focus of care in the family, medical, and educational systems is the same, there will always be areas of disagreement among the various professionals. Goals appropriate at the hospital may not mesh with the goals designed for the classroom. The school may wish a child to perform tasks that the hospital feels are unreasonable. In addition, parents may have expectations entirely different from those of the school or medical staff. Solutions for children with physical disabilities or complex health impairments are not simple and are dependent on effective communication among family, medical, and educational team members. Unfortunately, too often information is communicated only by the family and only after decisions on care or treatment have already been made. This kind of contact can lead to misunderstandings and hard feelings, particularly if the family has bias in one direction or another.

INSTRUCTIONAL CONSIDERATIONS

Frequent absences are a continual problem for children with chronic illnesses. Social adjustment is made more difficult by missing school with periodic episodes of illness or surgeries. The chronicity of their illnesses may cause more difficulties in adjustment and educational progress than the specific disease or condition. As the individual with chronic illness enters junior and senior high school, social experiences may become more complex. Peer rejection of teens who are chronically ill can be kept to a minimum if classroom activities are navigated to emphasize cognitive strengths. Using classmates as home tutors to assist students with health impairments who must miss classes has been found effective.

Gifted children with severe disabilities need modifications to their curriculum that is different from other children who are gifted. They also need more individualized planning for their educational programs than other children with the same primary disability diagnosis. However, many parents and teachers have described the difficulty of identifying children who are gifted when their communication skills are hampered by physical disabilities. Standardized testing (the usual method for identifying superior intellectual skills) is not appropriate for this population. Their limited motor abilities and impaired writing abilities preclude these students from easily communicating their special talents. Many children with communication difficulties cannot express themselves in a manner that makes their special talents or intelligence easily recognized. Intelligence tests usually require writing or other motor manipulation skills. Gifted individuals who cannot type or write because of physical and communication impairments are therefore discriminated against by the testing procedures. This situation has often caused incorrect labeling of students as mentally retarded when they really have normal to gifted intellectual skills. Likewise, many students with gifted abilities have been overlooked at a point in their lives when stimulation and intervention might have the greatest influence on their development. Whitmore (1981) reported that a reasonably accurate estimate of the occurrence of giftedness in combination with disabilities could be as high as 540,000—approximately 5% of the total population with disabilities (Johnsen & Corn, 1989).

Teachers and other educational staff today must be cognizant of herpes, hepatitis, cytomegalovirus, HIV infections, and other communicable diseases. These diseases have brought infection control efforts directly from hospitals into the public schools. Regrettably, many schools have not had sufficient resources directed to the comprehensive planning and development of appropriate programs. In the absence of clear universal regulations regarding the care and education of children with communicable diseases, these needs continue to be addressed in case-by-case, school-by-school fashion. This has resulted in great variations in the provision of care. In some cases teachers are performing intermittent catheterizations and suctioning procedures along with their daily teaching activities. In other reports, school nurses or instructional aides perform all of these procedures. Other schools have attempted to exclude children needing such care from attending school.

Training for this type of physical care has also shown considerable variation. Staff training is necessary for many different positions in schools to avoid the spread of communicable diseases to other students or staff. Bus drivers, cafeteria personnel, custodians, and those in frequent contact with these students must receive accurate information on infection control methods. The information should be conveyed along with the importance of protecting the confidentiality of involved children and their families. A valuable resource has been developed in response to this need by the Iowa Task Force on Children with Special Health Care Needs. This group has developed comprehensive training guidelines for special health care procedures (Task Force on Children with Special Health Care Needs, 1988).

While all of the educational considerations presented in this chapter and all the suggestions for safety and social considerations are important, proper hand-washing techniques have been identified as the single most effective procedure to decrease the spread of infections. Staff in all areas of schools must receive training in these methods. They should wash their hands frequently as they interact with different children and staff of the school.

The field of special education has steadily endorsed the education of students with disabilities in regular classrooms with students without disabilities. Separate facilities or classrooms are now recognized for the limitations they impose on all students. It has also been seen that major social and educational benefits can be attained by serving students with disabilities within their local communities and schools. The support necessary for successful inclusion programs for students with physical disabilities or other health impairments includes staff training, sufficient staffing levels for instructional and therapeutic staff, and strong backing from the principal of the school. When these ingredients are not present there is considerable chance for failure. Parents and teachers can grow resentful of the school's efforts, as successful inclusion may not become a reality in every attempt. Inadequate distribution of resources and space for the special needs of these children can also seriously hamper the program's objectives; for example, extra therapy sessions and additional space to store special adaptive equipment are essential for these children to receive the related services they need. With administrative commitment, instructional staff, a method to access expertise, a process allowing for cooperation, and development of transition and maintenance plans, these difficulties can be minimized (Thousand & Villa, 1993).

Transition Planning

Transition planning can minimize disruption in the family, ensure continuity of services, and help assure that children are prepared to function in the next class or placement outside of school. Planning for the next phase should begin early with the treatment team considering the range of placements that will be necessary for the student and sharing such discussions with the child and family. When the decision is made for moving to the next classroom or school or community placement, staff in the receiving program should share equally in the planning. The receiving professionals will know the environment of the new placement and can minimize the difficulties the student could encounter.

Recent assessments of the **transition** process have shown the critical nature of planning for students with physical disabilities or chronic illnesses. *Transition Planning for the 21st Century*, the report of the conferences in Minnesota sponsored by the National Center for Youth With Disabilities (1995), recommends that programs be based on the youth's abilities and competencies, have a family-centered focus with cultural sensitivity, and include a community-based emphasis with coordination and accountability built into the overall program.

Many specialists in transition planning now recommend that vocational specialists and other community-based professionals begin to attend IEP meetings well in advance of the time that the student will exit school. Psychologists are also recommended for these planning meetings to help the student, parents, and other members of the team understand changes that can be expected as the student moves into adolescence and then adulthood.

Transition planning should be seen as a process that changes and develops as the child grows. At an early age the student should become an integral part of the

There are many different positioning devices that can be used in the classroom.

creation of his or her own plan, and goals should list high expectations that encourage independence and self-reliance.

FAMILY PERSPECTIVES

Families of students with severe physical impairments, chronic illnesses, or terminal diseases obviously undergo many stresses. They can experience financial distress, social isolation, and behavioral difficulties with individual members in direct relation to the seriousness of the illnesses of the affected child. Some diseases, such as juvenile diabetes, may not be readily diagnosed and the symptoms of these illnesses can frustrate those seeking a remedy for the child's discomfort. It is important for teachers to ask about a family's experience and to use empathetic nonjudgmental listening to allow parents time to tell of their experiences within the health care system while searching for a definitive diagnosis of the child's condition.

The stresses on the siblings of children with chronic illnesses are important for teachers and support staff, including school counselors, social workers, and nurses to realize. Many siblings must provide relief for their parents by assisting with the care and supervision of their ailing sister or brother. These youngsters have responsibilities that are generally not imposed on their peers. Despite the nature of these responsibilities and other stresses that these children must contend with, it has been found that well siblings may not always experience a higher incidence of behavior and social competence problems (Gallo, Breitmayer, Knafl, & Zoeller, 1992). Similarly, there have been conflicting findings in studies reviewing family size in relation to coping abilities, although better adaptation was reported by Madan-Swain, Sexson, Brown, and Ragab (1993) in larger families that have a child with cancer. An interesting study by Bouma and Schweitzer (1990) compared stresses noted in families that have a child with a behavioral disorder (autism) with those in families having a child with chronic illness (cystic fibrosis). Their study did not show a relation between a family's stress and the number of well children in either of the family groups, but they found autism contributing more to family stress than cystic fibrosis.

Working With Families

Just as teachers need to use the expertise of the various rehabilitation therapists in structuring their classrooms and educational activities, the perspectives of social workers and other disciplines are required for dealing with families of students who are chronically ill. Effective communication between teachers and these professionals can greatly improve programming for students with disabilities and their families.

Teachers of toddlers, children, and young adults in all educational settings have learned how essential working with the parents or guardians of their students is to success in instructing their children. From the beginnings of early intervention efforts with infants with developmental delays, the teachers, therapists, and other developmental specialists have trained parents to provide therapy and stimulation activities to foster the growth and development of the child. Regular communication with those who interact most frequently with the infant or young child in need of early developmental programming—including the parents, siblings, and often members of the extended family—provides the greatest application of therapeutic and intervention approaches. In the case of children with chronic illnesses or physical impairments, communication and establishment of good working relationships with their families is critical for the child's success.

Thorne and Robinson (1988) describe a positive working relationship between parents and health care professionals as one in which both participants recognize and respect one another's differing points of view and negotiate mutually satisfying forms of care. They see the evolving relationship between families and health care providers as a dynamic process with three distinct stages—moving from naive trusting, to disenchantment, and subsequently to a guarded alliance. These authors define *naive trusting* as the stage in which a family assumes that its perspective on the child is shared with the professionals who care for the ill member of the family. As the *disenchantment* stage develops, trust decreases and the family may express frustration or anger with difficulty in obtaining information from health professionals. In this stage the family often becomes adversarial in an attempt to protect the sick member. *Guarded alliance* is the final stage seen by Thorne and Robinson—one that must be carefully sustained, which involves the rebuilding of trust and an agreement to work cooperatively with health professionals in order to accommodate the family and the professional medical points of view. This fragile nature of collaboration is similar between parents and educators. Parents may be skeptical of teachers' intentions to work with them for the child's benefit in a mutual communication arrangement. Teachers and other school staff must work together to show support to families undergoing the stresses of chronic illness in children.

In a review of nursing research on family adaptation to a child's chronic illness, Austin (1991) described how emotions related to shock, fear, guilt, and anger were common family responses. Families will develop their own methods of coping with the situation, but new illness episodes and other events may cause setbacks. When a well sibling reaches a developmental milestone it may trigger emotional reactions about the health status of the child with chronic conditions.

Many authors have described chronic sorrow since the term was coined by Olshansky in 1962 (Fraley, 1990). Olshansky used the term to depict the unending feelings of loss and fear that parents of children with mental retardation experience. In families with chronically ill children, a similar phenomenon is often seen. Over time the intensity of the emotions will fluctuate, but there remains a constant sense of sorrow in the daily lives of these parents.

A poor initial interaction with health care professionals prior to the child's diagnosis, or in cases with a missed diagnosis, can cause a family to feel victimized and then rescued by the system. Their frustrating experiences within the health care domain may be generalized to distrust of educational professionals.

Parents and families develop coping strategies to adjust to having a child with severe physical or health difficulties. When the need for care of a child in fragile health is extensive, parents may feel socially isolated and imprisoned by the situation. There is a loss of flexibility or spontaneity when the family is without adequate support and relief from the constant monitoring of the child, whom they may feel cannot be safely left in the trust of others. Parents often report experiencing a sense that they have the total responsibility for the life and health of the child.

Educators and health professionals can offer the family emotional support directly or by referrals. Team members must recognize and accept a family's hope for future research into cures or less intrusive treatments for children with chronic illnesses or medically fragile conditions.

It is vital for the teacher and other members of the student's treatment team to stay in close contact with the parents of these students. Warning signs that the parents have noticed prior to seizures, for instance, need to be clearly communicated to the entire team. Often children with heart ailments will exhibit fatigue or other symptoms that when recognized by the team can lessen the severity of an episode. Parents should be encouraged to provide the danger signs so that the school can rapidly notify them or the child's physician before a health-threatening event.

Working with the families of children with significant health care needs is a complicated and recent development for most educators. Coordination between the school and family is critical when the child has severe health impairments. Planning for the transition back and forth between the home and hospital and school is one key to the student's successful progression in times of illness, relapse, or other setbacks.

With the 1986 amendments to the Education for All Handicapped Children Act, an individualized family service plan (IFSP) was included for infants and toddlers found eligible for early intervention services. These plans should include help for families to obtain respite care for relief, especially when they are providing medical care and services to children with complex health care needs. The combination of continual care of a chronic condition of childhood and the financial and emotional stresses of health care procedures places strain on even the healthiest families.

Children who have acquired a brain or spinal cord injury may be very different from how they were prior to the incident. With TBI, families may grieve at first for the child's survival. Then they must face a recovering but often significantly changed member of the family who may be aggressive or even violent. Teachers and school social workers can provide referrals and other information regarding available community support services. Communications from the educational staff can be instrumental for the recovery of the child and support for his family.

CURRENT ISSUES AND FUTURE TRENDS

Technology-Dependent Children

Modern medical advances have allowed for the survival of persons who would not have lived in the recent past. Some of these affected individuals need continual mechanical intervention to sustain their lives. The federal Office of Technology Assessment has defined *technology-dependent* persons as those who use a medical technology (a medical device) to compensate for the loss of a vital body function, and who require substantial daily skilled nursing care to avert death or further disability (U.S. Congress, Office of Technology Assessment, 1987). In surveys conducted in Massachusetts (Palfrey et al., 1991) and New York (Millner, 1991) technologies that are now in common use with individuals who are technology-dependent included respirators, tracheotomies, oxygen, suctioning, gastrostomies, ostomies, genitourinary devices, intravenous devices, and dialysis. These studies and others have found children with a wide range of conditions—including cancer, chronic respiratory disorders, gastrointestinal malformations, muscular dystrophy, asthma, and others—who need such interventions to survive.

The advent of the portable ventilator has enabled persons using this technology to be mobile. Students on mechanical ventilation can routinely attend school, for instance, and adults can continue their employment. There has been a concentrated movement to care for children with such needs in their homes. Nevertheless, many of them continue to receive care primarily in hospitals due to equipment needs, financial constraints, the absence of dependable caretakers, and other limitations.

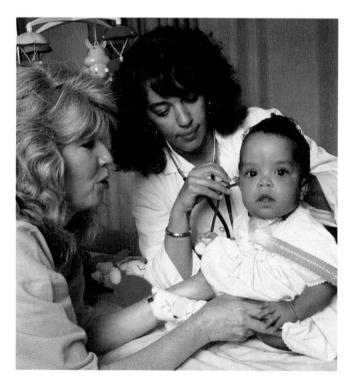

Although many technology-dependent children continue to receive care in hospitals, there has been a concentrated movement to care for children with such needs in their homes.

Most children on mechanical ventilation have attendants who know how to manage their special medical needs. However, teachers need to have basic knowledge of CPR techniques, and some awareness of how to assist the attendant in case of equipment failure.

Children on mechanical ventilation may not have audible speech because of the placement of the tracheostomy tube in the throat to assist in breathing and clearing secretions. Some mode of communication with teachers and classmates needs to be developed, if not already available when the child attends classes. Because so many of these children have other medical problems that often involve the ability to use the arms and hands, adapted communication devices may be necessary.

With ventilator-dependent students, the risk of power outages and other emergencies must be accounted for. Detailed planning for a safe exit from the facility (in case of fire or other dangers) must be strategized prior to the need for evacuation of the student and all the necessary equipment.

Communication with parents and the team of health care professionals for the person on mechanical ventilation is crucial. The classroom teacher may see the child as consistently as parents do and can serve as a valuable observer of the health and emotional status of the student.

The introduction into classrooms of modern machines to help with breathing or other basic functions can be disruptive and disconcerting for some students. Therefore, it is important for classmates to understand why specialized equipment is necessary for their affected classmates. Education of peers through discussions led by the student can promote understanding, acceptance, and integration of students who require the use of technology for life maintenance.

Attitudinal Barriers

Attitudinal barriers continue to limit the expectations and opportunities for individuals with physical disabilities. Bus drivers for special transit services and other line staff need routine training stressing the importance of treating individuals in a respectful manner. Individuals without clear verbal speech often encounter many people who assume they also have a low level of intellectual functioning. Despite the steady improvement in civil rights and integration of people with disabilities, there are daily instances of insensitivity to individual needs. Physicians and other health professionals have been known to talk past young adults with the communication difficulties of cerebral palsy, for instance, in order to direct queries to a parent.

Social restrictions are difficult to change. Nevertheless, the increased visibility of persons with physical disabilities in our society is helping increase integration in basic community activities. As adults and children with disabilities succeed in educational and vocational settings, the community at large should become more comfortable with their presence. Properly planned and administered inclusive education programs show promise in teaching children that they can play an important role in the lives of peers with physical and health-related disabilities. Likewise, they have the opportunity to learn that students with severe disabilities also have much to contribute when given the chance to fully participate in social and educational activities. The legal tenets of the Americans With Disabilities Act of 1990 (ADA) give recourse to persons with disabilities who perceive that discrimination and refusal to make modifications have denied them employment or educational opportunities (Bowman & Marzouk, 1992).

Environmental Modifications

In the past, persons with a disability or health impairment have been restricted in travel, entertainment, employment, and schooling opportunities due to physical and social barriers. But these limitations are now being addressed with federal legislation, including the following acts of Congress:

Architectural Barriers Act of 1968 (P.L. 90-480)

Section 504 of the Rehabilitation Act of 1973 (P.L. 93-112)

Americans With Disabilities Act of 1990 (P.L. 101-336)

Governmental action has been joined by organized, vocal advocacy groups working for equal access and a barrier-free community. Technological developments have made many goals attainable. Nevertheless, persons with physical disabilities or other health impairments often lack the spontaneity in their lives that most of us take for granted (e.g., shopping, visiting a library). For even short travel there is a great deal of planning necessary to manage their physical limitations or special routines (e.g., using public transportation with a wheelchair, managing colostomy care while spending the night at a friend's house). In addition, while adapted facilities may be available for the use of persons with a disability, public abuse of such arrangements may prevent access by the persons for whom they were designed; the frequent abuse of handicapped parking spaces by the general public is a good example.

Barrier-free environments are now legislated in all public buildings under the ADA. This means that schools, restaurants, museums, and other settings must have entrances, bathrooms, telephones, and water fountains accessible to persons with physical disabilities. In school settings, the presence of ramps, accessible buses, and accessible bathrooms have made general access easier for children with disabilities. The variability of needs within various disability groups means there is need for more individualized accommodation as well. Table 10.4 and Table 10.5 provide examples of environmental and task modifications for individual situations.

When a person with a disability or health impairment enters a new educational or vocational setting, advance planning involving the individual, the family, and all appropriate personnel (occupational and physical therapists, administrators, physical plant staff) is critical to ensuring that the environment meets the needs of the individual. Modifications often don't need to be expensive, and may only require simple rearrangement of space and materials or low-tech changes such as a speaker phone instead of a handset.

Assistive Technology

New developments in **assistive technology** have aided the quality of life of persons with disabilities in many ways. Smaller sized computers with larger memory capacities and lower cost translate into increased portability, greater potential for modifications, and facilitated purchase for individuals who are often financially stressed from medical bills. And as computers themselves are more portable, lightweight, and inexpensive, access devices for persons unable to directly use a keyboard are also becoming cheaper and more adaptable for a wider range of

Table 10.4   **Environmental Modifications**

Example:
A 14-year-old male with a spinal cord injury resulting in quadriplegia. Uses a power wheelchair driven by hand control, a computer with an adapted aid strapped to his hand to press the keys, and utensils strapped to his hand to eat.

Transportation and School Entry
- Bus or vehicle with power lift, wheelchair tie-downs and shoulder-to-floor harness for safety in the vehicle
- Curb cuts at home and school
- Entry door opening at home and school (another person or automated opener)
- Ramps if there are steps at home and school, both inside and outside
- Appropriate door width in all buildings and in all rooms

Classrooms
- Adequate wheelchair turning radius in each classroom
- Adequate aisle width within the classroom to drive, and a location socially and physically accessible to peers and the teacher
- Wheelchair-accessible computer station, with power strip, printer, disc storage, and on/off computer access within reach
- Wheelchair-accessible table or counter integrated with other students for reading, science experiments, group work, storage, etc.
- Lazy Susan or other mobile storage unit that allows access to materials
- Aide assigned to load printer paper and discs, put on adapted device for computer use, set up books, get books from book bag, help with classroom assignments, turn in homework, help with putting on and removing coats
- Bookstand to hold books upright
- Signal arranged with teacher for student to ask questions and give answers
- Cafeteria table that is wheelchair-accessible and allows student to sit with peers; aide or other help to put out lunch and set up adapted utensils, clear away after lunch
- Adapted PE setting that is wheelchair-accessible
- Auditorium and library accessibility

Health
- Cot or bed for lying down during the day to prevent pressure sores and to rest; aide to help with transfer
- Private area and aide to help with intermittent self-catheterization
- Aide or student to assist in regular pressure releases
- OT and PT services for problem solving and construction of devices to do schoolwork, teaching transfers, monitoring pressure releases

---

disabilities. One promising development is voice activation, which allows a person to operate a device with simple vocalizations. These units are becoming adaptable enough that persons with speech impairments are able to use them. While voice activation eliminates the need for an access device external to the computer, not all persons have voice capabilities. Breath activation switches, use of head or mouth movement, or virtually any body part can be used to control a computer or communication aid. Most of these types of aids can now be mounted on a wheelchair, allowing them to move with the individual.

Voice-activated devices have existed for some time and are being refined at present for greater accuracy. Combining access sources for multiple units (computers, power chair drive, and environmental controls) is becoming common. As the effectiveness of these integrated systems develop, the costs continue to escalate (Platts & Fraser, 1993; Thornett, Langner, & Brown, 1990). Increasing resources are being channeled into the development of robotic systems to augment and potentially replace the expensive human assistance currently necessary to assist persons with severe disabilities such as those with high level spinal cord injuries (Hammel, Van der Loos, & Perkash, 1992; Pullin & Gammie, 1991; Regalbuto, Krouskop, & Cheatham, 1992; Siddiqui, Ide, Chen, & Akamatsu, 1994).

Table 10.5   **Task Modifications**

Example:
A 6-year-old female with spastic quadriplegia. Has trouble holding onto objects, especially with the tips of her fingers. Task is cutting with scissors.

Position Modifications
- When seated, the hips should be flat against the back of the chair or wheelchair. A seat belt around the hips, not the waist, is used.
- Feet should be flat on a surface, either the floor or wheelchair footrest. Nonslip material may be needed on the floor to keep the feet from slipping.
- Arms on the classroom chair provide support to keep the body straight. A customized wheelchair has special pads that do this if needed.
- The table height should reach just above the waist. A table with a cut-out space to push or roll a chair into would help keep the body straight and give support for the arms as well.

Changes in Location of Materials and Equipment
- Scissors and paper the child uses should be placed on a shelf easily reached from the wheelchair.
- Scissors should be stored in a can or open container so a lid does not need to be moved to get to them.
- The paper or material to be cut should also be in an open box for easy access. Paper in a container keeps the other sheets from falling on the floor if grasp is inaccurate.

Work Surface Modifications
- The table surface should be adjustable so that it can be angled upward at about 25 to 30 degrees to help bring items into the visual field.
- A sheet of nonstick material on the table helps prevent the paper and the child's arms from slipping on the surface.

Object Modifications
- Spasticity causes this child to hold onto regular paper so tightly that it crumples. Stiff paper, like manila folders, helps prevent this problem and gives more sensory feedback when cutting.
- The material being cut should be in half-page size or smaller. The longer the distance to cut, the stiffer the child becomes, making success harder. Smaller sheets of paper give a better chance of success.
- When asked to cut on a line, use wide markers to draw the lines, making cutting easier. Two lines drawn any width apart can also be used to make cutting easier.

Manipulation Aids
- Instead of regular scissors, modified scissors might help. One type is *squeeze scissors*, which require a less precise grasp using all four fingers. These are operated by squeezing to cut, and relaxing the fingers to let go. Another kind is *voluntary opening scissors*, which spring open on their own after a cut is made. Either kind can make cutting an easier task.

A major concern in the area of assistive technology is the continuing high cost of the equipment. Coverage of funding must be addressed to allow equal access to technology for all persons with disabilities (O'Day & Corcoran, 1994). As a start in that direction, Congress passed legislation in 1988 to expand the availability and development of these technological advances. The Technology-Related Assistance for Individuals with Disabilities Act of 1988 (P.L. 100-407) provided states with grant funds to create a coordinated system of technological devices and services; the law was reauthorized in 1994 as P.L. 103-218. The clear legislative intent of this law is to utilize technological advances to assist individuals to become more functionally independent.

Communication devices, environmental control systems, and new kinds of power wheelchairs are other examples of assistive technology that benefits persons with disabilities. Many manufacturers are now combining computer access, environmental controls, and power chair controls into one unit that can be operated through a control box on a power chair, or through a computer system mounted on the chair. By combining complex operating systems into one unit, ease of access is

High-tech modifications, such as this computer with a specialized communication device, allow this boy to talk with his classmates.

greatly expanded for persons with conditions such as high level spinal cord injuries or muscular dystrophy.

While high technology systems have much to offer, simpler low-tech systems often serve just as well at considerably lower cost. Homemade switches (Burkhart, 1987) can operate toys, computers, and some environmental control systems. Touch lamps, available in most stores now, eliminate the need for a standard switch by turning off and on when the base is touched. Simple daily living aids, such as

INNOVATIVE IDEAS   WINNERS ON WHEELS

Winners on Wheels is an exciting and expanding social organization, designed especially for youngsters who use wheelchairs. Modeled somewhat on Girl Scouts and Boy Scouts, this growing organization is designed to improve the self-esteem and productivity of children aged 7 through 15.

WOW Circles are composed of up to 15 members (Winners) with Pit Crews (volunteers) in sites provided by churches, community organizations, corporate sponsors, and other groups. Members meet twice monthly to earn "wheel" awards, which are similar to scout merit badges. Groups and individuals must complete six "spokes" (objectives) to earn a wheel—with the objectives comprising

independent-living activities designed on topics of science and nature, sports and games, arts and crafts, entertainment, interpersonal skills, and community service. Winners generally work on 10 to 12 wheels each year.

Volunteer leaders are developing WOW Circles throughout the country and hundreds of Winners are participating. The Circle leaders are trained at WOW University to start and maintain Circles. WOW National provides guidance and support to their efforts.

Source: Winners on Wheels, 2842 Business Park Avenue, Fresno, CA 93727-1328; phone 209-292-2171, fax 209-292-7412.

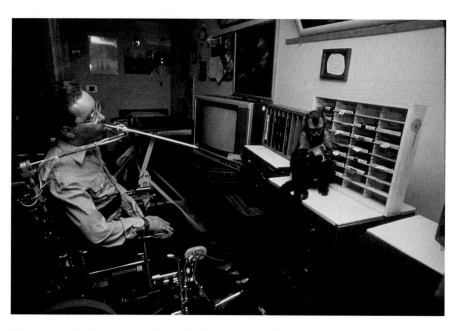

This monkey has been trained to assist his owner in his workplace.

attachments for eating utensils and dressing devices, can provide independence in areas where more sophisticated technology has limited application.

Pets are also being used to operate environmental controls. Dogs and monkeys can be trained to fetch, turn on appliances, open doors, and so on. While not cheap, animals offer the individual with a disability the added benefit of companionship and affection, and sometimes safety.

Recent advances in computerized communication devices have provided new opportunities for nonverbal individuals with physical disabilities. An ever expanding selection of equipment has made it possible to adapt these electronic communication devices for the most facile use of individuals with limited movements. The machine may actually "speak" for its operator or display the individual's written communications. As with other technological advances, these units may be mounted on wheelchairs or manually carried.

The ability to communicate with one's peers is critical to the development of healthy social interaction skills. These new communication devices have provided ways for individuals who are nonverbal to participate much more easily in social and business conversations.

Trauma Prevention

The high rate of childhood trauma, with its devastating outcomes, is a major concern in the United States. The intense focus of health care professionals on the matter is reflective of the magnitude of the problem. The U.S. Department of Health and Human Services has included injury prevention as one of its major goals, while the Centers for Disease Control have established a Center for Injury Control. The National Institute of Child Health and Human Development has formed a special research initiative on injury prevention, and the American Academy of Pediatrics (AAP) has added a division on Injury and Poison Prevention. In

1983, the AAP recommended that all children receive counseling regarding prevention of the most significant traumas. A set of guidelines, *Through the Injury Prevention Program (TIPP)*, available to all pediatricians, was developed by the AAP to help establish injury prevention programs.

In addition to professional and legislative organizations, community agencies have also been concerned with the issue of childhood trauma. Some of these programs are listed among the resources at the end of this chapter. Safety helmets for bicyclists and increased use of seat belts are important national trends for trauma prevention for people of all ages. Similarly the increasing availability of air bags has been identified in the survival of many individuals in serious motor vehicle accidents. (Refer again to Table 10.3, which lists strategies for prevention of trauma.)

Medical Advances

The promise of new medical treatments is one of the major trends for the future. Progress in surgery, medications, prenatal diagnosis, fetal surgery, newborn care (especially for premature infants), rehabilitation modalities, and gene therapy has been rapid, with many advancements in the early stages of development.

Lung transplants are now being used to treat persons with advanced cystic fibrosis, with a reported 1-year survival rate of about 64% (Shennib et al., 1992). Heart transplantation continues to be attempted in infants, with negligible outcomes as yet. Results are better in older children and are improving rapidly in adults. Kidney and liver transplants have been limited primarily by the lack of organ availability.

New surgeries are being developed for children with cerebral palsy. Selective dorsal rhizotomy, where selected nerve roots around the spine are cut, has been successful in reducing spasticity and increasing functional abilities in children with spastic diplegia. Outcomes in other kinds of cerebral palsy have shown more equivocal results.

The oncoming development of new medications, as well as new uses for previously existing drugs, is another area of promise. Steroids in high concentrations, used within 8 hours of spinal cord injury, have been shown to improve sensation and strength recovery in persons with paraplegia and quadriplegia (Hilton & Frei, 1991). Baclofen, used for the control of spasticity in traumatic brain injury, cerebral palsy, and spinal cord injury, appears promising. It has generally been administered into a tube in the spine through a small pump, strapped to the individual's body. Oral baclofen, especially in spinal cord injury, has not proven as useful (Lewis & Mueller, 1993). Prednisone has been used experimentally in children with muscular dystrophy (Fenichel et al., 1991), resulting in improvement in strength. Redfern and O'Dorisio (1993) discuss the promising use of peptides harvested from the gastrointestinal tract in managing such conditions as diabetes, asthma, spinal cord injury, and AIDS.

Amniocentesis and other diagnostic methods to determine conditions prior to birth have also offered the opportunity for development of prenatal surgeries. While such procedures to date have been limited, treatment for heart conditions and other congenital defects could soon be routinely carried out prior to birth. As genetic markers for inherited diseases are identified, it will be possible to diagnose these conditions with greater accuracy prenatally. Hemophilia, a genetic condition characterized by poor blood clotting, is the most recent condition to be diagnosed before birth (Peake et al., 1993). Eventually it may be possible to treat the fetus with gene therapy, altering the outcomes for some conditions.

Electrical stimulation is being used in spinal cord injuries, as well as in other disabilities, to improve breathing functions and bladder control (Yarkony, Roth, Cybulski, & Jaeger, 1992). This modality, like many of the others described in this section, continues to be used primarily on an experimental basis.

Of all the advances in medicine, gene therapy is the most exciting. The treatment of various cancers, acute leukemia, Duchenne's muscular dystrophy, cystic fibrosis, hemophilia, and liver disease have all been investigated with promising results (Akhtar & Ivanson, 1993; Crystal, 1992; Shapiro, 1993; Sivanandham, Scoggin, Sperry, & Wallack, 1992). This field is rapidly evolving and the potential for relief from the impairments caused by chronic diseases is enormous.

Five-Minute Summary

Physical disabilities and health impairments in individuals have been recognized throughout history. Records from numerous cultures identify members with cerebral palsy, epilepsy, and other types of physical or health impairments. Individuals with these types of disabilities often have been separated from the mainstreams of their cultures, and treated as if they threatened the overall culture.

In the 20th century, many Western cultures began seeking medical and habilitative treatments and developing special facilities for citizens with movement disorders or severe health conditions. Schools and residential living facilities were developed to house and educate these individuals separately from general public educational systems.

In the history of the United States, times of national crises have led to the development of treatment techniques and new efforts at habilitation. The Civil War was a period of great advancement in the development of surgical techniques, including amputations and the invention of prosthetics. This technology helped to aid in the daily lives of soldiers with the resultant physical impairments, caused by missing arms or legs. Both World Wars brought great social changes, including the creation of vocational and social services for veterans who were injured. Congressional efforts on behalf of war veterans also opened the door for medical rehabilitation services for others in American society, who had similar physical disabilities, brain injuries, or other health impairments.

As with the families of children with mental retardation, parents of children with cerebral palsy, a nonprogressive neurological and muscular disorder, were instrumental in the movement in the United States to provide multidisciplinary treatment and educational services to their children. This movement on behalf of children with disabilities has progressed in recent history to educate children with physical disabilities and severe, chronic health conditions in mainstream educational programs. Today's inclusion movement seeks to broaden the normalization approach that first began to take shape in the 1950s.

The causes of physical disabilities and other health impairments may be genetic, environmental, or caused by trauma. Today, special education and regular classroom teachers frequently encounter students with physical disabilities or combinations of severe health impairments and physical impairments. Some of the most commonly seen physical conditions of students with special education needs include cerebral palsy, spina bifida, muscular dystrophy, and traumatic brain injury, the fastest growing group of disabling conditions. Some of the most common health impairments that students and teachers encounter include asthma, diabetes, epilepsy, cystic fibrosis and other disabling conditions, characterized by chronic health concerns.

Continuous assessment of the individual student is necessary in order to measure the student against himself, over time for the most useful educational programming.

Parents of children with terminal illnesses or complex health needs encounter emotional and financial stresses, their children's frequent hospitalizations, and the imposing challenges of maintaining educational placements that they see as the most appropriate. Working with families of children with significant health care needs is a complicated recent development for most educators. Nevertheless, teachers are a vital part of the team and must coordinate the student's educational needs with other professionals working with the child. Coordination between the school and family is critical when the child has severe health impairments.

Study Questions

1. List four medical conditions that have a hereditary factor or genetic predisposition.
2. Discuss the changing context of HIV transmission in this country.
3. What is the procedure for managing tonic-clonic seizures?
4. Discuss two possible medical complications that can be seen in spina bifida and spinal cord injury.
5. Discuss two domains of technology advancement that have had major impact on the lives of persons with disabilities and/or other health impairments.
6. Where do multidisciplinary teams break down in planning programs for children with disabilities?
7. Discuss why including the family and child is important in planning individual educational objectives and programs.
8. Discuss five strategies for preventing trauma in children and adolescents.
9. What is the fastest growing disability group in the United States and what are the reasons for this?

For More Information

ORGANIZATIONS

American Burn Association
New York Hospital, Cornell University
525 East 68th Street, Room L706
New York, NY 10021
800-548-2876

American Juvenile Arthritis Organization
1314 Spring Street Northwest
Atlanta, GA 30309
404-872-7100

Asthma and Allergy Foundation of America
1125 15th Street, N.W., Suite 502
Washington, DC 20005
800-7-ASTHMA

Candlelighters Childhood Cancer Foundation
1312 18th Street, N.W., Suite 200
Washington, DC 20036
800-366-2223

Cystic Fibrosis Foundation
6931 Arlington Road
Bethesda, MD 29814-5200
800-FIGHT-CF

Epilepsy Foundation of America
4351 Garden City Drive, Suite 406
Landover, MD 20785
800-EFA-1000

In Touch With Kids
National Spinal Cord Injury Association
545 Concord Avenue, Suite 29
Cambridge, MA 02138
800-962-9629

Juvenile Diabetes Foundation International
432 Park Avenue South
New York, NY 10016
800-JDF-CURE

Leukemia Society of America
600 Third Avenue
New York, NY 10016
800-955-4LSA

Muscular Dystrophy Association, Inc.
3300 East Sunrise Drive
Tucson, AZ 85718
602-529-2000

National Head Injury Foundation
1140 Connecticut Avenue, Suite 812
Washington, DC 20036
800-444-6443

National Spinal Cord Injury Association
600 West Cummings Park, Suite 2000
Woburn, MA 01801-6379
800-962-9629

Pediatrics AIDS Foundation
2210 Wilshire Boulevard
Santa Monica, CA 90403-5784
800-552-0444

Spina Bifida Association of America
4590 MacArthur Boulevard, Suite 250
Washington, DC 20007
800-621-3141

United Cerebral Palsy Association
1522 K Street, N.W.
Washington, DC 20005
800-872-5827   202-842-1266 (Voice or TT)

BOOKS AND ARTICLES

Amado, A. N., Conklin, F., & Wells, J. *Friends: A manual for connecting persons with disabilities and community members.* Minnesota Governor's Planning Council on Developmental Disabilities, 300 Centennial Office Bldg., 658 Cedar Street, St. Paul, MN 55155; 612-296-4018.

Anderson, E. M., & Clarke, L. (1982). *Disability in adolescence.* New York: Methuen.

Bigge, J. L. (1991). *Teaching individuals with physical and multiple disabilities* (3rd ed.). Columbus, OH: Merrill.

Bloom, B., & Selijeskog, E. (1988). *A parent's guide to spina bifida.* Minneapolis: University of Minnesota Press.

Crocker, A. C., Lavin, A. T., Palfrey, J. S., Porter, S. M., Shaw, D. M., & Weill, K. S. (1994). Supports for children with HIV infection in school: Best practices guidelines. *Journal of School Health, 64,* 32–34.

Freeman, J., Vining, E., & Pillas, D. J. (1990). *Seizures and epilepsy in childhood: A guide for parents.* Baltimore: John Hopkins University Press (800-537-5487).

Geralis, E. (1991). *Children with cerebral palsy: A parent's guide.* Rockville, MD: Woodbine House.

Graff, J., Mulligan Ault, M., Guess, D., Taylor, M., & Thompson, B. (1990). *Health care for students with disabilities.* Baltimore: Paul H. Brookes.

Haynie, M., Proter, S., & Palfrey, J. (1989). *Children assisted by medical technology in educational settings: Guidelines for care.* Boston: Children's Hospital.

Kobrin, E. R. (1991). *Issues and answers: A guide for parents of teens and young adults with epilepsy.* Landover, MD: Epilepsy Foundation of America.

Larson, G. (Ed.). (1988). *Managing the school age child with a chronic health condition.* Wayzata, MN: DCI Publishing.

Panzarino, C., & Lash, M. (1994). *Rebecca finds a new way: How kids learn, play, and live with spinal cord injuries and illnesses.* Woburn, MA: National Spinal Cord Injury Association.

Phelps, W. M. (1948). Let's define cerebral palsy. *Crippled Child, 26,* 3–5.

Pollock, E., Fue, L. D., & Goldstein, S. (1993). *A teacher's guide: Managing children with brain injury in the classroom.* Salt Lake City: Neurology, Learning & Behavior Center.

VIDEO AND ELECTRONIC MEDIA

Inside Moves [Film].
1980, Goodmark Productions (ITC Home Video).

Mask [Film].
1985, Universal Pictures (MCA Home Video).

My Left Foot [Film].
1980, Miramax (HBO Home Video).

The Waterdance [Film].
1992, JBW Productions (Columbia Tri-Star Home Video).

World Wide Web

One of the most interesting places on the WWW is the *Yahoo* site. The section on "Society and Culture: Disabilities" is full of useful information:

http://www.yahoo.com/Society_and_Culture/Disabilities

Truthful to its name is the *Cornucopia of Disability:*

http://primes6.rehab.uiuc.edu/pursuit/disresources/inet-dis/inet-dis.html

Access to the Skies from the Paralysis Society of America is dedicated to dignified air travel for people with disabilities:

http://www.computek.net/access95

For extensive information on workplace accommodations for persons with musculoskeletal disorders:

http://janweb.icdi.wvu.edu/kinder/509skele

Disability-related information from the Rehabilitation Research and Training Center of West Virginia University:

http://www.icdi.wvu.edu/Others.html

Resources for research on disabilities from the University of Kansas:

http://www.sped.ukans.edu/speddisabilitiesstuff/speddisabilities-univs.html

The NCSA Mosaic AccessPage on use of the Internet and WWW by people with disabilities:

http://bucky.aa.uic.edu

Communications Technology for Everyone by Peter David Blanck:

http://www.law.indiana.edu/fclj/v47/no2/blanck.html

Disability Now, an electronic newsletter covering all disability issues:

http://www.pavilion.co.uk/Common Room/DisabilitiesAccess/D-Access/DN_News.html

Mark Nagler's reviews of books on disability:

http://www.books.com/releases/disab.htm

OTHER SOURCES

AT&T Accessible Communications Products Center
800-233-1222 (Voice and TT)

Centers for Disease Control
National AIDS Hotline
800-342-2437 (Voice-English)   800-344-7432 (Voice-Spanish)
800-243-7889 (TT)

National Child Abuse Hotline
800-422-4453

National Library Service for the Blind and Physically Handicapped
800-424-8567 (Voice)   800-424-9100 (TT-English)
800-345-8901 (TT-Spanish)

Pediatric AIDS Clearinghouse
310-395-9051 (Voice)

References

Akhtar, S., & Ivinson, A. J. (1993). Therapies that make sense [News]. *Nature Genetics, 4,* 215–271.

Anderson, V. E., & Hauser, W. A. (1988). Genetics. In J. Laidlaw, A. Richens, & J. Oxley (Eds.), *A textbook of epilepsy* (pp. 49–77). London: Churchill Livingstone.

Appleton, R. E., Bushby, K., Gardner-Medwin, D., Welch, J., & Kelly, P. J. (1991). Head circumference and intellectual performance of patients with Duchenne muscular dystrophy. *Developmental Medicine and Child Neurology, 33,* 884–890.

Austin, J. (1991). Family adaptation to a child's chronic illness. *Annual Review of Nursing Research, 9,* 103–120.

Bailey, R. B. (1991). Urologic management of spina bifida. In H. L. Rekate (Ed.), *Comprehensive management of myelodysplasia* (pp. 185–214). Boca Raton, FL: CRC Press.

Ball, J.D. (1988) *The nature of pediatric brain injury: Implications for educators.* Presentation to the Virginia Conference on Traumatic Brain Injury and the Student, Richmond, VA.

Bennett, T. L. (Ed.). (1992). *Neuropsychology of epilepsy.* New York: Plenum.

Berent, S., & Sackellares, C. (1989). Clinical monitoring of children with epilepsy: A neurologic and neuropsychological perspective. In B. P. Hermann & M. Seidenberg (Eds.), *Childhood epilepsies: Neuropsychological, psycho-social and intervention aspects* (pp. 15–32). Chichester, England: Wiley.

Blackman, J. (1990). Cerebral palsy. In J. Blackman (Ed.), *Medical aspects of developmental disabilities in children birth to three* (2nd ed., pp. 59–66). Rockville, MD: Aspen.

Bouma, R., & Schweitzer, R. (1990). Impact of chronic childhood illness on family stress: A comparison between autism and cystic fibrosis. *Journal of Clinical Psychology, 46*(6), 722–730.

Bowman, O. J., & Marzouk, D. K. (1992). Using the Americans with Disabilities Act of 1990 to empower university students with disability. *American Journal of Occupational Therapy, 46,* 450–460.

Bromfield, R., Weisz, J. R., & Messer, T. (1986). Children's judgments and attributions in response to the mentally retarded label: A developmental approach. *Journal of Abnormal Psychology, 95,* 81–87.

Brooke, M. H. (1986). *A clinician's view of neuromuscular diseases.* Baltimore: Williams & Wilkins.

Burkhart, L. J. (1987). *Simplified technology for the severely handicapped: Control for battery toys and computers.* College Park, MD: Linda Burkhart.

Butler, K. M., & Pizzo, P. A. (1992). HIV infection in children. In V. T. DeVita, Jr., S. Hellman, & S. A. Rosenberg (Eds.), *AIDS: Etiology, diagnosis, treatment, and prevention* (pp. 285–305). Philadelphia: Lippincott.

Caldwell, T. H., Todaro, A. W., & Gates, A. J. (1989). Special health care needs. In J. L. Bigge (Ed.), *Teaching individuals with physical and multiple disabilities* (pp. 50–74). Columbus, OH: Merrill.

Capute, A. J., & Accardo, P. J. (1991). Cerebral palsy: The spectrum of motor dysfunction. In A. J. Capute & P. J. Accardo (Eds.), *Developmental disabilities in infancy and childhood* (pp. 335–348). Baltimore: Paul H. Brookes.

Cavan, D. A., & Barnett, A. H. (1993). Genetic causes of insulin dependent diabetes mellitus. In R. D. Leslie (Ed.), *Causes of diabetes: Genetic and environmental* (pp. 3–21). New York: Wiley.

Centers for Disease Control. (1990). Regional variation in diabetes mellitus prevalence—United States, 1988 and 1989. *Morbidity and Mortality Weekly Report, 39,* 805–812.

Centers for Disease Control (1995, February 10). Update: AIDS among women—United States, 1994 (1995). *Morbidity and Mortality Weekly Report, 44*(5), 81–84.

Christensen, E., & Melchior, J. (1967). *Cerebral palsy: A clinical and neuropathological study.* Suffolk, England: Medical Information Unit of the Spastics Society.

Cole, D. A. (1986). Facilitating play in children's peer relationships: Are we having fun, yet? *American Educational Research Journal, 23,* 201–215.

Coultas, D. B., & Samet, J. M. (1993). Epidemiology and natural history of childhood asthma. In D. G. Tinkelman and C. K. Naspitz (Eds.), *Childhood asthma: Pathophysiology and treatment* (pp. 71–114). New York: Marcel Dekker.

Crocker, A. C., Lavin, A. T., Palfrey, J. S., Porter, S. M., Shaw, D. M., & Weill, K. S. (1994). Supports for children with HIV infection in school: Best practices guidelines. *Journal of School Health, 64,* 32–34.

Crockett, A. (1993). *Managing asthma in primary care.* Oxford, England: Blackwell Scientific Publications.

Crystal, R. G. (1992). Gene therapy for pulmonary disease. *American Journal of Medicine 92(6A),* 44S–52S.

Davidson, M. B. (1991). *Diabetes mellitus* (3rd ed.). New York: Churchill Livingstone.

Dreifuss, F. E. (1989). Childhood epilepsies. In B. P. Hermann & M. Seidenberg (Eds.), *Childhood epilepsies: Neuropsychological, psycho-social and intervention aspects* (pp. 1–14). Chichester, England: Wiley.

Dubowitz, V. (1989). *The color atlas of muscle disorders in childhood.* Chicago: Year Book Medical Publishers.

Fenichel, G. M., Mendell, J. R., Moxley, R. T., III, Griggs, R. C., Brooke, M. H., Miller, J. P., Pestronk, A., Robison, J., King, W., & Signore, L. (1991). A comparison of daily and alternate-day prednisone therapy in the treatment of Duchenne muscular dystrophy. *Archives of Neurology, 48,* 575–579.

Fraley, A. M. (1990). Chronic sorrow: A parental response. *Journal of Pediatric Nursing, 5* (4), 268–273.

Gallo, A. M., Breitmayer, B. J., Knafl, K. A., & Zoeller, L. H. (1992). Well siblings of children with chronic illness: Parents' reports of their psychologic adjustment. *Pediatric Nursing, 18* (1), 23–27.

Giancreco, M. F., Cloninger, C. J., & Iverson, V. S. (1990). *C.O.A.C.H.—Cayuga-Onondaga assessment for children with handicaps* (6th ed.). Stillwater: Oklahoma State University, National Clearing House of Rehabilitative Training Materials.

Graffi, S., & Minnes, P. M. (1988). Attitudes of primary school children toward the physical appearance and labels associated with Down syndrome. American Journal of Mental Retardation, 93, 28–35.

Hahn, H. (1988). The politics of physical differences: Disability and discrimination. *Journal of Social Issues, 44,* 39–47.

Hammel, J. M., Van der Loos, H. F., & Perkash, I. (1992). Evaluation of a vocational robot with a quadriplegic employee. *Archives of Physical Medicine & Rehabilitation, 73,* 683–693.

Hermann, B. P., Desai, B. T., & Whitman, S. (1988). Epilepsy. In V. B. Van Hassalt, P. S. Strain, & M. Hersen (Eds.), *Handbook of developmental and physical disabilities* (pp. 247–270). New York: Pergamon.

Hilton, G., & Frei, J. (1991). High-dose methylprednisolone in the treatment of spinal cord injuries. *Heart and Lung, 20,* 675–680.

Holt, P. J. (1990). The classification of juvenile chronic arthritis. *Clinical and Experimental Rheumatology, 8,* 331–333.

Howes, C. (1988). Peer interaction of young children. *Monographs of the Society for Research in Child Development, 53*, (1, Serial No. 217).

Interstate Research Associates. (1992). *Epilepsy: General information fact sheet number 6.* Washington, DC: National Information Center for Children and Youth With Disabilities.

Johnsen, S. K., & Corn, A. L. (1989, September). The past, present and futures of education for gifted children with sensory and/or physical disabilities. *Roeper Review, 12*(1), pp. 13–23.

Kahn, N. A., & Battle, C. U. (1987). Chronic illness: Implications for development and education. *Topics in Early Childhood, 6*(4), 25–32.

Knowler, W. C., McCance, D. R., Nagi, D. K., & Pettitt, D. J. (1993). Epidemiological studies of the causes of non-insulin dependent diabetes mellitus. In R. D. Leslie (Ed.), *Causes of diabetes: Genetic and Environmental* (pp. 187–218). New York: Wiley.

LaGreca, A. M., Satin Rapaport, W., & Skyler, J. S. (1991). Emotion: A critical factor in diabetes control. In M. B. Davidson (Ed.), *Diabetes mellitus* (3rd ed., pp. 403–417). New York: Churchill Livingstone.

Laplaza, F. J., Root, L., Tassanawipas, A., & Cervera, P. (1992). Cerebral palsy in twins. *Developmental Medicine and Child Neurology, 34*, 1053–1063.

Lehr, D. H. (1993) Providing education to students with complex health care needs. In E. L. Meyen (Ed.), *Challenges facing special education.* Denver: Love.

Leventhal, B. (1987). Neoplasms and neoplasm-like structures. In R. E. Behrman, V. C. Vaughan, & W. E. Nelson (Eds.), *Nelson's textbook of pediatrics* (13th ed., pp. 1079–1110). Philadelphia: Saunders.

Lewis, K. S., & Mueller, W. M. (1993). Intrathecal baclofen for severe spasticity secondary to spinal cord injury. *Annals of Pharmacotherapy, 27*, 767–774.

Little, W. J. (1861, October 19). Influence of abnormal parturition, difficult labour, premature birth, and asphyxia neonatorum on the mental and physical condition of the child, especially in relation to deformities. *Lancet.*

Madan-Swain, A., Sexson, S. B., Brown, R. T., & Ragab, A. (1993). Family adaptation and coping among siblings of cancer patients, their brothers and sisters, and nonclinical controls. *American Journal of Family Therapy, 21*(1), 60–70.

McCarthy, M., & Hilmen, G. A. (1993). The genetic aspects of non-insulin dependent diabetes mellitus. In R. D. Leslie (Ed.), *Causes of diabetes: Genetic and environmental* (pp. 158–183). New York: Wiley.

Michaud, L. J., Duhaime, A. C., & Bateshaw, M. L. (1993). Traumatic brain injury in children. *Pediatric Clinics of North America, 40*, 553–565.

Miller, G., Tunnecliffe, M., & Douglas, P. S. (1985). IQ, prognosis and Duchenne muscular dystrophy. *Brain and Development, 7*, 7–9.

Miller, J. R., Colbert, A. P., & Osberg, J. S. (1990). Ventilator dependency: Decision-making, daily functioning, and quality of life for patients with Duchenne's muscular dystrophy. *Developmental Medicine and Child Neurology, 32*, 1078–1086.

Millner, B. N. (1991). Technology dependent children in New York state. *Bulletin of the New York Academy of Medicine, 67*, 131–142.

Mills, J. L., & Simpson, J. L. (1993). Prospects for prevention of neutral tube defects by vitamin supplementation. *Current Opinion in Neurology & Neurosurgery, 6*, 554–558.

Molnar, G. B. (1991). Rehabilitation in cerebral palsy. *Western Journal of Medicine, 154*, 569–572.

Mulherin, D., & Fitzgerald, M. (1992). Cystic fibrosis in adolescents and adults: The coming of age of cystic fibrosis. *Digestive Digest, 10*(1), 29–37.

Mullins, J. B. (1986). Events influencing physically handicapped and health impaired people in the United States. *DPH Journal, 9*(1), 27–39.

Murphy, J. V., & Dehkharghani, F. (1993). *Handbook of pediatric epilepsy.* New York: Marcel Dekker.

National Center for Youth With Disabilities. (1995). *Transition planning for the 21st century.* Minneapolis: National Center for Youth With Disabilities.

National Head Injury Foundation. (1986). *Definition of traumatic head injury.* Washington, DC: National Head Injury Foundation.

National Institute of Neurological Disorders and Stroke. (1989). *Interagency head injury task force report.* Bethesda, MD: National Institutes of Health.

National Spinal Cord Injury Association. (1994). *Spinal cord injury statistical information* (NSCIA Fact Sheet #2) [Brochure]. Cambridge, MA: National Spinal Cord Injury Association.

O'Day, B. L., & Corcoran, P. J. (1994). Assistive technology: Problems and policy alternatives. *Archives of Physical Medicine & Rehabilitation, 75*, 1165–1169.

Olshansky, S. (1962). Chronic sorrow: A response to having a mentally defective child. *Social Casework, 43*, 190–193.

Palfrey, J. S., Walker, D. K., Haynie, M., Singer, J. D., Porter, S., Bushey, B., & Cooperman, P. (1991). Technology's children: Report of a statewide census of children dependent on medical supports. *Pediatrics, 87*, 611–618.

Peake, I. R., Lillicrap, D. P., Boulyjenkov, V., Briet, E., Chan, V., Ginter, E. K., Kraus, E. M., Ljung, R., Mannucci, P. M., & Nicolaides, K. (1993). Haemophilia: Strategies for carrier detection and prenatal diagnosis. *Bulletin of the World Health Organization, 71*, 429–458.

Pearson, M. L., Cole, J., & Jarvis, W. R. (1994). How common is latex allergy? A survey of children with myelodysplasia. *Developmental Medicine and Child Neurology, 36*, 64–69.

Platts, R. G., & Fraser, M. H. (1993). Assistive technology in the rehabilitation of patients with high spinal cord lesions. *Paraplegia, 31*, 280–287.

Pullin, G., & Gammie, A. (1991). Current capabilities of rehabilitation robots. *Journal of Biomedical Engineering, 13*, 215–216.

Quackenbush, M., & Sargent, P. (1990). *Teaching AIDS: A resource guide on Acquired Immune Deficiency Syndrome* (3rd ed.). (ERIC Document Reproduction Services No. ED 277 936)

Redfern, J. S., & O'Dorisio, T. M. (1993). Therapeutic uses of gastrointestinal peptides. *Endocrinology & Metabolism Clinics of North America, 22*, 845–873.

Reed, K. L. (1992). History of federal legislation for persons with disabilities. *American Journal of Occupational Therapy, 46*, 397–408.

Regalbuto, M. A., Krouskop, T. A., & Cheatham, J. B. (1992). Toward a practical mobile robotic aid system for people with severe disabilities. *Journal of Rehabilitation Research & Development, 29*, 19–26.

Rekate, H. L. (1991). *Comprehensive management of spina bifida.* Boca Raton, FL: CRC Press.

Rodriguez, J. G., & Brown, S. T. (1990). Childhood injuries in the United States. *The American Journal of Diseases of Children, 144*, 627–646.

Rush, D. (1994). Periconceptional folate and neural tube defect. *American Journal of Clinical Nutrition, 59*(Suppl. 2), 511S–515S, discussion 515S–516S.

Sandford, M. K., Kissling, G. E., & Joubert, P. E. (1992). Neural tube defect etiology: New evidence concerning maternal hyperthermia, health and diet. *Developmental Medicine and Child Neurology, 34*, 661–675.

Scheer, J., & Groce, N. (1988). Impairment as a human constant: Cross-cultural and historical perspectives on variation. *Journal of Social Issues, 44*, 23–37.

Schoub, B. D. (1994). *AIDS & HIV in perspective: A guide to understanding the virus and its consequences.* NY: Cambridge University Press.

Schwartz, R. H., Eaton, J., Bower, D., & Aynesley-Green, A. (1989). Ketogenic diets in the treatment of epilepsy: Short-term clinical effects. *Developmental Medicine and Child Neurology, 31*, 145–159.

Sears, M. R. (1991). Epidemiological trends in bronchial asthma. In M. A. Kaliner, P. J. Barnes, & C. G. Persson (Eds.), *Asthma: Its pathology and treatment* (pp. 1–49). New York: Marcel Dekker.

Seidenberg, M. (1989). Academic achievement and school performance of children with epilepsy. In B. P. Hermann & M. Seidenberg (Eds.), *Childhood epilepsies: Neuropsychological, psycho-social and intervention aspects* (pp. 15–32). Chichester, England: Wiley.

Senelick, R. C., & Ryan, C. E. (1991). *Living with head injury.* Washington, DC: Rehabilitation Hospital Services Corporation.

Shak, S., Capon, D. J., Hellmiss, R., Marsters, S. A., & Baker, C. L. (1993). Recombinant human DNase I reduces the viscosity cystic fibrosis sputum. *Proceedings of the National Academy of Sciences—USA 87*(230), 9188–9192.

Shapiro, L. J. (1993). Gene therapy: Possibilities and promise. *Pediatric Research, 33* (4 Pt 1), 321–322.

Shapiro, J., & Shumaker, S. (1987). Differences in emotional well-being and communication styles between mothers and fathers of pediatric cancer patients. *Journal of Psychosocial Oncology, 5*(3), 121–131.

Shaw, G. M., Schaffer, D., Velie, E. M., Morland, K., & Harris, J. A. (1995). Periconceptional vitamin use, dietary folate, and the occurrence of neural tube defects. *Epidemiology, 6*(3), 219–226.

Shennib, H., Noirclerc, M., Ernst, P., Metras, D., Mulder, M. S., Giudicelli, R., Lebel, F., & Dumon, J. F. (1992). Double-lung transplantation for cystic fibrosis. The Cystic Fibrosis Transplant Study Group. *Annals of Thoracic Surgery, 54*, 27–31.

Siddiqu, N. A., Ide, T., Chen, M. Y., & Akamatsu, N. (1994). A computer-aided walking rehabilitation robot. *American Journal of Physical Medicine & Rehabilitation, 73*, 212–216.

Sivanandham, M., Scoggin, S. D., Sperry, R. G., & Wallack, M. K. (1992). Prospects for gene therapy and lumphokine therapy for metastatic melanoma. *Annals of Plastic Surgery, 28*, 114–118.

Sollee, N. D., Latham, E. E., Kindlon, D. J., & Bresnan, M. J. (1985). Neuro-psychological impairment in Duchenne muscular dystrophy. *Journal of Clinical and Experimental Neuropsychology, 7*, 486–496.

Stine, G. J. (1993). *Acquired Immune Deficiency Syndrome: Biological, medical, social and legal issues.* Englewood Cliffs, NJ: Prentice-Hall.

Tajima, N., Matsushima, M., & La Porte, R. (1993). Population studies. In R. D. Leslie (Ed.), *Causes of diabetes: Genetic and environmental* (pp. 25–44). New York: Wiley.

Task Force on Children with Special Health Care Needs. (1988). *Recommendations: Services for children with special health care needs.* Des Moines: Iowa Department of Education.

THINK FIRST Foundation. (1993). *The national head & spinal cord injury prevention program.* Park Ridge, IL: THINK FIRST Foundation.

Thorne, S., & Robinson, C. (1988). Health care relationships: The chronic illness perspective. *Research in Nursing and Health, 11*, 293–300.

Thornett, C. E., Langner, M. C., & Brown, A. W. (1990). Disabled access to information technology—A portable, adaptable, multipurpose device. *Journal of Biomedical Engineering, 12*, 205–208.

Thousand, J. S., & Villa, R. A. (1993). Strategies for educating learners with severe disabilities within their local home schools and communities. In E. L. Meyen (Ed.), *Challenges facing special education.* Denver: Love.

Unsworth, L., & Howard, V. F. (1994). Children, youth and chronic illnesses: Cancer and AIDS in the classroom. *British Columbia Journal of Special Education, 18*, 70–80.

U.S. Congress, Office of Technology Assessment. (1987). *Technology dependent children: Hospital v. home care: A technical memorandum.* (TA-TM-H-38) Washington, DC: U.S. Government Printing Office.

Vandvik, I. H., & Hoyeraal, H. M. (1993). Juvenile chronic arthritis: A bio-behavioral disease. Some unanswered questions. *Clinical and Experimental Rheumatology, 11,* 669–680.

Wald, N. J. (1994). Folic acid and neural tube defects: The current evidence and implications for prevention. *Ciba Foundation Symposium, 181,* 192–208.

Weinberg, N. (1978). Preschool children's perceptions of orthopedic disability. *Rehabilitation Counseling Bulletin,* 183–189.

Weinberger, M. (1990). *Managing asthma.* Baltimore: Williams & Wilkins.

Whitmore, J. R. (1981). Gifted children with handicapped conditions: A new frontier. *Exceptional Children, 48*(2), 108–119.

Wolf, J. M. (Ed.). (1969). *Results of treatment in cerebral palsy.* Springfield, IL: Thomas.

Wolraich, M. L. (1990). Myelomeningocele. In J. A. Blackman (Ed.), *Medical aspects of developmental disabilities in children birth to three* (2nd ed., pp. 197–204). Rockville, MD: Aspen.

Yarkony, G. M., Roth, E. J., Cybulski, G. R., & Jaeger, R. J. (1992). Neuromuscular stimulation in spinal cord injury II: Prevention of secondary complications. *Archives of Physical Medicine & Rehabilitation, 73,* 195–200.

Zelinski, J. J. (1988). Epidemiology. In J. Laidlaw, A. Richens, & J. Oxley (Eds.), *A textbook of epilepsy* (pp. 21–48). London: Churchill Livingstone.

Chapter 11

Spacecraft and Family, acrylic on canvas, 60″ × 82″ (1989)

MENTAL RETARDATION

ANDREA M. LAZZARI AND JUDY W. WOOD

After studying this chapter, the reader will:

Be familiar with the historical influences that have shaped the
development of services for persons with mental retardation

Be able to define mental retardation

Know the common causes of mental retardation

Identify characteristics common to many individuals
with mental retardation

Understand the educational and vocational needs
of persons with mental retardation

Be aware of the measures that can be taken
to prevent mental retardation

Appreciate key issues and family concerns across the life spans
of persons with mental retardation

MENTAL RETARDATION

Ancient times   Infants born with severe or profound mental retardation were often killed, or sometimes (when older) sold into slavery.

5th–16th centuries   Many abandoned children, including those with mental retardation, were placed in church-supported hospitals and orphanages across Europe.

1547   Bethlehem Royal Hospital (later called Bedlam), was established in London.

1672   Thomas Willis published a treatise distinguishing the thought processes of "stupidity" (mental retardation) from those of "foolishness" (mental illness).

1773   The first separate public mental hospital in what was to become the United States was opened in Williamsburg, Virginia.

1798   The "Wild Boy of Aveyron" was found by hunters in France and taken to Dr. Jean Marc Itard. Itard's efforts to teach the boy marked the origin of special education.

1850   Samuel Gridley Howe established a school for "idiotic and feebleminded" children in Massachusetts.

Late 1800s   The first public school day classes for pupils with mental retardation were initiated in Providence, Rhode Island.

1905   Alfred Binet and Theodore Simon developed the first set of mental measurement tests.

1907   Indiana was the first state to pass legislation allowing eugenic sterilization to prevent "procreation of confirmed criminals, idiots, imbeciles, and rapists."

1946   The New York City Board of Education designated schools numbering in the 600s for "the handicapped," including disturbed and maladjusted pupils.

1958   P.L. 85–926 (Training of Professional Personnel) provided $1 million to colleges and universities to train professional educators to teach students with mental retardation.

1961   President John F. Kennedy appointed a special President's Panel on Mental Retardation (PPMR).

1971   *Pennsylvania Association of Retarded Children (PARC) v. Commonwealth of Pennsylvania* established a right to education for children with mental retardation.

1992   The American Association on Mental Retardation published its most recent definition of mental retardation.

INTRODUCTION

Andy, age 3, is lovable and adorable. He wakes up each morning smiling and takes off running. He is always into something—trying to bathe the cat in his wading pool, imitating his teenage brother's dance steps, or hiding in the laundry basket at bedtime. Andy goes to preschool each morning and to day care at a neighbor's home in the afternoon. He wants to be a policeman when he grows up, just like his grandpa.

Marla, age 9, has shiny dark hair and beautiful brown eyes. She loves to roller-skate, play dolls with her friends, and go to Girl Scouts. She is a good student although her mom often has to remind Marla to do her homework. Last year Marla played the part of a princess in a school play. Now, she wants to be an actress when she grows up. She often can be found in front of the bathroom mirror practicing her lines.

Tony, age 14, attends middle school. His favorite subjects are science and art. One of his drawings received second prize in a schoolwide art show. Tony spends his spare time hanging out with a friend from his class at school. Tony has a crush on a girl in his class, but he's too shy to approach her. His older brothers tease Tony about his girlfriend and that makes him mad. Tony has no idea of what he wants to do when he finishes school.

Donna, age 23, lives at home with her parents and her younger sister. Donna works for a local food distributing company, sorting damaged food. Although she wants to live in an apartment with a roommate, Donna does not earn enough money to leave home and support herself. Her parents do not feel Donna is ready to live independently. Donna's boss describes her as one of the company's hardest workers. Donna enjoys going to dances and movies in her spare time. She talks about getting married some day but right now is busy with her job, friends, and family.

What do Andy, Marla, Tony, and Donna have in common? Several things come to mind. Each of them is loved by his or her family and liked by friends, teachers, or bosses. Each is successful at school or work. They like to do the same things as others their own ages. And, each of them has been identified as a person with mental retardation.

In this chapter we will discuss the category of persons with mental retardation. The chapter will focus on the history of services for individuals with mental retardation, the evolution of definitions of mental retardation, causes and prevention of mental retardation, education of students with mental retardation, serving these students in inclusive settings, and current issues affecting persons with mental retardation and their families.

HISTORICAL OVERVIEW

It is important to keep in mind that early historical accounts no doubt refer to those individuals with only the most noticeable or severe disabilities. Individuals with mild or moderate mental retardation often did not stand out as being different from the rest of society, especially when most individuals did not read or write. In addition, early historical accounts make no distinction between persons with mental retardation and those with mental illness.

In ancient cultures, great emphasis was placed on physical beauty and mental ability. In ancient Greece, children with disabilities were killed or sold as slaves.

REAL PEOPLE   *Kelly Choularton*

At age 14, Kelly Choularton of Grand Prairie, Texas, has experienced more than many of us have in a lifetime. In addition to the typical things teenage girls do—go to school, play sports, hang out with friends, and experiment with hair and makeup, she has traveled to Europe, visited relatives on both coasts, and won a medal for her track performance. She has also had open-heart surgery, struggled with learning to speak, and spent months learning how to use her pincer grasp. Kelly has Down syndrome.

Although there was no reason to believe otherwise, Kelly's mom, Peggy Ellis, says she knew the entire time she was pregnant with Kelly that she was going to have a child with disabilities. "I made my husband promise that if we had a child with physical disabilities we would keep her, but that if she was mentally retarded we would put her up for adoption, because I just didn't think I could handle it. When Kelly was born she was not breathing nor did she have a heartbeat, but she was revived while on her way by ambulance to another hospital. My husband went to the hospital with her, and when he returned to me and told me of her prognosis, I told him I did not want to give her up—I wanted to keep her. I guess in those few minutes I had with her immediately after birth I fell in love with her and knew I could never give her up."

Kelly began "school" when she was 5 months old, when physical therapists tried to teach her to roll over. Because her heart was so weak (she had closed-heart surgery at 10 months and open-heart at 11 months) she wasn't able to do much but lie there, but she responded to faces and voices, and she "always had a twinkle in her eye," says Peggy. She began preschool at the lab school at San Diego State University where she played with children without disabilities, and also attended a regular first grade class. During elementary school, Kelly attended mostly special education classes, although she was mainstreamed into regular education classes in lower grades for some content areas, like science. Now in the seventh grade, Kelly is in a self-contained class and is mainstreamed for things like lunch. She rides the "regular" bus to and from school and stays home with her brother Sebastian, 12, until their mother gets home from work.

Kelly is also very active in sports. She plays soccer and baseball and until recently she also bowled. Not long ago she attended the state finals for the Special Olympics in Austin, where she won a bronze medal and a fourth place ribbon. She now has a pen pal from England who became enchanted with Kelly on a transcontinental flight. And she just went to her first boy/girl dance with her brother's friend.

Kelly's dreams include getting married, having two children, working, driving a car, and having a house. While Peggy realizes that not all these goals are attainable, she would like to see Kelly live on her own someday and have a job. When asked if she would "do it all over again," this was Peggy's response:

Oh definitely. I wouldn't change her for anything. Kelly has taught me what life is all about. We tend to take it for granted when kids reach normal milestones and achievements, but you really appreciate these achievements more when that child has worked so hard to reach them. For example, Kelly's speech was delayed until at least age 5 or 6 due to hearing problems. Then one day, right before Christmas, Kelly, Sebastian and I were shopping in Toys "R" Us. Kelly and Sebastian went off by themselves down an aisle where they saw a toy clown. She pointed at it and actually said "Clown." Sebastian came running back to me, all excited: "Mom, Kelly said 'clown'!" We were so excited— she had never done that before! A few weeks later I came across an article in the newspaper written by a man who had apparently witnessed this. He retold the story and then commented that Sebastian's excitement over Kelly's achievement reminded him of the true meaning of Christmas.

The Roman attitude was similar; Roman society had little tolerance for individuals who were weak or who could not make a contribution to the general welfare (Scheerenberger, 1983).

The Renaissance did not result in noticeable improvement in the treatment of persons with disabilities. People whose behavior was seen as deviant, including those with mental retardation, continued to be treated cruelly and often were kept in chains, cages, or dungeons.

The spread of Christianity brought some positive changes. Persons with mental retardation continued to be mistreated, but efforts were under way to protect them. As early as the 13th century, churches began to provide asylums for persons with mental disabilities, although most of these asylums simply served as a refuge and provided no form of treatment for their residents.

Treatment of persons with mental retardation was better in the Middle East than in western Europe during the medieval period (5th to 16th centuries). The Islamic physician, Avicenna, recognized different levels of intelligence, including what we refer to as mental retardation. Maimonides, a Jewish physician and scholar living in Egypt, advocated instruction for persons with mental retardation (Scheerenberger, 1983).

During the Reformation, many religious asylums for persons with mental disabilities were closed. Wars resulted in destruction and poverty throughout Europe. Individuals with mental disabilities who survived this difficult period remained with their families, although some resided in hospitals and workhouses. In the 17th and 18th centuries, however, the quality of care in such institutions was so deplorable that the death rate was very high (Scheerenberger, 1983).

Reformers such as Vincent de Paul worked during the 1600s and 1700s to bring about more humane treatment and care for people with mental retardation. The scientific method of inquiry, which provided a basis for the later scientific study of mental retardation, was also developed during this time. In America, colonists cared for family members with mental retardation, although some were placed in hospitals and almshouses (McGarrity, 1993).

In 1798, hunters found a boy of about 12 living in the woods near Aveyron, France. He was found naked, foraging for food, unable to communicate. The boy, later known as the "Wild Boy of Aveyron," was taken to a professor in Aveyron, who named him Victor, concluded that he was an incurable idiot, and sent him to Dr. Jean Marc Itard in Paris for further study.

Itard was able to make some changes in Victor's behavior through systematic training, but he did not progress as Itard had hoped. Itard's work is significant because it represents one of the first systematic attempts to teach a person with mental retardation. Although Victor was not successfully educated or socialized, he was the catalyst for more widespread acceptance of education and training as a goal for persons with mental retardation. Thus, the origins of the field of special education can be traced to Itard.

One of Itard's students, Edouard Seguin, emigrated to the United States in 1850 and established some of the early residential institutions for persons with mental retardation. He also defined mental retardation in terms of organic and physical defects.

Seguin's work provided a foundation for the work of Maria Montessori, director of the Orthophrenic School in Rome, a school for children with mental retardation. Montessori's teaching staff carried out systematic education programs using special materials and methods within a specially designed environment. Her

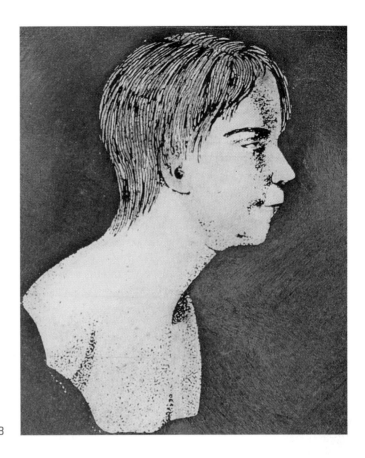

Victor, the "Wild Boy of Aveyron," 1798

curriculum methods evolved into the Montessori method, a movement that continues to have many advocates.

In the United States, progress was being made during this period in developing educational programs for children with mental retardation. In 1848, the Massachusetts legislature funded the first experimental school for students with mental retardation. Then in 1896, the first public school class for students with mental retardation was begun in Providence, Rhode Island. The **institutionalization** movement was gaining momentum during the middle to late 1800s, with the first residential institution for persons with mental retardation opening in Massachusetts in 1848.

Related to the institutionalization movement was an upsurge in interest in the relationship between heredity and intellectual development, partly as a result of the publication of Charles Darwin's *Origin of Species* in 1859. Darwin's theories on survival of the fittest were interpreted by some as a reason to remove certain undesirable segments of the population from society, a practice known as *eugenics*. Two studies of family histories fed into the frenzy. One was published in 1895 by R. L. Dugdale. He traced 709 descendants of the Jukes sisters over seven generations, beginning about 1792. He claimed to have found a preponderance of "poverty, crime and licentiousness" among the descendants (Dugdale, 1895). The significance of this work does not lie in its questionable findings, but rather that it is the first systematic study of the influence of heredity and environment across generations.

Another study of the effects of heredity was published in 1912 by H. H. Goddard. He claimed to have traced two lines of descendants of Martin Kallikak, a Revolutionary War soldier. One line resulted from Kallikak's liaison with a "feebleminded" woman. The second line descended from Kallikak and his legitimate wife, a "respectable" woman. Although his research was flawed, Goddard found that a significantly greater number of feebleminded persons resulted from the first line of descent. He concluded that feeblemindedness was hereditary and that it led to crime, prostitution, and poverty (Goddard, 1925).

One result of the eugenics movement was that many individuals with mental retardation were unwillingly placed in institutions and sterilized without their knowledge or consent, in an effort to "protect" society. Large, residential institutions were developed where residents spent their entire lives. Other persons with mental retardation continued to reside in local hospitals or workhouses.

The early 20th century saw several trends in the education and treatment of persons with mental retardation in the United States. Special education classes for students with mental retardation became more widely established in the public schools. The professions of special educator and clinical psychologist were established. Professional and advocacy groups began to spring up across the country. In 1922, the National Council for Exceptional Children (CEC) was established. In 1933, the first local Association for Retarded Children (now The Arc) was organized by parents.

As a result of widespread institutionalization resulting from the eugenics movement, expansion of public school special education programs was curtailed during the 1930s and 1940s. However, the screening of men and women for military service for World War II revealed that a significant number of American citizens had physical, mental, and emotional disabilities. Thus, the need for special education services for the nation's children once again came to the forefront in the 1940s.

In 1954, a landmark Supreme Court decision in *Brown v. Board of Education of Topeka* set the precedent for equal educational opportunity for all citizens. Although this case addressed racial discrimination and racially segregated educational programs, the principles established in this decision extended to other discriminatory classifications, including disabilities. The *Brown* decision provided a basis for including rather than excluding students with disabilities from the mainstream of public education (Sage & Burello, 1994).

In the 1960s, two societal events merged to enhance the status of persons with mental retardation in the United States. The civil rights movement, building on the foundation of the *Brown* decision, focused the nation's awareness on equal opportunities for all citizens, including those with disabilities. The "spillover" of the effects of the civil rights movement resulted in greater recognition of the rights of all citizens. In 1961, President John F. Kennedy appointed a President's Panel on Mental Retardation, which generated 112 recommendations for enhancing and improving services and programs for persons with mental retardation. These key events were enhanced when some public figures began open discussion of their family members with mental retardation.

The 1970s was a decade of progress for services for persons with mental retardation, as legislation and litigation opened new doors. In 1975, Public Law 94-142 mandated a free and appropriate public education for students with disabilities in the nation's public schools. By the 1980s, most public school divisions offered programs for students with mental retardation, although the quality of such programs varied considerably from one locality to another. Parents and advocacy groups continued to work hard to ensure equal access to a full range of educational services for students with mental retardation. As the 1990s began, attention turned to inclusion of students with mental retardation into the mainstream of school and community life. This "inclusion revolution," which continues to be a key issue, will be discussed later in this chapter.

The Kennedy clan, including Rosemary (second from right), who was diagnosed with mental retardation

DEFINITION OF MENTAL RETARDATION

As with most disability categories, defining **mental retardation** is not only a difficult task, but also one that has been much debated and many times changed. Over the years many definitions have been proposed and agreed on, only later to be discarded to make room for a new and more "descriptive" or "definitive" definition.

Early definitions (e.g., Tredgold, 1937) emphasized the medical or biological nature of mental retardation. Later definitions moved toward a more functional definition. In 1941, Doll presented six criteria essential to the definition of mental retardation, as follows: "social incompetence, due to a mental subnormality, which has been developmentally arrested, which obtains at maturity, is of constitutional origin, and is essentially incurable" (p. 215).

The American Association on Mental Deficiency (now AAMR—the American Association on Mental Retardation) has been a leader in defining and classifying mental retardation since the organization was founded in 1876. Its manual on definition, first published in 1921, is continually being revised. In the AAMR's 1959 definition, two significant changes set it apart from previous ones: The IQ ceiling was raised to approximately 85, and an adaptive behavior criterion (i.e., how a person copes with environmental demands) was introduced. The IQ ceiling was changed again in 1973 to approximately 70 and again in 1983, to approximately 75 (American Association on Mental Retardation, 1992).

With each revision of the definition, the focus shifted away from defining mental retardation strictly by IQ score toward a more functional definition of the disability category. The adaptive criterion has remained an integral part of the definition since it was added in 1959. It was expanded in 1992 to include 10 specific adaptive skill areas and reads as follows:

> Mental retardation refers to substantial limitations in present functioning. It is characterized by significantly subaverage intellectual functioning, existing concurrently with related limitations in two or more of the following applicable adaptive skill areas: communication, self-care, home living, social skills, community use, self-direction, health and safety, functional academics, leisure, and work. Mental retardation manifests before age 18. (American Association on Mental Retardation, 1992, p. 1)

The following four assumptions are essential to the application of the definition:

1. Valid assessment considers cultural and linguistic diversity as well as differences in communication and behavioral factors;

2. The existence of limitations in adaptive skills occurs within the context of community environments typical of the individual's age peers and is indexed to the person's individualized needs for supports;

3. Specific adaptive limitations often coexist with strengths in other adaptive skills or other personal capabilities; and

4. With appropriate supports over a sustained period, the life functioning of the person with mental retardation will generally improve. (American Association on Mental Retardation, 1992, p. 1)

As seen from the foregoing AAMR definition, three key components are central to defining mental retardation. They are (1) subaverage general intellectual functioning, (2) deficits in adaptive behavior, and (3) manifestation during the developmental period. Each criterion is discussed here. In applying these criteria, their interrelationship must be considered.

Subaverage General Intellectual Functioning. Intelligence level alone, as measured by a standardized IQ test, does not provide justification for labeling an individual as having mental retardation. The presence of intellectual limitations falling below the IQ level established by the definition is only one indication of a significant intellectual limitation. This information must be supported or refuted by consideration of the individual's adaptive skills (American Association on Mental Retardation, 1992).

Deficits in Adaptive Behavior. Adaptive difficulties experienced by persons with mental retardation can be considered in terms of deficits in practical intelligence and social intelligence. **Practical intelligence** is "the ability to maintain and sustain oneself as an independent person in managing the ordinary activities of daily living" (American Association on Mental Retardation, 1992, p. 15). This type of intelligence is key to adaptive skills such as self-care, safety, and sensorimotor skills. **Social intelligence** is "the ability to understand social expectations and the behavior of other persons and to judge appropriately how to conduct oneself in social situations" (American Association on Mental Retardation, 1992, p. 15). An individual may have deficits in some adaptive skill areas and not others. For example, a student may be limited in social skills and communication yet function effectively in each of the other areas. Another person may lack home living skills, yet perform adequately in the workplace.

Manifestation During the Developmental Period. The third part of the AAMR 1992 definition specifies that mental retardation manifests before age 18. American society typically considers the eighteenth birthday as passage into adulthood. Therefore, if an individual displays significant deficits in intellectual functioning and adaptive behavior prior to age 18, he would be considered to have mental retardation. If such deficits became apparent after age 18, the adult would be classified under a different disability category (e.g., traumatic brain injury; communication impairment as a result of a stroke, etc.).

The Individuals With Disabilities Education Act (IDEA) of 1990 (P.L. 101-476) also defines mental retardation for the purposes of identifying and categorizing students receiving special education and related services. This definition addresses the same key components as does the AAMR's 1992 definition. Students who are identified as having mental retardation under this definition may be found eligible for special education and related services, in accordance with state and local guidelines. It states:

> "Mental retardation" means significantly subaverage general intellectual functioning existing concurrently with deficits in adaptive behavior and manifested during the development period, which adversely affects a child's educational performance.

CLASSIFICATION SYSTEMS

Definitions establish boundaries into which one must "fit" in order to be classified or labeled. Classification may be defined as the way in which we sort people who qualify by definition for a label. Classification sorts the group on a specific variable such as cause, degree of impairment, and so forth. Although the 1992 AAMR definition established a new classification system, the traditional classification system will continue to be encountered in readings. Therefore, you should become familiar with both systems of classifying students with mental retardation.

Traditional Classification Systems

The classification of students with mental retardation has varied over the years. One system involves classifying according to cause, or **etiology.** This system has been and continues to be helpful to physicians but is of limited value to educators. Knowing the etiology of a disability, however, can be important to assist in early prevention (if possible) or in preventing the development of secondary characteristics associated with the disability.

Prior to the 1992 AAMR definition, students were classified according to levels of mental retardation (e.g., trainable, educable; or mild, moderate, severe, profound). A drawback to this system is that it limited how people (including educators) viewed this population of students. Movement between levels was almost impossible because emphasis was placed on IQ scores. Instruction and curriculum evolved around the classification system. Table 11.1 presents this traditional system with a brief explanation of each level.

New Classification System

By the new classification system, individuals with mental retardation are classified according to the levels of support they need within their environments, not by IQ

Table 11.1   **Traditional Classification System for Individuals With Mental Retardation**

LEVEL	IQ TEST SCORE	EXPLANATION
Mild	50–55 to approximately 70	• May not be identified until school age • May be initially placed in self-contained settings (classrooms) • Can function well in regular class settings • Should have curriculum that stresses reading, writing, arithmetic • Develop social and communication skills in a similar manner as students without disabilities • Can be functionally independent in adult life • Blend into traditional society after completion of school
Moderate	35–40 to 50–55	• Will exhibit developmental delays prior to entering school; discrepancies between this group and individuals without disabilities tend to increase with age • Usually starts out in self-contained classes and may remain there • Are focus of a national movement to place these students into regular education classrooms • Need more support than those with mild retardation • Should have curriculum emphasizing self-help and daily living skills; academics limited to functional activities such as learning "survival" words (*danger, stop, restroom,* etc.), counting, and making change • Will need supervision as adults
Severe Profound	20–25 to 35–40 Below 20–25	• Typically are identified at birth • Historically, have significant probability of medical complications • In the past were kept almost exclusively in institutions • Today may live at home and be served within their local schools • Can be taught simple life tasks • 24-hour supervision is necessary • Severe: May become semi-independent by adulthood • Profound: Will need constant supervision

scores. This system presents a more global view of these individuals. The levels of support include the following:

1. *Intermittent:* does not require constant support, but may need support on a short-term basis for special occurrences, such as help finding a new job.

2. *Limited:* requires certain supports consistently over time, such as with handling finances or may need time-limited support for employment training.

3. *Extensive:* needs daily support in some aspects of living, such as long-term job support.

4. *Pervasive:* requires constant, high-intensity support for all aspects of life. (Kozma & Stock, 1993, p. 10)

Unlike traditional classifications, the new classification system allows an individual to move up and down between levels. Services and support are adjusted to what the individual requires at any given point in time.

CHARACTERISTICS OF INDIVIDUALS WITH MENTAL RETARDATION

Developing an understanding of the characteristics of students with mental retardation assists in the identification process as well as in the teaching process. The various classification systems help focus on how a student with mental retardation acquires knowledge and skills and uses them in daily life. They also help us identify the areas in which a student may need support. By definition, the capacity for learning is a major deficit among the population of students with mental retardation. This section will cover cognitive or learning characteristics and social-emotional characteristics of students with mental retardation. Remember that these students' disabilities may range from mild to profound.

Cognitive Characteristics

Cognition is the mental process that we use to gain knowledge and an understanding of our environment. It includes several components or constructs that professionals in the field of special education should understand.

Learning is a term that is sometimes used to refer to cognition. It is a construct that cannot be measured with certainty. All children learn differently and at different rates. However, simply by the nature of the disability, students with mental retardation perform more slowly in the area of learning. Whatever skill area we focus on because of an identified need or deficit, information on how the individual with mental retardation functions helps to facilitate the learning or development of the skill.

Attention may be defined as the ability to focus on a stimulus and maintain that focus over time. Attention deficiencies in individuals with mental retardation have been reported in numerous studies (Brooks, McCauley, & Merrill, 1988; Merrill, 1990; Nugent & Mosely, 1987). Distractibility and inattentiveness are reported to be two of the characteristics most commonly seen in students with mental retardation (Patton, Beirne-Smith, & Payne, 1990). Early research by Zeaman and House (1961) comparing students with and without mental retardation concluded that the deficits of attention can be attributed to difficulties in cognitive processes. Bergen and Mosely (1994) also concluded that individuals with mental retardation experience significant difficulty in effortful processing and in the shift of attention. Attention deficits may be categorized in different ways: overattention, underattention, perseveration, and oversensitivity to information.

Overattention prevents the student from shifting attention from one task to another; making transitions is difficult. When a student has trouble moving from reading to math or if a student focuses on one small detail in a picture instead of the total picture, the student is exhibiting overattention.

Underattention (distractibility) occurs when an individual focuses on all information equally. Filtering out the unimportant and attending to the important information is difficult.

Some individuals with mental retardation **perseverate,** repeating an activity, word, or phrase over and over. The student becomes "stuck" on one word or topic, thinking or talking about it endlessly.

Oversensitivity to information received by the senses may distract these students. Oversensitivity to stimuli received by touching, smelling, hearing, and so forth can create situations where the student focuses on one aspect of a situation and blocks out all others. Often, the thing the student focuses on is not the most important aspect of the situation. For example, smelling popcorn from down the hall might receive the child's total attention while the teacher's instructions are blocked.

Beyond attention difficulties, there are deficits in other areas of cognition that make learning difficult for students with mental retardation. For instance, **memory**—"the ability to hold onto, store, and then retrieve information that has been learned" (Kozma & Stock, 1993, p. 14)—is another problematic area. When we learn, information is received by the senses and stored for later use. This information may be called up after a short period (short-term memory) or after a longer period (long-term memory). Learning small poems or factual information may take longer for a student with mental retardation when compared to children of the same chronological age. However, when compared to children of the same mental age (children of same IQ level who may be chronologically younger but mentally functioning about equally), these students remember about the same amount.

Rate and level of learning are reduced in students with mental retardation. This population will learn more slowly and will not reach as high a level as that of their peers without disabilities. As each year passes, the gap in level becomes more evident. This characteristic is quickly recognized by educators. When the student with mental retardation is placed in an inclusive environment, educators must be prepared to adjust their instruction to the student's slower rate and level of learning.

Generalization (the transfer of learning) refers to taking information learned in one situation and using it in a new situation. For example, the skills necessary for adding and subtracting are transferred to using the checkbook. Turner, Dofney, and Dutka (1994) found that "for students with mental retardation, strategy transfer was enhanced by the addition of attributional training" (p. 445). In this type of training, instruction focuses intentionally on similarities between information previously taught, now transferred to a new environment. New information is taught in context. For example, actually going to the bank and setting up a checking account assists in the transfer of skills more quickly than merely pretending to open a checking account in class.

Abstract thinking—the ability "to grasp concepts, principles, or processes that cannot be experienced directly through the senses" (Kozma & Stock, 1993, p .15)—is considered one of the most difficult areas for students with mental retardation, and an area that is crucial to learning. Students who have difficulty with abstract learning may recognize an apple as an apple and an orange as an orange, but cannot visualize that both are fruits and both grow on trees. For this reason, teachers of students with mental retardation must be aware of the need to present new concepts and ideas on a concrete level, using pictures, objects, demonstrations, and other visual examples to introduce and teach the concepts.

Problem solving refers to the ability to figure out new situations using prior knowledge (e.g., placing stones across a stream for crossing purposes). Problem solving requires abstract thinking and reasoning. For this reason, many students with mental retardation have difficulty solving problems. They also have difficulty trying new approaches to solving problems and tend to repeat past approaches, even though they have proved unsuccessful. Students with mental retardation can problem-solve at a rate similar to other students of equivalent mental age.

Social and Emotional Skills

Many students with mental retardation possess inferior or inappropriate social skills. These students do not pick up on social skills incidentally as others do, and therefore may not progress as rapidly as their peers without disabilities. This lack of skills must be addressed within the classroom and the workplace as well as in the home and community.

Students with mental retardation frequently show low levels of frustration tolerance. They often meet with failure not because they cannot do a task, but because they expect to fail when attempting the task *(failure set)*. Additionally, these

Students with mental retardation can learn appropriate social skills from their peers in the regular classroom.

individuals may feel that other people or events are a result or cause of their behavior, and thus they come to rely on external factors for problem solving.

Learned helplessness may occur when the student relies too much on others, and when people within the student's environment support this behavior. For example, a student may not dress himself because Mom or Dad always does this for him and does not encourage or allow independence. Parents and teachers must be willing to let the student try new things—and to fail occasionally—if he is to achieve maximum independence.

Speech and Language Characteristics

Speech (the process of producing sounds, combining these sounds, and putting the sounds into words) and *language* (communicating with others by combining words into sentences or by using another symbol system) are terms frequently used synonymously. However, they are different.

Language is crucial for communication. It must be understood before it is used. As Gioia (1993) notes: "The ability to understand spoken words, gestures, or written symbols is called *receptive language*, while the ability to use language to put thoughts into words is called *expressive language*" (p. 58). In general, children with mental retardation develop language at a slower rate (depending on functional level) than children without mental retardation. Children with severe or profound mental retardation may have very limited verbal output and rely on signs, gestures, and other augmentative communication systems. (See Chapter 7 for further discussion.)

CAUSES OF MENTAL RETARDATION

There are more than 350 identified causes of mental retardation (Special Olympics International, 1994a). It can result from influences during the prenatal or neonatal period, or from postnatal conditions. Hereditary factors account for only a very small portion of the cases. In about three fourths of the cases, especially those for which the effects are mild, the exact cause is unknown. The following discussion focuses on some of the most common causes.

Prenatal Causes

The first 3 months of pregnancy are critical to the development of the brain, nervous system, and sensory organs. During this period, many conditions arise that later may result in mental retardation. Some of these conditions are controllable by the mother; others are a result of genetic factors or unknown influences in the environment.

Maternal Infection.   Maternal infection during pregnancy is one prenatal cause of mental retardation. The probability of damage to the developing fetus is high, especially if the infection is acquired during the first 12 weeks of pregnancy. In the past, maternal rubella (German measles) was a significant cause of a variety of birth defects, among them mental retardation, deafness, blindness, heart defects, cerebral palsy, and other neurological problems. But widespread vaccination of children and prenatal screening of mothers has significantly decreased the incidence of this disease and the number of cases of mental retardation that result (Batshaw & Perret, 1992; Committee on Infectious Diseases, 1986; Scola, 1991).

Another maternal infection that can result in mental retardation is *toxoplasmosis*. This infection is caused by a protozoan organism and can be acquired if a pregnant woman has contact with animal fecal material or if she ingests raw meat. Sources of toxoplasmosis include cat litter, raw or undercooked meat, and dirt in flower beds. It can be prevented by taking care to avoid such substances during pregnancy (Scola, 1991).

Sexually transmitted diseases such as syphilis and herpes II are another source of maternal infection that can have negative consequences for the offspring. The fetus can acquire such infections if the virus or bacterium crosses the placenta, or they can be acquired during the birth process itself. Prevention is, however, possible. For example, if the mother is known to have syphilis, the fetus can be treated prenatally with drugs that cross the placenta (e.g., penicillin). Or, in other cases a Cesarean section can be performed to prevent the infant from acquiring an infection such as herpes II as it passes through the birth canal. Prenatal screening of mothers has reduced the number of cases of mental retardation acquired as a result of such infections (Scola, 1991).

Cytomegalovirus (CMV) is a very common viral infection in adults that can cause mental retardation in the developing fetus. The virus is passed through close personal contact, such as kissing, sharing eating utensils, wiping the nose of a child, or sexual contact. It is estimated that 75% of people in the United States will have had CMV by the time they become adults, although most will not be aware of it. CMV can cause *cytomegalic inclusion disease*, which can be contracted by the fetus before birth or by the infant as it passes through the birth canal. It affects approximately 1 in 100 babies born each year. The possible outcomes for infants who are infected include mental retardation, blindness, hearing loss, learning disabilities, and neurological impairments (e.g., spasticity, hyperactivity, seizures). Infants with severe infections may not survive the newborn period (Scola, 1991; Squires, 1991).

Since most people who have CMV do not show any symptoms and it is passed somewhat easily from one person to another, prevention is difficult. Those who are at particular risk include women in childbearing years who work in nursery schools and day care centers, mothers of children in day care, and health care work-ers. Since the worst outcomes seem to be among infants whose mothers acquire the infection for the first time during pregnancy, routine prenatal screening is critical to the prevention and early identification of infants with CMV.

Human immunodeficiency virus (HIV) infection is another possible cause of mental retardation. Developmental abnormalities, including cognitive deficits, have been reported in 75% to 90% of children with HIV (Batshaw & Perret, 1992). Children with HIV may display impaired brain growth, loss of previously acquired skills or failure to attain them at the typical ages, and general intellectual deficits. The nature of the causal relationship between HIV or AIDS and mental retardation among children has not been clearly established, but cognitive abilities do appear to decline as the disease progresses. It is often difficult to predict the course of cognitive development or eventual decline of cognitive skills in children with HIV or AIDS because the effects of the disease cannot be isolated from other health-related or environmental factors (Diamond & Cohen, 1992).

Substance Use and Abuse.   Prenatal substance use and abuse has been demon-strated to have potential harmful effects on neonatal outcome as well as having long-term effects on the offspring's subsequent development. Prenatal substance use and abuse places children at high risk for mental retardation and other develop-mental delays and disabilities. In recent years, we have become aware of the in-creased use of drugs (including alcohol and nicotine) by pregnant women and the potential harm of this behavior to fetal development. Even though reported esti-mates of drug use and abuse by women of childbearing age (15 to 44 years) have declined recently, in 1990 there were 4.8 million women of childbearing age esti-mated to have used some illicit drug during any given month. Estimates of cocaine use during pregnancy range from 8% (Gillogley, Evans, Hansen, Samuels, & Batra, 1990) to 31% (Ostrea, Brady, Gause, Raymundo, & Stevens, 1992). Use of legal drugs (e.g., alcohol and nicotine) is reported to be even higher, with an esti-mated 30.5 million women of childbearing age using alcohol, and an estimated 17.4 million women of childbearing age using nicotine during a given month (Khalsa & Gfroerer, 1991).

Children born to mothers who have used drugs during pregnancy may exhibit a range of cognitive and behavioral deficits. Offspring of mothers who ingest alcohol during pregnancy may suffer from **fetal alcohol syndrome (FAS)** or *fetal alcohol ef-fects (FAE)*. FAS is now acknowledged as the leading known cause of mental retar-dation in the Western world (Phelps & Grabowski, 1992). Babies born with FAS are unusually small at birth (weight, length, and/or head circumference fall below the 10th percentile), have small brains, display characteristic facial features (e.g., small eyes, a short upturned nose, thin upper lip, and flat cheeks), and may have body sys-tem abnormalities (e.g., heart murmurs or skeletal malformations). Most children with FAS have some degree of mental retardation, short attention spans, and behav-ioral problems. Children with FAE will display less severe effects, including small head size, poor heart and lung function, and minor physical abnormalities (e.g., pro-truding ears). Children who do not display the physical or behavioral characteristics of FAS or FAE as newborns may still have learning problems when they reach school age (March of Dimes Birth Defects Foundation, 1991; Shriver & Piersel, 1994).

Damage to children from prenatal alcohol abuse is reported in most coun-tries and among all socioeconomic and ethnic groups (Abel & Sokol, 1987). Since alcohol passes directly through the placenta, the fetus is not protected from its ef-fects. Most reported cases of infants with FAS are a result of heavy drinking

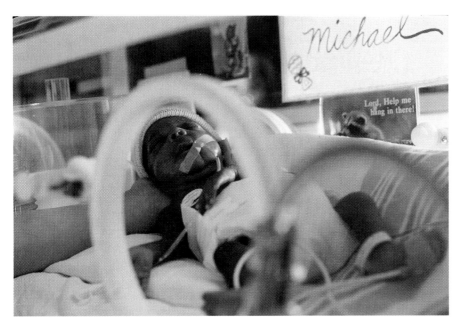

Although just newborn, this child already shows some of the characteristics of fetal alcohol syndrome.

throughout the pregnancy. It has been estimated that 5% to 10% of women who are pregnant drink at levels high enough to place their infants at risk (Rossett & Weiner, 1984). While there is no safe time for women to drink during pregnancy and no safe level of consumption, the severity of the effects of prenatal alcohol use can be reduced if the mother stops drinking as early as possible in the pregnancy.

While the most definitive relationship has been demonstrated between the offspring's intelligence and achievement and prenatal alcohol exposure (Shriver & Piersel, 1994), other studies have demonstrated a relationship between performance on intelligence measures and prenatal exposure to other drugs including methadone, nicotine, marijuana, heroin, and polydrug use (Carta et al., 1994).

Genetic Causes.   Genetic abnormalities in the form of chromosomal anomalies or defects of single genes can result in mental retardation. **Down syndrome** is the most common genetic disorder associated with mental retardation. It is named for John Langdon Down, who first described its characteristics in 1866 (Down, 1866). It is estimated that approximately 4,000 children with Down syndrome are born in the United States each year, or approximately 1 per 1,000 live births (National Information Center for Children and Youth With Disabilities, 1991).

The majority of individuals with Down syndrome have *trisomy 21*, in which three chromosomes of the 21st type are present in every cell of the body, resulting in a total chromosome count of 47 instead of the normal 46. Trisomy occurs in approximately 1 in 600 births and is present in 90% to 95% of the population with Down syndrome. A small percentage (4% to 6%) of individuals with Down syndrome have *translocation*, in which a part of one pair of chromosomes breaks off and becomes attached to a different chromosome. Parents who have given birth to a child with translocation may have a greater risk of conceiving another child with the same condition. *Mosaicism*, a third type of this syndrome, is very rare, occurring in 1% to 2% of the population with Down syndrome. Individuals with this type of Down syndrome have different chromosome counts within their individual cells. For example, their skin cells may have 46 chromosomes while their blood cells have 47. As a group, children with mosaicism are less severely retarded and have fewer characteristic features of Down syndrome (Pueschel, 1992; Pueschel & Thuline, 1991).

There are more than 50 clinical signs of Down syndrome. Characteristic physical features may include an upward slant to the eyes; an extra fold at the corners of the eyes (epicanthal folds); short, stubby hands with a single palmar crease (simian crease); light-colored specks in the iris (Brushfield spots); a round head; a short neck; a short nose; short, low-set ears; a small oral cavity that results in a protruding tongue; small physical stature; and low muscle tone (hypotonia). Children with Down syndrome often have related health problems, including congenital heart defects, gastrointestinal tract problems, visual problems, hearing loss, respiratory difficulties, and a misalignment of the top two vertebrae of the neck which makes them more prone to injury. The presence and extent of these various characteristics vary with each child (National Information Center for Children and Youth With Disabilities, 1993; Pueschel & Thuline, 1991).

Cognitive abilities, behavior, and developmental progress among children with Down syndrome vary widely. The majority of them function in the mild to moderate range of mental retardation and can acquire basic academic skills such as reading and arithmetic, and can later become gainfully employed (Pueschel & Thuline, 1991).

The life expectancy for individuals with Down syndrome has increased significantly since the middle of the 20th century. At that time, fewer than 50% of infants with Down syndrome survived the first year, and by age 5 only 40% were still living. Now, more than 80% of children with Down syndrome survive to age 5, and approximately 44% are still living at age 60. No doubt, improved medical treatment for associated conditions (e.g., heart defects) as well as more positive attitudes toward neonatal care of infants with Down syndrome have contributed to the increased survival rates (Sadovnick & Baird, 1992).

It is interesting to note that as more individuals with Down syndrome are surviving to middle age, it has become apparent that the majority of them over the age of 35 exhibit the characteristic features of dementia or Alzheimer disease. Older individuals with Down syndrome are found to be less proficient in daily living skills than younger persons with Down syndrome or same–age peers with other forms of mental retardation (Zigman, Schupf, Sersen & Silverman, 1996). Recent studies reveal that the onset of Alzheimer disease among persons with Down syndrome is almost inevitable, with an average age of onset in the mid-fifties. It is believed that the long arm of the 21st chromosome may prove to be the genetic link between the two diseases (Lai, 1992).

Whereas Down syndrome can result from extra chromosomal material, other genetic abnormalities may result from chromosomal deletion. This occurs when a segment of a chromosome is pulled off and lost during cell division, as in *cri du chat* ("cat-cry") syndrome. Children with cri du chat syndrome characteristically have high-pitched cries, microcephaly (small heads), widely spaced small eyes, low-set ears, and severe mental retardation.

Until the late 1960s, the most common known hereditary cause of mental retardation was not even identified. *Fragile X* syndrome is the result of an abnormal gene on the X chromosome. It was initially identified when researchers noted that individuals with mental retardation from families with long histories of mental retardation had an X chromosome that was fragile, tending to break. About one woman in 700 is a carrier of the fragile X genetic defect, which may be passed on to her offspring. Females who carry the fragile X gene have a 50-50 chance of passing it on to their daughter or son. Like other sex-linked disorders, the effects of fragile X syndrome are seen predominantly in males. Approximately 1 in 2,000 males are affected by fragile X (Dykens, Leckman, Paul, & Watson, 1988).

Males with fragile X usually display moderate to severe mental retardation. Other characteristics include delayed speech and language development, echolalic and perseverative speech, hyperactivity, short attention span, hand-flapping, hand-biting, impulsivity, and sensory–motor integration deficits. Characteristic physical features include long narrow faces, prominent ears, large head, high-arched palate, hyperextensive finger joints, large testicles, and a simian crease of the hand. Accompanying physical problems can include seizures, connective tissue problems, mitral valve prolapse, vision problems, and frequent ear infections (American Speech–Language–Hearing Association, 1990; Schopmeyer & Lowe, 1992; Smith, 1993).

The effects of fragile X in females are usually not as pronounced. It usually does not cause mental retardation, but affected females can display a range of learning problems including speech–language impairments and learning disabilities. Behavioral problems, particularly hyperactivity, may also be present.

The fragile X gene has also been linked with a small percentage of cases of autism in males. Although the majority of boys with fragile X display some features of autism (e.g., poor eye contact, perseveration, hand-flapping, stereotypic hand postures), most of them are able to relate to others socially, which is not consistent with a diagnosis of autism. It has been estimated that only about 15% of males with fragile X will display the full syndrome of autism (Schopmeyer & Lowe, 1992).

Other Prenatal Causes.   The developing brain and nervous system of the fetus are susceptible to a variety of prenatal influences (e.g., absence of certain nutrients or exposure to harmful substances) during the entire gestational period. Maternal undernutrition or malnutrition, Rh incompatibility between the mother's and fetus's blood, or exposure of the mother to radiation, carbon monoxide, lead, and mercury can all result in mental retardation in the developing fetus. Prenatal *anoxia*, in which there is a shortage of oxygen available to the fetus's blood, is another possible cause of mental retardation. Anoxia can be the result of an unusually long labor during which brain tissue is damaged, or by an umbilical cord that is twisted or becomes wrapped around the infant's neck.

Neonatal and Postnatal Causes

Although a significant number of cases of mental retardation are due to prenatal causes, mental retardation can also result from factors that occur after birth.

Substandard and Deprived Environments.   Many cases of mild mental retardation are attributed to a lack of positive social and cultural influences in the child's environment. Referred to as **cultural-familial retardation** or *psychosocial disadvantage*, the quality of the child's social and cultural experiences is inadequate for fostering normal cognitive development. The association between poverty, substandard and deprived environments, and children who are at risk is well documented. Studies have demonstrated greater incidence of mental retardation among children living in poverty (McDermott & Altekruse, 1994), higher incidence of mental retardation in poverty-stricken urban areas as compared to more affluent urban areas (Jackson, 1968), and associations between poverty and low birth weight and subsequent mental retardation among offspring (Baumeister, 1988).

Peterson (1987) identified a number of factors frequently associated with poverty that can have negative effects on children's development—including limited parental education and vocational skills, limited support systems for parents, and less emphasis on educational and intellectual activities in the home. These factors can result in a higher incidence of conditions known to threaten normal child development, such as the probability of lower parental competency in identifying the child's needs and providing adequate care; reduction of parental behaviors that foster cognitive development, language development, and school readiness skills; and increased probability for child abuse or neglect. These risk factors, in turn, can result in developmental delay and mental retardation among children, or can make it more difficult for a child to compensate for organic factors that might cause mental retardation.

Metabolic Disorders.   If untreated, some metabolic disorders can result in mental retardation. *Hypothyroidism* (underactivity of the thyroid gland) is an example of such a disorder. Replacement of the thyroid hormone does, however, significantly reduce the potentially harmful effects of this condition.

Phenylketonuria (PKU) is a metabolic disorder resulting from a single-gene defect that can be devastating to the child if not identified and treated early. Although phenylalanine is an essential amino acid found in common foods such as milk, children with PKU lack the enzyme needed to metabolize it. The phenylalanine then accumulates in the blood until it reaches a toxic level, resulting in progressive damage to the brain. Since no symptoms of PKU are present in infancy, children with PKU who are not identified are at high risk for mental retardation. Fortunately, a simple screening test performed in the hospital can identify infants who have inherited the defective gene that causes PKU. If started early, treatment in the form of a diet low in phenylalanine and vitamin supplements can prevent most of the negative consequences of PKU.

Postnatal Infections.   Mental retardation can result from infections acquired after birth. *Viral meningitis*, an infection that attacks the covering of the brain and spinal cord, can cause mental retardation if acquired during infancy. *Encephalitis*, an inflammation of the brain tissue, can also cause brain damage that results in mental retardation (Kozma & Stock, 1993).

Environmental Teratogens.   Increasingly, concerns are being raised about toxic agents in the environment and their effects on children, both prenatally and during their developmental years. Pesticides, including lawn care products and insect killers used in the home, have been implicated in cases of multiple disabilities, including mental retardation, in children exposed to them prenatally. Although the Environmental Protection Agency does not require that labels on pesticide packages warn pregnant women, and although companies claim their products are safe, some parents of children with multiple disabilities contend that the use of pesticides is the direct cause of their children's disabilities (Clavin, 1993).

Other environmental pollutants that are known to result in mental retardation in children include lead and mercury, which accumulate in the body over time, causing progressive damage to the brain and other body tissue. Lead poisoning is one of the most common and preventable pediatric health problems. It can result if a child inhales or swallows even small amounts of lead found in the soil, chipped paint or paint dust, water from lead contaminated pipes, auto exhaust, or other sources of air pollution. Even low blood levels of lead have been found to be associated with decreased intelligence and impaired neurobehavioral development in children (Centers for Disease Control, 1991; Schwartz, 1994).

PREVENTION OF MENTAL RETARDATION

In many cases, the causes of mental retardation are unknown; therefore, prevention is not an easy task. Prevention efforts in the form of public awareness and education continue to promote tactics such as prenatal care, routine health care and immunizations, accident prevention, child abuse prevention, child care education, and **early intervention** programs for infants and toddlers. Genetic screening, diagnosis, and counseling is a form of prevention for couples who may have inherited a genetic condition that could result in mental retardation in their offspring. Early and consistent prenatal care for mothers ensures the best possible outcomes for all infants, thereby reducing the incidence of mental retardation that is due to preventable prenatal causes. Routine screening of newborns can prevent or reduce the effects of some cases of mental retardation that result from metabolic errors, as in the case of PKU or hypothyroidism. Everyone can strive to prevent environmental causes of mental retardation and other disabilities and illnesses in children by reducing toxins in the environment and protecting young children from exposure to known environmental teratogens such as lead (Kasten & Coury, 1991).

Beyond these efforts, the most effective means of preventing mental retardation is the reduction of poverty. Reducing poverty and the environmental deprivations that children experience as a result can significantly reduce mental retardation among groups and individuals at risk (e.g., children and families with multiple risk factors). A multifaceted approach is needed that combines health care delivery and educational interventions for young children as well as their parents. For such efforts to be successful, public policy is needed that supports the importance of early intervention and the role that parents play in child development (McDermott & Altekruse, 1994).

ASSESSMENT OF MENTAL RETARDATION

A multidisciplinary assessment of individual strengths and weaknesses across a variety of developmental domains and in different environmental contexts is recommended when assessing children with mental retardation.

Evaluating Intelligence

Obviously, the assessment of intelligence is a key component in determining whether an individual has mental retardation. Standardized tests, including group and individual intelligence tests, are typically used to determine the extent to which a child's abilities are above or below average. Such tests yield standard scores that provide information on the child's overall cognitive abilities in comparison to other children of the same chronological age. Individual intelligence tests that are commonly used in the formal special education assessment process include the Stanford-Binet Intelligence Scale (4th ed.), the Weschler Intelligence Scale for Children–Revised (WISC-R), the Detroit Tests of Learning Aptitude–2 (DLTA-2),

INNOVATIVE IDEAS   SPECIAL OLYMPICS

President Bill Clinton at the opening of the 1995 Special Olympics

A long-standing concern of parents of children with mental retardation is that they have opportunities to enjoy the types of activities that other children do and experience feelings of success and accomplishment, as do their peers without mental retardation.

One program that has successfully addressed these parental concerns is Special Olympics. In 1968, Eunice Kennedy Shriver organized the first International Special Olympics Games. This year-round sports training and athletic competition for children and adults with mental retardation evolved from a day camp for people with mental retardation that Eunice Shriver started in the early 1960s. Since then, Special Olympics has grown and expanded to include programs in all 50 states, the District of Columbia, Guam, the Virgin Islands, American Samoa, and more than 130 countries around the world. The goal of Special Olympics, which relies on volunteers to organize and carry out training and competitions, is to give children and adults with mental retardation opportunities to develop physical fitness, greater self-confidence, a more positive self-image, new friendships, and to increase family and community support. Modeled after the Olympic Games, meets and tournaments are held in both summer and winter. Competition is held in 22 official sports including basketball, bowling, gymnastics, roller skating, softball, volleyball, tennis, equestrian sports, alpine and cross-country skiing, figure skating, speed skating, and floor hockey (Special Olympics International, 1994b).

Since its inception, Special Olympics has provided thousands of persons who have mental retardation with an avenue for success in sports and physical development. In July 1995, more than 7,000 athletes from more than 140 countries—supported by 45,000 volunteers and 2,000 coaches—competed at the ninth Special Olympics World Summer Games in New Haven, Connecticut. In spite of this and the many other positive opportunities that Special Olympics provides for athletes and their families, some have raised concerns that the games emphasize the differences between persons with and without mental retardation, and that media coverage tends to stigmatize Special Olympics and its athletes (Polloway & Smith, 1978).

In response, two of the guiding principles of Special Olympics address these concerns. They are (a) to help bring all persons with mental retardation into the larger society under conditions whereby they are accepted, respected, and given a chance to become productive citizens; and (b) to move its more capable athletes from Special Olympics training and competition into school and community competition, where they can compete in regular sports activities (Special Olympics International, 1994b). To help promote community integration, Special Olympics added the Unified Sports program in 1987. This program brings peers with and without mental retardation of comparable athletic abilities together on the same team, thereby fostering integration of persons with mental retardation into school and community sports programs.

the Kaufman Assessment Battery for Children, the McCarthy Scales of Children's Abilities, and the Woodcock-Johnson Psychoeducational Battery (Taylor, 1989).

Intelligence tests measure a sample of behaviors. Types of behaviors measured by intelligence tests include discrimination skills (finding which stimulus is different from the others), generalization skills (finding a stimulus that goes with another), motor skills (building block towers or tracing paths through a maze), memory, and abstract reasoning (Salvia & Ysseldyke, 1988). The formal testing process can also yield other valuable information including preferred learning modalities, the conditions under which the child learns best, the child's ability to remember information seen and heard on a short- and long-term basis, and attention, concentration, and independent work skills (Robinette, 1993).

The use of intelligence test scores as the main basis for classifying a student as mentally retarded is questionable, due to the controversy over what intelligence tests measure and to what extent a student's background experiences influence his or her performance. Although intelligence tests have been criticized for their potential bias against some groups (e.g., minorities), they are the most proven instruments in terms of predicting a student's academic skills related to school achievement. Their use is limited, however, in predicting a student's learning potential or future behavior other than in this narrow context of school achievement (Morgenstern & Klass, 1991).

Assessing Adaptive Behavior

As discussed previously in this chapter, a key component in the current definition of mental retardation is a deficit in adaptive behavior. **Adaptive behavior** has been defined as the way in which individuals cope with the natural and social demands of the environment (Heber, 1961). These coping skills enable a person to meet the daily demands of the environment and become integrated into the community (Lambert, Nihira, & Leland, 1993). Adaptive behaviors can be grouped under four broad headings:

1. Functional independent skills

2. Personal and social responsibility

3. Motivation

4. Cognitive development (Leland, 1991)

Assessment of adaptive behavior attempts to measure or characterize an individual's abilities in these domains and also includes more specific subskills such as peer relations, self-maintenance, economic activities/responsibilities, and domestic activities/responsibilities. Some scales also address an individual's maladaptive behavior, such as violent and destructive acts, eccentric habits, self-abusive practices, and inappropriate sexual conduct.

Assessment of adaptive behavior typically involves a scale or checklist that is completed by interviewing a parent or caregiver. Commonly used adaptive behavior scales include the AAMD Adaptive Behavior Scale, the AAMD Adaptive Behavior Scale–School Edition, the Vineland Adaptive Behavior Scales, the Scales of Independent Behavior from the Woodcock-Johnson Psychoeducational Battery, the Balthazar Scales of Adaptive Behavior, and the Adaptive Behavior Inventory for Children (Browder, 1987; Taylor, 1989).

While norm-referenced evaluation instruments are one means of assessing adaptive behavior skills, criterion-referenced instruments can yield helpful information for program planning and intervention, especially if they provide information in a hierarchy of skills mastered and not yet mastered. (See Figure 11.1 for examples of hierarchies for 11 specific self-care skills.) Interviews with the student or parents and observation of the student in different settings are also critical to obtaining an accurate picture of the student's adaptive skills (Reschly, 1989).

Naturalistic Assessment.   A recommended method of obtaining a better picture of how the child functions in and adapts to the real world is **naturalistic assessment.** Also referred to as *ecological assessment*, this approach assesses children and environments as a whole. For example, rather than assessing a student's motor skills while he is seated at a desk or during structured play times in the classroom, assessment would take place in the student's natural environment using familiar objects (Kozloff, 1994). For a young child, this might involve assessing his ability to grasp small objects while playing with his younger sister in the sandbox in his backyard rather than asking him to transfer blocks from one bucket to another while seated at a table in the classroom. For an older student, naturalistic assessment might involve observing the student in the cafeteria at school while she is engaged in conversation with her peers.

INCIDENCE AND PREVALENCE OF MENTAL RETARDATION

According to the World Health Organization, an estimated 156 million people, or 3% of the world's population, are thought to have mental retardation. In the United States, there are an estimated 7.5 million people, approximately 2.5% to 3% of the total U.S. population with mental retardation. Estimates of prevalence vary, however, according to place of residence. Higher rates are found in rural and inner-city areas—although the variation may actually reflect families' lower general economic status and related factors (e.g., poor nutrition, lack of prenatal care, deprived early environments) that can lead to mental retardation (Special Olympics International, 1994a).

Compared to other disabilities, mental retardation is 15 times more prevalent than cerebral palsy, 36 times more prevalent than total blindness, 50 times more prevalent than total deafness, and 30 times more prevalent than neural tube deficits such as spina bifida (Special Olympics International, 1994a).

According to the U.S. Department of Education, 553,992 students—11.6% of all students receiving special education and related services under Part B of the Individuals With Disabilities Education Act—received special education and related services in local school divisions during the 1993–94 school year. Between the school years 1992–93 and 1993–94, the percentage of students ages 6 through 21 who were served under the category of mental retardation increased by 4.1% (U.S. Department of Education, 1995).

SUGGESTIONS FOR ACCOMMODATING IN INCLUSIVE ENVIRONMENTS

Types and places for delivery of services for students with mental retardation have undergone major changes over the past 50 years—from expulsion from society and placement in institutions, to separate schools and separate classes, to regular class

INDEPENDENT FUNCTIONING

A. EATING

ITEM 1 — **Use of Table Utensils**
(Circle highest level)

Uses table knife for cutting or spreading 6
Feeds self neatly with spoon and fork (or appropriate alternate utensil, e.g., chopsticks) 5
Feeds self causing considerable spilling with spoon and fork (or appropriate alternate utensil, e.g., chopsticks) 4
Feeds self with spoon—neatly 3
Feeds self with spoon—considerable spilling 2
Feeds self with fingers 1
Does not feed self or must be fed 0

ITEM 2 — **Eating in Public**
(Circle highest level)

Orders complete meals in restaurants 3
Orders simple meals like hamburgers or hot dogs 2
Orders single items, e.g., soft drinks, ice cream, donuts, etc. at soda fountain or canteen 1
Does not order in public eating places 0

ITEM 3 — **Drinking**
(Circle highest level)

Drinks without spilling, holding glass in one hand 3
Drinks from cup or glass unassisted—neatly 2
Drinks from cup or glass unassisted—considerable spilling 1
Does not drink from cup or glass unassisted 0

ITEM 4 — **Table Manners**
(Circle all answers)

If these items do not apply to the individual, e.g., because he or she is bedfast and/or has liquid food only, place a check in the blank and mark "Yes" for all statements. _____

	Yes	No
Throws food	0	1
Swallows food without chewing	0	1
Chews food with mouth open	0	1
Drops food on table or floor	0	1
Does not use napkin	0	1
Talks with mouth full	0	1
Takes food off others' plates	0	1
Eats too fast or too slow	0	1
Plays in food with fingers	0	1

B. TOILET USE

ITEM 5 — **Toilet Training**
(Circle highest level)

Never has toilet accidents 4
Has toilet accidents only at night 3
Occasionally has toilet accidents during the day 2
Frequently has toilet accidents during the day 1
Is not toilet trained at all 0

ITEM 6 — **Self-Care at Toilet**
(Circle all answers)

	Yes	No
Lowers pants at the toilet without help	1	0
Sits on toilet seat without help	1	0
Uses toilet tissue appropriately	1	0
Flushes toilet after use	1	0
Puts on clothes without help	1	0
Washes hands without help	1	0

C. CLEANLINESS

ITEM 7 — **Washing Hands and Face**
(Circle all answers)

	Yes	No
Washes hands and face with soap and water without prompting	1	0
Washes hands with soap	1	0
Washes face with soap	1	0
Washes hands and face with water	1	0
Dries hands and face	1	0

ITEM 8 — **Bathing**
(Circle highest level)

Prepares and completes bathing unaided 6
Washes and dries self completely without prompting or helping 5
Washes and dries self reasonably well with prompting 4
Washes and dries self with help 3
Attempts to soap and wash self 2
Cooperates when being washed and dried by others 1
Makes no attempt to wash or dry self 0

ITEM 9 — **Personal Hygiene**
(Circle all answers)

If these items do not apply to the individual, e.g., because he or she is completely dependent on others, place a check in the blank and mark "Yes" for all statements. _____

	Yes	No
Has strong underarm odor	0	1
Does not change underwear regularly by self	0	1
Skin is often dirty if not assisted	0	1
Does not keep nails clean by self	0	1

ITEM 10 — **Toothbrushing**
(Circle highest level)

Cleans dentures appropriately 5
Applies toothpaste and brushes teeth with up and down motion 5
Applies toothpaste and brushes teeth with sideways motion 4
Brushes teeth without help, but cannot apply toothpaste 3
Brushes teeth with supervision 2
Cooperates in having teeth brushed 1
Makes no attempt to brush teeth 0
Does not clean dentures 0

D. APPEARANCE

ITEM 11 — **Posture**
(Circle all answers)

If these items do not apply to the individual, e.g., because he or she is bedfast or non-ambulatory, place a check in the blank and mark "Yes" for all statements. _____

	Yes	No
Mouth hangs open	0	1
Head hangs down	0	1
Stomach sticks out because of posture	0	1
Shoulders slumped forward and back bent	0	1
Walks with toes out or toes in	0	1
Walks with feet far apart	0	1
Shuffles, drags, or stamps feet when walking	0	1
Walks on tiptoe	0	1

Figure 11.1 **Examples of Skill Hierarchies for Assessing Adaptive Behavior**

Source: From Lambert, No., Nihira, K., and Leland, H. (1993). *Adaptive Behavior Scale-School.* 2nd edition, p. 4. Reprinted by permission of Pro-Ed.

Traditionally, students with mental retardation have been taught in separate classrooms.

placement and instruction delivered side by side with their peers without disabilities. In this section we will look at the traditional service delivery model and newer inclusive models and provide suggestions for teachers.

Traditional Service Delivery Model

Traditionally, students with mental retardation have been served in separate classrooms alongside other students with the same disorder. At one time it was not uncommon to find these self-contained classes on the regular school campus, but separated physically as much as possible from the other students. Trailers or basement rooms were frequently chosen for special education classes.

Today we find that separate classes are still the dominant placement; efforts are being made to include a greater number of students with mental retardation within regular classrooms, but progress is slow. Table 11.2 displays national data for students with mental retardation in six educational environments. The percentage of regular class placements increased less than 1 percentage point from 1989–90 to 1992–93, according to reported data for the 1992–93 school year (Davis, 1995). Overall, students with mental retardation are integrated less into regular classroom settings than are students with other disabilities. According to the U.S. Department of Education (1995), the most common placement for students with mental retardation is in separate, self-contained classrooms (56.8%), followed by resource room placements (26.8%). For the 1992–93 school year, only 7.1% of students with mental retardation were reported to have been served in regular classrooms, compared to 19.6% of students with serious emotional disturbance and 34.8% of students with specific learning disabilities.

Inclusive Service Delivery Model

As students with mental retardation increasingly are placed in regular class settings, a variety of teaching methods are being developed across the country to accommo-

Table 11.2   **Percentage of Students With Mental Retardation, Ages 6–21, Placed in Different Educational Environments**

ENVIRONMENT	SCHOOL YEAR 1989–90	SCHOOL YEAR 1992–93
Regular class	6.7	7.1
Resource room	20.1	26.8
Separate class	61.1	56.8
Separate school	10.3	7.9
Residential facility	1.4	0.8
Homebound/hospital	0.4	0.5
	100.0	100.0

Source: Data from *1995 Report Card on Inclusion in Education of Students With Mental Retardation,* by S. Davis, 1995, Arlington, TX: The ARC of the United States.

date these students. One popular model for teaching is that of **co-teaching.** In this model, the student is placed in the regular class setting and the special education teacher co-teaches with the regular class teacher. In some cases the special education teacher plans the lesson for the student and the regular education teacher implements it. Naturally, the student with mental retardation will be functioning at a different level academically, though the chronological ages of the students may be the same. The lesson for the student with mental retardation will parallel that of the students without disabilities. For example, the class may be learning multiplication facts, whereas the student with mental retardation may be learning to sequence numbers or do simple addition. Both groups are having a math lesson, but they are learning different things.

Suggestions for Teachers

Table 11.3 presents ideas for teaching students with mental retardation in relation to the specific learning characteristics discussed previously. Additional suggestions for teachers are also presented here.

Effective teachers of children with mental retardation need special sensitivity, knowledge, and skills that enable them to meet the needs of their students. First and foremost, regular education teachers need to realize that students with mental retardation are individuals who have strengths, needs, preferences, hopes, fears, and unique qualities just as all children do. Although students with mental retardation may not learn as quickly or as easily as their peers without disabilities, it doesn't mean that they are not motivated to learn or that they deserve less opportunity to achieve as their abilities allow. Nor does it mean that they should be protected from failure, or that teachers and other students should perform tasks for them that are challenging or difficult.

In addition to acquiring an appreciation for the potential of students with mental retardation and their capacity to learn and grow, regular education teachers need to be knowledgeable about the following factors:

- The effects of mental retardation on the family system and individual family members
- Medical problems that may accompany syndromes associated with mental retardation, and the implications these may have for individual students

Table 11.3   **Teaching Techniques That Address Learning Characteristics of Students With Mental Retardation**

LEARNING CHARACTERISTIC	SUGGESTED TEACHING TECHNIQUES
Deficits in Attention	• Focus attention to the task by using colors, bold print, etc. • Provide step-by-step directions, placing each direction on one 3-by-5 index card. • For younger children, use picture cards. • Use tape recorders to give directions, with a written checklist for the student to watch as directions are presented orally. • Use wall charts with pictures and word cues. • Review class outlines prior to class discussion. • Provide study guides prior to test. • Be clear with class objectives and structure. • Use a "rule list."
Deficits in Memory	• Present information in manageable units. • Assist students in developing a system of organizing information. • Use verbal and image rehearsal strategies (sing songs or use pictures for prompts). • Teach students to generalize memory strategies to a variety of situations.
Deficits in Rate of Learning	• State questions slowly and repeat them at least once before soliciting answers. • Present information in small sections. • Allow adequate "wait time" for student responses.
Deficits in Incidental Learning	• Be specific in providing directions. • Model skills to be taught. • Intentionally point out information that a student without disabilities may easily see or hear.
Deficits in Learning Transfer	• Have students practice skills beyond the point of initial mastery (overlearning). • Use simulation activities to encourage transfer of skills to other environments. • Return to skills previously taught to reinforce the same skill. • Use new and creative ways to teach the same skill. • Choose behaviors/skills for which there are naturally occurring cues, prompts, and reinforcers in the environment.
Deficits in Abstract Thinking	• Provide manipulatives or two- or three-dimensional models to assist students who have not reached the symbolic level of operations. • Monitor your instructional language to minimize your use of abstract terms and concepts. • Ask higher-level questions to stimulate abstract thinking.
Deficits in Problem Solving	• Guide students in defining the problem. • Teach sequential models of problem solving. • Remind students to evaluate strategies chosen at each step. • Do not always ensure success at problem solving so that students can learn from their errors. • Use "real life" instead of hypothetical problems.

- The effects of medication
- The limitations or risk factors in accurately predicting the IQ or academic achievement of any student
- The later age for plateau of mental age among students with mild mental handicaps (approximately 25 years) as compared to students without disabilities (16 to 18 years)

An understanding of these factors will enable regular educators to develop realistic expectations for each student's achievement and family involvement in the student's program, as well as to be aware of any limitations on activities that may be imposed by medical conditions.

Teachers also need to acquire certain skills to enable them to meet the individual needs of their students as specified by their IEPs. These skills should cover the following areas:

- How to accurately identify learning needs (e.g., self-help and independent living skills, survival skills, social skills, preacademic and academic skills, recreation/leisure skills)
- How to modify curriculum to make it more concrete and relevant to students' needs while using age-appropriate materials and activities
- How to modify instruction (e.g., pace, content, materials, evaluation techniques)
- How to correctly interpret students' behavior (e.g., not misinterpreting long-term memory deficits as laziness or short-term memory deficits as uncooperative behavior)
- How to function as a member of an interdisciplinary team and collaborate with special educators in developing programs and modifying instruction for students with mental retardation

In addition to basic reading, writing, and math skills, it is imperative that educators be aware of the different types of functional skills to be taught. Functional skills include knowledge of basic sight words (e.g., *restroom, men, women, danger, stop,* etc.), self-help skills (dressing, feeding), money skills, and community living (Berk, 1993). Table 11.4 presents functional-level expectations for students with mental retardation by the end of elementary and high school.

FAMILY PERSPECTIVES AND LIFE SPAN ISSUES

Being the parents or family member of an individual with mental retardation presents a lifetime of concerns. Even under ordinary circumstances, parenting and family living can be a difficult responsibility. When an individual with mental retardation comes into the family, a new set of issues arises and family relationships change. Parent concerns across the life span are presented in Table 11.5.

During infancy parents of children with disabilities have many questions and concerns and need tremendous support. The first time parents learn their child has mental retardation is typically an overwhelming and devastating event. As Jim Thornton (1995) recalls from his experiences as the parent of a son with Down syndrome, "Sometimes a new baby means sorrow as well as joy." In his recollection of when the doctor told him and his wife about their son's disability, Thornton states:

> I'd done the manly thing—acted strong, comforted my wife, pretended I was in control of the situation. That night, skimming through a pile of books about Down Syndrome, I cried like a baby. I would read until I couldn't see through the tears, stop and sob for a while, then read some more. (p. 55)

Information, resources, and support can be of tremendous help to parents in the early stages of trying to cope with and understand their child's disability. In many communities, individuals from organized support groups (e.g., Parents of Children With Down Syndrome) are available to come to the hospitals to help new parents begin the coping process. Some parents find it very helpful to talk to other parents as soon as possible. Others choose to wait until they have brought their

Table 11.4 Skills Typically Achieved by Children With Mental Retardation

BY THE END OF ELEMENTARY SCHOOL	BY THE END OF HIGH SCHOOL
Academic Skills Achieved by Children With Mild Mental Retardation • Core sight word vocabulary, with some ability to sound out unfamiliar words • Reading skills at about first grade to early third grade level • Literal reading comprehension (can understand surface meaning of sentences, but can't make inferences about what character is feeling, what might happen next, etc.) • Ability to identify main idea in simple paragraph • Ability to spell simple 3- to 4-letter words • Can write short sentences with help • Simple addition and subtraction using a calculator or objects • Can tell time on the hour and half-hour and understand time-related concepts such as "month," "tomorrow," "night"	**Academic Skills Achieved by Children With Mild Mental Retardation** • Reading skills at around fourth or fifth grade level • Expanded reading vocabulary (sight word reading) • Can follow written directions to complete a three- or four-step task • Literal comprehension of stories written at reading level; perhaps also some ability to make inferences • Can write simple letter, write out lists (e.g., groceries, things to do); may be able to complete forms such as job applications • Can use calculator in functional ways (to plan budget, balance checkbook) • Simple multiplication and division
Academic Skills Achieved by Children With Moderate Mental Retardation • At least, limited sight word vocabulary of "survival words" (*restroom, exit,* etc.) • Interest in looking through books independently and in being read to • Prewriting skills such as copying designs, circling choices • Can write own name • Addition and subtraction using objects • Can count to at least 10 or 20 • Basic understanding of money (e.g., which denominations are worth more)	**Academic Skills Achieved by Children With Moderate Mental Retardation** • Can follow directions on picture cards • Can write name in cursive; may be able to write other personal information such as address • Can copy written information (e.g., copy own address from a card onto a job application form) • Can understand that a written number represents a specific quantity (e.g., can get five bowls from cabinet) • Can match time on clock face (recognizes what 9:00 looks like and correlates it with time school begins)
Life Skills Achieved by Children With Mild Mental Retardation • Self-care skills such as bathing, grooming, and dressing (but may need help choosing appropriate clothes for weather conditions, etc.) • Understanding of basic safety rules (such as looking both ways before crossing street), but may still be impulsive at times • Early meal preparation skills (making self a snack, assisting in cooking, following a picture recipe)	**Life Skills Achieved by Children With Mild Mental Retardation** • Basic housekeeping skills, include making bed, vacuuming, washing clothes • More advanced meal preparation (following recipes involving measuring) • Basic financial management (budgeting, balancing checkbook) • Ability to use public transportation for familiar routes; may be able to qualify for driver's license • Basic independent job skills (arriving on time, staying on-task, interacting appropriately with coworkers) • Job-specific work skills acquired through on-the-job training (filing, typing, mopping, cooking, lawn care, etc.)
Life Skills Achieved by Children With Moderate Mental Retardation • Many self-care skills such as eating and toileting (but may need supervision of bathing and personal hygiene to ensure done adequately, or help with clothing fasteners) • Basic knowledge of home safety rules, but some childproofing may be necessary • Basic knowledge of neighborhood safety rules (can go down block to friend's house alone), but needs supervision • Early meal preparation skills, but needs supervision (can make peanut butter and jelly sandwich, but may prepare five sandwiches instead of one, or use half a jar of jelly)	**Life Skills Achieved by Children With Moderate Mental Retardation** • Housekeeping skills, with supervision or prompted by cue cards • Basic meal preparation skills (following picture cards to make a recipe) • Basic job skills (arriving on time, staying on-task, interacting appropriately with coworkers) • Job-specific work skills acquired through on-the-job training (usually involving a lot of repetition) • Ability to use public transportation with some supervision

Source: Adapted from *Children With Mental Retardation: A Parents' Guide* (pp. 195, 197), by R. Smith, 1993, Rockville, MD: Woodbine House. Used with permission.

EASY IDEAS FOR PRACTITIONERS

For the Teacher:

1. Focus on the child's strengths and accomplishments as well as deficit areas.
2. Present new information in concrete terms, providing tangible models and real-life examples.
3. Plan lessons that stress functional skills and concepts.
4. Advocate for your students to be included in all aspects of school activities.
5. Seek parents' input regarding objectives and approaches best suited for their child.

For Parents:

1. Look for and celebrate small successes.
2. Give your child responsibilities at home, just as you do with your other children.
3. Don't be afraid to allow your child to try and fail.
4. Provide opportunities for your child to interact with other children in the neighborhood and community outside of the school setting.
5. Be an advocate for early vocational planning for your child.

infant home and gotten to know him or her as an individual first, rather than focusing on the child's disability in the early weeks or months after birth. Early intervention programs available in many communities can provide both support to the family and appropriate services for the child. (See Chapter 13 for further discussion of early intervention and preschool programs.)

When the child reaches school age, new issues arise. For some children, this is the point of initial diagnosis of mental retardation. While infants with more severe mental retardation will be identified at birth or shortly thereafter, mild mental retardation may not be evident until the child enters school. Acceptance issues surface for the unsuspecting parent. Placement issues and the development of the Individualized Education Program (IEP) are extremely important to parents—especially if they feel that an integrated setting is the most appropriate for their child, but the IEP team recommends a more restrictive placement (e.g., self-contained class). Social skills and relationships with peers become important to both children and their parents during these early school years, especially as the children's social and cognitive skills begin to fall behind those of their peers. Another occurrence that can be stressful for the family during the child's school years is the point at which younger siblings begin to surpass the child with mental retardation in skills and accomplishments (Levitas & Gilson, 1990).

While adolescence is a stressful time for most children and parents, it may be even more so for parents of children with mental retardation. The gap between their children's sexual and psychosocial maturity causes concern for parents as they try to encourage independent behavior that is a natural part of adolescence, while providing the amount of supervision that their child continues to need. Many adolescents with mental retardation lack the social skills to date without a chaperone, or there may not be peers who are interested in dating them. It can be especially

Table 11.5   **Concerns of Parents of Children With Mental Retardation**

During Infancy	• What can we do for the child? • Where do we get help? • What does our child need? • Who will help our child? • Who educates us about this condition? • Who will pay for services? • How can we meet our child's needs and those of the rest of our family?
During Early Childhood	• Will our child grow out of this after getting help? • At what age can she begin to receive services? • Will she be in a regular or special education preschool class? • Will our child's teacher be educated in this field? • Who decides what services our child receives? • Will he receive help at home, as well as in school? • Will he be happy?
During School-Age Years	• Will our child go to a special school? • Can he go to the local school? • Is he protected by laws? • Will our child be in an integrated setting or "special" setting? • Will our child get better/intelligent from these services? • Will she be integrated into the community? • Is she going to be trained for transition from one school to the next, and from high school to the employment field? • Will our child be vocationally trained? • Will he learn socially acceptable behaviors? • Will our child be taught to control inappropriate behaviors? • Will she have friends?
During Adulthood	• Will he work? • Who will help him get a job? • Where will he be trained to work? • Will he work in competitive or supportive employment, or a workshop? • Will these jobs be in the mainstream, with people without disabilities? • Where will she live? Does she know enough to live there? • Will she be safe in a group home or supervised apartment? • Who decides where she lives and who she lives with? • Will our child be given choices? • Will he be educated about sexuality and marriage? • Will he be independent and self-sufficient?
During the Senior Years	• Will she have a "family" to belong to? • Who will take care of my child when I pass away? • Will he live with other senior citizens? • Will he be forced to work, or can he retire? • Will she be given opportunities to rest or perform in leisure activities of her choice? • Will he get ill? And if so, who will care for him and pay his medical bills?

Source: Adapted from information compiled in 1995 by B. Griffin, graduate student, Virginia Commonwealth University, Richmond, Virginia. Used with permission and special acknowledgment.

sad and stressful for the adolescent and the family if he or she is rejected by a chronological peer who is not retarded. Another source of stress during this period arises when siblings leave home to establish independent lives, leaving their brother or sister behind (Levitas & Gilson, 1990).

As their children move toward adulthood, parents face a set of new concerns regarding the end of formal schooling, the successful transition to the world of

Group homes are a good option for many adults with mental retardation.

work, the need for independence and adult relationships with peers, and acceptance as members of the community. Sometimes there is disappointment and frustration at the narrow range of job and training opportunities, housing options, and services available in the community. Although parental control and involvement is expected to diminish at this time, parents may continue to find themselves in the roles of caretaker and case manager for their children, roles they are often ready to relinquish (Thorin, Yovanoff, & Irvin, 1996). Parents whose adult children live away from them, such as in a group home or an institution, worry about the quality of care and supervision provided and about whether their children are being mistreated. (See Chapter 13 for an in-depth discussion of adult concerns such as community-based instruction and transition.)

The quality of life for individuals with mental retardation as they grow older is a major concern of family members. Not only are they concerned for their family member's physical health and safety, but also for his or her emotional well-being. Moss (1994) identifies the maintenance of autonomy, the potential to make choices, and the maintenance of close personal relationships as significant challenges to individuals with mental retardation in their later years. While these issues are not unlike those facing any older person, parents and family members of individuals with mental retardation may need to begin systematic planning while their children are still young in order to ensure the long-term quality of life for their children.

The pending senior years for individuals with mental retardation bring tremendous stress on parents as well as the family. Questions arise such as these:

Who will take care of the individual when the parent is gone?

Who will tend to his or her daily needs, medical bills, and so forth?

What responsibility must the siblings bear?

What resources are available in the community to ensure the necessary care and support?

And what will be the effects of these changes on the individual?

CURRENT ISSUES AND FUTURE TRENDS

Challenges facing families, educators, and other professionals in the area of mental retardation reflect those in the field of disabilities overall. Prevention, integration into school and community life, availability of funding, the delivery of appropriate instruction, and quality of life for persons with mental retardation are issues that concern parents, teachers, and advocates for persons with mental retardation.

Of particular concern to special educators is the need for their educational approaches to keep pace and be compatible with the approaches used in general education settings. Over the past decade, general education curriculum and instructional practices have been targeted for reform. A push has been under way to emphasize reasoning, problem solving, and higher order thinking skills in a movement away from the traditional emphasis on discrete, isolated skills and facts (Nolan & Francis, 1992). A salient characteristic of students with mental retardation is their limited ability to engage in abstract thinking, a factor that has focused the emphasis of curriculum and instruction for these students on acquisition of basic skills and knowledge. Thus, when designing or selecting curriculum for students with mental retardation, the need to provide students with the practical skills and knowledge they need to function in their future environments must be weighed against the curricular and instructional changes taking place in general education.

This difference in educational focus, in turn, raises questions about the feasibility and appropriateness of fully integrating students with mental retardation into general education settings. Many parents want their children totally integrated into general education classes. And in fact, during the early school years, when the curriculum emphasis is on acquiring skills and knowledge through concrete learning experiences, many students with mental retardation can be successfully educated alongside their peers without disabilities. As the children progress in school, however, the shift in curriculum and instructional methods toward higher level and more abstract skills may result in a mismatch between a student's needs and the general classroom environment. Parents may continue to want their children to be educated in general education settings, yet have concerns about the capacity of those settings to adequately prepare their children for the world beyond their school years. Thus, a future-focused curriculum is a key issue in education for students with mental retardation.

Some parents, who have struggled all during the school years to have their children with mental retardation fully integrated into school and community life, may suddenly find that their children's opportunities are severely restricted upon completion of high school. Not all communities have adequate vocational, recreational, and supported living opportunities available for young adults with mental retardation, especially those who require a high level of support to function successfully. This problem, however, is not solely that of parents and family members, but one that must be shared by a cross section of agencies and individuals in the community.

As the general population ages and as adults with mental retardation are living longer, a critical issue is that of the availability of programs and services for senior adults with mental retardation or developmental disabilities. Adult day care programs that accept participants with developmental disabilities can provide opportunities for interactions with peers (both with and without disabilities), recreation, physical conditioning, and nutritional meals (LePore & Janicki, 1991). In some communities, however, adults with developmental disabilities may not be accepted into such programs or their needs may be too complex to enable them to attend, especially if they have significant health problems. The question of how to care for older adults with mental retardation or developmental disabilities, particularly those without a family member to advocate for and support them, will continue to be a concern for individuals, families, communities, and social service agencies as the population ages. This problem will become greater as calls for cuts in funding for social services continue to be heard with each new demand for federal and state fiscal restructuring.

A look to the future for persons with mental retardation brings optimism as well as concern. Progress in the areas of prevention and determination of causes of mental retardation will continue to have a positive effect on incidence rates. Continued development and refinement of educational approaches will enable us to more appropriately meet each student's unique needs. Greater acceptance of differences by individuals and the general population will continue to open doors for persons with mental retardation in education, employment, and community living. However, decreased or eliminated funding sources for support and intervention programs may offset progress in other areas if needed services are not available to individuals with mental retardation of all ages across the nation.

Five-Minute Summary

The history of services for persons with mental retardation reveals centuries of abuse, mistreatment, and misunderstanding. Special classes for students with mental retardation began to be established in the late 1800s, but not until the 1970s were programs and services for all students with mental retardation available in all of the nation's public schools.

The definitions of mental retardation reveal an evolution in the view of persons with mental retardation. Early definitions focused on IQ scores. More recent definitions take into account not only an individual's intellectual functioning but also one's adaptive skills.

Characteristics of individuals with mental retardation include a slower rate of learning, deficits of attention and memory, difficulty transferring information learned to other situations, and weak or inappropriate social skills. These characteristics are displayed differently among the population of individuals with mental retardation.

Mental retardation can result from a variety of prenatal, neonatal, and postnatal influences. Hereditary conditions, viruses, diseases, and substance use and abuse during the mother's pregnancy are causes of mental retardation during the prenatal period. Physical trauma during birth can result in some cases of mental retardation. Metabolic disorders, infections, substandard and deprived environments, and environmental teratogens are postnatal factors that can lead to mental retardation. In the majority of cases, however, the causes of mental retardation are unknown.

It is estimated that up to 3% of the general population has mental retardation. Students with mental retardation make up just over 10% of all students receiving special education in U.S. public schools. Over the past two decades, there has been a decline in the percentage of students identified with mental retardation.

Assessment of students with mental retardation should be multidisciplinary in nature and should include an evaluation of the student's adaptive skills in different settings.

Attention deficiencies, distractibility, oversensitivity to information, and memory problems affect the rate and level of learning in individuals with mental retardation. Teachers need to acquire certain skills regarding each student's Individualized Education Program.

When teaching in an inclusive environment, teachers must maintain reasonable expectations for their students with mental retardation, while keeping the lessons for students with and without disabilities parallel.

Families of individuals with mental retardation must be provided with information, resources, and support as early as possible. The earlier the intervention, the greater the academic potential. Similarly, parents can help ensure quality of life for their children as they grow into their senior years if systematic planning is begun early.

Study Questions

1. List and discuss three of the most important events in the history of services for persons with mental retardation. How has each event influenced the current status of programs and services for students with mental retardation?

2. Paraphrase the current AAMD definition of mental retardation. What are key differences between this definition and earlier ones?

3. Discuss the common characteristics of persons with mental retardation. How do these characteristics mesh to influence their daily lives?

4. What is the prevalence of mental retardation in the general population? In the school-age population? What might be a reason for the greater prevalence of mental retardation among school-age children?

5. What are some common causes of mental retardation? Which ones are preventable and how can they be prevented?

6. What do you feel is the most important information to result from an assessment of a person with mental retardation? Why?

7. Define and give three examples of adaptive behavior skills. Should these skills be taught in school? Why or why not?

8. What are some considerations teachers should make when teaching students with mental retardation in inclusive environments?

9. Why is it important for a child with mental retardation to be identified as early as possible?

10. Explain why many educators prefer the new system for classifying individuals with disabilities rather than the traditional one.

11. What are some common concerns of family members of individuals with mental retardation? What can communities and individuals do to help alleviate these concerns?

For More Information

ORGANIZATIONS

American Association on Mental Retardation (AAMR)
444 North Capitol Street N.W.
Suite 846
Washington, DC 20001-1512

The Arc (Formerly the Association for Retarded Citizens)
2501 Avenue J
Arlington, TX 76005

The Association for Persons with Severe Handicaps (TASH)
7010 Roosevelt Way, N.E.
Seattle, WA 98115

National Down Syndrome Congress
1605 Chantilly Road
Atlanta, GA 30324
800-232-6372

National Down Syndrome Society
666 Broadway
New York, NY 10012
800-221-4602

National Fragile X Foundation
1441 York Street, Suite 215
Denver, CO 80206
800-688-8765   303-333-6155

Rehabilitation Research and Training Center
(RRTC)
Virginia Commonwealth University
1314 West Main Street, Box 2011
Richmond, VA 23284-2011

BOOKS AND ARTICLES

Cairo, S. (1985). *Our brother has Down syndrome.* Ontario, Canada: G. Allan Roeher Institute.

Cunningham, C. (1988). *Down syndrome: An introduction.* Cambridge, MA: Brookline Books.

Edwards, J. (1983). *My friend David.* Austin, TX: PRO-ED.

Kaufman, S. Z. (1988). *Retarded isn't stupid, Mom!* Baltimore: Paul H. Brookes.

Kingsley, J., & Levitz, M. (1994). *Count us in: Growing up with Down syndrome.* San Diego: Harcourt Brace.

Schloss, P. (1988). *Community integration for persons with mental retardation.* Austin, TX: PRO-ED.

Schwier, K. (1990). *Speakeasy.* Austin, TX: PRO-ED.

Smith, R. (1991). *Children with mental retardation.* Rockville, MD: Woodbine House.

Stray-Gunderson, K. (Ed.). (1986). *Babies with Down syndrome.* Rockville, MD: Woodbine House.

Trainer, M. (1991). *Differences in common.* Rockville, MD: Woodbine House.

Vitello, S. J. (1986). *Mental retardation.* Needham Heights, MA: Allyn & Bacon.

Wehman, P., & McLaughlin, P. J. (Eds.). (1996). *Mental retardation and developmental disabilities.* Austin, TX: PRO-ED.

JOURNALS, NEWSLETTERS, AND OTHER PUBLICATIONS

Mental Retardation (journal)
American Association on Mental Retardation
444 North Capitol Street, N.W., Suite 846
Washington, DC 20001-1512
202-387-1968

VIDEO AND ELECTRONIC MEDIA

Lily: A Story About a Girl Like Me [Video]
Davidson Films, Inc.
231 "E" Street
Davis, CA 95616
916-753-9604

Lily: A Sequel [Video]
Davidson Films, Inc.
231 "E" Street
Davis, CA 95616
916-753-9604

What's Eating Gilbert Grape? [Film]
1993, Paramount Pictures

References

Abel, E. L., & Sokol, R. J. (1987). Incidence of fetal alcohol syndrome and economic impact of FAS-related anomalies. *Drug and Alcohol Dependence, 19,* 51–70.

American Association on Mental Retardation (AAMR). (1992). *Mental retardation: Definition, classification, and systems of supports.* Washington, DC: American Association on Mental Retardation.

American Speech–Language–Hearing Association. (1990). Fragile X syndrome. *Let's Talk, 21,* 1–2.

Batshaw, M. L., & Perret, Y. M. (1992). *Children with disabilities: A medical primer.* Baltimore: Paul H. Brookes.

Baumeister, A. (1988). *The new morbidity and the prevention of mental retardation.* Nashville, TN: The John F. Kennedy Center for Research Progress at George Peabody College for Teachers.

Bergen, A. E., & Mosely, J. L. (1994). Attention and attentional shift efficiency in individuals with and without mental retardation. *American Journal on Mental Retardation, 95*(6), 688–743.

Berk, H. (1993). Early intervention and special education. In R. Smith (Ed.), *Children with mental retardation: A parents' guide* (pp. 1–49). Rockville, MD: Woodbine House.

Brooks, P. H., McCauley, C. M., & Merrill, E. M. (1988). Cognition and mental retardation. In P. J. Menolascino & J. A. Stark (Eds.), *Prevention and curative intervention in mental retardation* (p. 295–318). London: Brookes.

Browder, D. (1987). *Assessment of individuals with severe handicaps: An applied behavior approach to life skills assessment.* Baltimore: Paul H. Brookes.

Carta, J. J., Sideridis, G., Rinkel, P., Guimaraes, S., Greenwood, C., Baggett, K., Peterson, P., Atwater, J., McEvoy, M., & McConnel, S. (1994). Behavioral outcomes of young children prenatally exposed to illicit drugs: Review and analysis of experimental literature. *Topics in Early Childhood Special Education, 14*(2), 184–209.

Centers for Disease Control. (1991). *Preventing lead poisoning in young children.* Atlanta: Department of Health & Human Services.

Clavin, T. (1993, August). Danger on our doorstep. *McCall's*, pp. 95–103.

Committee on Infectious Diseases. (1986). *Report of the Committee on Infectious Diseases* (20th ed.). Elk Grove Village, IL: American Academy of Pediatrics.

Davis, S. (1995). *1995 report card on inclusion in education of students with mental retardation.* Arlington, TX: The ARC of the United States.

Diamond, G. W., & Cohen, H. J. (1992). Developmental disabilities in children with HIV infection. In A. Crocker, H. Cohen, & T. Kastner (Eds.), *HIV infection and developmental disabilities* (pp. 33–42). Baltimore: Paul H. Brookes.

Doll, E. A. (1941). The essentials of an inclusive concept of mental deficiency. *American Journal of Mental Deficiency, 46*, 214–229.

Down, J. L. (1866). Observations on an ethnic classification of idiots. *London Hospital Clinical Lectures and Reports, 3*, 259–262.

Dugdale, R. L. (1895). *The Jukes: A study in crime, pauperism, disease and heredity.* New York: Putnam.

Dykens, E., Leckman, J., Paul, R., & Watson, M. (1988). Cognitive, behavioral, and adaptive functioning in fragile X and non-fragile X retarded men. *Journal of Autism and Developmental Disorders, 18*, 41–51.

Gillogley, K. M., Evans, A. T., Hansen, R. L., Samuels, S. J., & Batra, K. K. (1990). The perinatal impact of cocaine, amphetamine and opiate use detected by universal intrapartum screening. *American Journal of Obstetrics and Gynecology, 163*, 1535–1542.

Gioia, G. (1993). Development and mental retardation. In R. Smith (Ed.), *Children with mental retardation: A parents' guide* (pp. 51–87). Rockville, MD: Woodbine House.

Goddard, H. H. (1925). *The Kallikak family.* New York: Macmillan.

Heber, R. (1961). A manual on terminology and classification in mental retardation (2nd ed.). *Monograph supplement to the American Journal of Mental Deficiency.* Pineville, LA: American Association on Mental Deficiency.

Jackson, R. N. (1968). Urban distribution of educable mental handicap. *Journal of Mental Deficiency Research, 12*, 312–316.

Kasten, E. F., & Coury, D. L. (1991). *Health policy and prevention of mental retardation.* In J. L. Matson & J. A. Mulick (Eds.), *Handbook of Mental Retardation* (pp. 336–344). New York: Pergamon.

Khalsa, J. H., & Gfroerer, J. (1991). Epidemiology and health consequences of drug abuse among pregnant women. *Seminars in Perinatology, 15*(4), 265–270.

Kozloff, M. A. (1994). *Improving educational outcomes for children with disabilities: Guidelines and protocols for practice.* Baltimore: Paul H. Brookes.

Kozma, C., & Stock, J. (1993). What is mental retardation? In R. Smith (Ed.), *Children with mental retardation: A parents' guide* (pp. 1–49). Rockville, MD: Woodbine House.

Lai, F. (1992). Life expectancy. In S. M. Pueschel & J. K. Pueschel (Eds.), *Biomedical concerns in persons with Down syndrome* (pp. 175–196). Baltimore: Paul H. Brookes.

Lambert, N., Nihira, K., & Leland, H. (1993). *AAMR Adaptive Behavior Scale—Examiner's manual* (2nd ed.). Austin, TX: PRO-ED.

Leland, H. (1991). Adaptive behavior scales. In J. L. Matson & J. A. Mulick (Eds.), *Handbook of mental retardation* (pp. 211–221). New York: Pergamon.

LePore, P., & Janicki, M. (1991). *The wit to win: How to integrate older persons with developmental disabilities into community aging programs.* Albany, NY: New York State Office for the Aging.

Levitas, A., & Gilson, S. (1990). Psychosocial crises in the lives of people with mental retardation. *Healthy Times, 2*(2), 1–5.

March of Dimes Birth Defects Foundation. (1991). *Drinking during pregnancy: Fetal alcohol syndrome and fetal alcohol effects.* White Plains, NY: Author.

McDermott, S., & Altekruse, J. (1994). Dynamic model for preventing mental retardation: The importance of poverty and deprivation. *Research in Developmental Disabilities, 15*(1), 49–65.

McGarrity, M. (1993). *A guide to mental retardation.* New York: Crossroad Publishing.

Merrill, E. C. (1990). Attentional resource allocation and mental retardation. In N. W. Bray (Ed.), *International review of research in mental retardation* (pp. 51–88). New York: Academic Press.

Morgenstern, M., & Klass, E. (1991). Standard intelligence tests and related assessment techniques. In J. L. Matson & J. A. Mulick (Eds.), *Handbook of mental retardation* (pp. 195–210). New York: Pergamon.

Moss, S. (1994). Quality of life and aging. In D. Goode (Ed.), *Quality of life for persons with disabilities: International perspectives and issues* (pp. 218–234). Cambridge, MA: Brookline.

National Information Center for Children and Youth With Disabilities. (1991). *General information about Down syndrome.* Fact Sheet No. 4 (FS4). Washington, DC: National Information Center for Children and Youth With Disabilities.

Nolan, J., & Francis, P. (1992). Changing perspectives in curriculum and instruction. In C. D. Glickman (Ed.), *Supervision in transi-*

tion: *1992 yearbook of the Association for Supervision and Curriculum Development* (pp. 44–60). Alexandria, VA: Association for Supervision and Curriculum Development.

Nugent, P. M., & Mosely, J. L. (1987). Mentally retarded and nonretarded individual's attention allocation and capacity. *American Journal of Mental Deficiency, 91,* 598–605.

Ostrea, E. M., Brady, M., Gause, S., Raymundo, L., & Stevens, M. (1992). Drug screening of newborns by meconium analysis: A large-scale, prospective epidemiological study. *Pediatrics, 89,* 107–113.

Patton, Jr., Beirne-Smith, M., & Payne, J. S. (1990). *Mental retardation.* Columbus, OH: Merrill.

Peterson, N. L. (1987). *Early intervention for handicapped and at-risk children.* Denver: Love.

Phelps, L., & Grabowski, J. A. (1992). Fetal alcohol syndrome: Diagnostic features and psychoeducational risk factors. *School Psychology Quarterly, 7*(2), 112–128.

Polloway, E. A., & Smith, J. D. (1978). Special Olympics: A second look. *Education and Training of the Mentally Retarded, 13,* 432–433.

Pueschel, S. (1992). Phenotype characteristics. In S. M. Pueschel & J. K. Pueschel (Eds.), *Biomedical concerns in persons with Down syndrome* (pp. 1–37). Baltimore: Paul H. Brookes.

Pueschel, S., & Thuline, H. (1991). Chromosome disorders. In J. L. Matson & J. A. Mulick (Eds.), *Handbook of mental retardation* (pp. 115–138). New York: Pergamon.

Reschly, D. (1989). Incorporating adaptive behavior deficits into instructional programs. In G. Robinson, J. Patton, E. Polloway, & L. Sargent (Eds.), *Best practices in mild mental disabilities* (pp. 39–66). Reston, VA: The Division on Mental Retardation of the Council for Exceptional Children.

Robinette, C. (1993). The multidisciplinary evaluation process. In R. Smith (Ed.), *Children with mental retardation: A parents' guide* (pp. 133–172). Rockville, MD: Woodbine House.

Rossett, H. L., & Weiner, L. (1984). *Alcohol and the fetus: A clinical perspective.* New York: Oxford University Press.

Sadovnick, A. D., & Baird, P. A. (1992). Life expectancy. In S. M. Pueschel & J. K. Pueschel (Eds.), *Biomedical concerns in persons with Down syndrome* (pp. 39–57). Baltimore: Paul H. Brookes.

Sage, D. D., & Burello, C. (1994). *Leadership in educational reform: An administrator's guide to changes in special education.* Baltimore: Paul H. Brookes.

Salvia, J., & Ysseldyke, J. (1988). *Assessment in special and remedial education.* Boston: Houghton Mifflin Company.

Scheerenberger, R. C. (1983). *A history of mental retardation.* Baltimore: Paul H. Brookes.

Schopmeyer, B. B., & Lowe, F. (1992). *The fragile X child.* San Diego: Singular Publishing Group.

Schwartz, J. (1994). Low-level lead exposure and children's IQ: A meta-analysis and search for a threshold. *Environmental Research, 65,* 42–55.

Scola, P. (1991). *Infections.* In J. L. Matson & J. A. Mulick (Eds.), *Handbook of mental retardation* (pp. 151–157). New York: Pergamon.

Shriver, M. D., & Piersel, W. (1994). The long-term effects of intrauterine drug exposure: Review of recent research and implications for early childhood special education. *Topics in Early Childhood Special Education, 14,* 161–183.

Smith, S. E. (1993). Cognitive deficits associated with fragile X syndrome. *Mental Retardation, 31*(5), 279–283.

Special Olympics International. (1994a). *Fact sheet: Mental retardation.* Washington, DC: Special Olympics International.

Special Olympics International. (1994b). *Fact sheet: What is Special Olympics?* Washington, DC: Special Olympics International.

Squires, S. (1991, July 16). Is your baby at risk for CMV? *Women's Day,* 46–50.

Taylor, R. L. (1989). *Assessment of exceptional students.* Englewood Cliffs, NJ: Prentice-Hall.

Thorin, E., Yovanoff, P., & Irvin, L. (1996). Dilemmas faced by families during their young adult's transitions to adulthood: A brief report. *Mental Retardation, 34*(2), 117–120.

Thornton, J. (1995, June 13). Matthew: Sometimes a new baby means sorrow as well as joy. *Style Magazine, 13*(24), 55.

Tredgold, A. F. (1937). *A textbook of mental deficiency.* Baltimore: Wood.

Turner, L. A., Dofny, E. M., & Dutka, S. (1994). Effect of strategy and attribution training on strategy maintenance and transfer. *American Journal on Mental Retardation, 98*(4), 445–454.

U.S. Department of Education. (1995). *Seventeenth annual report to Congress on the implementation of the Individuals With Disabilities Education Act.* Washington, DC: Author.

Zeaman, D., & House, B. J. (1961). *Role of attention in retardate discrimination learning: Progress Report No. 3.* Mansfield Depot, CT: Connecticut University Department of Psychology.

Zigman, W. B., Schupf, N., Sersen, E., & Silverman, W. (1996). Prevalence of dementia in adults with and without Down syndrome. *American Journal on Mental Retardation, 100*(4), 403–412.

Chapter 12

House in Jamaica, acrylic on canvas, 30″ × 40″ (1991)

AUTISM

ROBERT E. O'NEILL

After studying this chapter, the reader will:

Be familiar with the basic history of the definition
and use of the term *autism*

Know the current definitions used by researchers and practitioners

Recognize the behavioral characteristics exhibited
by children with autism

Be able to discuss theories and research about
possible causes of autism

Know how to carry out diagnostic and educational assessments

Know which teaching strategies have been shown to be
effective with children with autism

Understand the issues involved and the approaches to educational
placements and programs for children with autism

Understand areas of concern for parents and families, and be
familiar with related training and support strategies

Be able to describe other treatment approaches

Identify current issues of importance and controversy
concerning children with autism

Appreciate critical issues for future research and service efforts

AUTISM

1943	Characteristics of early infantile autism were first described in an article by child psychiatrist Leo Kanner.
1959	Psychologist Bruno Bettelheim published several papers on a parental causation theory of autism.
1964	Bernard Rimland, a psychologist whose son has autism, published *Infantile Autism,* a book that disputed the parental causation theory and proposed a neurobiological cause.
1965	The National Society for Autistic Children was founded by Rimland and other parents.
1965–1967	First reports on the application of behavioral techniques for teaching skills and dealing with problem behaviors were published by Lovaas, Hewett, Wolf, Risley, and others.
1966	Division TEACCH project was begun in North Carolina.
1973	Lovaas and colleagues presented results from the first long-term follow-up of children receiving behavioral treatment.
1980	Autism was included in third edition of the *Diagnostic and Statistical Manual* of the American Psychiatric Association.
1987	Lovaas published a study describing the apparent recovery of some children with autism following intensive behavioral treatment.
1988	The movie *Rain Man* was released, in which Dustin Hoffman portrayed a high-functioning adult with autism.
1990	Douglas Biklen published his first article describing facilitated communication as he observed it in Australia.
1993	Lovaas and colleagues published their follow-up report on children who received intensive behavioral intervention.

INTRODUCTION

Picture this: You have entered a classroom that is filled with a number of children, adolescents, and young adults. In one corner, some of the students are sitting on the floor, rocking back and forth, staring up at the room lights, and gazing intently at the hands and fingers they are flapping back and forth in front of their eyes. In another corner, others are repeatedly slapping themselves in the face, or banging their heads against the wall. Some students walk up to you calmly, put out their hands, and say "Hi, my name is Michael (or Caesar, or Mary); what's yours?" while other students walk up and say "Make a run for the border, at Taco Beeellll!" Others are rapidly walking around the room, pacing out repetitive patterns of squares or triangles on the floor. Still others are sitting quietly at a table, playing with toy trucks or blocks, or reading out loud from books. Sounds like a pretty confusing and chaotic situation, doesn't it? The interesting thing is that all of these students might have one thing in common; they may have all been labeled as having autism.

The point of imagining such a situation is that it gives you some idea of the wide range of behavioral characteristics that may be displayed by persons labeled as having autism. This is a disorder that can have a severe, lifelong impact on persons and their families. This chapter will describe the characteristics associated with autism and will talk about the strategies that have been shown to be effective for teaching and supporting students with autism and their parents and families.

HISTORICAL OVERVIEW

The term *early infantile autism* and a description of the characteristics of this syndrome were first presented in 1943 by Leo Kanner, an eminent child psychiatrist at Johns Hopkins University (Kanner, 1943). (The term *syndrome* means that a diagnosis of **autism** is given based on the presence of certain *behavioral* characteristics, as opposed to the presence of a particular physical or genetic feature.) In this article Kanner described his observations of 11 children, whom he believed demonstrated a unique set of characteristics that did not fit into diagnostic categories that were typically used at the time. These behavioral differences had become apparent at a very young age and included great difficulties in developing normal social interactions and relationships, significant delays and problems in language development and use, engagement in repetitive and stereotyped activities, and a desire for keeping their environment and routines consistent (Schreibman, 1988). Specific diagnostic criteria have changed in various ways since 1943, but these types of characteristics are still considered important in determining a diagnosis of autism.

Kanner initially considered both biological and environmental variables and their interaction as possible causes of autism (Sanua, 1990). He felt that the children seemed to have been born without the typical capacity for social and emotional development, perhaps due to some organic or neurological problem. However, based on the initial sample of 11 children, he also characterized their parents as highly intelligent, obsessive, cold, and lacking genuine interest in people. At that time Freudian and similar psychodynamic approaches were very pervasive in psychology and psychiatry. Because of this, many subsequent writers and researchers focused on the assumption that coldness, rejection, or other parental characteristics and behaviors were the primary causes of autism. Mothers in particular were implicated in this regard. This perspective was most prominently presented in the writings of Bruno Bettelheim. Bettelheim hypothesized that children

REAL PEOPLE

Ashley Page

Ashley is a 7-year-old with dark blonde hair and large blue eyes. She likes to play computer games, look at books, and have fun on swings and trampolines. She also enjoys being around and playing with other children, especially in her wading pool. Like most other kids, she sometimes gets frustrated with her twin brother, Brady, and expresses her frustration in not-so-loving ways! However, it is clear that the two siblings have a special relationship. Ashley's parents, Kerry and Valerie, describe Brady as Ashley's "best asset."

Ashley was diagnosed as having a pervasive developmental disorder (PDD), and later more specifically as having autism, at approximately 2 years of age. She has exhibited many of the behavioral symptoms often associated with autism, such as delays in language development, self-stimulatory behaviors (e.g., spinning objects, finger-flicking), and a lack of interest in social interactions and relationships. However, other difficult behaviors, such as tantrums, aggression towards others, and self-injury, have not been a consistent problem with Ashley.

Soon after her diagnosis, Ashley was enrolled in the Children's Behavior Therapy Unit, a preschool program for children with autism that provided structured, behaviorally oriented teaching and intervention. This program was successful in beginning to teach Ashley a variety of basic skills, such as paying attention to teachers, working on tasks, and communicating through sign language and initial speech. The program also provided information and training for Ashley's parents concerning autism in general, teaching Ashley and managing her behavior, and their legal rights in dealing with the public school system. Valerie and Kerry both feel strongly that this early intervention was very important both for Ashley's progress and their own learning. Along with their jobs and family life, they have both continued to be very involved in disseminating information and promoting awareness and understanding of autism. As a part of these activities, Kerry has served as the president of the chapter of the Autism Society of America in the state where the family resides.

For the last 2 years Ashley has attended classrooms for children with disabilities that are located on regular elementary school campuses. It took some work by Kerry and Valerie to convince their school district that this was a good thing to do, but they felt that it was very important for Ashley to have the opportunity to be around and interact with other children without disabilities. Ashley often imitates the behaviors of other children, which makes having good role models available extremely important. She enjoys being around and playing with other children at recess and other times, and Ashley's parents feel that these interactions will continue to be important as she learns and develops. In these classroom programs, Ashley has continued to receive instruction in areas such as language, identifying and labeling numbers, learning the alphabet, and fine motor skills (e.g., using scissors). She recently demonstrated her developing reading skills by labeling the letters printed on her father's T-shirt! She also continues to work on more general classroom skills, such as waiting her turn during games and activities. Along with classroom instruction, Ashley also works with a speech–language pathologist to further improve her communication skills.

Ashley continues to show positive changes in various ways. Like many children with autism, Ashley was substantially delayed in beginning to talk. In fact, some professionals who had evaluated Ashley told her parents they didn't think she would ever talk. However, over the past year she has substantially increased her use of one- or two-word phrases to communicate her wants and needs. When she is especially motivated she will produce even longer sentences. On a recent family outing she came out with "Go get ice cream!" when she saw a Wendy's restaurant. This effort was of course rewarded by pulling in and getting a tall, cool Frosty! Along with these increases in communication, Kerry and Valerie are also pleased with the progress Ashley is demonstrating in social interactions and relationships, and with her physical coordination.

It is clear that Ashley and her family will continue to struggle with the substantial difficulties and hurdles presented by the syndrome of autism. However, as we increase our understanding of how this disorder affects children and continue to improve our strategies for teaching and treatment, there is reason to be hopeful for Ashley and other children facing the challenge of autism.

with autism withdrew from contact with other persons and their environment because they were not receiving adequate and appropriate caregiving from parents (Bettelheim, 1967).

Even though it was not supported by empirical research, the psychodynamic approach was adopted by many doctors and therapists and had a number of unfortunate effects. Many parents experienced tremendous guilt and stress as a result of being told they were to blame for their children's difficulties. Therapeutic efforts were often focused on attempts to "analyze" the parents and their presumed problems, rather than directly helping or teaching the child. Bettelheim and others strongly supported the notion that many children could only be helped by separating them from their families and placing them in supposedly more therapeutic environments, which led to many children being institutionalized.

Significant challenges to the psychodynamic perspective began to arise in the mid- to late 1960s. In 1964, Bernard Rimland published a book titled *Infantile Autism*. Rimland was a research psychologist and the parent of a son with autism. In his book he reviewed a great deal of literature on the characteristics of children with autism and their parents. He argued that the evidence more strongly supported the hypothesis that autism resulted from biological causes. For example, he noted that many children with autism had parents that didn't fit the "typical" personality profile, and many parents that *did* fit such a profile often had other children without autism. In addition, behaviors characteristic of autism were noted to occur in children with known organic brain damage. As an alternative to the psychodynamic approach, Rimland presented a theory about the functions of particular brain structures and their possible role in autism.

Along with Rimland's work, a number of other researchers carried out and published well controlled scientific studies that demonstrated that parents of children with autism did not differ from other parents with regard to the occurrence of psychopathology, or in their personality and interaction characteristics (DeMyer, 1979; Koegel, Schreibman, O'Neill, & Burke, 1983; McAdoo & DeMyer, 1978; Schopler & Loftin, 1969). While there are still those who appear to believe in parental or psychogenic causes of autism, the current predominant perspective among most medical, educational, and mental health professionals is that it is a biologically based disorder (Gallagher, Jones, & Byrne, 1990; Gillberg & Coleman, 1992; Schopler & Mesibov, 1987). While the specific biological cause or causes have not yet been determined, some promising avenues of research in this area will be discussed later in the chapter.

As the emphasis on psychodynamic approaches decreased in the 1960s and 1970s, there was a concomitant increase in the development of educational and treatment strategies. In particular, approaches based on the principles and procedures of **applied behavior analysis** began to demonstrate substantial success in teaching children new skills and reducing the occurrence of problem behaviors. These approaches are still heavily used today and continue to show great promise in achieving positive outcomes for children with autism (Lovaas, 1987). The TEACCH program, begun in North Carolina in 1966, is another example of a structured educational approach that has produced positive results with many children (Schopler, Mesibov, & Hearsey, 1995). As children with autism and other disabilities have been given access to the public educational system, these behavioral and educational strategies have often served as the foundation for effective classroom programs. Other treatment approaches, such as the use of medications, have also been the focus of ongoing research and development since the 1960s.

Another important trend that began in the 1960s and is still influential is the acknowledgment and incorporation of parents in working with their children (in contrast to the previously popular psychodynamic model). The National Society for Autistic Children (now known as the ASA—Autism Society of America) was founded in 1965 as an organization to provide information and support to parents and family members. The ASA continues to be a very active organization with many state and local chapters that provide opportunities for parents to get information, receive support, and work with other parents to advocate for services for their children (Rimland, 1994). Structured teaching approaches, such as applied behavior analysis and the TEACCH program, have also consistently stressed the importance of directly involving parents in the teaching and treatment of their children, particularly in home environments (Lovaas, 1987; Schopler, Mesibov, Shigley, & Bashford, 1984).

The half century that has passed since the syndrome of autism was first identified has seen great changes in perspectives and approaches concerning the disorder. Many of these changes and the resulting current issues and approaches will be the focus of the remaining sections of this chapter.

DEFINITIONS AND DIAGNOSTIC CRITERIA

For many years, autism was considered to be an earlier manifestation of the severe mental disorders experienced by some adults, such as schizophrenia or psychosis (Rutter & Schopler, 1988). This led to confusion, as different labels—Kanner's syndrome, infantile autism, childhood schizophrenia, childhood psychosis—were used by writers and researchers to describe groups of children with similar behavioral characteristics (DeMyer, Hingtgen, & Jackson, 1981). Then in the 1970s, investigators began to delineate differences between autism and schizophrenia (Rutter & Schopler, 1988; Schopler, 1983). For instance, autism is considered to have an onset in infancy or very early childhood, while with childhood schizophrenia the onset is in later childhood or early adolescence. Children diagnosed with schizophrenia typically exhibit a number of years of normal or near-normal development prior to the appearance of symptoms such as delusions or hallucinations, which are rare in children diagnosed as having autism (Schopler, 1983). This evolution culminated in 1978 when Rutter (1978a) and Ritvo and Freeman (1978) published similar (but not identical) definitions of the syndrome, with emphases on early onset and severe disturbances in social relations, communication, and activity patterns.

In 1980, the American Psychiatric Association published the third edition of its *Diagnostic and Statistical Manual of Mental Disorders*, referred to as *DSM-III*. In this manual infantile autism was placed in a broader category labeled Pervasive Developmental Disorders, a term that was intended to indicate the broad range of behavioral domains that are affected and the fact that these difficulties become apparent in early stages of development. The *DSM* criteria included specific behavioral descriptions of symptoms in the areas of social interaction, communication, and a restricted range of activities and interests.

This diagnostic definition was further refined in *DSM-III-R*, a revised version of the *DSM-III* (American Psychiatric Association, 1987). Referred to as Autistic Disorder, it was still included in the category of Pervasive Developmental Disorders. However, research demonstrated that the definition had been broadened. In studies comparing the original and revised versions, more persons were typically diagnosed as having autism using the revised criteria (Volkmar, Bregman, Cohen, & Cicchetti, 1988). These issues led to further research and revision of the definition, which was recently published in **DSM-IV**, the fourth edition of the *DSM* (American Psychiatric Association, 1994). Table 12.1 lists the *DSM-IV* criteria for Autistic Disorder.

Children with autism have severe disturbances in social relations, communication, and activity patterns.

The *DSM-IV* criteria will most likely continue to be widely used in many research and clinical situations. The *DSM-IV* also includes diagnostic criteria for related disorders. Asperger's disorder is a diagnosis that is applied when a child displays severe social behavior deficits and a restricted pattern of interests and activities. However, children receiving this diagnosis typically do not display significant delays in language, general cognitive development, or self-help skills and adaptive behavior. Pervasive Developmental Disorder Not Otherwise Specified (PDDNOS) is a diagnosis that is applied when a child displays only some of the characteristics of a particular disorder (such as autism), but does not display enough symptoms, or symptoms severe enough, to warrant the more specific diagnosis. Several researchers and authors have begun to view autism and these related diagnostic categories as making up a continuum or spectrum of related disorders (Gillberg, 1990; Waterhouse, 1996; Wing, 1992).

Another recent definition of autism was presented in the federal regulations for the Individuals With Disabilities Education Act of 1990:

> Autism means a developmental disability significantly affecting verbal and nonverbal communication and social interaction, generally evident before age three, that adversely affects educational performance. Characteristics of autism include: irregularities and impairments in communication, engagement in repetitive activities and stereotyped movements, resistance to environmental change or change in daily routines, and unusual responses to sensory experiences. (Department of Education, 1991, p. 41271)

This definition and associated criteria are to be used by state educational personnel for determining eligibility for special education services. States must specify testing and assessment procedures to be followed in making such eligibility determinations (e.g., Utah State Office of Education, 1993).

There has been both change and continuity in the definitions of the syndrome of autism over the last several decades. For example, Leo Kanner originally felt that children with autism had normal cognitive or intellectual function that was

Table 12.1 *DSM-IV* **Diagnostic Criteria for Autistic Disorder**

A. A total of six (or more) items from (1), (2), and (3), with at least two from (1), and one each from (2) and (3):

(1) qualitative impairment in social interaction, as manifested by at least two of the following:

(a) marked impairment in the use of multiple nonverbal behaviors such as eye-to-eye gaze, facial expression, body postures, and gestures to regulate social interaction
(b) failure to develop peer relationships appropriate to developmental level
(c) a lack of spontaneous seeking to share enjoyment, interests, or achievements with other people (e.g., by a lack of showing, bringing, or pointing out objects of interest)
(d) lack of social or emotional reciprocity

(2) qualitative impairments in communication as manifested by at least one of the following:

(a) delay in, or total lack of, the development of spoken language (not accompanied by an attempt to compensate through alternative modes of communication such as gesture or mime)
(b) in individuals with adequate speech, marked impairment in the ability to initiate or sustain a conversation with others
(c) stereotyped and repetitive use of language or idiosyncratic language
(d) lack of varied, spontaneous, make-believe play or social imitative play appropriate to developmental level

(3) restricted repertoire and stereotyped patterns of behavior, interests, and activities, as manifested by at least one of the following:

(a) encompassing preoccupation with one or more stereotyped and restricted patterns of interest that is abnormal either in intensity or focus
(b) apparently inflexible adherence to specific, nonfunctional routines or rituals
(c) stereotyped and repetitive motor mannerisms (e.g., hand or finger flapping or twisting, or complex whole-body movements)
(d) persistent preoccupation with parts of objects

B. Delays or abnormal functioning in at least one of the following areas, with onset prior to age 3 years: (1) social interaction, (2) language as used in social communication, or (3) symbolic or imaginative play.

C. The disturbance is not better accounted for by Rett's Disorder or Childhood Disintegrative Disorder.

Source: From *Diagnostic and Statistical Manual of Mental Disorders* (4th ed.), 1994. Washington, DC: American Psychiatric Association.

being hidden by their severe withdrawal and isolation. It has become clearer over the years that the majority of children with autism also experience varying degrees of mental retardation as well. However, it is also clear that many of the aspects and characteristics described by Kanner continue to be important in defining the syndrome.

SPECIFIC BEHAVIORAL CHARACTERISTICS

In discussing specific characteristics it is important to keep in mind that even with the foregoing definitions and criteria, children diagnosed as having autism can demonstrate a very broad range in the type and severity of their behaviors. There is no such thing as a "typical" child with autism (recall that classroom we were in at the beginning of the chapter).

Social Behavior

Children with autism may display a wide range of differences or deficits in responding to other persons (Schopler & Mesibov, 1986). They may give very little attention to, or make very little eye contact with, other children or adults, unless specifically asked to do so. They will rarely seek out affection or physical contact from others, including their parents. If children or adults do initiate physical contact or social interactions with a child, they may be ignored or the child may actively resist or move away from them. Children with autism have been shown to be less likely to try to get others to pay attention to objects or events that interest them, or attempt to show or give objects such as toys to other persons (Sigman, 1994).

In the last 10 years there has been a great deal of research on the ability of children with autism to understand and respond to the social and emotional cues and behaviors of others. For example, in one study in which adults displayed facial expressions associated with fear, pain, or discomfort, children with autism only looked briefly at the actors, while typical children and children with mental retardation demonstrated considerable attention (Sigman, Kasari, Kwon, & Yirmiya, 1992). Other studies have involved asking children to identify emotions shown in photographs, slides, or videotapes. While children with autism who possess greater verbal abilities were able to label some of the emotions shown, they were significantly less accurate than children without disabilities (Ozonoff, Pennington, & Rogers, 1990; Sigman, 1994). Other research has focused on difficulties children with autism may have in understanding how other persons can have knowledge and beliefs that are different from their own (Happé & Frith, 1995).

Children with autism clearly have significant difficulties understanding and participating in the normal give-and-take of social interaction. These problems are very important to consider during assessment and planning for instructional activities.

Communication

A variety of deficits may be evident in this area (Schopler & Mesibov, 1985). Most estimates have indicated that approximately 50% of children with autism do not develop meaningful speech (Charlop & Haymes, 1994; Rutter, 1978b). Children who do develop spoken language may display a variety of characteristics, such as immature grammar and syntax, or immediate **echolalia,** in which the child repeats back what is said to him or her. Delayed echolalia may also occur, in which children will repeat words, phrases, or commercial jingles in a repetitive and stereotyped manner. While such repetitions may sometimes appear to be meaningless behavior, recent research has demonstrated that echolalic speech may serve various communicative functions for children, such as making requests. For example, a child may say "Do you want a cookie?" as a means of asking for a cookie (Charlop & Haymes, 1994). Pronoun reversal may be evident, such as when a child says "*You* want a drink" instead of "*I* want a drink."

As in social interaction, children with autism generally engage in very little spontaneous conversational give-and-take. Children who do speak may demonstrate a variety of differences in the intonation, pitch, and rhythm of their speech (Schreibman, Kohlenberg, & Britten, 1986). Along with these expressive aspects, children with autism most often have significant difficulties in comprehending language beyond the level of simple instructions or phrases (Rutter, 1978a; Schreibman, 1988).

High-functioning children who do develop more sophisticated verbal abilities also display a variety of language difficulties. They may do well with more concrete language that refers to specific and unambiguous objects and events, but may continue to have trouble with more abstract language that deals with such things as thoughts, feelings, double meanings, and humor (Baltaxe & Simmons, 1992; Siegel, Goldstein, & Minshew, 1996).

Restricted Interests and Activities

As already described, children with autism often do not engage in typical social-communicative interactions with other persons. In addition, they often do not develop typical play skills, particularly more imaginative or make-believe kinds of play (Dunlap, Koegel, & O'Neill, 1985). Their interactions with toys or other objects may primarily consist of repetitive, stereotypic manipulations, such as spinning the wheels of a car, stacking blocks, or sifting rocks through their fingers. They may also engage in a variety of repetitive or **self-stimulatory behavior** comprising motor movements such as body-rocking, flapping their hands, or facial grimacing.

Children may also spend a great deal of time engaging in ritualistic patterns of activity, such as lining up objects on a shelf, putting items away in drawers, or disassembling and reassembling toys or mechanical objects. On a more complex level, such activities may take the form of preoccupations with bus schedules, writing the letters of the alphabet, or memorizing calendars. A related characteristic, mentioned initially by Kanner, is an apparently strong resistance to changes in the environment or typical routines. Children may insist on eating only particular foods, following certain bedtime routines, or taking the same travel routes to school or the baby-sitter, and may become very upset if these routines are varied (Schreibman, 1988). Obviously, these types of preoccupations may place significant burdens on parents and teachers as they attempt to accommodate children in the typical chaos of daily routines.

Cognitive and Learning Characteristics

As mentioned earlier, current consensus in the literature indicates that roughly 75% of children diagnosed with autism will also exhibit varying degrees of mental retardation, as indicated by such characteristics as having a measured IQ below 70. Based on such criteria, approximately 50% of children with autism will score in the moderate, severe, or profound ranges of retardation (Wing, 1993). Children with autism differ from children with mental retardation in that their test performance may be relatively uneven. Children with mental retardation tend to score at lower levels across most or all areas of test performance. Children with autism may do poorly in some areas but obtain higher scores in others (Schreibman, 1988). Scores in areas involving manipulative or visual skills tend to be higher, while scores in areas involving linguistic skills or abstract or symbolic processes tend to be lower. Approximately 25% of children will score in the normal range of intelligence. While much research and clinical effort has been focused on children who are more severely impaired, in recent years there has been greater attention to the population of what are called high-functioning persons with autism (Schopler & Mesibov, 1992). Such persons may obtain normal scores on IQ tests, but still exhibit a variety of problems in social behavior, speech and language, emotional development and expression, and ritualistic or compulsive behaviors (Tsai, 1992).

Some children may exhibit exceptional abilities in isolated areas such as music, mathematics, mechanical abilities, or drawing (Sacks, 1995). Many readers of this book have seen the film *Rain Man*, in which Dustin Hoffman portrayed an adult with autism who displayed what are sometimes called **savant skills,** such as being able to instantly count the number of toothpicks that have spilled from the box to the floor. Other examples of these very rare skills include memorizing phone books, playing complex musical pieces after one hearing, or being able to specify the day of the week for a calendar date in the distant past or future (Rimland, 1978).

Information Processing and Learning.　　A great deal of research has been carried out to attempt to identify the kinds of problems that children with autism may have in processing information and learning (Schopler & Mesibov, 1995). The fact that children with autism are not always responsive to others in typical ways often leads parents and teachers to suspect they may be deaf, or have other sensory problems (Dunlap et al., 1985; Schreibman, 1988). However, this is typically not the case; in fact, the child who sometimes appears unresponsive may suddenly become *very* aware and responsive when he or she hears Mom unwrapping a favorite candy bar in the next room!

A number of studies have demonstrated that children may demonstrate what is called **stimulus overselectivity** (Lovaas, Koegel, & Schreibman, 1979)—that is, they may pay attention to only some parts of the environment at a given time. For example, if a teacher is presenting a picture and also presenting the verbal label for the picture, children may only attend to the picture, and miss the verbal label. This would prevent him from learning that the two things are related to one another. Other related research has demonstrated that these children may not be able to rapidly shift their attention from one aspect of the environment to another (Green, Fein, Joy, & Waterhouse, 1995). On a more complex level, children with autism appear to have difficulties with higher level, or *executive functions*, which include such things as problem solving, self-monitoring and self-correction, and inhibiting impulsive responding (Green et al., 1995; Ozonoff, 1995).

While they may often appear oblivious to their environment, it is clear that children with autism do pay at least some attention to what is going on around them. However, their ability to perceive, make sense of, and integrate this information in a typical way is what seems to be problematic (Ornitz, 1989). These kinds of problems are clearly related to their difficulties in areas such as language and social behavior. Further research will help us better understand what these problems are and develop strategies to help alleviate them.

Physical Characteristics

There are no particular external physical features or anomalies that appear to uniquely accompany the syndrome of autism. In fact, it has often been anecdotally noted in the literature that the children are considered to be quite good-looking. However, some writers have commented that years of engaging in problematic behaviors such as poor eating habits, abnormal posturing, or teeth-grinding may result in physical abnormalities by adulthood (Dunlap et al., 1985). Also, autism may be found in children with other identified genetic or chromosomal disorders, such as Down syndrome or fragile X (Folstein & Rutter, 1987). In such cases there may be a variety of physical characteristics present that are typical of these related disorders.

Other Characteristics

Seizure Activity.　　It has been reported that as many as 25% of children with autism will eventually display some evidence of seizure activity (Folstein & Rutter, 1987; Gualtieri, Evans, & Patterson, 1987; Rutter, 1978b). This becomes particularly likely as children go through puberty and move into adolescence. The causes responsible for this pattern of seizure development are not clear. In many children and adults with autism the seizures can be controlled with anticonvulsant medications; however, such medications may be required on an ongoing or lifelong basis, and require careful monitoring to detect and deal with potential serious side effects (Gualtieri et al., 1987).

Inconsistent Sensory Responses.   As mentioned earlier in the chapter, children with autism sometimes demonstrate inconsistent responses to sensory input (American Psychiatric Association, 1994; Schreibman, 1988). They may exhibit a high threshold for pain, demonstrate great sensitivity to being touched by others, or refuse to wear particular clothes due to their texture. With regard to vision and hearing, they may appear either underresponsive or overresponsive to particular lights or sounds. For example, some children may become very upset by particular noises, such as a smoke alarm or a siren. They may respond by covering their ears or getting very agitated (e.g., yelling, running around). There may also be an unusual interest in licking, mouthing, or sniffing objects that catch their attention.

Unusual or Affective Emotional Behaviors.   It has been noted that children with autism sometimes appear to express emotions or feelings in an unusual fashion. For example, they may suddenly begin to laugh or cry without apparent reason. They may show no signs of fear in dangerous situations, such as running out into the street. Conversely, they may demonstrate excessively fearful responses in response to apparently harmless objects. For example, one child would become very fearful and upset whenever cloth napkins were placed on the family dining table at mealtime.

Disruptive Behaviors.   Children with autism, like all children (including those with other developmental disabilities), engage in a variety of behaviors that are disruptive and upsetting for other people (Schopler & Mesibov, 1994). These include more typical problem behaviors such as crying and throwing tantrums, but they can also include more severe behaviors such as aggression towards other children and adults (hitting, kicking, biting) and throwing or destroying objects or materials (American Psychiatric Association, 1994; Schreibman, 1988). **Self-injurious behavior (SIB)** may also occur, in which children may hit or bite themselves or bang their heads on walls or other hard surfaces (Iwata, Zarcone, Vollmer, & Smith, 1994). These kinds of behaviors vary in intensity. For example, a teen-age boy with autism repeatedly slapped himself on the side of the jaw—but he did it just forcefully enough to be audible but not hard enough to cause bruising or other tissue damage. There are other children who bang their heads or bite themselves severely enough to cause bruises, scalp lacerations, and bleeding. While such severe behaviors are not necessarily very common, working with such children and their caregivers provides very significant challenges for teachers and others.

PREVALENCE OF THE AUTISM SYNDROME

Autism has been considered to be a relatively rare disorder. There have been a number of epidemiological studies over the last few decades examining the frequency of occurrence among children. Recent reviews of this literature indicate that it occurs in 4 to 5 children out of 10,000, or less than 0.5% (Locke, Banken, & Mahone, 1994; Ritvo et al., 1989; Wing, 1993). Different studies have reported prevalence figures ranging from 3 to 16 children per 10,000. This variability may be due to different factors, such as different definitions being used by different investigators, and greater attention to identifying high-functioning persons that still meet the diagnostic criteria (Wing, 1993).

With regard to gender differences, researchers have consistently reported that autism is diagnosed about three to four times more often in males than in females (Lord & Schopler, 1987). In addition, there is some indication in the literature that females diagnosed with autism tend to exhibit a more severe level of retardation (Wing, 1993). Lord and Schopler (1987) have pointed out the importance of guarding against gender bias in ensuring that all children have access to appropriate assessment and intervention. Because autism appears to be quite a bit more common in males, we need to make sure that those providing assessment, education, and treatment services don't overlook female children and adults in need of such services as well.

WHAT CAUSES AUTISM?

As described earlier, there is a strong consensus that the primary cause of the difficulties experienced by people with autism is some type of biological or neurophysiological abnormality or dysfunction (Gillberg & Coleman, 1992). This is supported by a wide range of investigations of neurobiological factors, and the fact that there appears to be a strong genetically related component to the disorder (Folstein & Rutter, 1987; Rutter, Bailey, Bolton, & Le Couteur, 1994). A specific causal factor of this type has not yet been identified. It has become clear, however, that different types of neurophysiological disorders can lead to the behaviors characteristic of autism. These disorders include tuberous sclerosis, congenital rubella, and fragile X syndrome (Rutter et al., 1994; Rutter & Schopler, 1988). Such issues have made it more difficult to try to pin down specific neurobiological factors that may be involved. It is also not clear when such a causal developmental problem might occur. Given that symptoms of autism may be displayed at very young ages (Baron-Cohen, Allen, & Gillberg, 1992), whatever does go wrong must begin to occur either before birth or very shortly thereafter.

Researchers have investigated a large number of possible problems in neurological structure. For example, a variety of studies have reported structural abnormalities or lesions in a number of different areas of the brain of people with autism, such as the cerebral ventricles, the cerebral cortex, the limbic system, the cerebellum, and the temporal lobes (Locke et al., 1994; Reichler & Lee, 1987). However, efforts to replicate these findings in larger groups of children have not been consistently successful. Neurochemical systems have also been extensively studied. Researchers have reported elevated levels of chemicals in the brain, such as serotonin and dopamine, in children with autism (Yuwiler & Freedman, 1987). Again, however, consistent findings in these areas have been difficult to come by. Some of these problems in attempting to replicate findings are most likely due to the heterogeneity of the children that may be diagnosed with autism and included in research studies. Investigators are increasingly moving in the direction of very carefully defining more specific subgroups of children for study (Coleman, 1987). For example, the studies by Courchesne and colleagues, discussed in the next paragraph, have typically involved high-functioning children and adults that are diagnosed with autism, but not mental retardation. While this is a smaller subgroup of the larger population of persons with autism, the results from such studies can potentially provide information relevant to the larger population.

Along with structural and chemical problems, researchers have investigated a variety of aspects of neurological functioning and how they may be related to the behaviors characteristic of autism. The investigations by Courchesne (1987) indicated that persons with autism have difficulties attending and responding in typical ways to auditory and visual stimuli. Courchesne hypothesized that periodic changes or intermittent "static" in neurological systems may undermine the ability to pay attention to and remember information effectively. Ornitz (1989) has proposed a similar model, which considers sensory and information processing difficulties as potentially responsible for the types of developmental and behavioral problems seen in children with autism.

Research in all these areas, as well as others, is ongoing. While there are no clear answers to the difficult puzzle of the cause of autism at this time, clear progress has occurred—providing strong hope for more positive results in the future.

ASSESSMENT ISSUES AND STRATEGIES

Diagnostic Assessment

Werry (1988) outlined several things that a good diagnosis should provide, as follows:

1. Information about how to treat or intervene with a child

2. A basis for telling parents or caregivers what the prognosis or expected outcomes may be in the shorter and longer terms

3. Information about the cause or causes of the disorder

4. Information about associated problems to watch for (e.g., seizures in children with autism)

5. Facilitation of communication among parents, professionals, and researchers

6. Information about how to prevent the disorder

Werry concluded that while a diagnosis of autism does not always tell us much about the critical issues of cause and specific effective treatments, it can provide us with a good deal of useful information and things to be aware of in working with a child and his or her family.

The diagnostic process often begins with parents approaching their pediatrician or other persons (e.g., teacher, psychologist) because they have concerns about their child's development and behavior. As the assessment process proceeds, a diagnosis of autism is typically arrived at through a variety of means, including structured interviews with parents and caregivers, observations of children, and the use of various standardized tests, checklists, and rating scales. For example, a practitioner might employ different strategies to collect information and then attempt to make a decision about whether the child's behavior meets particular criteria, such as those from the *DSM-IV.* It is *critical* that a variety of techniques be used to gather a broad array of information, rather than relying on a single approach. Schreibman and Charlop (1987) presented a structured interview format for gathering information about a child's developmental history and current patterns of behavior and functioning. Lord, Rutter, and Le Couteur (1994) presented a revised version of the Autism Diagnostic Interview (ADI), a standardized, semistructured format for interviewing parents and caregivers. The ADI provides scores indicating the level of severity in the areas of communication, social skills, and stereotyped behaviors, during both early development and at the time of evaluation. Compared to most interview formats, the ADI has the advantage of standardized scoring and interpretation criteria that can be used to arrive at a diagnosis.

Students diagnosed with autism may be observed in a variety of settings to obtain useful information on the student's behavior.

Lord and colleagues (1989) also developed and validated the Autism Diagnostic Observation Schedule (ADOS). The ADOS involves presenting children with a series of interactive situations and rating their behavior in areas such as social interaction and communication. As with the ADI, there are standardized procedures for scoring and interpreting the results of the assessment.

Other observational rating scales include the Real Life Rating Scale (RLRS) (Freeman, Ritvo, Yokota, & Ritvo, 1986) and the Childhood Autism Rating Scale (CARS) (Schopler, Reichler, & Renner, 1988). The RLRS requires an observer to watch a child for a 30-minute period, and then score the presence or absence of a number of behaviors in categories such as social interactions, sensory responses, and language. The CARS is similar in that raters observe a child in home, school, or other settings, and then rate his or her behavior on a number of diagnostic items. A child then receives a score that can be compared to cutoff scores for determining a diagnosis and the level of severity of impairment. In a recent review, Sturmey & Sevin (1994) compared research data on several autism rating scales and concluded that the CARS was currently the instrument of choice for use in diagnostic assessment. However, all of these types of measures need further research to improve their validity and usefulness to practitioners. For example, recent studies have indicated that all of these scales have difficulty identifying high-functioning children who meet diagnostic criteria for autism (Yirmiya, Sigman, & Freeman, 1994).

Along with these more structured techniques, a series of observations in a variety of settings (e.g., home, school) should also be done to obtain more detailed

INNOVATIVE IDEAS "WITH A LITTLE HELP FROM MY FRIENDS"

One of the primary areas in which children and adults with autism have difficulty is that of social interactions and relationships. A wide variety of strategies have been implemented in attempts to teach appropriate social interaction skills—including direct prompting and reinforcement by teachers, and group activities such as sociodramatic play and affection activities (Haring & Lovinger, 1989; McEvoy et al., 1988). But another set of approaches, called *peer-mediated interventions,* have gained popularity in recent years (Odom, McConnell, & Chandler, 1994). The primary focus of these approaches is on teaching nondisabled peers some basic strategies for initiating and maintaining ongoing interactions with children who have disabilities. In the case of autism, the aim is to increase the responsiveness of the children with autism as well as the likelihood that they will be more spontaneous and begin to *initiate* social interactions with other children. Peer-mediated interventions have produced substantial positive results in research studies, a large number of which have involved children with autism, particularly those in the preschool or early elementary age groups (Odom & Strain, 1984; Strain & Odom, 1986).

Before beginning to carry out such a program, appropriate children without disabilities must be selected to serve as interac-

information about a child's behavior. Such observations would yield more detail about a child's typical play and academic skills, social and communicative behavior, adaptive and self-help skills, and other indicators (Schreibman, 1988).

Assessment for Planning Specific Instruction and Treatment

Multidisciplinary Involvement. In the educational process teachers are typically the persons with primary responsibility for assessment and instructional planning. However, it's important to remember that focused assessments in a variety of areas can provide more specific information for developing educational and therapeutic goals. Related service professionals such as school psychologists, speech–language pathologists, physical or occupational therapists, and vision and hearing specialists can collect information that gives a clearer picture of a child's strengths and areas of need with regard to academic skills, language and communication, fine and gross motor behavior, and self-care and adaptive skills. However, it is critical to maintain appropriate communication and coordination among the members of a team (Westling & Fox, 1995). It is also very important to remember that parents and other significant caregivers are an integral part of such efforts and should be included in all steps of the process (Turnbull & Morningstar, 1993; also see Chapter 13 of this book). Parents are often the only consistent caregivers in a tion partners. Often this is done by having a teacher identify children that are cooperative and have reasonably good social skills. These children are then told about the program and their willingness to participate is determined. If they are willing, they participate in a series of short training sessions lasting about 15 to 30 minutes each, in which they are taught a variety of skills for initiating and maintaining interactions. These skills—such as sharing, or making requests to play with specific toys or games—are taught through a combination of discussion, role playing, and practice with feedback. Peers may also require training in areas such as how to be persistent without being pushy if other children are unresponsive, or how to respond to negative or disruptive behaviors. Training sessions can be conducted by teachers, school psychologists, or other relevant persons with appropriate background and experience. Once the peers demonstrate an adequate level of understanding and skill with the procedures, they are asked to carry them out in play sessions with the children who have disabilities.

A substantial number of studies have demonstrated that implementing peer-mediated procedures can result in increases in both responses and social initiations by children with autism. However, it has also become clear that peers without disabilities may require periodic prompting, encouragement, and reinforcement to continue to use the interaction strategies they have been taught. Peer-mediated interventions have been used by teachers and others in large numbers of schools and programs in the United States and other countries. More work is needed to determine the best approach for using peer-mediated strategies to achieve positive social interaction outcomes for children both with and without disabilities. However, the work in this area to date has demonstrated the powerful impact that using natural peer resources can have on the social interactions of children with autism. These types of strategies should be considered for use by anyone working to facilitate the appropriate social development of such children.

child's life and have the broadest knowledge about the child's behavior over time in different settings and situations.

INSTRUCTIONAL APPROACHES

The last 30 years have provided unequivocal evidence that structured educational programs produce the best outcomes for children with autism (Bartak, 1978; DeMyer et al., 1981; Koegel, Rincover, & Egel, 1982; Mesibov, Schopler & Hearsey, 1994; Rutter, 1985). Three areas of primary instructional importance are developing instructional goals, using effective instructional strategies and techniques, and managing problem behaviors.

Developing Instructional Goals

There have been great advances in the last two decades in the way educators and other practitioners go about establishing instructional goals and developing curricula for students with disabilities such as autism (Johnson & Koegel, 1982; Meyer, Peck & Brown, 1991; Morgan & Jenson, 1988; Snell, 1993; Westling & Fox, 1995; see also Chapters 1 and 2 of this book). In the past a developmental approach had been very common, in which children were taught skills chosen from a developmental continuum characteristic of normally developing children. There is now a substantial focus on educational objectives that teach students skills that are more immediately appropriate in the typical settings in which they participate—at school, at home, and in the community (Johnson & Koegel, 1982; Neel et al., 1983). For example, instruction for a younger child might focus on (among other things) learning appropriate toy-play and social-play skills, functional communication skills such as requesting desired items and objects, and a variety of self-care skills such as dressing, grooming, and so forth. An older child's curriculum might include some similar types of skills at an age-appropriate level, along with **community-based training** in real-world environments—including practice using public transportation, going to grocery stores, attending leisure/recreation activities, and developing job skills in work settings.

The critical overriding issue is that goals and objectives for students should be based on their *individual* needs. What seems reasonable and appropriate for one student may not be for others. Therefore, careful assessment is very important in the curricular planning process. A number of strategies have been developed for assessment, selection of goals and objectives, and development of a student's Individualized Education Program (IEP) (Brown & Snell, 1993; Johnson & Koegel, 1982). A variety of procedures as described by Westling and Fox (1995) are presented in Table 12.2.

Again, the end result should be a set of instructional goals and objectives that will result in the child acquiring skills that will be useful to him or her in various home, school, and community settings (Belfiore & Mace, 1994). Parents and teachers will want to keep in mind particular areas in which many children with autism would likely benefit from instruction, such as social and communication skills.

Effective Strategies and Techniques

Beginning in the mid-1960s, a number of groups began to produce evidence that structured, behaviorally oriented approaches could teach children new skills and

Table 12.2   **Strategies for Assessing and
Selecting Instructional Goals and Objectives**

---

1. Review child's previous records (e.g., IEPs, progress reports, etc.).
2. Interview parents to learn about the child's current skills, and the parents' desired goals.
3. Use curriculum or activity guides as sources of ideas.[*]
4. Conduct ecological assessments, in which the activities and skills important in the child's current and future environments are identified and used as instructional goals.[†]
5. Conduct direct observations of the child to identify potential goals and confirm the importance of present ones.
6. Directly assess the child's performance on skills potentially targeted for instruction (i.e., make sure there's a need for instruction).

---

[*]See, for example, Giangreco, Cloninger, & Iverson (1993); and Wilcox & Bellamy (1987).

[†]See Brown & Snell (1993).

Source: Adapted from *Teaching Students With Severe Disabilities,* by D. L. Westling & L. Fox, 1995, Englewood Cliffs, NJ: Prentice-Hall.

**Table 12.3 Common Features of Behavioral
              Approaches to Instruction and Intervention**

1. Careful assessment of the child's initial skills and abilities
2. *Task analysis*, or breaking skills to be taught into smaller, more manageable steps
3. Provision of brief, clear instructions suitable to the child's level
4. Use of effective verbal and physical prompts to guide the child's performance of the task
5. Fading out or removal of prompts to ensure independent performance
6. Provision of effective and appropriate consequences for success
7. Gradually shaping the child's behavior towards the desired goal
8. Combining or *chaining* behaviors to produce more complex skills
9. Collection and use of data to make decisions during instruction

Source: Information taken from "Pervasive Developmental Disorders," by G. Dunlap, R. L. Koegel, & R. E. O'Neill, 1985, in *Handbook of Clinical Child Behavior Therapy* (pp. 499–540), P. H. Bornstein & A. E. Kazdin (Eds.), Homewood, IL: Dorsey; "Educational Strategies in Autism," by S. L. Harris, 1995, in *Learning and Cognition in Autism* (pp. 293–309), E. Schopler & G. B. Mesibov (Eds.), New York: Plenum; "General Principles of Behavior Management," by L. Schreibman, 1994, in *Behavioral Issues in Autism* (pp. 11–38), E. Schopler & G. B. Mesibov (Eds.), New York: Plenum; "The Technology of Instruction," by T. S. Woods, 1987, in *Handbook of Autism and Pervasive Developmental Disorders* (pp. 251–272), D. J. Cohen, A. M. Donnellan, & R. Paul (Eds.), New York: Wiley.

reduce problem behaviors (Hewett, 1965; Lovaas, Berberich, Perloff, & Schaeffer, 1966; Risley & Wolf, 1967; Schopler, Brehm, Kinsbourne, & Reichler, 1971; Wolf, Risley, & Mees, 1964). These types of educational approaches were developed and implemented in large numbers of classrooms and programs in the United States and around the world. While specific teaching programs and approaches may differ somewhat, there are a number of features that are common across many of them. These are presented in Table 12.3. These kinds of instructional approaches have been used to teach skills in a broad variety of areas, including communication (Carr, 1985; Lovaas, 1977), social behavior (Matson & Swiezy, 1994), self-care (Snell & Farlow, 1993), academics (Browder & Snell, 1993), and community-based skills (Horner, McDonnell, & Bellamy, 1986).

While behaviorally oriented approaches have produced substantial positive results, there are still many challenging issues concerning instruction for children with autism. For instance, even though many children may acquire new skills in a particular setting (such as a classroom), **generalization** may not occur; that is, the children may not use those new skills with other persons or in other settings and situations (Lovaas, Koegel, Simmons, & Long, 1973; Schreibman, 1988). These types of problems have led to advances in behavioral technology, such as using more naturalistic teaching strategies that make use of activities and interaction styles more typical of the kinds of things a child might experience outside the structured teaching situation. For example, a child may be given more choice and control over the materials and activities, tasks may be varied to maintain interest and motivation, more natural and direct reinforcement may be used, the reinforcers themselves may be varied to maintain interest, or the child may be reinforced for attempting to respond even if he or she does not always get it exactly right (Schreibman, 1994).

General case programming is another strategy that has proven to be effective for teaching generalized skills (Horner & Albin, 1988). This approach involves determining the kinds of settings and situations in which the desired behaviors are supposed to occur. Instruction is planned and carried out so that it includes examples of a broad enough range of the identified situations so that generalized skills

Teachers can use technological applications for teaching children with autism.

will result. For example, a parent and teacher may want a child to learn to make communicative requests with different peers and adults in the classroom, cafeteria, and playground settings. Instruction would therefore need to take place with different peers and adults in situations across these settings (O'Neill, 1990).

Positive results have also been shown with the use of **self-management strategies** (Koegel, Frea, & Surratt, 1994). Children with autism have been taught to monitor their own behavior and earn rewards for increasing appropriate behaviors and decreasing inappropriate behaviors. For example, a child may be taught to keep track of positive social initiations toward other students by using a wrist counter, or marking on a piece of paper. Initially, the child earns rewards for particular numbers of positive responses. Over time the tracking procedure and external rewards can be gradually faded out as the child becomes more successful and independent. Such procedures can successfully promote the generalization of desired behaviors across different settings and situations (Stahmer & Schreibman, 1992).

A related approach that has been shown to be successful is that of teaching children with autism to use picture schedules to prompt them through activities. Children may be able to learn to use a series of pictures presented in a book as cues for engaging in particular behaviors. Once they have learned to respond to the pictures, the cues and prompts from others (e.g., parents, teachers) can be faded out. This approach has been successfully used to teach independent skills in areas such as leisure activities and domestic chores (Krantz, MacDuff, & McClannahan, 1993; MacDuff, Krantz, & McClannahan, 1993; Pierce & Schreibman, 1994).

In recent years different investigators have begun to study the impact of very intensive behavioral programs that are begun with children when they are at very young ages—as early as 2 or 3 years old. Reports of the successful outcomes of these programs have been both very promising and controversial. Later in this chapter, in the section on current issues and trends, this topic will be explored in more detail.

Managing Problem Behaviors

Part of the instructional assessment process should include identifying particular disruptive behaviors that are of concern to parents and teachers, and that may have an impact on a child's functioning in community settings (Gerhardt & Holmes, 1994). The child's educational program should include strategies for preventing and reducing the occurrence of such behaviors. In recent years there has been a shift away from primarily relying on consequence-oriented procedures (i.e., reinforcement and punishment) to bring about behavior change. The use of **consequences** (both positive and negative) is very important, but is increasingly seen as one piece of a broader approach that involves a number of components (Meyer & Evans, 1989).

There is now a much greater emphasis on conducting initial assessments to understand *why* problem behaviors are happening, and what events or influences are related to their occurrence. For example, what kinds of events or activities seem to consistently lead to problem behaviors? What kinds of potentially reinforcing outcomes seem to occur when the child engages in certain behaviors? Are there medical conditions (e.g., allergies, illness) that seem related to the occurrence of problem behaviors? This type of information collection process is referred to as **functional assessment** or *functional analysis* (Iwata et al., 1994; O'Neill, Horner, Albin, Storey, & Sprague, 1990). Interviews, questionnaires, direct observations, and direct manipulations of particular events are used to assess environmental influences on behavior. Once the critical variables are identified, a variety of strategies can be planned for preventing behavior problems and reacting effectively when they do occur (Dunlap, Robbins, & Kern, 1994). Such strategies might include the following:

- Changing or manipulating the events that typically precede problem behaviors
- Teaching new skills, such as communicative responses, that the student can use to achieve the same outcomes as the problem behaviors (e.g., get attention, get a break from a nonpreferred task or activity)
- Providing positive consequences for desired behaviors
- Minimizing payoffs and/or providing negative consequences for inappropriate behaviors

It is important to point out that this expanded approach is based on the perspective that we need to look more broadly at the activities and experiences to which children are exposed. Along with specific behavioral techniques, efforts need to be made to maximize their opportunities to make choices, engage in preferred activities, and generally lead a productive, enjoyable, and satisfying life (Dunlap et al., 1994; Horner et al., 1990; Meyer & Evans, 1989). From this perspective assessing and dealing with problem behaviors is not a separate set of approaches or techniques, but is rather something that is an integral part of the entire process of instructional and curricular planning (Horner, 1996).

Educational Program and Placement Options

During the 1970s the success of structured, behaviorally oriented teaching procedures and the implementation of the Education for All Handicapped Children Act (P.L. 94-142) combined to bring about opportunities for children with autism to attend public school programs from which they had previously been excluded. For example, research conducted by Koegel and his colleagues (Koegel & Rincover, 1974; Rincover & Koegel, 1977) demonstrated procedures for successfully teaching students with autism in both one-to-one and small group settings. At the same time, Schopler and his colleagues at the TEACCH program in North Carolina were developing and implementing an approach known as **Structured Teaching** (Schopler et al., 1995). These approaches, as well as school programs developed and implemented by others, made use of the types of effective instructional procedures described in this section to enable children with autism to participate and learn in public school and other classroom settings (Bailey, Owen, Hurd, & Conley, 1984; Krug, Rosenblum, Almond, & Arick, 1980).

The last two decades have seen a variety of trends and changes with regard to classroom programs and placements for all children with disabilities. Children with autism, like many children with disabilities, have typically attended self-contained or segregated educational programs in which they spend the majority of their time in the company of other students with disabilities. In recent years there has been a substantial movement towards educating students with disabilities in regular classroom settings. This trend has received a variety of labels, such as *inclusion, supported education,* and the *regular education initiative* (Lloyd, Singh, & Repp, 1991). While there are different conceptual approaches and procedures apparent in this trend, some of the primary issues include having students with disabilities attend their local or neighborhood school, be based in regular classes with age-appropriate peers, and receive as much instruction as possible in these integrated settings.

This movement toward inclusive education has generated tremendous amounts of controversy and debate about its appropriateness and effectiveness for children with autism and other disabilities (Fuchs & Fuchs, 1994). Many parents, teachers, and other professionals are concerned that children with autism and other disabilities will not receive the attention and instruction they need if they are placed in typical classroom settings. There is also concern that their educational needs and potentially disruptive behavior will have a negative impact on other students in the classroom. On the positive side, it is clear that children with autism can benefit from exposure to and interaction with students without disabilities. For example, research by Strain (1983) and others has indicated that integrated settings result in better outcomes with regard to children's social behavior. Advocates of inclusive education also emphasize the potential benefits for children without disabilities, such as developing greater understanding and acceptance of students with disabilities.

At this point, the main thing that seems clear is that families and school districts are approaching this issue in a variety of ways. Some students continue to be based in self-contained classrooms while being involved in a range of activities with peers without disabilities for some portions of their school day. Other students are primarily based in regular classrooms, but may spend some time in other settings for individualized instructional activities. Still others are spending virtually all of their time in the regular classroom where they receive their educational programming and instruction. At this point, there is a critical need for additional research and evaluation that can guide teachers and families in developing and implement-

Children with autism can benefit from integrated settings by observing their peers' appropriate behavior.

ing the most inclusive and effective programs possible for achieving positive social and skill acquisition outcomes. Such a database is developing (Meyer, 1994), but much work remains to be done.

As discussed earlier with regard to the issue of identifying instructional goals, the primary aspect of importance here is to make decisions based on the *individual* needs of students. Simpson and Myles (1993) exemplify such an approach in talking about effective supported education for students with autism. Simply dumping students into regular class environments is a recipe for failure. It is critically important that teachers receive initial and ongoing in-service training, that they have access to collaborative problem-solving resources, and that additional staffing resources are available as needed. There may also be a need for information and training for adults and nondisabled peers to facilitate the social acceptance and involvement of students with autism. In order to accomplish such outcomes, many programs and districts are implementing models that reallocate the resources available in special education programs to support students with disabilities in regular classroom settings. Such approaches are being viewed as part of broader school restructuring and reform efforts that are occurring within regular education systems (Fuchs & Fuchs, 1994).

Important Considerations for Supported Education. Clearly, students with autism are capable of participating in and benefiting from regular classroom settings. Again, what will be critical is that classroom programs be able to provide for the unique needs of individual students to the greatest extent possible. There are a number of resources available to guide parents, teachers, and others in developing curricular and instructional approaches for maximizing the success of students with disabilities (Giangreco, Cloninger, & Iverson, 1993; Stainback & Stainback, 1992).

It will be important to keep in mind particular issues that may arise in implementing such strategies with students who have autism. Some of the characteristics

EASY IDEAS FOR PRACTITIONERS

For the Teacher:

1. Organize the classroom layout so that it's clear which kinds of activities are supposed to occur in which areas; use picture or written labels or signs to mark different areas.
2. Use picture or written schedules to provide information and predictability to students concerning what is going to be happening, when, with whom, and so forth.
3. Present verbal instructions and directions in a brief, clear manner.
4. Determine whether verbal, visual, or physical prompts are most effective with particular students, and use them as appropriate.
5. Break tasks to be taught into smaller more manageable steps, and then combine them to develop more complex activities and routines.
6. Do your best to provide parents with relevant and helpful sources of information (e.g., books, newsletters, pamphlets, etc.) on their legal rights and their child's disability.

For Parents:

1. Visit and participate in your child's classroom often.
2. Maintain ongoing communication with the teacher via notes, phone calls, and informal and formal meetings.
3. Get involved with agencies and organizations which may be of help to you and your child (e.g., local chapter of the Autism Society of America).
4. Remember that you will always be the primary constant in your child's life.

of the Structured Teaching approach mentioned above provide good examples (Schopler et al., 1995). Children are likely to do better if the classroom is physically laid out and organized so that it is clear there are different locations in which particular activities take place (e.g., individualized instruction, free play, group activities). Part of this organization may involve providing areas that minimize things that might be distracting or aversive to students—like loud noise or bright lights. Providing information to students in the form of pictorial or written schedules can improve their ability to predict and understand what's going on in the classroom (Flannery & Horner, 1994). It will also be important to structure tasks so that what is supposed to be done, and in what sequence it is to be done, are as clear as possible. As with all effective teaching, clear instructions, effective prompts, and the use of appropriate feedback and consequences will always be critical.

Students with autism need maximum opportunities to interact with peers, in both the classroom and during less structured activities in other settings (e.g., cafeteria, playground). Effective strategies for conducting integrated group instruction have been identified (Kamps, Walker, Maher, & Rotholz, 1992). Most students will benefit from training in particular interactive **social skills** that will allow them to initiate and respond more appropriately in social situations (Matson & Swiezy, 1994). A large body of research has also demonstrated the effectiveness of providing information, training, and interaction experiences for nondisabled peers. These approaches increase the likelihood that peers will initiate and maintain interactions and relationships with their fellow students with disabilities (Kennedy & Itkonen, 1994; Strain & Odom, 1986).

The debate over inclusive school practices will be with us for some time. While we continue to grapple with the difficult issues involved, it will be important

Children with autism respond better to organized class-rooms that follow a predictable schedule.

not to lose our focus on supporting teachers and students to produce maximally positive benefits from schooling experiences, in whatever settings they occur (Trillingsgaard & Sorenson, 1994).

OTHER TREATMENT APPROACHES

Medically-Based Treatments

Psychoactive Drugs.   A wide range of medications have been evaluated for children with autism, including *neuroleptics* or major tranquilizers such as Thorazine, mood-altering drugs such as Lithium, stimulant drugs such as amphetamines, antidepressant medications such as Prozac, and opiate antagonists such as naltrexone (Campbell et al., 1993; Campbell, Perry, Small, & Green, 1987; Handen, 1993; Schreibman, 1988). Some drugs have yielded improvements in different areas of behavioral functioning for some children, such as reducing stereotyped behavior and increasing social responsiveness. However, there have not been consistent positive outcomes seen with any particular drug or class of drugs. Ideally, drugs should serve as a treatment component for producing positive effects on the more severe behavioral symptoms seen in autism, and for making children more responsive to effective educational interventions. However, given the mixed results obtained with most drugs, and the possibility of serious side effects, parents, teachers, and medical practitioners are best advised to proceed very cautiously and conservatively in considering and using drug treatments for children with autism.

Megavitamin Therapy.   There have been a number of studies that investigated the effects of giving large doses of vitamins (e.g., B vitamins) to children with autism. While some authors have been enthusiastic about the positive effects of such treatments (Rimland, 1987), others have been more cautious (Gualtieri et al., 1987). At this point it does appear that vitamin therapy may improve a variety of symptoms to some extent for some children. For example, different studies have reported reductions in problematic behaviors such as hyperactivity and self-stimulation, and increases in appropriate social and communicative behaviors. There is a clear need for additional well controlled studies of the effects of large doses of vitamins and other dietary supplements. Though not as serious as problems associated with psychoactive medications, large doses of vitamins and other supplements may also have problematic side effects. Therefore, proceeding with caution is important.

Auditory Training

In recent years there has been a great deal of attention to a method known as **auditory training** (sometimes referred to as *auditory integration training*, or AIT). This approach is based on procedures developed by French physicians Guy Berard and Alfred Tomatis. The basic concept of the approach is that persons with sensory processing difficulties can be helped by providing particular types of sensory experiences that result in more typical sensory functioning. (As mentioned earlier, persons with autism sometimes appear to have a variety of difficulties in the way they respond to sound, light, and other sensory stimulation.)

There are some different procedures used for carrying out auditory training. However, initially children are usually given a hearing test to try to determine what specific sound frequencies they are hypersensitive to. Then, a specific device is used to play music, which the children listen to through headphones. The device filters the sound so that the frequencies to which the children are hypersensitive are dampened or decreased. Children listen to the filtered music during a series of 10 sessions, each lasting 60 minutes. This experience is supposed to have the effect of reducing or eliminating the children's sensitivity to the problematic frequencies, as well as potentially improving their general hearing ability (Rimland & Edelson, 1995).

A variety of positive effects have been reported by parents and other caregivers, including reduced sensitivity to sounds, increased ability to focus and concentrate, and reduced levels of problem behaviors (Rimland & Edelson, 1995). However, it is critical to note that there has been very little scientific research done on the use of this method with children who have autism. Given that there is very little known yet about whether it is effective and for whom it might be helpful, parents, teachers, and other caregivers are well advised to be cautious about this approach. It is especially problematic because auditory training is currently often being offered at a substantial cost even though its potential benefit is not clear.

FAMILY NEEDS AND SUPPORT STRATEGIES

I knew only that my fourth child was not like the others, who needed me and loved me, as I loved them. . . . She dwelt in a solitary citadel, compelling and self-made, complete and valid. Yet we could not leave her there. We must intrude, attack, invade, not because she was unhappy inside it, for she was not, but because the equilibrium she had found, perfect as it was, denied the possibility of growth. (Park, 1972, p. 12)

Once, when I was about 12, my mom asked me if I ever wished Steve was different. I told her no, that he was just Steve, and I had never imagined him any other way. That is still true. Growing up with Steve has often been difficult and discouraging, but it has been gratifying too. I've learned a great deal not only about autism but about my own feelings and attitudes. And through all our different situations, through all the growing we've both done, I believe Steve and I are friends. That in itself has made my years with Steve wholly rewarding. (Fromberg, 1984, p. 353)

These eloquent words, written respectively by a mother and a sibling of a child with autism, illustrate some of the concerns and emotions that parents and family members must deal with on a day-to-day basis. The demands of living with a child who has autism can place a good deal of stress on all family members. Determining the supports that a family needs and helping to provide them is a critical function and challenge for teachers and persons from other relevant agencies and systems.

The area of autism has undergone a radical shift over the last 50 years—from viewing parents as a cause of their children's problems to viewing them as primary "experts" and important sources of help for their children. Beginning in the late 1960s and early 1970s, a number of programs in the field began to actively incorporate parents into the process of assessing and providing instructional and therapeutic programs for their children (Lovaas, 1978; Schopler et al., 1984). However, researchers and practitioners have gradually become more aware that family needs are often complex and require a range of helping strategies. Marital difficulties, anxiety and depression, stress related to their child, coping with school and other service systems, and concerns about siblings are examples of the range of issues with which families sometimes struggle to cope (DeMyer, 1979; Schopler & Mesibov, 1984). Educators, therapists, and other practitioners need to talk to parents about their needs and concerns for their child, themselves, and the larger family. Interviews, questionnaires, and observations can help provide useful information on the specific needs of individual families (Harris, 1984).

Early approaches to family involvement focused largely on training efforts, particularly in home settings. These types of training programs aimed to teach parents the behavior management and other skills they need to use with their children in order to increase appropriate behavior and decrease problem behaviors (Kozloff, 1973). Siblings of children with autism were also involved in such efforts (Schreibman, O'Neill, & Koegel, 1983). Such programs had a variety of positive effects with regard to changes in child behavior, family interaction, and parent satisfaction with the outcomes (Koegel, Schreibman, Britten, Burke, & O'Neill, 1982; Schopler, 1987; Schreibman, Koegel, Mills, & Burke, 1984).

Current approaches to family support have built on these effective strategies in incorporating a broader perspective in assessment and providing services (Bristol, Gallagher, & Holt, 1993; Howlin & Rutter, 1987; Singer & Irvin, 1989). Parents and other family members need to be actively invited and encouraged to participate in intervention and support efforts with their children in ways that are acceptable and helpful to them. For one family this may mean carrying out specific training activities in the home and providing access to support groups for siblings. Another family may need information about certain topics, as well as periodic respite care to get a much-needed break. Yet another family may require professional support from counselors or other therapists to deal with emotional difficulties. As with the children, support should be specifically tailored in ways that will make it maximally helpful for individual families (Singer & Powers, 1993). It has become very clear over time that successfully helping children with autism requires successfully understanding and supporting their parents and families as well.

Training efforts in home settings provide positive effects with regard to child behavior, family interaction, and parent satisfaction.

CURRENT ISSUES AND FUTURE TRENDS

Facilitated Communication

Many readers may be aware of the phenomenon of facilitated communication, as it has been the subject of a number of reports in the media, including television, newspapers, and weekly magazines. It is currently perhaps the single most controversial issue in the area of autism. **Facilitated communication (FC)** is a method for assisting persons with disabilities such as autism to communicate by pointing to pictures or letters on communication boards or on the keyboards of typewriters or computers. This assistance typically involves a person, known as a *facilitator*, standing or sitting next to the person with disabilities and providing physical support by holding on to the hand, wrist, or elbow while the person points to letters or pictures on the communication board, or types on the keyboard. Over time, attempts are supposed to be made to fade out the physical support and move to independent pointing or typing. Facilitators are supposed to provide physical support and stability to allow the person to respond; they are not supposed to guide the selections that the person makes.

This kind of approach is not really new, as similar methods have been used and reported in the past (e.g., Oppenheim, 1974). However, it is only in recent years that FC has received such widespread attention. Douglas Biklen of Syracuse University is credited with initiating the current popularity of this technique. In 1990, Biklen described his observations of persons with disabilities in Australia communicating via FC (Biklen, 1990). He reported that persons who had been considered to have severe disabilities and/or mental retardation were communicating very sophisticated messages through FC, and showing unexpected reading and spelling skills. And it is this aspect of FC that has received the most attention; that is, FC has sometimes been promoted as a technique for accessing or revealing unsuspected skills and abilities for persons considered to have severe disabilities. Since Biklen's earlier reports, FC has been used with literally thousands of persons with

Much controversy surrounds Facilitated Communication as a way for people with autism to express themselves.

autism and other disabilities. Advocates have claimed that it has allowed them to display unexpected literacy and communication concerning their thoughts, feelings, and experiences. For some students, use of FC has resulted in dramatic changes in classification, placement, and participation in general education. Adding to the controversy is the fact that a number of instances have arisen in which allegations of physical and sexual abuse have been made through FC against parents, teachers, and other caregivers. These situations have resulted in severe personal and financial consequences for some families, and extended legal debates and proceedings.

In support of the validity of FC, most proponents point to large numbers of anecdotal descriptions by teachers, parents, and others, and the results of descriptive studies by researchers (Biklen, 1993). However, more controlled experimental evaluations of FC have painted a much more pessimistic picture (Bomba, O'Donnell, Markowitz, & Holmes, 1996; Green & Shane, 1994; Simon, Whitehair, & Toll, 1996). These studies have typically involved situations in which students were asked to respond to questions, describe activities, label pictures, or provide other information to which facilitators did not have access. For example, a student might go to Burger King or be shown an object from the classroom while the facilitator is not present, and then be asked to describe the outing or object when the facilitator returns.

Dozens of such studies have been published or reported at professional conferences and have consistently provided clear evidence of the following: (1) When facilitators don't know the correct information or responses, the students' responses are almost always incorrect. (2) The responses sometimes correspond to things the facilitators see or information that the facilitators *do* have, even if it's different from what the students are experiencing. (3) Facilitators report being unaware of exerting such influence over the students' responses. (4) There have been no validated demonstrations of the kinds of sophisticated communication that is described in the more informal anecdotal reports. These consistently negative results have led to widespread skepticism on the part of many parents and professionals and have prompted a variety of professional organizations—American Psychological Association, American Speech–Language–Hearing Association, American Association on Mental Retardation, American Academy of Pediatrics, and American Academy of Child and Adolescent Psychiatry—to adopt formal resolutions that are critical of FC. Supporters of FC have responded to these empirical studies by suggesting that the methods used are problematic and may be contributing to the negative results obtained (Biklen & Duchan, 1994).

What are teachers, parents, and others to make of these differing perspectives? There is a clear need for further research to determine under what, if any, conditions FC might be effective and with whom. Every opportunity must be given for students with disabilities to communicate and express themselves. However, we must also be extremely cautious about a method that is so clearly vulnerable to influence and control by others and that has received virtually no scientific support. How should parents, teachers, and others proceed in situations in which FC is being considered or used? The issue of who is authoring facilitated messages is of primary importance. There should be regular opportunities to assess whether the communications are coming from students or are being influenced by the facilitator. This would be extremely important in situations involving controversial communications such as allegations of abuse, or major life-affecting decisions such as changes in school placement, living situations, and so forth. Such assessments can be done through situations in which students are asked to provide information unknown to facilitators. In addition, multiple facilitators can periodically be used to assess the consistency of information that is provided.

Even when FC is being used, students must continue to receive training in other more independent communication strategies that are appropriate for them, including vocal speech and other augmentative or alternative communication approaches such as sign language, communication boards, or electronic devices (see Chapter 7). These proven approaches should not be abandoned, even in the face of apparent success with FC. All students should have ongoing access to multiple ways of communicating in the different settings and situations in which they are involved. No one wants to deprive students of opportunities to communicate and make themselves heard—but we must be sure that we are providing opportunities through well supported approaches, rather than techniques that may lead to false hopes and miscommunications.

Early Identification and Intensive Intervention

Our technologies of instruction and opportunities for education and training of students with autism have improved in recent decades. But still, while most children will generally make some progress in their behavior and functioning over time, the general long-term outcomes for many persons with autism are still less positive than would be hoped. The large majority of persons with autism require continuous supervision and support in areas such as domestic living, employment, and other community activities (Paul, 1987; M. D. Smith, 1990). Continued efforts to improve these outcomes are very important.

In 1987, Ivar Lovaas published the results of a long-term study in which a group of children with autism received up to 40 hours per week of intensive behavioral treatment, beginning when they were approximately 3 years old (Lovaas, 1987). This group was compared with two other groups of children that received either 10 hours per week of treatment, or no treatment from the Lovaas program.

The intensive treatment employed the types of behavioral methods described earlier in the chapter to teach language skills, appropriate play, preacademic and academic skills, emotional expression, and interactions with peers. Parents were heavily involved in the planning and implementation of the treatment. When the children were assessed at 7 years of age, 47% of the students in the intensive treatment group (9 out of 19) obtained average or above average scores on IQ tests, and had passed first grade in a regular education setting without extra supports from the research program. These children were characterized by Lovaas and his colleagues as *recovered*, in that the researchers considered them to be normal with regard to intellectual and educational functioning. Other children in this group had varying and less positive outcomes in terms of performance and educational placement. Only 1 child of the 40 in the two comparison groups demonstrated a normal level of functioning. Follow-up assessments conducted when the children reached the age of 13 indicated that 8 of the 9 "recovered" children from the intensive treatment group had remained in regular classes and scored in the normal range on standardized tests of intelligence, adaptive behavior, and personality (McEachin, Smith, & Lovaas, 1993). Lovaas and his colleagues have characterized the results as consistent with the large body of previous research on the use of behavioral methods with children with developmental disabilities.

These results have generated substantial controversy. Schopler, Short, and Mesibov (1989) raised the issue of whether the children in the treatment group had begun the study already functioning at a higher level than most children with autism. They also had concerns about the measures used to assess the children's behavior, and whether they truly indicated "normal" functioning: Did the treatment truly eliminate all signs or characteristics of autism? These concerns have been echoed by others (Foxx, 1993; Mesibov, 1993; Mundy, 1993). Lovaas, Smith, and McEachin (1989) responded to many of these issues and reasserted their belief that the children had achieved a truly normal level of functioning. It is worth noting that other studies in recent years have reported substantial positive results from early intervention efforts with children with autism (Anderson, Avery, DiPietro, Edwards, & Christian, 1987; Fenske, Zalenski, Krantz, & McClannahan, 1985; Perry, Cohen, & DeCarlo, 1995; Strain, Hoyson, & Jamieson, 1985; see also Chapter 14 of this book). There have also been accounts from parents describing the recovery of their children after involvement in intensive behavioral treatment (Maurice, 1993).

Further research is needed to evaluate outcomes and optimal strategies for early and intensive intervention for children with autism. A number of efforts are currently under way to attempt to replicate the findings of Lovaas and his colleagues (Birnbrauer & Leach, 1993). Advances are also being made in screening and identifying very young children at risk for problems associated with autism (Stone, Hoffman, Lewis, & Ousley, 1994). Together these developments inspire optimism concerning our ability to have a powerful positive impact on the development and functioning of these children. The history of evidence demonstrating the effectiveness of structured, behaviorally oriented approaches, together with the recent results from early intervention studies, provide strong support for the use of these kinds of educational strategies with children with autism (Smith, 1993).

The Future?

Major changes have occurred in the half century since autism was first delineated as a specific syndrome. It is now clear that the primary causes of the disorder will be

Early intervention programs consisting of intensive behavioral treatments show promise, but are still controversial.

found in neurobiological structure and functioning, rather than in parenting styles and characteristics. Research has provided us with effective approaches for teaching new skills and dealing with problem behaviors. Children with autism are participating more than ever in typical school, work, and other community environments.

While there are many reasons for optimism, there are still tremendous needs to be dealt with. Continued research in areas such as biological conditions and treatments and effective behavioral interventions is very important. Equally or perhaps more important, however, is the need to make effective education and support services available to the children and families that need them. Children with autism continue to present major challenges and demands for parents, teachers, and other service providers. We have learned much about effective teaching and support strategies, but the resources and systems for making these strategies available for children and families are often lacking. As M. D. Smith (1990) has pointed out, there is far too much of a gap between what we know is possible for persons with autism (and other disabilities) and the realities that they and their families are faced with on a daily basis. Working to bridge that gap will provide some of our most significant and important challenges in the years ahead.

Five-Minute Summary

Autism was defined as a specific syndrome, or set of characteristics, in 1943. Children and adults with autism typically exhibit a lack of skills in areas such as social behavior, speech and communication, play, and other in-

teractions with their environment. They may also exhibit disruptive behaviors such as tantrums, aggression, or self-injury. At one time, it was thought that parents may have been in some way responsible for their children's problems. However, it is now clear that autism is caused by some type of neurobiological dysfunction, which has not yet been consistently identified.

Autism is diagnosed through a combination of interviews with parents, standardized questionnaires, and observations of the child in different settings. Children with autism, like all children, require individualized assessment to determine the educational goals and objectives that will be best for them.

Behaviorally oriented educational approaches have been demonstrated to be the most effective methods for teaching new skills and reducing problem behaviors. Children with autism have been educated in a variety of segregated and integrated environments. They can be

successful in typical classrooms, but both children and teachers require training and support for this to be successful. Parents and families also require individualized assessment and support in order to help them and their children to do well together.

There are currently some controversial issues in the field, such as the use of facilitated communication strategies to help children communicate, and the application of intensive behavioral intervention methods with young children. Continued research efforts are very important, along with efforts to do a better job of providing effective education and help for children and their families.

Study Questions

1. How has thinking changed about what causes autism?
2. List the primary behavioral characteristics that are seen in children with autism.
3. What are the basic strategies used to assess a person for a possible diagnosis of autism?
4. What are the strategies that can be used to determine appropriate educational goals and objectives for a child with autism?
5. What are characteristics of effective teaching strategies for children with autism?
6. What are important issues to consider in determin-

ing the most appropriate educational placement for a child?
7. Describe some of the problems faced by parents and families of children with autism and strategies that may be helpful to them.
8. What is facilitated communication? Why is it such a controversial issue?
9. Why is early and intensive behavioral intervention being promoted as an effective approach for helping children?
10. What are some of the pressing challenges that need to be met in the future for children and families?

For More Information

ORGANIZATIONS

Autism Research Institute
Dr. Bernard Rimland, Director
4182 Adams Avenue
San Diego, CA 92116
619-281-7165
(An information sharing network for parents and professionals. Has information packets available on many topics.)

Autism Society of America (ASA)
7910 Woodmont Avenue, Suite 650
Bethesda, MD 20814
301-565-0433

(Oldest and largest support group for parents and professionals. Has an information and referral service, and offers books and tapes that can be ordered. Coordinates a national network of affiliated chapters.)

Division TEACCH
310 Medical School Wing E
University of North Carolina
Chapel Hill, NC 27599
919-966-2174

Autism National Committee (AUTCOM)
7 Teresa Circle
Arlington, MA 02174
(Can offer information and referrals for parents.)

BOOKS AND ARTICLES

Brill, M. T. (1994). *Keys to parenting the child with autism.* Haupaugge, NY: Barron's.

Gerlach, E. K. (1993). *Autism treatment guide.* Eugene, OR: Four Leaf Press.

Grandin, T. (1992). An inside view of autism. In E. Schopler & G. B. Mesibov (Eds.), *High-functioning individuals with autism* (pp. 105–126). New York: Plenum.

Grandin, T., & Scariano, M. M. (1986). *Emergence labeled autistic.* Novato, CA: Arena.

Harris, S. L. (1995). Educational strategies in autism. In E. Schopler & G. B. Mesibov (Eds.), *Learning and cognition in autism* (pp. 293–309). New York: Plenum.

Hart, C. A. (1993). *A parent's guide to autism.* New York: Simon & Schuster.

Maurice, C. (1993). *Let me hear your voice.* New York: Knopf.

Powers, M. D. (1989). *Children with autism: A parent's guide.* Rockville, MD: Woodbine House.

Sacks, O. (1993, Dec. 27). An anthropologist on Mars. *The New Yorker,* pp. 106–125.

Schopler, E., & Mesibov, G. B. (Eds.). (1983–1995). *Current issues in autism* book series. New York: Plenum.

Woods, T. S. (1987). The technology of instruction: A behavior analytic approach. In D. J. Cohen, A. M. Donnellan, & R. Paul (Eds.), *Handbook of autism and pervasive developmental disorders* (pp. 251–272). New York: Wiley.

JOURNALS, NEWSLETTERS, AND OTHER PUBLICATIONS

The Advocate
Autism Society of America
7910 Woodmont Avenue, Suite 650
Bethesda, MD 20814
301-565-0433

Autism Research Review International (quarterly newsletter)
Autism Research Institute
4182 Adams Avenue
San Diego, CA 92116
619-281-7165

The Communicator (newsletter)
Autism National Committee
7 Teresa Circle
Arlington, MA 02174

OTHER SOURCES

Autism Mailing List
LISTSERV@SJUVM.STJOHNS.EDU
(Subscribe by sending message "subscribe autism firstname lastname.")

World Wide Web Site
http://web.syr.edu/~jmwobus/autism/

References

American Psychiatric Association. (1980). *Diagnostic and statistical manual of mental disorders* (3rd ed.). Washington, DC: American Psychiatric Association.

American Psychiatric Association. (1987). *Diagnostic and statistical manual of mental disorders* (3rd ed., rev.). Washington, DC: American Psychiatric Association.

American Psychiatric Association. (1994). *Diagnostic and statistical manual of mental disorders* (4th ed.). Washington, DC: American Psychiatric Association.

Anderson, S. R., Avery, D. L., DiPietro, E. K., Edwards, G. L., & Christian, W. P. (1987). Intensive home-based early intervention with autistic children. *Education and Treatment of Children, 10,* 352–366.

Bailey, S. L., Owen, V. E., Hurd, D. S., & Conley, C. A. (1984). *Instructional procedures for educating students with autism in the communication disorders program.* DeKalb, IL: Northern Illinois University.

Baltaxe, C. A. M., & Simmons, J. Q. (1992). A comparison of language issues in high-functioning autism and related disorders with onset in childhood and adolescence. In E. Schopler & G. B. Mesibov (Eds.), *High-functioning individuals with autism* (pp. 201–225). New York: Plenum.

Baron-Cohen, S., Allen, J., & Gillberg, C. (1992). Can autism be detected at 18 months? The needle, the haystack, and the CHAT. *British Journal of Psychiatry, 161,* 839–843.

Bartak, L. (1978). Educational approaches. In M. Rutter & E. Schopler (Eds.), *Autism: A reappraisal of concepts and treatment* (pp. 423–438). New York: Plenum.

Belfiore, P. J., & Mace, F. C. (1994). Self-help and community skills. In J. L. Matson (Ed.), *Autism in children and adults: Etiology, assessment, and intervention* (pp. 193–211). Pacific Grove, CA: Brooks/Cole.

Bettelheim, B. (1967). *The empty fortress.* New York: Free Press.

Biklen, D. (1990). Communication unbound: Autism and praxis. *Harvard Educational Review, 60,* 291–314.

Biklen, D. (1993). *Communication unbound.* New York: Teachers College Press.

Biklen, D., & Duchan, J. F. (1994). "I am intelligent": The social construction of mental retardation. *Journal of the Association for Persons with Severe Handicaps, 19,* 173–184.

Birnbrauer, J. S., & Leach, D. J. (1993). The Murdoch Early Intervention Program after 2 years. *Behaviour Change, 10,* 63–74.

Bomba, C., O'Donnell, L., Markowitz, C., & Holmes, D. L. (1996). Evaluating the impact of facilitated communication on the communicative competence of fourteen students with autism. *Journal of Autism and Developmental Disorders, 26,* 43–58.

Bristol, M. M., Gallagher, J. J., & Holt, K. D. (1993). Maternal depressive symptoms in autism: Response to psychoeducational intervention. *Rehabilitation Psychology, 38,* 3–10.

Browder, D. M., & Snell, M. E. (1993). Functional academics. In M. E. Snell (Ed.), *Instruction of students with severe disabilities* (4th ed.). (pp. 442–479). New York: Merrill.

Brown, F., & Snell, M. E. (1993). Meaningful assessment. In M. E. Snell (Ed.), *Instruction of students with severe disabilities* (4th ed.). (pp. 61–98). New York: Merrill.

Campbell, M., Anderson, L. T., Small, A. M., Adams, P., Gonzalez, N. M., & Ernst, M. (1993). Naltrexone in autistic children: Behavioral symptoms and attentional learning. *Journal of the American Academy of Child and Adolescent Psychiatry, 32,* 1283–1291.

Campbell, M., Perry, R., Small, A. M., & Green, W. H. (1987). Overview of drug treatment in autism. In E. Schopler & G. B. Mesibov (Eds.), *Neurobiological issues in autism* (pp. 341–356). New York: Plenum.

Carr, E. G. (1985). Behavioral approaches to language and communication. In E. Schopler & G. B. Mesibov (Eds.), *Communication problems in autism* (pp. 37–57). New York: Plenum.

Charlop, M. H., & Haymes, L. K. (1994). Speech and language acquisition and intervention: Behavioral approaches. In J. L. Matson (Ed.), *Autism in children and adults: Etiology, assessment, and intervention* (pp. 213–240). Pacific Grove, CA: Brooks/Cole.

Coleman, M. (1987). The search for neurological subgroups in autism. In E. Schopler & G. B. Mesibov (Eds.), *Neurobiological issues in autism* (pp. 163–178). New York: Plenum.

Courchesne, E. (1987). A neurophysiological view of autism. In E. Schopler & G. B. Mesibov (Eds.), *Neurobiological issues in autism* (pp. 285–324). New York: Plenum.

DeMyer, M. K. (1979). *Parents and children in autism.* Washington, DC: Winston.

DeMyer, M. K., Hingtgen, J. N., & Jackson, R. K. (1981). Infantile autism reviewed: A decade of research. *Schizophrenia Bulletin, 7,* 388–451.

Department of Education. (1991). Notice of proposed rulemaking. *Federal Register, 56,* 41271.

Dunlap, G., Koegel, R. L., & O'Neill, R. E. (1985). Pervasive developmental disorders. In P. H. Bornstein & A. E. Kazdin (Eds.), *Handbook of clinical child behavior therapy* (pp. 499–540). Homewood, IL: Dorsey.

Dunlap, G., Robbins, F. R., & Kern, L. (1994). Some characteristics of nonaversive intervention for severe behavior problems. In E. Schopler & G. B. Mesibov (Eds.), *Behavioral issues in autism* (pp. 227–245). New York: Plenum.

Fenske, E. C., Zalenski, S., Krantz, P. J., & McClannahan, L. E. (1985). Age at intervention and treatment outcome for autistic children in a comprehensive intervention program. *Analysis and Intervention in Developmental Disabilities, 5,* 49–58.

Flannery, K. B., & Horner, R. H. (1994). The relationship between predictability and problem behavior for students with severe disabilities. *Journal of Behavioral Education, 4,* 157–176.

Folstein, S. E., & Rutter, M. L. (1987). Autism: Familial aggregation and genetic implications. In E. Schopler & G. B. Mesibov (Eds.), *Neurobiological issues in autism* (pp. 83–105). New York: Plenum.

Foxx, R. M. (1993). Sapid effects awaiting independent replication. *American Journal on Mental Retardation, 97,* 375–376.

Freeman, B. J., Ritvo, E. R., Yokota, A., & Ritvo, A. (1986). A scale for rating symptoms of patients with the syndrome of autism in real life settings. *Journal of the American Academy of Child Psychiatry, 25,* 130–136.

Fromberg, R. (1984). The sibling's changing roles. In E. Schopler & G. B. Mesibov (Eds.), *The effects of autism on the family* (pp. 343–353). New York: Plenum.

Fuchs, D., & Fuchs, L. S. (1994). Inclusive schools movement and the radicalization of special education reform. *Exceptional Children, 60,* 294–309.

Gallagher, B. J., Jones, B. J., & Byrne, M. M. (1990). A national survey of mental health professionals concerning the causes of early infantile autism. *Journal of Clinical Psychology, 46,* 934–939.

Gerhardt, P. F., & Holmes, D. L. (1994). The Eden decision model. In E. Schopler & G. B. Mesibov (Eds.), *Behavioral issues in autism* (pp. 247–276). New York: Plenum.

Giangreco, M. F., Cloninger, C. J., & Iverson, V. S. (1993). *COACH: Choosing options and accommodations for children: A guide to planning inclusive education.* Baltimore: Paul H. Brookes.

Gillberg, C. (1990). Autism and pervasive developmental disorders. *Journal of Child Psychology and Psychiatry, 31,* 99–119.

Gillberg, C., & Coleman, M. (1992). *The biology of the autistic syndromes* (2nd ed.). New York: Cambridge University Press.

Green, G., & Shane, H. C. (1994). Science, reason, and facilitated communication. *Journal of the Association for Persons With Severe Handicaps, 19,* 151–172.

Green, L., Fein, D., Joy, S., & Waterhouse, L. (1995). Cognitive functioning in autism: An overview. In E. Schopler & G. B. Mesibov (Eds.), *Learning and cognition in autism* (pp. 13–31). New York: Plenum.

Gualtieri, T., Evans, R. W., & Patterson, D. R. (1987). The medical treatment of autistic people: Problems and side effects. In E. Schopler & G. B. Mesibov (Eds.), *Neurobiological issues in autism* (pp. 373–388). New York: Plenum.

Handen, B. L. (1993). Pharmacotherapy in mental retardation and autism. *School Psychology Review, 22,* 162–183.

Happé, F., & Frith, U. (1995). Theory of mind in autism. In E. Schopler & G. B. Mesibov (Eds.), *Learning and cognition in autism* (pp. 177–197). New York: Plenum.

Haring, T. G., & Lovinger, L. (1989). Promoting social interaction through teaching generalized play initiation responses to preschool children with autism. *Journal of the Association for the Severely Handicapped, 14,* 58–67.

Harris, S. L. (1984). Intervention planning for the family of the autistic child: A multilevel assessment of the family system. *Journal of Marital and Family Therapy, 10,* 157–166.

Hewett, F. M. (1965). Teaching speech to autistic children through operant conditioning. *American Journal of Orthopsychiatry, 34,* 927–936.

Horner, R. H., & Albin, R. W. (1988). Research on general case procedures for learners with severe disabilities. *Education and Treatment of Children, 11,* 375–388.

Horner, R. H., Close, D. W., Fredericks, H. D. B., O'Neill, R. E., Albin, R. W., Sprague, J. R., Kennedy, C. H., Flannery, K. B., & Heathfield, L. T. (1996). Supported living for people with profound disabilities and severe problem behaviors. In D. H. Lehr & F. Brown (Eds.), *People with disabilities who challenge the system* (pp. 209–240). Baltimore: Paul H. Brookes.

Horner, R. H., Dunlap, G., Koegel, R. L., Carr, E. G., Sailor, W., Anderson, J., Albin, R. W., & O'Neill, R. E. (1990). Toward a technology of "nonaversive" behavioral support. *Journal of the Association for Persons With Severe Handicaps, 15,* 125–132.

Horner, R. H., McDonnell, J. J., & Bellamy, G. T. (1986). Teaching generalized skills: General case instruction in simulation and community settings. In R. H. Horner, L. H. Meyer, & H. D. B. Fredericks (Eds.), *Education of learners with severe handicaps: Exemplary service strategies* (pp. 289–314). Baltimore: Paul H. Brookes.

Howlin, P., & Rutter, M. (1987). *Treatment of autistic children.* New York: Wiley.

Iwata, B. A., Zarcone, J. B., Vollmer, T. R., & Smith, R. G. (1994). Assessment and treatment of self-injurious behavior. In E. Schopler & G. B. Mesibov (Eds.), *Behavioral issues in autism* (pp. 131–159). New York: Plenum.

Johnson, J., & Koegel, R. L. (1982). Behavioral assessment and curriculum development. In R. L. Koegel, A. Rincover, & A. L. Egel (Eds.), *Educating and understanding autistic children* (pp. 1–32). San Diego: College-Hill Press.

Kamps, D., Walker, D., Maher, J., & Rotholz, D. (1992). Academic and environmental effects of small group arrangements in classrooms for students with autism and other developmental disabilities. *Journal of Autism and Developmental Disorders, 22,* 277–293.

Kanner, L. (1943). Autistic disturbances of affective contact. *Nervous Child, 2,* 217–250.

Kennedy, C. H., & Itkonen, T. (1994). Some effects of regular class participation on the social contacts and social networks of high school students with disabilities. *Journal of the Association for Persons With Severe Handicaps, 19,* 1–10.

Koegel, R. L., Frea, W. D., & Surratt, A. V. (1994). Self-management of problematic social behavior. In E. Schopler & G. B. Mesibov (Eds.), *Behavioral issues in autism* (pp. 81–97). New York: Plenum.

Koegel, R. L., & Rincover, A. (1974). Treatment of psychotic children in a classroom environment. I. Learning in a large group. *Journal of Applied Behavior Analysis, 7,* 45–59.

Koegel, R. L., Rincover, A., & Egel, A. L. (Eds.). (1982). *Educating and understanding autistic children.* San Diego: College-Hill Press.

Koegel, R. L., Schreibman, L., Britten, K. R., Burke, J. C., & O'Neill, R. E. (1982). A comparison of parent training to direct child treatment. In R. L. Koegel, A. Rincover, & A. L. Egel (Eds.), *Educating and understanding autistic children* (pp. 260–279). San Diego: College-Hill Press.

Koegel, R. L., Schreibman, L., O'Neill, R. E., & Burke, J. C. (1983). The personality and family interaction characteristics of parents of autistic children. *Journal of Consulting and Clinical Psychology, 51,* 683–692.

Kozloff, M. A. (1973). *Reaching the autistic child: A parent training program.* Champaign, IL: Research Press.

Krantz, P. J., MacDuff, M. T., & McClannahan, L. E. (1993). Programming participation in family activities for children with autism: Parents' use of photographic activity schedules. *Journal of Applied Behavior Analysis, 26,* 137–138.

Krug, D. A., Rosenblum, J. F., Almond, P. J., & Arick, J. R. (1980). *Autistic and severely handicapped in the classroom: Assessment, be-*

havior management, and communication training. Portland, OR: ASIEP Education Co.

Lloyd, J. W., Singh, N. N., & Repp, A. C. (1991). *The regular education initiative: Alternative perspectives on concepts, issues, and models.* Sycamore, IL: Sycamore Press.

Locke, B., Banken, J. A., & Mahone, C. H. (1994). The graying of autism: Etiology and prevalence at fifty. In J. L. Matson (Ed.), *Autism in children and adults: Etiology, assessment, and intervention* (pp. 37–57). Pacific Grove, CA: Brooks/Cole.

Lord, C., Rutter, M., Goode, S., Heemsbergen, J., Jordan, H., Mawhood, L., & Schopler, E. (1989). Autism Diagnostic Observation Schedule: A standardized observation of communicative and social behavior. *Journal of Autism and Developmental Disorders, 19,* 185–212.

Lord, C., Rutter, M., & Le Couteur, A. (1994). Autism Diagnostic Interview–Revised: A revised version of a diagnostic interview for caregivers of individuals with possible pervasive developmental disorders. *Journal of Autism and Developmental Disorders, 24,* 659–685.

Lord, C., & Schopler, E. (1987). Neurobiological implications of sex differences in autism. In E. Schopler & G. B. Mesibov (Eds.), *Neurobiological issues in autism* (pp. 191–211). New York: Plenum.

Lovaas, O. I. (1977). *The autistic child: Language development through behavior modification.* New York: Irvington.

Lovaas, O. I. (1978). Parents as therapists. In M. Rutter & E. Schopler (Eds.), *Autism: A reappraisal of concepts and treatment* (pp. 369–378). New York: Plenum.

Lovaas, O. I. (1987). Behavioral treatment and normal educational and intellectual functioning in young autistic children. *Journal of Consulting and Clinical Psychology, 55,* 3–9.

Lovaas, O. I., Berberich, J. P., Perloff, B. F., & Schaeffer, B. (1966). Acquisition of imitative speech in schizophrenic children. *Science, 151,* 705–707.

Lovaas, O. I., Koegel, R. L., & Schreibman, L. (1979). Stimulus overselectivity in autism: A review of research. *Psychological Bulletin, 86,* 1236–1254.

Lovaas, O. I., Koegel, R. L., Simmons, J. Q., & Long, J. S. (1973). Some generalization and follow-up measures on autistic children in behavior therapy. *Journal of Applied Behavior Analysis, 6,* 131–166.

Lovaas, O. I., Smith, T., & McEachin, J. J. (1989). Clarifying comments on the young autism study: Reply to Schopler, Short, and Mesibov. *Journal of Consulting and Clinical Psychology, 57,* 165–167.

MacDuff, G. S., Krantz, P. J., & McClannahan, L. E. (1993). Teaching children with autism to use photographic activity schedules: Maintenance and generalization of complex response chains. *Journal of Applied Behavior Analysis, 26,* 89–97.

Matson, J. L., & Swiezy, N. (1994). Social skills training with autistic children. In J. L. Matson (Ed.), *Autism in children and adults: Etiology, assessment, and intervention* (pp. 241–260). Pacific Grove, CA: Brooks/Cole.

Maurice, C. (1993). *Let me hear your voice.* New York: Knopf.

McAdoo, W. G., & DeMyer, M. K. (1978). Personality characteristics of parents. In M. Rutter & E. Schopler (Eds.), *Autism: A reappraisal of concepts and treatment* (pp. 251–267). New York: Plenum.

McEachin, J. J., Smith, T., & Lovaas, O. I. (1993). Long-term outcome for children with autism who received early intensive behavioral treatment. *American Journal on Mental Retardation, 97,* 359–372.

McEvoy, M. A., Nordquist, V. M., Twardosz, S., Heckman, K., Wehby, J. H., & Denny, R. K. (1988). Promoting autistic children's peer interaction in an integrated early childhood setting using affection activities. *Journal of Applied Behavior Analysis, 21,* 193–200.

Mesibov, G. B. (1993). Treatment outcome is encouraging. *American Journal on Mental Retardation, 97,* 379–380.

Mesibov, G. B., Schopler, E., & Hearsey, K. A. (1994). Structured Teaching. In E. Schopler & G. B. Mesibov (Eds.), *Behavioral issues in autism* (pp. 195–207). New York: Plenum.

Meyer, L. H. (1994). Editor's introduction to the special issue: Understanding the impact of inclusion. *Journal of the Association for Persons With Severe Handicaps, 19,* 251–252.

Meyer, L. H., & Evans, I. M. (1989). *Nonaversive intervention for behavior problems.* Baltimore: Paul H. Brookes.

Meyer, L. H., Peck, C. A., & Brown, L. (Eds.). (1991). *Critical issues in the lives of people with severe disabilities.* Baltimore: Paul H. Brookes.

Morgan, D. P., & Jenson, W. R. (1988). *Teaching behaviorally disordered students: Preferred practices.* New York: Merrill.

Mundy, P. (1993). Normal versus high-functioning status in children with autism. *American Journal on Mental Retardation, 97,* 381–384.

Neel, R. S., Billingsley, F. F., McCarty, F., Symonds, D., Lambert, C., Lewis-Smith, N., & Hanashiro, R. (1983). *Teaching autistic children: A functional curriculum approach.* Seattle: Department of Special Education, University of Washington.

Odom, S. L., McConnell, S. R., & Chandler, L. K. (1994). Acceptability and feasibility of classroom-based social interaction interventions for young children with disabilities. *Exceptional Children, 60,* 226–236.

Odom, S. L., & Strain, P. S. (1984). Peer-mediated approaches to promoting children's social interaction: A review. *American Journal of Orthopsychiatry, 54,* 544–557.

O'Neill, R. E. (1990). Establishing verbal repertoires: Toward the application of general case analysis and programming. *Analysis of Verbal Behavior, 8,* 113–126.

O'Neill, R. E., Horner, R. H., Albin, R. W., Storey, K., & Sprague, J. R. (1990). *Functional analysis of problem behavior: A practical assessment guide.* Pacific Grove, CA: Brooks/Cole.

Oppenheim, R. (1974). *Effective teaching methods for autistic children.* Springfield, IL: Thomas.

Ornitz, E. M. (1989). Autism at the interface between sensory and information processing. In G. Dawson (Ed.), *Autism: Nature, diagnosis, and treatment* (pp. 174–207). New York: Guilford.

Ozonoff, S. (1995). Executive functions in autism. In E. Schopler & G. B. Mesibov (Eds.), *Learning and cognition in autism* (pp. 199–219). New York: Plenum.

Ozonoff, S., Pennington, B. F., & Rogers, S. J. (1990). Are there emotion perception deficits in young autistic children? *Journal of Child Psychology and Psychiatry, 31,* 343–361.

Park, C. C. (1972). *The siege.* Boston: Atlantic-Little, Brown.

Paul, R. (1987). Natural history. In D. J. Cohen, A. M. Donnellan, & R. Paul (Eds.), *Handbook of autism and pervasive developmental disorders* (pp. 121–130). New York: Wiley.

Perry, R., Cohen, I., & DeCarlo, R. (1995). Case study: Deterioration, autism, and recovery in two siblings. *Journal of the American Academy of Child and Adolescent Psychiatry, 34,* 232–237.

Pierce, K. L., & Schreibman, L. (1994). Teaching daily living skills to children with autism in unsupervised settings through pictorial self-management. *Journal of Applied Behavior Analysis, 27,* 471–481.

Reichler, R. J., & Lee, E. M. C. (1987). Overview of biomedical issues in autism. In E. Schopler & G. B. Mesibov (Eds.), *Neurobiological issues in autism* (pp. 13–41). New York: Plenum.

Rimland, B. (1964). *Infantile autism.* New York: Appleton Century Crofts.

Rimland, B. (1978). Inside the mind of an autistic savant. *Psychology Today, 12,* 68–80.

Rimland, B. (1987). Megavitamin B6 and magnesium in the treatment of autistic children and adults. In E. Schopler & G. B. Mesibov (Eds.), *Neurobiological issues in autism* (pp. 389–405). New York: Plenum.

Rimland, B. (1994). The modern history of autism: A personal perspective. In J. L. Matson (Ed.), *Autism in children and adults: Etiology, assessment, and intervention* (pp. 1–11). Pacific Grove, CA: Brooks/Cole.

Rimland, B., & Edelson, S. M. (1995). A pilot study of auditory integration training in autism. *Journal of Autism and Developmental Disorders, 25,* 61–70.

Rincover, A., & Koegel, R. L. (1977). Classroom treatment of autistic children. II. Individualized instruction in a group. *Journal of Abnormal Child Psychology, 5,* 113–126.

Risley, T. R., & Wolf, M. M. (1967). Establishing functional speech in echolalic children. *Behaviour Research and Therapy, 5,* 73–88.

Ritvo, E. R., & Freeman, B. J. (1978). National Society for Autistic Children definition of the syndrome of autism. *Journal of Autism and Childhood Schizophrenia, 8,* 162–167.

Ritvo, E. R., Freeman, B. J., Pingree, C., Mason-Brothers, A., Jorde L., Jenson, W. R., McMahon, W. M., Peterson, P. B., Mo, A., & Ritvo, A. (1989). The UCLA–University of Utah epidemiological study of autism: Prevalence. *American Journal of Psychiatry, 146,* 194–199.

Rutter, M. (1978a). Diagnosis and definition of childhood autism. *Journal of Autism and Childhood Schizophrenia, 8,* 139–161.

Rutter, M. (1978b). Diagnosis and definition. In M. Rutter & E. Schopler (Eds.), *Autism: A reappraisal of concepts and treatment* (pp. 1–25). New York: Plenum.

Rutter, M. (1985). The treatment of autistic children. *Journal of Child Psychology and Psychiatry, 26,* 193–214.

Rutter, M., Bailey, A., Bolton, P., & Le Couteur, A. (1994). Autism and known medical conditions: Myth and substance. *Journal of Child Psychology and Psychiatry, 35,* 311–322.

Rutter, M., & Schopler, E. (1988). Autism and pervasive developmental disorders: Concepts and diagnostic issues. In E. Schopler & G. B. Mesibov (Eds.), *Diagnosis and assessment in autism* (pp. 15–36). New York: Plenum.

Sacks, O. (1995, Jan. 9). Prodigies. *The New Yorker,* pp. 44–65.

Sanua, V. D. (1990). Leo Kanner (1894–1981): The man and the scientist. *Child Psychiatry and Human Development, 21,* 3–23.

Schopler, E. (1983). New developments in the definition and diagnosis of autism. In B. B. Lahey & A. E. Kazdin (Eds.), *Advances in clinical child psychology: Vol. 6* (pp. 93–127). New York: Plenum.

Schopler, E. (1987). Specific and nonspecific factors in the effectiveness of a treatment system. *American Psychologist, 42,* 376–383.

Schopler, E., Brehm, S., Kinsbourne, M., & Reichler, R. J. (1971). The effect of treatment structure on the development of autistic children. *Archives of General Psychiatry, 24,* 415–421.

Schopler, E., & Loftin, J. (1969). Thinking disorder in parents of young psychotic children. *Journal of Abnormal Psychology, 14,* 281–287.

Schopler, E., & Mesibov, G. B. (Eds.). (1984). *The effects of autism on the family.* New York: Plenum.

Schopler, E., & Mesibov, G. B. (Eds.). (1985). *Communication problems in autism.* New York: Plenum.

Schopler, E., & Mesibov, G. B. (Eds.). (1986). *Social behavior in autism.* New York: Plenum.

Schopler, E., & Mesibov, G. B. (Eds.). (1987). *Neurobiological issues in autism.* New York: Plenum.

Schopler, E., & Mesibov, G. B. (Eds.). (1992). *High-functioning individuals with autism.* New York: Plenum.

Schopler, E., & Mesibov, G. B. (Eds.). (1994). *Behavioral issues in autism.* New York: Plenum.

Schopler, E., & Mesibov, G. B. (Eds.). (1995). *Learning and cognition in autism.* New York: Plenum.

Schopler, E., Mesibov, G. B., & Hearsey, K. (1995). Structured Teaching in the TEACCH system. In E. Schopler & G. B. Mesibov (Eds.), *Learning and cognition in autism* (pp. 243–268). New York: Plenum.

Schopler, E., Mesibov, G. B., Shigley, H., & Bashford, A. (1984). Helping autistic children through their parents: The

TEACCH model. In E. Schopler & G. B. Mesibov (Eds.), *The effects of autism on the family* (pp. 65–81). New York: Plenum.

Schopler, E., Reichler, R. J., & Renner, B. R. (1988). *The Childhood Autism Rating Scale (CARS).* Los Angeles: Western Psychological Services.

Schopler, E., Short, A., & Mesibov, G. B. (1989). Relation of behavioral treatment to "normal functioning": Comment on Lovaas. *Journal of Consulting and Clinical Psychology, 57,* 162–164.

Schreibman, L. (1988). *Autism.* Newbury Park, CA: Sage.

Schreibman, L. (1994). General principles of behavior management. In E. Schopler & G. B. Mesibov (Eds.), *Behavioral issues in autism* (pp. 11–38). New York: Plenum.

Schreibman, L., & Charlop, M. H. (1987). Autism. In V. B. Van Hasselt & M. Hersen (Eds.), *Psychological evaluation of the developmentally and physically disabled* (pp. 155–177). New York: Plenum.

Schreibman, L., Koegel, R. L., Mills, D. L., & Burke, J. C. (1984). Training parent–child interactions. In E. Schopler & G. B. Mesibov (Eds.), *The effects of autism on the family* (pp. 187–205). New York: Plenum.

Schreibman, L., Kohlenberg, B., & Britten, K. R. (1986). Differential responding to content and intonation components of a complex auditory stimulus by nonverbal and echolalic autistic children. *Analysis and Intervention in Developmental Disabilities, 6,* 109–125.

Schreibman, L., O'Neill, R. E., & Koegel, R. L. (1983). Behavioral training for siblings of autistic children. *Journal of Applied Behavior Analysis, 16,* 129–138.

Siegel, D. J., Goldstein, G., & Minshew, N. J. (1996). Designing instruction for the high-functioning autistic individual. *Journal of Developmental and Physical Disabilities, 8,* 1–19.

Sigman, M. (1994). What are the core deficits in autism? In S. H. Broman & J. Grafman (Eds.), *Atypical cognitive deficits in developmental disorders* (pp. 139–157). Hillsdale, NJ: Erlbaum.

Sigman, M., Kasari, C., Kwon, J. H., & Yirmiya, N. (1992). Responses to the negative emotions of others by autistic, mentally retarded, and normal children. *Child Development, 63,* 796–807.

Simon, E. W., Whitehair, P. M., & Toll, D. M. (1996). A case study: Follow-up assessment of facilitated communication. *Journal of Autism and Developmental Disorders, 26,* 9–18.

Simpson, R. L., & Myles, B. S. (1993). Successful integration of children and youth with autism in mainstreamed settings. *Focus on Autistic Behavior, 7,* 1–13.

Singer, G. H. S., & Irvin, L. K. (Eds.). (1989). *Support for caregiving families: Enabling positive adaptation to disability.* Baltimore: Paul H. Brookes.

Singer, G. H. S., & Powers, L. E. (Eds.). (1993). *Families, disability, and empowerment: Active coping skills and strategies for family interventions.* Baltimore: Paul H. Brookes.

Smith, M. D. (1990). *Autism and life in the community: Successful interventions for behavioral challenges.* Baltimore: Paul H. Brookes.

Smith, T. (1993). Autism. In T. R. Giles (Ed.), *Handbook of effective psychotherapy* (pp. 107–133). New York: Plenum.

Snell, M. E. (Ed.). (1993). *Instruction of students with severe disabilities* (4th ed.). New York: Merrill.

Snell, M. E., & Farlow, L. J. (1993). Self-care skills. In M. E. Snell (Ed.), *Instruction of students with severe disabilities* (4th ed.). (pp. 380–441). New York: Merrill.

Stahmer, A. C., & Schreibman, L. (1992). Teaching children with autism appropriate play in unsupervised environments using a self-management treatment package. *Journal of Applied Behavior Analysis, 25,* 447–459.

Stainback, S., & Stainback, W. (1992). *Curriculum considerations in inclusive classrooms: Facilitating learning for all students.* Baltimore: Paul H. Brookes.

Stone, W. L., Hoffman, E. L., Lewis, S. E., & Ousley, O. Y. (1994). Early recognition of autism: Parental reports vs. clinical observation. *Archives of Pediatric and Adolescent Medicine, 148,* 174–179.

Strain, P. S. (1983). Generalization of autistic children's social behavior change: Effects of developmentally integrated and segregated settings. *Analysis and Intervention in Developmental Disabilities, 3,* 23–34.

Strain, P. S., Hoyson, M. H., & Jamieson, B. J. (1985). Normally developing preschoolers as intervention agents for autistic-like children: Effects on class deportment and social interaction. *Journal of the Division for Early Childhood, 9,* 105–115.

Strain, P. S., & Odom, S. L. (1986). Innovations in the education of preschool children with severe handicaps. In R. H. Horner, L. H. Meyer, & H. D. B. Fredericks (Eds.), *Education of learners with severe handicaps: Exemplary service strategies* (pp. 61–98). Baltimore: Paul H. Brookes.

Sturmey, P., & Sevin, J. A. (1994). Defining and assessing autism. In J. L. Matson (Ed.), *Autism in children and adults: Etiology, assessment, and intervention* (pp. 13–36). Pacific Grove, CA: Brooks/Cole.

Trillingsgaard, A., & Sorenson, E. U. (1994). School integration of high-functioning children with autism: A qualitative interview study. *European Child and Adolescent Psychiatry, 3,* 187–196.

Tsai, L. Y. (1992). Diagnostic issues in high functioning autism. In E. Schopler & G. B. Mesibov (Eds.), *High-functioning individuals with autism.* New York: Plenum.

Turnbull, A. P., & Morningstar, M. E. (1993). Family and professional interaction. In M. E. Snell (Ed.), *Instruction of students with severe disabilities* (4th ed.). (pp. 31–60). New York: Merrill.

Utah State Office of Education. (1993). *Special education rules.* Salt Lake City: Utah State Office of Education.

Volkmar, F. R., Bregman, J., Cohen, D. J., & Cicchetti, D. V. (1988). DSM-III and DSM-III-R diagnoses of autism. *American Journal of Psychiatry, 145,* 1404–1408.

Waterhouse, L., Morris, R., Allen, D., Dunn, M., Fein, D., Feinstein, C., Rapin, I., & Wing, L. (1996). Diagnosis and classification in autism. *Journal of Autism and Developmental Disorders, 26,* 59–86.

Werry, J. S. (1988). Diagnostic classification for the clinician. In E. Schopler & G. B. Mesibov (Eds.), *Diagnosis and assessment in autism* (pp. 49–58). New York: Plenum.

Westling, D. L., & Fox, L. (1995). *Teaching students with severe disabilities.* Englewood Cliffs, NJ: Prentice-Hall.

Wilcox, B., & Bellamy, G. T. (1987). *The activities catalog.* Baltimore: Paul H. Brookes.

Wing, L. (1992). Manifestations of social problems in high-functioning autistic people. In E. Schopler & G. B. Mesibov (Eds.), *High-functioning individuals with autism* (pp. 129–142). New York: Plenum.

Wing, L. (1993). The definition and prevalence of autism: A review. *European Child and Adolescent Psychiatry, 2,* 61–74.

Wolf, M. M., Risley, T. R., & Mees, H. (1964). Application of operant conditioning procedures to the behavior problems of an autistic child. *Behaviour Research and Therapy, 1,* 305–312.

Yirmiya, N., Sigman, M., & Freeman, B. J. (1994). Comparison between diagnostic instruments for identifying high-functioning children with autism. *Journal of Autism and Developmental Disorders, 24,* 281–291.

Yuwiler, A., & Freedman, D. X. (1987). Neurotransmitter research in autism. In E. Schopler & G. B. Mesibov (Eds.), *Neurobiological issues in autism* (pp. 263–284). New York: Plenum.

Chapter 13

Red Room, acrylic on canvas, 24″ x 30″ (1994)

THE FAMILY PERSPECTIVE

NONA FLYNN AND CHERIE TAKEMOTO

After studying this chapter, the reader will:

Know about the major changes of the 20th century for
families of children with disabilities

Understand how families react when children's
disabilities are identified

Appreciate families as unique systems, needing individualized
support and assistance to learn to advocate effectively
for their children with disabilities

Know how family-focused services and parent–professional
partnerships are changing systems

Be aware of the critical issues facing families in the 21st century

THE FAMILY PERSPECTIVE

1880–1930 The eugenics movement, dedicated to "improving the human race," promoted institutionalization of "the feebleminded and delinquents."

1950s Parents began to organize services and schools for their children in their communities. National organizations were formed and political action initiated.

1972 The landmark case of *Pennsylvania Association for Retarded Citizens v. Commonwealth of Pennsylvania* established that all children with mental retardation are entitled to free public education.

1975 P.L. 94-142, the Education for All Handicapped Children Act (later incorporated into IDEA), established parents' roles as decision makers.

1980s Grassroots support for parent-to-parent support groups increased.

1983 Legislation established a national program of Parent Training and Information Centers to provide assistance for families.

1986 P.L. 99-457 (later incorporated into IDEA) mandated that families—not just the infants and toddlers with disabilities— were to be the focus for services.

1990s Advocacy movements—early childhood, inclusion, transition, and self-advocacy—grew in numbers and influence.

HISTORICAL OVERVIEW

The rapid changes in the field of special education mirror the changes in how children with disabilities are perceived by society. This dramatic evolution (or revolution), initiated by parents[1] in partnership with professionals, continues today, permanently changing the perspective of the family's role throughout the child's life. In the 21st century, working cooperatively with families will be an important aspect of teachers', therapists', and counselors' careers from the early childhood years of children with disabilities through adulthood. Knowledge about this evolution—a brief review of major landmarks and movements in the 20th century—leads to increased understanding of today's issues. Looking back also prepares for looking forward: to realize that lasting change takes time.

At the beginning of the 20th century, public attitude toward children with disabilities was one of pity and charity. A permanent residential care model was considered necessary to "protect" them. Families were urged to do the "best" thing for children with more severe disabilities, which meant putting them in institutions. This attitude was fostered by the *eugenics movement* (1880–1930), which was dedicated to "improving" the human race through institutionalization and selective breeding (Scheerenberger, 1983). Feeblemindedness and delinquent behaviors were linked to heredity—the parents' fault. Policies of residential institutions, both state and private, evolved over time to severely limit children's contact with their parents. Visiting hours were brief, home visits often denied, and information was difficult to obtain. Families were encouraged to abdicate their responsibilities, with the exception of financial support. These attitudes and policies persisted into the 1970s in some parts of the country (Gartner, Lipsky, & Turnbull, 1991).

Parents who elected to keep their children at home were often blamed for their children's problems, especially in cases of maladaptive behavior. In the case of autism, for instance, as late as the 1960s, parents were considered by the most

An infantile paralysis ward, Beacon, New York, 1916

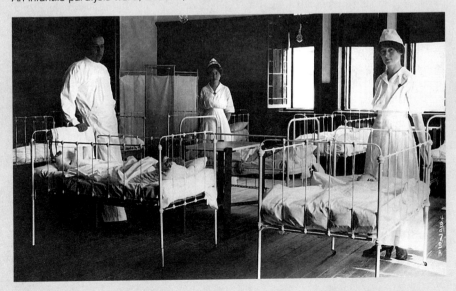

---

[1]The term *parent* in this chapter refers to anyone who is in charge of the care and well-being of a child. Included are single parents, parents by birth or adoption, guardians, grandparents, foster parents, or surrogate parents.

"Having Elise in our lives has turned out to be the best thing that could have happened to us (next to the birth of her brother, Brian, of course). I haven't always felt this way. From her premature birth, ultimate diagnosis of cerebral palsy, and the misery of her first few years of life, often I wished that I could simply disappear.

"There's no question that Elise has significant disabilities due to her premature birth. She takes a lot of work—much of it guesswork. But, she also has brought such joy and fullness to our lives. No one has a smile like hers, a giggle like hers, or spirit like hers. I don't know anyone who has the patience, tenacity, and determination to enjoy every moment of life the way Elise does.

"To say that she has given us a new perspective on life is an understatement. And, she has pushed us all to grow in unexpected and wonderful ways. We've learned to be Elise's champions and to fight for her right to be fully valued and included in our community. Not only because it is simply the right thing to do, but because Elise rightfully demands it. She wants the same things out of life as any other person. If anyone is deserving of all that life has to offer, it is Elise."

respected professionals in the field to be responsible for their children's disability (Bettelheim, 1967). By 1977, research and clinical observation established that autism was caused by "no known factors in the psychological environment" (National Society for Autistic Children, 1977).

Though research has now shown that there are genetic causes for some disabilities, there is no justification for blaming parents. There is ample evidence that guilt trips are counterproductive, impeding parents from working effectively with their children. Ann and H. Rutherford Turnbull, writing as parents and professionals, advise as follows:

> Although causation theories have declined over the last 20 years, each of us can help eradicate erroneous accusations wherever they occur—whether in professional literature, teachers' lounges, or parent–professional conferences. Through our professional and personal experiences, we have come to the conclusion that parents do the best they can in the difficult circumstances they are facing, and that it is impossible to judge another person until we have "walked a mile in his moccasins." (Turnbull & Turnbull, 1986, pp. 4–5)

The major changes—increased knowledge and understanding of disabilities occurring in the 1970s—were largely the result of parents' work in the 1950s and 1960s. Frustrated and unwilling to institutionalize their children, they began to organize. At first they supported each other at the local level, developing parent-sponsored community services and schools for their children. State and national organizations were formed according to type of disability, and political action was initiated. Two of the early national organizations were the National Association for Retarded Citizens (now The Arc), started in 1950, and the United Cerebral Palsy Association (UCP) organized in 1955.

A Legislative Victory

In the 1970s, many professionals joined with parents to seek political action through legislative mandates. Paving the way for state and then national legislation was a landmark lawsuit, *Pennsylvania Association for Retarded Citizens v. Commonwealth of Pennsylvania* (1972). This court decision established that, under the **equal protection clause** of the Fourteenth Amendment to the U.S. Constitution, all children with mental retardation must be provided with a free public program of education and training.

In 1975, as a result of parents and professionals working together, Public Law 94-142, the Education for All Handicapped Children Act, was passed (now incorporated as a part of current legislation, the Individuals With Disabilities Education Act, known as IDEA). Under this law, all children with disabilities, including more than a million who were receiving no services, were entitled to a free appropriate public education. Further, the law established the role of parents as decision makers in the education of their children. This role is twofold: to be active participants in the education process, and to be advocates for their children.

Clarifying the intent of the law, testimony in the *Congressional Record* states that parents have both a regulatory role with procedural safeguards and the right to contribute their own unique understanding throughout the special education process. This was a revolutionary change. No longer were parents to be passively told by professionals *what* to do with their children, *if* their children would be accepted, or *how* they would be educated. Not only did their children have a right to be educated, but parents had the right to be directly involved in decisions and to work cooperatively with administrators and teachers as partners.

Changing Perspective of Parent Involvement

As with any revolutionary education movement, change does not happen immediately or spontaneously. The struggle for both professionals and parents to define and learn their roles and to make needed systemic changes continues today. Why

This family attended a candlelight vigil to advocate for more rights for individuals with disabilities.

has it been a struggle and why is it taking so long? The reasons are multiple and complex for both parents and professionals. These will be addressed briefly—with the major emphasis placed on the current status of relationships between parents and professionals, and how partnerships can be fostered in the future.

From the professional perspective, special educators welcomed the new legislation while most regular educators viewed the changes as having very little to do with them directly. Special education, still in infancy as a profession, was striving to learn how to effectively meet the needs of children with a wide variety of disabilities. Categorical, self-contained classrooms were considered the "best" way to meet the needs of exceptional children. The term used in P.L. 94-142, **least restrictive environment,** was widely interpreted as giving children as much time as possible with their peers without disabilities, without interfering with their special education. In their eagerness to educate children with disabilities, special educators organized a separate complex educational system, saying "we know best, give us all of the children with special needs" (Skrtic, 1991). Most regular educators were only too happy to oblige, removing the more "difficult" children from their classrooms. Special educators struggled with how to implement the new federal and state regulations.

It was the 1980s before states were ready to focus on the "active parent participation" portion of the law. The majority of school systems were concerned with meeting the letter of the law, making sure that parent signatures were in place and that parents were invited to meetings. Individualized Education Programs (IEPs), though initially heralded positively, soon were considered merely as paperwork instead of useful plans or blueprints for each child's education (Anderson, Chitwood, & Hayden, 1996).

In 1982, the first edition of a guide for parents captured the frustrating parental dilemma:

> School personnel complain of being overburdened with paperwork, scheduling problems, over-demanding parents, and lack of money. Parents, hoping to realize the promise of cooperation with the schools for their child's well-being, feel like unwelcome intruders if their participation is more than passive acceptance of what the school people prescribe. The complicated process of referral, assessment, and selection of services too often has parents caught in the posture either of compliant recipient or hostile critic. What they have heard over the years from school systems urging more parent involvement now echoes with the wish that parents go away and leave the job of education to the educators. (Anderson, Chitwood, & Hayden, 1982, p. 3)

Legislation gave parents the role of decision maker, but this new role was a demanding one. From the parents' perspective, to be advocates for their children in this complex process meant acquiring a whole new set of skills. This meant learning the special education process, their legal rights and responsibilities, and how to communicate effectively with professionals. The learning needs of parents were soon recognized at the national level and pilot information centers for families were initiated in several states. In 1983 a federal law established a national program of Parent Training and Information Centers, with a goal of having at least one in every state (Ziegler, 1992). Several states organized local networks of community-based Parent Resource Centers (Flynn, 1987). Parent-to-parent support groups were organized as statewide systems in many states, regions, and local communities.

However, though parents now have some resources available, for many families active involvement is still a challenge. In a time when family structures have changed, when both parents are working, and when there are many single-parent homes, the role of educational decision maker may be overwhelming and time-consuming. Prior to the 1980s parents' roles focused primarily on the needs of their children with disabilities. Now the realities of family life are causing the focus to shift to the family as a whole.

A FAMILY SYSTEMS APPROACH

Major strides have been made in the study of family life in the past 50 years. *Family systems* theorists have viewed the family as an open interactional system, operating according to the rules and principles applying to all systems—including considerations of interrelatedness, interactional patterns, different rates of growth, different responses to stress, varied means of communication, different family rules, and flexibility to adapt to internal and external change (Walsh, 1984).

Another theoretical perspective considers the entire ecosystem of the family. The *ecosystem approach* broadens the scope of study, including not only family members, but peers and all persons who have a significant effect on the child's behavior. Hobbs (1980) described this approach as "ecological to take into account the situational, developmental, the transactional character of the demands on a service delivery system" (p. 275). Fewell (1986) explained it as follows:

> Development, both biological and social, is a process of continual adaptation due to the constant state of change in the individuals and the environment. While changes and accommodations are inevitable and indeed essential, extreme situations and events can create a discontinuity that affects the entire ecosystem, requiring a closer examination of transactions in order to support families in their predestined roles. (pp. 5–6)

Ann Turnbull and her colleagues (Turnbull, Summers, & Brotherson, 1984) adapted family systems theory to focus specifically on families of a child with disabilities. Their family systems conceptual framework includes these elements:

1. **Family resources:** All the characteristics of a family—their cultural background, financial well-being, size, location, abilities and disabilities, and so forth

2. **Family interactions:** The daily relationships between and among family members

3. **Family functions:** The needs and interests of family members met by the family—may be social, emotional, educational, or physical such as health care or child care

4. **Family life cycle:** All the changes that affect families and influence family resources, interactions, and functions

In 1986, Ann Turnbull and H. Rutherford Turnbull encouraged professionals to apply family systems theory by individualizing their relationships with each family, just as they individualize their work with each child with disabilities.

The major change in shifting professionals' focus from the child to the family is a very significant one in terms of professionals' attitudes and training. Administrators, teachers, and specialists who have been trained to meet the needs of the child are now required to develop broader skills for working with families. Significant changes in preservice and in-service training are required.

An extended family group provides the extra social, emotional, and physical support needed for families with children with disabilities.

Working With Individual Families

Addressing professionals, parent Cory Moore writes:

> We need respect, we need to have our contribution valued. We need to partici-pate, not merely be involved. It is, after all, the parent who knows the child first and who knows the child best. Our relationship with our sons and daughters is personal and spans a lifetime. (1993, p. 49)

A major factor in learning to respect parents is developing an understanding of their perspectives as individuals and as members of a family system and of communities. Because of the changing configuration of the American family, it is important to think in terms of different family pictures: many with only one parent; large extended families; foster, adoptive, and blended families; and families that include parents with disabilities. (Cultural differences are addressed in another segment of this chapter.) Although the intact nuclear family is still representative of a majority of U.S. households, an increasing percentage of chil-dren with disabilities are being raised in nontraditional families from diverse back-grounds, with varying degrees of expertise. These families may have special needs, which should be addressed by professionals in a respectful and understanding manner.

One caution for professionals is not to make assumptions based on the family picture. An adoptive parent who had chosen a child with disabilities gave the fol-lowing perspective:

> Before Adam came I had read everything I could get my hands on about cere-bral palsy. I was prepared for his not walking and speech difficulties. However, read-ing about a disability and living with a child on a daily basis who has that disability are two different things. . . . I was overwhelmed with it all . . . fear and guilt and tremen-dous feelings of failure. (Gilman, 1987, p. 211)

INNOVATIVE IDEAS   PARENT OR FAMILY RESOURCE CENTERS

In communities throughout the country, families' needs for information and training are being addressed by local centers housed in schools, community centers, libraries, or wherever there is space available. Some centers are simply lending libraries with parent volunteers working as liaisons between parents and educators within a school. In other settings parent liaisons coordinate their school's activities as part of a county or district network. In four states (Maryland, Kentucky, Virginia, and West Virginia) parents' need for a place to visit or call within the community has resulted in a statewide network of centers. The centers are staffed by a team—a parent of a child with special needs and an educator—reflecting the emphasis on collaboration, on parent–professional partnerships in education.

More than 150 centers in these four states offer a wide variety of training opportunities as well as individual assistance to thousands of families who have children with disabilities. The centers, serving rural, urban, and suburban communities, have some similar features, but are also unique, reflecting the needs of the individual communities they serve. When a parent center opens, the new parent–educator team takes the pulse of the community to find out what kinds of information and assistance parents, educators, and students need. Then they attempt to meet those needs through personal contacts, informal gatherings, workshops, conferences, support groups, publications, information packets, videotapes, radio talk shows, and any other means limited only by human imagination. Here are some examples:

Serving rural areas: The Montgomery County (VA) Parent Resource Center offered a workshop titled "Positive Parenting of Adolescents." Participants so enjoyed the 7-week course that they decided to form a mini-support group. In Calvert County (MD) the Parent Information and Training Center recently invited parents of infants and toddlers to an "Afternoon at the Movies." Families enjoyed free popcorn, child care by infant/toddler teachers, and the video "1-2-3 Magic!" which teaches parents how to manage children ages 2 through 12 without arguing, yelling, or hitting. The Putnam County (WV) Parent/Education Resource Center helps parents of children with disabilities find adaptive equipment by maintaining a list of items available for sale or trade, their description, and their price.

Serving urban, suburban areas: At the Franklin County (KY) Parent Resource Center in Frankfort, a workshop titled "At Your Wit's End" was created to relieve family stress during the holiday period. Each year in Norfolk (VA), the Parent Resource Center sponsors "The Possibilities Tour" to give students and their families a look at adult life after high school. The 4-hour session includes an overview of adult services at the center, followed by a bus tour to work sites and residential options.

Staff of the centers are trained to provide empathetic support and assistance to families to enhance parents' abilities to work with professionals in the best interests of their children. Phone calls range from simple information requests to crisis calls from parents who desperately need assistance.

As the need for family support has grown, many centers are now serving a broader spectrum of families. In Kentucky, in many communities, Family Resource Centers have now incorporated the centers that serve parents of children with disabilities. In the other states, many centers are being expanded to serve all families with needs related to their children's education.

Information about these centers may be obtained from each state's Department of Education, Director of Special Education.

UNDERSTANDING THE PARENTS' PERSPECTIVE

For effective working relationships to be formed, it is necessary for both professionals and parents to strive for a basic understanding of the other's perspective.

For professionals, the responsibility is to learn what it is like to walk in the parents' shoes—to at least know the demands parents face physically and emotionally.

Reaction to the Diagnosis

Before the Niedermeyers' daughter Emma was born, Stephanie and her husband Paul expected a normal home delivery. The pediatrician, concerned with Emma's birth complications as well as her lack of muscle tone and inability to nurse, hospitalized the infant immediately. In the beginning there was no time to grieve. Their focus was on protecting and bonding with their child. In Stephanie Niedermeyer's words:

> Suddenly, after the intensity of a home birth and a flurry of activity, everyone was gone. Instead of the three of us being together and bonding, my husband and the baby were at the hospital, and I was totally alone at home and overwhelmed with sadness. At that point, all of our rosy expectations were suddenly irrelevant. Emma had taught us our first and most important lesson—to accept and value her as a unique individual. (Miller, 1994, p. xxiii)

Just as every child is unique, family reactions to the news of a child's disability are unique. Reactions may depend on family values, perceptions, and resources (Turnbull & Turnbull, 1986, p. 304). There are also diverse cultural interpretations—that may vary from explaining the child's disability as resulting from a curse someone placed on a family (faulting the outside world), to its being punishment for past sins (internalizing responsibility or guilt), or even a gift from God.

Common emotions experienced by parents include any or all of the following:

- *Denial or disbelief:* Some parents cannot immediately accept their child's disability and must be allowed time to adapt at their own pace.
- *Guilt:* Many parents experience this emotion even if others believe the feeling is not justified.
- *Sadness:* A recognition that many of the parents' hopes and dreams for their child will not be realized brings sadness. Some parents are also sad that their children will not be able to do many of the things their peers do.
- *Fear:* There are many real threats to the child's life and safety, and there is also fear of the unknown.
- *Loneliness:* Parents sometimes feel isolated from friends and relatives who may be uncomfortable about how to respond after a diagnosis has been made.
- *Vulnerability:* After a child's diagnosis, many parents feel that anything can happen to them. Before that time, they might have believed that misfortune always happened to someone else.
- *Anger:* Feelings of anger may stem from a number of sources. Parents may be angry at relatives or friends who do not know how to offer help or respond to a family that includes a child with special needs. Sometimes it might be a reaction to a professional they consider to be insensitive. Anger may be channeled in positive directions, however, motivating a parent to take action.

As a way of studying emotions and understanding what happens to families, Marilyn Segal (1988) interviewed family members together and individually. She found that while each family's experiences are unique and personal, there are some common themes. Feelings of sadness, loss of the expected "normal" child, can re-occur even at unexpected times. Anger and frustration are often present and may be directed toward anyone, everyone, or no one in particular. Sometimes these frustrations may result from unmet needs for support.

The "grief cycle" developed by Elisabeth Kübler-Ross to explain typical reactions to death and dying have often been used to describe a parent's reaction to the birth of a child with a disability. This grief cycle may be on target for some families, but is not applicable for all (Segal, 1988). For instance:

> Sure I know and have experienced the emotions in the grieving process—denial, anger, guilt, depression, acceptance. Yet I have not experienced a cycle or process. These feelings don't come in stages. And between all those emotions are impatience, joy, pride, reflection, love, defensiveness, protectiveness, and happiness—just to name a few. My son is very much alive and lets me know it every day, thank you. (cited in Anderson & Takemoto, 1992, p. 2)

Segal further states as follows:

> The natural cycle of mourning does not tell the whole story. It is not just that parents go through a series of predictable states and end up accepting the baby. The baby plays a vital dynamic role . . . feelings of pain and anguish do not always disappear, but in time and with love, feelings of joy prevail. (1988, p. 13)

A study conducted by Able-Boone and Stevens (1994) of 30 families whose children were graduates of intensive care nurseries found some differences in coping styles between families of children with disabilities and families whose children had no identified disabilities. The primary coping strategy of families of children without identified disabilities was primarily day-to-day problem solving. When families have to cope with disability, they also rely on assistance from extended family, taking one day at a time, and their faith in God.

While there have been many studies of parental reaction to the diagnosis of a disability at birth, for many parents the discovery of their child's disability may come more gradually. These parents often experience concerns when their child does not meet developmental milestones or seems different from other children of the same age. For some, it may be an intuitive feeling that something is wrong. For others, it may be a child who is not learning to read or is failing in school. After the anxiety of not knowing what or even if something is wrong, to some parents the diagnosis of a disability may come as somewhat of a relief. For other parents, the reaction may be similar to what many parents feel upon the birth of a child with disabilities (Turnbull & Turnbull, 1990). Regardless of when the diagnosis is made, the family equilibrium will be changed.

Family Roles

The time and energy required to care for a child with disabilities may be intensive and exhausting, stressing a family's ability to function effectively. The entire family becomes vulnerable, with parents feeling especially unprepared for the task. Their search for information and services taxes their reserves even further. When parents finally do locate services or a program for their child, they may need a period of respite before becoming actively involved in the program. They also may not understand why their participation is important.

Mother and Father.   As the traditional primary caregiver, the mother's role becomes immensely complicated when her child has disabilities. Responsibilities and demands on her time often are doubled or tripled. Not only are these mothers faced with more work, but they must learn new skills in caring for the special needs of the child and must learn to navigate the service systems. This all happens at a time when the mother's own emotions may be in turmoil. It is a time when a mother needs support from her immediate and extended family. For single mothers, this may be a time of isolation, and she may benefit greatly from a parent-to-parent support group.

Although there is general agreement in the field that fathers' roles in the education of their children with disabilities should be expanded (Gallagher et al., 1983), for the most part, it has not happened. In the past 10 years, however, model programs and studies have provided direction and paved the way for broad-scale implementation. Programs especially designed for fathers have proven effective in lessening stress, pessimism, and depression. In general, these programs (1) reflect fathers' expressed concerns, (2) are held at convenient times, (3) include topical discussions to broaden understanding, and (4) provide time to share attitudes and feelings. A program for fathers of preschoolers was conducted in a treatment/no-treatment study at the University of Washington and was proven to be highly effective (Vadasy, Fewell, Meyer, & Greenberg, 1985). This program encouraged a father to do the following:

- Learn to read his child's cues and interpret the child's behavior
- Develop an awareness of activities, materials, and experiences suitable to the child's current stage of development
- Practice his skill as the child's caregiver
- Learn more about the nature of the child's disability
- Discuss his concerns with other fathers in a similar situation
- Develop an awareness that he, as a parent, will be his child's primary educator and advocate
- Explore the changing role of the father in today's society
- Examine the impact of the child's disability on the entire family (Meyer, 1986, p. 63)

Though progress has been made in developing programs for fathers, Lillie (1993) encourages further research and refinement of roles for fathers.

Studies of marital relationships in families of children with disabilities indicate mixed findings. The divorce rate is higher, with couples experiencing greater emotional stress, more demands on their time, and communication difficulties. However, many couples report that having a child with special needs has strengthened their marriage (Turnbull & Turnbull, 1986). Although professionals cannot make assumptions about the needs of parents, they should be sensitive to the need for respite care and should be considerate of their time limitations when scheduling evening meetings or home visits.

Siblings.   Especially stressful times for siblings of a child with disabilities generally occur at points in their own lives when friends make fun of the child or ask questions about the disability, when they start to date, or if problems related to the child are handled in secrecy. Milestones in the life of the child with disabilities—

Having a sibling with disabilities can be stressful, but also can provide many rewarding experiences.

such as when the child starts school or when the child is critically ill—cause stress on siblings (Powell & Ogle, 1985).

Alper (1994) reported that siblings enumerated several pluses for having a brother or sister with disabilities, including having greater empathy, more tolerance, and more patience with others. They also felt they had learned to be helpful, were more mature and responsible, and had developed pride in their sibling's accomplishments. On the negative side, they expressed resentment, jealousy, guilt, fear, shame, and feelings of rejection. There is a need for these children to receive assistance, support, guidance, and opportunities to meet with other siblings of children with disabilities.

The Extended Family.   Extended family members in today's mobile society are just as often friends or neighbors as grandparents and other relatives. Unless these members have had some experience dealing with disabilities, they will need information and direction. They will be at a loss of what to say or what to do to help family members. Professionals should provide materials about the disability for parents to share; they should talk with parents about the need to widen their immediate family circle and to anticipate the reactions they may encounter; and they should offer to meet with the extended family.

Parents of Children With Exceptional Gifts and Talents

Though children who are identified as gifted and talented are not included under the federal special education and nondiscrimination laws unless they also have a disability, some states do consider these children under special education. Challenges faced by parents may be similar to those facing families of children with disabilities. The need for assessment of the child's strengths, weaknesses, and interests is essential if the child's potential is to be realized. A child who is gifted may be considered by peers to be different and may be isolated, lonely, and frustrated. There is danger of the child either withdrawing or becoming aggressive as the feeling of frustration and not belonging builds.

The role for professionals who work with parents of a student who is gifted and talented calls for helping them decide what type of program is best suited to their child's unique abilities. Families may need suggestions regarding how to plan appropriate activities and other ways they can meet the child's needs in the home and community. Professionals should encourage parents to do the following:

- Openly discuss the value of diversity, and demonstrate the need to respect everyone's differences even when others do not.
- Provide a variety of stimuli and experiences tailored to the child's natural interests.
- Select games, toys, books, and stories that enrich imagery, allow for creativity, challenge the child's abilities, or encourage the development of perceptual and motor skills.
- Allow ample time for thinking and daydreaming.
- Give these children space of their own to keep their possessions and work on their own projects.
- Assign household tasks that relate to or spark the child's interests (when possible).
- Take their child to enrichment activities in the community, such as to the library, museums, theater, and concerts.
- Encourage new interests, such as drama or music instruction (Fine & Carlson, 1992; Oakes & Lipton, 1990).

Families From Different Cultures

Although in American culture the 1970s marked the end of the time when having a child with disabilities was considered something to hide, in some cultures parents are still stigmatized when their child is identified as having disabilities. In contrast, other cultural lifestyles may strengthen and support families who are facing major problems related to a child's disabilities. Cultural roots influence family values and self-image. Differences in values may result in real disparity between parent and professional expectations for a child with disabilities.

For example, in traditional Native American families, learning to talk is expected sometime between the child's third and fourth birthday, not between the first and second birthday. A valued developmental milestone is when the child first laughs. In Latino cultures there is most often a high degree of nurturing of young children accompanied by indulgence, with less emphasis on individual achievement. Close family interdependence is promoted, and it is normal for members to sit close to each other and to have physical contact regardless of age.

As cultural diversity increases in this country, professionals may be working with parents who are still living with feelings of shame, superstitions, fear of the unknown, or a lack of understanding of intervention and school programs. When these parents appear reluctant to participate in their child's education, an insensitive and superficial conclusion is that the family "is not motivated." However, Harry (1992) offers a more thoughtful observation regarding family motivation. Lack of involvement is not caused by lack of concern for their child's needs. Rather, parents may be reluctant to participate in activities that make them feel uncomfortable, or that might not be in their native language (and with no interpreter provided).

Communication difficulties can be especially evident for Asian ethnic groups, whose language is situation centered or context bound. A Vietnamese mother ignores her newborn baby because she believes a baby is in grave danger when first born. To recognize the child's presence by fussing over the baby would bring too much attention, placing the baby in jeopardy. The nurse who is unaware of the reason is very disapproving of the mother's behavior and records a mother–child bonding score of O on the chart (Dresser, 1996). A primary value in some Asian cultures is preserving harmony and face in human relationships. Entering a new, strange situation—with an interpreter they do not know—may be viewed with apprehension by Asian families.

Both knowledge and skills are needed by professionals to work effectively with parents from diverse cultures. Lynch and Hanson (1992) put it this way:

> Achieving cross-cultural competence requires that we lower our defenses, take risks, and practice behaviors that may feel unfamiliar and uncomfortable. It requires a flexible mind, an open heart, and a willingness to accept alternative perspectives. It may mean setting aside some beliefs that are cherished to make room for others whose value is unknown; and it may mean changing what we think, what we say, and how we behave. (p. 35)

The first step in learning to be more culturally competent is to explore one's own culture and become aware of the values, attitudes, and customs of one's own family. The second step is learning as much as possible about the child's family and other culture-specific information. This step is critical to successfully complete the third step: identifying effective cross-cultural communication strategies (Lynch & Hanson, 1992). Similar points are described by Gartner, Lipsky, and Turnbull (1991) and McCracken (1993), who stress that providing appropriate supports for parents of a child with disabilities requires cultural understanding of the meaning of disability, the nature and roles of families, and the ways in which they can be supported. The combination of dealing with acculturating stresses and coping with their child's disabilities doubles the difficulties families from other cultures must face in American society.

Family Coping Strategies

Recently, there has been a growing interest in the relationship between family resiliency and positive outcomes for children with disabilities. Patterson (1991) identified key characteristics of family resiliency and noted that these perspectives help a family not merely to cope, but to thrive. Included are the following:

- *Balancing the demand of the disability with other family needs.* The child's special needs are balanced with the child's normal developmental needs and the needs of the family. The resilient family is able to set priorities and maintain normal routines.

- *Maintaining clear family boundaries.* Parents work together as a team to solve problems and make decisions. They are in charge, working hard to develop competence in caring for their child.

- *Developing communication competence.* Resilient families learn as much as possible about their child's disability. They learn new terms, how to

The special needs of the child with disabilities must be balanced with the needs of the rest of the family.

express their feelings in an open yet constructive manner. They share their feelings—anger, frustration, gratitude, caring, and commitment.

• *Attributing positive meanings to the situation.* The positive attributes and contributions of the child with disabilities are emphasized. Many resilient families have recognized how they have grown and changed, becoming stronger and closer as a family unit.

• *Maintaining family flexibility.* Flexibility is a major key to resilience. A changing of roles, responsibilities, and expectations is often required. Willingness to take risks and to try new things promotes growth and resiliency.

• *Making a commitment to family cohesion.* Pulling together to face the crises of a child with disabilities strengthens the family unit. Without this commitment and working together in a supportive manner, families may become dysfunctional and break apart.

Similarly, the philosophy at the Beach Center of Families and Disability (1989) at the University of Kansas stems from six important values that they have identified through their research and the experiences of parents and professionals:

1. *Positive contributions:* People with disabilities enrich their families, their communities and society.

2. *Great expectations:* Visions can become realities. Families need to have dreams and to be supported in realizing their expectations.

3. *Full citizenship:* People with disabilities and their families deserve full participation in American life.

4. *Choices:* Giving families choices builds on their strengths.

EASY IDEAS FOR PRACTITIONERS

For the Teacher:

1. Use phrases like "Help me understand . . . " in order to obtain a nonjudgmental understanding of the parents' perspective.
2. Help parents to capitalize on their strengths.
3. Facilitate linkages with other parents, support groups, or organizations.
4. Avoid using labels or categorizing parent emotions.
5. Suggest counseling if a parent is "stuck" in overwhelming sadness, anger, or some other emotion that is keeping him or her from moving on.
6. Support parents as they try to balance the needs of the whole family.
7. Build a parent's confidence and self-sufficiency.

5. *Relationships:* Family members need to be connected to each other and to friends in the community.

6. *Inherent strengths:* Families may need support, but they have many natural abilities and make many positive contributions to their communities.

REALIZING THE PARENT–PROFESSIONAL PARTNERSHIP

In describing what the parent–professional relationship should be, a publication of the U.S. Department of Education (1994) states that mutual trust, respect, and open communication are essential elements. Partnership implies equal status and responsibility. Dunst and Paget (1991) define the parent–professional partnership as an association between a family and one or more professionals who agree to collaborate to pursue a joint interest and common goal. The partnership is further outlined in terms of the following minimum requirements:

1. Both the family and professional contribute resources and expertise to the partnership that are pooled and used collaboratively.

2. Both the family and professional want and agree to enter into a collaborative arrangement.

3. The partnership must be built upon loyalty, trust, and honesty and must involve full disclosure of any and all "material facts" affecting the joint venture.

4. The powers of the partners must be established at the point of entry into a collaborative arrangement, and the locus of decision making clearly stated. . . . A major duty and responsibility of the professional is to provide all necessary information to assist the family to . . . make informed decisions. (pp. 29–30)

Early Childhood Family Advocacy

In 1986 the passage of Part H of P.L. 99-457, later incorporated into the Individuals With Disabilities Education Act (IDEA), was a major victory for family advocates. Under this legislation, services for infants and toddlers with disabilities are to be family centered, with parents making decisions and with their concerns, priorities, and resources included in the service plans. Furthermore, not only are parents decision makers along with professionals, but their family needs must be met, and their wishes should drive many aspects of the **Individualized Family Service Plan**

(IFSP). For educators this change means leaving behind the medical model that focuses only on the child, with professionals as decision makers, and moving toward a family-centered model with professionals working in partnership with parents.

The focus of early intervention partnerships is to build on family strengths and capabilities, to promote their growth and strengthen family functioning. Dunst, Trivette, and Deal (1988) enumerate seven characteristics of the parent–professional relationship that are essential to effectively promote the abilities of families to meet their needs:

1. A trusting relationship

2. Effective communication

3. Honesty, with all interactions including a clear statement about the purpose of the exchange, and being "up front" with families

4. Understanding families' concerns and interests, focusing on what is important to them

5. Emphasis on solutions rather than causes

6. Movement from concerns to actions as rapidly as possible

7. Confidentiality—sharing no information with others without the family's permission

Advocacy for Inclusive Schools

In the 1980s the **inclusion** movement gained momentum, advocating that children with disabilities attend their neighborhood schools. Parents and professionals initiated this move away from self-contained special education classes to the least restrictive environment. As reasons, the movement cited lack of efficacy in research findings for segregated classes, parent dissatisfaction with their children's progress, and isolation from peers in the children's neighborhoods and community life. Baker, Wang, and Walberg (1995) reported that "considerable evidence from the last 15 years suggests that segregation of special students in separate classrooms is actually deleterious to their academic performance and social adjustment, and that special students generally perform better on average in regular classrooms" (p. 34).

A series of court decisions have upheld the right of children with disabilities to be educated in regular classrooms with their peers without disabilities. The *Oberti v. Clementon* (1993) decision placed the burden of proof on school districts to demonstrate that a segregated special education placement is the best educational approach for the individual student. Other decisions, such as *Clyde K. and Sheila K. v. Puyallup School Districts* (1994), have supported the exclusion of children with disabilities if their behavioral problems interfere with the education of the whole class.

This movement is not without controversy. Placement of children with disabilities in regular classrooms without preparation and appropriate supports leads to stressful failures for everyone—the child, teachers, classmates, and families. Because of such cases, Maloney (1994) advocates continuing alternative placements, with a continuum of services—the position supported in 1993 by the Learning Disabilities Association of America.

There are many moving examples of school systems, individual schools, and classrooms where children with disabilities are now successfully learning alongside their peers without disabilities. In the Newark School District in Delaware, an inclusive classroom model—"Team Approach to Mastery"—has operated for 20 years with strong support from parents (Johnston, Proctor, & Corey, 1994). Five years of planning and careful implementation by all major stakeholders in Montgomery County, Virginia, culminated in returning special education students to their neighborhood schools (Flynn, 1993). Parent initiative has often led to major change, not only for the child but also for the school or system. In the case of Montgomery County, for instance, a handful of parents and special educators began the movement, but now regular education teachers, administrators, and parents of students without disabilities are strong supporters of inclusion—which is the pattern found in successful inclusive schools throughout the country. Here are other testimonials:

> We need these young people and we need to continue in the American way by including rather than excluding.
>
> > Superintendent of Schools
> > Des Moines, Iowa
> > ("Inclusion Award," 1993, p. 15)

> If the worth of a person's life is judged by the effect they had on others, Catherine's presence will be felt for a lifetime in the hearts of many people. I speak not only for me but all the children she came in contact with. She fostered a deep caring and love, but maybe a longer lasting effect will be the understanding and compassion in the hearts and minds of everyone who came in contact with her.
>
> > Regular education teacher
> > St. Paul, Minnesota
> > (Vandercook, 1991, p. 9)

From the parents' perspective there is another positive outcome of having their children in regular education classrooms:

> As happy as we are with the warm welcome given to Elise, I can't help but reflect on the long term benefits to her classmates from having her in their class. When these children grow up, the likelihood that they will have a person with a disability in their lives is strong. Either they may have a child with a disability or a family member may become disabled. How much better prepared these children will be to deal with this challenging reality. And it will be so much better for their special family member, that they knew Elise as a child and learned to be unafraid of her differences and to value her as a friend and full member of their school community. (Rebhorn & Takemoto, 1994, p. 7)

The full impact of this movement has yet to be realized. Successful inclusion of children with disabilities in regular education classrooms requires teamwork among professionals and parents, including parents as vital members of the team. Carlos Oberti, after spending 3 years fighting for public school inclusion for Rafael, his 8-year-old son who has Down syndrome, writes: "The best way for children to succeed is to have a coherent, organized effort from parents and educators working together" (1993, p. 20).

Navigating the Service Maze

While parents may not refer to themselves as the "service coordinator" or "case manager," they frequently are the ones who locate, coordinate, and manage services. For instance:

Having a son or daughter with disabilities often requires reading small print, filling in forms, attending meetings, making phone calls, explaining information to new program staff, explaining information to old program staff, etc. Parents do all those activities. From experience, they have learned that important information and vital services can fall through the cracks if they are not involved. (Beckett, 1993a)

Able-Boone and Stevens (1994) found that a major need identified by parents is help in finding community services; in their study, only 34% of the parents of children with identified disabilities who left the intensive care nursery received information about services from the hospital or their child's pediatrician. Even after a service is identified, frustrations often continue. One mother described her experience of navigating the maze as follows: "It took 3 weeks to get all the application forms completed, and then we were referred to another service 2 weeks later because we were ineligible for the service" (Able-Boone & Stevens, 1994, p. 108).

Often parents obtain information about available services and support from other parents. Parent support groups, parent-to-parent linkages, and other formal or informal opportunities for parents to share information can be invaluable. Electronic databases and bulletin boards open up additional opportunities for parents to find out about services and help each other solve problems concerning care for their children with disabilities.

Most states have training and information centers funded by the U.S. Department of Education to assist parents who have children with disabilities (or suspected disabilities) from birth through age 21. There are also national clearinghouses—such as the National Information Center for Children and Youth With Disabilities (NICHCY) and the National Organization for Rare Disorders—that can provide parents with information about services or organizations serving children with a particular disability. (See "For More Information" at the end of this chapter.)

Educators may collaborate with parents as they navigate the service maze in the following ways:

- Working in partnership with parents in understanding the system and making informed decisions for their children
- Being familiar with information and referral resources in the community
- Helping parents develop skills in organizing information about their child and communicating with service providers
- Facilitating the coordination of services by providing service coordination, linking parents with service coordination, and/or helping parents develop their own service management skills
- Facilitating linkages among parents, support groups, and computer bulletin boards that may be able to support the search for services

Finding Financial Help

It felt like my baby was part of a tug-of-war between the hospital and our insurance company. After spending three months in the hospital, Suzy was on a ventilator, but in stable condition. We agreed with the hospital that home was the best place for Suzy. But our insurance company didn't cover the in-home care that she would require and we couldn't afford it. (Takemoto & King, 1993, p.21)

Once families find needed services, the financial burdens for care must still be faced. On top of the time and energy required, caring for children with disabilities

The average middle-class American family may face extra financial burdens and worries about insurance when they have a child with disabilities.

also means added expenses. Some of these expenses may include respite or child care, medical procedures or therapies, therapeutic or assistive equipment or supplies, and special diet or medication.

At the same time, families may have fewer resources to cover these expenses. In two-parent families, it is not uncommon for one parent to stay home in order to care for the child. Fear of losing medical insurance may keep a parent in a low-paying job. Even if a family has some insurance coverage, a child's disability may be considered by the insurance company to be a preexisting condition that is not covered.

In 1993, there were 39.3 million Americans who were uninsured. Furthermore, there were between 50 and 70 million Americans who were underinsured, with coverage that would leave them bankrupt if they had to face a major illness (White House Domestic Policy Council, 1993). With rising health care costs and shrinking insurance coverage, families experience additional stress worrying about whether their child will be able to receive a needed service or how they will pay for it.

A number of financing options include private insurance, Medicaid, Supplemental Security Income (SSI), state or local programs for children with special health care needs, state family support subsidy programs, charities, or loan programs. However, parents may still be faced with denial of coverage and/or burdensome debt from medical care.

Available assistive technology for mobility, communication, and other functional endeavors can increase independence for people with disabilities. Unfortunately, many of these devices are expensive. Some insurance companies as well as Medicaid, vocational rehabilitation programs, and maternal/child health programs will consider paying for assistive technology. Also, assistive technology is specifically included as a special education service under IDEA. However, although there are many possible funding sources, the high cost of some technologies and the reluctance of insurance companies and others to pay for equipment that might possibly be funded elsewhere can make it difficult for parents to obtain what their child needs.

The chances of successfully securing funding for medical services, assistive technology, and other supports increase dramatically when parents and professionals work as a team to problem-solve, locate possible funding sources, and convince them to pay. Professionals can focus on making sure that parents have and understand the information they need, and that they know what to do with it. Educators can collaborate with parents on financial issues in the following ways:

- Exploring less expensive options for services or care
- Linking parents with possible financing options
- Encouraging parents to prevent financial difficulties by checking about sliding fee scales, revised payment schedules, or insurance preapproval procedures
- Advising parents to use the appeal process when a request for financial assistance or payment is denied
- Helping parents to pursue other funding options
- Helping parents to document their need in such a way that the funding source is more likely to pay

SELF-ADVOCACY FOR ADULTS WITH DISABILITIES

It had been in the back of my mind for years, soon after I found out my son Samuel had this lifelong disability. What would the future hold for him when I wasn't there anymore to be his advocate, friend, and supporter? It was both a big and little worry. Big, because it gave me a hole in my gut whenever the questions crept in. And little, in the sense that I tried not to think about it. I'd think: I'll worry about that tomorrow, next week, when he's older, when I'm older. (Frolik, 1992, p. 5)

Many children with disabilities will require lifelong support by a parent, sibling, or other responsible adult. Responding to the needs of a person with disabilities from birth throughout their life span is an ever changing process of adaptation. Miller (1994) describes the following stages of adaptation that parents of children with disabilities experience:

- *Surviving:* Reacting and coping, and experiencing uncomfortable feelings that may include fear, confusion, guilt, blame, shame, and anger. This period is unique for each individual. Parents know that they have survived when they begin to feel a sense of control, optimism, and hope.
- *Searching:* Looking for a diagnosis and services, and trying to understand what the child's disability means to the parent's identity.
- *Settling in:* When the searching becomes less intense. The child's situation is stabilized, and parents may begin to pay more attention to themselves as a family within the community.
- *Separating:* A gradual process that begins at birth. Parents let go and adjust to their child's growing need for independence.

Although Miller presents these stages in a linear fashion, she describes them as a circular, dynamic process. Just as parents are "settling in," for example, there may be a change in personnel or programming, sending them back to the "searching" phase. Or perhaps parents have worked through "separating," as their adult child goes to work or live outside the home. But if the child's job or housing situation becomes disrupted, it can send the parents back into the "surviving" stage.

As a child moves into adult life, Beckett (1993b) describes four areas of concern that parents experience:

1. *Finances:* Parents worry whether their child with a disability will have a self-supporting job or may need government benefits such as Supplemental Security Income (SSI). This concern also includes financial planning that recognizes the limits of federal and state financial assistance programs.

2. *Living arrangements:* In the past, many people with disabilities lived at home, in group homes, or institutions. While these options are still available, there is a trend to open up more choices for adults with disabilities that include supported housing (attendant care, roommates, physical or technological adaptations, communication assistance, agency support, and so forth).

3. *Health care:* Insurance coverage often ceases once the child becomes an adult. Parents must seek other health care options, such as private health insurance, Medicaid, or some other alternative. In addition, parents are faced with the need to encourage self-advocacy for their children.

4. *Quality of life:* Parents often have concerns in the areas of finances, housing, autonomy and choice, physical and mental health, safety, appearance and hygiene, relationships with others, meaningful activities, and mobility. In each area, the highest possible quality of life should be sought.

One of the largest barriers to independence and self-sufficiency for adults with disabilities remains obtaining employment. A 1994 survey by Louis Harris and Associates indicated that two thirds of Americans with disabilities between the ages of 16 and 64 are not working, while only 11% are working part-time and 20% full-time. This finding showed no improvement since 1986 (National Organization on Disability, 1994).

As a child with disabilities grows older, the whole family must adjust to the child's need for increased independence and **self-advocacy.** Self-advocacy supports the rights of persons with disabilities to achieve the following:

• To live with dignity and respect

• To have the same opportunities to fail and to succeed as people without disabilities

• To no longer be seen as individuals perpetually dependent on welfare and charity (Beckett, 1993a)

With increased independence and self-advocacy for the person with disabilities may come tension for the family, as members adjust to their changing roles. There may also be tension between the parents' desire for their children to make their own decisions and the parents' desire to protect their children.

Professionals who understand life span issues and the need for self-advocacy by people with disabilities can help parents to prepare for these transitions and

All parents would like their children to become independent adults; group homes can offer some autonomy to adults with disabilities.

changing roles throughout their child's life. Specifically, educators may collaborate with parents around life span issues in the following ways:

- Helping parents to anticipate and plan for changes
- Encouraging parents to investigate available housing and long-term care options, including waiting lists, costs, benefits, and drawbacks of each
- Including goals and objectives for transition and self-advocacy into IEPs as early as possible, so parents can become comfortable with the level of independence achievable for their child
- Discussing with parents how specialized wills or estate plans can protect future benefits and services

CURRENT ISSUES AND FUTURE TRENDS: A PARENT'S PERSPECTIVE

Cherie Takemoto, one of this chapter's authors, has two young children—Margaret, age 8, and Peter, age 6. Positive experiences with parent–professional partnerships have led Cherie Takemoto to her current position as executive director of the Parent Educational Advocacy Training Center, the federally funded parent training and information center in Virginia.

My two children will be entering their teens as the 21st century begins. When Peter was born, my husband and I were tossed in the turmoil of neonatal intensive care nursery, tests, needles, and fears that Peter was not going to make it. Though we still do not have a diagnosis, we do know that Peter has developmental delays. Many professionals have given us hope and encouragement. Peter continues to surprise us and exceed our expectations. He is a sensitive and friendly child, and he is learning to read, write, add, and subtract. He also is teaching his friends how to be considerate and caring for others. My husband and I celebrate each accomplishment with the professionals who are our partners in helping Peter to realize his potential.

In my work, I have researched issues, learned from parents and advocates who are veterans in the parent movement, and listened to self-advocates. My vision for the future is based on my hopes, current trends, and my experience with parents and professionals.

Parent–professional partnerships will become accepted and expected practice, with professionals becoming more comfortable in their role and parents becoming more knowledgeable and skilled in theirs. More parents will enter the work force in educational and disability-related fields. Current models of empowerment for parents will metamorphose into models for parents and professionals to combine their mutual expertise and power. Parent support groups, parent-to-parent programs, computer bulletin boards, and other opportunities for parents to share information will expand, disseminating information about best practices to professionals as well. This will occur at the national, state, and local levels where decisions about families are made.

Self-advocacy will expand its scope from a movement for youth and adults with disabilities to include practices that help families and professionals listen closer to the desires, hopes, and dreams of even younger children. Parents and professionals will begin attending to these desires and preferences when the children are very young, and they will help these children learn to communicate their messages in a responsible way. Families and professionals will better understand interdependence and that relationships with people with disabilities are more reciprocal than one-sided.

Innovations in technology, education, and medicine will improve the functional capabilities of children with disabilities to a level that we can only dream about today. The vista of possibilities and expectations for the future of children with disabilities will widen. Families and professionals will have expanded access to information about best practices and increasing opportunities to communicate via telecommunications and the Internet.

Increased acceptance by the general public of people with disabilities and their families will follow the lead of the Americans With Disabilities Act as well as school and community inclusion efforts of the 1980s and 1990s. As children, youth, and adults become more successfully included in our schools and communities, the stigmatization often faced by children with disabilities and their families will begin to fade.

Service systems and funding streams will be structured to make more sense for individuals with disabilities and their families. Decision makers and practitioners will have a better understanding of how to combine private and public funding in order to provide goods and services (often at a lower cost), based more on what is needed than on what can be funded. Parents and professionals will become more comfortable with supports available through the extended family, friends, and the community. Service systems will encourage and bolster these "natural supports" with respite, training, and funding that is flexible enough to cover the gaps. Furthermore, families will be able to go to one place, such as a family resource center, to receive information, support, and assistance throughout their child's lifetime. These service systems will respond to the diversity of culture, family structure, and preference for the families they serve.

Five-Minute Summary

In the 20th century, major changes have occurred in how families and their children with disabilities are perceived and treated. In the first half of the century, professionals advised parents to institutionalize children with disabilities. Families who elected to keep their children at home were often "blamed" for the disabilities and were responsible for the total care and education of the children if any occurred. During the 1950s and 1960s, parents began to assist each other and to advocate for their children by actively opposing institutionalization and by organizing groups according to type of disability.

In 1975, landmark legislation for children with disabilities was passed, mandating a free, appropriate public education for all children. The legislation also introduced the concept of parent involvement in decision-making. To assist parents in learning about the special education process and about their role and responsibilities in that process, additional legislation was passed a few years later to establish a national program of Parent Training and Information Centers. In recent years, with the changing of family structures and the realities of family life, the narrow focus on the needs of the child with disabilities has broadened to include the family as a whole.

Study of the roles of family members and how they cope with crises in the context of a family systems approach must be an important element in preparing to work in special education and related fields. As society becomes increasingly diverse, cross-cultural competence is also needed. Knowing about one's own culture—recognizing family attitudes, biases, and values—is necessary in order to acquire new skills and techniques to work with culturally and linguistically diverse families.

Parents and professionals working together as partners provide the most productive approach for achieving the common goal of an appropriate education for each child with disabilities. To form effective working relationships, both parties must strive for a basic understanding of the other's perspective. Parents verbalize the need for additional understanding from professionals. Families' reactions to the news of a child's disability are unique and depend upon their values, culture, perceptions, and resources. There are some common emotions experienced by parents such as disbelief, guilt, sadness, anger, fear, and loneliness. Families cope with these emotions and with many health and education problems with varying degrees of success. Studies of resilient families have identified some key characteristics including balancing the demand of the disability with other family needs, developing communication competence, and making a commitment to family cohesion.

Major current issues professionals now face are: the delivery of family-centered services for young children; the movement toward inclusive schools; the navigation of service systems; family issues related to transition into adulthood, financial problems, and self-advocacy. Services for infants and toddlers should focus upon building family strengths and capabilities and requiring professionals to work in partnership with families. Successful inclusion of children with disabilities in regular education classrooms requires teamwork among regular educators, special education professionals, and parents. A major need identified by parents is finding community services, including financial assistance. Professionals may help parents develop skills in organization of information about their child and communication with service providers. Facilitating coordination of services and linking parents to other parents and resources are other ways to assist families. As children grow into young adults, new skills of self-advocacy are required. Both the young adult and his or her family members must adjust to the need for increased independence and the challenges of employment and housing.

Study Questions

1. To increase your understanding of the dramatic changes occurring for families of children with disabilities in the 20th century, imagine walking in parents' shoes and answer the following questions:
   a. If you were a parent of a child with cerebral palsy in 1930, how would you feel about your child, his future?
   b. If you were a parent of a child with Down syndrome in 1960, how would you feel about your child, her future?

c. If you were a parent of an infant born in 1990 with major physical disabilities, how would you feel about your child, his future?
2. What is meant by a family systems approach to working with families of children with disabilities?
3. How may professionals help fathers become more involved in their child's education?
4. How would you prepare to work with a family from a culture that was new and strange to you?

5. Drawing from your own experience as well as the chapter's information, what do you consider the strongest arguments in favor of inclusive schools? Why is there opposition?
6. Remember your own struggle for independence as a young adult. What additional barriers does a young adult with a significant disability face? (Think of a particular disability.)

For More Information

ORGANIZATIONS

National Information Center for Orphan Drugs and Rare Diseases (NICODARD)
P.O. Box 1133
Washington, DC 20013
703-522-2590 (in Virginia)   800-336-4797

National Organization for Rare Disorders (NORD)
P.O. Box 8923
New Fairfield, CT 06812
203-746-6518   800-999-6673

Parent Information and Training Centers
Each state has a Parent Information and Training Center funded by the U.S. Department of Education "to provide training and information to parents to enable them to participate more effectively with professionals in meeting the educational needs of their children with disabilities."
The Technical Assistance for Parent Programs (TAPP) project provides technical assistance to the Parent Training and Information Centers.
For the address or phone number of a particular program, call TAPP at 617-482-2915 or the National Information Center for Children and Youth with Disabilities (NICHCY) at 800-695-0285.

BOOKS AND ARTICLES

Anderson, W., Chitwood, S., & Hayden, D. (1996). *Negotiating the special education maze: A guide for parents and teachers* (3rd ed.). Rockville, MD: Woodbine House.

Beckman, P. J., & Boyes, G. B. (1993). *Deciphering the system: A guide for families of young children with disabilities.* Cambridge, MA: Brookline.

Fine, M. J. (1991). The handicapped child and the family: Implications for professionals. In M. J. Fine (Ed.), *Collaboration with parents of exceptional children* (pp. 3–24). Brandon, VT: Clinical Psychology Publishing Company.

Fish, M. C. (1991). Exceptional children in nontraditional families. In M. J. Fine (Ed.), *Collaboration with parents of exceptional children* (pp. 45–60). Brandon, VT: Clinical Psychology Publishing Company.

Gallagher, J. J., Beckman, P., & Cross, A. H. (1983). Families of handicapped children: Sources of stress and its amelioration. *Exceptional Children, 50,* 10–19.

Grossman, F. K. (1972). *Brothers and sisters of retarded children: An exploratory study.* Syracuse, NY: Syracuse University Press.

Hayden, D. (1993). Establishing respectful partnerships: A parent-advocate's view. *EDLAW Briefing Paper, 3*(5), 1–9.

MacKinnon, L., & Marlett, N. (1984). A social action perspective: The disabled and their families in context. In J. C. Hansen (Ed.), *Families with handicapped members* (pp. 111–126). Rockville, MD: Aspen.

Martin, R. (1991). *Extraordinary children—Ordinary lives: Stories behind special education case law.* Champaign, IL: Research Press.

Miller, N. B., Burmester, S., Callahan, D. G., Dieterle, J., & Niedermeyer, S. (1994). *Nobody's perfect: Living and growing with children who have special needs.* Baltimore: Paul H. Brookes.

Powell, T. H., & Gallagher, P. A. (1993). *Brothers and sisters: A special part of exceptional families* (2nd ed.). Baltimore: Paul H. Brookes.

Putnam, J. W. (1993). *Cooperative learning and strategies for inclusion: Celebrating diversity in the classroom.* Baltimore: Paul H. Brookes.

Rosenfeld, L. R. (1994). *Your child and health care: A "dollars & sense" guide for families with special needs.* Baltimore: Paul H. Brookes.

Russell, L. M., Grant, A. E., Joseph, S. M., & Fee, R. W. (1993). *Planning for the future: Providing a meaningful life for a child with a disability after your death.* Evanston, IL: American Publishing.

Sonnek, I. M. (1986). Grandparents and the extended family of handicapped children. In R. R. Fewell & P. F. Vadasy (Eds.), *Families of handicapped children.* Austin, TX: PRO-ED.

Spiegle, J. A., & van den Pol, R. A. (1993). *Making changes: Family voices on living with disabilities.* Cambridge, MA: Brookline.

Takemoto, C. (1994, Spring). Educating my Peter too. *PEATC Press,* 4.

Wehman, P. (1992). *Life beyond the classroom: Transition strategies for young people with disabilities.* Baltimore: Paul H. Brookes.

VIDEO AND ELECTRONIC MEDIA

Educating Peter [Video]
Produced by Home Box Office (1989)
Available from:
Ambrose Video Publishing
1290 Avenue of the Americas, Suite 2245
New York, NY 10104

Facing Inclusion Together [Video]
Produced by CASE Research Committee (1993)
Available from:
Council for Exceptional Children
1920 Association Drive
Reston, VA 22091

Family and the IFSP Process: Training in Family-Centered Approaches [Video]
Produced by Project Copernicus (1993)
Available from:
Kennedy Krieger Institute
2911 East Biddle Street
Baltimore, MD 21213

How Difficult Can This Be? A Learning Disabilities Workshop [Video]
Produced by Eagle Hill School and Peter Rosen Productions (1989)
Available from:
PBS Video
1320 Braddock Place
Alexandria, VA 22314

Kids Belong Together [Video]
Produced by People First Association of Lethbridge, Alberta (1990)
Available from:
Centre for Integrated Education and Community
24 Thorne Crescent
Toronto, Ontario M6H 2S5 CANADA

References

Able-Boone, H., & Stevens, E. (1994, Spring). After the intensive care nursery experience: Families' perceptions of their well being. *Children's Health Care, 23*(2), 99–114.

Alper, S. K. (1994). *Families of students with disabilities: Consultation and advocacy.* Needham Heights, MA: Allyn & Bacon.

Anderson, W., Chitwood, S., & Hayden, D. (1982). *Negotiating the special education maze.* Englewood Cliffs, NJ: Prentice-Hall.

Anderson, W., Chitwood, S., & Hayden, D. (1996). *Negotiating the special education maze.* Rockville, MD: Woodbine House.

Anderson, W., & Takemoto, C. (1992). *Beginning with families: A parents' guide to early intervention.* (Available from the Parent Educational Advocacy Training Center, 10340 Democracy Lane, Suite 206, Fairfax, VA 22030)

Baker, E. T., Wang, M. C., & Walberg, H. J. (1995). The effects of inclusion on learning. *Educational Leadership, 52*(4), 33–39.

Beach Center of Families and Disability. (1989, Spring). A positive vision. *Families and Disability Newsletter, 1*(1), 2.

Beckett, C. (1993a). *Transition series 3: Self-advocacy and supports: Keys to independence,* 8. (Available from the Parent Educational Advocacy Training Center, 10340 Democracy Lane, Suite 206, Fairfax, VA 22030)

Beckett, C. (1993b). *Transition series 6: Planning ahead: Future finances and supports,* 9. (Available from the Parent Educational Advocacy Training Center, 10340 Democracy Lane, Suite 206, Fairfax, VA 22030)

Bettelheim, B. (1967). *The empty fortress: Infantile autism and the birth of self.* London: Collier-MacMillan.

Dresser, N. (1996). *Multicultural Manners.* New York: Wiley.

Dunst, C. J., & Paget, K. D. (1991). Parent–professional partnerships and family empowerment. In M. J. Fine (Ed.), *Collaboration with parents of exceptional children* (pp. 25–44). Brandon, VT: Clinical Psychology Publishing Company.

Dunst, C. J., Trivette, C. M., & Deal, A. G. (1988). *Enabling and empowering families: Principles and guidelines for practice.* Cambridge, MA: Brookline.

Fewell, R. R. (1986). A handicapped child in the family. In R. R. Fewell & P. F. Vadasy (Eds.), *Families of handicapped children: Needs and supports across the life span* (pp. 3–34). Austin, TX: PRO-ED.

Fine, M. J., & Carlson, C. (Eds.). (1992). *The handbook of family–school intervention: A systems perspective.* Boston: Allyn & Bacon.

Flynn, N. (1987, November/December). Parent–professional partnership: Parent Resource Centers. *Counterpoint,* 7–8.

Flynn, N. (1993, Summer). A community's success story: Educating Peter and other children with special needs. *PEATC Press, 2,* 1–2.

Frolik, L. A. (1992). Overview of estate planning issues. *NICHCY News Digest, 2*(1), National Information Center for Children and Youth with Disabilities, 5.

Gartner, A., Lipsky, D. K., & Turnbull, A. P. (1991). *Supporting families with a child with a disability.* Baltimore: Paul H. Brookes.

Gilman, L. (1987). *The adoption resource book.* New York: Harper & Row.

Harry, B. (1992). *Cultural diversity, families, and the special education system: Communication and empowerment..* New York: Teachers College Press.

Inclusion award. (1993). *Exceptional Parent, 23* (7), 15.

Johnston, D., Proctor, W., & Corey, S. (1994). Not a way out: A way in. *Educational Leadership, 52*(4), 46–49.

Lillie, T. (1993). A harder thing than triumph: Roles of fathers of children with disabilities. *Mental Retardation, 31,* 438–443.

Lynch, E. W., & Hanson, M. J. (1992). *Developing cross-cultural competence.* Baltimore: Paul H. Brookes.

Maloney, J. (1994). A call for placement options. *Educational Leadership, 52*(4), 25.

McCracken, J. B. (1993). *Valuing diversity: The primary years.* Washington, DC: National Association for the Education of Young Children.

Meyer, D. J. (1986). Fathers of handicapped children. In R. R. Fewell & P. F. Vadasy (Eds.), *Families of handicapped children* (pp. 35–72). Austin, TX: PRO-ED.

Miller, N. B. (1994). *Nobody's perfect: Living & growing with children who have special needs.* Baltimore: Paul H. Brookes.

Moore, C. (1993). Maximizing family participation in the team process. In L. Kupper (Ed.), *Second national symposium on effective communication for children and youth with severe disabilities: Topic papers, reader's guide & videotape* (pp. 43–54). McLean, VA: Interstate Research Associates.

National Organization on Disability. (1994, July). *A Louis Harris and Associates survey on employment and disability.* (Available from the National Organization on Disability, 910 16th Street, N.W., Washington, DC)

National Society for Autistic Children. Board of Directors and Professional Advisory Board. (1977). *A short definition of autism.* Albany, NY: National Society for Autistic Children.

Oakes, J., & Lipton, M. (1990). *Making the best of schools: A handbook for parents, teachers, and policymakers.* New Haven, CT: Yale University Press.

Oberti, C. (1993). A parent's perspective. *Exceptional Parent, 23*(7), 18–21.

Patterson, J. (1991, September). Family resilience to the challenge of a child's disability. *Pediatric Annals, 20*(9), 491.

Powell, T. H., & Ogle, P. A. (1985). *Brothers and sisters: A special part of exceptional families.* Baltimore: Paul H. Brookes.

Rebhorn, T., & Takemoto, C. (1994). *Unlocking the door: A parent's guide to inclusion.* (Available from the Parent Educational Advocacy Training Center, 10340 Democracy Lane, Suite 206, Fairfax, VA 22030)

Scheerenberger, R. C. (1983). *A history of mental retardation.* Baltimore: Paul H. Brookes.

Segal, M. (1988). *In time and with love.* New York: Newmarket Press.

Skrtic, T. M. (1991). The special education paradox: Equity as the way to excellence. *Harvard Educational Review, 61*(2), 148–206.

Takemoto, C., & King, C. (1993). *Taking charge: A parents' guide to health care for children with special needs.* (Available from the

Parent Educational Advocacy Training Center, 10340 Democracy Lane, Suite 206, Fairfax, VA 22030)

Turnbull, A. P., Summers, J. A., & Brotherson, M. J. (1984). *Working with families with disabled members: A family systems approach.* Lawrence: Kansas University Affiliated Facility.

Turnbull, A. P., & Turnbull, H. R., III. (1990). *Families, professionals, and exceptionality* (2d ed.). Columbus, OH: Merrill.

U.S. Department of Education. (1994). *Strong Families, Strong Schools.*

Vadasy, P. F., Fewell, R. R., Meyer, D. J., & Greenberg, M. T. (1985). Supporting fathers of handicapped young children: Preliminary findings of program effects. *Analysis and Intervention in Developmental Disabilities, 5,* 125–137.

Walsh, F. (1984). Conceptualizations of normal family functioning. In F. Walsh (Ed.), *Normal family processes* (pp. 3–42). New York: Guilford.

White House Domestic Policy Council. (1993). *Statistical abstract 1993.*

Ziegler, M. (1992). Parent advocacy and children with disabilities: A history. *OSERS News in Print, 5*(1), 4–6.

Chapter 14

Flabbergasted, acrylic on canvas, 48″ × 72″ (1993)

EARLY CHILDHOOD INTERVENTION

MARY BETH BRUDER

After studying this chapter, the reader will:

Know the definition of early childhood intervention

Be able to list legislative initiatives that support early childhood intervention for individuals with disabilities

Be able to describe the elements of the service delivery process for young children

Know the major components of an Individualized Family Service Plan

Be aware of the issues critical to the improvement and expansion of early childhood intervention for individuals with disabilities

EARLY CHILDHOOD INTERVENTION

1930   The White House Conference on Child Health and Protection recommended federal funding of programs for "crippled children."

1935   The Social Security Act was passed, including Title V: Maternal and Child Health Services (Part I) and Services for Crippled Children (Part II).

1965   Head Start was established by Congress to serve preschool children living in poverty.

1968   The Handicapped Children's Early Education Assistance Act was passed by Congress, funding model demonstration programs for infants and preschool children with disabilities.

1973   The Division for Early Childhood was established within the Council for Exceptional Children.

1986   The Education for All Handicapped Children Act (P.L. 99-457) amended P.L. 94-142 by mandating special education for children ages 3 to 5 and establishing a voluntary program for infants and toddlers and their families.

1988   The Federal Family Support Act was passed, ensuring that children receive financial support from their parents.

1991   The Child Care and Development Block Grant was passed.

INTRODUCTION

Early childhood is an important time in any student's life. For children with disabilities, the early years are critical for a number of reasons. First, the earlier a child is identified as having a developmental delay or disability, the greater the likelihood that the child will benefit from intervention strategies designed to meet the child's needs. Second, families benefit from the support given to them through the intervention process. Third, schools and communities benefit from a decrease in costs because more children come to school ready to learn.

As a field, early childhood intervention has been defined as the provision of educational or therapeutic services to children under the age of 8 (Sigel, 1972). Legislatively, **early intervention** is used to describe the years from birth to age 3, while the term *early childhood special education* (or sometimes *preschool special education*) has been used to describe the period of preschool years from ages 3 to 5. For purpose of ease, this chapter will use Sigel's (1972) definition of early childhood intervention as a description of services provided to children from birth to age 5 under the Individuals With Disabilities Education Act of 1990 (Part H for infants and toddlers; Part B for 3- to 5-year-olds).

Who Receives Early Childhood Intervention?

Early childhood intervention service providers have identified at least three separate groups of children who warrant early childhood intervention:

1. Children at *established risk* who are diagnosed with conditions known to result in disability or delay (e.g., genetic conditions)

2. Children at *biological risk* because of prenatal, perinatal, or postnatal histories suggesting increased vulnerability to disability or delay (e.g., prematurity or birth trauma)

3. Children at *environmental risk* because of conditions in their surroundings that might result in disability or delay (e.g., poverty) (Tjossem, 1976)

While children with established conditions are usually recognized during the first weeks of life, children at risk for delay or disabilities can be identified any time between birth and age 5. It has been estimated that 30% of these children from "at-risk" groups subsequently demonstrate delays in development (Scott & Masi, 1979).

One concern for both early childhood intervention programs and families is the lack of conformity regarding eligibility criteria for services across age groups and states (Snyder, Bailey, & Auer, 1994). Under current legislation, services for infants and toddlers can be made available to a broad range of children, and each state can determine its own eligibility criteria. These criteria can also differ from preschool services under Part B, both across and within states. Thus, efforts to identify eligible children and their families are somewhat idiosyncratic to each state and locality.

HISTORICAL OVERVIEW

The history of early childhood intervention spans many disciplines and fields of study. The child development literature has provided a theoretical focus for early

Mitchell Andrew Levitz is a bright, engaging young man with an impressive list of honors and awards to his credit. He was born on April 10, 1971, to Jack and Barbara Levitz and grew up in Peekskill, New York. He graduated with a regular diploma from Walter Panas High School in June 1991 and received awards for community service, school service, and academic achievement in business education, as well as legislative commendation and a varsity letter for soccer.

During his high school years, Mitchell toured Canada, Hawaii, California, and the Midwest with a social club for young adults. Mitchell has a strong interest in politics, government, world affairs, and public service. His hobbies include reading newspapers, downhill skiing, boating, water skiing, tennis, and Ping-Pong.

Mitchell has interned for two State Assembly members and has served on the Legislative Action Committee for the Board of Education. He has worked as a busboy, a bank teller at the Summit Trust Bank, and as an office assistant at the Peekskill/Cortlandt Chamber of Commerce.

Mitchell is employed as Consumer Empowerment Ombudsman in White Plains, New York, where he lives on his own. He is an active member of the First Hebrew Congregation of Peekskill.

Mitchell has appeared many times on television and radio, including interviews and appearances in documentary films. He has been a keynote speaker at more than 100 local, state, and national conferences, and he has presented congressional testimony a number of times in Washington, D.C.—most recently on the twentieth anniversary of the passage of IDEA. Mitchell has coauthored (with Jason Kingsley) his first book, and has completed a national book promotion tour.

What makes Mitchell's achievements especially noteworthy is the fact that he has Down syndrome. After his diagnosis, his pediatrician recommended to his parents that he be placed in an institution. Instead, his mother, who was a special education teacher, began to devise an early intervention program for him. When his home county later opened up its early intervention program, Mitchell became the first child enrolled.

Mitchell's book, *Count Us In: Growing Up With Down Syndrome,* was published by Harcourt Brace in January 1994. It has received the National Media Award from the National Down Syndrome Congress, a special EDI Award from the National Easter Seals Society, a Media Access Award from the Governor's Office of the State of California, the TASH National Media Award in Print, and Honorable Mention from the National Rehabilitation Week Awards. *Count Us In* is listed on the Westchester Library Association 1995 Washington Irving Booklist and on the Books for the Teen Age 1995 Booklist of the New York City Public Library.

Mitchell has presented a paper to the International Symposium on the Rights of Persons With Intellectual Disabilities at Yale Law School. In June 1995, Mitchell begins a new position with the National Down Syndrome Congress working on a self-advocacy leadership project, "Resources for America's Future," located at the Cincinnati Center on Developmental Disorders/UAP.

childhood intervention that has evolved from the transactional model of development (Sameroff & Chandler, 1975). At one time child development theory was polarized into two competing schools of thought: a biologically based view of development, versus one that stressed behavioral and environmental factors. The current transactional developmental model represents a synthesis of the two theories, emphasizing the interactive nature of child development.

The transactional model of development recognizes the fact that the interaction between the child and the environment is a continual process in which neither the child's status nor the environmental effects on that status can be separately addressed. This developmental model suggests that the environment can be used to modify a child's biological limitations—and conversely, a deficient environment can lead to delays in a child's development. This focus has greatly influenced both early childhood intervention strategies and early childhood intervention service models—most notably on the emphasis placed on a child's relationship with his caregiver (Beckman, Robinson, Rosenberg, & Filer, 1994).

The maternal and child health field has emphasized the role of government in designing and supporting practices to promote the well-being of children. The Children's Bureau, established by Congress in 1912, collected data on such issues as institutional care, mental retardation, and the care of crippled children (Lesser, 1985). The Social Security Act, enacted in 1935, established maternal and child health services as well as services for crippled children. Lastly, the Social Security Act amendments of 1965 included Medicaid services for children. In particular, the Early and Periodic Screening Diagnosis and Treatment (EPSDT) program was initiated for all children under age 21 who qualified for Medicaid. EPSDT was funded to assist in the early identification and treatment of children's health and developmental needs.

The field of early childhood education was also an important contributor to current early childhood intervention service models. Many early childhood programs were developed to serve children from lower socioeconomic backgrounds and, to some extent, their parents (Kagan, 1991). The concept of kindergarten was established in the early 1800s by proponents such as Friedrich Froebel in Germany, and by the mid 1800s many privately run kindergartens were operating in Europe and North America. The first public kindergarten program was established in the United States in 1873. At the turn of the century, half of all kindergartens in the United States were operated by public school systems—with the major focus on the potential benefits of such programs for children from deprived backgrounds.

The concept of preschool or nursery school was firmly established in the early 1900s, and as with kindergarten, the concept was developed in Europe. In England, the MacMillan sisters began nursery schools to provide for the emotional and physical well-being of needy children. In Rome, Maria Montessori also established early education programs for needy children. She had initially worked with children who had mental retardation and used educational practices that emphasized learning through active involvement with the environment.

Both the Depression and World War II resulted in the government providing assistance to expand early education opportunities (both day programs and kindergarten) for young children in the United States, primarily as a support for working mothers. However, early childhood programs remained stagnant until the 1960s (Peterson, 1987).

The largest government-funded early childhood program, Head Start, was established in 1965. Head Start began as a compensatory program for low-income 4- and 5-year-old children. It provided comprehensive early childhood services focusing on health, education, social services, and parent involvement. This program has been expanded to serve infants and toddlers.

More recently, the federal Family Support Act (1988) and the Child Care and Development Block Grant (1991) recognized the importance of early care and education programs. States are now authorized to coordinate such programs to ensure accessibility by families in need of child care, Head Start, or other children's services. Rather than drawing a distinction between nursery school, compensatory programs, and child care, proponents have recently recommended the development of integrated systems of early care and education. However, fragmentation and dwindling resources continue to hamper efforts to build capacity and enhance the quality of early childhood education so that all children may benefit from such programs (Kagan, 1991).

Lastly, the field of special education contributed to the development of early childhood intervention through its emphasis on remedial and compensatory services and instructional techniques. Special education history began in the late 1700s in France with the story of Victor, a child who had grown up with wolves. Jean-Marc Itard developed and provided an intensive education program to teach Victor (who was known as the "Wild Boy of Aveyron") language and behavior skills. Shortly thereafter, Edourd Seguin, a student of Itard, developed a physiological method of education for children with disabilities. This method emphasized the importance of early education and the use of detailed assessment information with which to develop a remediation plan. Unfortunately, the techniques used by Itard and Seguin were not universally adopted. The preferred treatment for people with disabilities until the 1960s in both Europe and the United States was institutionalization and segregation from society.

During the Kennedy administration, the government became more involved in providing services to school-age children with disabilities. This commitment was formalized by Congress in 1966 when the Section for Exceptional Children was expanded and renamed the Bureau of Education for the Handicapped within the U.S. Office of Education. A number of legislative initiatives also began in this era, including the 1968 Handicapped Children's Early Education Assistance Act. The act provided federal funds to support model demonstration programs to educate infants and preschool children with disabilities. This impetus began to raise awareness about the importance of early childhood intervention, and an early childhood branch was developed in the Office of Special Education and Rehabilitation Services within the U.S. Department of Education. It wasn't until 1986, however, that a federal mandate was established to make special education services available to all eligible preschool children with disabilities. This mandate was established as P.L. 99-457, which was a set of amendments to P.L. 94-142 (the Education for All Handicapped Children Act of 1975, later reissued as the Individuals With Disabilities Education Act of 1990, or IDEA).

P.L. 99-457 added a number of significant components specific to children under age 5. First, services for eligible young children ages 3 to 5 were mandated under the provisions for free and appropriate public education (Part B of P.L. 94-142). Second, the amendments created incentives for states to develop early intervention entitlement programs for children from birth through age 2 (Part H). Through Part H, Congress identified an "urgent and substantial need" (1) to enhance the development of infants and toddlers with disabilities, (2) to minimize the likelihood of institutionalization and the need of special education services after this group reaches school age, and (3) to enhance the capacity of families to meet the special needs of their infants and toddlers with disabilities. To meet this need, federal financial help was made available to the states to develop programs for the delivery of interagency, multidisciplinary services to all eligible children. Since 1986, statewide systems have been designed, implemented, and refined. As of 1996, all states and territories were participating in Part H services.

THE EFFECTIVENESS OF EARLY CHILDHOOD INTERVENTION

There are more than 50 years of research findings to support the effectiveness of intervention for infants and young children with disabilities. In the 1930s, a series of studies were completed on the impact of the environment on young children who were described as having mental retardation (Skeels & Dye, 1939). In the first study, two children from an orphanage had been placed in an institution for persons with mental retardation because of a lack of space in the orphanage. In the institution, they received attention from women who were labeled "mentally deficient." The stimulation provided by these women over a 2-year period resulted in a significant rise in the intelligence quotient of the children. This finding provided the impetus for a second study, in which 13 more children from the orphanage were placed on a ward with adolescent women who were mentally retarded. These young women became surrogate mothers. Each woman was assigned one child to care for, after being given limited training on how to care for and play with the children. A comparison group of 12 children remained in the orphanage where they received no individualized attention. After a period of 18 to 36 months, the children who were assigned the surrogate mothers had a mean gain of 27.5 IQ points, and the children in the orphanage showed a mean loss of 26.2 points. Follow-up research completed 25 years later documented long-term gains in the treatment group. There were significant differences in quality-of-life indicators such as marriages, educational level (all of the experimental group had completed twelfth grade), and employment. In contrast, the orphanage group had a mean educational level of third grade, one member had died, and four were institutionalized. All but one of the seven noninstitutionalized adults were working as unskilled laborers.

Research conducted in the late 1950s also strengthened the concept of early childhood intervention. Samuel Kirk (1958) measured the effects of preschool experience on 43 children who were identified as having mental retardation, in comparison to 38 children who did not have preschool experiences. The children who received early childhood intervention gained between 10 and 30 IQ points, while the comparison group showed losses in IQ scores.

Other studies during the 1940s and 1950s documented the effects of the environment on development. Comparisons were made between infants who grew up in sensory-deprived environments as opposed to infants who received stimulation. The infants who were sensory deprived had substantial decreases in their health, as well as their mental capacity. One study followed up and looked at a group of such infants at ages 10 to 14, finding that the children who were raised in a sterile environment demonstrated deficiencies across all developmental and behavioral domains (Spitz, 1947).

A number of studies conducted in the 1960s investigated the effects of early childhood intervention on children from low-income backgrounds. After a much publicized study that questioned the effectiveness of Head Start (Westinghouse Learning Corporation, 1969), a number of other studies applied more rigorous methodology to study the effect of early childhood intervention on preschool children. These later studies documented positive gains in IQ and socioemotional development and fewer later placements in special education among well run or model programs (Lazar & Darlington, 1978; Richmond, Stipek, & Zigler, 1979). One of the most comprehensive studies of this nature was conducted on the Perry Preschool Project, which served low-income children. This study has followed enrolled children into adulthood, and significant differences were found between these children and a control group of children on quality-of-life indicators such as employment and incarceration (Schweinhart, Barnes, & Weikart, 1993). Similar findings have also been documented in other well controlled studies (Lally, Mangione, Honig, & Wittmer, 1992).

Many reviews of early childhood intervention literature involve scores of studies completed during recent years (Guralnick, 1988; Meisels, Dichtelmiller, & Liaw,

1993). While many problems have been identified in regard to methodological limitations within these data (e.g., lack of control groups; narrowly defined outcome measures), it is still a universally held belief that early childhood intervention is effective. Most recently, it has been suggested that studies should expand their impact by systematizing designs and improving methodology to focus more specifically on both input and outcome variables. For example, it has been suggested that studies incorporate analyses that allow for greater application of a systems approach. This approach has been articulated by Guralnick (1989), and it includes a focus on (1) child and family characteristics, (2) program features, and (3) goals and objectives.

Two recently completed longitudinal efficacy studies have incorporated this perspective into their methodology. The Early Intervention Collaborative Study (Shonkoff, Hauser-Cram, Krauss, & Upshur, 1992) has followed a group of 190

Table 14.1   **A Comparison of Interventions With Infants, Preschoolers, and Elementary-Age Children With Special Needs**

	DOMAIN	INFANTS AND TODDLERS (0–36 MONTHS)	PRESCHOOLERS (36–60 MONTHS)	ELEMENTARY (5–12 YEARS)
Characteristics of Children	Population parameters	Noncategorical; developmentally delayed, conditions that typically result in delay, at risk of substantial delay; results in wide range of ability levels and types of disabilities	Noncategorical; wide range of ability levels and disabilities (some states, however, will choose categorical descriptions)	Categorical; more restricted range of ability levels and disability types; formal eligibility criteria
	Goals for intervention	Behavior and motor organization, differentiated responses to environmental cues, cause and effect, early communication and social skills, attachment	Cognitive, self-help, social, fine motor, communication, behavior, toy play, gross motor	Reading, spelling, mathematics, appropriate social behavior
	Schedule regularity	Low—almost entirely determined by infant	Moderate—some adult determination of schedules, but requires flexibility depending on children's needs and interest	High—preset routine and time allocation for tasks; very little in the way of child-initiated activities
	Endurance	Short—interactions typically last less than 2–3 minutes	Moderate—interactions may last 5–15 minutes	Long—interactions may last 30 minutes to 2 hours
	Motivation	Must come from inherent appeal of material or activity; based on infant's interest	Begin to follow adult expectations, but high-interest toys and activities are critical	Based on adult expectations for compliance; reliance on self-regulation and response to rules
The Intervention Context	Context of teaching	Parent–child interactions; feeding, bathing, diapering, and dressing routines; object play	Object play, peer interactions, adult–child interactions, routines	Classroom instruction, written materials

infants and their families who received services within 29 community-based programs in Massachusetts and New Hampshire. Results suggested that developmental change in the participating children was influenced by gestational age and health characteristics, as well as the severity of the child's psychomotor impairment at entry. Different correlates of adaptive change were demonstrated within and among subsamples of children, but also within and among mothers and fathers. Another longitudinal intervention study, the Infant Health and Development Program (Brooks-Gunn, Gross, Kraemer, Spiker, & Shapiro, 1992; Ramey et al., 1992) was a multisite, randomized project that included low birth weight premature infants. The intervention infants received 3 years of home visits, child care, medical care, and parent groups. Results at age 3 showed that the intervention infants scored higher on tests of mental ability than did the control infants who only received health-related services.

Table 14.1   Continued

	DOMAIN	INFANTS AND TODDLERS (0–36 MONTHS)	PRESCHOOLERS (36–60 MONTHS)	ELEMENTARY (5–12 YEARS)
	Sites for intervention/services	Homes, day care centers, family day homes, specialized developmental centers, developmental evaluation centers, hospital settings (NICU, pediatrics ward)	Specialized developmental center/classrooms, day care centers, homes, development evaluation centers, hospital settings	Elementary schools (regular classroom, resource room, self-contained classroom)
	Responsible agencies	Mental health centers, hospitals, public health services, private day care, specialized nonprofit agencies, public schools	Public schools, mental health centers, Head Start, day care	Public schools
	Team functioning	Often involves multiple professionals from multiple agencies; considerable role overlap, requiring extensive communication and coordination	Moderate blending of roles, but work in isolation is possible	Differentiated and specific roles; isolation likely
Family Role	Mandated family role	Essential and family-focused—IFSP requires documentation of family needs and strengths, a statement of family goals, and the provision of family services, including case management	Very important—IEP provisions pertain, all parents' rights protected, and parent training encouraged when necessary	Important—IEP provisions pertain, all parents' rights protected

Source: Adapted from "Issues and Directions in Preparing Professionals to Work With Young Handicapped Children and Their Families," by D. B. Bailey, 1989, in *Policy Implementation and P.L. 99-457: Planning for Young Children With Special Needs* (pp. 97–132), ed. by J. Gallagher, P. Trohanis, & R. Clifford, Baltimore: Paul H. Brookes.

CHARACTERISTICS OF EARLY CHILDHOOD INTERVENTION

Early childhood intervention services and programs are different from services for school-age children in a number of ways. These differences include the heterogeneous characteristics of the children served, the developmental nature of intervention goals, and the need for a flexible intervention schedule and service delivery approach (Bailey, 1989; Peterson, 1987). These characteristics, as delineated by Bailey, are on Table 14.1. Particularly unique to early childhood intervention programs are the role of the family in early childhood intervention, the need for a team-based model of service delivery, and the variety of intervention environments. Following is an overview of these three characteristics.

Family-Centered Orientation

Every child is a member of a family (however it defines itself) and has a right to a home and a secure relationship with an adult or adults. These adults create a family unit and have ultimate responsibility for caregiving, supporting the child's development, and enhancing the quality of the child's life. The caregiving family must be seen as the constant in the child's life and the primary unit for service delivery. Early childhood interventionists must respect the individual families they serve and the decisions of these families in directing their children's early childhood intervention programs.

Parents of young children with disabilities rarely take on this parenting role with any amount of preparation for the special challenges they will face. Rather, the early days, weeks, and months of parental responsibility may be spent in a blur of visits to the hospital, physician's office, and special clinics with little or no opportunity to adapt to the significant change that has taken place in their lives. While most parents report an increase in their level of stress after the birth of a child, the parents of an infant with disabilities must deal with additional unanticipated pressures and responsibilities that can make the parenting role seem overwhelming.

It has been suggested that the primary goal of early childhood intervention should be to promote the parents' awareness of and adaptation to their primary role of parenting a child with disabilities (McBride, Brotherson, Jaonning, Whiddon, & Demmitt, 1993; Turnbull & Turnbull, 1990). One key to accomplishing this goal is to recognize the ongoing stress of parents and help them to find support networks (Beckman, Newcomb, Frank, Brown, & Filer, 1993; Dunst, Trivette, & Deal, 1994). Support should be both formal (e.g., assisting with insurance and financial needs; identifying respite services; training on medical equipment) and informal (e.g., identifying existing community resources; facilitating family involvement within the school). The overriding premise of such support is that it must be individually matched to the needs of the family, and the use of such strategies should be directed by the family (Murphy, Lee, Turnbull, & Turbiville, 1995). By changing the focus from child change to parent/family adaptation, both programs and parents have seen beneficial results (Affleck et al., 1989; Beckman et al., 1994; Dunst et al., 1994).

Family-centered care is the name of a set of beliefs, attitudes, and principles that have been applied to the care of children with special health care needs and their caregiving families (Shelton et al., 1987). The philosophy of family-centered care is based on the premise that the family is the enduring and central force in the life of a child and has a large impact on the child's development and well-being.

In order to work effectively with infants and young children with disabilities, early childhood interventionists must become aware of each caregiving family's

The Ronald McDonald House is an example of family-centered care that has become a well known institution.

priorities, concerns, and resources. Furthermore, staff must be able to communicate with the family in order to establish collaborative goals for the child and to design appropriate interventions that can be delivered in the context of the family. A family-centered approach is thus dependent on a relationship between early childhood interventionists and families that is based on mutual trust and respect.

Just as the population of children who are considered to have special needs is not a homogeneous group, neither are the children's families. The early childhood intervention professional serving young children with disabilities will no doubt work with a diversity of families who vary by background and economic conditions, as well as by family structure (Lynch & Hanson, 1992).

Specifically, the early childhood interventionist must become more sensitive to the cultural background of the enrolled families. This important variable contributes to the composition and operation of a family system. The families of infants and toddlers in the early childhood intervention system represent all the facets of American society and cultural backgrounds. The basic cultural components that must be considered as professionals interface with families include language, communication style, religious beliefs, values, customs, food preference, and taboos. Any one of these factors may affect the family's perception of disabilities. Professionals who work in early childhood intervention must have the ability to understand the similarities and differences between their own cultural beliefs and values and those of the families they serve (Bruder, Anderson, Schutz, & Caldera, 1991). The influence of cultural norms can be more significant than the influence of a specific intervention. Professionals must develop sensitivity to the unique role these parameters play in each family system. Each family will bring unique resources to the task of parenting their child with special needs, and each family will identify unique needs that must be addressed through early childhood intervention.

Team-Based Service Delivery

While infants and young children with disabilities may require the combined expertise of numerous professionals providing specialized services, the coordination of both people and services is frequently overwhelming. For example, personnel having medical expertise, therapeutic expertise, educational/developmental expertise, or social service expertise traditionally have been involved in the provision of services to infants and young children with disabilities and their families. Each of these service providers may represent a different professional discipline and a different philosophical model of service delivery. In fact, each discipline has its own training sequence (some require undergraduate, while others require graduate degrees), licensing and/or certification requirements (most of which do not require age specialization for young children), and treatment modality (e.g., occupational therapists may focus on sensory integration techniques). In addition, many disciplines have their own professional organization that addresses the needs of persons across the entire life span, unlike organizations focused on a single age group (e.g., National Association for the Education of Young Children). Nonetheless, as services for young children with disabilities continue to grow, so too does the need for professionals. Table 14.2 contains an overview of the professional disciplines most typically involved in services for young children with disabilities and their families.

In order to improve the efficiency of the individuals providing early childhood intervention, it has been suggested that services be delivered through a team approach. A group of people become a team when their purpose and function are derived from a common philosophy with shared goals (Maddux, 1988). The types of teams that typically function within service delivery models for young children with disabilities have been identified as multidisciplinary, interdisciplinary, and transdisciplinary.

The *transdisciplinary approach* originally was conceived as a framework for professionals to share important information and skills with primary caregivers (Hutchinson, 1978). This approach integrates a child's developmental needs across the major developmental domains. The transdisciplinary approach involves a greater degree of collaboration than other service models, and for this reason may

Table 14.2   Professional Disciplines in Early Childhood Intervention

Audiologist

Early childhood special educator

Nutritionist

Nurse

Occupational therapist

Physician

Psychologist

Physical therapist

Social worker

Speech–language pathologist

Vision specialist

be difficult to implement. Nevertheless, it has been identified as ideal for the design and delivery of early childhood intervention services for infants and young children with disabilities (Bruder, 1995; Garland & Linder, 1994; McGonigel, Woodruff, & Roszmann-Millican, 1994).

A transdisciplinary approach requires the team members to share roles and systematically cross discipline boundaries. The primary purpose of the approach is to pool and integrate the expertise of team members so that more efficient and comprehensive assessment and intervention services may be provided. The communication style in this type of team involves continuous give-and-take between all members (especially the parents) on a regular, planned basis. Professionals from different disciplines teach, learn, and work together to accomplish a common set of intervention goals for a child and his or her family. The role differentiation between disciplines is defined by the needs of the situation, as opposed to discipline-specific characteristics. Assessment, intervention, and evaluation are carried out jointly by designated members of the team. Other characteristics of the transdisciplinary approach are joint team effort and joint staff development to ensure continuous skill development among members (Bruder, 1995; Woodruff, 1994).

In the transdisciplinary approach, the child's program is primarily implemented by a single person or a few persons with ongoing assistance provided by team members from the various disciplines. In most early childhood intervention

---

EASY IDEAS FOR PRACTITIONERS

For the Teacher:

1. Always use "person-first" language when writing or talking about children or adults with disabilities. For example, say "child with speech impairment" instead of "speech-impaired child."
2. Write realistic goals on IFSPs and IEPs, goals that serve a useful purpose to the child and the child's family.
3. Remember that parents are the best informants concerning their child's daily needs, strengths, and challenges.
4. Stay in touch with current research and resources in the field of disabilities and use these resources in your interactions with children and families.
5. If using a transdisciplinary approach, remember to pool and integrate the expertise of the team members.

For Parents:

1. Keep your child's next environment in mind when looking at his or her current program.
2. Be sure to include the functional goals and objectives that are important to you and your child when writing IFSPs and IEPs with the intervention team.
3. Keep a cumulative file of information and resources (e.g., people, places, documents, etc.) concerning all events occurring in your child's educational life.
4. Try to familiarize yourself with all medical and educational terms being used concerning your child.
5. Give educators a true picture of your child from your own perspective, including strengths and challenges.

programs, it is the teacher and program assistants who take on the primary service delivery role. It is also appropriate for this role to be assumed by a special education teacher who may provide services within the early childhood program on a regular basis. Related service support staff, most commonly therapists, often serve as consultants to the teachers. In this way, the child's therapy and other needs are integrated into the daily routine of the classroom. This strategy facilitates the delivery of appropriate interventions across developmental domains, as opposed to having a specific speech group, fine motor group, gross motor group, and so on. This does not mean that therapists stop providing direct services to children. In reality, in order for therapists to be effective, they need to maintain direct contact with the child.

Although collaborative, transdisciplinary service delivery teams appear simple in concept, implementation of this strategy can be difficult because of its departures from more familiar, structured, discipline-specific intervention structures. In particular, the time commitment required to implement a collaborative team model effectively may be difficult for some early childhood intervention programs (Bruder, 1994).

Varied Intervention Environments

A variety of factors influence the decision about the optimum service setting for an infant or young child with disabilities. These include the location of the intervention program (e.g., urban versus rural), the program's space allocation, the needs of the child, the transportation resources of the family and program, and the preference of the family. Early childhood intervention can be provided in a hospital setting, a child care setting (a center, family day care home, or baby-sitter's house), the home, or elsewhere in the community. Not all services have to be provided at the same location; the settings may change over time as the needs of the family and child change. Clearly, there is no standard setting for early childhood intervention. No matter where the intervention services occur, the intervention techniques and services (including assistive technology) must be transferable within all of the settings in which the child and family participate.

Many times, families are restricted from participating in community activities and everyday routines if their child has a disability. Early childhood interventionists should help the family identify the natural community environments and activities the family would like to pursue (e.g., shopping, church, library)—and then intervention routines should be developed to empower the family to participate in as many of these natural environments as they wish.

Children with disabilities benefit from participating in group settings with children without disabilities; in fact, this practice, termed **inclusion** (Salisbury, 1991; Thousand, Villa, & Nevin, 1994), has been cited as a quality indicator of early childhood and early childhood intervention services (McDonnell & Hardman, 1988). Support for the practice of inclusive early childhood intervention services was derived from a conceptual base that emphasizes the social, ethical, educational, and legal reasons for integrating young children with disabilities and young children without disabilities (Bricker, 1978). As a result, both families and professionals have stated the importance of providing interventions to young children with disabilities within group settings that also serve young children without disabilities. In particular, a number of interrelated service delivery developments support the expansion of early childhood intervention into natural group environments. They will each be summarized.

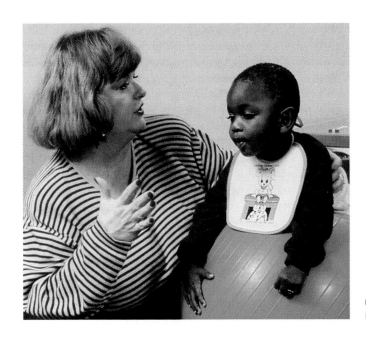

One of the roles of the early childhood interventionist is to help the child acquire life skills in normal environments.

The first development is the issue of inclusive preschool environments. Families have become increasingly vocal about their expectations for their children with disabilities. It has been well documented that parents of young children with disabilities want their children to have the opportunity to receive services in the mainstream (J. J. Guralnick, Connor, & Hammond, 1995; M. Guralnick, 1994; Turnbull & Winton, 1983). These parents have also suggested that one of the most important outcomes of special education should be the development of friendships between their children and children without disabilities (Buswell & Schaffner, 1990). Special educators, as well as other service providers for children with disabilities, are responding to expectations like these by revamping special education curricula to focus on the facilitation of social competence and friendships between children with and without disabilities (Guralnick, 1990; Odom, McConnell, & McEvoy, 1992). A collateral finding in this research has been that parents of young children without disabilities who have participated in inclusive preschool programs have reported positive attitudes toward this practice (Green & Stoneman, 1989; Peck, Carlson, & Helmstetter, 1992).

Second is the need for day care for children with disabilities. More than 11 million preschool children attend early care or school programs (Blank, 1993). This is not surprising since statistics show that 53% of women with an infant under 1 year of age are in the labor force (U.S. Census Bureau, 1990) and therefore in need of ongoing child care. This large number includes women who have children with disabilities. In order to meet this growing need, it has been suggested that early childhood intervention programs collaborate with child care programs and deliver services within those settings. Model demonstration projects have given evidence for this model, providing that appropriate supports are in place (Bruder, Deiner, & Sachs, 1990). In particular, training resources are needed to increase the availability and access to these programs by families of children with disabilities (Bruder, 1993; Wesley, 1994).

The third development involves service delivery in a child's natural environment. Part H of IDEA (now reauthorized as a part of P.L. 102-119) emphasizes the rights of eligible infants, toddlers, and preschool-aged children to receive early childhood intervention services within natural environments—such as in the home, or in environments in which typical children participate. The definitions under Part H further clarify that, when group settings are used for intervention, the infant or toddler with a disability should be placed in groups with same-aged peers without disabilities, such as play groups, day care centers, or whatever typical group settings exists for infants and toddlers without disabilities.

Fourth, children with disabilities have a legal right to government-operated services. The Americans With Disabilities Act of 1990 (P.L. 101-336) prohibits discrimination against individuals with disabilities by state and local governments (Title II) and in public accommodations (Title III). All state and local government-operated services for children—such as child care centers, preschools, park and recreation services, or library services—cannot exclude from participation in or deny the benefits of their services, programs, or activities, or otherwise discriminate against a child with disabilities.

And the final development influencing delivery of early childhood intervention services is that young children ages 3 to 5 who are eligible for special education and related services have the right to receive these services in inclusive environments, as ordered through two memorandums issued by the Office of Special Education and Rehabilitation Services, U.S. Department of Education. These memos reinforce a child's right to both part- and full-time placement in programs that serve preschool children who do not have disabilities. Use of both private and public programs (such as Head Start) for typical children and as special education placements for children with disabilities is one strategy that has been identified to ensure a least restrictive setting (OSEP Memo 87-17, 6/2/87; OSERS Preschool Grants Memorandum, n.d.).

The foregoing developments, in combination, underscore the need to expand inclusionary educational services to young children with disabilities and their families (Smith & Hawkins, 1992). The Division for Early Childhood of the Council for Exceptional Children has released a position statement supporting inclusion for young children with disabilities (DEC, 1993); it is presented in Table 14.3.

Table 14.3 DEC Position on Inclusion

Inclusion, as a value, supports the right of all children, regardless of their diverse abilities, to participate actively in natural settings within their communities. A natural setting is one in which the child would spend time had he or she not had a disability. Such settings include but are not limited to home and family, play groups, child care, nursery schools, Head Start programs, kindergartens, and neighborhood school classrooms.

DEC believes in and supports full and successful access to health, social service, education, and other supports and services for young children and their families that promote full participation in community life. DEC values the diversity of families and supports a family guided process for determining services that are based on the needs and preferences of individual families and children.

To implement inclusive practices DEC supports: (a) the continued development, evaluation, and dissemination of full inclusion supports, services, and systems so that options for inclusion are of high quality; (b) the development of preservice and in-service training programs that prepare families, administrators, and service providers to develop and work within inclusive settings; (c) collaboration among all key stakeholders to implement flexible fiscal and administrative procedures in support of inclusion; (d) research that contributes to our knowledge of state of the art services; and (e) the restructuring and unification of social, education, health, and intervention supports and services to make them more responsive to the needs of all children and families.

Source: "DEC Position on Inclusion," by the Division for Early Childhood, Council for Exceptional Children, 1993, *DEC Communicator, 19*(4), p. 4.

SERVICE ELEMENTS IN EARLY CHILDHOOD INTERVENTION

Current practices in early childhood intervention are dictated to a large extent by federal and state regulations. Part H of IDEA contains a listing of services that can be made available to eligible infants and toddlers (see Table 14.4). Part B of IDEA dictates the services available to eligible preschool-aged children (the same as for children ages 5 through 21). These services are delivered in a variety of ways, depending on the unique needs of the child. Following are descriptions of service elements included in the early childhood intervention process.

Assessment and Identification of Eligible Children

Assessment is the process of gathering information in order to make a decision. Assessment is an important component of early childhood intervention, yet traditional assessment models that are discipline specific, occur in a novel setting with contrived activities, and are conducted by a stranger prove inadequate when working with infants and young children with disabilities (Meisels & Provence, 1989). Effective early childhood intervention assessment protocols rely on a sensitivity to the age of the child as well as the nature of the delay or disability (McLean, Bailey, & Wolery, 1996).

It has been noted that early childhood assessment offers a unique opportunity to facilitate parent participation and partnership in the intervention process (Campbell, 1991). For one thing, parents are most knowledgeable about their children, and children are most comfortable with their parents. A comprehensive assessment process includes gathering a wide range of information about a child's abilities. Parents have the most extensive information in such areas as motivation, interactive abilities, learning style, and tolerance for learning. Furthermore, if assessment is viewed as an integral part of intervention, then parent participation in assessment introduces the parent as an equal partner in fostering the child's development.

Assessment instruments include a variety of standardized and criterion-referenced instruments that provide information across developmental areas

---

Table 14.4 **Services in Early Intervention**

- Family training, counseling, and home visits
- Special instruction
- Speech pathology and audiology
- Occupational therapy
- Physical therapy
- Psychological services
- Case management services
- Medical services only for diagnostic or evaluation purposes
- Early intervention, screening, and assessment services
- Health services necessary to enable the infant or toddler to benefit from the other early intervention services
- Social work services
- Vision services
- Assistive technology devices and assistive technology services
- Transportation and related costs that are necessary to enable an infant or toddler and the infant's or toddler's family to receive early intervention services

---

Source: From the Individuals With Disabilities Education Act of 1990 (P.L. 101-336), Part H.

including cognition, fine and gross motor development, receptive and expressive communication development, social and emotional development, and self-help. Professionals representing different disciplines may use assessments that focus on specific developmental areas. It is most important that the instruments used match the intended outcomes of the assessment. In early childhood intervention, three separate assessment purposes have been identified: screening, eligibility for services, program planning.

Screening.   Developmental **screening** is the process through which children are identified as having a possible developmental need or delay, and therefore will require additional assessment. The major goal of screening is to reduce the time that elapses before intervention begins (Meisels & Wasik, 1990). For screening to be effective, it must be accurate, comprehensive, and cost effective. Screening can occur through a variety of methods, including parent interviews, observations of the child, or the use of a specific instrument or checklist. However, because of wide range and variations in normal development and behavior during the early years, infants and young children are difficult to screen. Parent involvement in the screening process may alleviate some of these difficulties. One technique that has been used to do this is the parent-completed screening questionnaire.

Determining Eligibility.   A second purpose of assessment is for diagnostic or **eligibility** purposes. Usually this assessment is comprehensive and includes a variety of measures (sometimes using standardized tools) and professionals with discipline-specific expertise. When diagnosing the nature and extent of a child's disability, it is important for this early assessment to provide a foundation for more finely tuned assessment procedures that may follow (McLean & McCormick, 1993). And, as with screening, parents should participate in the assessment.

Recent recommendations in regard to diagnostic assessment include a focus on the *process*, as opposed to focusing merely on the product of assessment (McLean & Odom, 1993). One method by which to do this is by using a *play-based assessment protocol* (Linder, 1990). This protocol supports observation in a play-based situation that allows the child to demonstrate his or her behavioral repertoire. Parents are an integral part of this play-based assessment, and it should occur in a natural environment. Professionals from different disciplines can jointly collect information about specific development areas, as well as noting the interaction and integration of these areas within the child. An integrated assessment report is then completed by the participating professionals, including input from the family.

Program Planning.   A third purpose of assessment is to determine intervention outcomes, goals, objectives, and strategies. Assessments conducted for program planning should use a variety of instruments and discipline-specific professionals, as needed. It is most important that the family participates actively in the assessment to ensure the validity of the outcomes or goals.

An important component of assessing for program planning is an inventory of the sequences of skills needed by the child to participate in a variety of natural environments. This strategy is called an **ecological inventory.** It gathers information that has relevance to enhancing the child and family's quality of life (Noonan & McCormick, 1993b).

The IFSP and IEP Process

The **Individualized Family Service Plan (IFSP)** and the **Individualized Education Program (IEP)** are planning documents that shape and guide the day-to-day provision of early childhood intervention services. The IFSP is required for the provision of early intervention services for eligible infants and toddlers (age from birth to 3) and their families. The IEP is used for special education services delivered to eligible children age 3 and older. Table 14.5 contains the elements that must be included in an IFSP and those that must be in an IEP. Unlike the IFSP, the IEP does not require a statement of the family's resources, priorities, and concerns, nor does it require a designated service coordinator. The requirement within the IFSP for a statement of the natural environments where services will be provided is replaced in the IEP by a statement on the extent of the child's regular classroom participation.

While the content of both the IFSP and IEP seem somewhat similar, the concept is different. The IFSP relies very much on a family-centered and community-based orientation to service delivery, while the IEP is more grounded in a school-based model. Many states are trying to remedy this philosophical discrepancy by using IFSPs for both early childhood intervention and preschool special education. This practice is supported by the U.S. Office of Special Education Programs in regard to compliance to the regulations of IDEA.

It has been suggested that the IFSP and IEP contain individualized outcomes, goals, and intervention strategies that are functional and embedded within daily activities and routines and delivered in accordance to the families' wishes (Bruder, 1995; Kramer, McGonigel, & Kaufmann, 1991). One way to articulate these outcomes is to use the Individualized Curricula Sequencing Model (Guess & Horner, 1978; Mulligan & Guess, 1984). This type of planning incorporates the many naturally occurring events and opportunities that exist in a young child's life as "intervention opportunities" (Noonan & McCormick, 1992; Peterson, Leroy, Field, & Wood, 1992). When this method is used, the IFSP and IEP can be developed according to the family's (or other environmental) routines and priorities. The parent can help a child learn turn taking during games at bath time, and learn

---

Table 14.5 Requirements of the IFSP and IEP

INDIVIDUALIZED FAMILY SERVICE PLAN (IFSP)

1. A statement of the child's present level of functioning in cognitive development, communication development, social or emotional development, physical development, and adaptive development
2. A statement of the family's resources, priorities, and concerns
3. A statement of expected intervention outcomes—including criteria, procedures, and time lines
4. A description of the services that the child and family need—including method, frequency, and intensity
5. A statement of the natural environments in which early intervention services shall be provided
6. Projected dates for initiation of services and expected duration
7. The name of the service coordinator who will be responsible for implementation of the plan and coordination with other agencies and persons
8. The procedures to ensure successful transition from infant services to preschool programs

---

INDIVIDUALIZED EDUCATION PROGRAM (IEP)

1. A statement of the child's present levels of educational performance
2. Annual goals and short-term objectives
3. A statement of the special education and related services the child will receive
4. The extent to which the child will participate in programs along with typically developing children
5. Projected dates for when services will begin and how long those services are expected to continue
6. Evaluation procedures, schedules and objective criteria
7. Statement of needed transition services (beginning at age 16)

---

motor movement and self care during dressing routines. The IFSP or IEP should incorporate specific intervention strategies within the activities, with adaptations as necessary. These adaptations should be focused on enabling the child to participate in all of the activities and routines in the environment (Halvorsen & Sailor, 1990). For example, during snack time or meal time, objectives from several developmental domains may be implemented. The child could be supported in a position by an adaptive chair (motor), while they are asked to vocalize for food (communication), using adaptive eating utensils. Table 14.6 contains a planning sequence based on this model for IFSP/IEP development. Figure 14.1 is an example of an IFSP.

Curriculum for Early Childhood Intervention

Curriculum provides a basis for intervention. In particular, curriculum addresses the content of the intervention, the teaching and learning strategies, and the means for assessing intervention (Bailey, Jens, & Johnson, 1983). The designation of "best practice" in curricula for infants and young children with disabilities has been evolving for a period of years, with input coming from theories of normal child development and from research with both typical and atypical children and their families (Bruder, 1996).

Child curricula reflect a developmental focus. This is not surprising, since most eligibility criteria for early childhood intervention emphasize the discrepancy between a child's chronological age and developmental abilities. A widely used descriptor of early childhood curriculum is "developmentally appropriate practice." This approach refers to a set of guidelines that set forth appropriate practices for early education (Bredekamp, 1987). Two core beliefs within these guidelines are age appropriateness and individual appropriateness. Within early childhood intervention, curriculum models that emphasize developmentally appropriate practices are usually insufficient without some adaptations and the use of teaching techniques individually tailored to a child's needs (Carta, 1994; Wolery & Bredekamp, 1994).

Two other important practices in organizing and delivering the curriculum for an infant or young child are the use of intervention objectives (usually done in conjunction with the IFSP/IEP) and systematic instruction. Basically, objectives represent learning expectations and are based on a child's strengths, needs, and preferences. Objectives differ from goals or outcomes in that they separate the goal

---

Table 14.6 **IFSP Planning Sequence**

---

1. Assist the family to identify their resources, priorities, and concerns.
2. Identify the child's strengths and abilities.
3. Elicit desired IFSP outcomes from the family.
4. Determine intervention strategies to support the IFSP outcomes.
5. Identify the daily routines and activities of the natural environments in which the child and family participate.
6. Imbed IFSP outcomes and strategies within the routines and activities of the natural environments.
7. Identify the adaptations and supports needed by the child to participate in the routines and activities in the natural environments.
8. Assign responsibilities and roles to all who interact with the child.
9. Implement intervention.
10. Evaluate intervention.

---

into smaller components. Each objective should be written so that there is little or no doubt of the intervention target. Principles of systematic instruction include the use of antecedents and consequences. **Antecedents** include prompts such as cues, signals, or other methods of gaining the child's attention; **consequences** include reinforcements (individual for each child and as natural as possible) or correction procedures. There are a variety of instructional systems that can be used to enhance a child's learning. These include incidental teaching, time delay, mand-model, systematic commenting, and milieu teaching (Hemmeter & Kaiser, 1994).

Interventionists do not have to sacrifice structure in order to provide a responsive learning environment (Noonan & McCormick, 1993a). It is possible, and often advisable, to implement systematic instructional procedures within a responsive learning environment. The key to using these procedures in naturalistic teaching situations lies in tailoring intervention to the needs of each child, using the least intrusive strategies to promote learning and embedding instruction within developmentally appropriate routines and activities such as play.

Evaluation of Early Childhood Intervention

One element that must be highlighted within early childhood intervention programs is program evaluation. As previously described, the effectiveness of early childhood intervention programs has received much attention during recent years. The result of such scrutiny has been an increased awareness of the importance of evaluation in improving and expanding the early childhood intervention service system.

A number of issues must be considered when designing evaluation plans. First and foremost is the heterogeneity of the population. This factor may limit the

Section I, Page 1

CONNECTICUT BIRTH TO THREE SYSTEM
INDIVIDUALIZED FAMILY SERVICE PLAN

☐ Referral date _____   ☐ Initial IFSP/date _____   ☑ Annual IFSP/date __8/26/96__
☐ 6 Month Review/date _____   ☐ Transition Meeting/date _____   ☐ Interim IFSP/date _____

Child's Name: ___Allison Montgomery___   Sex: __F__ Date of Birth: __10/27/94__

Parent/Guardian/Family Member   Parent/Guardian/Family Member

Name ___Bill and Tina Montgomery___   Name _____

Address _____2 Orchard Lane_____   Address _____

City ____Katonal____ State _CT_ Zip _06001_   City _____ State ____ Zip _____

Phone (Day) ( ) _233-3333_ (Evening) ( ) _244-4444_   Phone (Day) ( ) _____ (Evening) ( ) _____

Primary Language _____English_____   Primary Language _____

Physician or Health Care Provider: _Bob Greenstein_ Address _____ Phone ( ) _____

Insurance Carrier/Medicaid: _____BC/BC_____   Policy #: _____

   Health Status Code: _____2_____   Medicaid #: _____

Referral concerns and/or diagnosis: _cerebral palsy due to an intercranial hemorrhage; born at 29 weeks_

gestation, ventilator dependent for 5 weeks; bilateral sensorineural hearing loss

Service Coordinator/Program: ___Eileen Kaminer — Beginnings___

Address ____1100 Albany Ave.; Hartford____   Telephone ____688-8888____

Surrogate Parent Name: _____   Address: _____

Phone: ( ) _____

School District: _____   Contact Person/Telephone: _____

Child's Name: _____Allison Montgomery_____ Date: _8/26/96_ DOB: _10/27/94_   Section II, Page __2__ of __5__

II. FAMILY'S CONCERNS, PRIORITIES AND RESOURCES
AS THEY RELATE TO ENHANCING THEIR CHILD'S DEVELOPMENT
(This information is optional for the Family to include in the plan)

1 What, if any, are your concerns? _____Allison's speech and language_____

_____

_____

2. What do you want the Team to know about your child? Suggestions:
* Pregnancy and birth history   * History of child's growth and development   * Medical Information
* The important people in your child's life   * Child's favorite and least favorite activities   * Opportunities to interact with peers

Allison is a very happy child and she loves other children. She is an only child. She was 10 weeks

premature and needed a ventilator for 5 weeks. She has cerebral palsy (diplegia) and a moderate

hearing loss. She has been in early intervention since she came home from the hospital.

_____

_____

_____

3. What do you want the team to know about your family? Suggestions:
* Who is part of your family   * Helpful people and agencies
* Other important events that have occurred   * Family activities   * Effect of child's needs on the family

Bill (dad) travels all over the world 10 days a month. Tina (mom) also travels all over the country

to visit friends and relatives with Allison about once every two months.

_____

_____

_____

_____

                                                        Attach additional pages as needed

---

Child's Name: _____Allison Montgomery_____ Date: _8/26/96_ DOB: _10/27/94_   Section III, Page __3__ of __5__

III. SUMMARY OF CHILD'S PRESENT ABILITIES, STRENGTHS AND NEEDS

* Summarize below observations by family and other team members of the child's abilities, strengths and needs in day-to-day routines. Include information on formal assessments as well as the child's interests, motivators and frustrations. Areas of development to include:

• Bathing, feeding, dressing, toileting — Adaptive/Self-Help Skills
• Thinking, reasoning and learning — Cognitive Skills
• Moving, hearing, vision, health — Physical Development
• Feelings, coping, getting along with others — Social/Emotional Development
• Understanding, communicating with others and expressing self with others — Communication Skills

Summary

Allison has just begun to walk when held at hips or hands. She can also walk pushing a weighted

carriage or chair. Allison has new hearing aid molds which fit her so that she can put them in and

take them out by herself. Allison manipulates toys with both hands and picks up and places small

objects (puzzles, crayons, pegs) with either hand. Allison vocalizes and is beginning to babble

(cv). Her ability to understand simple signs and verbal language has improved so that she can follow

one-step directions in context. Allison points and grabs to get her wants met. Allison can feed her-

self with a spoon and uses a fork when seated in a supportive high chair (high sides, strapped hips,

strapped feet).

_____

_____

List Reports, Assessments and dates which were used to develop this plan: ___Battelle, PLS, Peabody Motor Scale during home

visit in a playbased procedure; Environmental Inventory Home Child Care Center

_____

                                                        Attach additional pages as needed

Child's Name: _____Allison Montgomery_____ Date: _8/26/96_ DOB: _10/27/94_   Section IV, Page __4__ of __5__

IV. OUTCOME # _1_

What we want for our child or family is:

_____Allison to start using words_____

What is happening now: (including child or family resources and concerns) _Allison points, gestures, and babbles_

What are the next steps to reach this outcome (objectives)?	By when?	Done ✔
1.1 Allison will use consistent gestures combined with vocaliza-tions for 5 different needs across three people and two settings	1.1 10/15/96	
1.2 Allison will use a word approximation and sign for 5 different needs across three people and two settings	1.2 11/30/96	

HOW	**WHO**	**WHERE**
(Ideas and activities we will do to make this happen)	*(Who will be involved?)*	*(The places where this will happen)*
Present opportunities to Allison (favorite games, toys, activities) Model gesture and word Provide access to game, toy, activity	mom dad	home grocery store child care church mom and me swimming library tales for tots

Progress Toward Outcome	Projected Review Date _____ Date Reviewed _____
_____ Finished _____ Ongoing _____ Revised	Comments:
Progress Toward Outcome	Projected Review Date _____ Date Reviewed _____
_____ Finished _____ Ongoing _____ Revised	Comments:

Child's Name: _____Allison Montgomery_____ Date: _8/26/96_ DOB: _10/27/94_   Section V, Page __5__ of __5__

V. EARLY INTERVENTION SERVICES

ICD 9 Code(s) _____

Check One:
____ Interim ____ Initial ____ Review ____ Annual

What's Going to Happen: (e.g. Homevisits, Play Groups, Assistive Technology)	By Whom: (the discipline(s) responsible)	Where:	Indiv.=I Group=G	How Often	How Long	Start Date	Stop Date	Outcome #
Home visit	teacher/PT	home	I	twice week	30 min	9/1/96	3/30/97	1
Child care visit	teacher	child care center	I	every week	90 min	9/1/96	3/30/97	1
Sat. play group	speech/lang	YMCA	G	every week	90 min	9/1/96	3/30/97	1
Child care visit	speech/lang	child care center	I	every other week	60 min	9/1/96	3/30/97	1

PAYMENT ARRANGEMENTS (If Any:)

Justification for services offered in settings other than child's natural environment:

I HAVE REVIEWED THIS INDIVIDUALIZED FAMILY SERVICE PLAN. I CONFIRM THE APPROPRIATENESS OF THE DIAGNOSIS(es) AS STATED (ICD-9 CODE) AND THE RECOMMENDATIONS FOR THE TREATMENT SERVICES AS THEY ARE WRITTEN.

Physician Signature_____ DPH Lic. # _____ Date _____

Print Name _____

VI. OTHER SERVICES

These services are not covered by the Connecticut Birth to Three System

Other Resources and Supports	Payment

types and scope of variables that can be measured across the group of program participants (Garwood, 1982). The second factor relates to the first. Few standardized tools are available that either meet the diverse developmental needs of the population or identify small rates of growth over time (Dunst, 1985). A third factor to consider when planning an evaluation is the inherent methodological limitations that may compromise evaluation efforts of programs serving children with severe disabilities. These limitations may include subject characteristics that affect both the internal and external validity of the plans, sample or group size, the lack of rigorous designs, misuse of statistical procedures, and the lack of detail about both independent and dependent variables.

In order to remedy these inherent problems, it has been suggested that evaluation in early childhood intervention programs be multidimensional (Johnson & LaMontagne, 1994). For the enrolled child, the measurement and outcome procedures should match the specific goals of the interventions. This could include measures that focus on interactional competence, contingency awareness, or engagement with the environment. In addition, programs should measure the outcomes of various family variables such as resource management or support networks. Last, the program should measure aspects of the environment, including staff status. All measures should be conducted on both a formative (during program operation) and a summative (at the completion of services) schedule.

One often overlooked yet vital aspect of the program evaluation process is an assessment of the intervention environment. The Early Childhood Environment Rating Scale (Harms & Clifford, 1980) assesses the quality of center-based environments for young children. This scale is organized around basic categories, with content areas including furnishings, routines, learning activities, interaction, program structure, and adult needs. This type of environmental assessment provides immediate feedback about the nature and the quality of the environment, which in turn has a direct impact on the quality of early childhood intervention services.

A comprehensive evaluation plan should represent the scope of the most important features of intervention: the child, the family, and the program. Without this critical feedback on all of these interlocking components, early childhood intervention services can never fully meet the individual needs of children and toddlers with disabilities and their families.

Transition

The importance of transition has been addressed in state and federal legislation, federal funding initiatives, and professional literature (e.g., Bruder & Chandler, 1996; Rosenkoetter, 1992). A successful transition is a series of well planned steps that result in the placement of the child and family into another setting. Successful transitions are a primary goal of early childhood intervention (Fowler, 1992; Salisbury & Vincent, 1990). Needless to say, the type of planning and practices that are employed can influence the success of transition and satisfaction with the transition process.

Within the field of early childhood intervention, **transition** is defined as "the process of moving from one program to another, or from one service delivery mode to another" (Chandler, 1992, p. 246). Others have emphasized the dynamic process of transition, as children with disabilities and their families will have repeated moves among different service providers, programs, and agencies as the child ages (Healy, Keesee, & Smith, 1989). While formal program transitions for young children with disabilities typically occur at age 3 (into preschool) and age 5 (into kindergarten), informal transitions between services, providers, and programs also can occur throughout these early years. Part H of IDEA, the provision of early childhood intervention services, increases the potential number of transitions. For example, transition can begin for some children at the moment of birth, if it is determined that their health status requires transfer to a special care nursery (Bruder & Walker, 1990).

According to Wolery (1989), transition should fulfill four goals:

1. To ensure continuity of services

2. To minimize disruptions to the family system by facilitating adaptation to change

3. To ensure that children are prepared to function in the receiving program

4. To fulfill the legal requirements of P.L. 99-457

In order to achieve these goals, it is necessary to plan for transition. The responsibility for transition planning should be shared across the sending and receiving programs, and should involve families (Bruder & Chandler, 1996). Transition procedures should assist families and their children and promote collaboration between the families and program staff who make up the transition team.

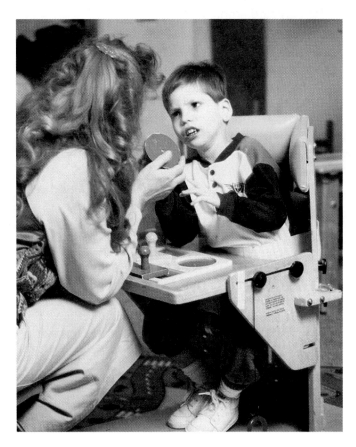

One of the goals of early childhood intervention is to help the child make a successful transition into the next environment—in this case, the regular classroom.

INNOVATIVE IDEAS   EARLY INTERVENTION FOR PREMATURE INFANTS

There has been an increase in the survival rates for low birth weight and premature infants. Infants born as early as 24 weeks gestation (i.e., 16 weeks early) now have a 79% chance to live. These increases in survival rates have focused attention on decreasing the likelihood that these babies will have continued medical or developmental needs. This has resulted in the expansion of early intervention to the Neonatal Intensive Care Nursery (NICU) where these babies are cared for.

Heidi Als at Children's Hospital in Boston and Harvard Medical School has been conducting research for more than 5 years on the impact of early intervention on low birth weight and premature infants. The early intervention model she has developed is called the Newborn Individualized Developmental Care and Assessment Program (NIDCAP). Infants and families who participate in the NIDCAP intervention show significant differences from those who don't participate in the program. These include physiological outcomes (faster weaning off respirators and supplemental oxygen and tube feedings, shorter hospital stays, improved weight gain) as well as developmental outcomes (behavioral organization and developmental progress) and family outcomes (parent competence, pleasure and ability to facilitate the child's completion of a learning task). These differences have persisted until the age of 7.

NIDCAP intervention is individualized for each infant and family, and it is carried out by a team that includes interdisciplinary staff. The components of the intervention include the following:

- The structuring of the physical environment in the NICU in support of the co-regulation of infant and family (e.g., decreasing light and noise)

- The appropriate timing and organization of medical, nursing, and other interventions in support of the individuality of the infant's need for regulation of physiological status (e.g., sleep–wake cycles)

- The support and nurturance of the parents in their appreciation of their infant as an individual and in their confidence in supporting their infant's development and care

- The development of early intervention support services that will continue until the child goes home and begins community-based programs

NICU staff must be trained to provide NIDCAP services in order to implement the earliest intervention appropriately. It seems reasonable to suggest that all low birth weight and premature infants and their families have the opportunity to benefit from early intervention from the earliest time possible.

CURRENT ISSUES AND FUTURE TRENDS

While early childhood intervention is an accepted program of services and supports for infants and young children with disabilities, it is an area that is constantly improving and changing. Most recently, an attempt was made by the Division for Early Childhood (DEC) of the Council for Exceptional Children to identify recommended practices in the field of early childhood intervention (DEC Task Force on Recommended Practices, 1993; McLean & Odom, 1996). Fourteen programmatic areas were identified, and work groups identified practices within each area that met six criteria: research-based or value-based; family-centered; multicultural emphasis; cross-disciplinary; developmentally and chronologically age-appropriate; and normalized (McLean & Odom, 1993).

A national sample of 500 randomly selected DEC members, persons in higher education, and family members was used as a validation sample. These individuals were surveyed to assess whether they were in agreement with the items in the recommended practices. They were also asked to indicate whether the practices were used. It is not surprising that while the practices were validated by the sample, there was discrepancy in what practices were actually used in service delivery (Odom, McLean, Johnson, & LaMontagne, 1995). Most importantly, this points out that while many in the field agree on what constitutes a recommended practice in early childhood intervention, the programs and service providers are not always implementing them.

Besides the importance of continually building and improving early childhood intervention, there are a number of other critical issues that must be addressed in the future. Two of these, to be discussed here, are the use of assistive technology and the development of collaborative service models.

Assistive Technology

The use of **assistive technology** as a tool for children with disabilities is an area receiving attention. IDEA lists assistive technology as both an early intervention service and a special education service. Assistive technology may be termed either "low-tech," such as velcro strips or paintbrushes with extended handles, or "high-tech." High-technology devices include computers, CD-ROM, adapted keyboards, graphic tablets, input devices such as switches, and output devices such as speech synthesizers. Additionally, many types of seating and mobility devices are also considered assistive technology.

Research in this area has supported the fact that assistive technology can be used to promote learning in young children with disabilities (Hutinger, 1987; Hutinger & Ward, 1988; McCormick, 1987; Spiegel-McGill, Zippiroli, & Mistrett, 1989; Sullivan & Lewis, 1990). It has therefore been suggested that a greater emphasis on assistive technology be incorporated into early childhood intervention (Hutinger, Robinson, & Clark, 1990; Odom & Warren, 1988; Sullivan & Lewis, 1993) since technology expands a child's options and independence (Reed & Bowser, 1991; Sullivan & Lewis, 1990).

In addition, medical assistive devices are a necessity for many children with complex health care needs (Baroni, Tuthill, Feenan, & Schroeder, 1994). These devices replace or augment inadequate bodily functions (Levy & Pilmer, 1992) and include respiratory technology assistance (e.g., oxygen supplementation, mechanical ventilation, positive airway pressure devices), surveillance devices (e.g., cardiorespiratory monitors, pulse oximeters), nutritive assistive devices (e.g., tube-feedings, ostomies), intravenous therapy (e.g., nutrition, medication infusion), and kidney dialysis. The field of early childhood intervention must be prepared to use any technology necessary to enhance a child's development.

Collaborative Service Models

Early childhood intervention requires that many agencies work together to develop joint activities focused on the development of collaborative service models (Trohanis, 1989). A logical extension to this requirement for services for young children with disabilities is the design of collaborative service models to encompass the early care and education needs of all young children (Kagan, 1991). The challenge is to identify the various agencies, professionals, and payment sources currently involved in the provision of such services. While interagency and cross-disciplinary collaboration is the first step toward building collaborative service models, the ultimate goal would be a seamless system of service delivery that

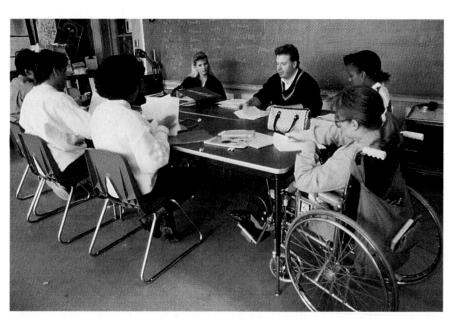

This special chair is an example of assistive technology being used in early childhood settings today.

fluctuates around the family's and child's needs, as opposed to artificially imposed program limitations reflective of agency and funding constraints.

There are many benefits to collaborative service delivery models (Baldwin, Jeffries, Jones, Thorp, & Walsh, 1992; Bruder & Bologna, 1993). Most important is the efficient and effective use of service providers and funding streams across agencies, resulting in improved service delivery. These models also result in a reduction in service duplication. Collaborative models enable parents and service providers to efficiently locate and manage the services required by the family. Lastly, collaborative models eliminate the need for formal transitions, as services are integrated, comprehensive, and longitudinal.

Unfortunately, the development of collaborative early childhood service systems remains an elusive goal for many states. This is not surprising considering that the service delivery system is composed of independent agencies, institutions, and organizations—each providing a specific service or function. As a result, each participating provider has its own orientation toward the service system, thus creating the need for transition points for families and their children.

A collaborative model would not, however, negate the need for the practices and processes cited in this chapter. Many of the practices reflect effective service delivery principles that will, in fact, support the movement of children and families within a seamless, collaborative service model. The challenge facing the field is to redefine service priorities to support families and their children as they make choices in service delivery reflection of their needs.

Five-Minute Summary

Early childhood intervention is a dynamic field focused on the enhancement of a child's abilities and development. Families are also an important component of interaction with the goal being to enable them to adapt to their child's ongoing needs. The issues facing eligible young children and their families are complex, demanding a commitment by early childhood interventionists to build comprehensive coordinated community service systems. These systems must be family centered, team based, and delivered in natural and inclusive environments in order to provide the best start possible to infants and young children with disabilities. A number of service elements have been identified as critical to the success of early intervention programs. These include identification and assessment process for eligible infants and young children, the IEP or IFSP process, curriculum development, the evaluation process, and transitions into the next environment. These elements provide a foundation for service delivery systems that are flexible and responsive to individual child and family needs. Future service delivery issues include the utilization of assistive technology to expand learning opportunities for children and the development of collaborative early childhood models for both children with disabilities and children without disabilities.

Study Questions

1. How would early intervention create a positive effect in the life of a child with disabilities?
2. How do early intervention services differ from services for school-age children?
3. List several reasons for respecting and including the family in providing early intervention services.
4. Which professional disciplines are involved in delivering early intervention services?
5. What is a transdisciplinary approach to early intervention?
6. Explain the major components of the Individualized Family Service Plan.
7. What are the drawbacks to using formal, standardized assessment instruments with very young children?
8. Name some natural environments for delivering early intervention services to young children.

For More Information

ORGANIZATIONS

American Association of Psychiatric Services for Children
1133 15th Street, N.W., Suite 1000
Washington, DC 20005

American Bar Association Child Advocacy Center
1800 M Street, N.W., Suite 200
Washington, DC 20036

BOOKS AND ARTICLES

Abraham, M. R., Morris, L. M., & Wald, P. J. (1993). *Inclusive early childhood education.* Tucson, AZ: Communication Skill Builders.

Beaty, J. J. (1992). *Preschool appropriate practices.* Fort Worth: Holt, Rinehart and Winston, Inc.

Goodman, J. F. (1992). *When slow is fast enough.* New York: The Guilford Press.

Lazzari, A. (1991). *The transition sourcebook.* Tucson, AZ: Communication Skill Builders.

Urbano, M. T. (1992). *Preschool children with special health care needs.* San Diego: Singular Publishing Group, Inc.

Urbano, M. T. (1994). *Meeting early intervention challenges.* Baltimore: Paul H. Brookes.

References

Affleck, G., Tennen, H., Rowe, J., Roscher, B., Walker, L, & Higgins, P. (1989). Effects of formal support on mothers' adaptation to the hospital-to-home transition of high risk infants: The benefits and costs of helping. *Child Development, 60,* 488–501.

Bailey, D. B., Jr. (1989). Case management in early intervention. *Journal of Early Intervention, 13* (120–134).

Bailey, D. B., Jr., Jens, K., & Johnson, N. (1983). Curricula for handicapped infants. In S. Garwood & R. Fewell (Eds.), *Educating handicapped infants* (pp. 387–415). Germantown, MD: Aspen.

Baldwin, D. S., Jeffries, G. W., Jones, V. H., Thorp, E. K., & Walsh, S. A. (1992). Collaborative systems design for Part H of IDEA. *Infants and Young Children, 5*(1), 12–20.

Baroni, M. A., Tuthill, P., Feenan, L., & Schroeder, M. (1994). Technology-dependent infants and young children: A retrospective case analysis of service coordination across state lines. *Infants and Young Children, 7*(1), 69–78.

Beckman, P. J., Newcomb, S., Frank, H., Brown, L., & Filer, J. (1993). Providing support to families of infants with disabilities. *Journal of Early Intervention, 17*(4), 445–454.

Beckman, P. J., Robinson, C. C., Rosenberg, S., & Filer, J. (1994). Family involvement in early intervention: The evolution of family-centered service. In L. J. Johnson, R. J. Gallagher, M. J. LaMontagne, J. B. Jordan, J. J. Gallagher, P. L. Hutinger, & M. B. Karnes (Eds.), *Meeting early intervention challenges: Issues from birth to three.* Baltimore: Paul H. Brookes.

Blank, H. (1993). *Investing in our children's care: An analysis and review of state initiatives to strengthen the quality and build the supply of child care funded through the Child Care and Development Block Grant.* Washington, DC: Children's Defense Fund.

Bredekamp, S. (Ed.). (1987). *Developmentally appropriate practice in early childhood programs serving children from birth through age 8.* Washington, DC: National Association for the Education of Young Children.

Bricker, D. (1978). Rationale for the integration of handicapped and nonhandicapped preschool children. In M. Guralnick (Ed.), *Early intervention and the integration of handicapped and nonhandicapped preschool children.* Baltimore: University Park Press.

Brooks-Gunn, J., Gross, R. T., Kraemer, H. C., Spiker, D., & Shapiro, S. (1992). Enhancing the cognitive outcomes of low birth weight, premature infants: For whom is the intervention most effective? *Pediatrics, 89*(6), 1209–1215.

Bruder, M. B. (1993). *Child care for children with disabilities: Needs assessment of Connecticut.* Farmington, CT: Division of Child and Family Studies, University of Connecticut.

Bruder, M. B. (1994). Working with members of other disciplines: Collaboration for success. In M. Wolery & J. S. Wilbers (Eds.), *Including children with special needs in early childhood programs* (pp. 45–70). Washington, DC: National Association for the Education of Young Children.

Bruder, M. B., Anderson, R., Schutz, G., & Caldera, M. (1991). Ninos Especiales Program: A culturally sensitive early intervention model. *Journal of Early Intervention, 15*(3), 268–277.

Bruder, M. B., & Bologna, T. M. (1993). Collaboration and service coordination for effective early intervention. In W. Brown, S. K. Thurman, & L. Pearl (Eds.), *Family-centered early intervention with infants and toddlers: Innovative cross-disciplinary approaches.* Baltimore: Paul H. Brookes.

Bruder, M. B., & Chandler, L. (1996). Transition. In S. Odom & M. McLean (Eds.), *Recommended practices in early intervention.* Austin, TX: PRO-ED.

Bruder, M. B., Deiner, P., & Sachs, S. (1990). Models of integration through early intervention/child care collaboration. *Zero to Three, 10*(3), 14–17.

Bruder, M. B., & Walker, L. (1990). Discharge planning: Hospital to home transitions for infants. *Topics in Early Childhood Special Education, 9*(4), 26–42.

Buswell, B., & Schaffner, C. B. (1990). Families supporting inclusive schooling. In S. Stainback & W. Stainback (Eds.), *Support networks for inclusive schooling* (pp. 219–230). Baltimore: Paul H. Brookes.

Campbell, P. H. (1991). Evaluation and assessment in early intervention for infants and toddlers. *Journal of Early Intervention, 15*(1), 36–45.

Carta, J. J. (1994). Developmentally appropriate practices: Shifting the emphasis to individual appropriateness. *Journal of Early Intervention, 18*(4), 342–343.

Chandler, L. K. (1992). Promoting young children's social competence as a strategy for transition to mainstreamed kindergarten program. In S. L. Odom, S. R. McConnell, & M. A. McEvoy (Eds.), *Social competence of young children with disabilities* (pp. 245–276). Baltimore: Paul H. Brookes.

DEC. (1993). DEC position statement on inclusion. *DEC Communicator, 19*(4), 4.

DEC Task Force on Recommended Practices. (1993). *DEC recommended practices: Indicators of quality in programs for infants and young children with special needs and their families.* Reston, VA: Council for Exceptional Children.

Dunst, C. (1985). Rethinking early intervention. *Analysis and Intervention in Developmental Disabilities, 5*, 165–201.

Dunst, C. J., Trivette, C. M., & Deal, A. G. (1994). *Supporting and strengthening families: Vol. 1. Methods, strategies and practices.* Cambridge, MA: Brookline.

Fowler, S. A. (1992). Transition from preschool to kindergarten for children with special needs. In K. E. Allen & E. M. Goetz (Eds.), *Early childhood education: Special problems, special solutions* (pp. 309–330). Rockville, MD: Aspen.

Garland, C. W., & Linder, T. W. (1994). Administrative challenges in early intervention. In L. J. Johnson, R. J. Gallagher, M. J. LaMontagne, J. B. Jordan, P. L. Hutinger, J. J. Gallagher, & M. B. Karnes (Eds.), *Meeting early intervention challenges: Issues from birth to three* (pp. 133–166). Baltimore: Paul H. Brookes.

Garwood, G. (1982). Early childhood intervention: Is it time to change outcome variables? *Topics in Early Childhood Special Education, 1*, ix–xi.

Green, A. L., & Stoneman, Z. (1989). Attitudes of mothers and fathers of non-handicapped children towards preschool mainstreaming. *Journal of Early Intervention, 13*(4), 292–304.

Guess, D., & Horner, R. D. (1978). The severely and profoundly handicapped. In E. L. Meyer (Ed.), *Exceptional children and youth—An introduction* (pp. 218–268). Denver: Love.

Guralnick, J. J., Connor, R. T., & Hammond, M. (1995). Parent perspectives of peer relationships and friendships in integrated and specialized programs. *American Journal on Mental Retardation, 99*(5), 457–476.

Guralnick, M. (1988). Efficacy research in early childhood intervention programs. In S. Odom & M. Karnes (Eds.), *Early intervention for infants and children with handicaps: An empirical base* (pp. 75–88). Baltimore: Paul H. Brookes.

Guralnick, M. (1989). Recent developments in early intervention efficacy research: Implications for family involvement in P.L. 99-457. *Topics in Early Childhood Special Education, 9*(3), 1–17.

Guralnick, M. J. (1990). Social competence and early intervention. *Journal of Early Intervention, 14*(1), 3–14.

Guralnick, M. J. (1994). Mothers' perceptions of the benefits and drawbacks of early childhood mainstreaming. *Journal of Early Intervention, 18*(2), 168–183.

Halvorsen, A., & Sailor, W. (1990). Integration of students with profound disabilities: A review of the research. In R. Gaylord-Ross (Ed.), *Issues and research in special education* (pp. 110–172). New York: Teachers College Press.

Hanson, J., & Lynch, E. (1989). *Early intervention: Implementing child and family services for infants and toddlers who are at-risk or disabled.* Austin, TX: PRO-ED.

Harms, T., & Clifford, R. (1980). *The Early Childhood Environment Rating Scale (ECERS).* New York: Teachers College Press, Columbia University.

Healy, A., Keesee, P. D., & Smith, B. S. (1989). *Early services for children with special needs: Transactions for family support* (2nd ed.). Baltimore: Paul H. Brookes.

Hemmeter, M. L., & Kaiser, A. P. (1994). Enhanced milieu teaching: Effects of parent-implemented language intervention. *Journal of Early Intervention, 18*(3), 269–289.

Hutchinson, D. (1978). The transdisciplinary approach. In J. Curry & K. Peppe (Eds.), *Mental retardation: Nursing approaches to care* (pp. 65–74). St. Louis: Mosby.

Hutinger, P. (1987). Computer-based learning for young children. In J. L. Roopnarine & J. E. Johnson (Eds.), *Approaches to early childhood education* (pp. 213–234). Columbus, OH: Merrill.

Hutinger, P., Robinson, L., & Clark, L. (1990). *Technology applications to meet training challenges.* Macomb, IL: Macomb Projects, Western Illinois University.

Hutinger, P., & Ward, E. (1988). *Technology for the preschool handicapped classroom: New learning tools to assist the teacher.* Paper presented at CEC/TAM Conference on Special Education and Technology, Reno, NV.

Johnson, C. B. (1993). Developmental issues: Children infected with human immunodeficiency virus. *Infants and Young Children, 6*(1), 1–10.

Johnson, L. J. (1988). Program evaluation: The key to quality programming. In J. Jordan, J. Gallagher, P. Hutinger, & M. Karnes (Eds.), *Early childhood special education: Birth to three* (pp. 183–212). Reston, VA: Council for Exceptional Children.

Johnson, L. J., & LaMontagne, M. J. (1994). Program evaluation: The key to quality programming. In L. J. Johnson, R. J. Gallagher, M. J. LaMontagne, J. B. Jordan, J. J. Gallagher, P. L. Hutinger, & M. B. Karnes (Eds.), *Meeting early intervention challenges: Issues from birth to three* (pp. 185–216). Baltimore: Paul H. Brookes.

Kagan, S. L. (1991). *United we stand: Collaboration for child care and early intervention and education services.* New York: Teachers College Press.

Kirk, S. A. (1958). *Early education of the mentally retarded: An experimental study.* Urbana: University of Illinois Press.

Kramer, S., McGonigel, M. J., & Kaufmann, R. K. (1991). Developing the IFSP: Outcomes, strategies, activities, and services. In M. J. McGonigel, R. K. Kaufmann, & B. H. Johnson (Eds.), *Guidelines and recommended practices for the individualized family service plan* (pp. 57–66). Bethesda, MD: Association for the Care of Children's Health.

Lally, J. R., Mangione, P., Honig, A. S., & Wittmer, D. S. (1992). More pride, less delinquency: Findings from the ten-year-follow-up study of the Syracuse University Family Development Research Program. In *Zero to Three Child Care Anthology.* Arlington, VA: Zero to Three.

Lazar, I., & Darlington, R. (1978). *Lasting effects after preschool* (DHEW Publication No. 79-30178). Washington, DC: U.S. Department of Health, Education, and Welfare, Office of Human Development Services, Administration for Children, Youth, and Families.

Lesser, A. J. (1985). The origin and development of maternal and child health programs in the United States. *American Journal of Public Health, 75,* 590–598.

Levy, S. E., & Pilmer, S. L. (1992). The technology-assisted child. In M. C. Batshaw & Y. M. Perret (Eds.), *Children with disabilities: A medical primer* (pp. 137–157). Baltimore: Paul H. Brookes.

Linder, T. W. (1990). *Transdisciplinary play-based assessment.* Baltimore: Paul H. Brookes.

Lynch, E., & Hanson, M. (1992). *Developing cross cultural competence: A guide for working with young children and their families.* Baltimore: Paul H. Brookes.

Maddux, R. B. (1988). *Team building: An exercise in leadership.* Los Altos, CA: Crisp Publications.

McBride, S. L., Brotherson, M. J., Jaonning, H., Whiddon, D., & Demmitt, A. (1993). Implementation of family-centered services: Perceptions of families and professionals. *Journal of Early Intervention, 17*(4), 414–430.

McCormick, L. (1987). Comparison of the effects of a microcomputer activity and toy play on social and communication behaviors of young children. *Journal of the Division for Early Childhood, 11*(3), 195–205.

McDonnell, A., & Hardman, M. (1988). A synthesis of "best practice" guidelines for early childhood services. *Journal of the Division for Early Childhood, 12*(4), 328–341.

McGonigel, M. J., Woodruff, G., & Roszmann-Millican, M. (1994). The transdisciplinary team: A model for family-centered early intervention. In L. J. Johnson, R. J. Gallagher, M. J. LaMontagne, J. B. Jordan, P. L. Hutinger, J. J. Gallagher, & M. B. Karnes (Eds.), *Meeting early intervention challenges: Issues from birth to three* (pp. 95–131). Baltimore: Paul H. Brookes.

McLean, M., Bailey, D., & Wolery, M. (1996). *Assessment of infants and preschoolers with special needs*. Englewood Cliffs, NJ: Merrill/Prentice-Hall.

McLean, M., & McCormick, K. (1993). Assessment and evaluation in early intervention. In W. Brown, S. K. Thurman, & L. F. Pearl (Eds.), *Family-centered early intervention with infants and toddlers: Innovative cross-disciplinary approaches* (pp. 43–79). Baltimore: Paul H. Brookes.

McLean, M. E., & Odom, S. L. (1993). Practices for young children with and without disabilities: A comparison of DEC and NAEYC identified practices. *Topics in Early Childhood Special Education, 13*(3), 274–292.

Meisels, S., & Provence, S. (1989). *Screening and assessment: Guidelines for identifying young disabled and developmentally vulnerable children and their families*. Washington, DC: National Center for Clinical Infant Programs.

Meisels, S. J., Dichtelmiller, M., & Liaw, F. (1993). A multidimensional analysis of early childhood intervention programs. In C. H. Zeanah (Ed.), *Handbook of infant mental health* (pp. 361–385). New York: Guilford.

Meisels, S. J., & Wasik, B. A. (1990). Who should be served? Identifying young children in need of early intervention. In S. J. Meisels & J. P. Shonkoff (Eds.), *Handbook of early childhood intervention*. New York: Cambridge University Press.

Mulligan, M., & Guess, D. (1984). Using an individualized curriculum sequence model. In L. McCormick & R. L. Schiefelbusch (Eds.), *Early language intervention* (pp. 300–323). Columbus, OH: Merrill.

Murphy, D. L., Lee, I. M., Turnbull, A. P., & Turbiville, V. (1995). The Family-Centered Program Rating Scale: An instrument for program evaluation and change. *Journal of Early Intervention, 19*(1), 24–42.

Noonan, M., & Kilgo, J. L. (1987). Transition services for early age individuals with severe mental retardation. In R. Ianacone & R. Stodden (Eds.), *Transition issues and directions* (pp. 25–37). Reston, VA: Council for Exceptional Children.

Noonan, M., & McCormick, L. (1992). A naturalistic curriculum model for early intervention. *The Transdisciplinary Journal, 2*(3), 147–159.

Noonan, M., & McCormick, L. (1993a). *Early intervention in natural environments: Methods and procedures*. Belmont, CA: Wadsworth.

Noonan, M. J., & McCormick, L. (1993b). Naturalistic Curriculum Model. In *Early Intervention in Natural Environments: Methods & Procedures* (pp. 129–161). Pacific Grove, CA: Brooks/Cole.

Odom, S., McConnell, S., & McEvoy, M. (1992). *Social competence of young children with disabilities: Issues and strategies for intervention*. Baltimore: Paul H. Brookes.

Odom, S., & Warren, S. (1988). Early childhood special education in the year 2000. *Journal of the Division of Early Childhood, 12*(3), 263–273.

Odom, S. L., McLean, M. E., Johnson, L. J., & LaMontagne, M. J. (1995). Recommended practices in early childhood special education: Validation and current use. *Journal of Early Intervention, 19*(1), 1–17.

Peck, C. A., Carlson, P., & Helmstetter, E. (1992). Parent and teacher perceptions of outcomes for typically developing children enrolled in integrated early childhood programs: A statewide survey. *Journal of Early Intervention, 16*(1), 53–63.

Peterson, M., Leroy, B., Field, S., & Wood, P. (1992). Community-referenced learning in inclusive schools: Effective curriculum for all students. In S. Stainback & W. Stainback (Eds.), *Curriculum considerations in inclusive classroom* (pp. 207–228). Baltimore: Paul H. Brookes.

Peterson, N. (1987). *Early intervention for handicapped and at-risk children*. Denver: Love.

Ramey, C. T., Bryant, D. M., Wasik, B. H., Sparling, J. J., Fendt, K. H., & LaVange, L. M. (1992). The Infant Health and Development Program for low birthweight, premature infants: Program elements, family participation, and child intelligence. *Pediatrics, 89*, 454–465.

Reed, P., & Bowser, G. (1991). *The role of occupational and physical therapy in assistive technology*. Ralston, VA: Center for Special Education Technology.

Richmond, J. B., Stipek, D. J., & Zigler, E. (1979). A decade of Head Start. In E. Zigler & J. Valentine (Eds.), *Project Head Start: A legacy of the war on poverty*. New York: Free Press.

Rosenkoetter, S. E. (1992). Guidelines from recent legislation to structure transition planning. *Infants and Young Children, 5*(1), 21–27.

Salisbury, C. L. (1991). Mainstreaming during the early childhood years. *Exceptional Children, 58*(2), 146–155.

Salisbury, C. L., & Vincent, L. J. (1990). Criterion of the next environment and best practices: Mainstreaming and integration 10 years later. *Topics in Early Childhood Special Education, 10*(2), 78–79.

Sameroff, A., & Chandler, M. (1975). Reproductive risk and the continuum of caretaking casualty. In F. Horowitz (Ed.), *Review of child development research*. Chicago: University of Chicago Press.

Schweinhart, L. J., Barnes, H. V., & Weikart, D. P. (Eds.). (1993). *Significant benefits: The High/Scope Perry Preschool study through age 27*. Ypsilanti, MI: High/Scope Press.

Scott, K., & Masi, W. (1979). The outcome from the utility of registers of risk. In T. Field, A. Sostek, S. Goldberg, & H. Shuman (Eds.), *Infants born at risk* (pp. 485–496). Jamaica, NY: Spectrum.

Shelton, T., Jeppson, E., & Johnson, B. (1987). *Family-centered care for children with special health care needs* (2nd ed.). Washington, DC: Association for the Care of Children's Health.

Shonkoff, J. P., Hauser-Cram, P. Krauss, M. W., & Upshur, C. C. (1992). Development of infants with disabilities and their families: Implications for theory and service delivery. *Monographs of the Society for Research in Child Development, 57*(6, Serial No. 230).

Sigel, I. (1972). Developmental theory: Its place, the relevance in early intervention programs. *Young Children, 27,* 364–372.

Skeels, H. M., & Dye, H. B. (1939). A study of the effects of differential stimulation on mentally retarded children. *Proceedings and Addresses of the American Association on Mental Deficiency, 44,* 114–136.

Smith, A., & Hawkins, P. (1992). State-wide systems change: A federal strategy for integration and inclusion. In P. Karasoff, M. Alwell, & A. Halvorsen (Eds.), *Systems change: A review of effective practices* (pp. ii–iv). San Francisco: San Francisco State University.

Snyder, P., Bailey, D. B., & Auer, C. (1994). Preschool eligibility determination for children with known or suspected learning disabilities under IDEA. *Journal of Early Intervention, 18*(4), 380–390.

Spiegel-McGill, P., Zippiroli, S. M., & Mistrett, S. G. (1989). Microcomputers as social facilitators in integrated preschools. *Journal of Early Intervention, 13*(3), 249–260.

Spitz, R. A. (1947). Hospitalism: A follow-up report. In *Psychoanalytic Studies of the Child.* New York: International Universities Press.

Sullivan, M., & Lewis, M. (1990). Contingency intervention: A program portrait. *Journal of Early Intervention, 14*(4), 367–375.

Sullivan, M. W., & Lewis, M. (1993). Contingency, means-end skills, and the use of technology in infant intervention. *Infants and Young Children, 5*(4), 58–77.

Thousand, J. S., Villa, R. A., & Nevin, A. I. (Eds.). (1994). *Creativity and collaborative learning: A practical guide to empowering students and teachers.* Baltimore: Paul H. Brookes.

Tjossem, T. D. (1976). Early Intervention: Issues and approaches. In T. D. Tjossem (Ed.), *Intervention strategies for high risk infants and young children.* Baltimore: University Park Press.

Trohanis, P. L. (1989). An introduction to P.L. 99-457 and the national policy agenda for service young children with special needs and their families. In J. J. Gallagher, P. L. Trohanis, & R. M. Clifford (Eds.), *Policy implementation and P.L. 99-457.* Baltimore: Paul H. Brookes.

Turnbull, A., & Turnbull, H. (1990). *Families, professionals and exceptionality: A special partnership.* Columbus, OH: Merrill.

Turnbull, A., & Winton, P. (1983). A comparison of specialized and mainstreamed preschools from the perspectives of mothers of handicapped children. *Journal of Pediatric Psychology, 8*(1), 57–71.

Wesley, P. W. (1994). Providing on-site consultation to promote quality in integrated child care programs. *Journal of Early Intervention, 18*(4), 391–402.

Westinghouse Learning Corporation. (1969). *The impact of Head Start: An evaluation of the effects of Head Start on children's cognitive and affective development: Executive summary.* (Reports to the Office of Economic Opportunity). Athens: Ohio University. (ERIC Document Reproduction Service No. ED 036 321)

Wolery, M. (1989). Transition in early childhood special education: Issues and procedures. *Focus on Exceptional Children, 22,* 1–16.

Wolery, M., & Bredekamp, S. (1994). Developmentally appropriate practices and young children with disabilities: Contextual issues in the discussion. *Journal of Early Intervention, 18*(4), 331–341.

Wolery, M., & Sainato, D. M. (1996). General curriculum and intervention strategies. In S. Odom & M. McLean (Eds.), *Recommended practices in early intervention.* Austin, TX: PRO-ED.

Woodruff, G. (1994). Serving the needs of children with AIDS and their families: A case for comprehensive community-based and family-centered programs. *Teaching Exceptional Children, 26*(4), 45–48.

Chapter 15

World Unity, acrylic on canvas, 38″ × 50″ (1992)

TRANSITION FROM SCHOOL TO ADULTHOOD

PAUL WEHMAN

After studying this chapter, the reader will:

Be able to define and describe the importance of
transition from school to adulthood

Be able to discuss how a core transition team works together
in the community for planning transition services

Describe the major components of an Individualized Education
Program and an Individualized Transition Plan

Know the critical characteristics of an effective
vocational training program

TRANSITION FROM SCHOOL TO ADULTHOOD

1983

The U.S. Department of Education identified transition from school to work as a major federal priority.

1986

Through passage of the Rehabilitation Act, supported employment emerged as a national work option for people with severe disabilities.

1990

The Individuals With Disabilities Education Act (IDEA) was passed, mandating individual transition planning for all young people with disabilities.

1993

The School to Work Opportunities Act was passed, making $300 million annually available to the states for transition planning for individuals with disabilities.

INTRODUCTION

Michael is a 20-year-old man with mental retardation. He has always needed some help and support from his family and the community. Michael will leave his school program in the upcoming year. Michael's teacher, Mr. Wilson, is concerned about what he will do after he leaves school, but no formal plans have been made to get the local rehabilitation services agency involved. In fact, Michael is receiving no specific job training other than an hour each day in a simulated sheltered workshop program in the classroom, putting paper clips into a box and then taking them out. Michael's teacher knows this "job" isn't like working in the community, but he doesn't know what to do differently.

Michael's parents are worried because they don't want him to sit at home all day after he reaches age 21, and they know that Michael is not legally entitled to any services after he leaves school. At the local sheltered workshop they visited, they were told that Michael was probably not skilled enough to be placed on the workshop's permanent production client load. The workshop indicated, however, that Michael may be able to receive a work evaluation in conjunction with the rehabilitation services agency. At the local adult day center, Michael's parents learned that the center provides no opportunity for competitive employment and that 20 people were already on a waiting list ahead of him. Michael and his parents attended a national conference of the Association for Persons in Supported Employment and learned that supported employment is a way to help individuals like Michael enter the competitive job market. However, they did not know of any such programs where they lived.

EASY IDEAS FOR PRACTITIONERS

1. Reach out to all local and four-year community colleges in the area to establish visitation experiences, internship experiences, selected course offerings, exchange programs, and guidance counselor and admission counselor training options.
2. Closely network with the County Chamber of Commerce, as well as the Retail Merchants Association, and other possible employers in the local area for youth with disabilities.
3. Working agreements need to be established, if they have not been already, with the County Community Services Board as well as the Department of Vocational Rehabilitation, Department of Social Services, and any other relevant agencies to help in the successful transition from school into adulthood.
4. Establish agreements and connections with local trade schools, business schools, and training centers who will enroll local youth with disabilities who are in their final years of education as interns or students.
5. Commit to including students with disabilities, to the extent that is best for the student, into general education classroom and activities.
6. All youth with disabilities in the county should have transition plans as part of the individual education plan that highlights some or all of these specific points above.
7. The county public schools should track the post-21 outcomes of students with disabilities that are leaving their program.

Larry is a 21-year-old male who has a disability label of intermittent explosive disorder and mental retardation. He has a history of behavioral and emotional difficulties and uncontrollable anger with repeated psychiatric hospitalizations since he was 5 years old. Larry has attended special education classes for emotionally disturbed students since the fourth grade, and during his last 5 years of school he attended a special education center for students with disabilities. He participated in a work experience through his school as a food service worker in a cafeteria. At age 17, Larry was referred for vocational evaluation through the vocational rehabilitation agency. Unfortunately, this experience was terminated prematurely due to aggressive and inappropriate behaviors. He also participated in short-term work adjustment training and assessment at a sheltered workshop.

During his last year in school, Larry was referred for supported employment services by his vocational rehabilitation counselor. The job coach conducted a home visit, community assessment, and situational assessment. Larry repeatedly expressed a desire to work as a bagger in a grocery store, and the job coach was able to find such a position within a short amount of time. Larry began working 20 hours a week, earning $4.35 an hour. He received training for his job duties by coworker mentors as well as the company supervisor and job coach. Additional supports were provided through the purchase of a raincoat, an umbrella, and a lock (so Larry could store

some personal possessions at work). In addition, the job coach provided training and advocacy in response to Larry's hanging out with coworkers during work hours and frequently requesting to leave work. Within 3 months, Larry received a raise to $4.55 an hour and began working 25 hours a week. However, he was terminated after approximately 6 months for stealing an item from the store.

Larry received assistance and found a second job within a month. He was hired as a back line cook at McDonald's, working 25 hours a week and earning $4.25 an hour. Training was provided by coworkers as well as the job coach. A discussion with Larry following an explosive episode at work (and Larry's near hospitalization) indicated a desire to have some weekend nights off. The job coach advocated with the employer to give Larry one weekend night off a month, which was color-coded on a small calendar to be carried in Larry's wallet. In addition, a proactive effort to avoid Larry's typical pattern of hospitalizations was implemented through negotiations with the employer. Arrangements were made and scheduled in advance for Larry to take one week's vacation without pay every 3 months. This was also color-coded on the calendar, as a reminder that time off was close at hand when frustration or dissatisfaction at work escalated. The employer gave Larry the option to increase or decrease the amount of time off as he wanted; however, at the first scheduled time Larry only took 3 days, and since then he has chosen not to take advantage of the prearranged time off.

The flexibility and support offered to Larry have enabled him to continue transitioning into the world of work.

Unfortunately, Michael's situation is not unusual. Although the goal of our educational system is to help students become productive members of society as adults, few schools have guided students with disabilities into meaningful employment opportunities appropriate for their abilities. Because most students who have a disability—especially those with severe disabilities—do not benefit from the systematic transition from school to work, approximately 50% to 75% of all adults with disabilities are unemployed (Louis Harris Poll, 1991). Until recently, most parents of children with disabilities rarely considered the possibility of a career for their children after graduation. A career was viewed as highly unlikely or impractical, and even as irresponsible in the sense that expectations are falsely raised for the student.

For a transition such as Michael's to proceed smoothly, a number of changes must occur in the way we help our citizens who have disabilities to secure meaningful, competitive employment, as well as move into adulthood with minimal difficulties. First, school programming must be revamped to include a functional curriculum that reflects community-based job training or paid employment. Second, parents and professionals must develop formal written Individualized Transition Plans (ITPs) (e.g., Wehman, 1995) that will serve as a blueprint for the future, much like an architect would write a plan for building a house. These plans serve as part of the legally mandated Individualized Education Program (IEP), which is the written overall program for the student. Third, schools and community agencies will have to work with businesses and other agencies in the community to develop a variety of meaningful employment and living options for citizens with disabilities.

It is the purpose of this chapter to help educators, parents, and students learn the importance of transition planning for young adults like Michael.

HISTORICAL OVERVIEW

It has been two decades since the implementation of Public Law 94-142, the Education for All Handicapped Children Act of 1975—revised in 1990 and renamed the Individuals With Disabilities Education Act (IDEA). The first generation of students served by legally mandated and federally funded educational services is now graduating from school. These young adults, as well as their parents and the professionals who work with them, have begun to realize that "appropriate" education does not always translate into meaningful employment and community living opportunities. Individuals who have grown accustomed to legally mandated educational services are often shocked to learn that adult services are not automatically provided by vocational rehabilitation agencies, community mental health agencies, or mental retardation agencies to the citizen with disabilities. Employment, which is often an assumed outcome of American public education, is not a reality for an estimated 50% to 75% of adults with disabilities (Harris, 1994).

As thousands of young adults leave school, they are turning to their local community for additional vocational training, community college experience, trade schools, and job placement assistance. Although funding sources and the services provided by these programs differ from state to state, research shows that the majority of individuals are still in segregated day programs, on waiting lists, or are underemployed in low-paying jobs with no career path. Furthermore, special day centers promote dependence, with participants receiving zero or very low wages, slow or no movement into less restrictive employment options, and segregation from peers without disabilities and community resources (Braddock, 1994; Hayden & Abery, 1994; Wilcox & Bellamy, 1982a). In the United States today, well over 65% of all adults with disabilities are currently unemployed (Bowe, 1993). Additionally, the more severe the disability, the more unlikely it is that the individual will gain competitive employment.

Parents, politicians, and professionals have not ignored this lack of a coordinated and systematically planned transition from school to work. A growing body of literature, in both the education and rehabilitation fields, has begun to focus on the need to provide formal and longitudinal transition services throughout the school years and during the transition from school to adult services for individuals with disabilities. On the federal level, both the Office of Special Education and Rehabilitative Services (OSERS) and the Administration on Developmental Disabilities (ADD) have made it clear that transition from school to adult services is a very

This man is working in a sheltered workshop for adults with disabilities.

important priority. Congressional hearings were held for much of 1994 as the House Subcommittee on Select Education and Civil Rights considered IDEA reauthorization. In addition to IDEA, Congress has also passed the School to Work Opportunities Act of 1993, (P.L. 103-239), a $300 million a year program for all young adults with disabilities, to be administered by the U.S. Department of Labor. The purpose of this law is to expand career opportunities for students during their transition from school to adulthood. It is particularly important because it provides significant resources to local communities and businesses to foster employment and vocational training.

The issues and legislation described here point to increasing awareness of the problems in making the transition from school to adulthood for young people with disabilities. It is perhaps one of the more significant initiatives of the past decade and represents an issue that all educators in the field of disabilities will encounter. IDEA mandates that one of the purposes of the annual IEP meeting for students with disabilities reaching 16 years of age will be to plan needed transition services. Sections 300.346 and 300.18 of the law state:

> The IEP for each student, beginning no later than age 16 (and at a younger age, if determined appropriate), must include a statement of transition services. (Individuals With Disabilities Education Act of 1990, Sec. 300.346)

> (a) As used in this part, "transition services" means a coordinated set of activities for a student, designed within an outcome-oriented process that promotes movement from school to post-school activities, including postsecondary education, vocational training, integrated employment (including supported employment), continuing and adult education, adult services, independent living, or community participation.

> (b) The coordinated set of activities described in paragraph (a) of this section must:

(1) Be based on the individual student's needs, taking into account the student's preferences and interests; and

(2) Include (i) instruction, (ii) community experiences, (iii), the development of employment and other post-school objectives, and (iv) if appropriate, acquisition of daily living skills and functional vocational evaluation. (Individuals With Disabilities Education Act of 1990, Sec. 300.18)

In effect, this means that, at a minimum, for *all* identified students with disabilities who have reached the age of 16, the educational team must consider each student's **transition** needs in the areas of instruction, community experiences, employment, and other post-school goals.

THE TRANSITION PROCESS

The IEP and the ITP

The **Individualized Education Program (IEP)** has been required since P.L. 94-142 was passed in 1975. It is a legally binding document that describes the student's annual goals and short-term objectives, along with a detailed level of performance assessment and whatever diagnostic data are necessary. The IEP can be enforced through due process and an entire range of complaints that can advance to the federal court level. The IEP is a very important document because of the legal requirements associated with it, and most school systems have learned that they must be responsible for what is on the IEP.

On the other hand, the **Individualized Transition Plan (ITP)** is new. The ITP is not legally required in the same way as an IEP, nor does it hold the specificity of structure that the IEP holds. Furthermore, the concept of an ITP was only recently introduced, in the 1990 passage of IDEA; previously, the concept of transition was discussed in a more general or theoretical way. School systems do not have a statutory responsibility to provide any form of written transition plan.

Conversations with many teachers and other educational personnel have made it patently clear that the ITP is all too often only a stepchild to the IEP. It is not uncommon in a school system for the IEP meeting to last an hour or more—and then be followed by a 15- to 30-minute ITP meeting. This practice is most unfortunate, because the idea underlying the ITP is to create a design or blueprint with a futures orientation and in collaboration with the student and family. This task can hardly be achieved in 15 or 30 minutes.

The development of functional and highly useful goals for a student is the most important aspect of the ITP. In Virginia, Elizabeth Getzel and her associates (personal communication, April 16, 1994) reviewed more than 1,700 ITPs and found that more than half did not include a career objective goal. This is precisely the problem with ITPs in most parts of the United States. The typical ITP team is not using this planning time with parents and families to identify important employment, career education, financial, social, transportation, and other goals necessary for success in adulthood. A major focal point of this chapter is the inclusion of significant numbers of useful goals for the diverse population of students with disabilities.

An individualized transition plan is developed and implemented to ensure systematic transition from school to supported employment and adult services once students leave school. The ITP may be incorporated as part of a student's Individualized Education Program during the secondary years. By targeting a student early

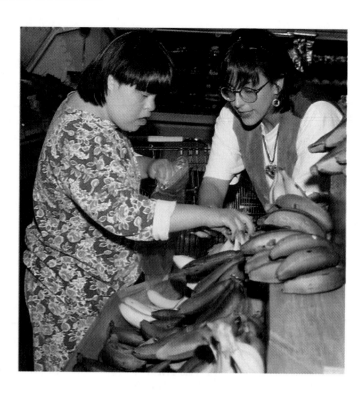

One of Susan's goals is learning to choose healthy foods.

in the secondary years for transition services, parents, school personnel, and adult services providers from various disciplines and agencies will be required to work together in the decision making and service provision required for successful transition. To illustrate, consider the ITP for Susan, shown in Figure 15.1. What follows is a description of how Susan received transition services.

Susan is a 19-year-old student with Down syndrome who is enrolled in a self-contained special education classroom in a regular high school. Her native language is Spanish. Psychological testing has placed her in the low to moderate range of mental retardation. She has been a student in a classroom for students with mental retardation for 13 years. Susan is involved 4 days a week in a community-based vocational training program in which she is learning some of the skills required for food service occupations. Her teacher feels that Susan has demonstrated much progress in the food service training program and thinks that competitive employment might be possible.

Susan's parents have never given much thought to competitive employment but rather have been planning for Susan to attend the local sheltered workshop. Lately, however, they have become discouraged about a place for Susan at the sheltered workshop, as there is currently a waiting list of approximately 30 individuals. Even more individuals from her graduating class will be competing with Susan for the slots. Her parents have also looked into a day activity center in their community. They were very disappointed to find out that they would have to pay a fee for Susan to be able to go to the day activity center. Because school had always been a free service, they were surprised to find out that Susan would not necessarily be entitled to free services as an adult.

Susan's teacher has not yet talked with the parents about post-school plans for Susan. She also has not contacted the rehabilitation counselor assigned to the school, as this is a routine task handled by a guidance counselor who works with the

Figure 15.1   **Sample ITP (for Susan)**

INDIVIDUALIZED TRANSITION PLAN

Student's Name: _____Garcia_____ _____Susan_____ ___L.___

  Last **First** **M.I.**

Birthdate: _____8/11/76_____ **School:** _____Reedsville_____

Student's I.D. #: _____652_____ **ITP Conference Date:** _____9/10/94_____

Participants

Name	Position
Jake & Linda Garcia	Parents
Amanda Jones	Teacher
Sharon Silvia	Case Manager
Berta Lowe	Interpreter

	Date Initiated	Date Completed
1. Referral to Vocational Rehabilitation Services	9/94	
2. SSI/SSDI	9/94	
3. Medical/Medicine		
4. Referral to Local Social Services		
5. Application for Special Transportation		
6. Referral to Residential Services for Housing Placement		
7. Referral to Center for Independent Living (CIL)	9/94	
8. Referral to Rehabilitation Engineering Services		
9. Referral to MH/MR Case Management Services	6/91	

INDIVIDUALIZED TRANSITION PLAN

STUDENT PROFILE

Susan is an 18-year-old student with Down syndrome. She moved from Mexico to the United States with her family 3 years ago. Susan's native language is Spanish but she has limited routine utterances in both Spanish and English. She cannot read and has no math skills. Her family is large and of low income. Susan has a limited array of community living skills and very little confidence in her ability to be an independent worker yet wants to have a job. She has a diabetic condition, in addition to mental retardation, which will require her to become capable of maintaining an appropriate diet.

INDIVIDUALIZED TRANSITION PLAN

I. CAREER AND ECONOMIC SELF-SUFFICIENCY

1. **Employment Goal:** Susan will work in the hospitality industry, initially as a food service worker.

Level of Present Performance: Susan has worked in the dishrooms of two area restaurants as a member of school work crews.

Steps Needed to Accomplish Goal: (1) Schedule time for counselor to observe Susan while she's working. (2) Arrange for transportation. (3) Make connection with another employee who speaks Spanish to be a "mentor" to Susan.

Date of Completion: 10/1/94

Person(s) Responsible for Implementation: Rehabilitation counselor, teacher.

2. **Vocational Education/Training Goals:** Susan will work independently in a school cafeteria dishroom approx. 3 hours per day and receive pay via work-study.

Level of Present Performance: Susan has worked at a variety of unpaid sites as part of a 4-member work crew. She works for approximately 2-hour sessions.

Steps Needed to Accomplish Goal: (1) Contact cafeteria manager. (2) Train Susan at designated site. (3) Systematically fade supervision and assistance. (4) Obtain necessary I.D. information for payroll.

Date of Completion: 12/1/94

Person(s) Responsible for Implementation: Work coordinator (if available) or vocational teacher.

3. **Postsecondary Education Goal:** Susan will continue to add to her English vocabulary.

Level of Present Performance: Susan has communication deficits and speaks very little English. Her native language is Spanish, which is the dominant language at home.

Steps Needed to Accomplish Goal: (1) Enroll in an English class offered by County Dept. of Adult Ed. (2) Attend class with family member.

Date of Completion: 1/1/95

Person(s) Responsible for Implementation: Case manager, family.

4. **Financial/Income Needs Goal:** Susan will partially provide for her personal needs such as recreation and clothing.

Level of Present Performance: Susan currently does not have an income. She has many recreational interests. Her family is large and has a low income.

Steps Needed to Accomplish Goal: (1) Apply for SSI. (2) Assist her in opening savings account. (3) Assist her in the maintenance of the account.

Date of Completion: 3/1/95

Person(s) Responsible for Implementation: Family, case manager.

Individualized Transition Plan
II. Community Integration and Participation

5.   **Independent Living Goal:** To live in a supervised apartment with 1–2 housemates near her family.

Level of Present Performance: Susan is the youngest of a large supportive family. She is independent in daily self-care and domestic chores. She cannot cook or budget money.

Steps Needed to Accomplish Goal: (1) Locate an appropriate residential placement. (2) Apply for occupancy. (3) Provide initial training for Susan in the apartment once placed.

Date of Completion: 5/1/95

Person(s) Responsible for Implementation: Case manager, designee for Center for Independent Living.

6.   **Transportation Mobility/Goal:** Susan will be able to use public transportation independently to travel to and from work.

Level of Present Performance: Susan walks from her home to nearby convenience stores. She is dependent for all other travel.

Steps Needed to Accomplish Goal: (1) Provide bus training to and from work. (2) Provide bus training to 2 community-based instruction sites currently used.

Date of Completion:

Person(s) Responsible for Implementation: Rehabilitation counselor, teacher.

7.   **Social Relationship Goal:** She will interact appropriately with male acquaintances.

Level of Present Performance: Susan is very sociable and often inappropriately affectionate with male classmates and staff.

Steps Needed to Accomplish Goal: (1) Continue to attend Family Life classes at school. (2) Attend CIL workshop on Human Sexuality with parent.

Date of Completion: 3/95

Person(s) Responsible for Implementation: Family, teacher.

8.   **Recreation/Leisure Goal:** Participate weekly in integrated sports activities.

Level of Present Performance: Susan has no physical limitations, is energetic, but lacks skills to fully participate in sports.

Steps Needed to Accomplish Goal: (1) Learn 2 sports activites (swimming, bowling). (2) Arrange for transportation to facilities. (3) Budget funds for swimming and bowling fees.

Date of Completion: 12/94

Person(s) Responsible for Implementation: Physical education teacher, family.

INDIVIDUALIZED TRANSITION PLAN

III. PERSONAL COMPETENCE

9.   **Health/Safety Goal:** Susan will maintain proper diet to control diabetes.

   Level of Present Performance: Susan eats healthy foods and proper proportions but likes to use vending machines for snacks. She depends on others to prepare meals.

   Steps Needed to Accomplish Goal: (1) Teach Susan to choose diet sodas in vending machines. (2) Use picture list to make healthy choices in restaurants and grocery stores. (3) Continue instruction in simple meal preparations.

   Date of Completion: 10/94

   Person(s) Responsible for Implementation: Teacher.

10.   **Self Advocacy/Future Planning:** Provide an interpreter for Susan at all significant meetings that affect her receiving of services.

   Level of Present Performance: Susan's native language is Spanish. Her father speaks English but her mother does not. Susan has language deficits evident in her native tongue. She uses approximately 10 words in English.

   Steps Needed to Accomplish Goal: (1) Access interpreters. (2) Document need for interpreter for adult service meetings.

   Date of Completion: 6/95

   Person(s) Responsible for Implementation: Case manager.

STUDENT'S CAREER PREFERENCE: Working in hospitality industry.

STUDENT'S MAJOR TRANSITION NEEDS:	
	1. Employment as a dishwasher with Supported Employment Services.
	2. Public transportation training.
	3. Increased use of English.
	4. Financial resources.
	5. Regular integrated recreational activities.
	6.
	7.
	8.
	9.
	10.
	11.
	12.

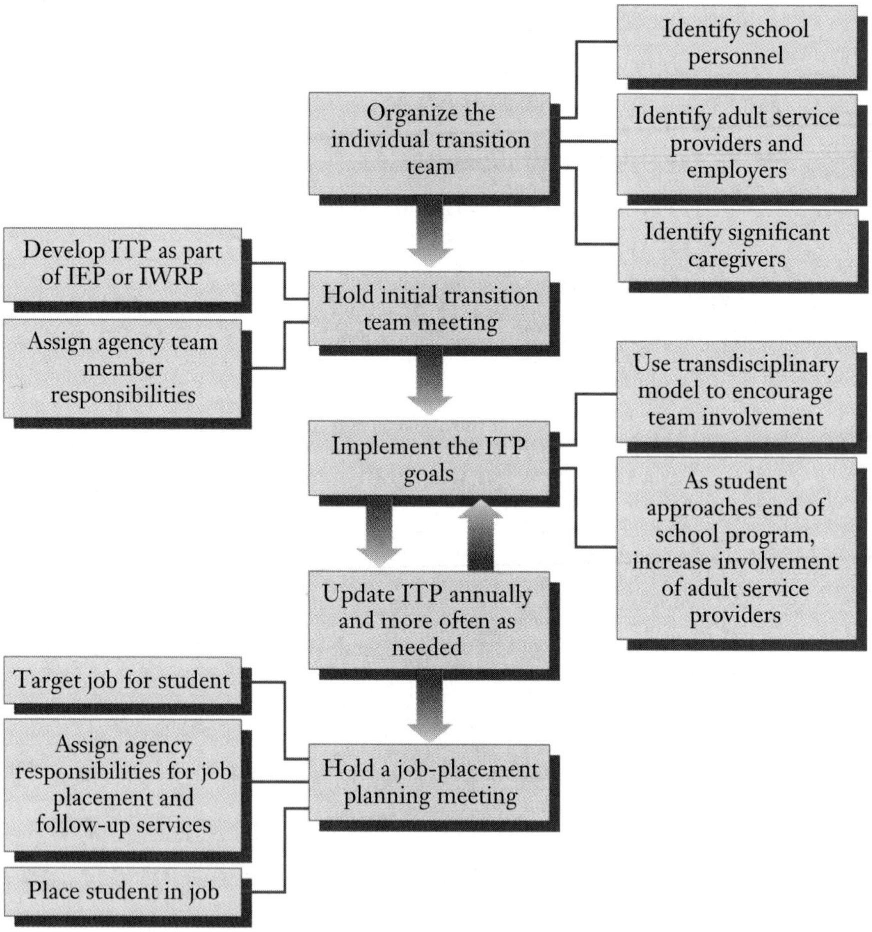

Figure 15.2   **Individualizing the Transition Process**

students in special education. The rehabilitation counselor is contacted for all students in special education who are thought to have "employment potential" in their last year of school.

The teacher wants to do something to offer Susan some better alternatives for adulthood, but does not know the best way to achieve the outcome she wants for Susan and that she feels Susan wants.

There are many students, parents, and teachers currently facing problems similar to Susan's. The youths with disabilities coming out of the schools today and their parents are finding that adult services are not automatically available. The schools and adult service agencies must work together to develop a plan for the desired post-school outcomes of employment and independent living in the community. Figure 15.2 illustrates this transition process.

Steps in the Transition Process

Organize the Transition Team.   Organize the transition team when the individual reaches the beginning of the targeted age span. As stated earlier, age 16 is generally the age of a student when the school system establishes a transition team for him or her. However, Susan's team will be organized when she is 19, since the school realized her need after she passed the targeted age. Based on her needs, Susan's team consists of Susan, her parents, her teacher, the speech–language pathologist, a representative from the rehabilitation services agency, and a representative from the mental retardation service agency.

Hold the Initial Transition Team Meeting.   The initial transition team meeting should take place as part of the IEP meeting. Since Susan is still in school, her transition plan (ITP) is included in her IEP and is developed at the annual IEP meeting. If she had already left school, the ITP would be a part of her **Individualized Written Rehabilitation Plan (IWRP).** The goals in an ITP include training in job skills as well as job-related areas such as transportation, handling money, communication, and socialization.

Implement the ITP Goals.   The next step is to implement the transition plan goals—with updates annually or as needed, with the attendance of appropriate transition team members. Using a transdisciplinary model, Susan's teacher will function as the primary service provider during Susan's remaining years in school. The teacher will provide programming, while other team members will serve as information resources. For example, Susan may need assistance in communicating her needs to her supervisor at the job training site. The speech–language pathologist would target communication goals for Susan and develop a plan for teaching her the necessary skills. The therapist would then show the teacher how to teach Susan to communicate at work so that the teacher, in turn, could train the skills on a daily basis in the natural environment.

Hold a Job-Placement Planning Meeting.   Next, team members should hold a job-placement planning meeting to target a specific job for the student and assign responsibilities to team members and adult service agencies. At the next annual IEP meeting when Susan is 20 years old, for instance, the transition planning team might make job placement in a part-time food service position Susan's employment goal for the year. By arranging for a real employment situation before Susan leaves school, there will be a period of time when the school and adult service agencies can work together on the employment goal. The rehabilitation counselor might be able to locate a job for Susan. The vocational teacher and the special education teacher could work together to provide for training on the job site. This cooperative effort requires administrative support in that one or the other needs to accompany Susan to the job site for one-to-one training until she begins to demonstrate independence in performing the job skills. A developmental disabilities case manager might be able to work out transportation arrangements to and from the job site with school personnel providing the training for independent traveling. As long as Susan is receiving school services and employment is written into the IEP, she is able to remain on the school's enrollment.

If the part-time employment placement is successful, then Susan's teacher will continue to assess Susan's progress periodically by observing at the job site and soliciting feedback from employers and coworkers for continuous evaluation information. If there is a problem, the teacher will be aware of it through the data and observations, and more training can be provided. If the first employment placement is not successful, the transition planning team should have adequate time to analyze the problems that occurred and try again while all of the support systems are still available. At the final transitional IEP meeting, plans should be made for a smooth transfer of service responsibilities, so that there are no gaps in the services provided to Susan as she exits the school system.

COMPONENTS OF TRANSITION PLANNING

A successful transition from school to adulthood requires individuals, schools, agencies, and programs to coordinate their efforts. There must be longitudinal vocational training throughout the primary, middle, and secondary school years; cooperative and interagency transition planning; parent, student, and employer involvement in the transition planning process; and multiple employment and/or postsecondary college options in the community. The transition may be viewed as a three-step process involving work preparation training during the school years, identification and development of meaningful career development and community lifestyle options, and planning for the individual's transition from school to work (Clark & Kolstoe, 1994; Wehman, 1992).

Figure 15.3 illustrates how this process is enacted by professionals working together locally in the community. This group is called the **transition core team** (Wehman, 1992). This section describes how to establish interagency transition core teams as well as the other components necessary to implement a community system of transition for students with severe disabilities.

Start-Up and Procedural Decisions

The first step a community must take to devise a system for the transition of individuals with disabilities from school programs into employment is to form the transition core team. In most localities this responsibility will be assumed by the *local education agency (LEA)* since it is ultimately responsible for students until age 22. The primary function of the core team is to develop the foundation on which individualized transition teams will build. As previously stated, team members should include professionals representing special education, vocational rehabilitation, vocational education, developmental disabilities, mental health/mental retardation, social services, medical services, parents, and employers from local businesses.

Conducting a Needs Assessment.   The initial task of the core team is to conduct a needs assessment of the community to review the status of existing services. The assessment should identify preemployment training options, supported employment options, and support services (e.g., housing, transportation, and medical treatment available to individuals with disabilities).

Determining the Target Age/Population for Transition.   After the core team completes the needs assessment, it begins establishing procedures and other elements to be incorporated in the community's transition process. Generally the most efficient method is to designate a small group of students for a pilot study. The team would identify a target age group and/or population in order to field-test the transition process. For example, during the first 2 years a school system may concentrate on developing the transition process with all 19-year-old students who have a diagnosis of severe mental retardation. At the end of the 2-year trial period, the transition process could be extended to include all students with severe disabilities from 16 to 21 years of age. By gradually expanding the process to include more students, the school and post-school programs will not be overwhelmed with the transformation of service delivery.

Planning the ITP Format.   Next, the core team plans the format of the Individualized Transition Plan (ITP) that the community will use. As previously discussed,

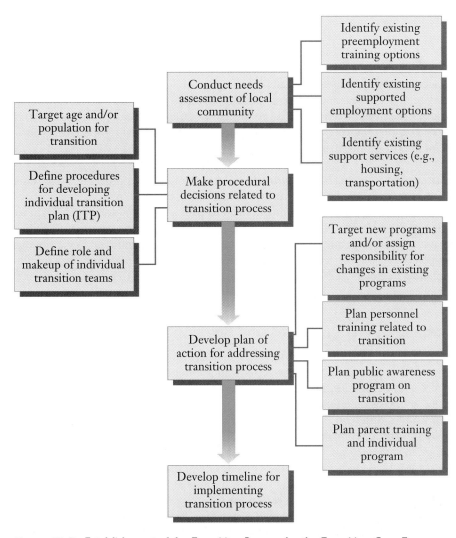

Figure 15.3 **Establishment of the Transition Process by the Transition Core Team**

the ITP should include goals related to all aspects of work (e.g., job skills, transportation, handling of a paycheck). It may be a portion of or an addendum to the student's Individualized Education Program (IEP) and/or part of his or her Individualized Written Rehabilitation Plan (IWRP). Usually the ITP is written when students are 16 years old, but each community will decide for itself at what point in the student's program the plan should be written (Wehman, 1992, 1995). As long as the individual is of school age, updates of the ITP should coincide with the annual IEP meeting.

Establishing Procedures for Selecting a Transition Team.   Another task of the core team is to establish procedures for selecting the transition team for an individual student, and to define the role of each member of that team. For example, a student with severe mental retardation and autism may have a transition team composed of the student, a special education teacher, a vocational rehabilitation counselor, a psychologist, the parent or guardian, a vocational education teacher, and a case manager from the mental health/mental retardation (MH/MR) agency.

The special education teacher would serve as the team coordinator during the school years, with the responsibility switching to the MH/MR case manager when the student turns 21. On the other hand, the transition team for a student with cerebral palsy and average intelligence may include a regular education teacher, a teacher certified in orthopedically handicapped (OH), a vocational rehabilitation counselor, a physical and/or occupational therapist, a rehabilitation engineer, and a vocational education teacher. The coordinator of the team during the school years would be the OH teacher, and would change to the vocational rehabilitation counselor in post-school years.

Taking the Plan to the Community. After the foregoing procedural decisions have been made, the transition teams serving during the pilot study can begin operation. Meanwhile, the core team will need to plan a public awareness program to address the adoption of the transition process throughout the community. Other major topics to be addressed include (1) targeting new programs and/or assigning responsibility for changing existing programs, (2) planning personnel training for potential members of the transition teams, and (3) developing a parent training and involvement program. These tasks will now be discussed.

Targeting New Programs and Revising Old Ones

Employment Training During the School Years. Although some school districts have made major efforts to develop appropriate vocational programs for students with disabilities, many systems need to revamp their existing programs to place emphasis on employment training. Quality high school training can make a tremendous difference in how early in adulthood a person with disabilities will be able to work for competitive wages. A major element of an effective employment program is training on job sites in business and industry. Business leaders indicated in a recent U.S. Department of Labor study (1995) that work experience was one of the three top reasons they would hire a job candidate; the other two were attitude and communication skills. The reason for training on actual jobs is to sidestep the problem with generalization of skill acquisition from the school to the job site, which many persons with severe cognitive impairments experience.

Supported Work Options. In most states, the current array of "work" options for adults with disabilities are often federally funded programs. These options are designed for individuals to be guided through a continuum of services toward the goal of regular competitive employment. However, too often these programs include merely adult activity centers and work activity centers, which may or may not provide job preparation and where, unfortunately, the major emphasis is rarely work. Ideally, the expectation is that the person will move from these programs into a sheltered workshop and eventually into regular competitive employment as he or she gains the necessary work skills. Historically, this transition has not occurred for persons with disabilities. In many instances, these individuals never even meet the entrance requirements posed by sheltered workshops.

In recent years, several work options have become available that are designed to enhance success in regular competitive employment. The employee who has several disabilities, including maladaptive behaviors, low cognitive abilities, and/or physical disabilities, generally needs some form of **supported employment.** Supported employment includes the use of an on-site job counselor who helps the individual overcome barriers faced at the job. This approach has been highly

The vocational training this young man is receiving will help him find gainful employment when he finishes school.

successful and popular because it has been so effective (Revell, Wehman, Kregel, West, & Rayfield, 1994; Wehman, Sale, & Parent, 1992).

Since most severe disabilities are lifelong, recurring difficulties on the job can be lessened through the follow-along component of the supported employment model. Current supported employment alternatives for persons with disabilities include supported competitive employment (Wehman et al., 1992), enclaves or small groups of people with disabilities in industry (Rhodes & Valenta, 1985), and mobile work crews (Bourbeau, 1985).

Personnel Training

In most communities, professionals need training in order to serve efficiently as members of a transition team. Many professionals have only a vague knowledge of the structure of other agencies; yet, some understanding across disciplines is necessary for an effective interdisciplinary approach. Training for the team members should cover topics including (1) the growing need for a transition process to be developed, (2) definitions related to transition from school to work, (3) legislation and funding issues, (4) implementation of an interagency transition process, and (5) solutions to barriers that professionals may face while developing preemployment training, supported work options, and transition teams. The format may involve a training session prior to service on a team, ongoing in-service programs, and publications such as newsletters and monographs.

Parent Training and Involvement

An essential element to a smooth transition into work for a person with disabilities is the involvement of the parents/guardians. They often need training in order for them to know what can be expected of their offspring and know which agencies

INNOVATIVE IDEAS "TAKING CHARGE" WITH COMPUTER TECHNOLOGY

The complexity of the employment process can be daunting for students who have little or no knowledge about the world of work. A new and innovative product has been developed to ease students with the transition from school to work. "Taking Charge" is a multimedia computer-assisted training product (available on both Macintosh and IBM platform, on CD and diskette) developed by Karen Flippo and Amy Armstrong from Virginia Commonwealth University. Its purpose is to inform individuals with disabilities about the steps they must take to find a quality job of their choice.

Many employment novices believe that the primary effort in finding a job is the job interview. "Taking Charge" methodically breaks down the job-seeking process by first identifying individuals who can support the job seeker (parent, teacher, employment specialist, friend) and describing their support roles. Next, the program features 200 photos of various jobs in a variety of occupational areas. The program cautions the user that the only way to find a job of choice is to visit a workplace and, ideally, try the job out. "Taking Charge" can help the user identify interest areas that can lead to development of work experiences and situational assessments. Additional content areas stress the importance of the consumer directing the planning and implementation of the job-seeking process.

Content is described through brief case studies and concise explanations about informational interviewing, preparing applications and resumes, and identifying transportation, job accommodation, and salary requirements. At the conclusion of the program, the user completes an Employment Wish List. Users are prompted to answer a series of questions that identify interest and ability. For example, they are asked to list their job of choice, salary, and job characteristics such as part-time or full-time, indoors or outdoors, and formal or relaxed work environment. Additional questions allow them to rate their skills, identify job accommodation needs, and determine the individuals (by name) who they want to work with during the job search. Once printed, the wish list can serve as a blueprint for a successful job or work experience process.

Since computer technology is quickly becoming a tool for communication and information access, it is necessary for students to be comfortable with hardware and software. A secondary objective of the program is to encourage using computers for learning. "Taking Charge" is user-friendly, operated by a mouse or touch screen, and allows the user to choose content areas and repeat sections. Text is brief, with information presented through animation, photographs, and audio narration. This computer program is one in a series of four that explain career planning and job development for individuals with disabilities.

should have representatives on the transition team. A major area to be included in training is a discussion of the capabilities of individuals with disabilities. Because professionals and family members often tell parents that their child will never be able to develop skills for independent living, particularly for competitive work, parents often have low expectations. Therefore, they need to be made aware of how persons with disabilities can be productive on a job through a supported work model involving a proper job match, the use of systematic instruction, the development of adaptations, and ongoing follow-along.

Convincing parents that their children with disabilities will be able to work is often difficult because of the history of receiving information that conflicts with competitive employment as an outcome. Therefore, teachers and other professionals who work with elementary-age students need to be educated in the work prognosis of persons with severe disabilities. In this manner, the parents' early contact with professionals will provide more positive projections in independence.

INDIVIDUALIZING THE TRANSITION PLAN

Once the core team in a community has developed a general process for student transition from school to supported employment, the involved professionals need to individualize this process for each student. The individual's unique characteristics, experiences, and environment must be considered when a transition team is developed in order to make appropriate long-range goals. This section will use the example of Susan to demonstrate how this process can be individualized.

Transition Goals for Youth With Disabilities

What educators and families who are involved in transition planning must remember is that a major purpose of school is to help students become more competent, independent, and capable of managing their own lives and affairs in such a way that they will become productive citizens. The subsections that follow discuss many of the key transition goals and what their role is when developed on an Individualized Transition Plan. These 10 key goals were listed on Susan's ITP; some of them are described here. It should also be emphasized that not all students will necessarily require all 10 of these planning goal areas. In fact, it is probably somewhat unlikely that the educational team would identify 10 goals every year for every student. The ITP should be individualized to that student's particular needs, and it must transcend educational achievement/classroom performance.

Employment and Work Training. Most students should have employment as an Individualized Transition Plan goal. Not in all cases will employment be full-time, and for some students it will be only a temporary stepping-stone before they move on to community college, trade school, or perhaps a four-year university environment. However, there are compelling data from many research studies (e.g., Peraino, 1992), which demonstrate that when students work in paid employment before they exit school, the probabilities dramatically escalate for permanent employment after their school years. In other words, students aged 16 to 21 who have held jobs—that were not make-work jobs, and that were not sheltered work, but instead were real jobs in the community—were much more likely to be successful in adulthood jobs.

Postsecondary Education. Fortunately, in recent years the doors are swinging open wider than ever at community colleges, four-year colleges, and major universities for people with disabilities. Through the Americans With Disabilities Act, there has been an increased push to allow students with disabilities an opportunity to go to college. There was a time, for example, when students with any significant level of disability would never dream of going to college. However, students with traumatic brain injury, learning disabilities, communication impairments, sensory impairments, severe physical disabilities, and behavior and intellectual disabilities are all applying in increasing numbers for some form of higher education.

The educational team and family need to aim high in terms of their goals and expectations. If the student does not target for a high level at a younger age, the likelihood that the student will do so when he or she is older is unlikely. There are a number of ways to overcome the barriers that seem, at least initially, to be insurmountable to students who are severely cognitively disabled, or who did not do particularly well in high school, or who are uncertain about what type of college education plans they might have. Furthermore, there are increasing amounts of student support and funds available to help individuals with disabilities.

Organizing these snack containers is a necessary and rewarding job.

Independent Living.   The independent living goal is sufficiently broad for the educational team to make any decisions that they and the family think are necessary, primarily in the context of home living, residential support, domestic skill training, or other areas that directly pertain to stability and satisfaction in the home environment. While an extensive amount of time needs to be devoted to the employment, vocational aspirations, and career outlook for young adults with disabilities, where they live and how satisfied they are in their living arrangements will be absolutely paramount to any successes they are able to enjoy. One only needs to look at the problems faced by thousands of youngsters living in blighted urban and rural areas to realize that no amount of schooling will easily overcome these problems.

Therefore, an independent living goal may turn out to be for some students *the* major goal. This will require the individual transition team to research the different types of living arrangements in a given community as well as make some difficult decisions about the quality of parenting and family support that is available. It may be the mutual decision of the family and the transition team that continued placement of the student in that home is at complete cross-purposes for an effective transition into adulthood and, therefore, an alternative supported living or alternative foster home arrangement may be a more viable option.

On the other hand, there may simply be a decision made by the family and educational team that the student's behavior in the home environment is totally unacceptable and must be substantially improved in terms of sibling relationships, relationships with one of the parents, or personal responsibility for jobs or different activities around the house. Hence, it might not be unusual to find a transition goal that was reflective of an independent living competency that did not take place in the school, but rather in the home or neighborhood environment.

Transportation.   Getting to and from places in the community is a major aspect of transitioning from childhood/dependence to adulthood/independence. This is a

Group home living is often a natural step in the transition into adulthood.

goal that is all too often passed over by educators and left to family members or others. Although most schools have driver education programs in which all students want to enroll, what about youngsters who are unable to drive due to the nature or severity of their disability?

The transportation goal needs to reflect a continuum of mobility options ranging from selection of an appropriate wheelchair to use of a specially equipped vehicle. Transportation goals may also include use of public transportation, gaining a driver's license, finding one's way around the community, using a map, or learning how to ask for help.

The type of IEP or ITP goals that might be listed under transportation would include ones like these:

- When approaching a traffic-light-controlled intersection, Keesha will stop at curb, observe lights, watch for traffic, and cross safely within the crosswalk 100% of the time across 20 trials.

- At 8:00 a.m. on school days, John will leave home and walk directly to the public bus stop on nine of ten consecutive school days.

- When in Sears department store, Sally will appropriately use the escalator to reach the second floor on three consecutive shopping trips.

- When told to get into the automobile, Carlos will open door, sit in passenger seat, close door, lock door, and fasten seat belt on nine of ten trips to the store.

Social Relationships.   There are three points to remember in crafting appropriate social relationship goals. First, these goals must be developed in a positive and constructive manner and not exclusively with a focus on managing "bad" behavior. Positive and constructive interventions are the ways to teach social skills, as opposed to simply trying to extinguish or eliminate inappropriate behaviors. Second, the student and family should have major input as to the most important social relationship goals they believe should be identified in the transition process. Remember, in writing an Individualized Transition Plan, it is not necessary to identify every social goal, but rather the one or ones that appear to be the greatest impediment to making a smooth transition from school to adulthood. Third, there should be an emphasis on inclusion or establishing social relationships with nondisabled people whenever appropriate. Once again, however, this will depend on the context.

For example, the student who has spent 14 years in a special or segregated school will necessarily have a greater need to learn social interaction skills with peers without disabilities. On the other hand, the student who has had the benefit of regular class participation and/or normal school activities may be able to develop other areas of socialization. Finally, it may be that a student does not have a specific social goal that is paramount in the transition process. Some of the students will do just fine socially. In fact this may turn out to be one of their assets. If this is the case, the team can move on and leave this area blank.

Health/Safety.   There has never been a generation that did not experience serious health problems and epidemics. Throughout history there have always been challenges to maintaining health. Despite the impact of cancer, heart disease, childhood injuries, and AIDS on the health of all Americans, more than ever there are surgical procedures and drugs available to help alleviate pain and suffering. Medical and health researchers report every day of new ways to detect illnesses, prevent injuries, lengthen lives, and reduce hospitalization.

When making the decision as to which types of health and safety goals to focus on, the team must draw especially heavily on the insights of the student and family. Is this student at risk for HIV? Is this student prone to seizures unless daily medication is taken? Has this student had a head injury? Will this student work at a job where the workplace environment could put him at risk? These are among the types of questions a futures oriented and holistic approach would pull out in a team meeting. In short, one does not identify goals in this area randomly off a packaged curriculum—instead there must be an accounting of the unique home, work, and daily living environments in which this student functions, with the health needs then assessed accordingly.

Self-Advocacy.   The goal of self-advocacy as a part of a transition plan would probably not have been included as recently as 10 years ago. It has really been only since the passage of the Americans With Disabilities Act in 1990 and publication of literature within the last 5 to 7 years documenting the consumer movement in disability that self-advocacy has come to the fore. Self-advocacy is grounded in the roots of freedom, choice, and self-determination—all of which are fundamental American values that all citizens of the country are entitled to enjoy. Unfortunately, too many of the nearly 49 million people who are labeled as having a disability by the United States Bureau of Census (1990) do not know how to advocate for themselves in an appropriate fashion. Many individuals with disabilities, particularly severe disabilities, have been taken care of or made to be highly dependent on others. This type of dependence has fostered a great deal of what psychologists call **learned helplessness.** The entire concept of learned helplessness—that is, not being able to be independent on behalf of yourself and your needs—is widespread in the disability community, and the only way to begin to offset this debilitating way of life is for schools and other service providers to promote greater personal competence.

The self-advocacy goal needs to be a highly practical one that is directly tied to the local community services and other needs on the ITP of the particular student. For some students this goal may not be necessary, but it would appear that most students could benefit, since it is likely that at some point they will need to know how to best advocate for services or for help within the community.

CRITICAL CHARACTERISTICS OF VOCATIONAL TRAINING PROGRAMS

Critical program characteristics that contribute to effective vocational training and successful job placement have been identified by a number of authors (Wehman, Bates & Renzaglia, 1985; Wilcox & Bellamy, 1982b). These critical characteristics are summarized in Table 15.1 and discussed below.

Community Analysis

A thorough and ongoing process of community analysis is used to identify local industry and job trends and to develop a vocational curriculum that reflects skills identified in the local community. Community analysis or community assessment is the first step in the development of an appropriate vocational training program. A thorough and ongoing community analysis requires the vocational trainer to make telephone contact with potential employers in the local community, to visit potential job sites, observe employees, task-analyze the jobs being performed, and assess physical and cognitive skills needed to complete each job. Information gathered by the vocational trainer during community analysis enables the trainer to make decisions about the content of vocational curricula.

A community analysis enables a vocational trainer to select career awareness activities at the elementary level that reflect community values and trends, to select equipment and core skills for school-based acquisition at the middle school level, and to provide community-based training sites for the practices and refinement of job skills at the secondary level. Employer contacts made and maintained through the community analysis process often turn into job placement contacts for transition-aged students.

Longitudinal Training Program

A longitudinal training program is used that begins at the elementary level and is systematically expanded throughout the school years. Successful vocational training culminates only after a student in his or her last years of school is employed in a full- or part-time job that pays a decent wage and provides maximum benefits.

Table 15.1   **Critical Characteristics of Vocational Training Programs**

1. A thorough and ongoing process of community analysis is used to identify local industry and job trends and to develop a vocational curriculum that reflects skills identified in the local community.
2. A longitudinal training program is used that begins at the elementary level and is systematically expanded throughout the school years.
3. Systematic and behavioral training procedures including a commitment to data-based programming are implemented.
4. Students develop and practice work skills with nondisabled workers in integrated community job sites.
5. An Individualized Transition Plan is developed and implemented to ensure systematic transition from school to supported employment and adult services once students leave school.

Table 15.2 **Guidelines for Vocational Training at the Elementary Level**

1. Become familiar with state, federal, and local regulations regarding vocational training and employment of citizens with disabilities. The earlier you become an advocate of mandated services in this area, the more likely your children/students are to receive proper training. Lobby for legislation that enhances employment opportunities.

2. Make sure that vocational training is part of the IEP in the earliest school years.

3. Visit upper-level school vocational programs and adult training programs and see if they match the variety of model programs that exist throughout the country. If local programs are good, determine what skills you need to teach to assure your student's entry into these programs.

4. Make certain that the IEP addresses self-care and independent living skills and functional academic and social skills that are needed in the workplace. Such skills include eating, toileting, dressing, grooming, communication, independent mobility, money and time management, physical fitness, and appropriately using leisure time. If these skills are taught early, there will be more time for specific job training in later years.

5. Emphasize the importance and rewards of work and create opportunities for students to see and learn about different vocations. Get students into the community to see and be seen by nondisabled workers. Be certain to encourage realistic vocations such as office helper, receptionist, maid, orderly, janitor, auto mechanic helper, food service worker, farm labor, and entry-level communications assistant.

6. Let students sample at school and at home a wide array of "work skills" applicable to realistic jobs such as cleaning tables, washing dishes, taking messages to other people, emptying trash, or answering the phone. Creating a schedule of work duties and demanding completion of duties within a time frame teaches young students the importance of work quality and rate.

7. Begin training skills in all curriculum areas outside the classroom. Integration into the community and training in natural settings at early stages of learning will promote generalization of learning and acceptance by other people.

School vocational training programs that begin in the elementary years and emphasize job placement before graduation are critical to reducing the high unemployment rate of citizens who are disabled (Wehman, 1985).

The following guidelines are provided to help both educators and parents fulfill a goal of meaningful employment for young adults with disabilities once they leave school.

Training at the Elementary Level. During the elementary years, students with disabilities should be exposed to a variety of vocational and vocationally related experiences that concentrate on the development of independent living and self-care skills, social and communication skills, awareness of vocational training opportunities at the upper grade levels, and specific skill clusters that are necessary to work in a variety of potential job settings (Moon & Beale, 1984; Wehman & Pentecost, 1983).

Table 15.2 provides more detailed guidelines teachers and parents may follow to ensure appropriate vocational preparation at the elementary level.

Training at the Middle School Level. During the middle school years, vocational training for students with disabilities should be provided during a large portion of the school day (e.g., 2 to 3 hours daily). Students should be given the opportunity to practice specific job skills in a variety of community-based settings. These experiences should include the opportunity to acquire a variety of independent living, social, language, functional academic, and community mobility skills. Money and time management, independent travel around the community, social interactions, and the ability to follow instructions and ask for help are skills that are associated with holding a job.

Table 15.3 provides specific training guidelines for teachers and parents during the middle school years.

Table 15.3   **Guidelines for Vocational Training at the Middle School Level**

1. Continue to train communication, self-care, mobility, independent living, and recreation skills. Teach all of them within the context of job training whenever possible.
2. Make sure the IEP addresses specific vocational training in a variety of potential jobs related to realistic employment options in the local labor market.
3. Provide job training in real job sites such as hotels, restaurants, hospitals, and local businesses. At the very least, train in a variety of school sites as the grounds, cafeteria, office, and overall building.
4. Begin working with high school personnel to identify possible permanent job placements. Make sure the transition from middle school to high school programs is smooth and appropriate.
5. Identify a "vocational track" for each student so that more specific job training can occur at the high school level. This can only be done after a student shows preferences, strengths, and weaknesses in a variety of job categories that have been trained in community-based settings.
6. Continue to work on general work habits such as neatness, promptness, and responding to criticism—but within the context of specific job training. Use systematic instructional methodology and a data-based system to monitor the learning of general work habits and specific skills. Documentation of learning can be used later to assure appropriate job entry.
7. Continue to get students into the community for training in all curriculum areas.
8. Contact rehabilitation and mental retardation adult service providers to identify who will be working with your students after graduation.

Training at the Secondary Level.   By the time a student with disabilities is 16 years old, a minimum of 3 hours of the school day should be devoted to vocational training and related vocational skills in a community job site. Students should be given the opportunity to practice and refine specific job skills. The training emphasis should begin to move away from acquisition of new skills to productivity, endurance, and refinement of skills. Through the development of a formal and individualized transition process, the parents, the student, the school, and adult service professionals should discuss and target a supported employment placement, a residential option as needed, and additional support services or training as required. The goal of vocational training at the secondary level is to eliminate a lapse in services by providing an employment opportunity that coincides with the student leaving school.

Table 15.4 summarizes the components of vocational training for students with disabilities at the secondary level.

Systematic and Behavioral Training Procedures

An effective vocational training program uses systematic and behavioral training procedures, including a commitment to data-based programming. Classroom and community-based vocational training should begin with the development of *task analyses* to describe the step-by-step process needed to complete each skill identified for specific jobs. A good task analysis states this step-by-step process in terms of observable behavior with words stated in the second person, so that when spoken, the step may be used as a verbal prompt.

Once task analyses are written, the next step is to write a *vocational objective*. A vocational objective should include two components: (1) the criteria for mastery, and (2) the conditions under which mastery must be met. Criteria must be defined in measurable terms—for example, percentage of correctly completed steps in a task analysis, or frequency or rate of desired behavior over a specified period of time. The conditions under which mastery must be met should be defined to include materials, setting, or time. An example of a vocational objective is: "Given the

Table 15.4   Guidelines for Vocational Training at the High School Level

1. Develop a *transition team* composed of the student, parents/guardians, teacher, rehabilitation counselor, MR case manager, and other appropriate professionals to ensure movement from school to an appropriate job or post-school training program.

2. The transition team must formulate a formal, written plan that specifies how a student will be trained and placed in a permanent job upon graduation. This *transition plan* specifies who is responsible for each goal/objective of this plan and a time line for completion of each goal/objective of the plan.

3. As part of the development of the transition plan, identify existing job options and target needed ones. Work with adult service providers and businesses to create new jobs.

4. Provide daily training at community job sites in several job categories that are realistic permanent job possibilities for the students. These categories should have been identified earlier in conjunction with middle school personnel.

5. Within the context of community-based job-site training, focus on improving work quality and production rate. As well, make sure that a student has the endurance and stamina to work all day.

6. Prepare job placement files with references, descriptions of acquired skills, work history, and community assessment information.

7. Follow up on all graduates to make sure they are either employed or are receiving job placement services.

verbal cue 'The floor needs to be mopped,' John will mop the floor with 100% accuracy."

Systematic and behavioral training procedures, including a commitment to data collection, are necessary to evaluate and document student and worker progress. The observation and data-based evaluation of students in real work situations allows the trainer to make a comprehensive assessment of the student's work skills. *Baseline data*, collected for several days prior to providing instructional training, will give the trainer input on how much of the skill the student can perform independently prior to formal instruction. In community training sites, it will be more difficult to collect data and observe baseline conditions, but every effort should be made to collect a minimum of one day of baseline data. *Probe data*, or assessment data, should be collected weekly according to a predetermined schedule. A probe should be conducted after approximately every third training session prior to daily instruction.

CURRENT ISSUES AND FUTURE TRENDS

In many ways the future lives of young adults with disabilities will be influenced by the economic, social, and political forces in American society more than any specific technological or instructional breakthroughs. More than ever, teachers and other helping professionals know how to help individuals with disabilities to gain employment, enter the community successfully, and enjoy a good quality of life. The fact that this knowledge is not more significantly implemented is due more to certain dynamics in American society and local communities than to anything else.

For example, those young people with disabilities who have learned what their rights are and how to advocate for those rights are more likely to be able to take advantage of the opportunities that exist in many communities today. Those young adults with disabilities who live in communities with thriving businesses and industry and a growing economy that calls for a diverse labor force are more likely to share in the fruits of meaningful employment than those who live in impoverished economic areas. Those young people with disabilities who have had the benefits of stable families and progressive schools and communities are more likely to have a greater degree of hope and courage to try new ideas and innovations.

The future can be very rich for young adults with disabilities, even though they face many of the same challenges that confront all youths in American society. This generation of young people has spawned a Miss America, Heather Whitestone, who has a hearing impairment; it has lifted Chris Burke, a young person with Down syndrome, into the national media spotlight as a star of the television series *Life Goes On;* and there are many other examples of young people with disabilities greatly succeeding. The challenge awaits people with disabilities, their families, and teachers to help fully attain their potential.

Five-Minute Summary

The use of a community-derived and community-based vocational training program for students with disabilities combined with behavioral and systematic training procedures ensures the following outcomes: (1) the provision of longitudinal training throughout the school years, (2) the collection and evaluation of data-based vocational assessment and training, (3) the coordination and cooperation of service provision among professionals, and (4) the development and implementation of an outcome-oriented transition from school to adult life plan.

Transition is an essential and natural passage for all youth as they move from school into greater independence in the community and work. The challenges of growing up are difficult for many students. Some of these difficult issues include dealing with disabilities, low self-esteem, mobility, financial concerns, employment, and sexuality. The school, along with family members and the community, must all play a coordinated role in helping students make this important transition.

Study Questions

1. What are the major issues concerning adults with disabilities in seeking employment?
2. What are the benefits of on-site job counselors in helping individuals with disabilities?
3. Summarize the components of the definition of transition from school to adult services contained in IDEA.
4. Who should serve as members of a transition team for a student at the secondary level who will be transitioning to the workplace in several years?
5. Describe supported employment services.
6. Identify three ways in which a school system can improve opportunities for the future success of a teenager with a disability to secure and maintain employment.
7. Describe critical characteristics for vocational training and instruction activities.
8. How might vocational training differ for students at the middle school and secondary levels?

For More Information

ORGANIZATIONS

Administration on Developmental Disabilities
U.S. Department of Health and Human Services
Program Operations Division
200 Independence Avenue, S.W., Room 329D
Washington, DC 20201
(202) 245-2897 (voice)
(202) 245-2890 (TDD)

American Association for Persons in Supported Employment
5001 W. Broad Street
Richmond, VA 23230-3003

The Dole Foundation for Employment of People with Disabilities
1819 H Street, N.W., Suite 850
Washington, DC 20006
(202) 457-0318 (voice and TDD)

National Association of Rehabilitation Facilities
1910 Association Drive, Suite 200
Reston, VA 22091-1502
(703) 648-9300 (voice only)

National Council on Disability
800 Independence Avenue, S.W., Suite 814
Washington, DC 20591
(202) 267-3846 (voice)
(202) 267-3232 (TDD)

National Institute on Disability and Rehabilitation
Research
U.S. Department of Education
400 Maryland Avenue, S.W.
Washington, DC 20202-2572
(202) 732-1134 (voice)
(202) 732-5079 (TDD)

National Organization on Disability
910 16th Street, N.W., Suite 600
Washington, DC 20006
(202) 293-5960 (voice)
(202) 293-5968 (TDD)

National Rehabilitation Information Center
(NARIC)
8455 Colesville Road, Suite 935
Silver Spring, MD 20910
(301) 588-9284 (voice and TDD)
(800) 346-2742 (voice and TDD)

President's Committee on Employment of People
with Disabilities
1331 F Street, N.W., Third Floor
Washington, DC 20004
(202) 376-6200 (voice)
(202) 276-6205 (TDD)

BOOKS AND ARTICLES

Everson, J. (1993). *Youth with disabilities: Strategies for interagency transition programs.* Austin, TX: PRO-ED.

Everson, J. M. (1995). *Supporting young adults who are deaf-blind in their communities: A transition planning guide for service providers, families, and friends.* Baltimore: Paul H. Brookes.

Hayden, M. F., & Abery, B. H. (1994). *Challenges for a service system in transition: Ensuring quality commu-nity experiences for persons with developmental disabilities.* Baltimore: Paul H. Brookes.

Moon, M. S. (1994). *Making school and community recreation fun for everyone: Places and ways to integrate.* Baltimore: Paul H. Brookes.

Moon, M. S., Inge, K. J., Wehman, P., Brooke, V., & Barcus, J. M. (1990). *Helping persons with severe mental retardation get and keep employment.* Baltimore: Paul H. Brookes.

Szymanski, M. (1996). *Work and disability: Issues and strategies in career development and job placement.* Austin, TX: PRO-ED.

Wehman, P. (1992). *Life beyond the classroom: Transition strategies for young people with disabilities.* Baltimore: Paul H. Brookes.

Wehman, P. (1993). *The ADA mandate for social change.* Baltimore: Paul H. Brookes.

Wehman, P., Sale, P., & Parent, W. (1992). *Supported employment: Strategies for integration of workers with disabilities.* Austin, TX: PRO-ED.

JOURNALS, NEWSLETTERS, AND OTHER PUBLICATIONS

Creating Schools for All Our Students: What 12 Schools Have to Say
Council for Exceptional Children
Reston, VA 22070
(800) 232-7323

Issues and Options in Restructuring Schools and Special Education Programs
Council for Exceptional Children
Reston, VA 22070
(800) 232-7323

Winners All: A Call for Inclusive Schools
NASBE
Alexandria, VA 22314-2465
(703) 684-4000

VIDEO AND ELECTRONIC MEDIA

It's Your Life, Take Control [Video]
Available from:
Minnesota Education Services
70 County Road B2 West
Little Canada, MN 55116

References

Bourbeau, P. E. (1985). Mobile work crews: An approach to achieve long term supported employment. In P. McCarthy, J. Everson, S. Moon, & M. Barcus (Eds.), *School to work transition for youth with severe disabilities* (pp. 151–166). Richmond: Virginia Commonwealth University, Rehabilitation Research & Training Center.

Bowe, F. (1993). Statistics, politics, and employment of people with disabilities: Commentary. *Journal of Disability Policy Studies, 4*(2), 83–89.

Braddock, D. (1994). Presidential address 1994: New frontiers in mental retardation. *Mental Retardation,* 434–439.

Clark, G., & Kolstoe, O. (1994). *Career education and transition.* Boston: Allyn & Bacon.

Harris, L. & Associates (1994). *N.O.D./Harris Survey of Americans with Disabilities.* New York: L. Harris & Associates.

Hayden, M., & Abery, B. (Eds.). (1994). *Challenges for a service system in transition.* Baltimore: Paul H. Brookes.

Individuals With Disabilities Education Act of 1990 (October 30, 1990), Public Law 101-476. Title 20, U.S.C. 1400-1485. *U.S. Statutes at Large, 104,* 1103–1151.

Louis Harris Poll. (1991, January). *Americans Respond to People With Disabilities.* Washington, DC: Louis Harris & Associates.

Moon, M. S., & Beale, A. (1984). Vocational training and employment: Guidelines for parents. *The Exceptional Parent, 14*(8), 35–38.

Peraino, J. M. (1992). Post-21 follow-up studies: How do special education graduates fare? In P. Wehman (Ed.), *Life beyond the classroom: Transition strategies for young people with disabilities* (pp. 27–70). Baltimore: Paul H. Brookes.

Revell, W. G., Wehman, P., Kregel, J., West, M., & Rayfield, R. (1994). Supported employment for persons with severe disabilities: Positive trends in wages, models, and funding. *Education and Training in Mental Retardation and Developmental Disabilities,* 256–264.

Rhodes, L. E., & Valenta, L. (1985). Industry based supported employment. *Journal of the Association for Persons With Severe Handicaps, 10,* 12–20.

Wehman, P. (1992). *Life beyond the classroom: Transition strategies for young people with disabilities.* Baltimore: Paul H. Brookes.

Wehman, P. (1995). *Individual transition plans: A curriculum guide for teachers and counselors.* Austin, TX: PRO-ED.

Wehman, P., Bates, P., & Renzaglia, A. (1985). *Functional living skills for moderately and severely handicapped individuals.* Austin, TX: PRO-ED.

Wehman, P., & Pentecost, J. H. (1983). Facilitating employment for moderately and severely handicapped youth. *Education and Treatment of Children, 6*(11), 69–80.

Wehman, P., Sale, P., & Parent, W. (1992). *Supported employment: Toward integration of workers with disabilities.* Austin, TX: PRO-ED.

Wilcox, B., & Bellamy, G. T. (1982a). *A comprehensive guide to the activities catalog: An alternative curriculum for youth and adults with severe disabilities.* Baltimore: Paul H. Brookes.

Wilcox, B., & Bellamy, G. T. (1982b). *Design of high school programs for severely handicapped students.* Baltimore: Paul H. Brookes.

Epilogue

Lost Paradise, acrylic on canvas, 30″ × 24″ (1994)

EPILOGUE

ANDREA M. LAZZARI

After studying this epilogue, the reader will:

Be aware of the significant progress that has been made in service
provision to individuals with disabilities, especially
in the past two decades

Cite factors that have led to changes within the field of disabilities

Discuss current trends that are likely to affect our society, specifically
in relation to individuals with disabilities,
over the next two decades

Articulate a personal view of the future as it might unfold
for individuals with disabilities

EPILOGUE

As we look to the future, let us place ourselves once more in the past. Consider the following questions:

- In 1900, how many young persons with physical disabilities who used wheelchairs ever dreamed that they could play basketball competitively?
- In 1910, how many individuals with communication disorders attempted to enter the fields of entertainment or politics?
- In 1920, how many individuals who were blind ever considered entering reading-intensive professions such as law, university teaching, or publishing?
- In 1930, how many persons with epilepsy were encouraged to marry and have children?
- In 1940, how many individuals who were deaf were able to communicate with one another by telephone?
- In 1950, how many parents of babies with Down syndrome ever expected that their children could attend their local public schools or even be raised at home, outside of an institutional setting?
- In 1960, how many persons with disabilities were positively portrayed in television shows, movies, advertisements, and commercials?
- In 1970, what proportion of general education teachers had ever experienced teaching a student with a disability in their classrooms?
- In 1980, how many employers considered the provision of accommodations for workers with disabilities as their responsibility?

Although all of these accomplishments are now possible—and some even commonplace—at the times specified, the answer to each of these questions was "none" or "very few."

CHANGES WITHIN THE FIELD OF DISABILITIES

After reading and discussing each of the chapters in this text, we can see that the field of disabilities has undergone tremendous changes over the past century, especially in the past two decades. Change has been fueled by many factors, including research into the causes of and, in some cases, treatments and cures for disabilities; increased public education and awareness regarding the prevention of disabilities; the development of new professional fields, resulting in new intervention and rehabilitation approaches; legislation; litigation; broad-scale societal changes (e.g., the civil rights movement); grassroots movements that have led to self-advocacy and parent advocacy; technological developments; and medical and scientific breakthroughs.

CURRENT TRENDS

A look at recent trends that are likely to have a direct or indirect effect on individuals with disabilities—and the persons who provide services to them and interact with them in their schools, workplaces, and communities—may help us formulate new questions and possible answers as we approach the next century. The following general trends have been identified as potentially affecting all individuals in our society, regardless of age, income, gender, area of residence, occupation, political persuasion, or other characteristics (Cetron & Gayle, 1990; United Way of America, 1989).

The Maturation of America

By the year 2000 the elderly will make up 13% of the American population. As a group, they will be better educated, healthier, wealthier, more challenging of authority, and more likely to seek social change than the elderly have been in previous generations. The numbers of older people entering their peak earning years at the same time will have a noticeable effect on the economy. The remaining group of workers will be less educated and poorer (Montgomery & Herer, 1994).

Multiculturalism and Changing Family Lifestyles

An increasingly multicultural and diverse society will necessitate a redefinition of individual, family, and societal roles. The concept of family is being redefined to include many configurations other than the "traditional" family. Two trends that are leading to redefinition of family are the reduced earning power of young adults, resulting in more adult children living with their parents, and the increase in the number of elderly Americans, resulting in more parents living with their adult children.

By the year 2000, it is projected that fewer than 4% of families will conform to the so-called "norm" of a father working outside the home, a mother who is a homemaker, and two children. It is increasingly likely that both partners in a family unit will work—a figure that may increase to 75% by the year 2000. The number of single-parent families is projected to continue to increase, and poverty rates will continue to rise among female-headed families (Cetron & Gayle, 1990).

Although the links between childhood disability and poverty have often been overlooked and unaddressed, there are a significant number of children living in poverty who have disabilities. For example, 8% of children receiving Aid to Families With Dependent Children have disabilities. Unless support in the form of prevention and intervention programs is provided, as the number of children living in poverty increases, a concomitant increase can be expected in the number of children with disabilities (Administration on Developmental Disabilities, Administration for Families and Children, 1995). Many of these same families are among the almost 38 million Americans who do not have health insurance. One recognized outcome of restricted access to quality health care is the waning of immunizations that prevent children from acquiring preventable diseases, such as polio or rubella (Montgomery & Herer, 1994). If this trend continues, it is possible that we could face an increase in diseases that result in disabilities among our children.

Currently, a large number of the more than 3 million Americans with developmental disabilities represent racial and ethnic minority groups. Many of these individuals are unable to gain access to or benefit from the service systems already in place to provide needed supports. As demographic shifts in society result in a population that is even more linguistically, culturally, and ethnically diverse, the service systems that can benefit these individuals must develop the knowledge, skills, and competencies needed to serve a culturally diverse constituency (Administration on Developmental Disabilities, Administration for Families and Children, 1995).

Actor Christopher Reeve with his wife Dana. After suffering a broken neck from a horse riding accident, Reeve has quadriplegia; his celebrity status has brought new exposure to the need for more research in the area of spinal cord injury.

The changing face of America has brought about positive changes for persons with disabilities. As individual and cultural diversity have become more widely accepted and even encouraged, high-profile, positive representations of persons with disabilities are becoming more common (Fuchs & Fuchs, 1995). Individuals with disabilities are positively portrayed in advertisements, movies (e.g., *My Left Foot, Forrest Gump*), and television shows; they hold positions of responsibility in local, state, and federal government and in private industry; and they make significant contributions in the arts, sciences, and business sectors. As the diversification of the American population continues, a greater acceptance of differences, including disabilities, is a promising trend that hopefully will continue.

Information-Based, Global Economy

The growing economic relationship between the United States and other nations and the competition we face from other major industrial countries will continue to reshape the economy. One need that is emerging as we shift from an industrial economy to one that is information based and technology driven is that of a better trained work force (Montgomery & Herer, 1994). Schools will be called on to turn out graduates who are better prepared to meet the demands of the new economy. This need for adequately educated employees with a knowledge base in information processing (e.g., collecting, compiling, synthesizing, analyzing, and storing data, text, or graphics) and other technological skills may motivate businesses to enter into partnerships with schools: Businesses will reduce remediation costs as schools develop technical skills among the potential work force (Cetron & Gayle, 1990). This can affect both general and special education programs, because as businesses invest their time, expertise, and money in local schools, they are likely to have a greater interest in educational reform, particularly in local education policy and practices (e.g., curriculum). This, in turn, could weaken the decision-making power of state and local education agencies.

Another likely effect of the trend toward a global economy is that of more limited fiscal resources for education. Since 1975, when P.L. 94-142 was passed, fewer dollars have been allocated for special education funding each successive year. In 1990 P.L. 94-142 was reissued as P.L. 101-476 (IDEA)—but currently the federal government contributes only 8% of the average per pupil expenditure for students served under IDEA (approximately $400 per student receiving special education services), compared to the 40% originally pledged by Congress in 1975. The greater portion of the financial burden of educating students with disabilities (from $7,000 to $10,000 per year per student) falls on state and local governments (Council for Exceptional Children, 1995a; Montgomery & Herer, 1994).

Not only is the amount of funding of concern to special educators, but the form the funding may take is of concern as well. Some governors have proposed that funding for discretionary programs—such as the Preschool Grants Program (Section 619 of IDEA), which extends the requirements of a free, appropriate public education to all eligible preschool children—be cut and the funds turned over to states in the form of block grants. Thus, monies that have traditionally been earmarked for specific special education programs could be funneled into other educational programs at the discretion of individual states.

FUTURE DEVELOPMENTS

A look at recent developments in conjunction with the foregoing trends can lead us to predict future developments that we can expect as we enter the next century. Consider the areas of education, family and community living, technology, and medicine.

Educational Developments

Significant educational developments have occurred over the past two decades in the areas of policy and legislation. As discussed in Chapter 1, we have seen the passage of key legislation mandating and expanding opportunities for appropriate education for students with disabilities in public school settings. Although the development of supportive policies and practices has lagged somewhat behind these legislative mandates, the effects of legislation have slowly filtered down to local school divisions and to individual school buildings, students, and their families (e.g., individualized education at no cost to identified students with disabilities; early intervention services for infants, toddlers, and their families; special education as a preparation for life beyond school; education for students with disabilities in inclusive settings).

Not all trends in the education arena are necessarily positive, however. The education system is faced with significant problems that will push it beyond its limits if changes are not forthcoming. Montgomery and Herer (1994) have identified major concerns facing the U.S. educational system, including illiteracy, a high dropout rate, diminishing science and math capabilities, the growing need for technological literacy in the work force, multicultural and multilingual school populations, increased numbers of high-risk children entering school, poorer achievement in urban schools, limited availability of teachers, and adequacy and relevancy of teacher preparation.

These major concerns have fueled calls for educational reform. Forces both within and outside of the education profession have called for educational reforms that have begun to affect not only general education practices but those in special education as well. Criticisms of special education practices include the lack of validity in special education assessment, placement procedures, and curriculum practices, as well as the significant proportion of local school budgets that must be allocated to special education (Fuchs & Fuchs, 1995).

A strong driving force behind calls for special education reform is the steady growth in the number of students identified as needing special education services. Nationally, the special education population has grown 1% to 2% a year over the last decade. These larger numbers mean a significant proportion of the total school population is in need of special education services. For example, in Massachusetts, the state serving the largest percentage of special education students in the country, 17% of the school-age population receives special education services (Fafard, 1995). When one considers the commonly accepted prevalence figure that from 8% to 10% of the total population has a disability, legitimate questions can be raised about the numbers of students receiving special education and related services.

Furthermore, not only are we seeing a change in the numbers of students with disabilities being identified and served in special education programs, but a change is also evident in the characteristics of the student population in special education. Although proportionately more students are being identified with milder disabilities (i.e., learning disabilities), the diversity and intensity of the needs of individual students is also increasing. Shrag (1990) identified a range of reasons for these changes, including these:

1. An increase in the number of births affected by substance abuse

2. An increase in the number of medically fragile children in the schools, as a result of advanced medical technology and knowledge that is enabling more premature infants who are medically fragile and more infants with disabilities to survive

3. New medications for cancer, epilepsy, and emotional problems that appear to have a permanent effect on learning skills

4. A greater survival rate of students with traumatic brain injury

5. Longer survival rates for children with cystic fibrosis, muscular dystrophy, and heart defects

6. Increased numbers of children with HIV or AIDS

7. Younger and more significantly affected children with emotional problems

8. A younger special education population overall, as states fully implement early childhood special education mandates for preschoolers and expand programs for infants and toddlers with disabilities

The increasing numbers of students in special education in conjunction with increases in the complexity of the needs of many of these students have resulted in a shortage of special education teachers and related service providers in many areas of the country. This problem is especially critical in rural areas. The limited pool of candidates who seek to enter teacher training and the higher attrition rates among special education teachers (almost twice that of general educators) have also contributed to the mismatch between supply and demand of special educators. Another challenge related to supply and demand is that of the discrepancy between the number of minority students and minority teachers. Whereas approximately

30% of the school-age population comprises minority students, minority teachers represent only about 13% of public school teachers. As our population becomes more ethnically diverse, this discrepancy may become even greater unless efforts to recruit teachers from minority groups are successful (Ludlow & Lombardi, 1992; Shrag, 1990).

Equal access to core curriculum by all students is the basis of many reform efforts. Educators are being charged with the responsibility for educating all students, regardless of the characteristics a student brings to the learning setting. Within the field of special education, calls for "full inclusion" (i.e., doing away with all special education settings and special placements) have met with resistance from general administrators and teachers as well as many special educators. They fear that full-time placement in general education settings of all students with disabilities (particularly those with significant physical, cognitive, and sensory impairments) will prevent some students with disabilities from obtaining the appropriate education guaranteed to them under the Individuals With Disabilities Education Act (Fuchs & Fuchs, 1995) as well as interfere with the rights of general education students to receive maximum benefit from the classroom setting.

Another facet of special education reform has been the shift toward noncategorical models in both service delivery and teacher preparation. Some states (e.g., California) are already using a classification system based on a student's level of need for service rather than a diagnostic category or categorical label. Proponents of noncategorical approaches maintain that sound instructional practices can be applied across categorical labels, including mild mental retardation, learning disabilities, behavior disorders, and students deemed at risk. Opponents of noncategorical models point out that the special needs of many students with disabilities would go unrecognized and unmet without categorical labels and that the range of special education services and programs would become too limited if students with disabilities were educated in general education classes (Ludlow & Lombardi, 1992).

Both the inclusion movement and the shift toward noncategorical service delivery are leading us away from the traditional educational practices of students receiving instruction in one room from one teacher. Instead, students in both general and special education are receiving instruction from teams of educators in a variety of learning environments, including community settings. This, in turn, necessitates more flexible scheduling and modification of curriculum approaches designed for large group instruction.

Calls for change extend far beyond the level of local school districts or even state departments of education. The issue of the federal government's role in education is central to the current educational reform movement. Traditionally, decisions about what students are to be taught have been left to the discretion of states and localities. This changed in 1991, when, for the first time in U.S. history, President George Bush and the nation's governors established six national education goals and a strategy—AMERICA 2000—to achieve them (Alexander, 1992). Enacted by Congress as the Goals 2000 bill in the spring of 1994, it represented a new approach for the federal government in helping states and local school divisions raise their educational standards and enact plans for school reform (Jennings & Stark, 1995). The long-term effects of the federal government's direct involvement in education remains to be seen. It is likely, however, that targeting educational practices and policies as a political and social agenda will continue as long as schools are viewed as both a cause and a cure for the problems facing society.

One of the keys that has been identified to recovering the lost quality in our schools is that all stakeholders (parents, businesspersons, community members) must accept responsibility for the performance of their local school system by volunteering their time and talents, by working to raise school budgets, and by providing informed input into educational issues and decisions (Cetron & Gayle, 1990). The success of reform efforts will, in part, depend on the willingness of stakeholders to invest their time, money, and expertise into strengthening the schools. Today, children make up only 26% of the population (Coontz, 1995), a figure that is likely to decline as the population ages. It remains to be seen whether older Americans will be willing to make these contributions to an educational system that no longer directly serves them or their offspring, or if they will instead delegate these responsibilities to a younger generation that is likely to be poorer and have less time and fewer resources available to contribute to school reform and improvement.

Family and Community Living

Over the past 20 years, children and adults with a wide range of disabilities and chronic illnesses have increasingly become a regular part of family and community life. Through a range of public programs and individual efforts, families have been provided with the support needed to enable their children or adult members with disabilities to live at home rather than in institutional settings, to have their children with disabilities educated in local public schools, and to encourage their family members with disabilities to participate in a range of community activities (U.S. Department of Health and Human Services, 1994).

Changes in family structure will bring about changes in the characteristics of communities and in the characteristics of the student population in our local schools. Schools and other social service agencies will need to be responsive to the different needs of these new families and their children, necessitating a redefinition of their roles. Local public schools will be seeing children with diverse needs: those who are medically fragile, those who speak English as a second or third language, infants and toddlers with a range of developmental disabilities who are in need of early intervention, and children who are at risk due to a variety of social, economic, and health factors. Schools may be asked to provide increasingly diverse programs—such as family aid (e.g., health care, nutrition services), preschool education, child day care, adult day care, parenting classes, and a variety of prevention efforts. As school budgets are strained to accommodate the special needs of these diverse groups, their ability to continue to provide the level of special education and related services to students with disabilities may be strained as well.

Technological Developments

The integration of technology into our daily lives has been rapid over the past decade. The magnitude of this infiltration becomes apparent when one considers that microcomputers were found in only 16% of U.S. public schools in 1981, but nearly *all* of the nation's schools used computers in some way just a decade later (Okolo, Bahr, & Reith, 1993). Or consider that from 1985 to 1995, the proportion of households that had VCRs increased from 17% to 85%, those having telephone answering devices increased from 5% to 54%, and the proportion having personal computers increased from 13% to 33% (Electronic Industries Association, 1995). The availability of affordable technology to assist people with disabilities in their daily activities at school, work, and home has paralleled the development and influence of technology in general. Technological developments have enabled many persons for the first time to live independently, to perform tasks needed for

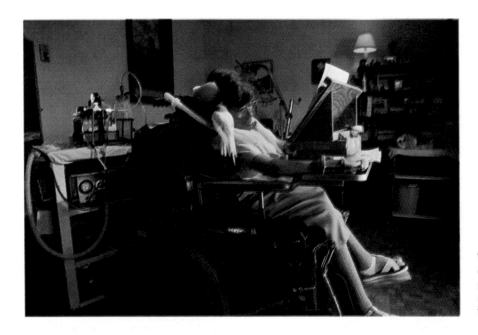

With the advent of more sophisticated computer devices, even people with the most severe disabilities can now communicate with their families and friends.

employment, and to have access to a range of educational, recreational, social, and financial opportunities.

In the schools, technology applications are opening many doors for students with disabilities. Developments in technology-based assessment within special education (i.e., using computer technology to assess and evaluate individual student needs and progress) are enabling educators to more accurately diagnose, assess, and prescribe educational interventions for individual students. Augmentative communication devices allow students who are nonverbal to actively participate in general education classrooms. For example, nonverbal students with limited fine motor control can communicate with others using a variety of input/output options such as touch screens, pointing stylus tools, speech and handwriting interpreters, scanning devices, and bar code readers (Greenwood & Reith, 1994; Irvin & Walker, 1993). Although assistive technology is usually discussed in the context of students with physical and sensory impairments, it also has exciting potential for the 75% to 80% of the students in special education programs who have mild disabilities.

We can expect to see a number of new technological applications in the schools of the future—laptop computers with built-in voice synthesizers that have alternate input capabilities; computer-assisted instruction that allows teachers to work simultaneously with students at different skill levels; electronic cooperative learning; devices that can scan printed text and convert it into another language or another medium (e.g., braille); telecommunication capabilities that enable students and teachers to access the Internet; voice output devices that will also serve as computer input devices; use of virtual reality to teach students skills before they attempt them in the actual environment (e.g., how to maneuver wheelchairs) or to interact with a variety of new environments in unique ways (e.g., enabling a student with severe physical disabilities to experience hiking up a mountain); holographic teleconferences that can bring images of speakers right into the classroom; distance learning provided at an affordable cost that enables any student to receive instruction from a worldwide expert; and locally created textbooks using publisher-supplied materials that are adapted for local school divisions or individual students (Bruder, 1990; Council for Exceptional Children, 1995b).

Virtual reality isn't just for fun any more; we're only just beginning to explore the possibilities of this medium for students with disabilities.

New technologies are being developed and refined at a rapid pace. By the time this book is printed, new technological devices and applications that were not available when the text was written will be in use. However, a major restraining force to accessing new technology—being able to afford and acquire the devices—remains a barrier to many persons with disabilities.

Medical Developments

The development of new medical treatments that can alleviate or prevent disabilities is one of the most promising future trends. Medical advances are enabling children with disabilities to live longer, many surviving to adulthood who previously would not have.

We have already begun to see the outcomes of recent advances in medicine: prenatal screening, diagnosis, and genetic counseling; fetal surgery; newborn screening for risk factors that could result in disabilities (e.g., otacoustic emissions hearing tests for newborns before they leave the hospital); advances in neonatal care for high-risk babies; improvements in treatments for chronic diseases; advances in surgery (e.g., organ transplants); new rehabilitative and therapeutic techniques (e.g., bionic prostheses, portable and inexpensive life-support systems); genome mapping to reduce or eliminate certain disabilities and diseases (e.g., discovery of a gene for one type of Alzheimer disease); and gene therapy (a promising treatment for curing inherited diseases such as cystic fibrosis). Each of these developments has been enabled through rapid advances in medical technology that have led to techniques and treatments that would have been thought impossible even a decade ago and deemed "science fiction" by most practitioners in the first half of this century.

A LOOK TO THE FUTURE

A consideration of the current issues and future trends facing education, family and community life, medicine and technology, and the field of disabilities in general raises more questions about the future. What does the future hold for individuals with disabilities and their families, friends, classmates, and colleagues? What future developments and major changes can we expect to see in the field of disabilities in general and in the related fields of rehabilitation, medicine, and education? Past events and current trends lead us to pose many questions for which the answers remain to be seen . . .

Will developments in the education of students with disabilities continue along the upward spiral that we have experienced since the passage of P.L. 94-142 in 1975, or will the needs of students with disabilities place such a financial burden on local school divisions that appropriate services cannot be provided?

Will the pool of skilled professionals trained to provide educational, medical, therapeutic, and rehabilitation services be sufficient to meet the needs of persons with disabilities, especially in rural areas, or will shortages continue to be experienced?

Will the high standards of professional training for teachers and therapists be upheld in the face of significant personnel shortages, or will standards be lowered in an attempt to meet the demand for personnel?

Will legislation and litigation continue to support the progress that has been made in enabling full and equal access to educational, community living, and vocational opportunities for citizens with disabilities, or will discrimination flourish in a climate of legal and legislative indifference?

Will medical and technological advances continue to be made at the rapid rate they have been over the past decade, or will lack of financial resources impede progress?

Will funding from governmental sources and private foundations continue to be available to support the various educational, medical, rehabilitation, and research programs that are under way, or will these efforts be lost in large-scale budget cuts and program revisions?

Will society at large and individual citizens embrace the ideal of welcoming individuals with disabilities into all facets of school and community living, or will they open their doors only because it has been mandated or deemed politically correct?

Although we can expect to experience setbacks as the political and social climate changes and as the effects of these changes ripple through various segments of our culture, we can look to the future with hope that, as the next generation is born and grows to adulthood, the following wish list will be fulfilled:

Recognition of the individual capabilities and competencies of persons with disabilities and the potential contributions they can make to families, communities, schools, the arts, and various professional and occupational fields

Inclusion of individuals with disabilities in the full range of educational, vocational, economic, and community living opportunities

Empowerment of families and individuals with disabilities to define their own needs and priorities and make informed choices on the full range of decisions affecting their own lives and the development of their children with disabilities

Refinement of the existing service delivery system to eliminate the patchwork of programs that fail to cover some individuals with disabilities or do not provide adequate coverage for long-term rehabilitation

Development of partnerships among individuals, direct service providers, private and public agencies and funding sources, communities, and legislators that cross traditional agency boundaries and result in a coordinated, responsive service delivery system

Funding of research and development projects to continue and expand current efforts in medicine, technology, education, and rehabilitation and to initiate new and innovative efforts

Development of effective, timely, and appropriate public policy and legislation to uphold the rights of citizens with disabilities to become contributing members of society at large and of their state and local communities and families

Recruitment and retainment of a qualified pool of professionals to provide needed medical, educational, therapeutic, and other supportive services in all localities to individuals with disabilities and their families

Elimination or reduction in the incidence of certain disabilities through advances in genetic counseling, medical intervention, and wide-scale prevention efforts

Reduction of the handicapping effects of certain disabilities through advances in technology, which will be available and affordable to all persons with disabilities who can benefit from them

These outcomes are not likely to come to fruition without the continued and persistent efforts of advocates for individuals with disabilities. The progress that has been made thus far in providing equal access to the full range of educational, vocational, spiritual, recreational, family life, and community living experiences by children and adults with disabilities has resulted from work on many different levels by a variety of individuals. As can be realized from a look at key events in the history of special education and the areas it encompasses, change agents have taken on various forms over the years. Advocates have included individuals with disabilities, parents and other family members of children with disabilities, educators, therapists, nurses, physicians, researchers, writers, legislators, judges, and professional organizations. The common thread connecting these individuals is that their efforts to change the events in the present have also shaped the future.

As the change agents of the future, we have the advantage of learning from the past. As we enter the next century, we may not be able to predict with certainty what is about to unfold. What we do know is that change is inevitable. As we strive to shape the future for individuals with disabilities, we must keep sight of the fact that any significant and lasting changes will be the result of human efforts, creativity, and persistence.

Five-Minute Summary

The field of disabilities has undergone tremendous changes over the past century. Many of these changes have been influenced by broader-scale changes in society. A look at current trends in our society may help us prepare for future changes that are likely to affect programs and services for individuals with disabilities. These trends include the maturation of America, an increasingly multicultural society with diverse lifestyles, and a shift to an information-based, global economy.

Future developments in the field of education are likely to result from the current calls for educational reform. Lack of accountability for educational outcomes is a common concern voiced by critics of current educational practices. For the first time in U.S. history, the federal government has gotten involved in decisions about what students should be taught.

Key factors that have fueled calls for reform in special education are the steady increase in the numbers of students identified as needing special education services, the changing characteristics of the student population, and personnel shortages. The movement toward full inclusion of all students with disabilities in general education settings and the practice of noncategorical service delivery are current trends that will continue to shape the future of special education services in the schools.

The changes in schools are both a reflection of and a reaction to demographic changes in families and communities. As families increasingly comprise family structures other than the traditional two-parent, two-child "norm," their needs will evolve as well. Schools are likely to be called on to fulfill more and varied roles for families and communities—including child care, family aid, parenting education, and prevention efforts. If financial support is not forthcoming from other sources in the community, the ability of schools to meet the needs of their students as well as those of other community members may be restricted.

Technological and medical developments are occurring at a rapid rate. Many of these accomplishments have made tremendous differences in the lives of persons with disabilities. We can look forward to the continued and often rapid development of technological and medical innovations with the hope that they can be made affordable to all individuals who can benefit from them.

Regardless of the high-tech nature of many developments we can predict or hope for in the future, we must not lose sight of the fact that all of these accomplishments must be spurred by human effort, creativity, and perseverance. As history demonstrates, the efforts of many individuals have brought the field of disabilities to the place it is today and will continue to be the driving force behind future changes.

References

Adminstration on Developmental Disabilities, Administration for Families and Children. (1995). Developmental disabilities: Request for public comments on proposed developmental disabilities funding priorities for projects of national significance for Fiscal Year 1995, 95 C.F.R. 615.

Alexander, L. A. (1992). The best education for *all* children. *Teaching Exceptional Children, 25*, 1, 5.

Bruder, I. (1990). Education and technology in the 1990s and beyond: Visions of the future. *Electronic Learning, 9*, 24–30.

Cetron, M. J., & Gayle, M. E. (1990, September–October). Educational renaissance: 43 trends for U.S. schools. *The Futurist*, 33–40.

Coontz, S. (1995). The American family and the nostalgia trap. *Phi Delta Kappan, 7*(76), K1–K20.

Council for Exceptional Children. (1995a). CEC fights to include special education in assessment. *CEC Today, 1*(9), 1, 10.

Council for Exceptional Children. (1995b). Educational technology creates new frontiers. *CEC Today, 1*(10), 1, 9–10.

Electronic Industries Association. (1995, April). *Household penetration of consumer electronics products.* Arlington, VA: Electronic Industries Association.

Fafard, M. B. (1995). Twenty years after Chapter 766: The backlash against special education in Massachusetts. *Phi Delta Kappan, 76*(7), 536–537.

Fuchs, D., & Fuchs, L.S. (1995). What's special about special education? *Phi Delta Kappan, 76*(7), 522–529.

Greenwood, C. R., & Reith, H. J. (1994). Current dimensions of technology-based assessment in special education. *Exceptional Children, 61*(2), 105–113.

Irvin, L. K., & Walker, H. M. (1993). Improving social skills assessment of children with disabilities: Construct development and applications of technology. *Journal of Special Education Technology, 12*(1), 63–70.

Jennings, J., & Stark, D. (1995). Education facing new challenges. *Phi Delta Kappa Washington Newsletter, 4*(2), 1.

Ludlow, B. L., & Lombardi, T. P. (1992). Special education in the year 2000: Current trends and future developments. *Education and Treatment of Children, 15*(2), 147–162.

Montgomery, J. K., & Herer, G. R. (1994). Future watch: Our schools in the 21st century. *Language, Speech, and Hearing Services in Schools, 25*, 130–135.

Okolo, C. M., Bahr, C. M., & Reith, H. J. (1993). A retrospective view of computer-based instruction. *Journal of Special Education Technology, 12*, 1–27.

Shrag, J. (1990). Charting the course for the 1990's. In L. M. Bullock & R. L. Simpson (Eds.), *Critical issues in special education: Implications for personnel preparation* (monograph). Denton, TX: University of North Texas, Programs in Special Education.

United Way of America. (1989). *What lies ahead: Countdown to the 21st century.* Alexandria, VA: United Way of America.

U.S. Department of Health and Human Services. (1994). Children's disability research issues, 94 C. F. R. 12160.

GLOSSARY

acceleration: the practice of moving a student through the curriculum at a rapid pace, so that the result is advanced placement or credit.

acculturation: the process of acquiring culture in education; the term often refers to students' unique background experiences and opportunities.

adaptive behavior: the way in which an individual copes with his or her environment.

addition: an articulation error made when an extra sound is added to a word.

adventitious: a disorder or disability acquired after birth.

amblyopia: commonly known as "lazy eye," a vision impairment in which the brain suppresses the use of one eye to eliminate confusing signals to the brain caused by unequal acuities or misalignment of the eyes.

American Sign Language (ASL): a gestural communication system whereby thoughts and messages are conveyed using a system of formal finger, hand, and arm movements.

Americans With Disabilities Act of 1990 (ADA): an act of Congress (P.L. 101-336) that prohibits discrimination against individuals with disabilities, including employment practices and accessibility to public vehicles and accommodations.

anophthalmia: a relatively rare condition that is characterized by an absence of the globe of the eye.

antecedents: prompts such as cues, signals, or other methods of gaining a student's attention during instruction.

aphonia: the absence or loss of one's voice either temporarily, due to a condition such as laryngitis, or permanently.

applied behavior analysis: a system of principles and procedures used to arrange stimuli and consequences, to teach and promote positive behaviors, and reduce the frequency of problem behaviors; often referred to as *behavior management* or *behavior modification*.

articulation disorder: a communication disorder that occurs when a person cannot correctly produce one or more sounds of his or her spoken language.

assistive technology: various manual and electronic devices, including computers and other physical modifications, that enhance the quality of life of persons with disabilities.

asthma: a respiratory condition with resistance to air flow in the lungs for short periods of time; also referred to as *reactive airway disease*.

astigmatism: a visual impairment caused by an irregularly shaped cornea (eye surface).

attention: the ability to focus on a stimulus and maintain that focus over time.

attention deficit disorder (ADD): a persistent pattern of inattention and/or hyperactivity-impulsivity that presents itself before age 7. The symptoms must occur in at least two settings and must interfere with social, academic, or occupational functioning.

audiogram: a graph of a person's hearing pattern.

audiologist: a professional trained to assess hearing problems.

audiometer: the most common instrument used to assess hearing.

auditory brainstem response (ABR): a procedure to test the hearing of individuals who are very young, cognitively impaired, or unable to voluntarily respond to pure tone testing. Electrodes are placed on the scalp, and neural responses to sound are detected.

auditory training: activities to help children learn to use their residual hearing and improve their listening abilities and their recognition of environmental and speech sounds.

augmentative communication system: a gestural or mechanical alternative or supplement to verbal communication skills.

autism: a pervasive developmental disability represented by a syndrome of behaviors that typically appear during the first 3 years of life. Such behaviors involve disturbances in social behavior and communication, as well as restricted interests and activities.

behavioral models: conceptual models of emotional and behavioral disorders that focus on causal explanations and formal principles, replicable and effective interventions, and a scientific approach.

bibliotherapy: the use of carefully selected reading materials, matched to the child's needs, that enable gifted learners to identify with a character, real or imaginary, who has faced similar problems and resolved them.

bilateral hearing loss: a hearing loss in both ears.

bilingual/bicultural deaf education: education that recognizes that many students who are deaf communicate in both ASL and printed English, making them bilingual; they must adapt to both hearing and deaf cultures, and so are bicultural as well; also referred to as "DBiBi" education.

bilingual special education: the use of the home language and the home culture along with English in an individually designed program of special education for a student.

braille: a system of raised dots by which blind individuals are able to read text tactually. Individual braille cells comprise different combinations of six dots to represent letters, whole words, parts of words, numbers, or punctuation.

cataract: a cloudiness in the typically clear lens of the eye, which blocks light entering the eye.

central auditory dysfunction: hearing loss resulting from damage to the auditory nerve leading from the inner ear to the brain or in the brain itself.

cerebral palsy: a condition caused by an injury or insult to the brain, causing disorganized communication between the brain and muscles often resulting in physical impairments.

cochlear implant: an electronic device that directly stimulates nerve fibers in the inner ear.

community-based training: instruction that occurs in natural environments such as community, work, home, etc.

conductive hearing loss: a hearing loss resulting from damage, disease, or injury to the external ear, the ear canal, the eardrum, or any part of the middle ear.

congenital: a disability present at birth.

consequences: reinforcements (individual for each child and as natural as possible) or correction procedures used during instruction.

contingent reinforcement: the principle that states that immediate consequence either weakens or strengthens a behavior.

cortical visual impairment (CVI):   bilateral vision loss associated with damage to the visual pathways to the brain.

co-teaching: a system whereby a student with disabilities is placed in a general education classroom and the general education teacher co-teaches with the special education teacher.

cued speech: a method of visually supplementing oral communication with eight hand shapes placed near the mouth.

cultural-familial retardation: developmental delays resulting from inadequate social and cultural experience that fail to foster normal cognitive development; sometimes referred to as *psychosocial disadvantage*.

cultural pluralism: a view of multiple cultural subgroups living together in a way that maintains subsocietal differences, thereby continuing each group's cultural or ethnic traditions.

culture: a way of perceiving, believing, evaluating, and behaving that is shared by a group of people. Culture includes institutions, language, values, religion, ideals, habits of thinking, artistic expressions, and patterns of social and interpersonal relationships.

cystic fibrosis: a disease affecting the endocrine system characterized by the production of abnormal mucus, progressive lung damage, and impaired absorption of fats and proteins.

deaf: a term referring to hearing loss in the severe to profound range.

developmental apraxia of speech (DAS): lack of voluntary control of the oral mechanism needed for clear speech production.

developmental disability: a severe chronic disability attributable to a mental or physical impairment or combination of mental and physical impairments manifested before age 22 and likely to continue indefinitely, resulting in substantial function limitations in three or more of the following areas of major life activities: self-care, receptive and expressive language, learning, mobility, self-direction, capacity for independent living, and economic sufficiency. These reflect a need for special interdisciplinary or generic care, treatment, or other services that are of lifelong or extended duration.

deviance perspective: belief that emotional and behavioral disorders and problem behavior are due to learned experience and are affected by environmental influences.

diabetes: a health impairment caused by the continuous presence of increased glycogen in the body and the disturbance of metabolism of carbohydrate, fat, and protein from poor insulin secretion.

disability: a physical or mental impairment that substantially limits a person in some major life activity such as walking, talking, breathing, or working.

disability perspective: belief that emotional and behavioral disorders is caused by intra-psychic (within the individual) or biological phenomena.

disfluency: halting speech filled with many interruptions, pauses, or repetitions; also referred to as *stuttering*.

disorder: a broad term used to refer generally to an impairment of mental, physical, or psychological processes, such as a hearing loss or mental disorder.

distortion: an articulation error made when a sound is produced incorrectly.

distractibility: the inclination to attend to everything but the matter at hand.

diversity: variety in values and behavioral styles, language and dialects, nonverbal communication, awareness of one's own cultural distinctiveness, frames of reference, and identification. Diversity also includes gender, age, language, backgrounds, religious beliefs, politics, the work world, physical and mental abilities, and experiences.

Down syndrome: the most common genetic disorder associated with mental retardation; caused by a chromosomal abnormality.

dysarthria: a disorder in which individuals exhibit abnormal motor movements when attempting to speak.

dyslexia: an inability to read; usually, an inability to decode words.

early intervention: the provision of programs and services to infants and toddlers with disabilities and their families.

echolalia: repetition of words or phrases already heard, either immediately after hearing them or after some delay; a characteristic of many children with autism and some children who are blind.

ecological assessment: the assessment of environmental characteristics and conditions that have an impact on the learning of an individual student.

ecological inventory: an inventory of the sequences of skills needed by an individual with disabilities to enable their participation in a variety of natural environments.

ecological models: conceptual models of emotional and behavioral disorders that focus on causal explanations and formal principles, replicable and effective interventions, and a scientific approach.

eligibility: determination if a child qualifies to receive special education and related services.

emotional and behavioral disorder (EBD): a disability in which students display externalizing and internalizing behaviors that are chronic, severe, and disturbing to the school community. They are particularly resistant to standard or typical classroom and behavior management practices, and they interfere with the student's educational performance; also referred to as *serious emotional disturbance* or *behavior disorder*.

encoding: the storing of incoming stimuli.

enrichment: curricular modifications for gifted students that increase the depth and breadth of learning beyond that in the regular curriculum but do not result in advanced placement.

epilepsy: a neurological disorder characterized by unprovoked, recurrent seizures of a chronic nature.

equal protection clause: the section of the Fourteenth Amendment to the U.S. Constitution that guarantees "equal protection of the laws" to all.

ESL (English as a Second Language):   a curriculum that promotes English proficiency for students whose native language is not English. ESL instruction relies exclusively on English as the medium of teaching and learning.

esophageal speech: an alternate method of voice production used when the larynx is removed.

ethnicity: a term referring to the common history, values, attitudes, and behaviors that bind a group of people together.

ethnocentrism: the belief in the superiority of one's own culture, leading to judgment of others in terms of one's own cultural norms. Those who do not conform to such norms may be found lacking.

etiology: the cause of a disability or illness.

exceptional: a term used to describe individuals who differ from the norm in some way; can refer to individuals who are gifted as well as individuals with disabilities.

expressive language: the outward expression of a message, using written or spoken words, signs or symbols.

externalizing behavior: behavior that is generally characterized as acting out, aggressive, and excessive.

facilitated communication: a system of communication whereby a facilitator provides support to the communicator's forearm, wrist, and/or fingers as the communicator types responses on a keyboard or points to pictures or words.

family-centered care: a set of beliefs, attitudes, and principles based on the premise that the family is the enduring and central force in the life of a child and has a significant impact on the child's development and well-being.

family life cycle: all changes that affect families; these changes may influence family resources, interactions, and functions.

family resources: all the characteristics of a family including their cultural background, financial well-being, size, location, abilities and disabilities, etc.

fetal alcohol syndrome (FAS):   the leading preventable cause of mental retardation in the United States; caused by expectant mothers who ingest alcohol during pregnancy. *Fetal alcohol effects (FAE)* is a less severe form.

fluency disorder: a communication disorder exhibiting the abnormal flow of verbal expression characterized by impaired rate and rhythm of speech that is often accompanied by struggle behavior.

fluency shaping therapy: teaching a speaker to replace stuttering with fluent speech in a variety of situations.

free appropriate publication education (FAPE):   a guarantee set forth in P.L. 94-142 that enables all children with disabilities to receive an appropriate education at no cost.

functional assessment: an assessment process in which the function or purpose of problem behavior is identified and studied in order to design and implement a uniquely appropriate program that promotes positive behaviors and reduces the problem behaviors.

functionally blind: an educational term describing students who are unable to benefit from visual modes of learning and/or visual educational materials.

generalization: the ability to perform a skill or behavior in situations or with persons that are different from those of the initial training.

glaucoma: an increased pressure in the eye causing a loss of vision.

handicap: a limitation imposed by a disability, encountered during interaction with one's environment.

hard-of-hearing: a term for hearing loss in the mild to moderate range.

health impairments: conditions that require ongoing medical attention.

hearing loss: a hearing deficit of any degree or type.

hydrocephalus: accumulation of excess fluid in the ventricles of the brain caused by blockage of the normal flow of cerebrospinal fluid.

hyperactivity: an excess of nonpurposeful motor activity.

hyperopia: farsightedness; persons with hyperopia can clearly see objects at a distance but are unable to clearly focus on nearby objects.

impulsivity: spontaneous activity without forethought; often characterized by interruption in activities or conversations.

inattentiveness: inappropriate shifting of attention from one activity or stimuli to another.

incidence: the number of new cases identified within a population over a certain period of time; typically reported in a ratio (e.g., 1 in 500 chance).

inclusion: including students with disabilities in classrooms and other school activities alongside their peers without disabilities; also refers to integration of individuals with disabilities in a full range of family and community activities.

Individualized Education Program (IEP): a written statement of the resources and services to be provided in a child's special education program; also used by parents and school personnel to monitor a child's progress.

Individualized Family Service Plan (IFSP): a written statement for each infant or toddler receiving early intervention services which includes outcomes for the child and family and a transition plan for the child into services for children over age 2.

individualized instruction: the practice of identifying an individual's preferred learning modality strengths and weaknesses and planning and delivering instruction accordingly.

Individualized Transition Plan (ITP): a written statement, including goals related to all aspects of work, of the steps for moving a student from school to the workplace.

Individualized Written Rehabilitation Plan (IWRP): a document required by the federal government that provides vocational rehabilitation for individuals residing in institutions or community-based living arrangements, such as group homes.

Individuals With Disabilities Education Act (IDEA): the groundbreaking law (P.L. 101-476) originally passed in 1975 (P.L. 94-142) and amended in 1990, which guarantees the right to a free appropriate public education, nondiscriminatory evaluation, procedural due process, an Individualized Education Program, and education in the least restrictive environment.

institutionalization: the practice of placing individuals with mental retardation and other disabilities in institutions rather than supporting them in their local communities.

integrated therapy: speech-language therapy and other supportive services that are delivered in classroom settings instead of in isolated therapy rooms or settings.

internalizing behavior: behavior that is generally characterized as withdrawn, depressed, and deficient.

juvenile rheumatoid arthritis (JRA): a chronic disease involving one or more joint structures characterized by pain and swelling in the joints.

language: a system of common rules used by a group of people to communicate.

language disorder: the impairment or deviant development of comprehension and/or use of a spoken, written, and/or other symbol system.

LEP: a term denoting limited English proficiency.

learned helplessness: an overreliance on others in one's environment for assistance or for cues on how to act or what to do.

learning disability: a disorder in one or more of the basic psychological processes involved in understanding or in using language, spoken or written, that may manifest itself in an imperfect ability to listen, think, speak, read, write, spell, or do mathematical calculations.

learning strategy: a structured approach to a learning task.

learning styles: the internal structures and processes that affect an individual's reception, interrelation, and use of information.

least restrictive environment (LRE):   a component of P.L. 94-142 that requires a child to be placed with his or her peers without disabilities as much as possible.

legal blindness: legal classification referring to individuals with a visual acuity of 20/200 or less in the better eye with correction or a visual field of 20 degrees or less in the better eye.

low incidence disability: a disability with prevalence in 1% or less of the total population.

low vision: an educational term referring to students with visual impairments who are able to benefit from visual modes of learning.

mainstreaming: the practice of placing students with disabilities in general education classrooms for part of the day. Such students may still leave the regular class to receive special services.

measurement bias: unfairness or inaccuracy of assessment results due to cultural background, gender, or race.

memory: the ability to hold on to, store, and then retrieve information that has been learned.

mental retardation: subaverage intellectual function with deficits in adaptive behavior, manifested during the developmental period.

metacognition: the self-regulation of cognitive processes, characterized by self-monitoring of learning, use of strategies to facilitate learning, and self-evaluation of learning outcomes.

microphthalmia: a small eyeball, approximately two-thirds of the normal size.

most appropriate placement (MAP):   an educational placement decision based on considerations of both developmental needs and disability-specific needs of the student with a visual impairment; the MAP is chosen from a full array of program options and may vary over time according to the students' needs.

multichannel auditory brainstem implant: an implant that transmits sound, via electrodes, directly to the auditory region of the brainstem.

multicultural education: the provision of equal opportunities for students from diverse cultural and ethnic backgrounds by promoting positive contacts between groups and cultural enrichment for all students, while emphasizing the value of cultural diversity.

myopia: nearsightedness; persons with myopia can see objects that are close by, but distant objects are out of focus.

naturalistic assessment: assessment of children and their environments taken as a whole.

nondiscriminatory evaluation: methods that attempt to eliminate errors or bias in the classification and placement of students suspected to have disabilities.

nystagmus: a disorder characterized by involuntary rapid eye movements.

occupational therapist: a professional trained to assess and treat strength and joint motion, primarily of the hands and upper limbs, and to assess and treat sensory perception, processing, organizational skills, activities of daily living, manipulative skills, and computer access.

omission disorder: an articulation error made when a speaker leaves out sounds from words.

otitis media: a buildup of fluid in the middle ear that can cause conductive hearing loss, especially in young children.

ototoxic: a term used to describe any agent capable of causing damage to the nerves associated with hearing and balance.

overattention: difficulty shifting attention from one task to another.

oversensitivity: an attention problem in which virtually all stimuli received by the senses distract an individual from paying attention to the most important aspect of the situation.

paraplegia: a type of spinal cord injury resulting in partial or complete loss of use of the lower half of the body.

partially sighted: a legal classification referring to individuals who have a visual acuity between 20/70 and 20/200 in the better eye with correction.

Carl D. Perkins Vocational Education Act of 1984: legislation requiring that federal funds must be used to integrate academic and vocational education for students with disabilities.

perseverate: to repeatedly perform an action or repeat a word or phrase.

person-first language: the practice of referring to the person before the disability (e.g., "an individual with disabilities," rather than "disabled individual").

phonological processing: a cluster of skills related to interpreting the sounds within words that includes mapping component sounds to specific letters, breaking words into component parts, and blending sounds together to make words.

physical disabilities: acquired or congenital impairments of the body's neurological or muscular systems that affect basic movement functions.

physical therapist: a professional trained to improve an individual's mobility skills, strength, endurance, and movement at the joints.

pitch disorder: a voice that is too high or low for the speaker's age, size or gender, or that is monotone or has excessive or limited variation in pitch.

postlingual: hearing loss acquired after the acquisition of language.

practical intelligence: the ability to maintain and sustain oneself as an independent person in managing the ordinary activities of daily living.

precorrection: prevention strategy that focuses on arranging the instructional and/or social environment to increase the probability or opportunity for the student to make correct responses instead of exhibiting a problem behavior.

prelingual: hearing loss acquired before the acquisition of language.

presbycusis: the sum of hearing loss that results from physiological degeneration of the hair cells in the inner ear over a person's life span.

prevalence: total number of cases throughout the population that exists at a certain time or in a certain place; typically reported as a percentage (e.g., 3% of the population).

preventive counseling: the use of counseling techniques to prevent likely emotional problems before they occur.

problem-solving instruction: the active teaching of strategies to recognize and address problems in various domains and of various types.

procedural due process: a component of P.L. 94-142 that guarantees safeguards to children with disabilities and their parents in all areas relating to identification, evaluation, and educational practices.

processing disorder: disorder related to how an individual processes or uses information for learning.

psychoeducational models: conceptual models of emotional and behavioral disorders that focus on internal causation, past events, formal explanatory principles, and a wide range of interventions.

psycholinguistic teaching: the practice of using an individual's modality strengths and weaknesses to plan individualized instruction.

quadriplegia: a type of spinal cord injury resulting in partial or complete loss of control over both legs, both arms, and the trunk of the body.

receptive language: an individual's understanding of his or her language code.

Regular Education Initiative (REI): a movement to blend regular and special education by diminishing the physical and curricular boundaries between the two settings.

resonance disorder: a voice disorder created when air does not resonate in the nasal passages when the nasal sounds (/m/, /n/, /ing/) are produced or when too much air resonates in the nasal passages when non-nasal sounds are produced.

retinitis pigmentosa (RP):   a hereditary condition in which the retina gradually degenerates over time.

retinoblastoma: a malignant tumor in the retina; one of the ten most frequent causes of visual impairment in children in the United States.

retinopathy of prematurity (ROP):   a vision impairment caused by the administration of too much oxygen to premature, low birthweight infants placed in incubators for extended periods of time. Such large amounts of oxygen can cause scar tissue in the retina.

savant skills: rare and unusual abilities that may be displayed by persons with autism, such as being able to play musical pieces after hearing them once, to perform complex mathematical calculations unaided, or to draw in a sophisticated manner without formal training; these skills may exist even though the person shows other characteristics of severe impairment (e.g., mental retardation).

screening: the process by which children are identified as having a possible developmental delay. Additional assessment may be required.

Section 504:   a component of the Vocational Rehabilitation Act of 1973 (P.L. 93-112) that applies to all Americans with disabilities, regardless of age; it states that no person with a disability may be excluded, on the basis of the disability, from a program benefiting from federal financial assistance.

selection: the sorting of processed stimuli for later use.

self-advocacy: the process by which persons with disabilities make others aware of their abilities, needs, and concerns in effort to reduce discrimination and prejudice and increase opportunities to participate fully in a range of educational, economic, and social activities.

self-injurious behavior: behavior exhibited by some persons with autism and other disabilities that can result in tissue damage or injury (e.g., head banging, biting fingers and hands).

self-management strategies: a set of strategies for teaching children with autism (and other disabilities) to monitor, record, and provide consequences for their own behavior and accomplishments.

self-stimulatory behavior: behavior exhibited by some persons with autism whose primary function appears to be providing some kind of internal sensory input or stimulation (e.g., hand flapping, rocking, spinning and staring at objects).

sensorineural hearing loss: a hearing loss resulting from damage to the inner ear.

severe discrepancy: a criterion for identifying individuals with learning disabilities indicated by a significant difference between the individual's potential for learning and actual achievement in one or more academic areas.

signed language system: a system of formal finger, hand, and arm movements used to express thoughts and convey messages.

social intelligence: the ability to understand social expectations and the behavior of other persons and to judge appropriately how to conduct oneself in social situations.

social skills: those behaviors that, within a specific situation, result in socially important outcomes (peer acceptance).

speech: the expression of a language by using one's voice.

speech disorder: an impairment of voice, articulation of speech sounds, and/or fluency.

speech-language pathologist: a professional who is certified to diagnose and treat speech, language, and voice disorders; also referred to as *speech-language clinician* or *therapist*.

speechreading: interpreting spoken words by watching the speaker's mouth; also known as *lip reading*.

spina bifida: a group of disorders affecting the spinal column, spinal cord, and skin, usually causing partial or complete paralysis of the muscles and sensory organs at and below the spinal cord lesion.

spinal cord injury (SCI):   a trauma to the spinal cord that results in paralysis and loss of sensation.

standardized assessment: formal assessment that is administered and scored according to specific protocols.

stereotypic behaviors: self-involved movements such as body rocking, eye poking, and finger flicking, which are thought to develop initially to meet a need for additional sensory stimulation; also known as *mannerisms.*

stimulus overselectivity: a characteristic demonstrated by some persons with autism in which they appear unable to focus on more than one aspect of a situation at a given time.

strabismus: a misalignment or turning of the eyes either inward or outward; commonly called *cross-eye.*

stress reduction techniques: methods to recognize and alleviate the causes and symptoms of anxiety in one's life.

stuttering: speech that is notably disfluent much of the time and in many different speaking situations.

stuttering modification therapy: a technique whereby a speaker learns to monitor his or her own speech production and use new speech patterns and control techniques to maintain fluent speech in a variety of speaking situations.

substitution disorder: an articulation error made when a speaker replaces a sound that belongs in a word with a different sound.

successive approximation: the breaking down of a task into smaller tasks and reinforcing each step toward the final goal.

supported employment: use of a job coach to help an individual with disabilities work successfully at a real job.

tactual defensiveness: a negative or overly emotional response to the sensation of touch.

task persistence: the motivation to stay with something even when it becomes difficult.

test bias: an unfair testing procedure or instrument that gives one group a particular advantage or disadvantage.

threshold of hearing: a measure of the quietest sound heard at a particular frequency.

Total Communication (TC): a philosophy that incorporates the use of a variety of methods of receiving and sending messages—including speech, speechreading, writing, gesturing, American Sign Language, and fingerspelling.

transition: the process of moving from one environment to another (e.g., from preschool to elementary school or from school to work and the community).

transition core team: a team consisting of representatives from special education, vocational rehabilitation, vocational education, developmental disabilities, mental health/mental retardation, social services, medical services, parents, and employers from local businesses that supports a student in transition from school to the work place.

traumatic brain injury (TBI): an injury to the brain caused by an external force that results in significant impairment of cognitive, physical, or psychosocial functional abilities.

tympanometry: a procedure to determine how well the middle ear is functioning.

underattention: an attention problem in which an individual focuses on all information equally, unable to filter out what is unimportant.

visual acuity: a measurement that refers to the distance from which an individual can clearly see an object; a person with typical vision has a visual acuity of 20/20.

visual field: the area that can be seen while gazing directly forward.

vocational education: formal training designed to prepare individuals to work in a certain job or occupational area.

voice disorder: the absence or abnormal production of voice quality, pitch, loudness, resonance, and/or duration.

CREDITS AND ACKNOWLEDGMENTS

Impact Visuals, **509**; © Spencer Grant / Photo Researchers, **512**; © Cathlyn Melloan / Tony Stone Images, **517**; © David Young-Wolff / PhotoEdit, **520**; © Lawrence Migdale / Tony Stone Images **525**; © Robin Sachs, **528**

Chapter 14 Flabbergasted, by Nelson Rivera, **536**; Courtesy of the Levitz family, **540**; © Jeff Greenberg / PhotoEdit, **547**; © Robin Sachs, **551**; © Robin Sachs, **561**; © Robert E. Daemmrich / Tony Stone Images, **564**

Chapter 15 Pierre Anthony, "World Unity" 48″ × 72″ 1992, Collection: Robert Wood Johnson Foundation, Princeton, N.J., **570**; © John Coletti / Stock, Boston, **576**; © Robin Sachs, **578**; © Robert E. Daemmrich / Tony Stone Images, **589**; © Robin Sachs, **592**; © Alan Carey / The Image Works, **593**

Epilogue Lost Paradise, by David Hill, **602**; AP / Mark Lennihan / Wide World Photos, **606**; © A. Ramey / Stock, Boston, **611**; © Geoff Tompkinson / Science Photo Library / Photo Researchers, **612**

LITERARY ACKNOWLEDGMENTS

Chapter 1
13 Figure 1.3 Reprinted by permission of the Hanover County Public Schools.

Chapter 2
48 Figure 2.1 Reprinted by permission of U.S. News and World Report.
48 Figure 2.2 From "Nonstandardized instruments the assessment of Mexican American children for gifted and talented programs" by J. H. Garcia in Sernaz B. Garcia (ed.), *Addressing cultural and linguistic diversity in special education*, 1994, p. 30. Copyright 1994 by The Council for Exceptional Children, Division for Culturally and Linguistically Diverse Exceptional Learners. Reprinted with permission.
51 Figure 2.3 From *Preventing Inappropriate Referrals of Language Minority Students to Special Education* (New Focus Series, No. 5), by S. B. Garcia and A. A. Ortiz, 1988, Wheaton, MD: National Clearinghouse for Bilingual Education. Reprinted by permission.
54 Table 2.1 Learning Styles Inventory by Jerry Brown and Richard Cooper, copyright 1981, revised 1994. Permission to use this segment granted by Educational Activities, Inc., P.O. Box 392, Freeport, NY 11520.
55 Table 2.2 Sternberg, R. J. "Allowing for thinking styles." *Educational Leadership*. Reprinted by permission of the Association for Supervision and Curriculum Development and Robert J. Sternberg. Copyright © 1994 by ASCD. All rights reserved.

Chapter 3
81, 97, 100 Figures 3.1, 3.3, 3.4 Reprinted by permission of Creative Learning Press.
94 Figure 3.2 Used with permission of Mary M. Frasier.
104 Figure 3.5 Reprinted by permission of Jenkins-Friedman and Anderson, 1985.

Chapter 5
167, 174, 175 Tables 5.1, 5.4, 5.5 Produced by the Utah State Office of Education, 1992. Used with permission.
170 Table 5.3 A special thanks to Ann B. Welch, the Council for Exceptional Children's 1993 National Teacher of the Year.
178 Figure 5.1 Used with the permission of Judy W. Wood.

Chapter 7
242 Real People Box. Daniel R. Levine, reprinted with permission from the February 1992 Reader's Digest. Copyright 1992 by The Reader's Digest Association, Inc.
246 Figure 7.2 Reprinted by permission of the American Speech-Language-Hearing Association and E. K. Sander.
257 Table 7.2 Reprinted with permission from "How to React When Speaking with Someone Who Stutters," Stuttering Foundation of America.
265 Figure 7.3 Reprinted with permission. Kleiman, L. *Functional Communication Profile*. East Moline, IL: LinguiSystems, Inc., 1994, p. 5.
271 Figure 7.4 Reprinted by permission of Mayer-Johnson Company.

Chapter 8
288 Real People Box. Reprinted with permission from Parade, copyright © 1994. Sheryl Flatow is a San Francisco-based writer whose work appears in many national publications.
290 Figure 8.1 Reprinted by permission of the National Information Center on Deafness, Gallaudet University.
299 Figure 8.2 Reprinted by permission of the American Academy of Audiology.
306 Figure 8.6 Reprinted by permission of Woodbine House, from *Choices in Deafness: A Parents' Guide* by Sue Schwantz, Ph.D.
309 Figure 8.8 Copyright 1993 by Modern Signs Press, Inc., Los Alamitos, CA from "Signing Exact English." Used by permission. All rights reserved.
315 Figure 8.9 Reprinted by permission of Ann Hughes.
321 Innovative Ideas Reprinted by permission of Dogs for the Deaf.

Chapter 9
337 Figure 9.2 From Prevent Blindness America.

Chapter 11
447 Figure 11.1 Reprinted by permission of Pro-Ed.
449 Table 11.2 Reprinted by permission of The Arc.
452 Table 11.4 Smith, R., ed. *Children With Mental Retardation: A Parent's Guide*. Bethesda, MD: Woodbine House, 1993. Reprinted with permission of Woodbine House.
454 Table 11.5 From Griffin, B. (1995). Graduate student, Virginia Commonwealth University, Richmond, VA. With permission and special acknowledgment.

Chapter 12
470 Table 12.1 Reprinted by permission of American Psychiatric Association: *Diagnostic and Statistical Manual of Mental Disorders, Fourth Edition*. Washington, DC: American Psychiatric Association, 1994.

Chapter 14
545 Table 14.1 Bailey, D.B. (1989) Issues and directions in preparing professionals to work with young handicapped children and their families. In J. Gallagher, P., Trohanis & R. Clifford (Eds.) *Policy implementation and P.L. 99-457: Planning for young children with special needs* (pp. 97–132). Baltimore: Paul H. Brookes Publishing Co. Reprinted by permission of Paul H. Brookes Publishing Co. and Donald B. Bailey.

Chapter 15
579 Figure 15.1 Reprinted by permission of Pro-Ed Inc.

NAME INDEX

SUBJECT INDEX